# HOLIDAY HOMES

## Finest Real Estate Worldwide

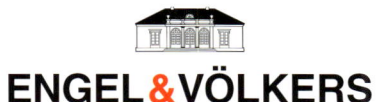

**ENGEL&VÖLKERS**

**teNeues**

# FOREWORD
## Christian Völkers

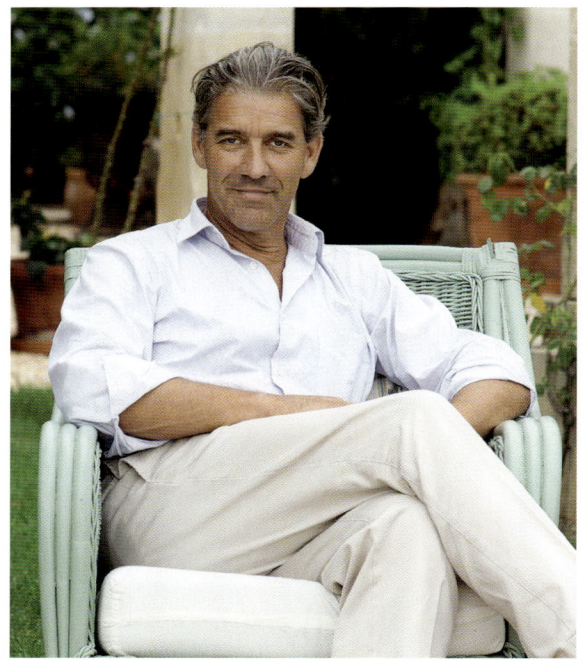

Dear Reader,

AS A SPECIALIST in exceptional homes situated in prime locations, Engel & Völkers has built up a name for itself around the world over the course of the last three decades. Operating from more than 500 different places in 38 countries also qualifies us with a particularly extensive pool of expertise in the field of exclusive holiday residences and second homes as well. An expertise driven by an incredible passion. In fact, there is hardly anything that lies closer to our hearts than the combination of holidays and properties. Whether you are looking to rent a beautiful home for a few days or are thinking of buying for longer-term stays, this book will carry you off to places simply made for escaping from everyday life – be it in the heart of nature, right by the sea or set against a breathtaking mountain backdrop. Be inspired by the 31 properties featured from our extensive portfolio – and enjoy a mix of fascinating architecture and international flair, modern design and feel-good comfort!

ALS SPEZIALIST für besondere Immobilien in den besten Lagen hat sich Engel & Völkers im Laufe der letzten drei Jahrzehnte weltweit einen Namen gemacht. Mit einer Präsenz von mehr als 500 Standorten in 38 Ländern verfügen wir auch und gerade im Hinblick auf exklusive Ferien- und Zweitwohnsitz-Objekte über eine profunde Expertise. Eine Expertise, die von einer großen Leidenschaft geprägt ist – gibt es doch kaum eine Konstellation, die unsere Seele so zuverlässig zum Schwingen bringt wie die aus Ferien und Immobilien. Ob Sie Ihr Wunschdomizil für ein paar Tage mieten oder für längerfristige Aufenthalte eines kaufen möchten: Dieses Buch entführt Sie an Orte, die wie geschaffen sind für eine unvergessliche Auszeit vom Alltag – inmitten ursprünglichster Natur, direkt am Meer oder vor imposanter Bergkulisse. Lassen Sie sich von 31 ausgewählten Angeboten aus unserem umfangreichen Portfolio inspirieren – und von einer Melange aus spannender Architektur mit internationalem Flair, modernem Design und unvergleichlichem Wohlfühl-Komfort begeistern!

COMO ESPECIALISTA en inmuebles excepcionales en las mejores localizaciones, Engel & Völkers ha sabido hacerse un nombre en todo el mundo durante las últimas tres décadas. Nuestra experiencia operativa en más de 500 lugares diferentes de 38 países también nos otorga cierta calificación como expertos en el campo de los inmuebles vacacionales y las segundas residencias; una experiencia impulsada por una inmensa pasión. De hecho, casi no hay nada que nos apasione e inspire más que poder combinar vacaciones e inmuebles. Tanto si desea alquilar por unos días la casa de sus sueños o si prefiere comprarla para disfrutar de estancias más largas, este libro le llevará a lugares capaces de convertir cualquier escapada de la vida cotidiana en una vivencia memorable, bien en plena naturaleza, frente al azul del mar o entre valles y montañas. Aquí tiene 31 propiedades seleccionadas para usted entre las maravillas de nuestra amplia cartera: una seductora mezcla de arquitectura fascinante y toque internacional, diseño moderno y confortable bienestar.

Sincerely,

Christian Völkers
CEO and Founder

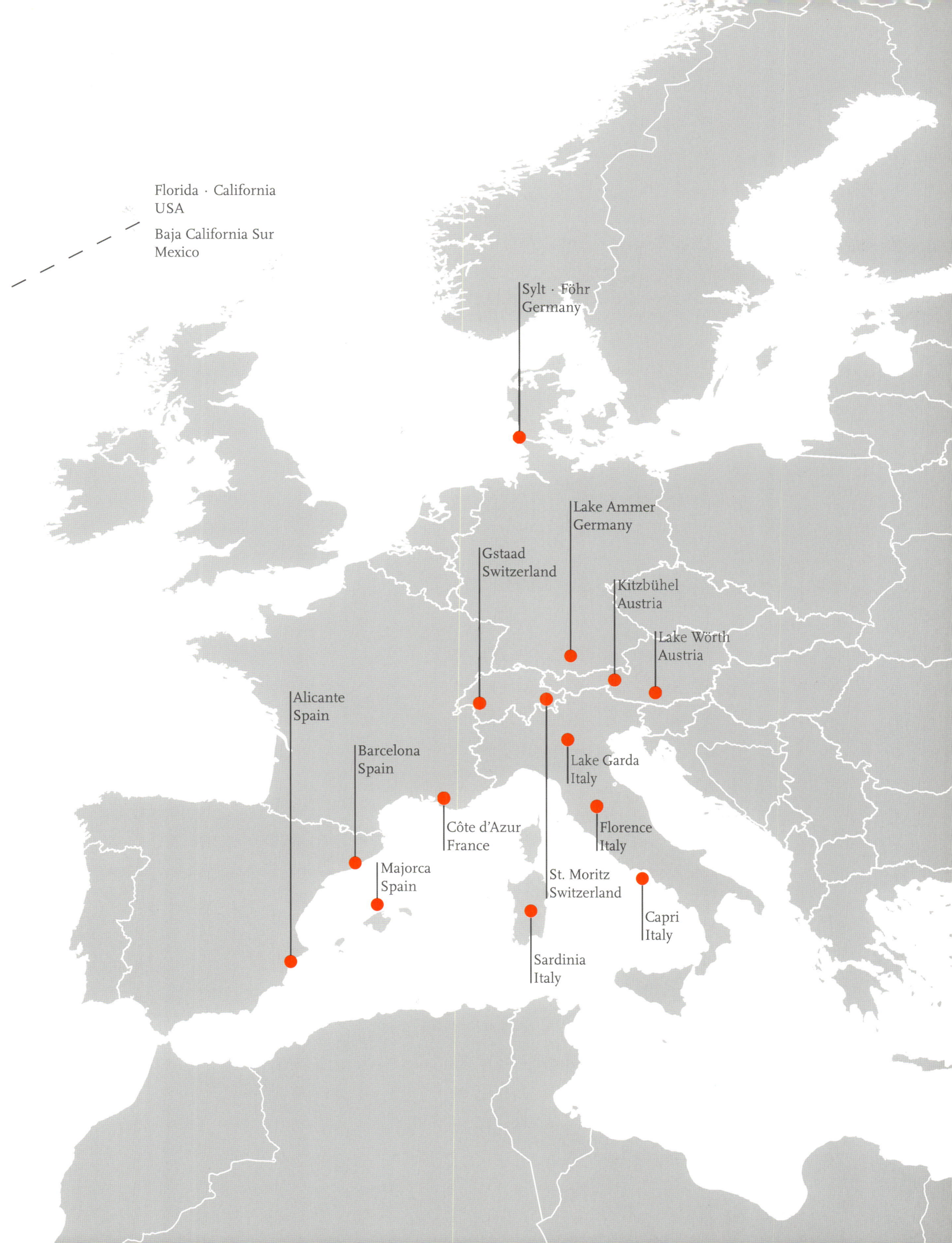

Florida · California
USA

Baja California Sur
Mexico

Sylt · Föhr
Germany

Lake Ammer
Germany

Gstaad
Switzerland

Kitzbühel
Austria

Lake Wörth
Austria

Alicante
Spain

Barcelona
Spain

Lake Garda
Italy

Côte d'Azur
France

Florence
Italy

Majorca
Spain

St. Moritz
Switzerland

Capri
Italy

Sardinia
Italy

# CONTENTS
## Holiday Homes

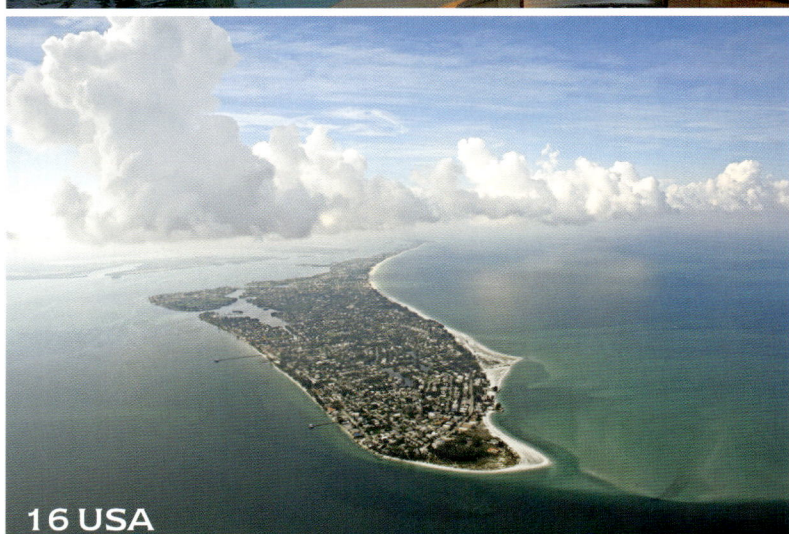

08 MEXICO

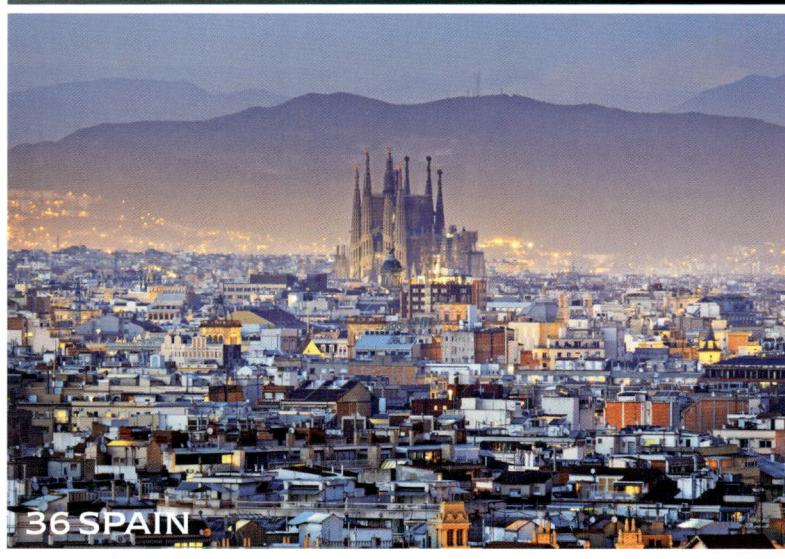

16 USA

36 SPAIN

Let us carry you off to places that are so unique they are destined for unforgettable holidays. Be inspired by magnificent mansions in the south of Mexico, California and Florida. Savour the finest quality of life the Mediterranean has to offer in Spain and Italy. Enjoy the relaxed sophistication of the Côte d'Azur, fall in love with luxurious Alpine chalets in Switzerland and Austria – and with Germany's wealth of scenic and architectural treasures.

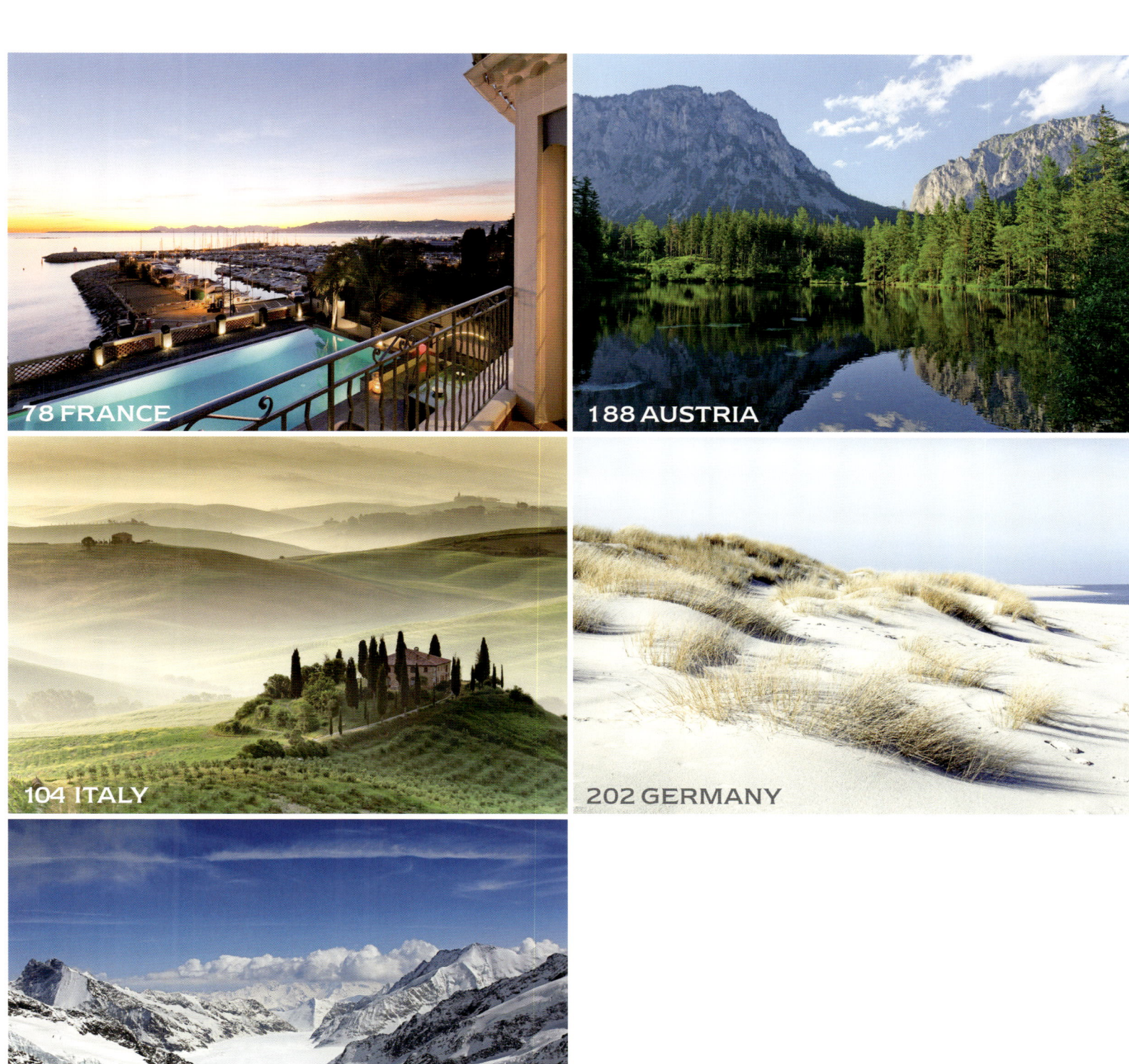

78 FRANCE

188 AUSTRIA

104 ITALY

202 GERMANY

162 SWITZERLAND

E&V – Be inspired ...

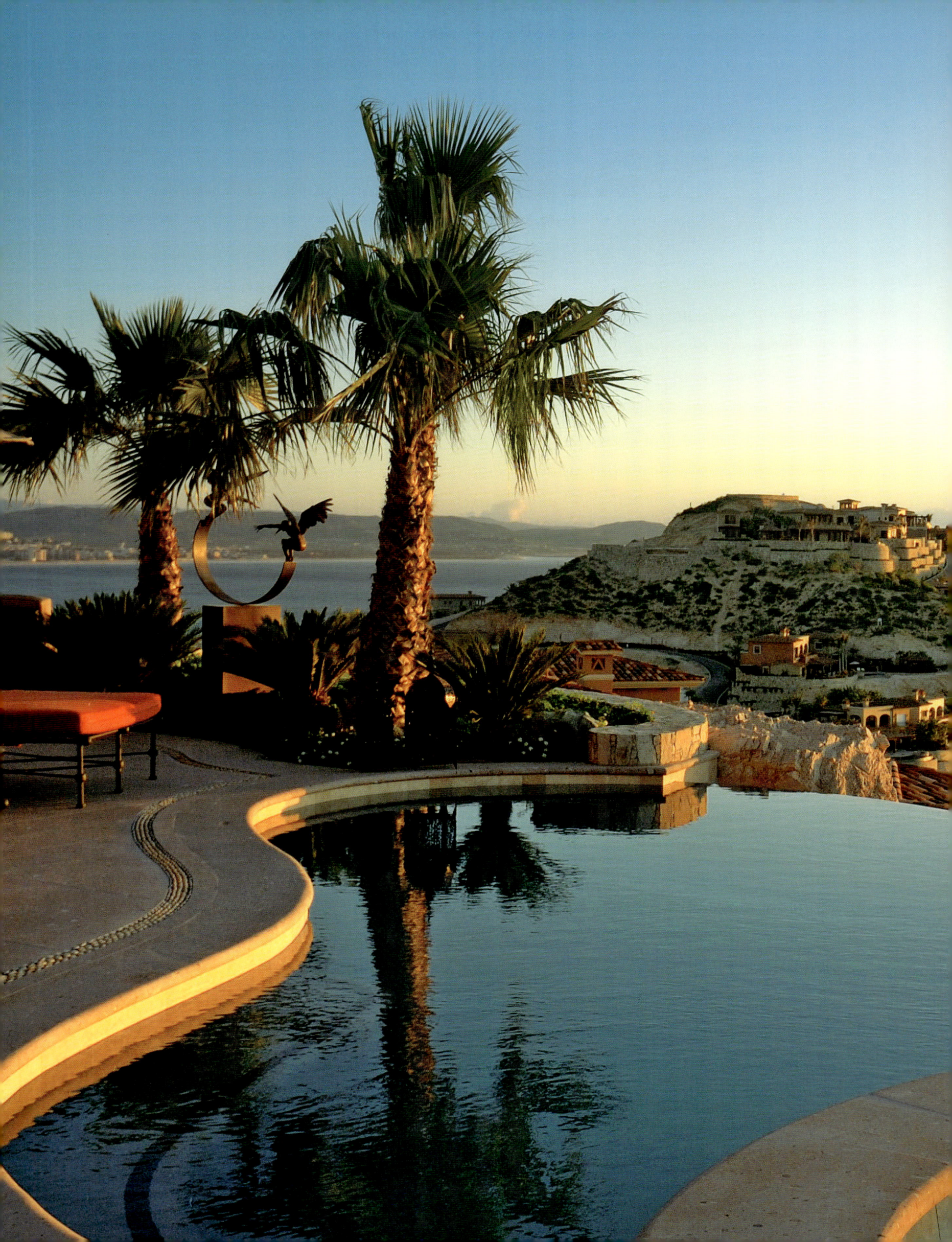

# MEXICO

## San José del Cabo

An eldorado for connoisseurs on the southernmost tip
of the Baja California Sur peninsula, San José del Cabo is a
lavish Mexican paradise with abundant charm.

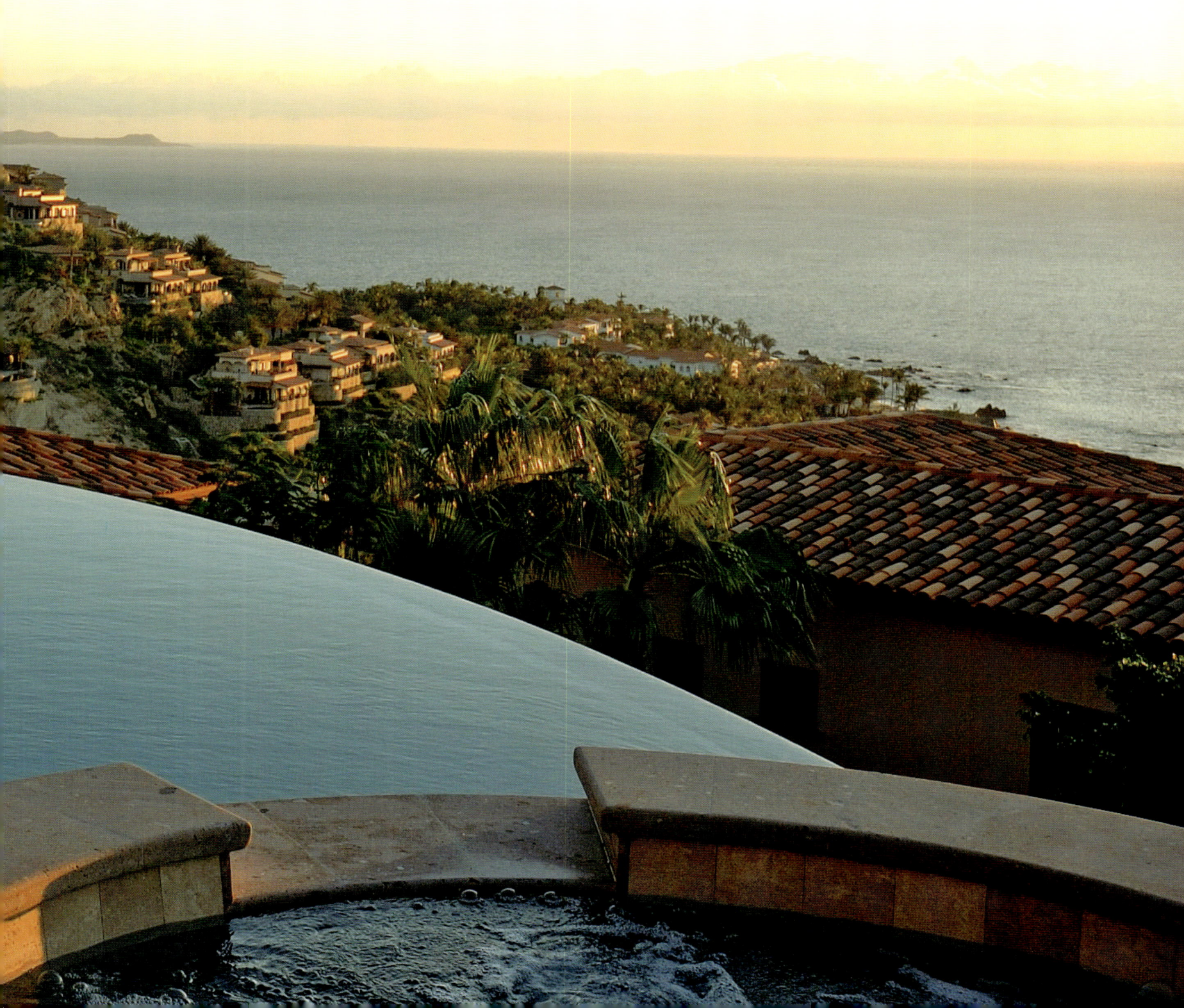

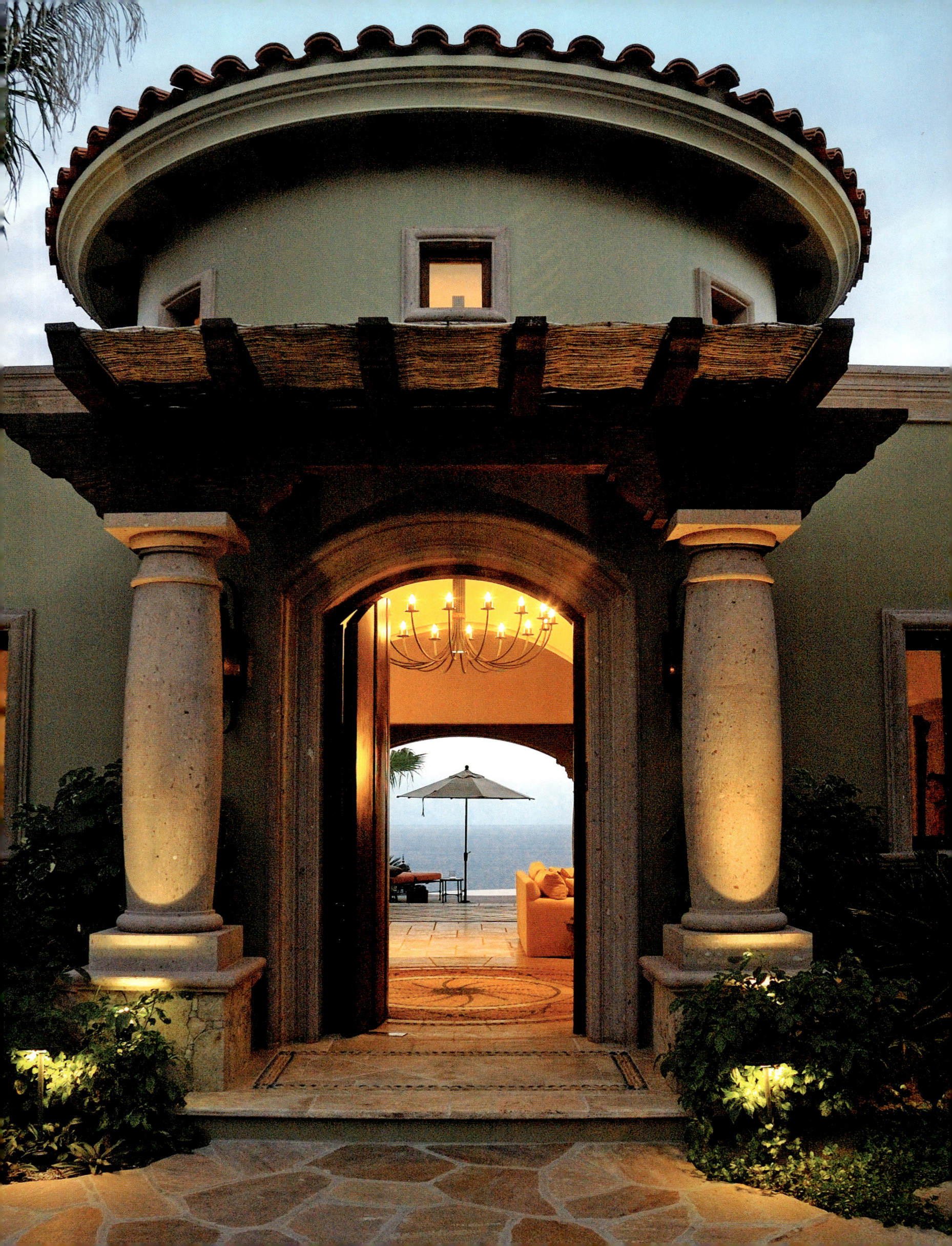

# Coastal Splendour

With its hypnotic fusion of classic Mexican style
and sleek contemporary elegance, this mansion by
San José del Cabo is a true architectural gem.

A HIGH-CLASS HOME at the peak of perfection: enjoying an exquisite hilltop location in La Montaña – a prestigious residential enclave in Villas del Mar, Palmilla, on the southernmost tip of the Baja California Sur peninsula – "Casa Adriana" is blessed with panoramic views of the Sea of Cortez and the beaches of San José del Cabo. All the property-management services needed for enjoying a life of luxury are close at hand, as well as access to a members-only fitness club, a private beach club and the 27-hole Jack Nicklaus Championship Palmilla Golf Course. As if this were not enough, the spacious one-level dwelling is of astounding beauty and grandeur. Its hacienda-style living areas provide seamless transitions between the inside and outside, and the five lavish bed- and bathrooms all boast seaside vistas. Enjoying a private walk-out lounge area with a fountain and a fire pit, the master suite is blissful indeed. And heavenly hours are sure to be spent on the landscaped patio surrounding the infinity pool – ideal for entertaining, relaxing or stargazing …

EIN HIGH-CLASS-ANWESEN in Perfektion: Das „Casa Adriana" liegt auf einem Hügel in La Montaña – einer Wohnsiedlung in Villas del Mar, Palmilla, an der Südspitze der Halbinsel Baja California Sur – und ist mit einem beeindruckenden Panoramablick über das Meer und die Strände von San José del Cabo gesegnet. Neben vielfältigen Dienstleistungen genießen die Eigentümer exklusiven Zugang zum Fitnessclub, einem privaten Beachclub und dem 27-Loch Jack Nicklaus Championship Palmilla Golfplatz. Die einstöckige Villa selbst zeichnet sich durch stilvolle Erhabenheit aus, mit Räumlichkeiten im Hacienda-Stil, fließenden Übergängen der Innen- und Außenbereiche sowie prachtvoll ausgestatteten Schlaf- und Badezimmern mit Meerblick. Vor allem die Master-Suite mit Terrassenzugang lädt dazu ein, den Alltag hinter sich zu lassen. Selbiges gilt auch für den Patio rund um den Infinity Pool, der zum Verweilen mit Freunden oder zu zweit einlädt – ob bei einem Barbecue oder beim Betrachten des mexikanischen Nachthimmels mit seinen zahllosen Sternen …

UN HOGAR DE ALTO NIVEL en la cima de la perfección: es Casa Adriana, sobre una exquisita colina de La Montaña –el prestigioso residencial de Villas del Mar, Palmilla, en el extremo sur de la península de Baja California Sur–, bendecida con inspiradoras vistas panorámicas al mar de Cortés y las playas de San José del Cabo. Todos los servicios de administración de propiedades para disfrutar una vida de lujo están a mano, así como el acceso al gimnasio sólo para miembros, al club de playa privado y al Jack Nicklaus Championship Palmilla Golf Course, de 27 hoyos. Por si fuera poco, la espaciosa vivienda en un nivel es de una asombrosa y gran belleza. Sus zonas de día en estilo hacienda lucen transiciones sin fisuras entre interior y exterior, y los cinco lujosos dormitorios y baños cuentan todos con fabulosas vistas al mar; la *suite* principal con su *lounge* exterior privado con una fuente y lar de fuego, es pura dicha. Culminando la experiencia al aire libre, el patio paisajístico envuelve la piscina de horizonte, un oasis para el ocio, el relax o la contemplación de las estrellas…

MEXICO, SAN JOSÉ DEL CABO **PURCHASE PRICE** USD 9.85 MILL. **INTERIOR APPROX.** 5,800 ft² **NO. OF BEDROOMS** 5
**LAND APPROX.** 16,700 ft² **E&V ID** E-0014Z8 **CONTACT** LOS CABOS (MX), SNELL VENTURES S DE RL DE C.V.,
LICENCE PARTNER OF ENGEL & VÖLKERS RESIDENTIAL GMBH **TEL.** +52 624 105 81 21
**E-MAIL** LOSCABOS@ENGELVOELKERS.COM

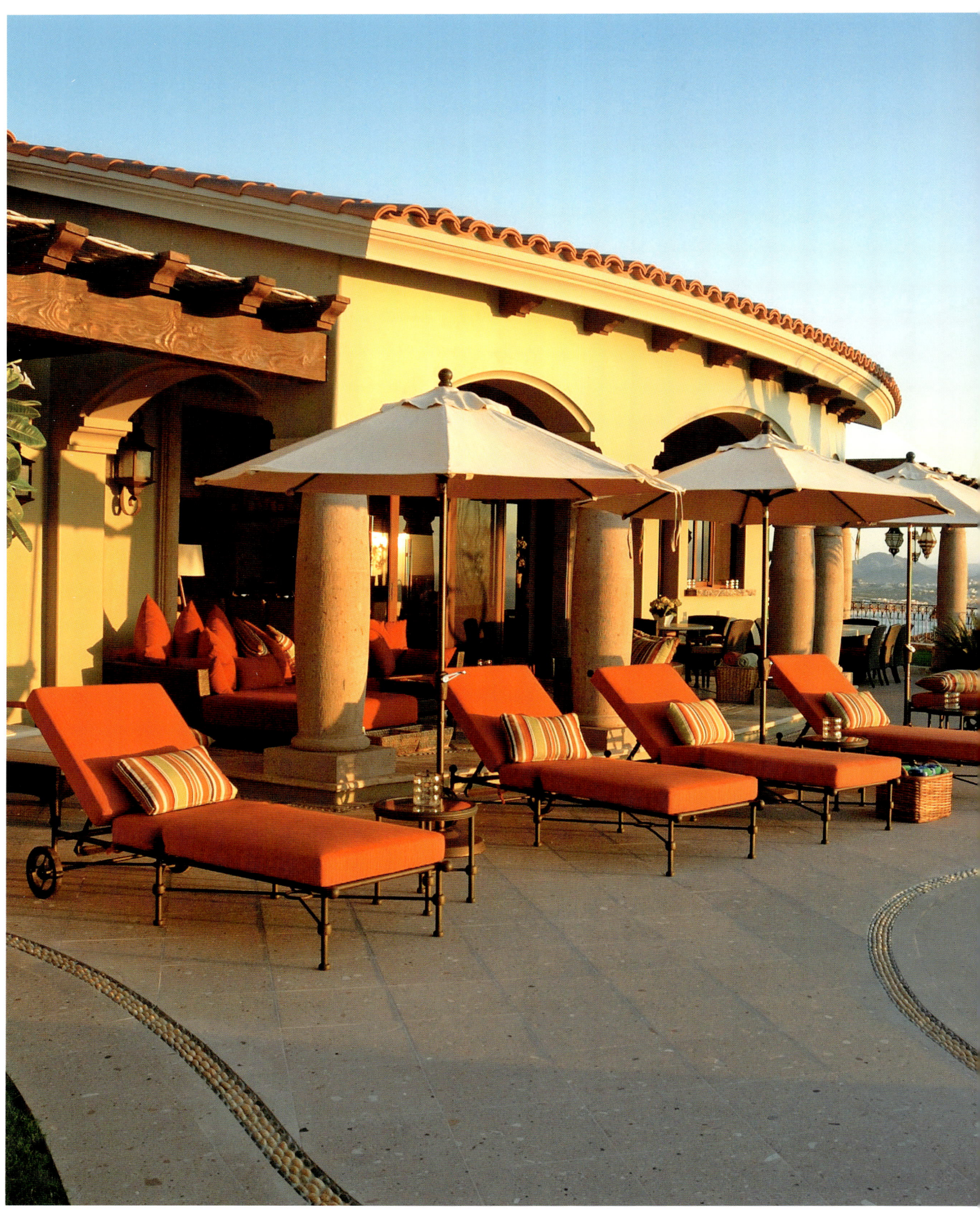

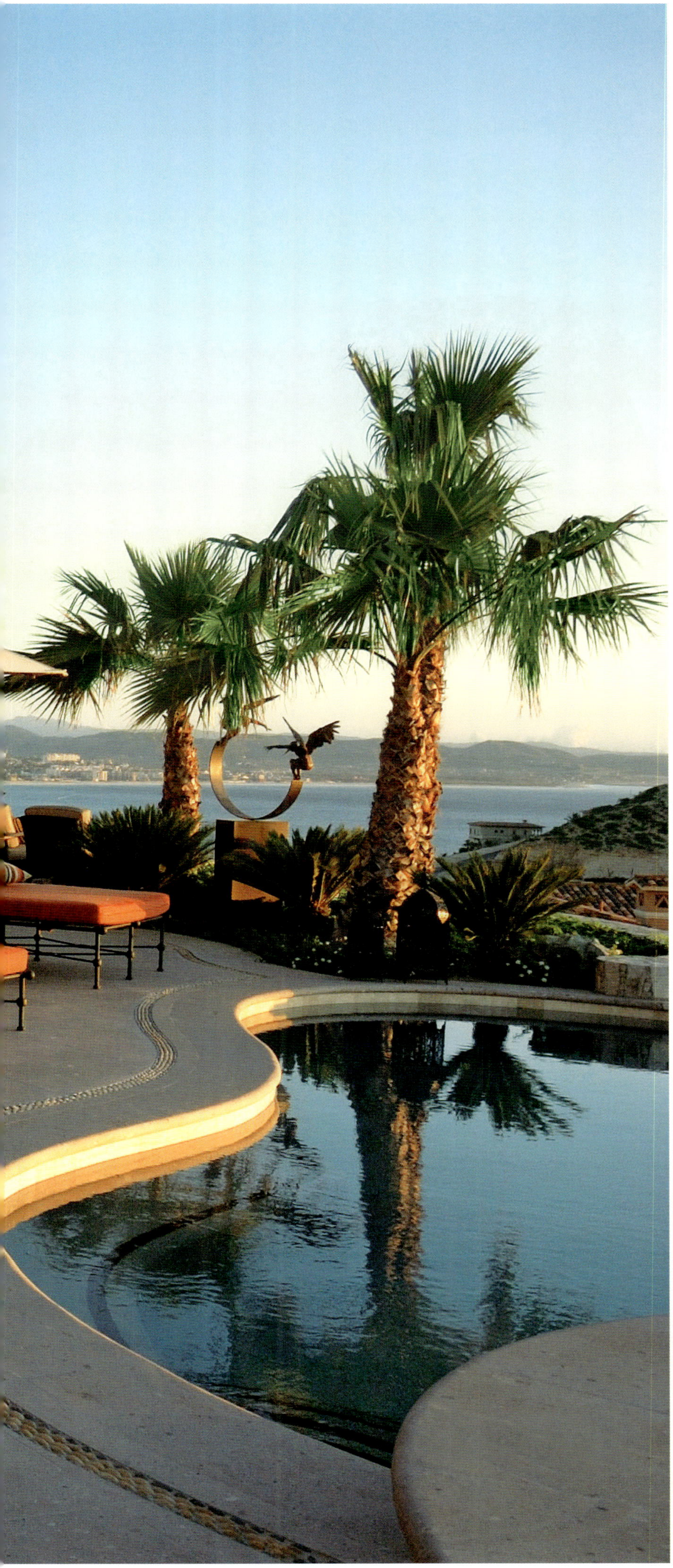

&lt;

Basking in the glory of a coveted location, this private hilltop sanctuary is a dream come true.

Himmlische Aussichten: Die Lage dieses exklusiven Hideaways ist kaum zu überbieten.

Tomar el sol en este santuario privado que corona la colina es un sueño hecho realidad.

The region's mile-long white sandy beaches are every beach lover's delight.

Die kilometerlangen, weißen Sandstrände begeistern nicht nur Sonnenanbeter.

Las playas de arenas blancas de una milla de largo hacen las delicias de los fans de la playa.

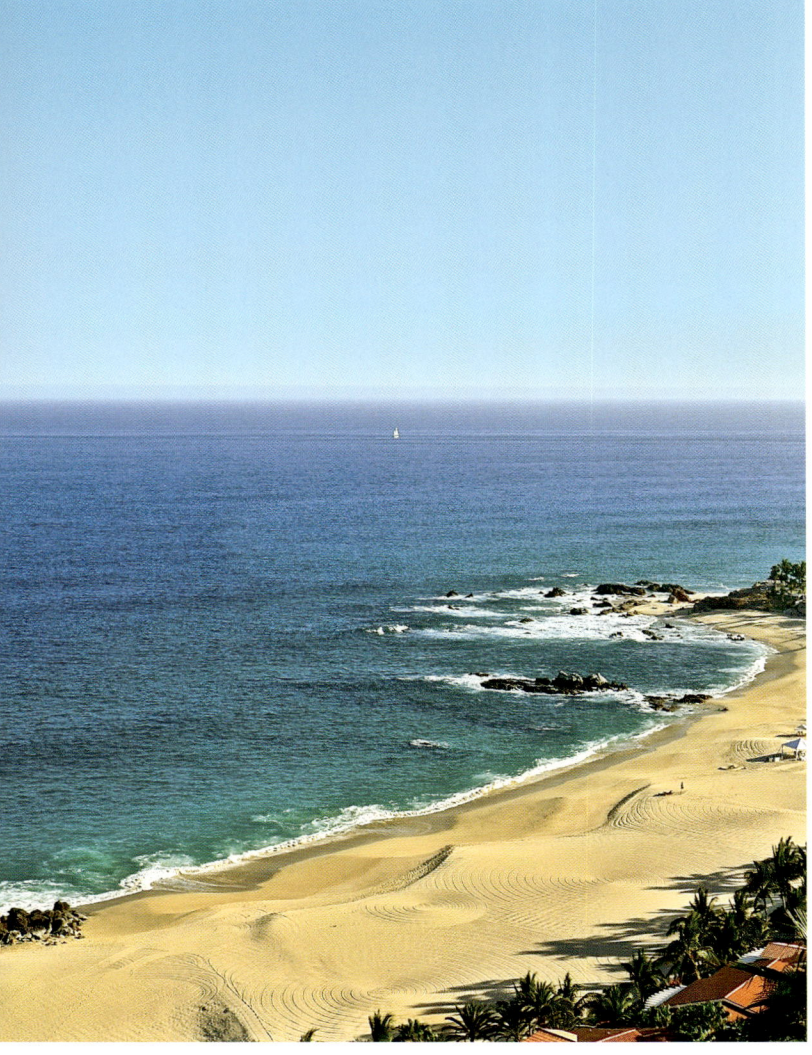

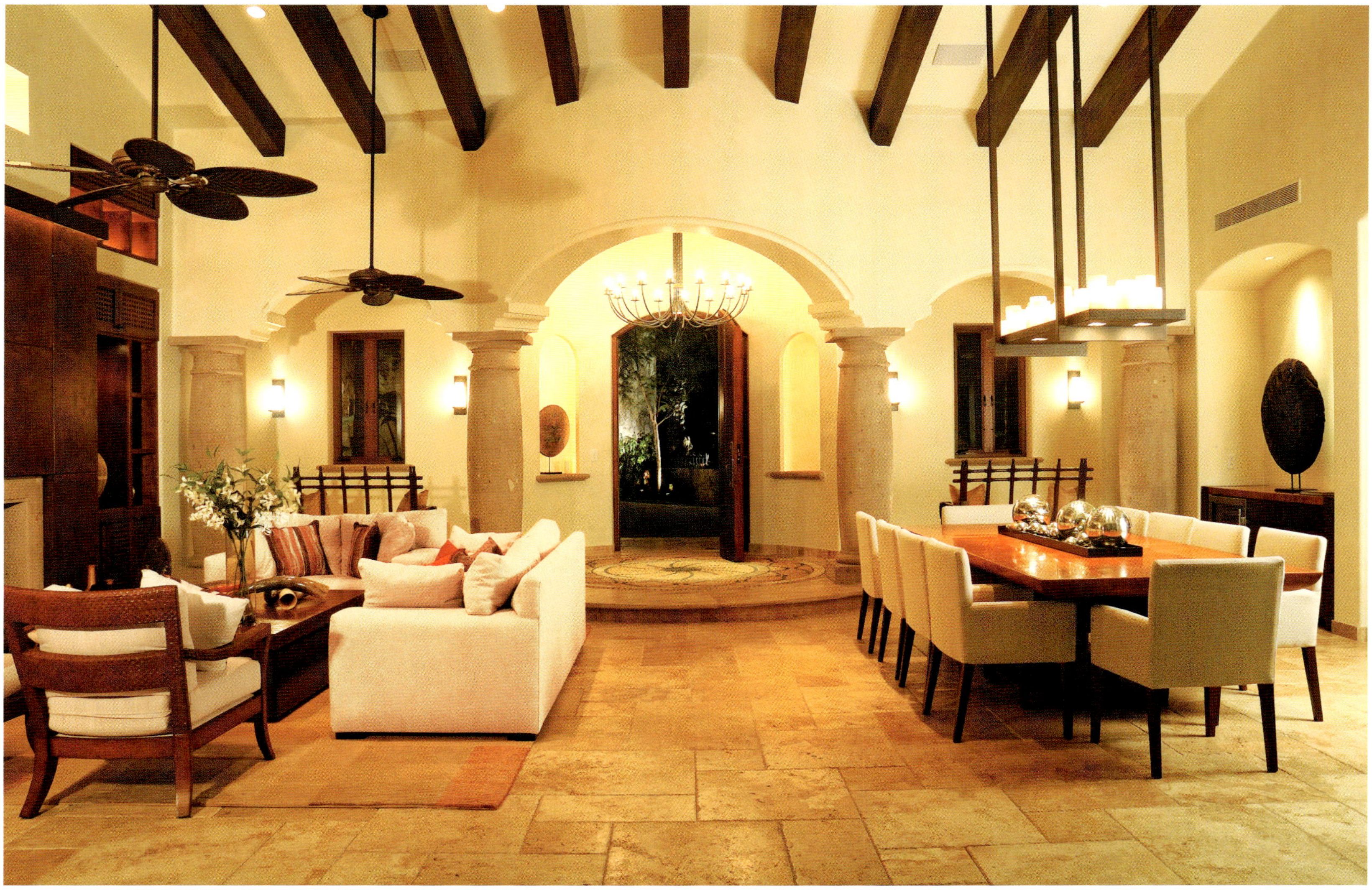

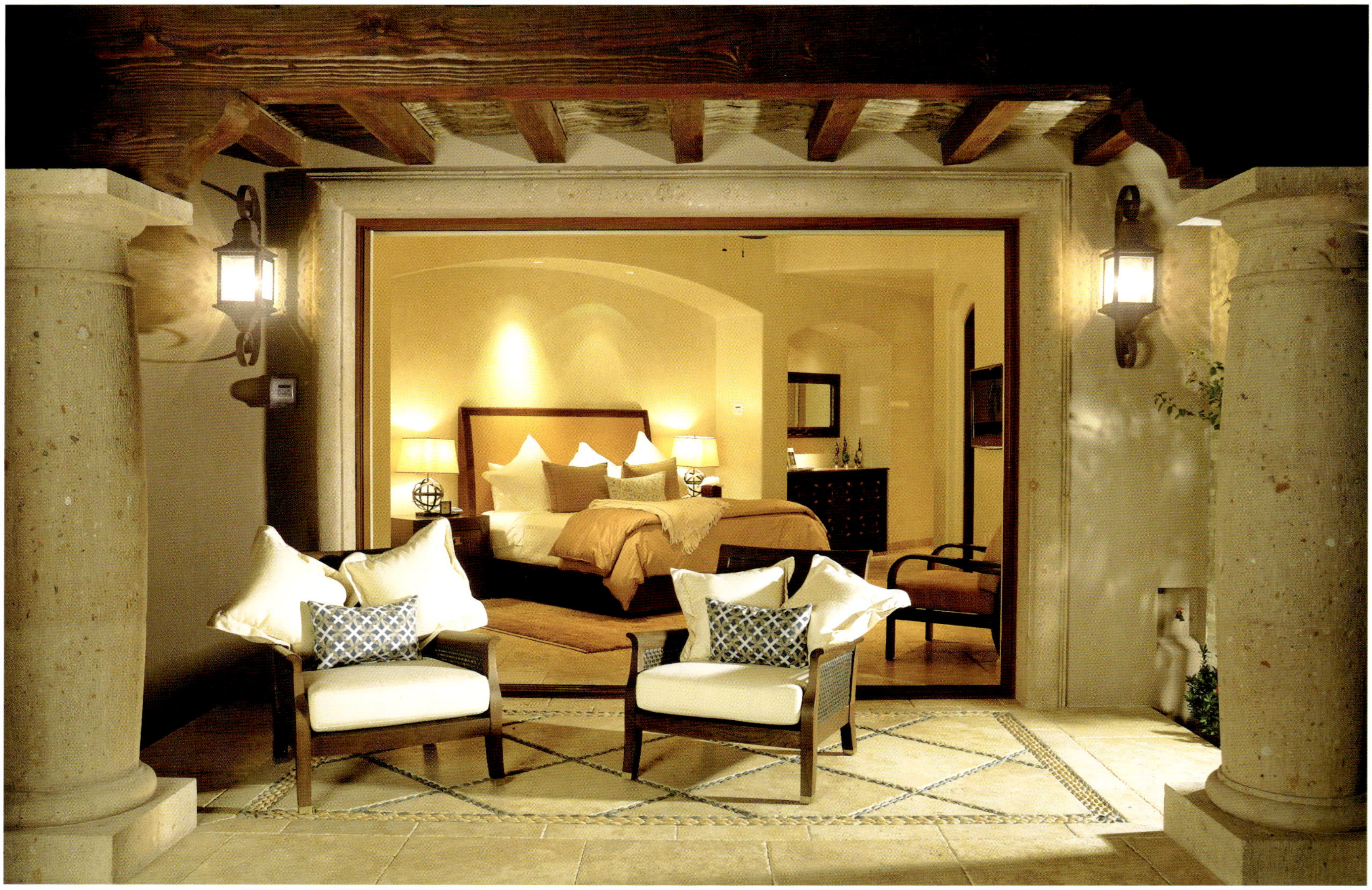

<

Gracious interiors: finest marble floors and
high-vaulted ceilings with wooden beams.

Wohnliche Eleganz: Edle Marmorböden treffen
auf gewölbte Decken mit Holzbalken.

Interiores refinados: suelos de mármol y
altas bóvedas con vigas vistas de madera.

The heated infinity pool, Jacuzzi and wet bar
are located high above the Sea of Cortez.

Hoch oben über dem Meer von Cortez: der
beheizte Infinity Pool mit Jacuzzi und Pool Bar.

Piscina climatizada, Jacuzzi y bar son un oasis
en alto sobre el nivel del mar de Cortés.

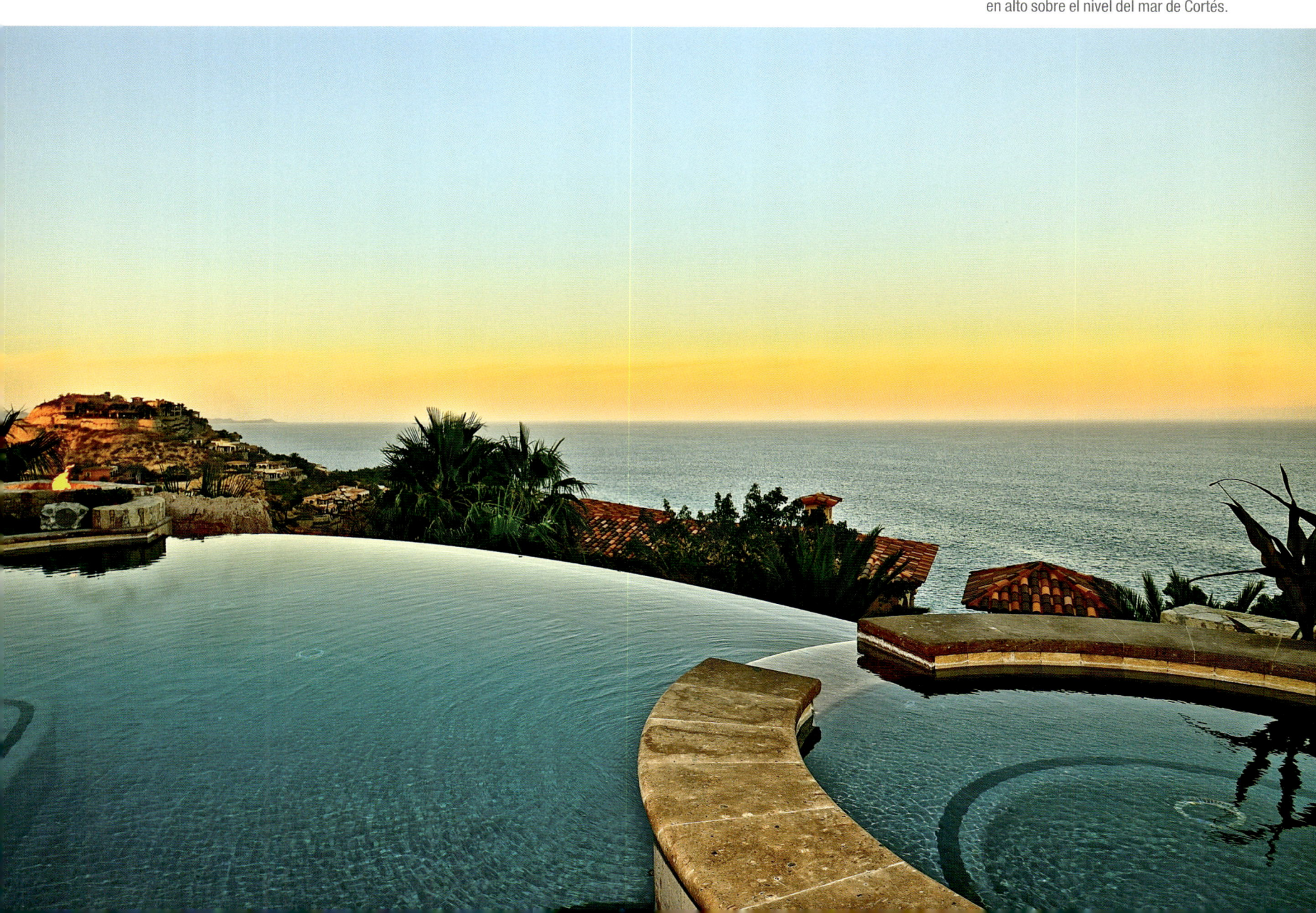

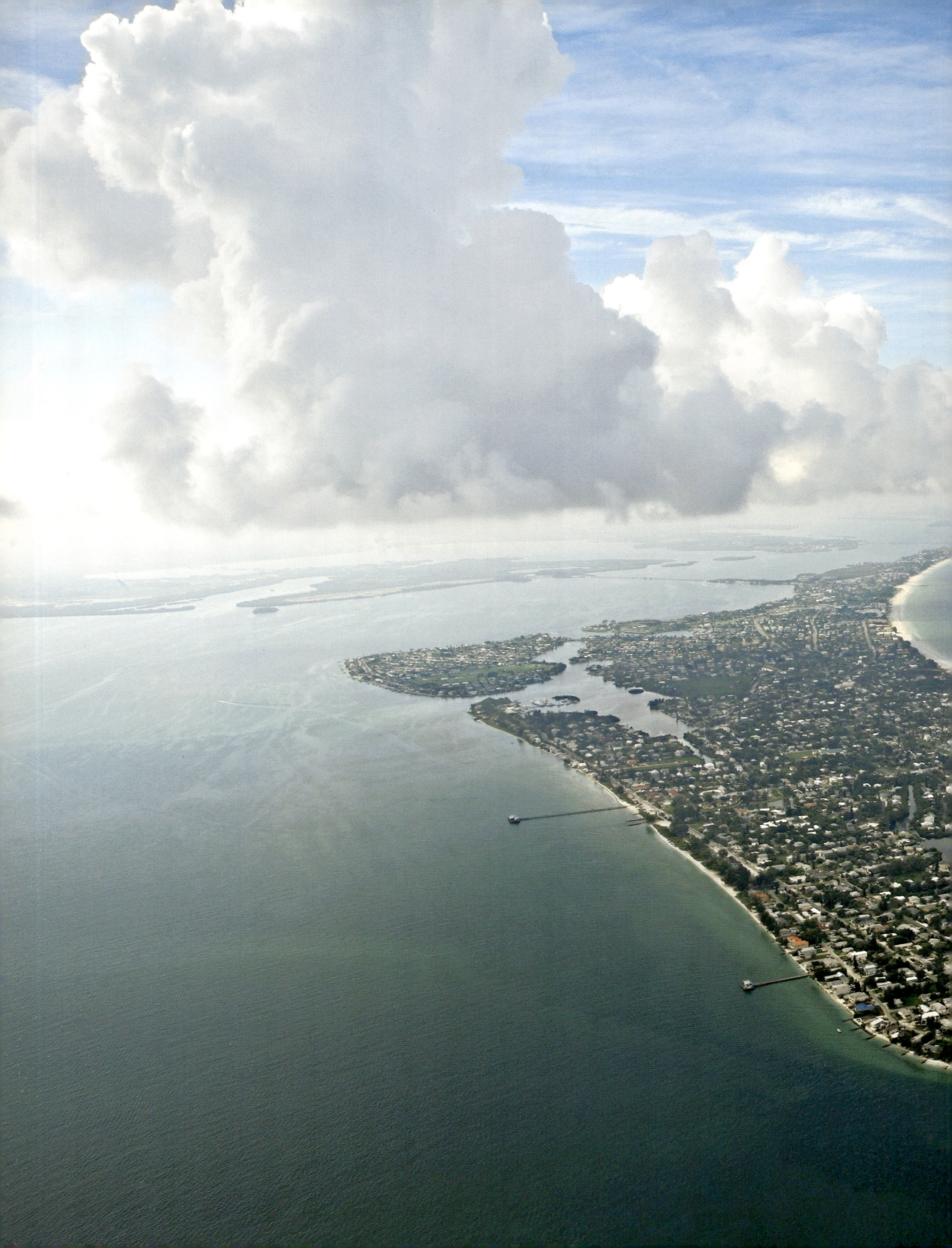

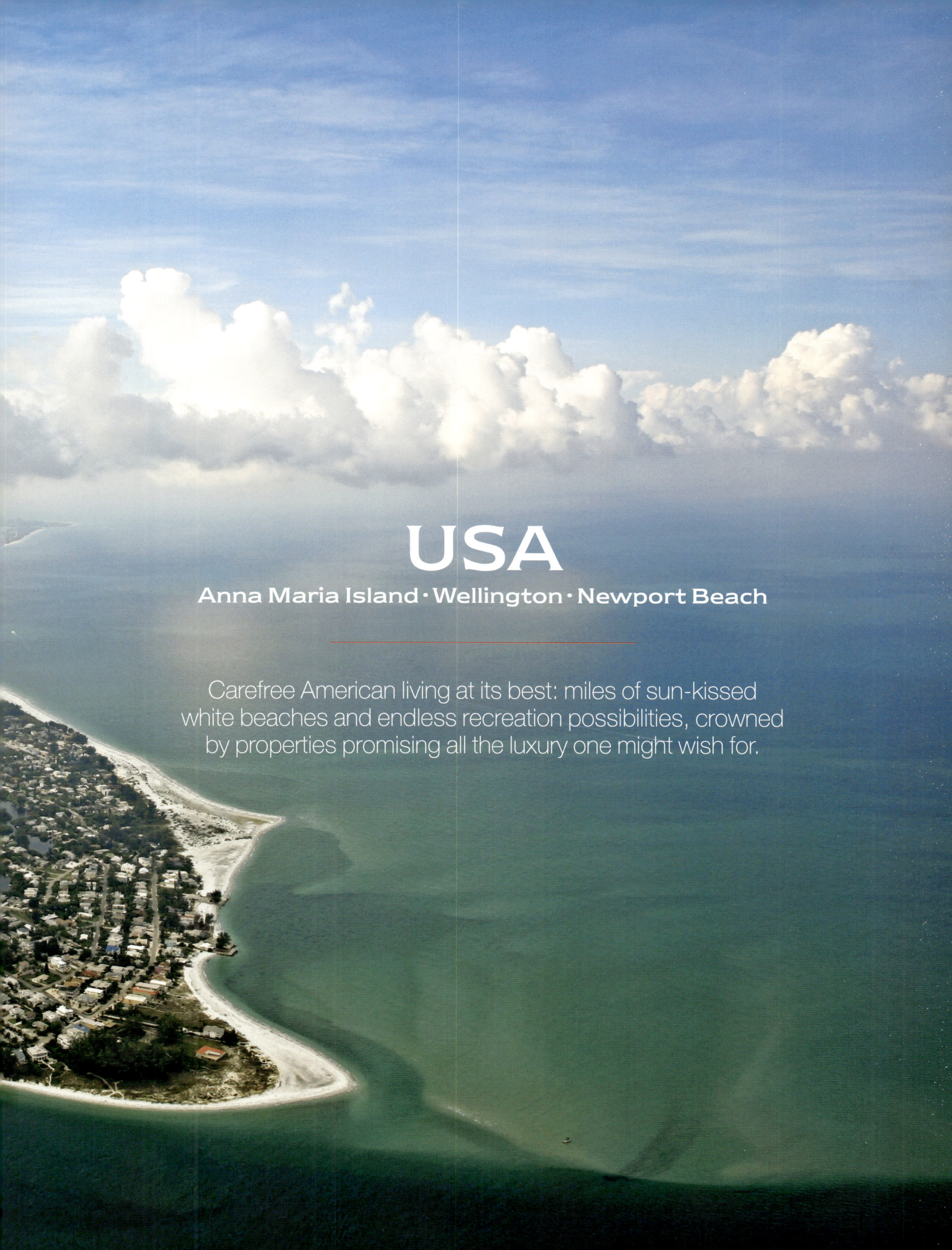

# USA

**Anna Maria Island · Wellington · Newport Beach**

Carefree American living at its best: miles of sun-kissed
white beaches and endless recreation possibilities, crowned
by properties promising all the luxury one might wish for.

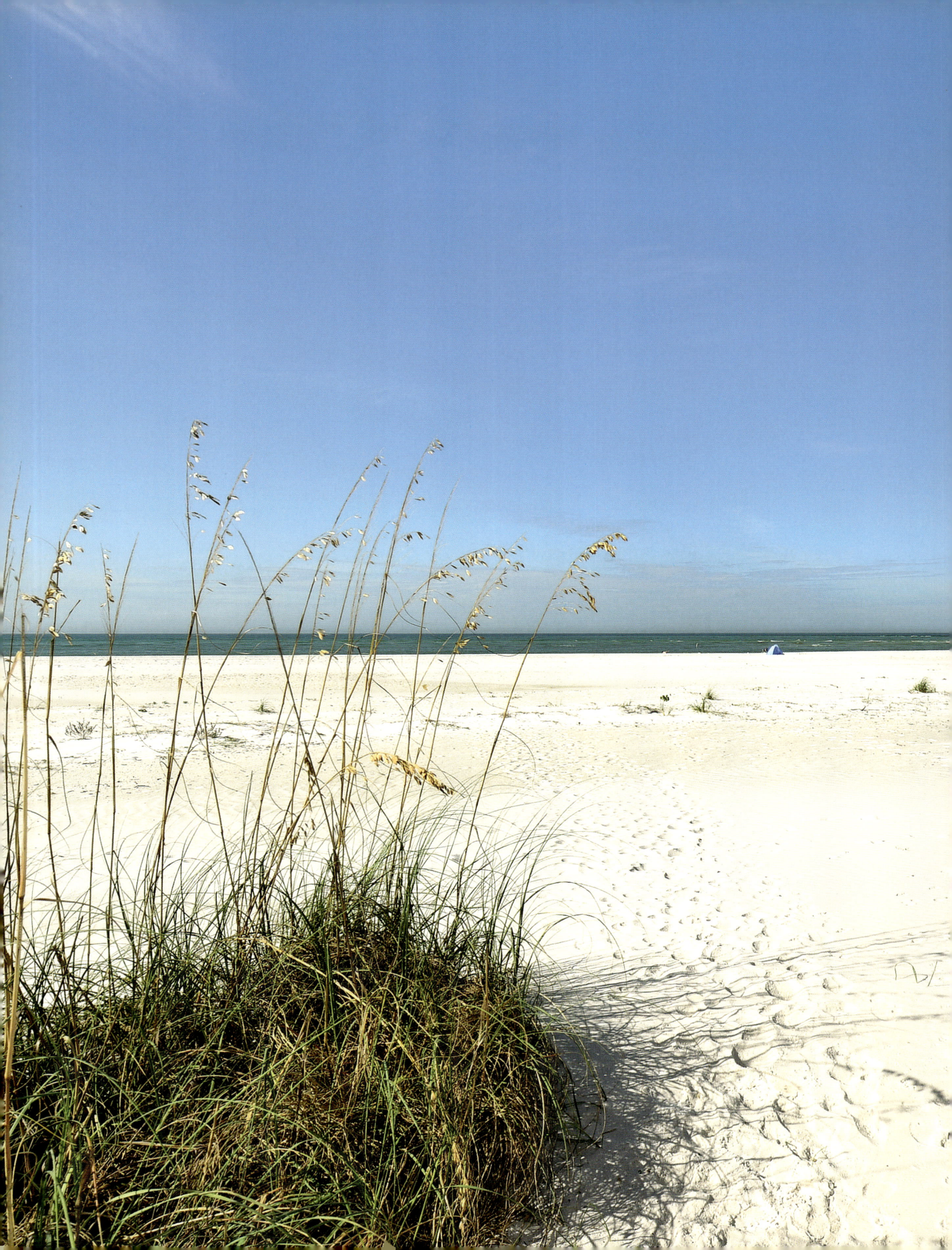

# Florida Island Escape

Nestled on the shores of the Gulf of Mexico, this seaside retreat on Anna Maria Island provides stunning views, charming comfort and gracious interiors.

WITH ITS LONG white sandy beaches, abundant wildlife and extremely mild year-round climate, Anna Maria Island is the perfect destination just south of Tampa for those in search of an idyllic holiday. Enjoying views of the Gulf of Mexico's crystal-blue waters, this spacious beachfront villa has a distinctive "Old Florida" feel and could easily be one of the loveliest homes on the island. With its upscale furnishings and decor, every moment spent in "Villa Marisol" is bound to be filled with joy. Upon entry, the visitor is welcomed by a fountain-graced garden and a patio. The inviting open-plan living room features an exquisitely appointed kitchen and an adjacent dining area with panoramic vistas of the gulf. A beauty to behold is the romantic master bedroom that has a sitting area with a fireplace, a private balcony and a large bathroom with a sauna. Three further lovingly furnished bedrooms provide abundant space for accommodating friends and family in a comfortably stylish manner. This is a true holiday jewel in the sunny state of Florida!

MIT ENDLOS LANGEN weißen Stränden, einer artenreichen Tierwelt und dem ganzjährig milden Klima ist Anna Maria Island südlich von Tampa die ideale Destination für idyllische Ferien in ursprünglicher Natur. Neben der Traumaussicht auf den kristallblauen Golf von Mexiko fasziniert die „Villa Marisol" vor allem durch ihr spezielles „Old-Florida-Feeling", was sie zu einer der schönsten Immobilien der Insel macht. Gleich beim Betreten des Grundstücks wird man von dem einladenden Garten mit Springbrunnen und einem hübschen Patio begrüßt. Von hier aus gelangt man in den offenen Wohnbereich, zu dem auch eine voll ausgestattete Küche und ein einladender Essbereich gehören. Das romantische Hauptschlafzimmer verfügt über eine Sitzecke mit Kamin, einen Balkon und ein großes Bad mit Sauna. Mit drei weiteren liebevoll eingerichteten Zimmern bietet die Villa auch für die Unterbringung von Freunden und Verwandten genügend Platz – perfekt, um die Auszeit vom Alltag im Sonnenstaat Florida gemeinsam mit seinen Lieben zu genießen!

CON INFINITAS playas de arena blanca, abundante vida silvestre y clima templado todo el año, Anna Maria Island es el destino ideal, justo al sur de Tampa, para quienes van en busca de unas vacaciones idílicas. Las impresionantes vistas a las cristalinas aguas azules del golfo de México hacen de esta espaciosa villa frente al mar y su distintivo toque *Old Florida* uno de los hogares con más encanto de la isla. Y con el mobiliario y la decoración de lujo, cada momento pasado en Villa Marisol viene cargado de alegría. Nada más entrar, el patio y el jardín con su fuente cantarina dan la bienvenida. La atractiva zona de estar de plano abierto luce también la cocina decorada exquisitamente y el comedor adyacente; las vistas panorámicas al golfo invaden cada flanco. El romántico dormitorio principal dispone de un gran cuarto de baño con sauna, sala de estar con chimenea y de su propio balcón. Tres dormitorios más, amorosamente decorados, proporcionan mucho espacio para alojar a la familia y los amigos de manera elegante y confortable en esta joya de vacaciones en la soleada Florida.

USA, ANNA MARIA ISLAND **RENTAL PRICE/WEEK** USD 5,000 **INTERIOR APPROX.** 3,684 ft² **NO. OF BEDROOMS** 4
**E&V ID** E-001535 **CONTACT** HOLMES BEACH (US), TAG REAL ESTATE VENTURES, INC.,
LICENCE PARTNER OF ENGEL & VÖLKERS FLORIDA RESIDENTIAL, LLC. **TEL.** +1 941 704 21 68
**E-MAIL** ANNAMARIAISLAND@EVUSA.COM

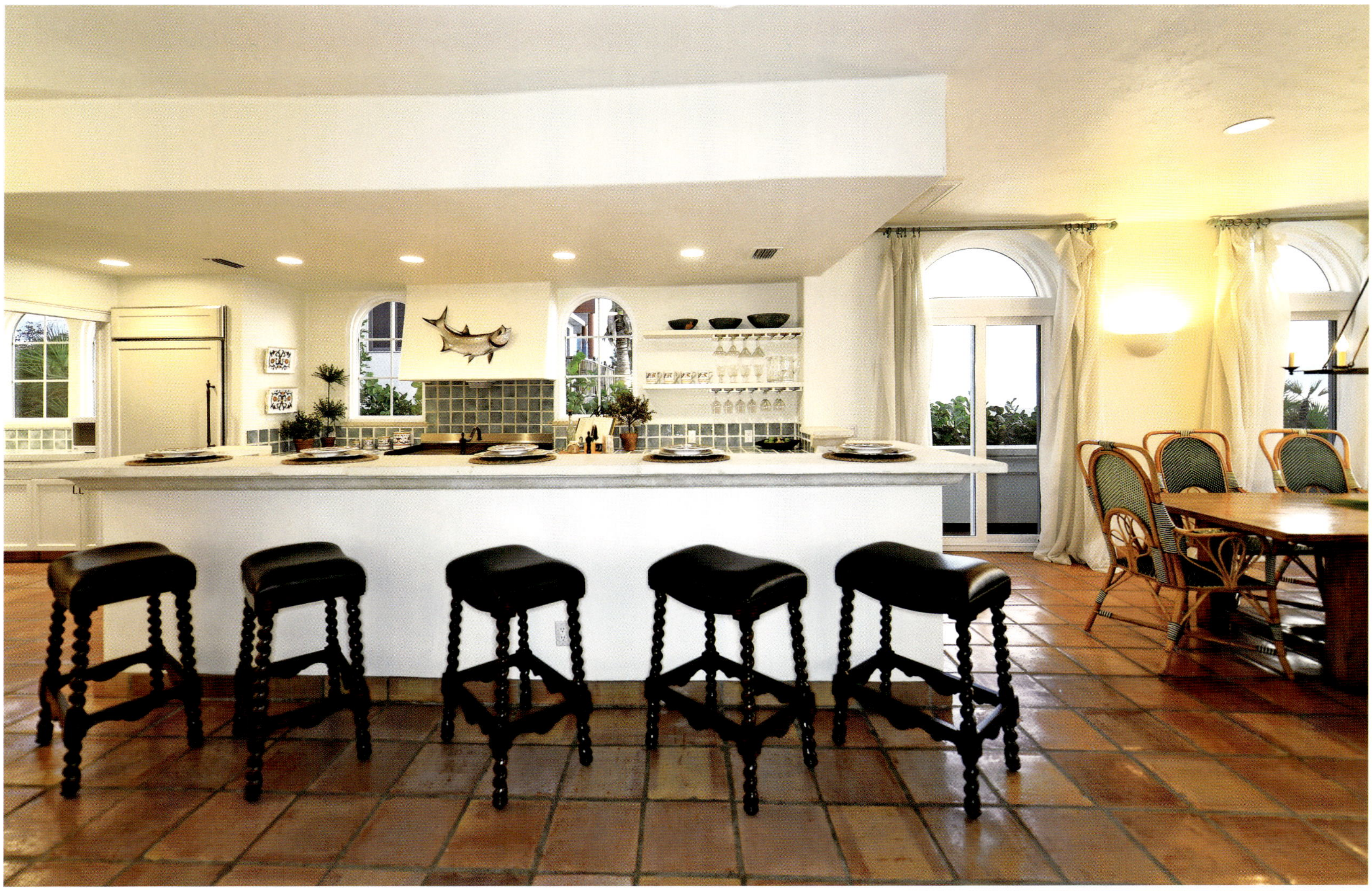

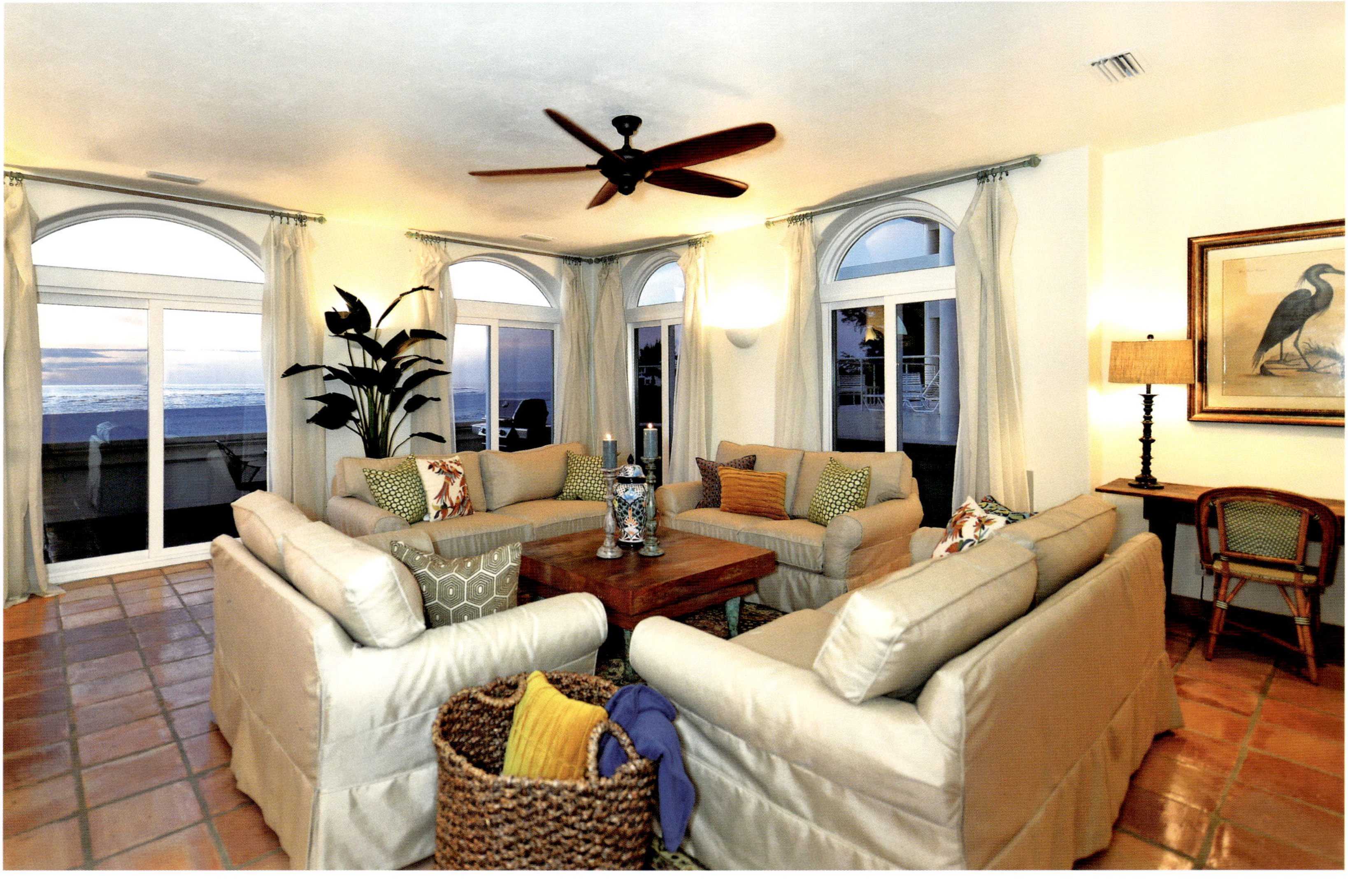

Enhanced by the glorious views, the villa's relaxed interiors are inviting and refreshing.

Das einladende Interieur wird gekrönt von der Aussicht auf die reizvolle Umgebung.

Tan acogedor como refrescante, el interior de la villa queda realzado con las panorámicas.

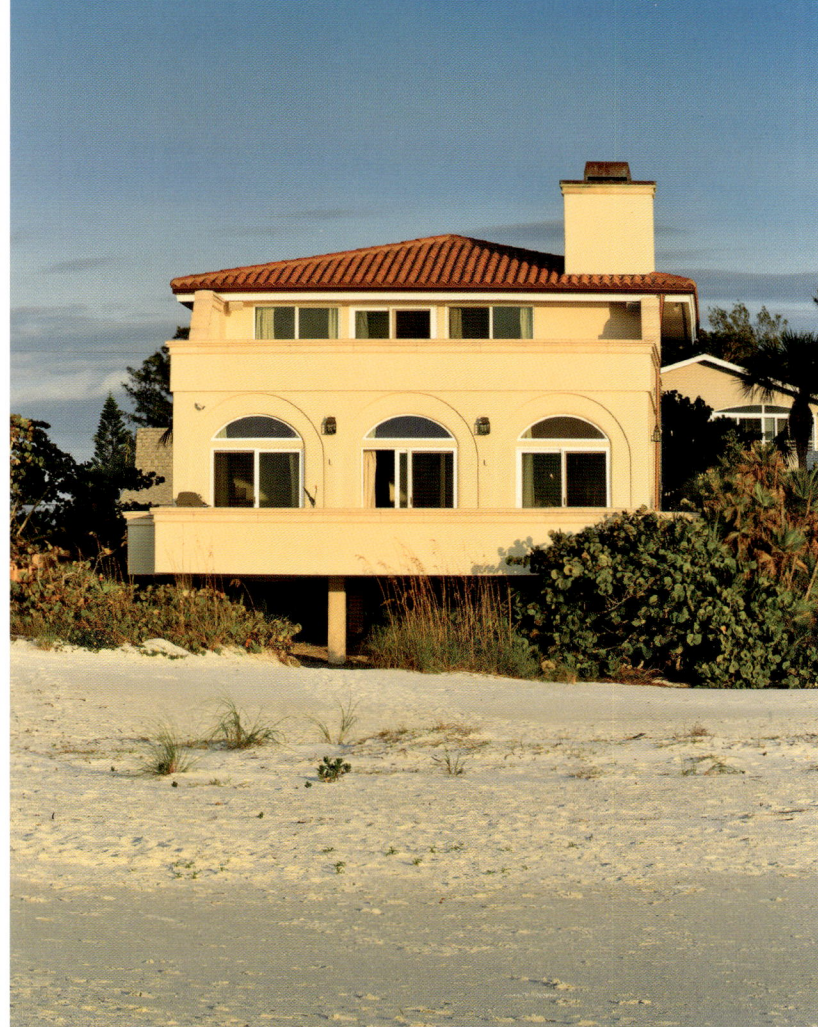

Just steps from the sea: this holiday hideaway is blessed with an unrivalled location.

Nur wenige Schritte zum Meer: Diese Villa überzeugt durch ihre konkurrenzlose Lage.

A pocos pasos del mar: un escondite de vacaciones en una ubicación inmejorable.

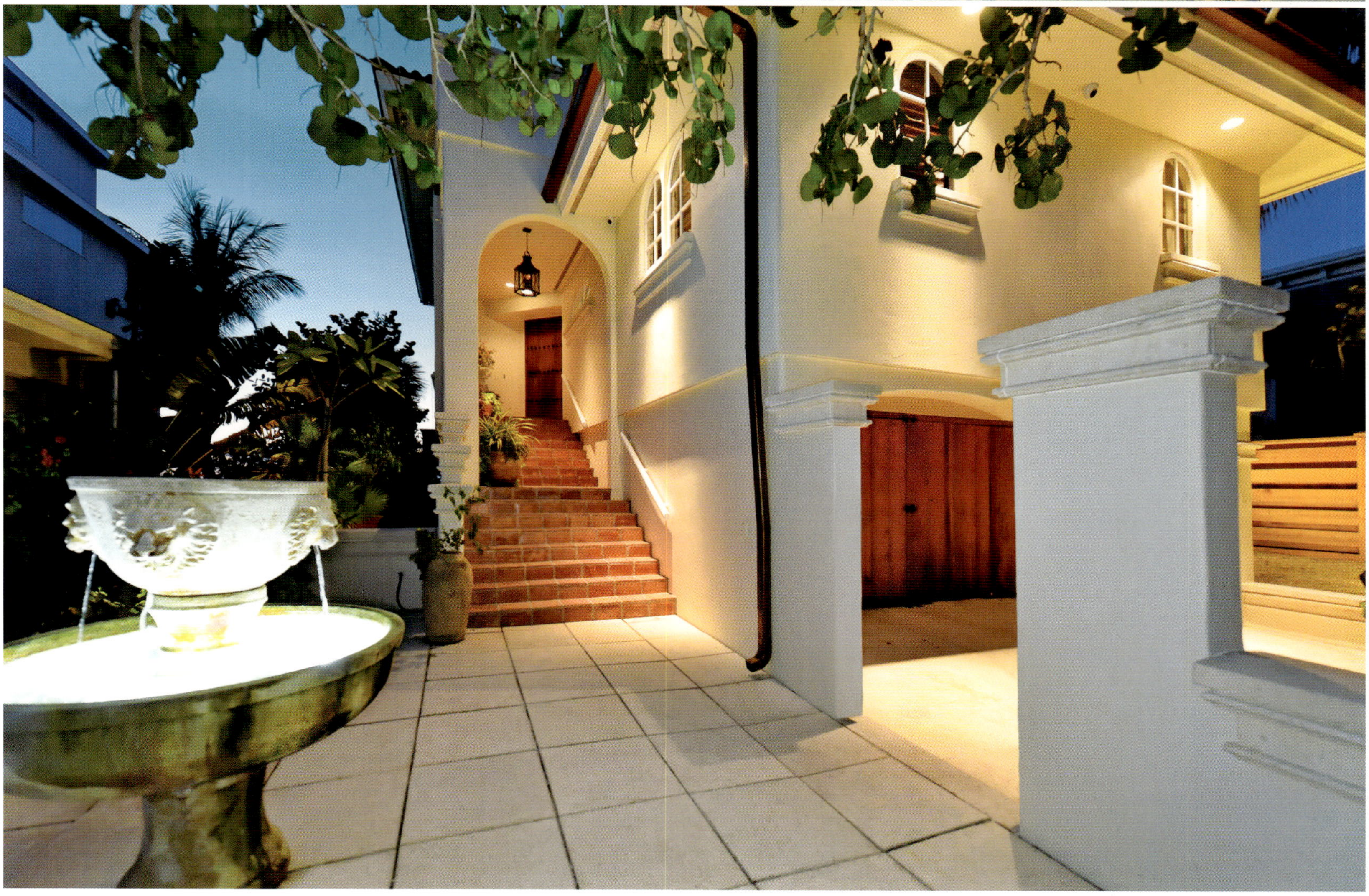

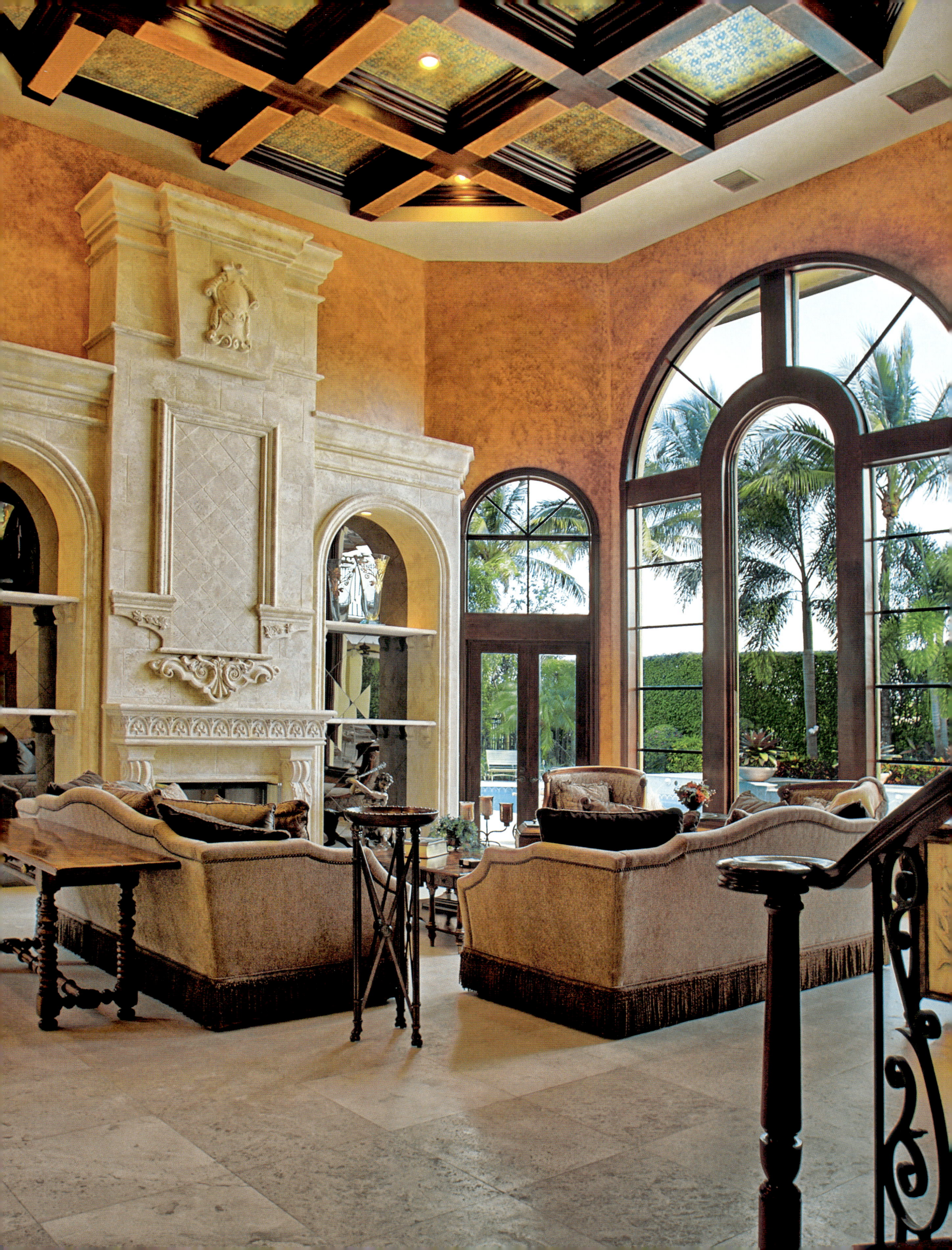

# Golfers' Delight

This splendid estate is the perfect venue to enjoy
a relaxing lifestyle in sunny South Florida – replete with
generous living space and golf course vistas.

SET IN A QUIET cul-de-sac in the prestigious Palm Beach Polo and Country Club in Wellington, Florida, this elegant two-storey home features a stately interior design and beautiful outdoor areas. Newly renovated, the property is striking with its keen sense of detail and luxury – seen, for example, in the opulent interiors or the elaborate designs adorning the ceilings. The dignified villa comprises a glorious master suite on the ground floor and five additional bedrooms. Furthermore, there are seven full bathrooms and a spacious gourmet kitchen with state-of-the-art appliances, granite countertops and bar seating that opens to the living room. Balconies overlooking the pool area and the adjacent golf course are among the further highlights of this truly enchanting home. Whether when relaxing after a round of golf, entertaining friends by the poolside or simply enjoying the sunset with a cool drink, it will be easy to savour the day's finest moments on the premises of a masterpiece like this – and best of all, with gorgeous golf course views all around.

IN EINER RUHIGEN Straße innerhalb des prestigeträchtigen Palm Beach Polo und Country Clubs in Wellington gelegen, verspricht dieses zweistöckige, frisch renovierte Villenanwesen entspannten Lifestyle mit mondäner Note. Diese spiegelt sich vor allem in der herrschaftlichen Innenausstattung wider: So fällt einem beim Betreten der Räumlichkeiten sofort der Sinn für prachtvolle Details ins Auge – was sich unter anderem in der aufwändigen Deckengestaltung zeigt. Die Villa verfügt über ein Haupt- und fünf weitere Schlafzimmer sowie sieben Bäder, ergänzt von einer modernen Einbauküche mit Granitoberflächen und State-of-the-Art-Geräten, die in den repräsentativen Wohnbereich übergeht. Zu den weiteren Highlights gehören die Balkone mit Blick auf den Poolbereich und den benachbarten Golfplatz. Ob beim Relaxen mit Freunden oder bei einem Sundowner nach einer Runde Golf: Dieses architektonische Meisterwerk bietet unzählige Gelegenheiten und Plätze, um die schönsten Momente des Tages voll auszukosten – Golf-Panorama inklusive.

EN UNA TRANQUILA calle sin salida del prestigioso Palm Beach Polo & Country Club de Wellington, Florida, la elegante residencia de dos pisos cuenta con un diseño interior señorial y preciosas áreas al aire libre. Recientemente renovada, la mansión sorprende con su marcado sentido del detalle y del lujo, como denotan los elaborados diseños que adornan los techos de las salas o la opulencia del mobiliario. La fabulosa villa cuenta con una gran *suite* principal en la planta baja y otros cinco dormitorios. Además, hay siete cuartos de baño completos y una amplia cocina *gourmet* con electrodomésticos de última generación, encimeras de granito y una tipo bar, hacia la sala de estar. Los balcones con vistas al *spa* y al campo de golf adyacente se cuentan entre los diversos hitos de esta encantadora casa. Bien después de la partida con los amigos en la piscina o tomando algo fresco mientras se contempla la puesta de sol, saborear los mejores momentos del día en una obra maestra arquitectónica como esta es una bendición... envuelta en magníficas panorámicas al campo de golf.

USA, WELLINGTON **PURCHASE PRICE** USD 4.75 MILL. **INTERIOR APPROX.** 9,017 ft² **NO. OF BEDROOMS** 6
**LAND APPROX.** 24,393 ft² **E&V ID** E-0014JJ **CONTACT** WELLINGTON (US), CARR SOLLAK REALTY, LLC,
LICENCE PARTNER OF ENGEL & VÖLKERS FLORIDA RESIDENTIAL, LLC **TEL.** +1 561 791 22 20
**E-MAIL** WELLINGTON@EVUSA.COM

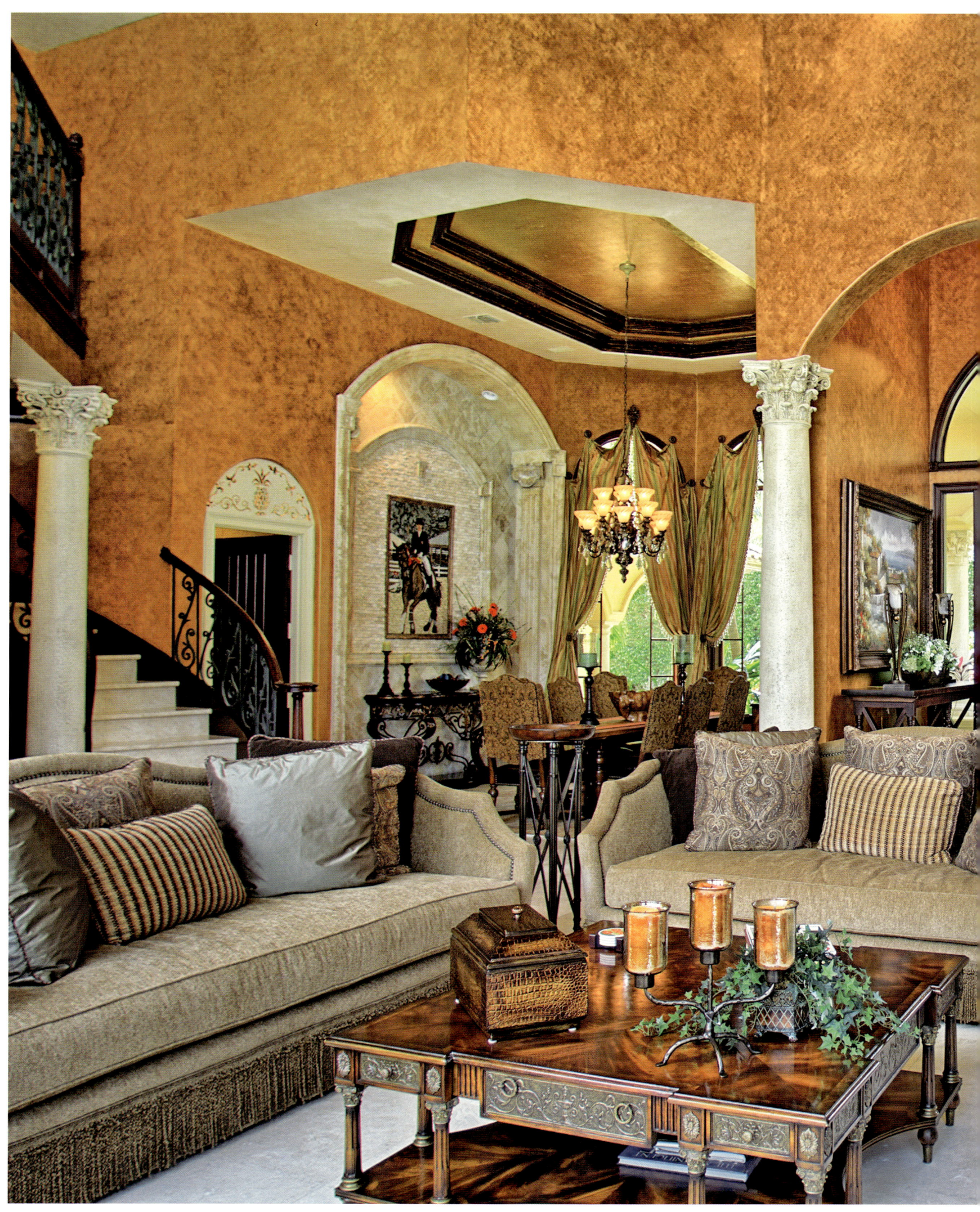

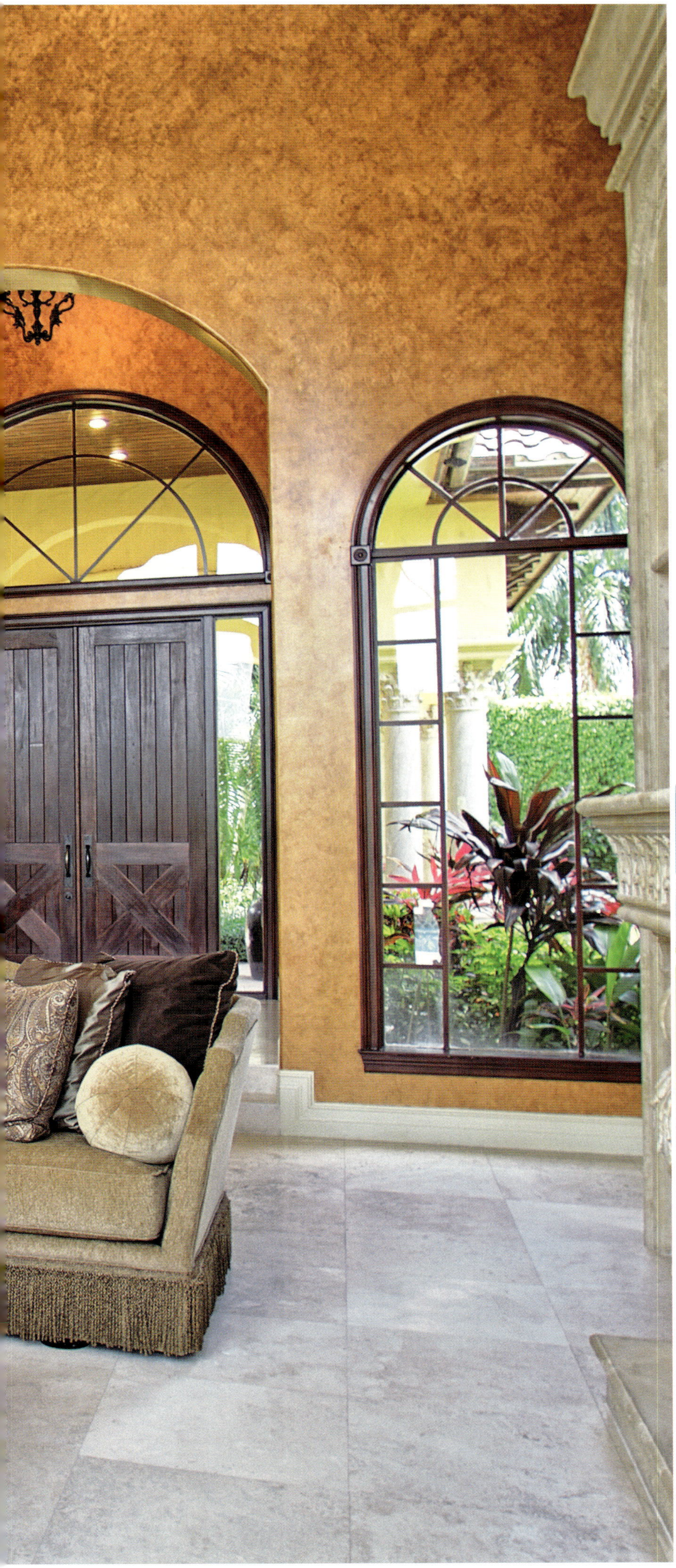

&lt;

Muted colours provide a high-class,
country-style flair to the living areas.

Die stilvolle Opulenz in gedämpften Farben
vermittelt mondänes Country-Flair.

Los colores mitigados otorgan un ambiente
rústico de alto nivel a las zonas de día.

The spacious pool is the perfect place to
entertain guests and enjoy the Florida sun.

Der elegant angelegte Pool lädt zum
Sonnenbaden und Entspannen ein.

El sitio ideal donde entretener a los invitados y
disfrutar del sol de Florida: la gran piscina.

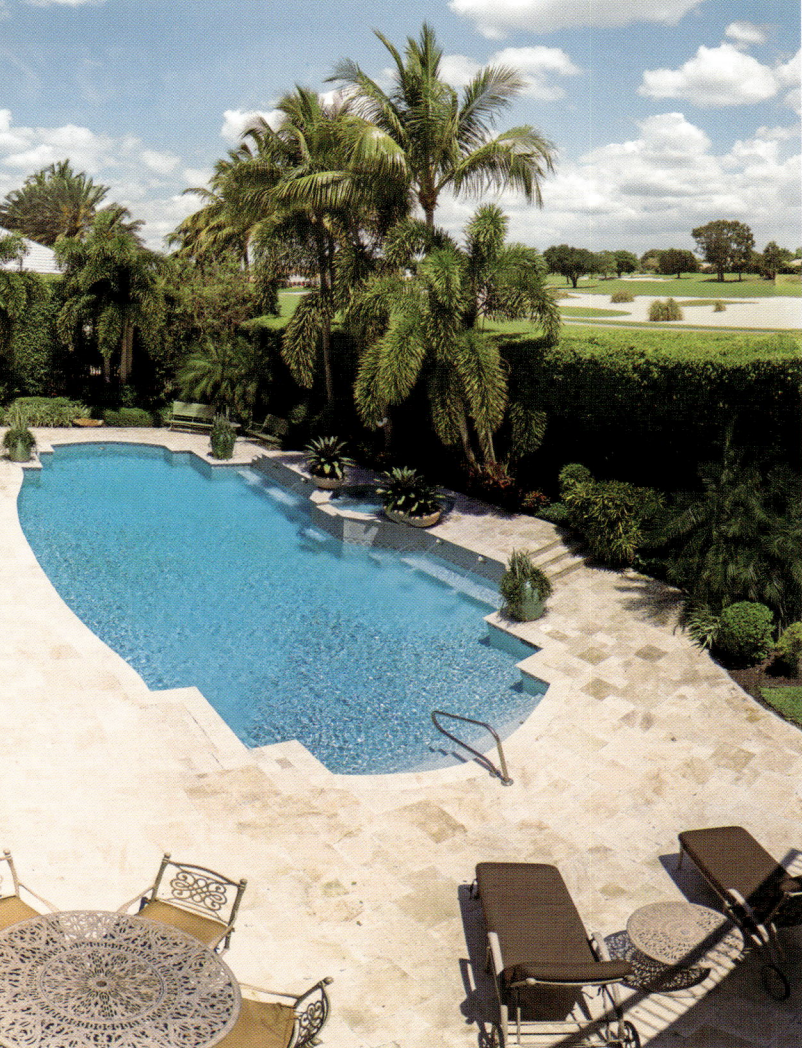

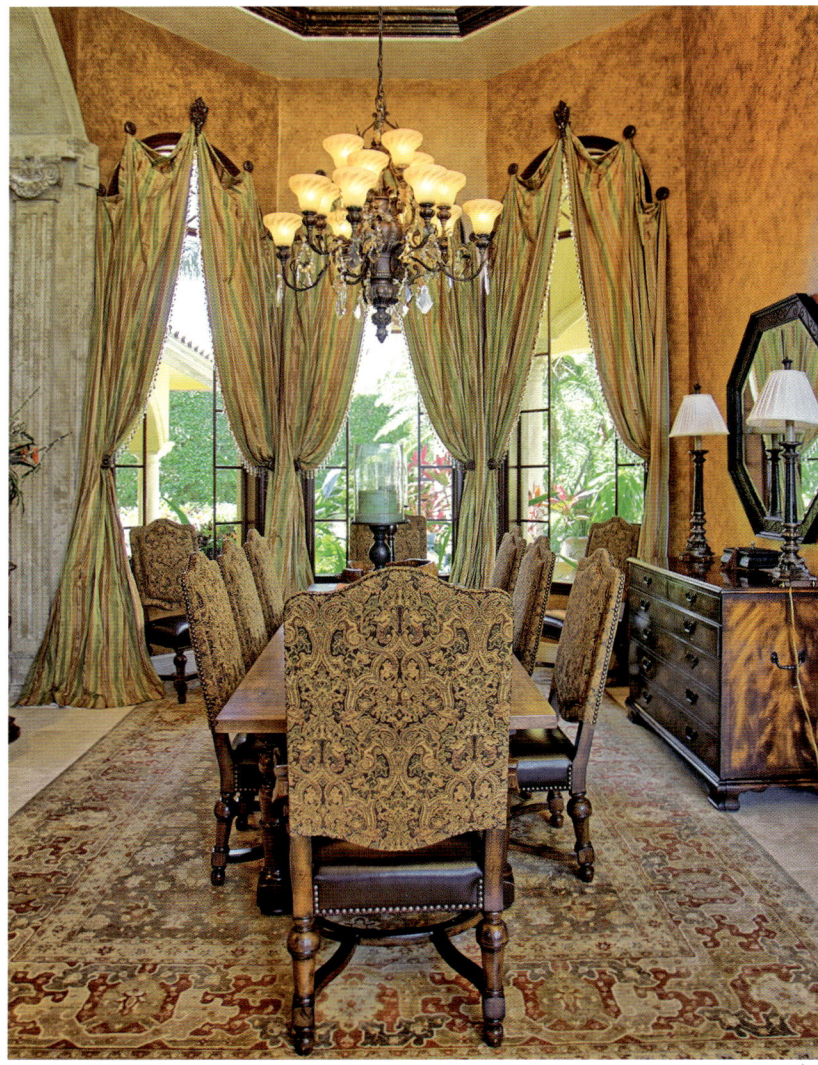

Ample space and luxurious design contribute
to the mansion's distinguished atmosphere.

Gediegen und von eleganter Noblesse:
die großzügigen Räumlichkeiten der Villa.

Espacios amplios y diseño lujoso contribuyen
al ambiente distinguido de la mansión.

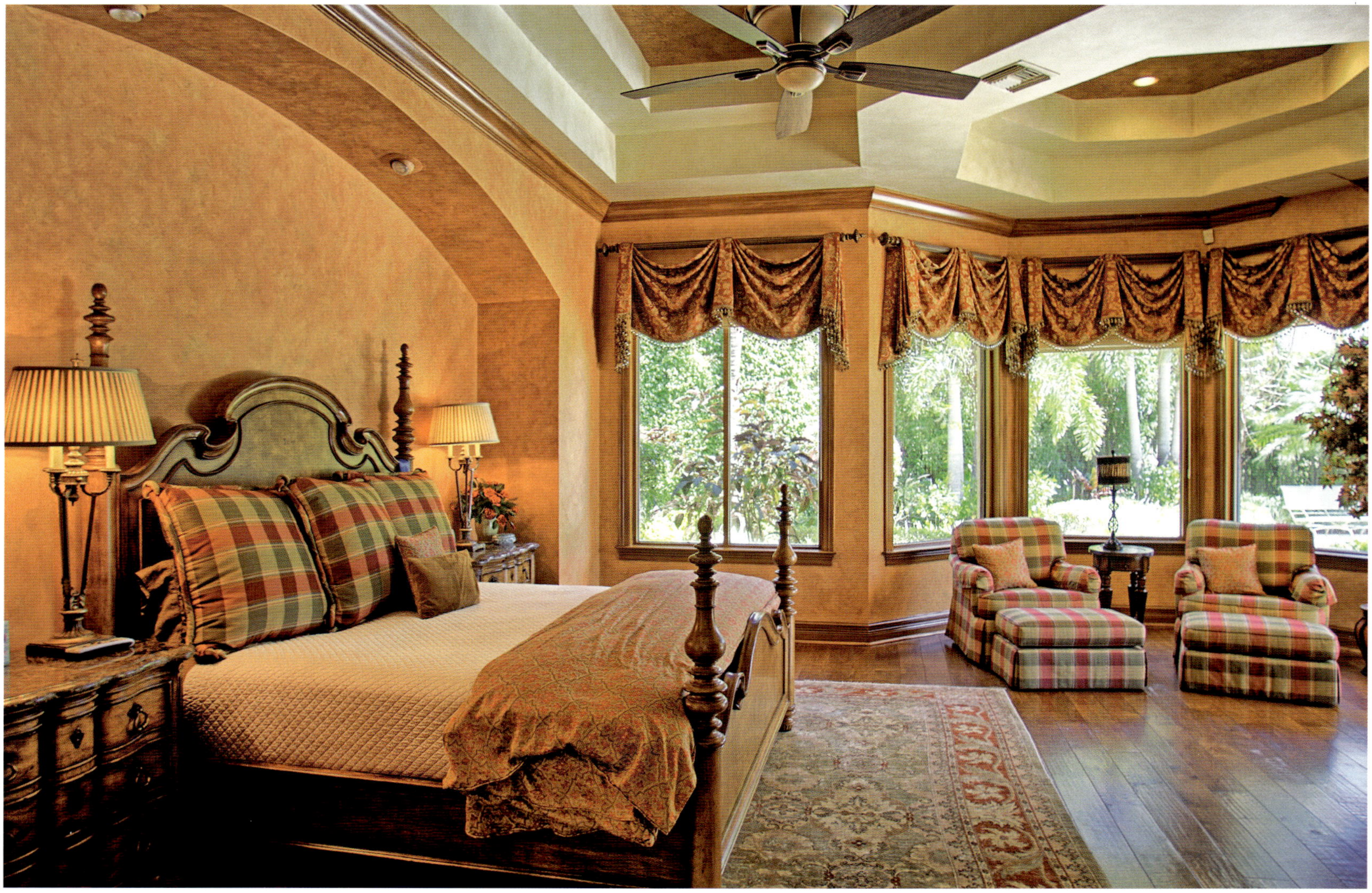

Verdant gardens and shady places ensure
delightful outdoor living at its best.

Eine grüne Oase mit vielen schattigen
Plätzen: der paradiesische Gartenbereich.

Verdes jardines y muchos lugares sombrea-
dos garantizan lo mejor de la vida al aire libre.

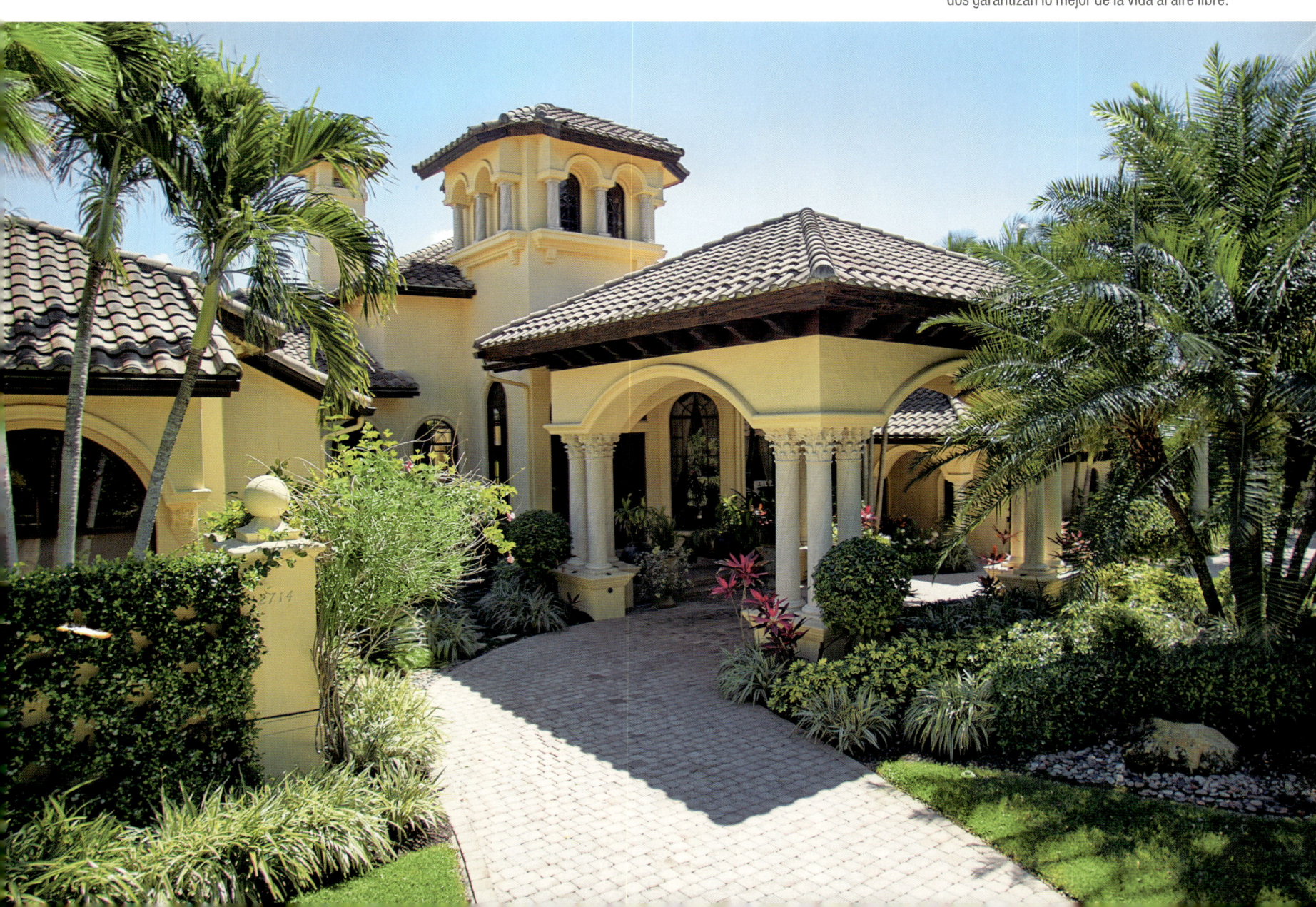

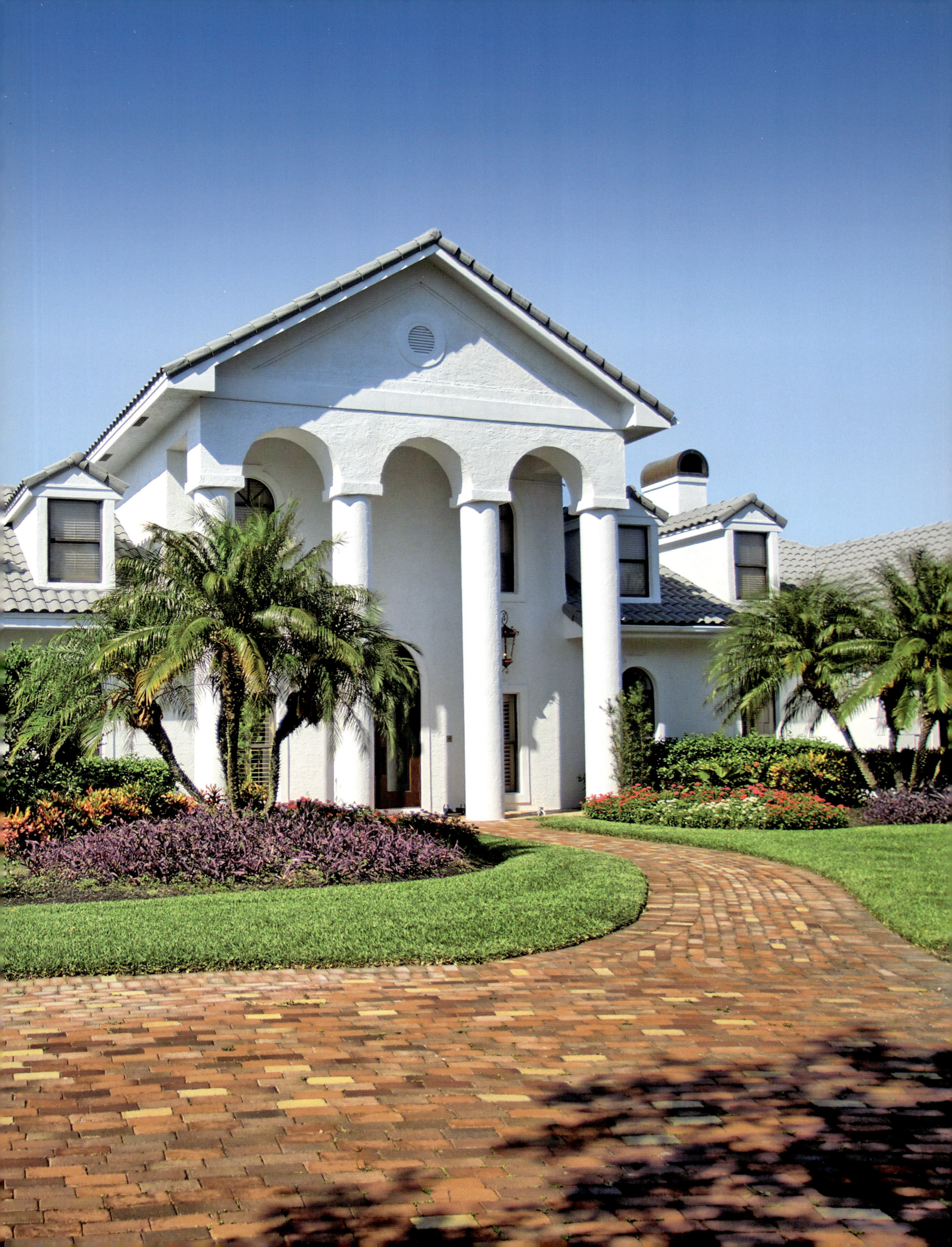

# Horse Lovers' Estate

Extensive grounds, elegant design and fine equestrian facilities – this noble villa comprises some truly remarkable features that will cheer the heart of any horse lover.

THE VILLAGE of Wellington, Florida, is world-famous for its equestrian community. This magnificent estate is situated in Wellington's most exclusive location within walking distance to Palm Beach International Equestrian Center. Set on a plot of 4.15 acres, the dignified home includes four bedroom suites, four bathrooms, a custom wood-panelled office and a large custom granite kitchen. What is immediately striking are the high ceilings and the many fine details such as the bespoke wall trims, cabinets and woodwork throughout. The generous exterior areas include covered porches, a loggia, an outdoor California kitchen with grill and a swimming pool plus Jacuzzi amidst lush landscaped gardens. Yet the sensational equestrian facilities are an undisputed highlight: the new sixteen-stall barn includes a four-bedroom grooms' quarter, a custom tack room and ample storage space, complete with an outdoor entertaining area, an upper-level viewing lounge with wrap-around porch, a large all-weather ring and numerous paddocks. This is a dream come true for connoisseur equestrians!

ALS ELDORADO des Reitsports hat sich Wellington in Florida weltweit einen Namen gemacht. In exklusiver Lage direkt im Herzen der Stadt befindet sich dieses Anwesen mit seinem rund 1,68 Hektar großen Grundstück. Nur wenige Gehminuten vom Palm Beach International Equestrian Center entfernt, verfügt die Villa über vier Schlafzimmer-Suiten, ein maßgefertigtes holzgetäfeltes Büro und eine Maßküche mit Granitoberfläche. Zu den besonderen Ausstattungsdetails gehören die hohen Decken mit stuckähnlichen Zierleisten und die komfortablen Schrankeinbauten. Die Außenbereiche glänzen mit überdachten Veranden, einer Loggia, einem Grillplatz sowie einem Gartenbereich mit Pool und Jacuzzi. Das unbestrittene Highlight stellen jedoch die Reitanlagen dar: Dazu gehören eine Scheune mit 16 Pferdeboxen, ein Vier-Zimmer-Schlafbereich für Stallburschen, eine Sattelkammer, umfassende Stauräume sowie großzügige Außenanlagen mit großer Zuschauertribüne, professionellem Allwetter-Reitrondell und zahlreichen Koppeln. Ein Traum für jeden Pferdeliebhaber!

LA LOCALIDAD de Wellington, Florida, es mundialmente famosa por su carácter ecuestre. Esta magnífica finca está situada en la zona más exclusiva de Wellington, a un paseo de distancia del Palm Beach International Equestrian Center. En un terreno de unas 1,68 hectáreas, la noble vivienda incluye cuatro dormitorios, cuatro baños, un despacho revestido en madera natural y la gran cocina de granito. Llaman la atención los techos altos y los muchos y refinados detalles artesanales como las molduras, armarios y ebanistería por doquier. Las zonas al aire libre incluyen porches, galería, cocina de California con parrilla y una lujosa piscina con Jacuzzi entre exuberantes jardines paisajísticos. Aún entre tanta maravilla, las instalaciones ecuestres destacan indiscutiblemente. El nuevo granero de dieciséis establos incluye un apartamento de cuatro habitaciones, cuarto de arreos y muchos trasteros, redondeado con un área exterior de ocio, sala audiovisual con porche alrededor, una gran pista cubierta y diversos potreros. Con todo, es un sueño hecho realidad para los *connoisseurs* de lo ecuestre.

USA, WELLINGTON **PURCHASE PRICE** USD 15 MILL. **INTERIOR APPROX.** 4,900 ft² **NO. OF BEDROOMS** 4
**LAND APPROX.** 180,000 ft² **E&V ID** E-0014PO **CONTACT** WELLINGTON (US), CARR SOLLAK REALTY, LLC,
LICENCE PARTNER OF ENGEL & VÖLKERS FLORIDA RESIDENTIAL, LLC. **TEL.** +1 561 791 22 20
**E-MAIL** WELLINGTON@EVUSA.COM

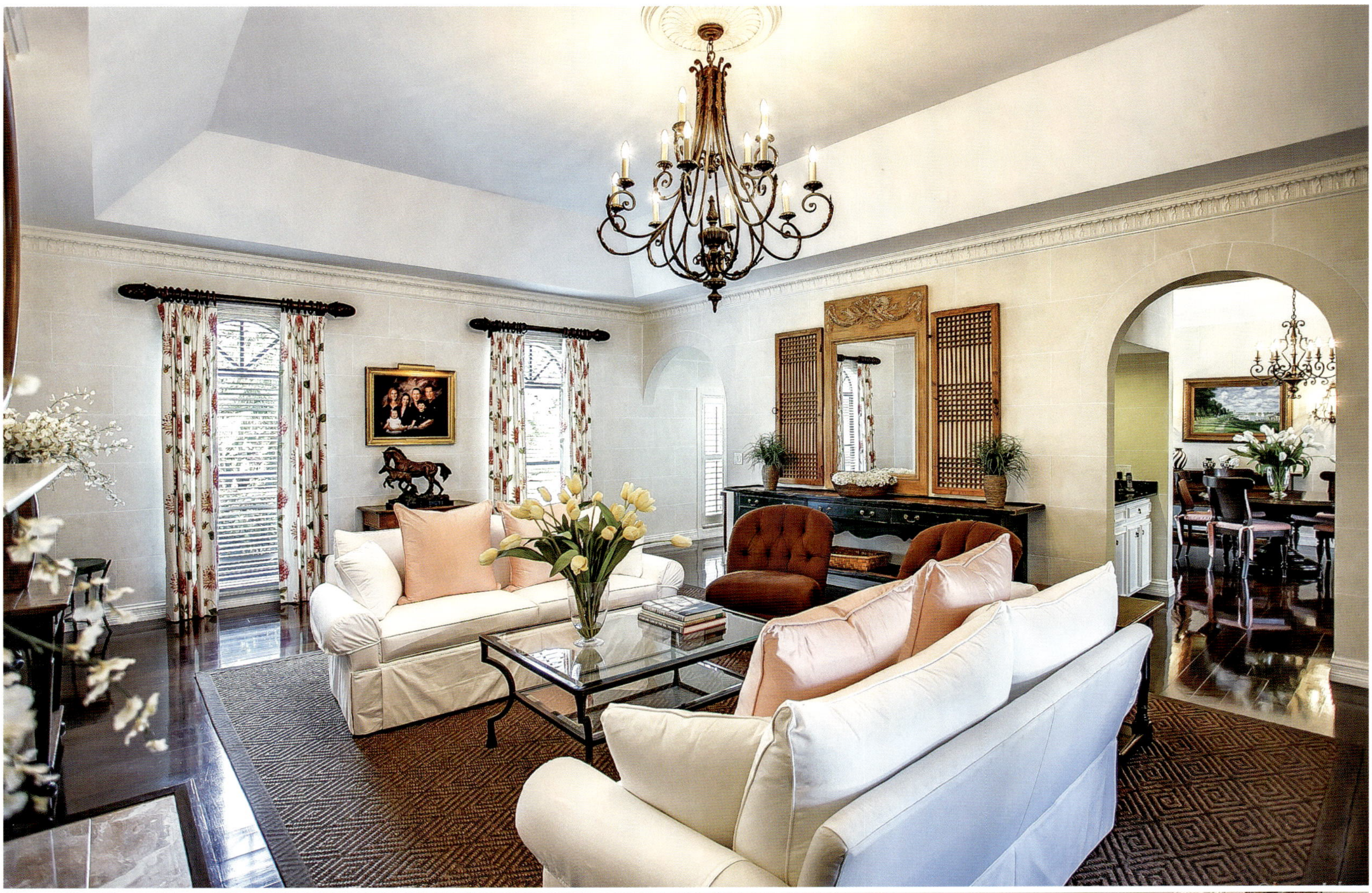

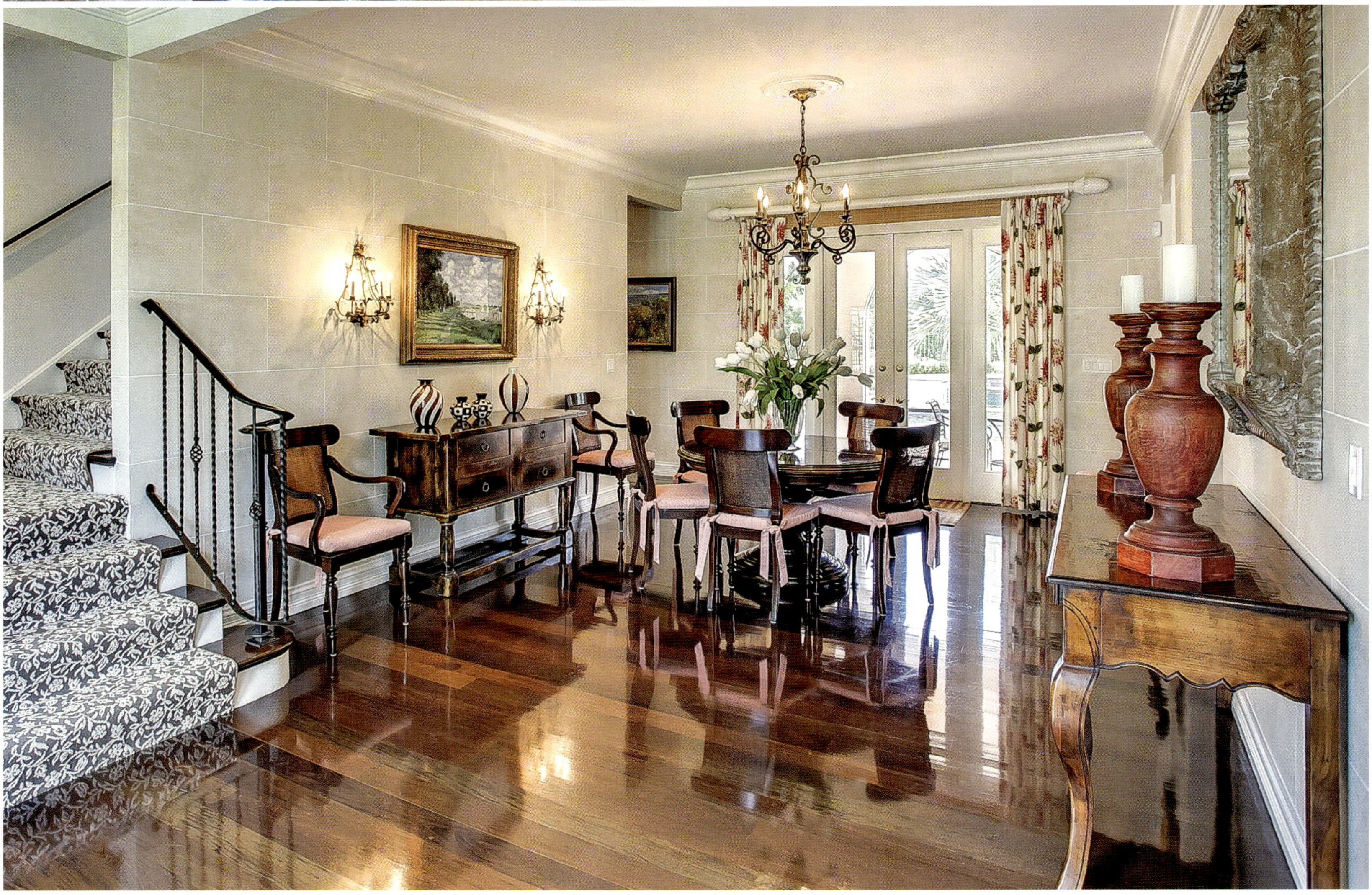

Brazilian hardwood, Berber carpets and
marble floors enhance the exclusive interiors.

Brasilianisches Holz, Berberteppiche und
Marmorböden prägen die edle Ausstattung.

Madera brasileña, alfombras bereberes y
suelos de mármol realzan los interiores.

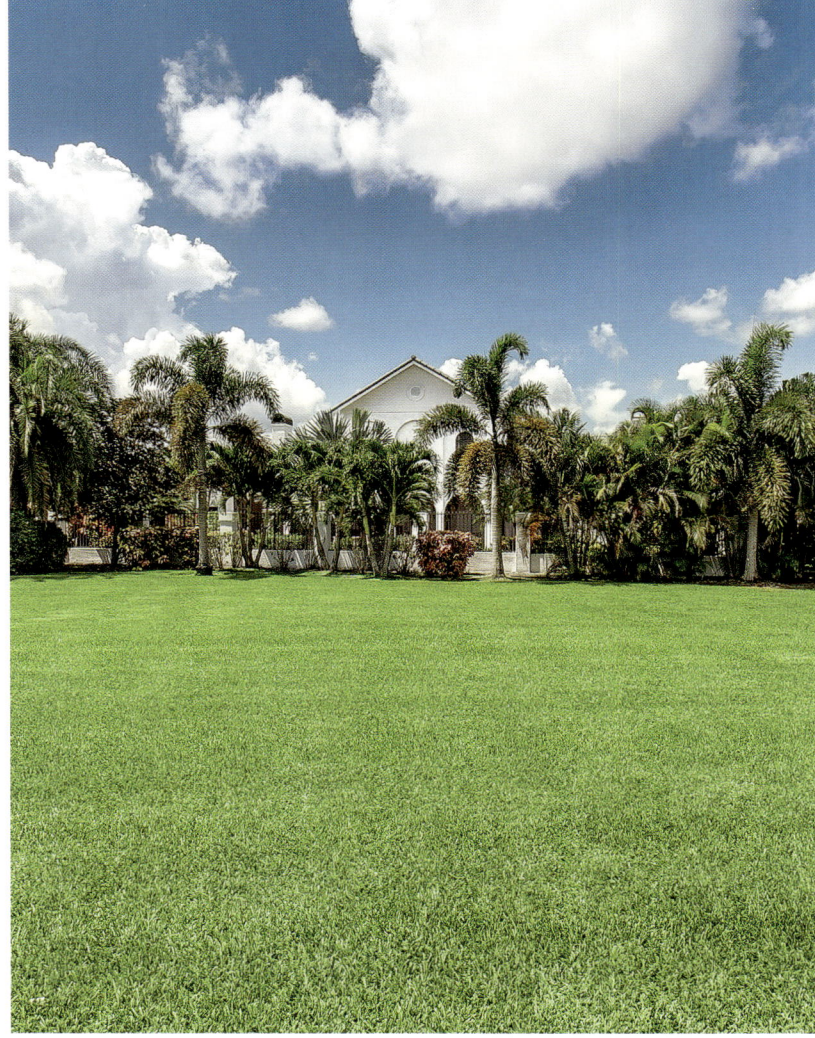

An oasis of green and blue: the lovely pool is
nestled amidst splendidly manicured gardens.

Grün-blaue Oase: Der Pool ist harmonisch in
den schön gestalteten Garten eingebettet.

Oasis de verde y azul: la coqueta piscina entre
espléndidos e impecables jardines.

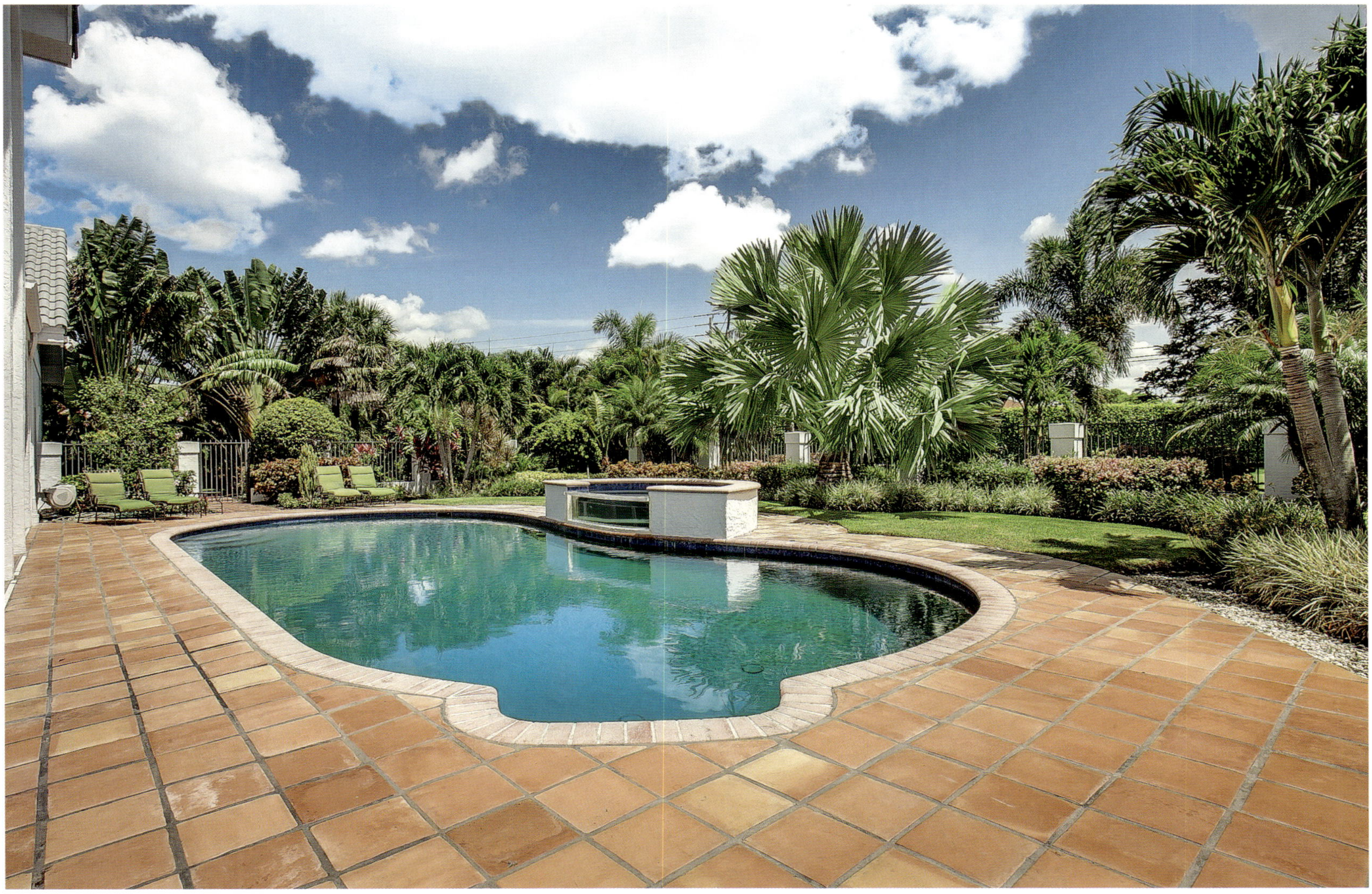

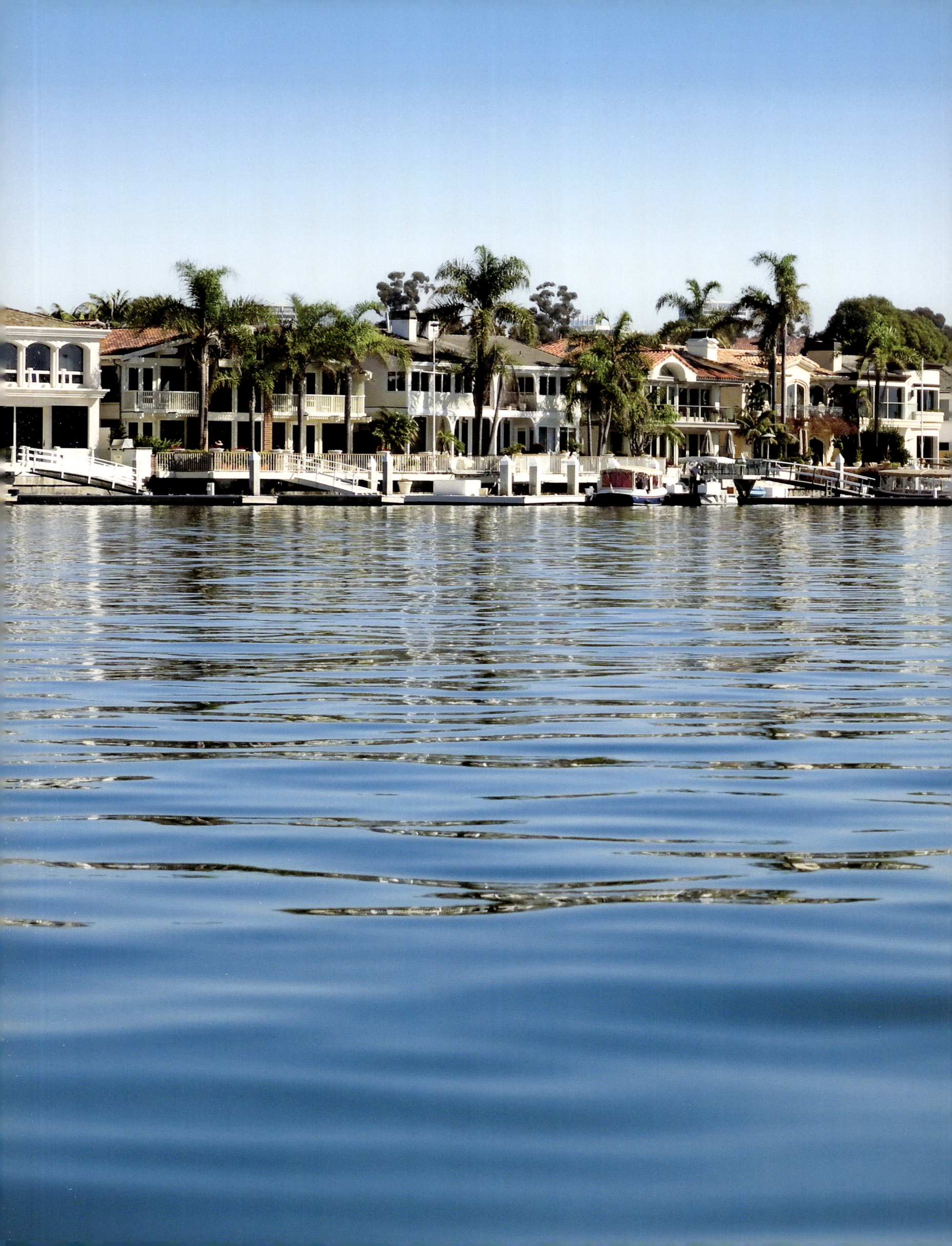

# Pacific Glamour

Enjoying a coveted setting in Newport Beach
just south of Los Angeles, this elegant waterfront estate
represents classy Pacific living at its most exclusive.

IMMEDIATELY UPON entering this stunning Californian residence, the visitor will be overcome by its special allure. The unparalleled location as well as the magnificent gardens with a lagoon-style pool make this estate so exceptional – but it could also be the palpable air of history permeating every part of the premises. The house was built in the 1970s for the philanthropists Robert and Shirlee Guggenheim to accommodate their dynamic social and high-profile lifestyle. A true entertainers' dream, it is equipped with five bedrooms and seven bathrooms plus a luxurious spa. Looking out onto the main channel and the Pacific Ocean, the master suite features a cosy morning room with a fireplace as well as two full bathrooms. One of the outstanding highlights is the gorgeous water frontage with terraces and a private pier large enough to accommodate an 85-foot vessel. All this within the ultra-exclusive residential community of Linda Isle. In short, this is the ideal home to enjoy a sophisticated lifestyle by the Pacific Ocean.

DER BESONDERE REIZ dieser kalifornischen Villa erschließt sich einem schon beim ersten Anblick: Die unvergleichliche Lage und der hübsche Garten mit dem lagunenförmigen Pool machen sie so einzigartig – und ein Hauch ihrer legendären Geschichte ist hier nach wie vor spürbar. Das Anwesen wurde in den Siebzigerjahren für die Philanthropen Robert und Shirlee Guggenheim gebaut, um ihrem dynamischen und hochkarätigen gesellschaftlichen Lebensstil einen adäquaten Rahmen zu geben. Eine Traum-Location für Gastgeber, die über insgesamt fünf Schlaf- und sieben Badezimmer sowie ein luxuriöses Spa verfügt. Zur Master-Suite mit ihrem herrlichen Blick über den Main Channel und den Pazifik gehören zudem ein einladendes Frühstückszimmer mit Kamin und zwei Bäder. Unübertroffenes Highlight dieser Residenz ist aber sicherlich die Lage am Wasser samt Terrassen und einer privaten Anlegestelle, die Platz für eine 25-Meter-Yacht bietet – und den Lifestyle im exklusiven Umfeld von Linda Isle perfekt macht.

BASTA ENTRAR en esta impresionante residencia californiana para verse superado por su especial encanto. La irrepetible ubicación frente al mar así como los magníficos jardines con la piscina estilo laguna hacen de ésta una finca excepcional, pero también puede ser la causa ese palpable aura de historia que destila por cada uno de sus cuatro costados. La casa fue construida en la década de los 70 por los filántropos Robert y Shirlee Guggenheim, de acuerdo con su estilo de vida social dinámico y de perfil alto, un verdadero sueño para quienes gustan de recibir en casa, equipado con cinco dormitorios, siete baños y un *spa* de lujo. Mirando hacia el Main Channel y el océano Pacífico, el dormitorio principal cuenta con una acogedora sala mañanera con chimenea, así como con dos baños. Pero es la fachada marítima la perla del inmueble, con terrazas y su muelle privado con cabida para una nave de 85 pies. Todo ello en el residencial ultra exclusivo de Linda Isle, haciendo de ésta la casa ideal donde disfrutar de un sofisticado estilo de vida frente al Pacífico.

USA, NEWPORT BEACH **PURCHASE PRICE** USD 11.895 MILL. **INTERIOR APPROX.** 6,587 ft² **NO. OF BEDROOMS** 5
**LAND APPROX.** 7,500 ft² **E&V ID** E-00150D **CONTACT** LOS ANGELES (US), AVENUE REAL ESTATE INTERNATIONAL,
LICENCE PARTNER OF EV REAL ESTATE INC. **TEL.** +1 323 937 51 01 **E-MAIL** LOSANGELES@EVUSA.COM

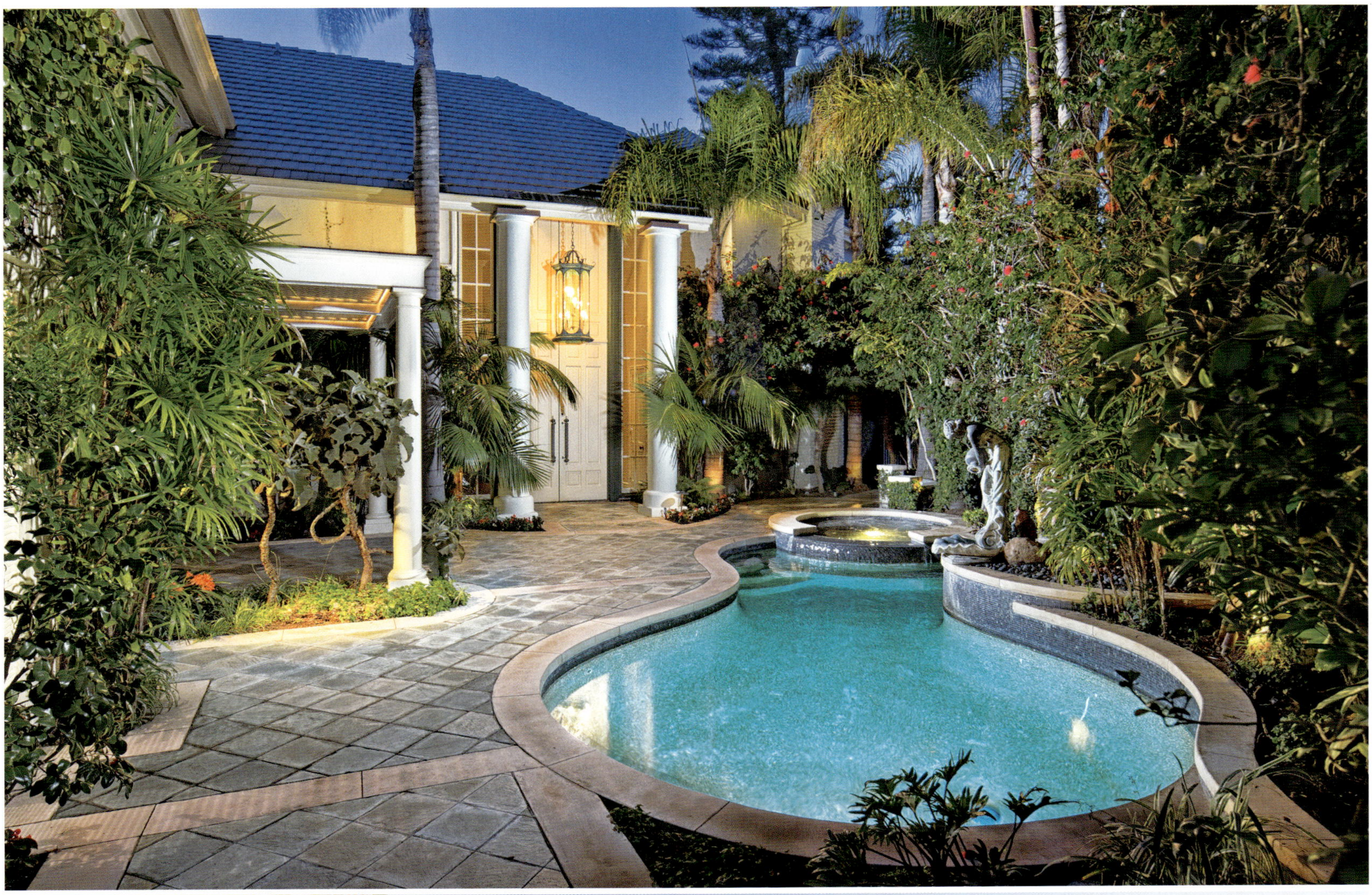

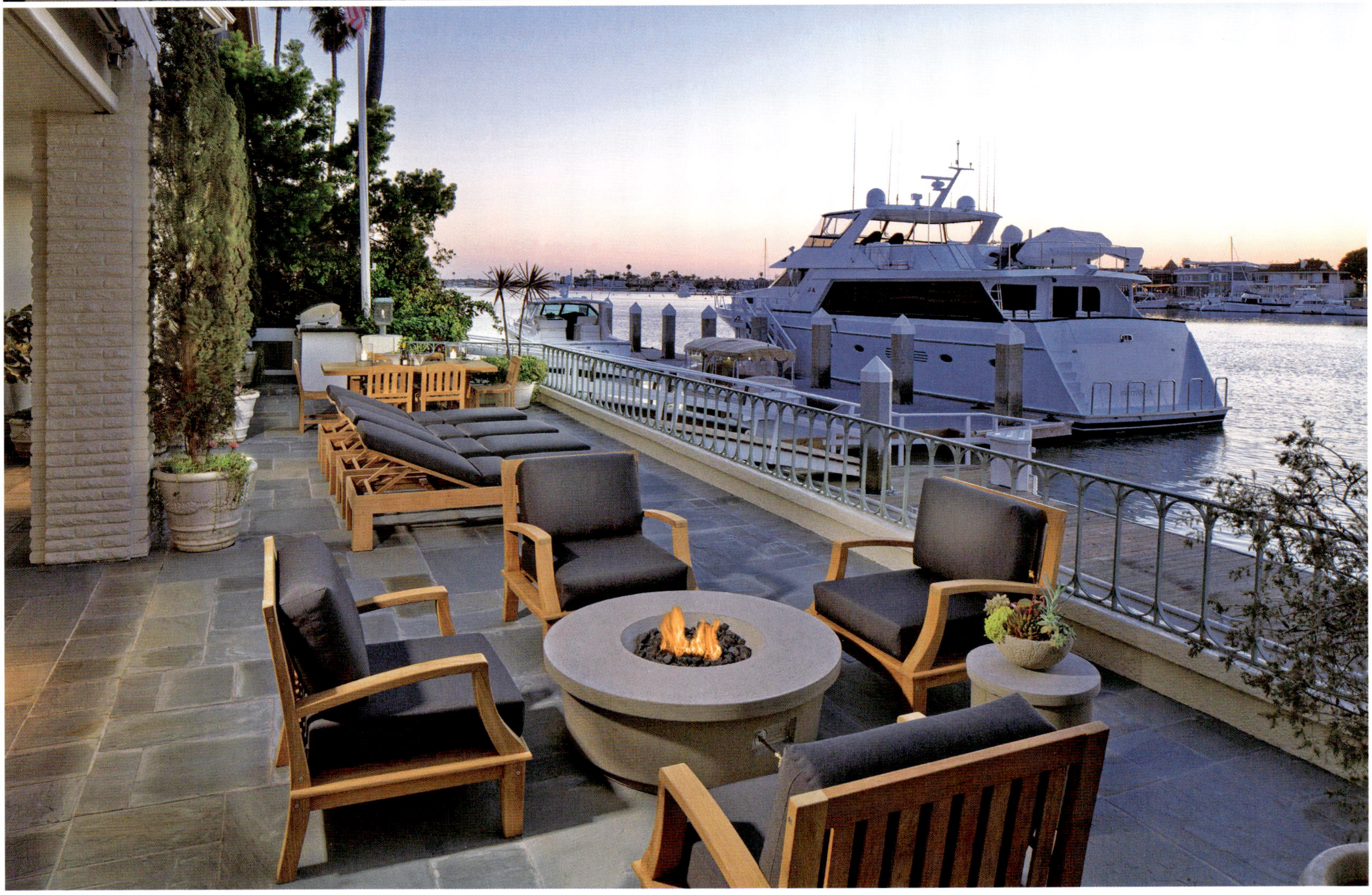

The attractive, lagoon-style pool blends in with lush gardens in a magnificent manner.

Der lagunenförmige Swimmingpool fügt sich wunderbar in das idyllische Gartenareal ein.

La atractiva piscina-laguna se funde con exuberantes jardines de forma magnífica.

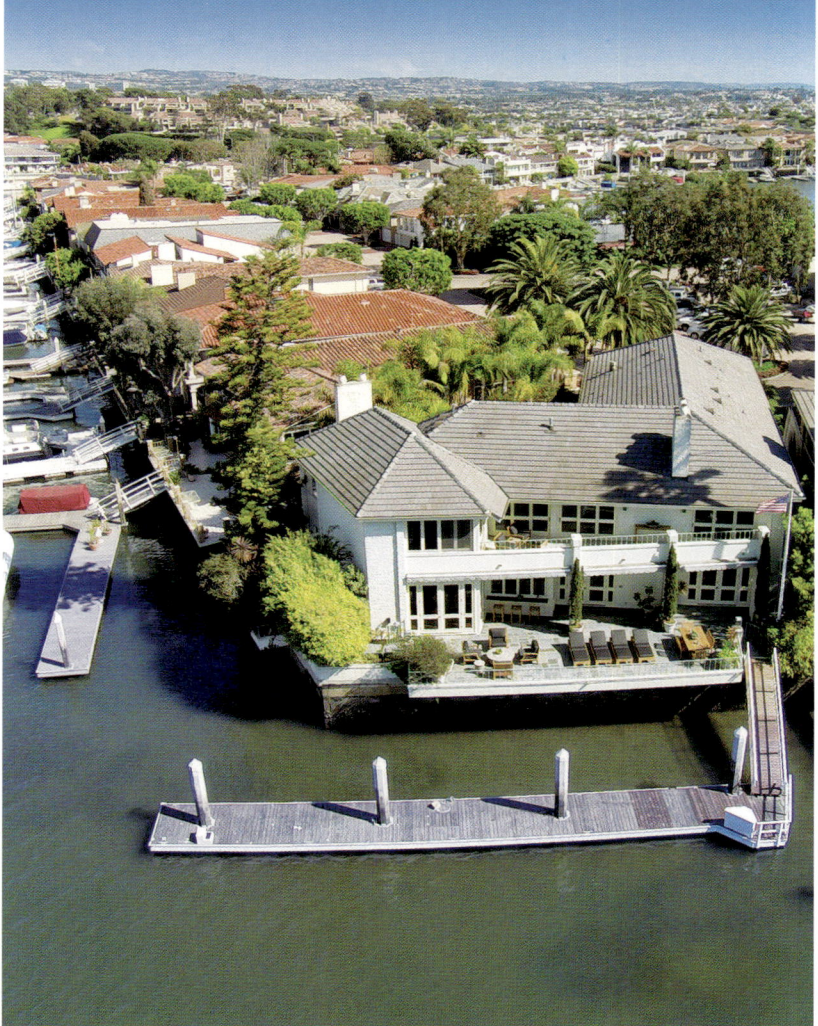

The bay-front location is perfect for relishing the Californian sunset.

Hier lässt sich der kalifornische Sonnenuntergang direkt am Wasser genießen.

Ubicada frente a la bahía, es inevitable gozar las puestas de sol californianas.

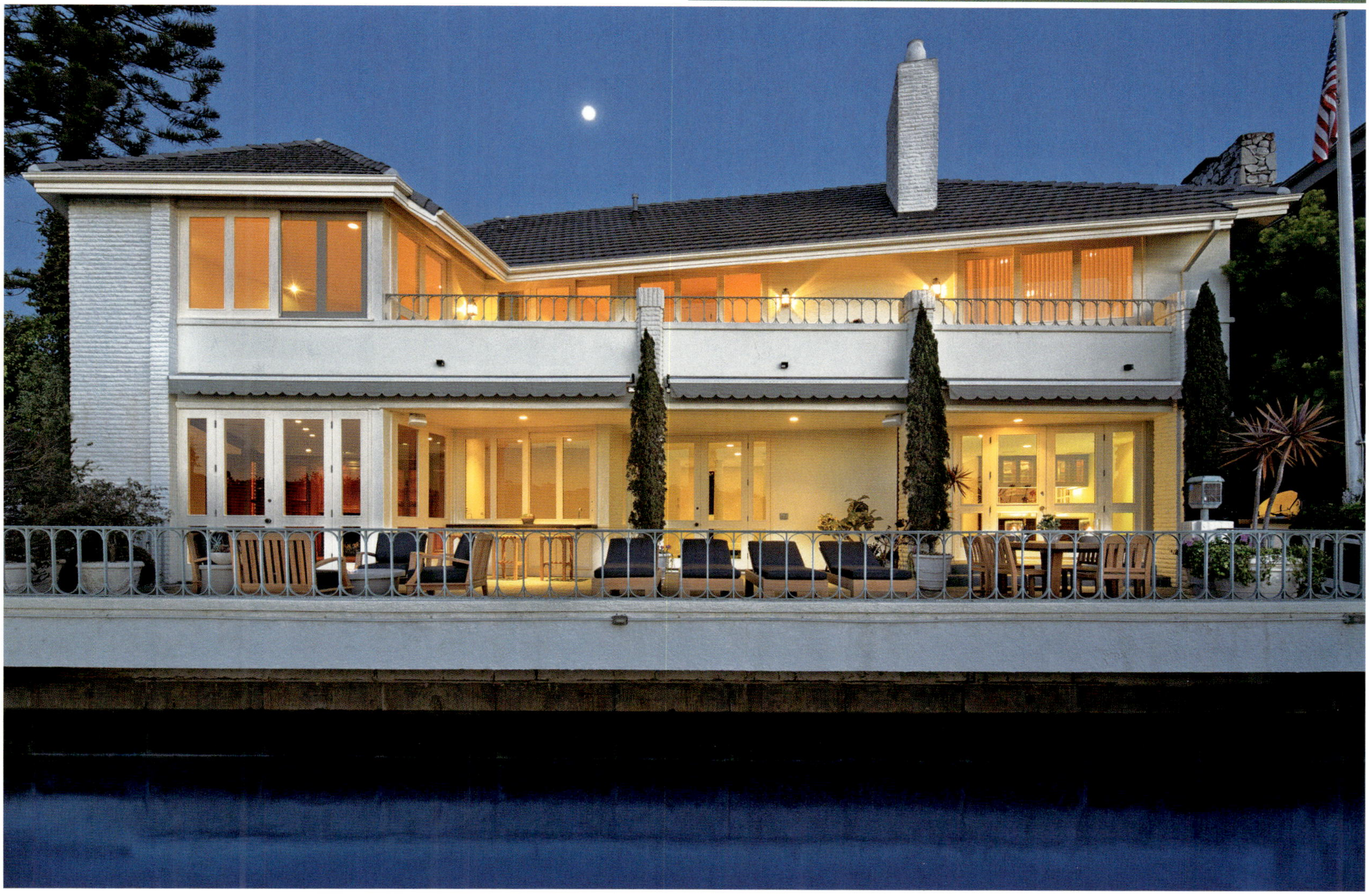

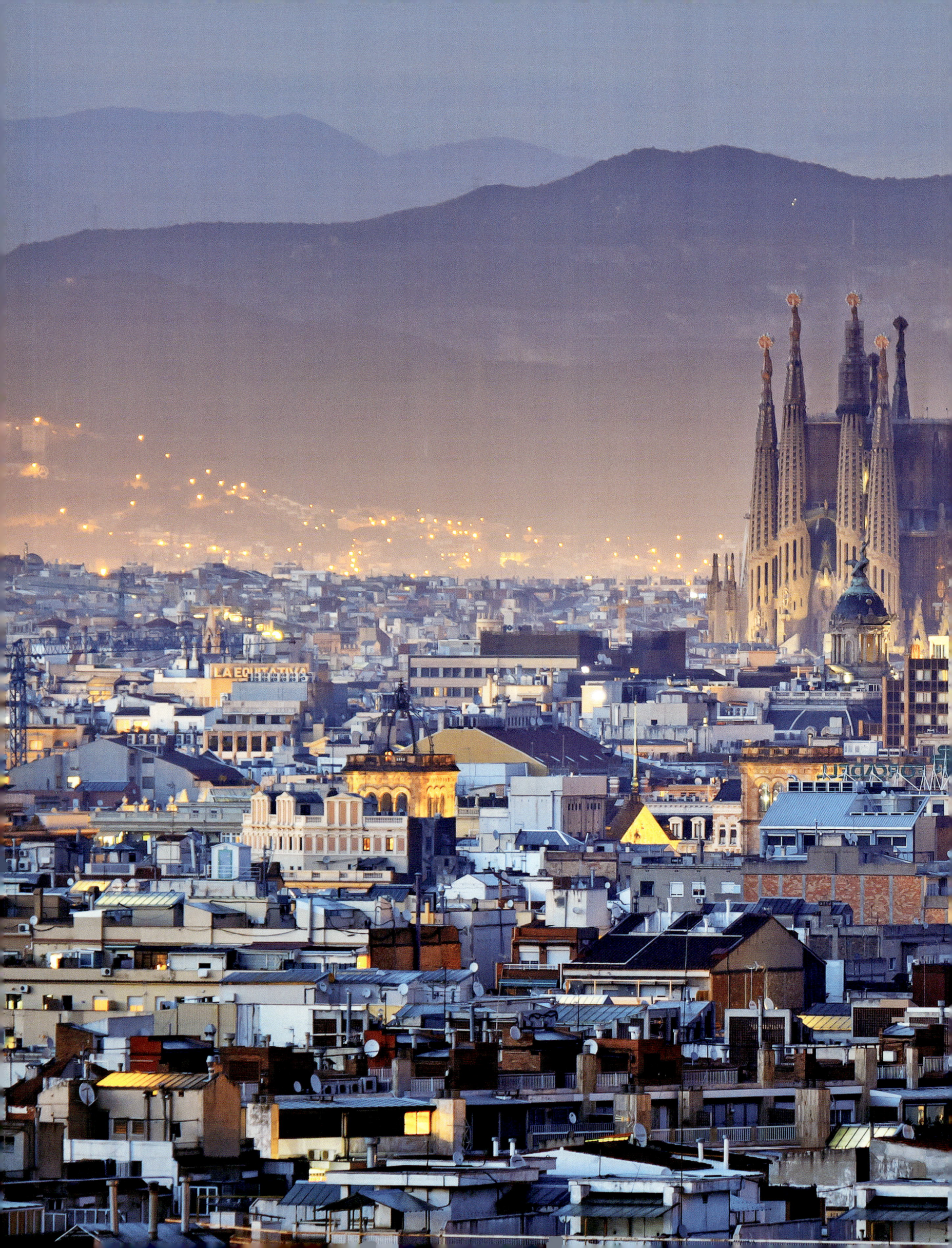

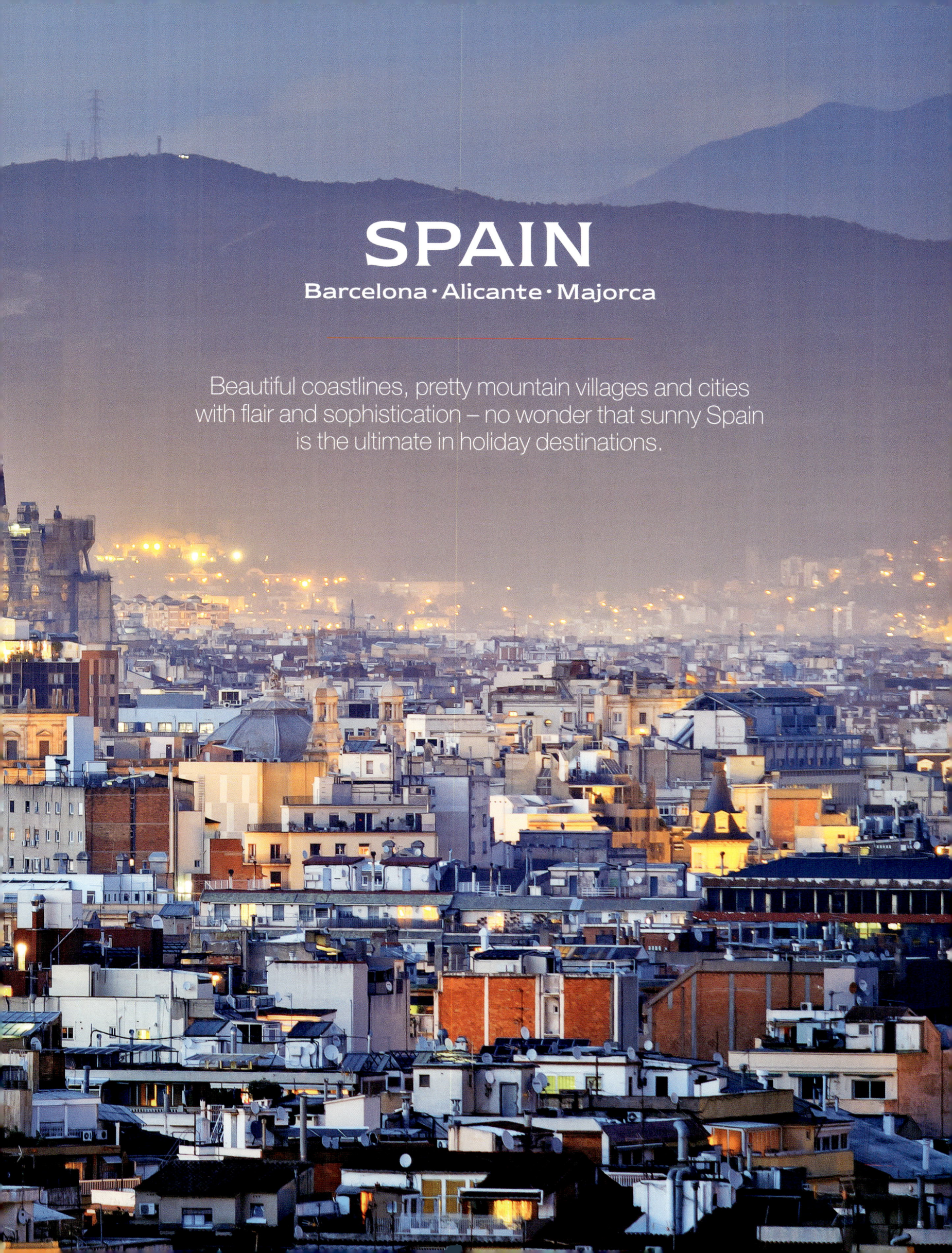

# SPAIN

**Barcelona · Alicante · Majorca**

Beautiful coastlines, pretty mountain villages and cities
with flair and sophistication – no wonder that sunny Spain
is the ultimate in holiday destinations.

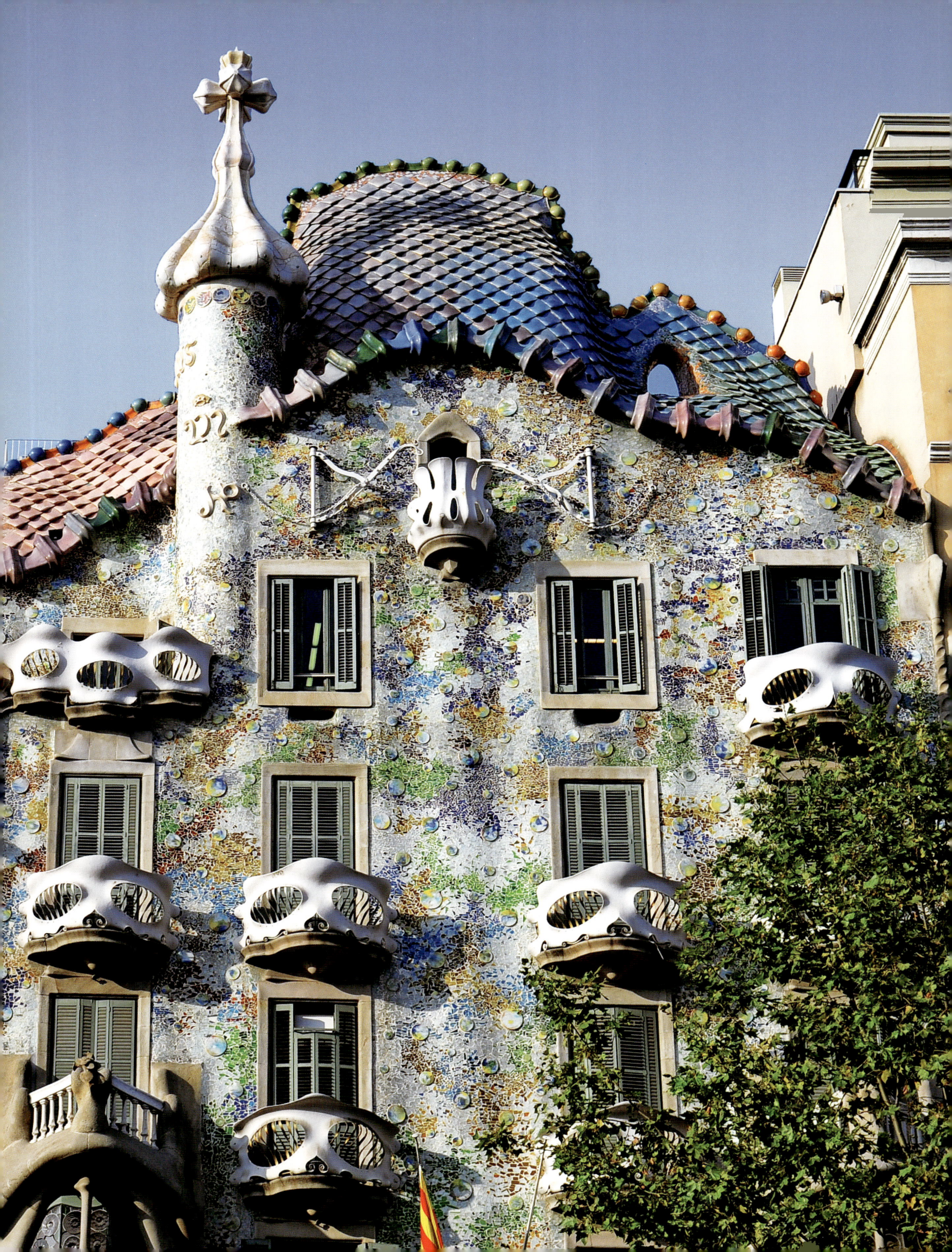

# Palatial Apartment

This exquisite dwelling in downtown Barcelona is an architectural masterpiece of grand proportions, complete with many fine details and luxurious elements.

FAMOUS FOR ITS impressive art nouveau architecture, vibrant nightlife and thriving cafe culture, the district of Eixample is a high-class residential area in central Barcelona – and the location of this exclusive ground-floor apartment with true cosmopolitan flair. Offering a superlative level of comfort on around 533 square metres of living space, it is a homage to noble elegance and stately design with abundant gracious details: absolutely everything in this flat has been conceived with a loving attention to detail, and nothing left to chance. With 20 rooms in total – including a spacious living room, a dining room, two offices, a library, a bar, four en-suite bedrooms and a truly spectacular dressing room – it also includes high-tech amenities such as a sauna and a private gym. Delightful highlights are the four balconies and a terrace that is no less than 192 square metres in size, complete with a chill-out area, a Jacuzzi and a swim-current pool. The final touch: this urban jewel comes with six parking spaces, a luxury in downtown Barcelona that is second to none!

DER BEZIRK Eixample, ein High-Class-Wohnviertel im Zentrum von Barcelona, ist neben seiner beeindrucken-den Jugendstil-Architektur bekannt für seine lebendige Cafékultur und ein pulsierendes Nachtleben. Inmitten dieses faszinierenden Umfeldes befindet sich dieses Erdgeschoss-Apartment mit seinem sehr kosmopolitischen Flair. Auf 533 Quadratmetern Wohnfläche bietet es geradezu herausragenden Komfort voll exquisiter Details und nobler Eleganz. Alles wurde hier mit viel Liebe gestaltet, nichts dem Zufall überlassen. Das Apartment verfügt über insgesamt 20 Zimmer – darunter ein geräumiges Wohnzimmer, ein Esszimmer, zwei Büros, eine Bibliothek, eine Bar, vier behagliche Schlafzimmer mit En-suite-Bad und ein spektakulärer Ankleideraum. Zu den weiteren Annehmlichkeiten gehören eine Sauna, ein Fitnessraum sowie eine große Terrasse mit überdachtem Ruhebereich, Jacuzzi und Pool mit Gegenstromanlage, ergänzt von sechs eigenen Parkplätzen – in der Innenstadt von Barcelona definitiv ein Luxus, der seinesgleichen sucht!

FAMOSO POR SU fascinante arquitectura modernista, vibrante vida nocturna y próspera *café-culture*, el Eixample es más que un barrio residencial de clase alta en el centro de Barcelona, y la singular ubicación donde se esceni-fica esta exclusiva planta baja con verdadero acento cosmopolita. Ofreciendo un nivel superlativo de comodidad en unos 533 metros cuadrados habitables, el inmueble es un homenaje a la noble elegancia y al diseño señorial donde abundan elementos característicos, todos concebidos con una atención primorosa por el detalle, sin dejar nada al azar. En un total de 20 habitaciones incluye una espléndida sala de estar, comedor, dos despachos, biblio-teca, bar, cuatro dormitorios en *suite* y un vestidor realmente espectacular, todo equipado con elementos de alta tecnología, sauna y gimnasio. Destacan los cuatro románticos balcones y la terraza de 192 metros cuadrados con la zona *chill-out* cubierta, Jacuzzi y piscina con contracorriente. El toque final: esta peculiar joya urbana viene con seis plazas de aparcamiento, todo un lujo en el centro de Barcelona. ¿Alguien da más?

SPAIN, BARCELONA **PURCHASE PRICE** EUR 8 MILL. **INTERIOR APPROX.** 533 m² **NO. OF BEDROOMS** 4
E&V ID W-01I34W **CONTACT** BARCELONA (ES), ENGEL & VÖLKERS BARCELONA MANAGEMENT, S.L., & CÍA., S.EN C.,
LICENCE PARTNER OF ENGEL & VÖLKERS RESIDENTIAL GMBH **TEL.** +34 93 515 44 44
**E-MAIL** BARCELONAMMC@ENGELVOELKERS.COM

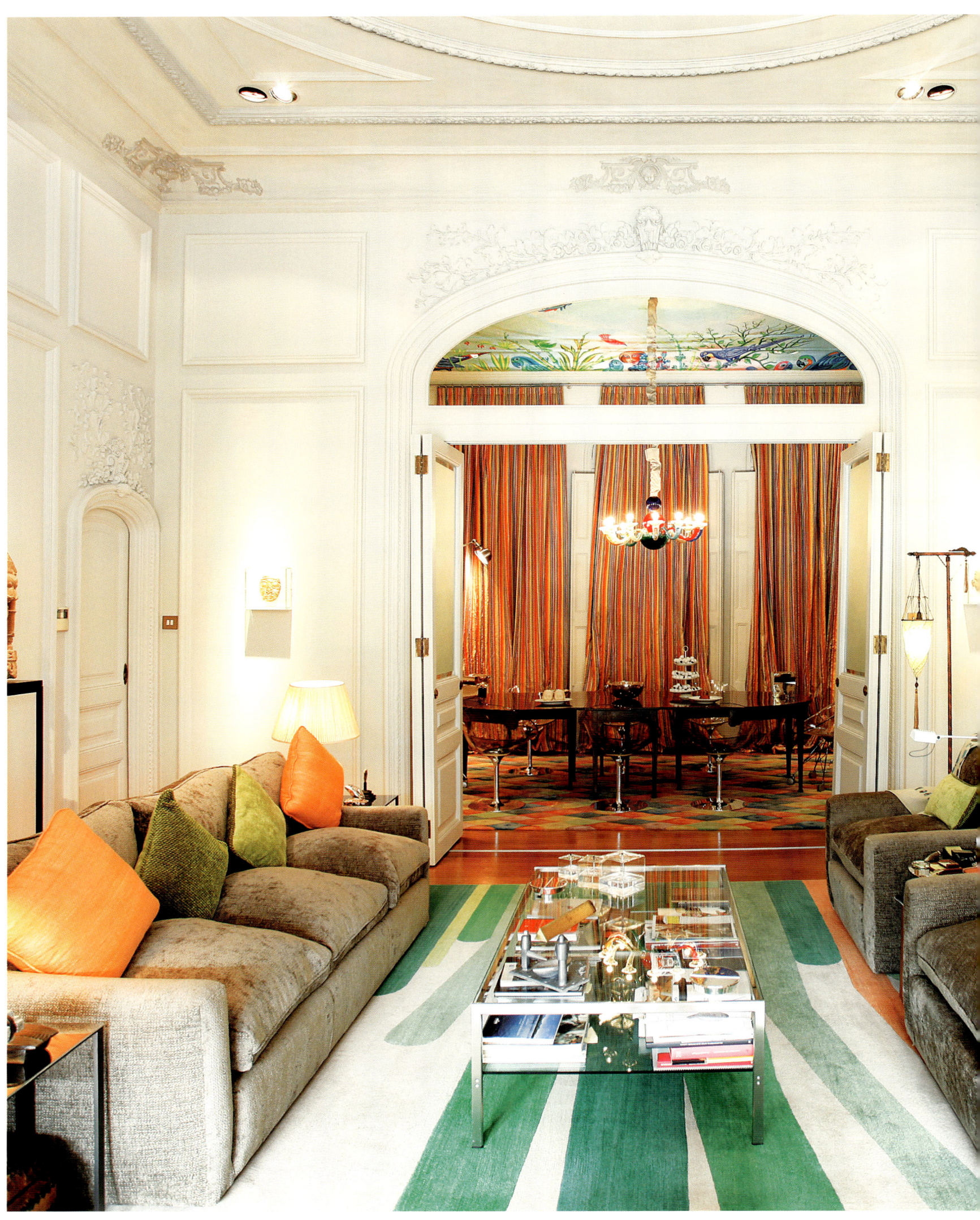

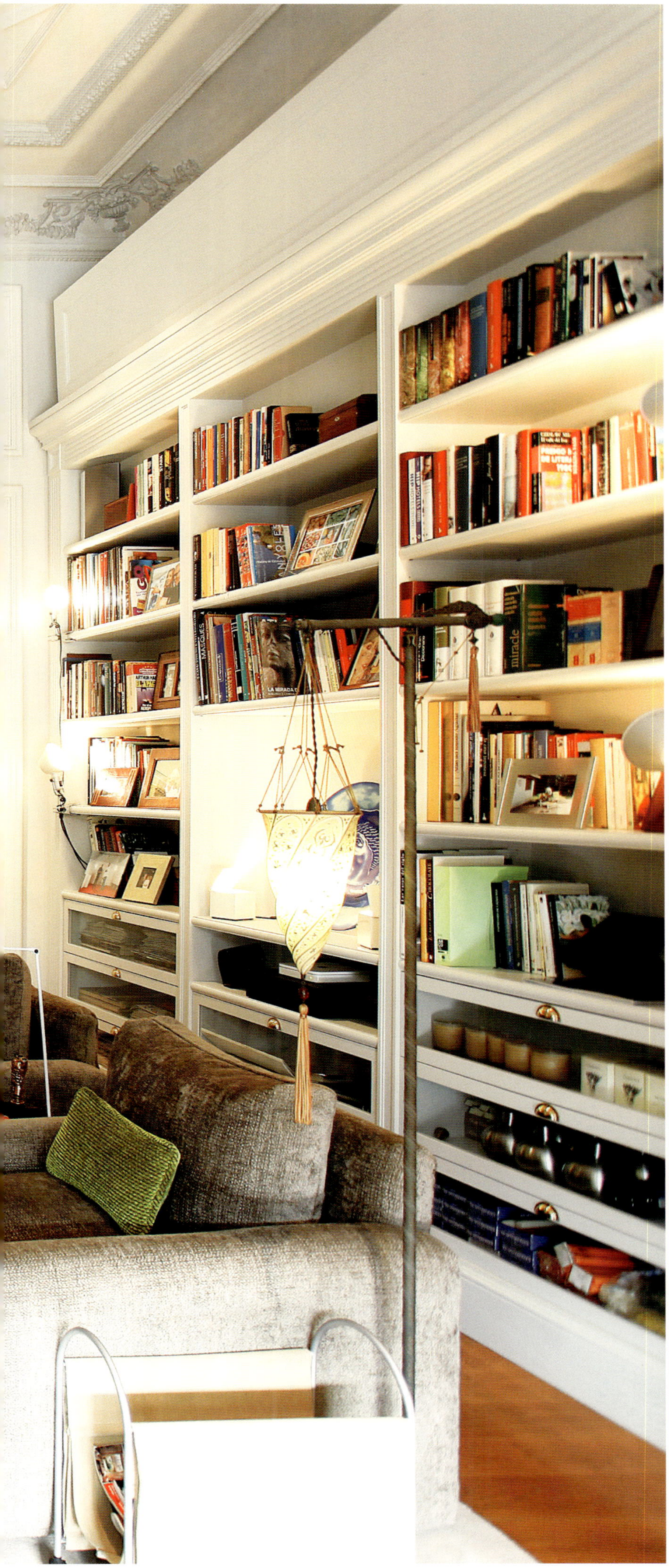

<

Lavish opulence permeates the elegant
interiors of this capacious apartment.

Das geräumige Apartment ist durchdrungen
von verschwenderischer Opulenz.

Opulencia y esplendor impregnan los
interiores de este piso monumental.

Small yet beautiful: the charming,
fully appointed country-style kitchen.

Klein aber fein: die charmante,
komplett ausgestattete Landhausküche.

Pequeña pero matona: la cocina rústica bien
pensada y completamente equipada.

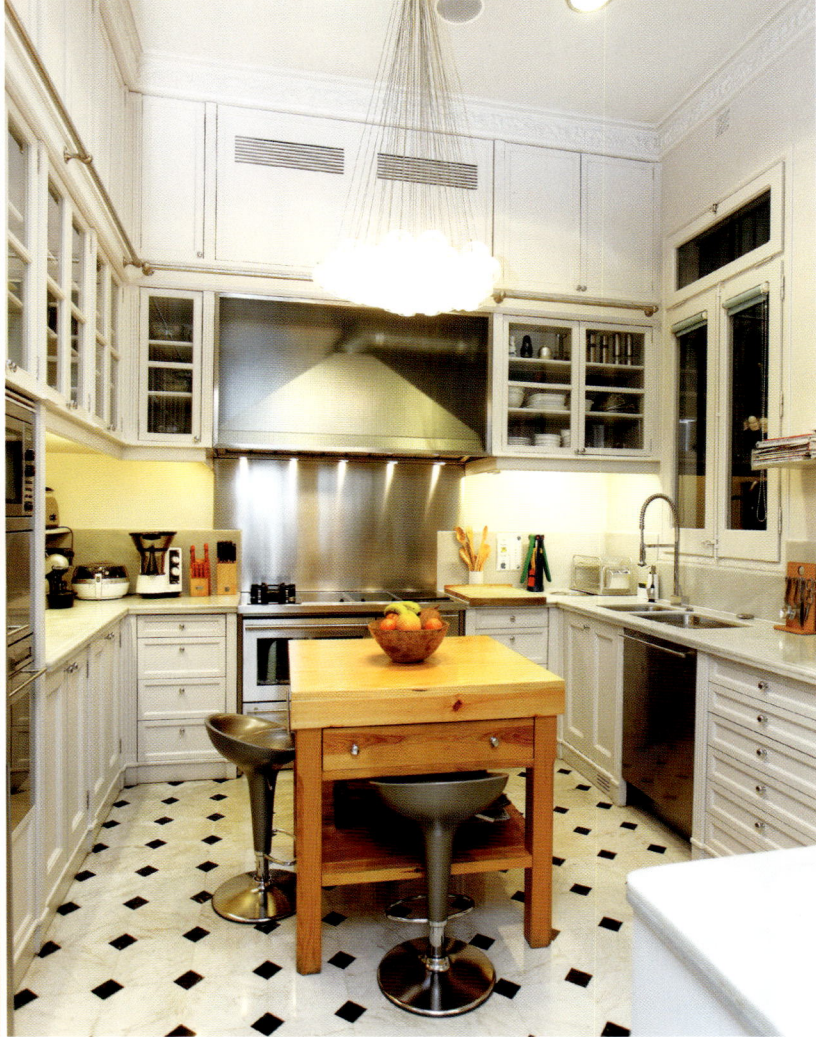

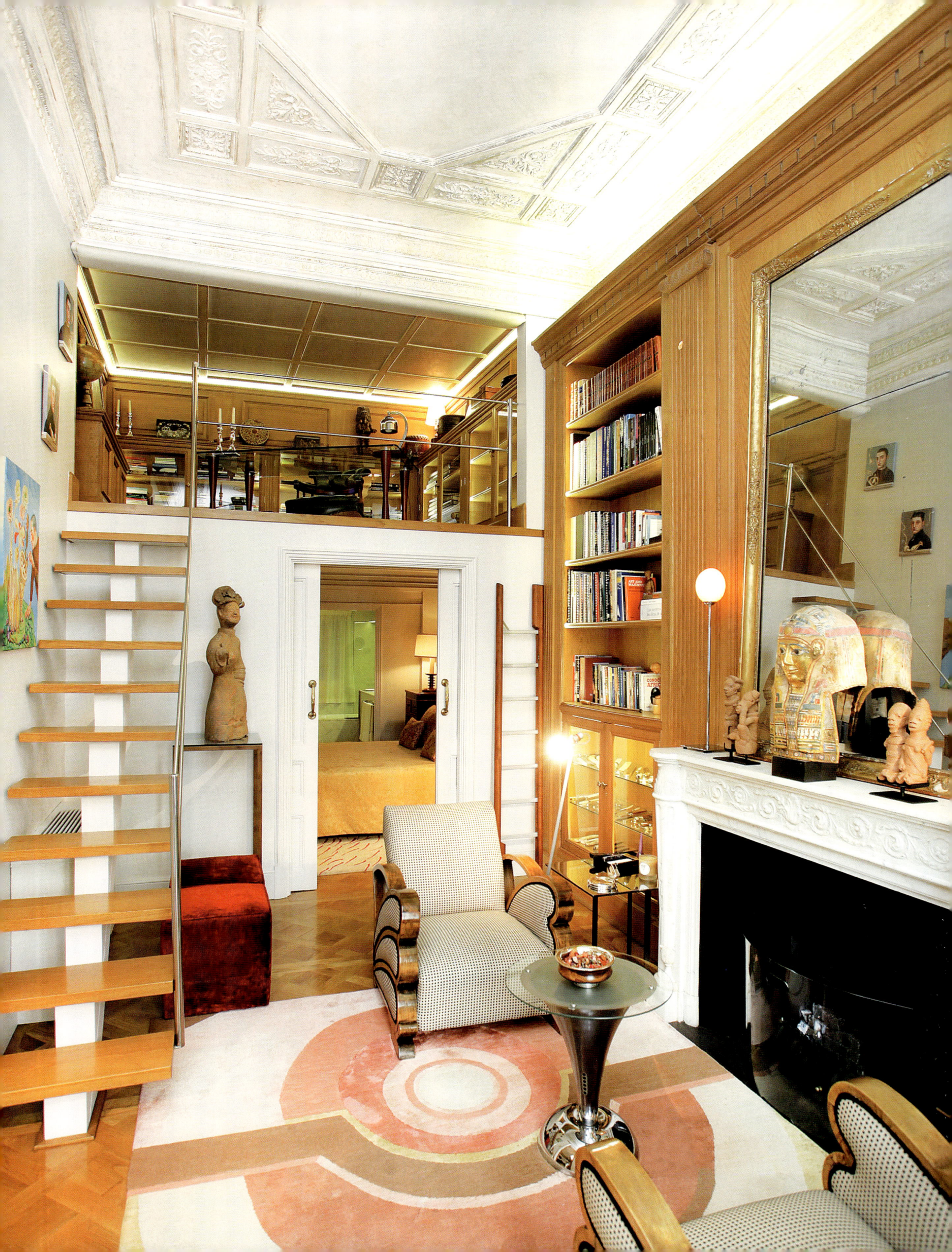

High ceilings and multilevel spaces create
an impressive and stately atmosphere.

Hohe Decken und Räume mit mehreren
Ebenen vermitteln herrschaftliches Flair.

Techos altos y espacios multinivel crean una
imponente y majestuosa atmósfera.

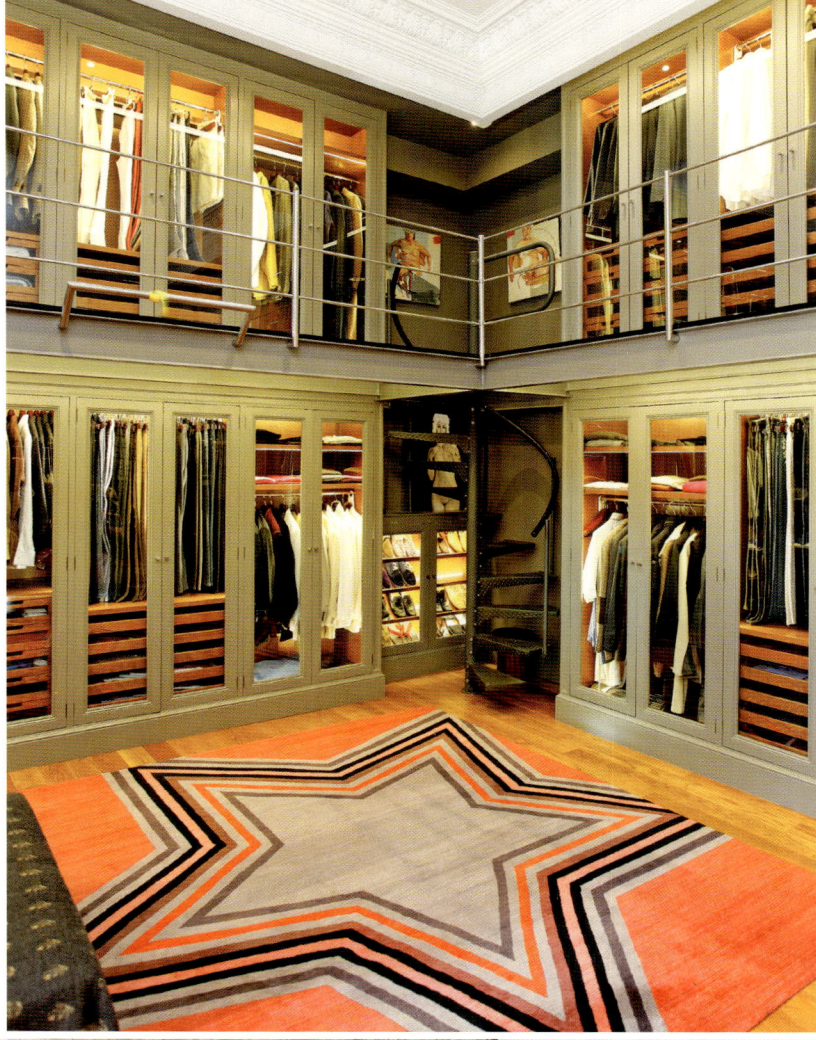

A real highlight: the stunning two-storey
dressing room with a spiral staircase.

Ein echtes Highlight: der zweistöckige
Ankleideraum mit Wendeltreppe.

Sobresaliente: el impresionante vestidor de
dos plantas unidas con la escalera de caracol.

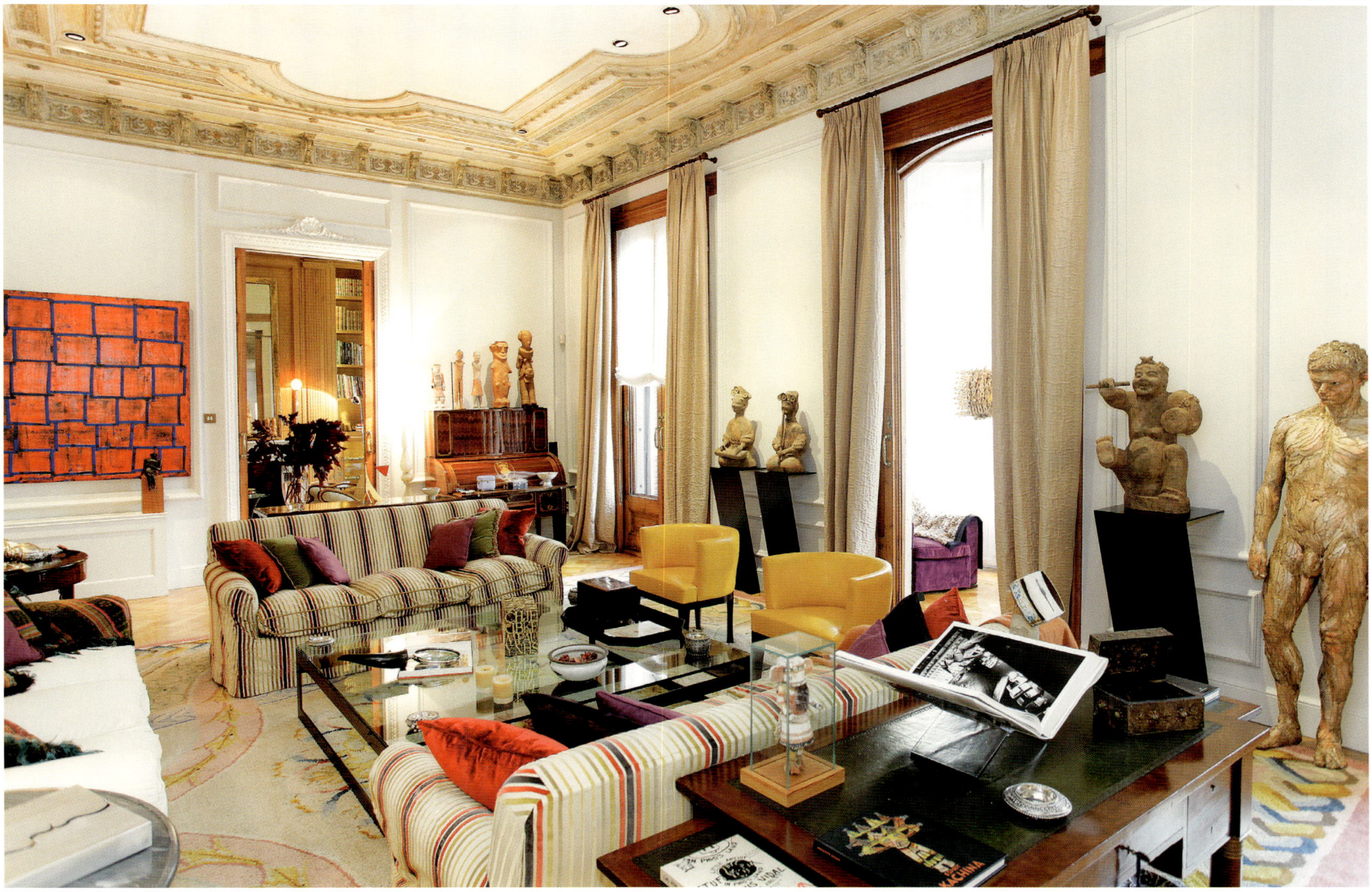

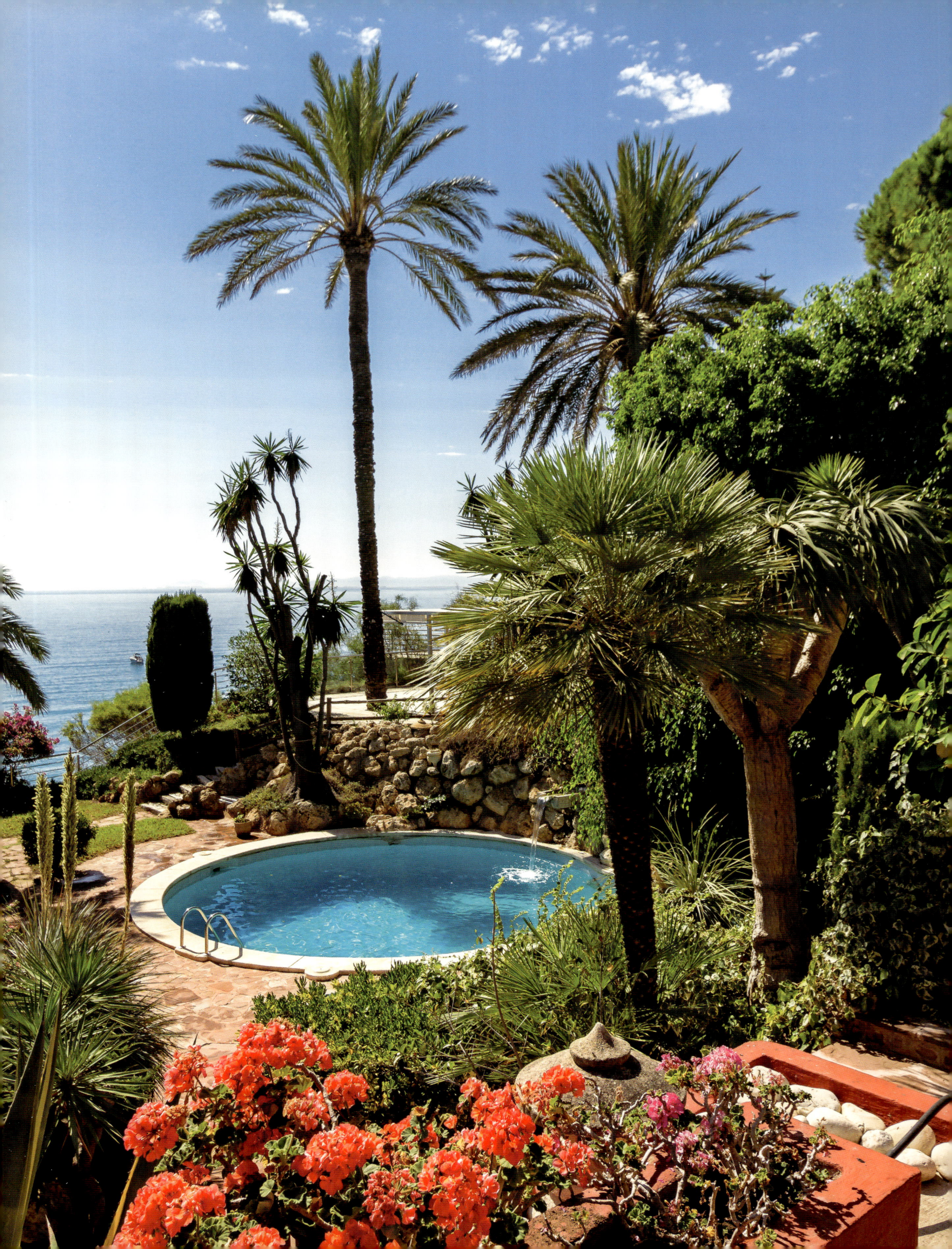

# Spanish Holiday Idyll

With private access to the beach of Cabo Roig on the southern Costa Blanca, this spacious villa is surrounded by a magnificently lush and verdant garden paradise.

BLESSED WITH a mild year-round climate and over 300 days of sunshine a year, the south-eastern region of Spain is a perfect holiday destination – for families, sun worshippers and sports enthusiasts alike. Long sandy white dream beaches, miles of craggy coastline and picturesque coves as well as marinas are never far away. And good news for golf lovers: some of the top golf courses in the Mediterranean region are located here. Ideally situated on a large property by the finest beach of Orihuela Costa, this exquisite villa caters to the most discerning of tastes. With 350 square metres of living space spread across three floors, the air-conditioned dwelling has six en-suite bedrooms and a living room with designer furniture, a fireplace and a large open-plan kitchen. Further highlights are a home cinema, a games room, a wine cellar, a private gym and a spa area with a Turkish hammam. The basement garage for several cars, many high-tech features and, most certainly, the splendid views make this seaside home a coveted holiday haven.

MIT SEINEM ganzjährig milden Klima und über 300 Sonnentagen im Jahr ist Spaniens Südosten als Urlaubs-ziel für Familien, Sonnenanbeter und Sportler wie geschaffen. Feinsandige Traumstrände wechseln sich ab mit schroffen Küsten, malerischen Buchten und mondänen Yachthäfen – und auch einige der Top-Golfplätze der Mittelmeerregion befinden sich hier in der Gegend. Am schönsten Strand der Orihuela-Küste gelegen, dürfte diese großzügige Ferienvilla auch dem anspruchsvollsten Geschmack gerecht werden. Auf 350 Quadrat-metern Wohnfläche, verteilt auf drei Etagen, verfügt sie über sechs Schlafzimmer mit En-suite-Bad, ein großzügiges, modern möbliertes Wohnzimmer mit Kamin sowie eine große offene Küche. Zu den weiteren Highlights gehören ein Heimkino, ein Spielezimmer, ein Weinkeller, ein Fitnessstudio, ein Spa-Bereich mit türkischem Hammam, eine Tiefgarage für mehrere Autos sowie diverse High-Tech-Extras – ergänzt von einer Aussicht, die dieses Refugium am Meer zu einem wahren Sehnsuchtsort macht.

BENDECIDO CON un clima templado todo el año y más de 300 días anuales de sol, el sudeste de España es un destino de vacaciones perfecto, para disfrutar en familia o para quienes anhelan disfrutar del sol o el deporte por igual. Hay bellísimas playas, kilómetros de costas escarpadas y calas pintorescas o sofisticados puertos deporti-vos al alcance de la mano. Y buenas noticias también para los golfistas: algunos de los mejores campos de golf del Mediterráneo también están aquí. En un extenso terreno idílicamente situado en la mejor playa de Orihuela Costa, esta exquisita villa satisfará los gustos más exigentes: en cerca de 350 metros cuadrados habitables en tres plantas con aire acondicionado cuenta con seis dormitorios con sus baños, un gran salón con muebles de diseño, chimenea y una espaciosa cocina abierta, además de sala de cine y otra de juegos, bodega, gimnasio y un espec-tacular *spa* con *hammam* turco. Se añaden el garaje, equipamiento técnico de vanguardia y, cómo no, las esplén-didas vistas alrededor que hacen de este refugio junto al mar un paraíso de vacaciones.

SPAIN, ALICANTE **RENTAL PRICE/WEEK** EUR 5,500 **INTERIOR APPROX.** 350 m² **NO. OF BEDROOMS** 6
**LAND APPROX.** 1,100 m² **E&V ID** W-01U2BX **CONTACT** TORREVIEJA (ES), TORREVIEJA & ORIHUELA RES,
LICENCE PARTNER OF ENGEL & VÖLKERS RESIDENTIAL GMBH **TEL.** +34 965 70 45 83
**E-MAIL** TORREVIEJAORIHUELA@ENGELVOELKERS.COM

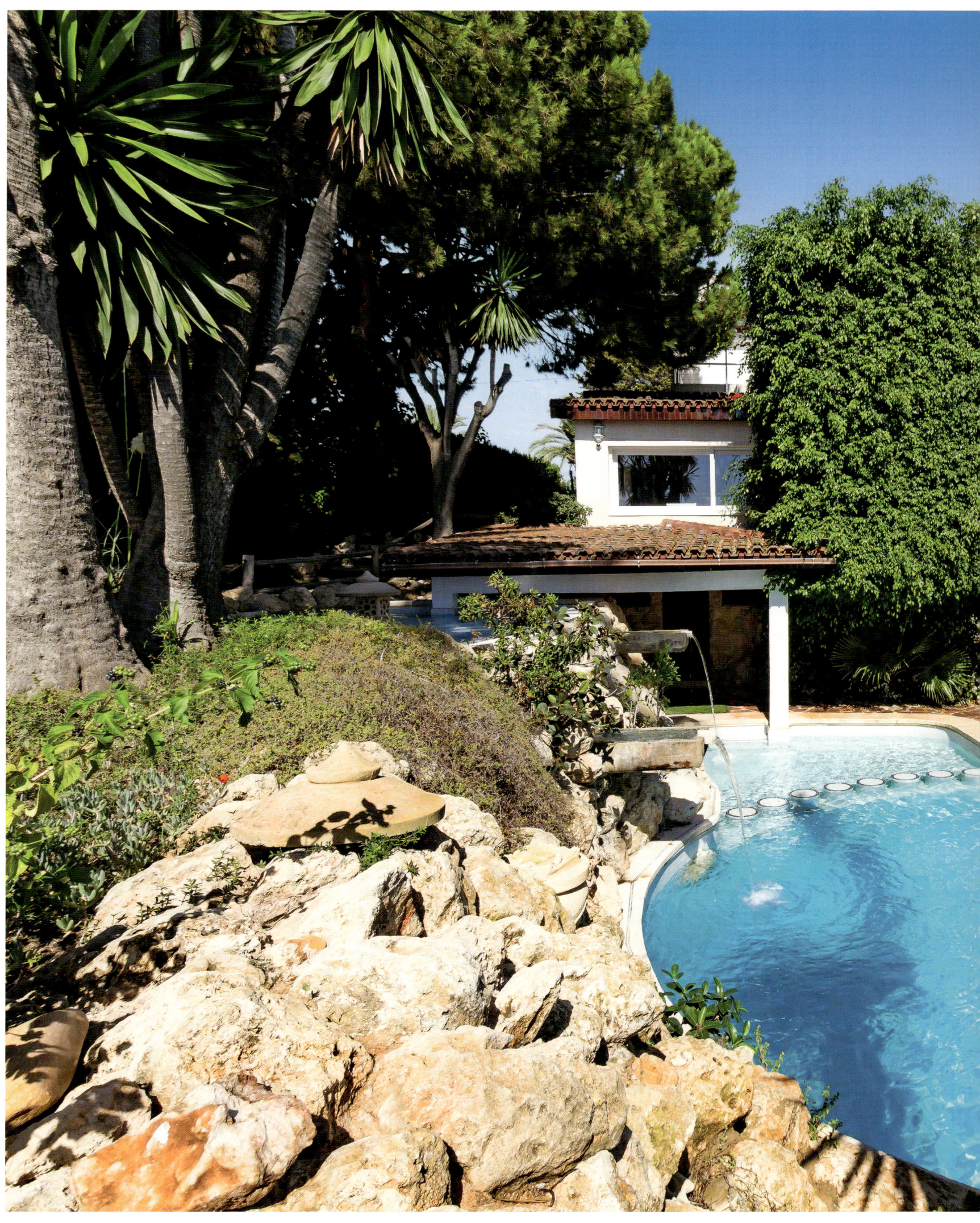

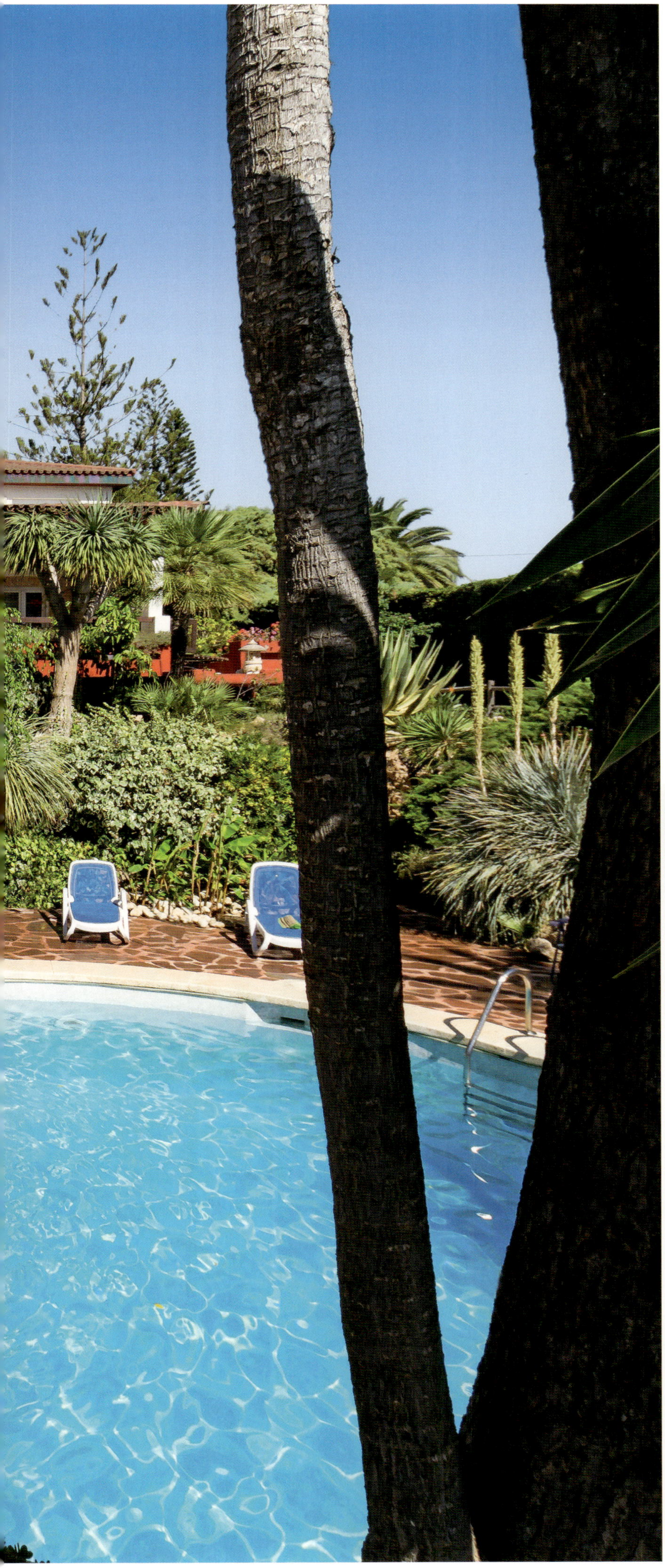

Idyllic poolside relaxation with a blissful sound, thanks to the two different waterfall jets.

Der Pool mit seinen zwei Wasserfalldüsen erfrischt und beruhigt die Sinne.

Relax en la idílica piscina que despierta los sentidos gracias a las dos cascadas.

A decadent experience for body and soul is provided by the Turkish hammam.

Pure Entspannung für Körper und Seele verspricht der türkische Hammam.

El *hammam* turco promete un espacio de pura relajación para cuerpo y alma.

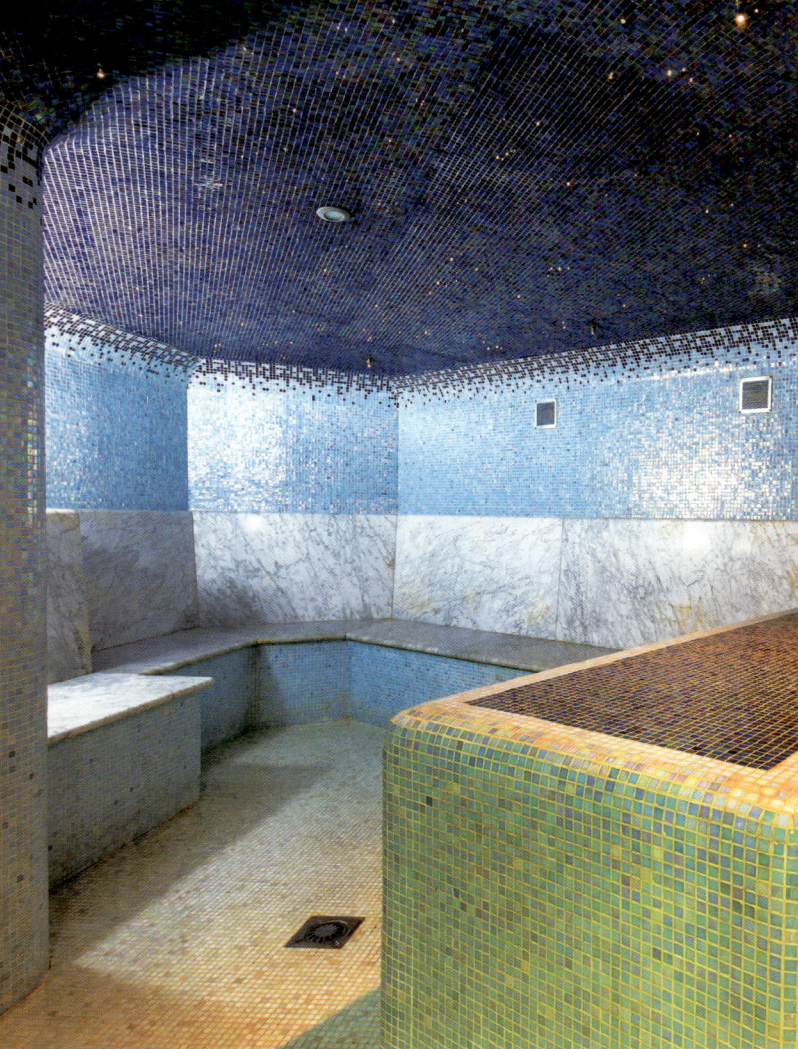

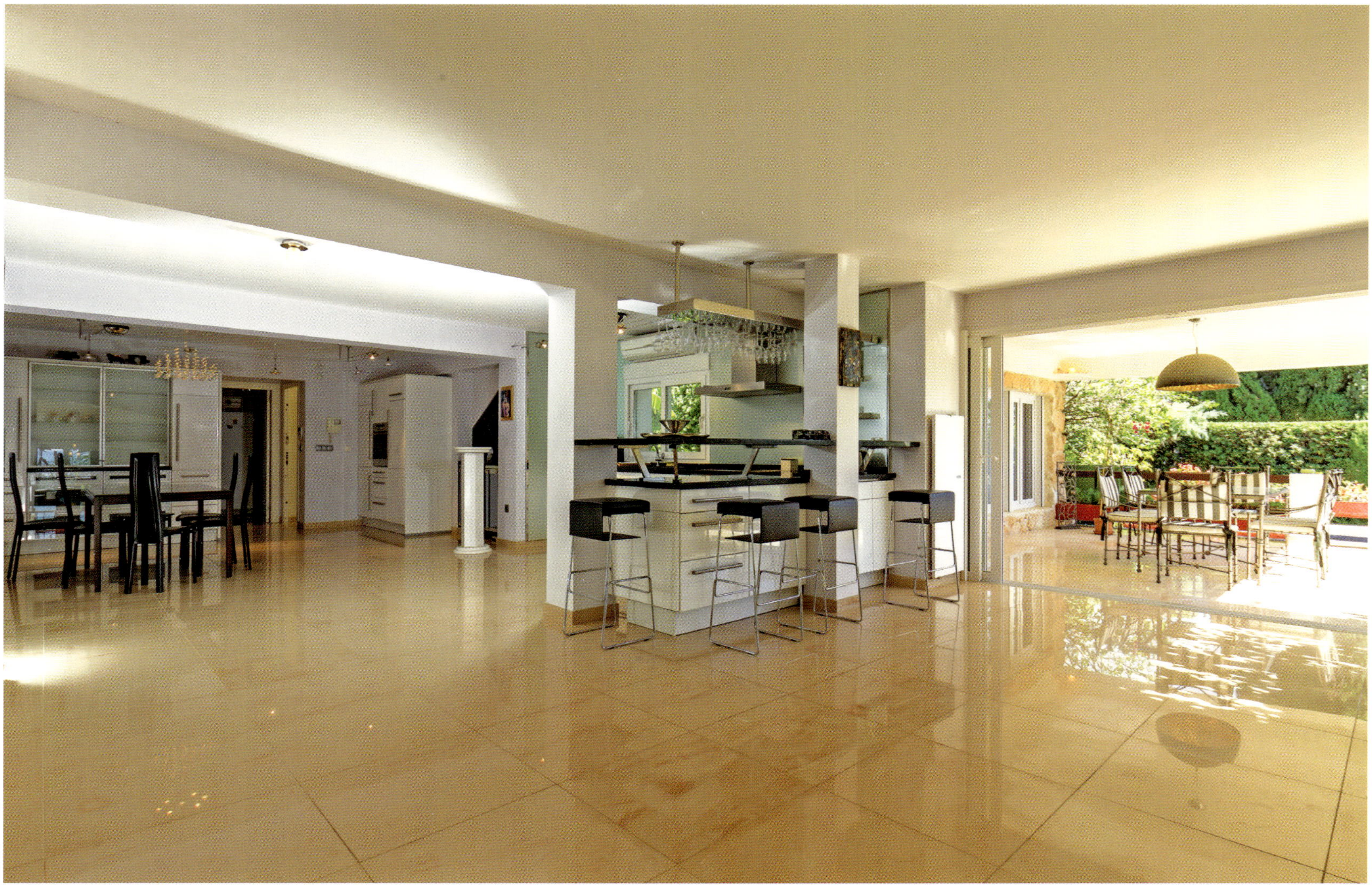

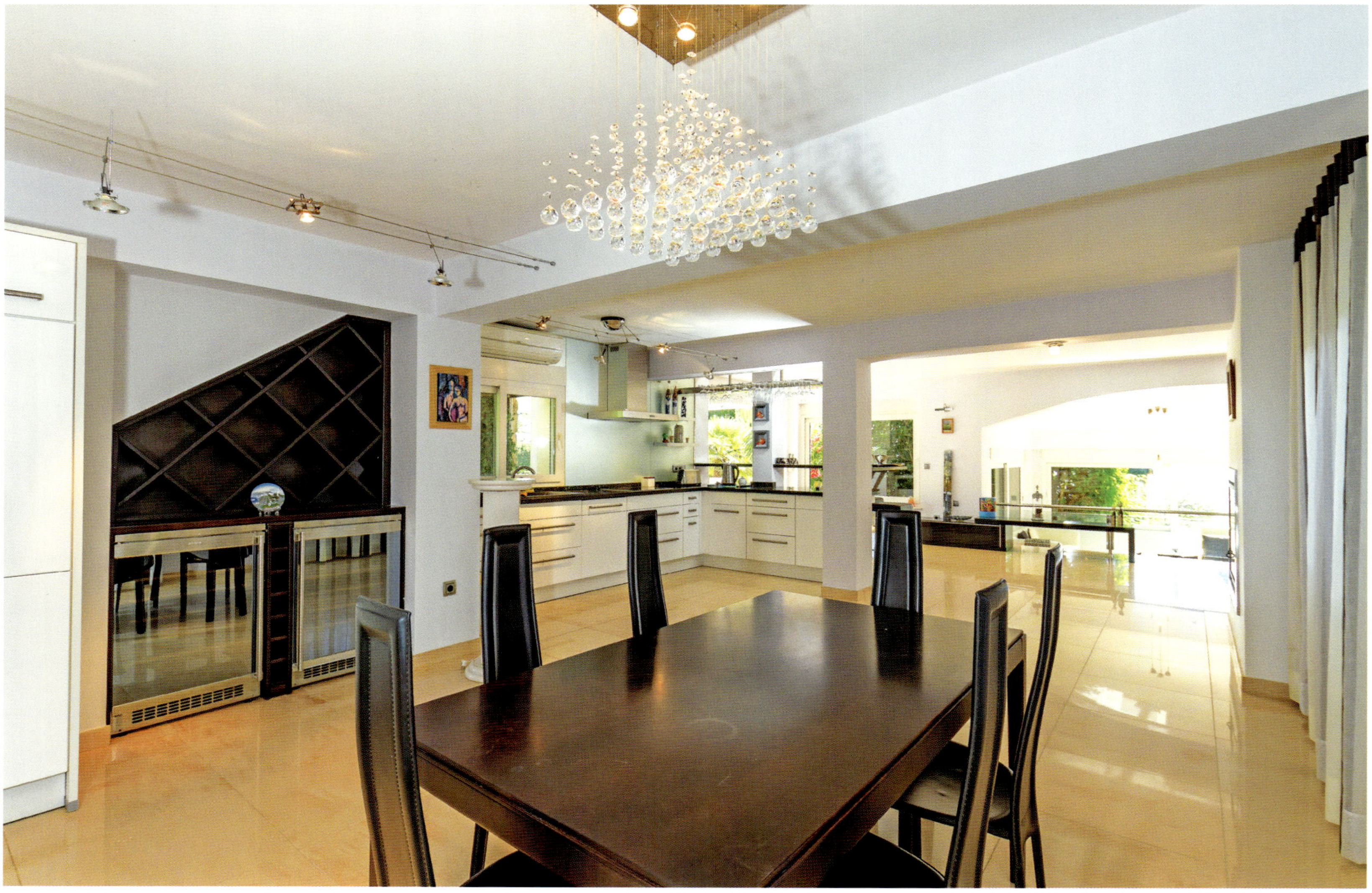

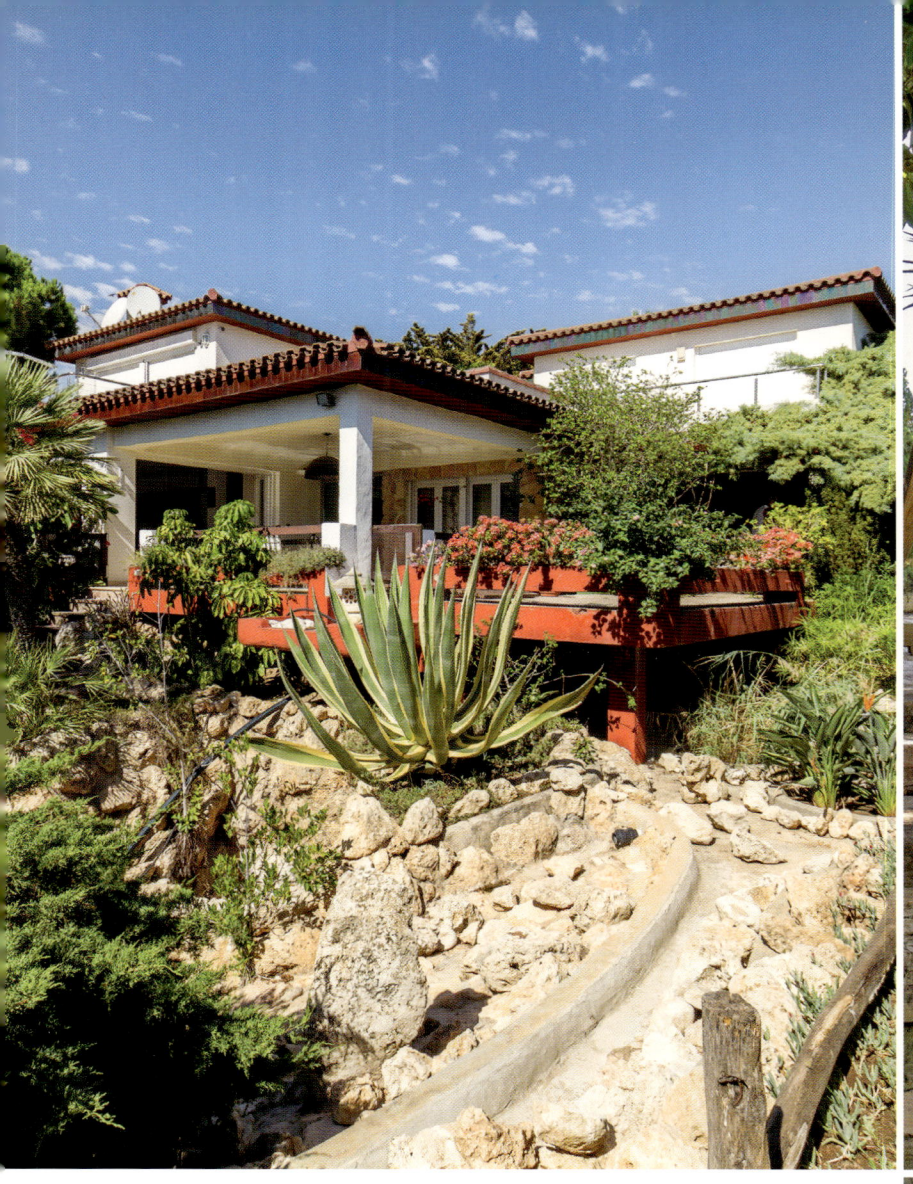

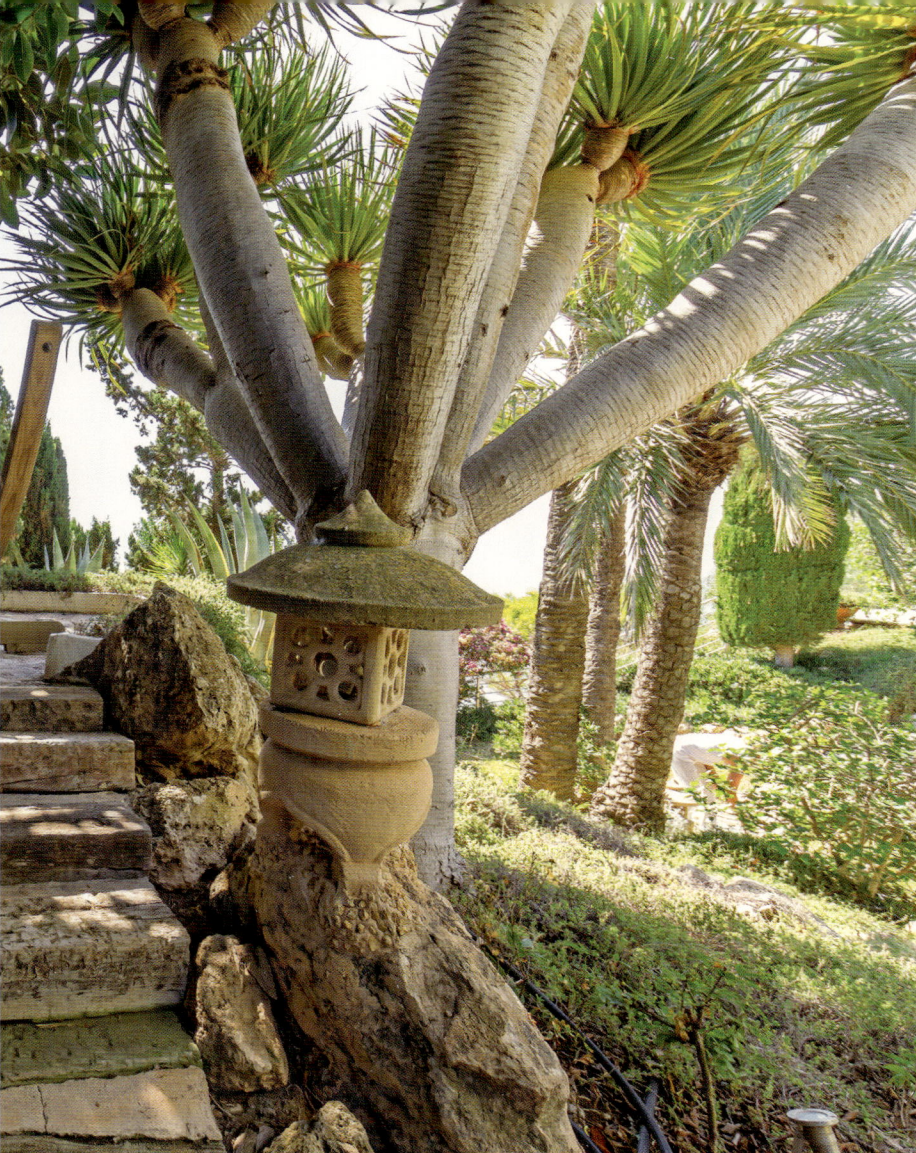

The extensive landscaped gardens are a real highlight of this attractive holiday home.

Die weitläufigen Gärten sind ein besonderes Highlight dieses mediterranen Feriendomizils.

Los extensos jardines son un verdadero hito de belleza en esta atractiva casa de vacaciones.

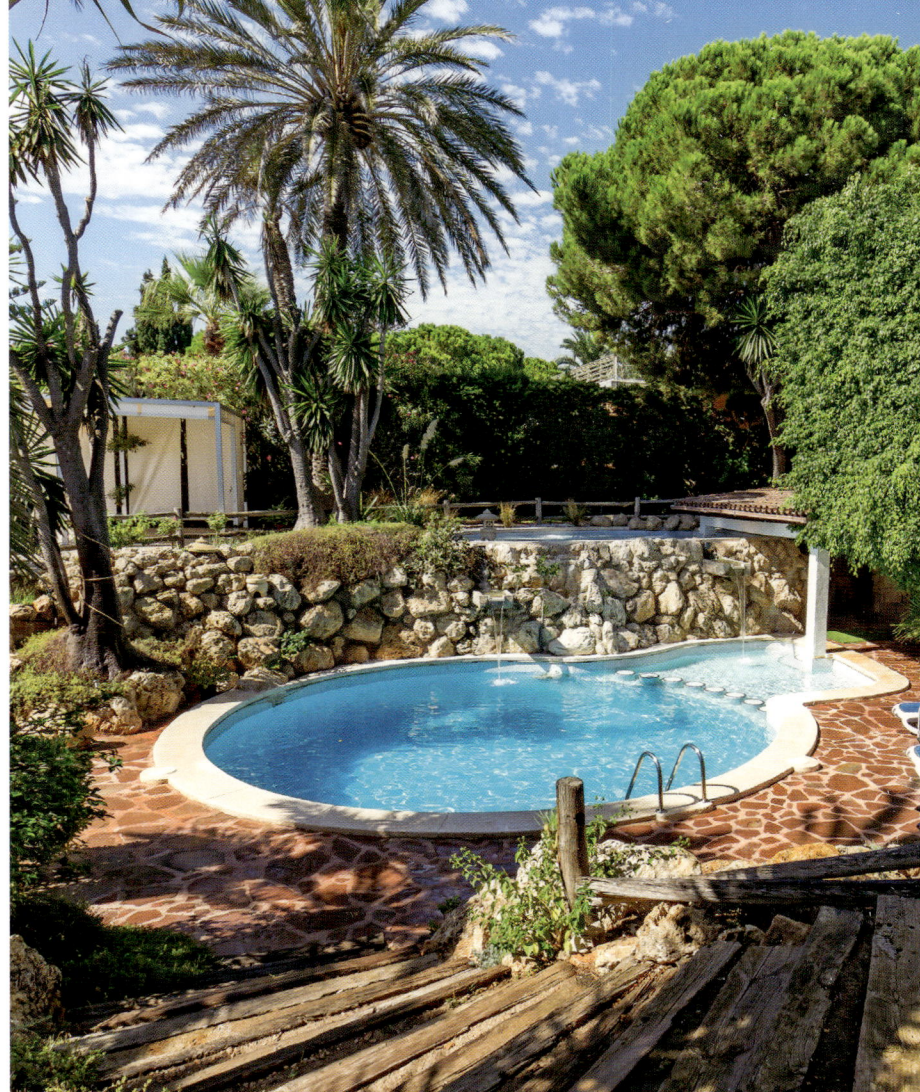

<

The atmosphere of the well-appointed villa is distinctly cool, clean and very modern.

Die gut ausgestattete Villa besticht durch ihre klare, gepflegte und moderne Atmosphäre.

La atmósfera de su bien decorado interior es singularmente fresca, limpia y muy moderna.

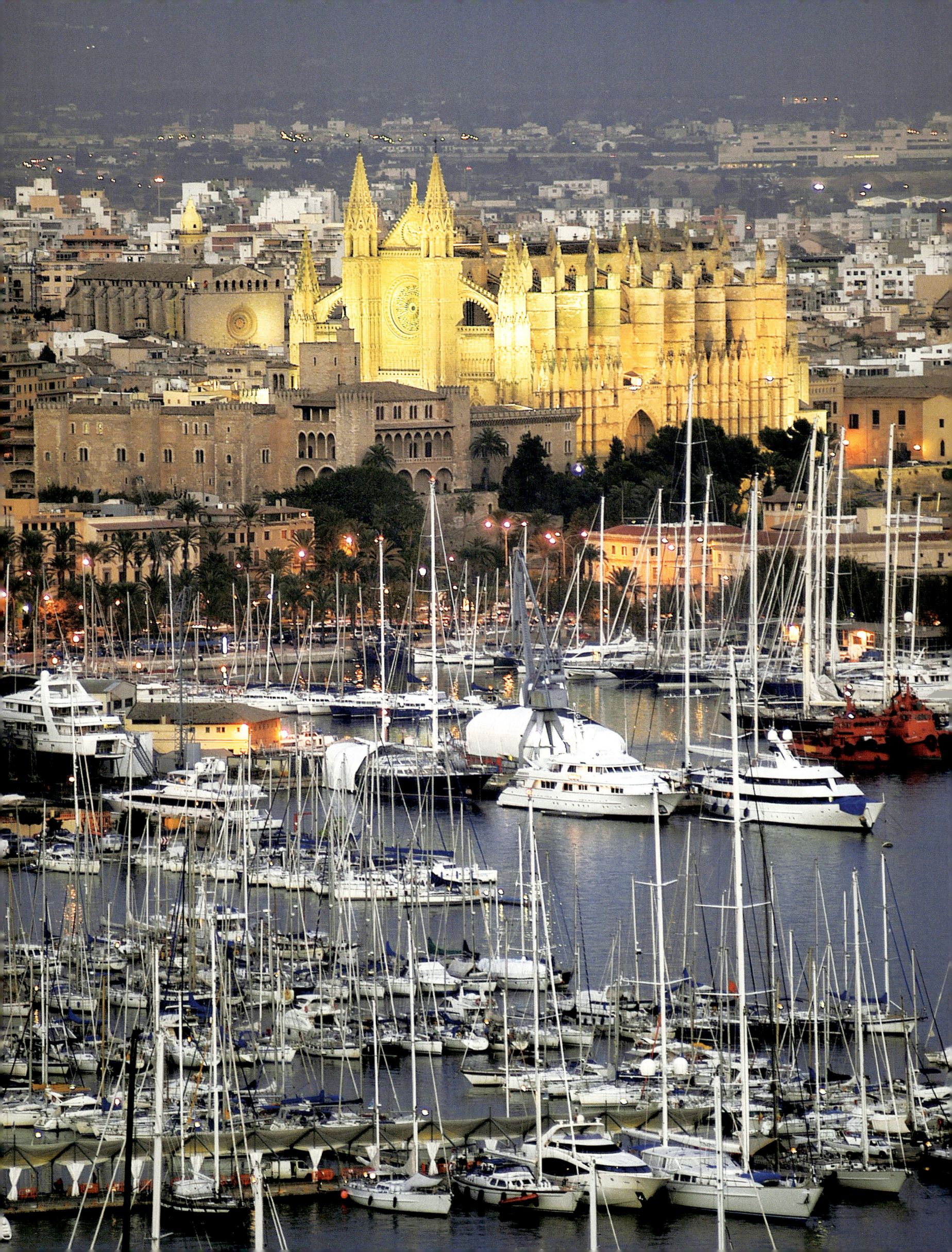

# Townhouse in Palma

A Gothic palace in former days, this lovingly restored home boasts a mix of stylish urban design, Mediterranean elements and beautiful, state-of-the-art comfort.

RIGHT IN THE HEART of Palma's charming old town with its delightful winding alleys, this modern townhouse affords stunning views of the magnificent cathedral La Seu and the sea. Extensive renovation work has transformed it into the ideal residence for all those who appreciate a lively cosmopolitan setting and, at the same time, close proximity to the sea. With 700 square metres of tasteful living space spread across four floors, it is very easy to relax and feel at home here. Comprising a total of four bedrooms and five bathrooms, the house also offers a living and dining area of extremely spacious proportions and a well-equipped kitchen with a separate service area. Today, the marvellous historic cistern, a relict of the former Gothic palace, accommodates the exclusive spa and pool area, a blissful sanctuary of peace and quiet to restore the tired soul. To top off this symbiosis of luxurious living comfort and Mediterranean lifestyle, there is a spectacular roof terrace high above the gables of the picturesque old town – simply divine!

IM HERZEN von Palmas charmant-verwinkelter Altstadt gelegen, beeindruckt dieses moderne Townhouse mit einem großartigen Ausblick auf die prachtvolle Kathedrale La Seu und das Meer. Nach aufwändigen Sanierungs- und Modernisierungsmaßnahmen ist es heute ein ideales Domizil für alle, die das lebendige Großstadtflair und die Nähe zum Meer zu schätzen wissen. Auf rund 700 Quadratmetern und vier Etagen laden die stilvoll ausgestatteten Räumlichkeiten zum Verweilen und Entspannen ein. Insgesamt verfügt das Ausnahmeobjekt über vier Schlaf- und fünf Badezimmer, einen großzügigen Wohn-Essbereich sowie eine hochwertig ausgestattete Küche nebst separatem Service-Bereich. Ein Relikt aus dem ehemals gotischen Palast ist die historische Zisterne, in der sich heute ein Spa- und Poolbereich befindet – hier lässt sich der Alltag auf schönste Weise abstreifen. Abgerundet wird diese Symbiose aus Wohnkomfort und mediterraner Lebensqualität von der im wahrsten Sinne des Wortes himmlischen Dachterrasse hoch oben über den Dächern der Altstadt.

EN PLENO CORAZÓN del encantador casco antiguo de Palma, con sus evocadoras y sinuosas callejuelas, esta moderna finca urbana ofrece unas impresionantes vistas a La Seu, la magnífica catedral de Palma, y al mar. Tras una exhaustiva reforma, la propiedad luce idónea para quienes saben apreciar el ambiente animado y cosmopolita y, al mismo tiempo, la siempre inspiradora proximidad del mar. Con 700 metros cuadrados de exquisito buen gusto en cuatro plantas, resulta muy fácil relajarse y sentirse en ella como en casa. Consta de cuatro dormitorios y cinco baños, y se sobrentienden la zona de estar y comedor sobredimensionada y la cocina perfectamente equipada con zona de servicio independiente. En la actualidad, la fabulosa cisterna histórica, vestigio del antiguo palacio gótico, aloja la exclusiva zona de *spa* y la piscina, un dichoso santuario de serenidad y silencio donde restaurar el alma cansada. Para rematar esta simbiosis de lujoso confort residencial y estilo de vida mediterráneo, la espectacular azotea sobre los tejados del pintoresco casco antiguo: ¡simplemente divina!

SPAIN, MAJORCA **PURCHASE PRICE** EUR 4.8 MILL. **INTERIOR APPROX.** 605 m² **NO. OF BEDROOMS** 4
**E&V ID** W-01GZC6 **CONTACT** PALMA CENTRE (ES), ENGEL EN PALMA S.L.,
LICENCE PARTNER OF BALEAREV GMBH **TEL.** +34 971 21 41 40 **E-MAIL** PALMACENTRE@ENGELVOELKERS.COM

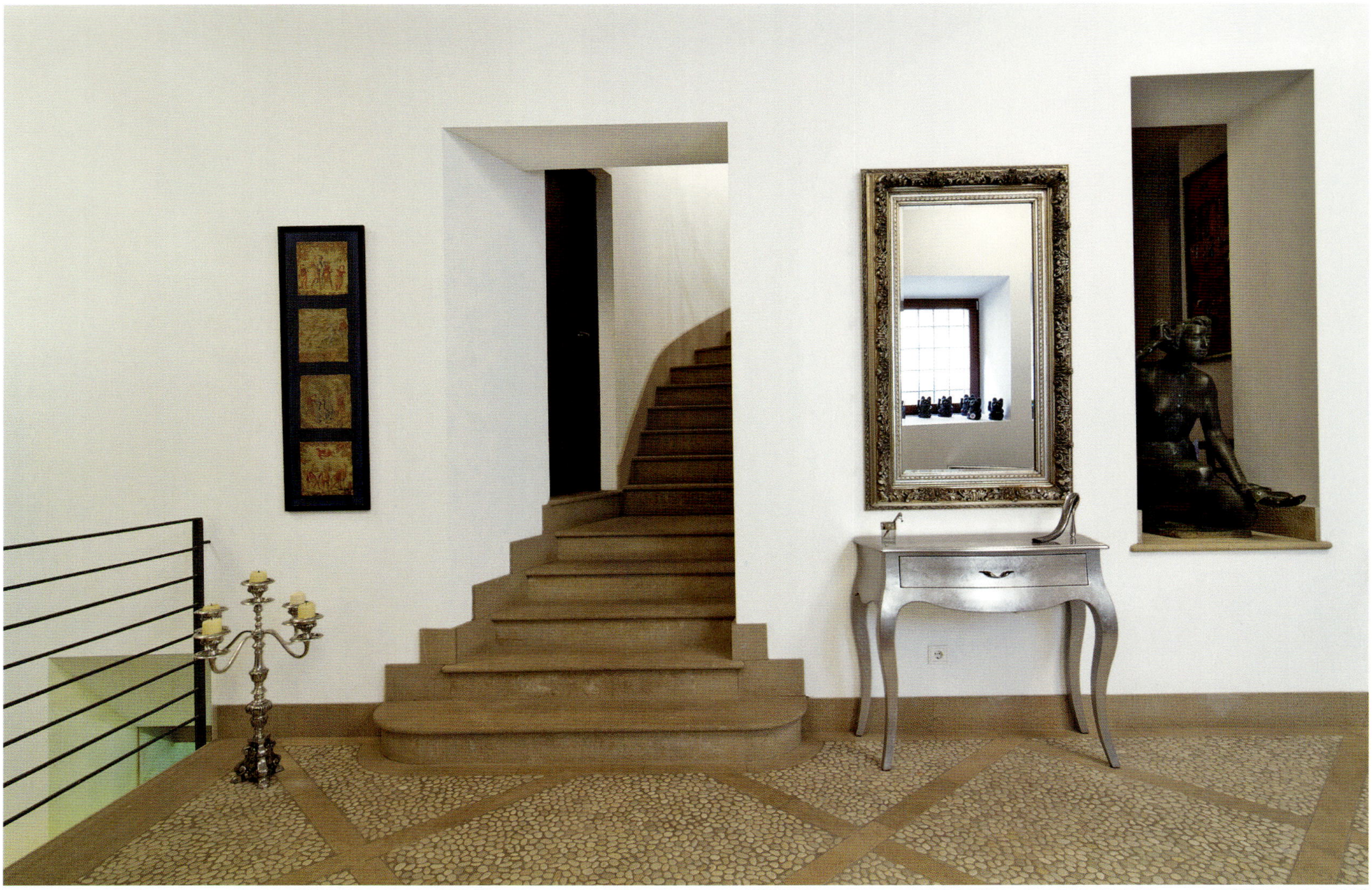

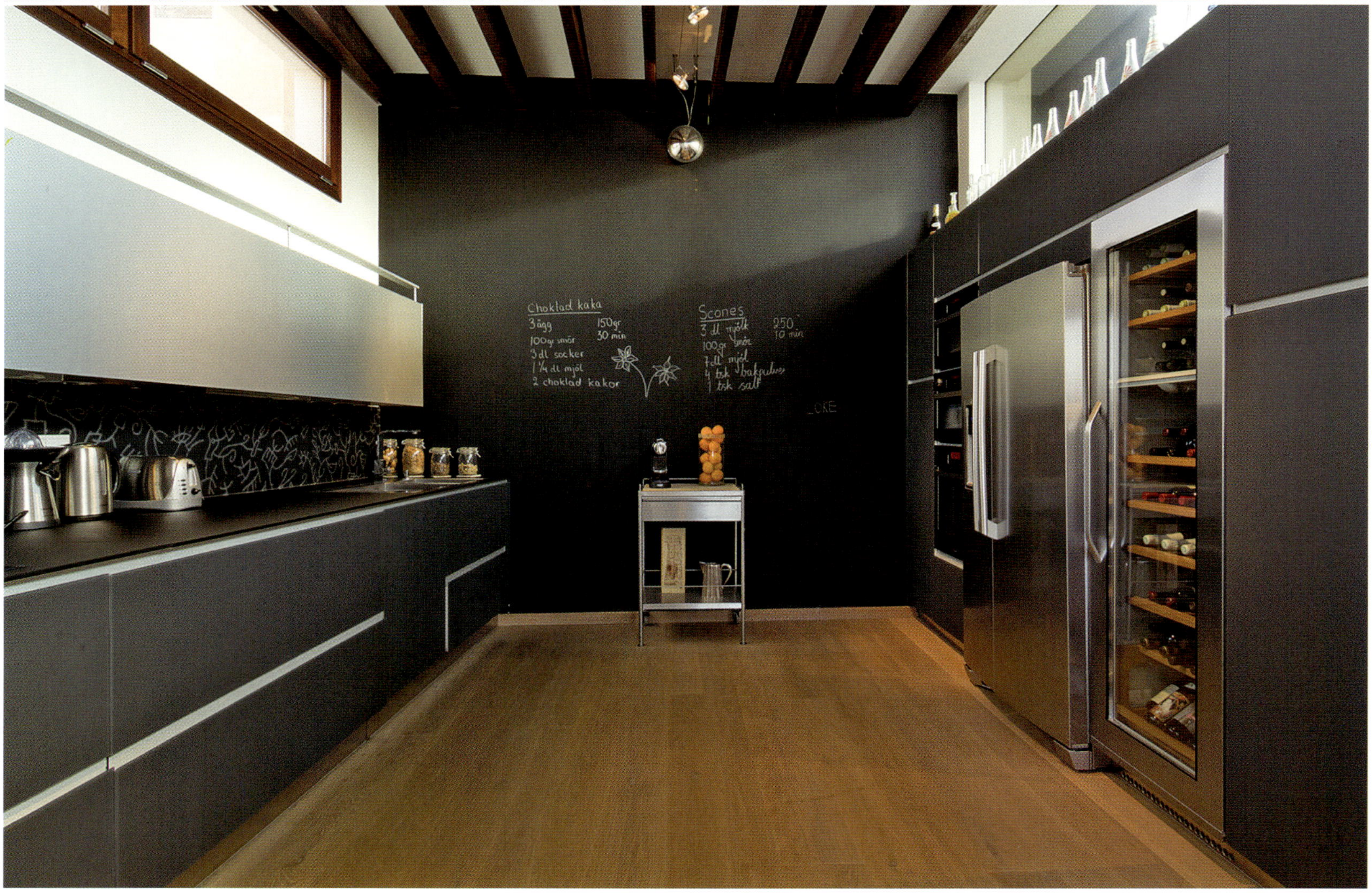
Choklad kaka
3 ägg
100gr smör
3 dl socker
1 1/4 dl mjöl
2 choklad kakor
150gr
30 min
Scones
3 dl mjölk
100gr smör
7 dl mjöl
4 tsk bakpulver
1 tsk salt
250°
10 min

<

Puristic elegance and bright, generous
dimensions form the ambience of the interiors.

Puristische Eleganz und helle Großzügigkeit
bestimmen das Ambiente im ganzen Haus.

Elegancia purista y generosas dimensiones
aireadas forman el ambiente de los interiores.

Simply sublime: the view of Palma's
iconic landmark, the cathedral La Seu.

Einfach sagenhaft: der Blick auf das
Wahrzeichen Palmas, die Kathedrale La Seu.

Simplemente sublime: las vistas a
la icónica catedral de Palma, La Seu.

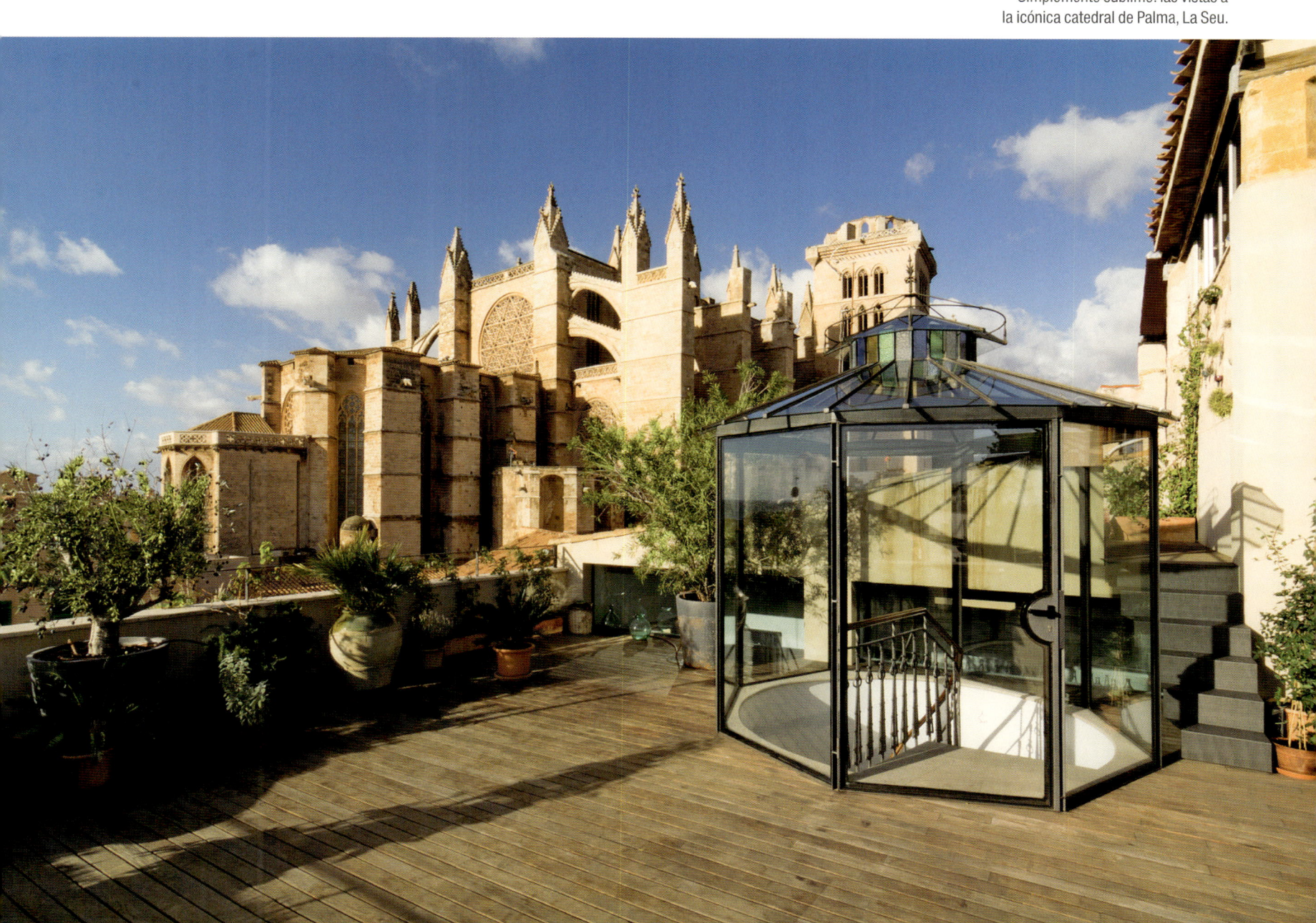

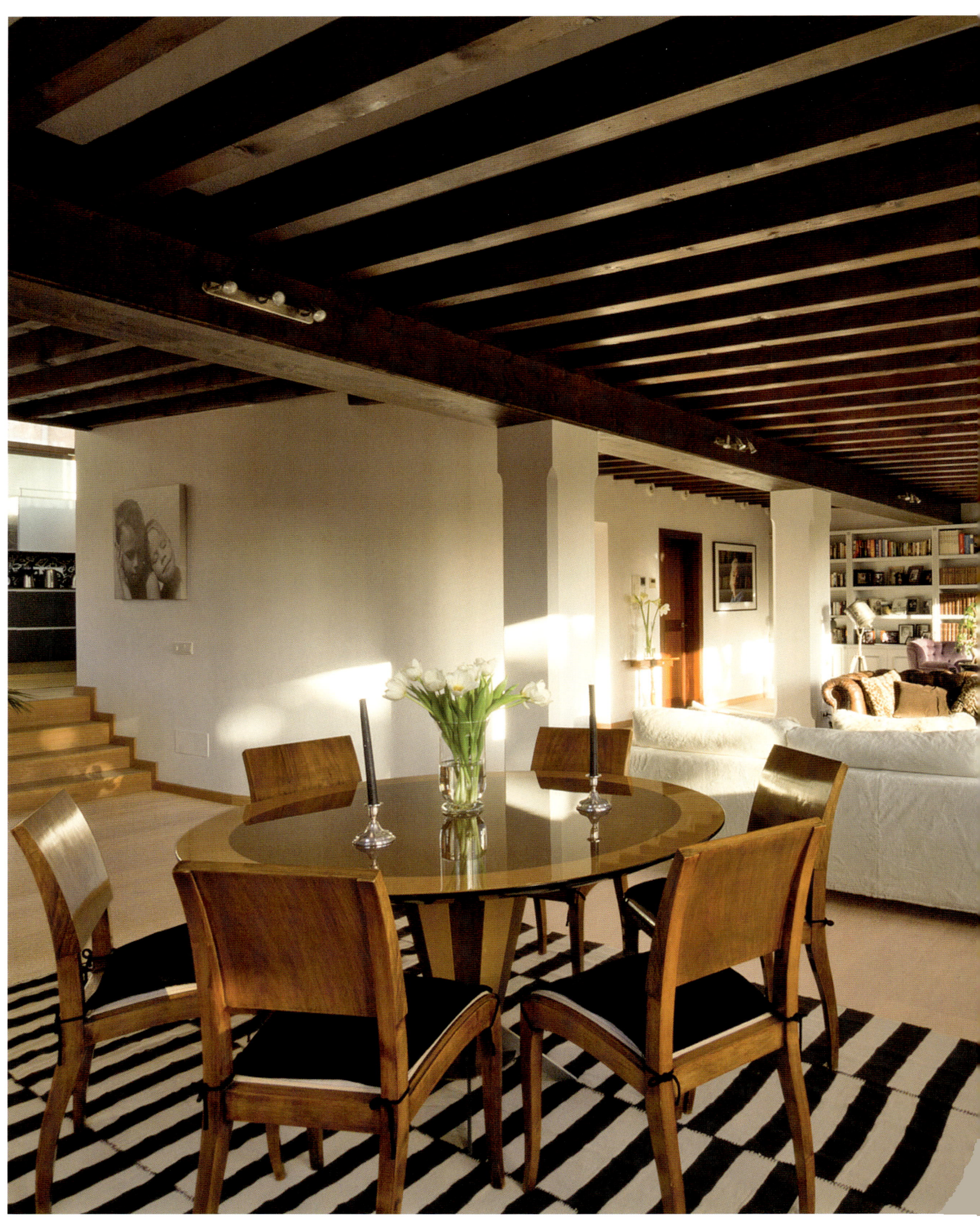

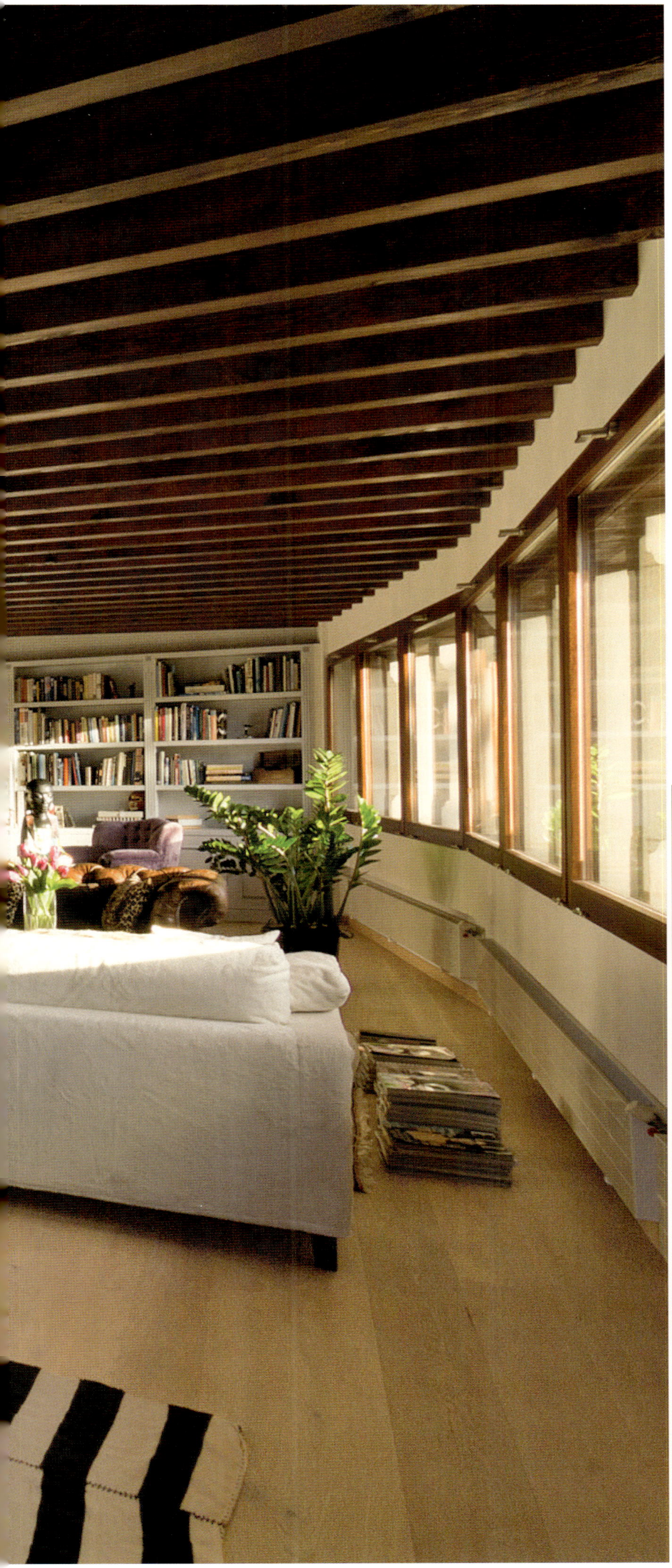

A characteristic element: the wooden ceiling beams create a rustic, Mediterranean flair.

Charakterisches Element: Die Deckenbalken sorgen für ein rustikal-mediterranes Flair.

Un elemento característico: las vigas de madera dan ese toque rústico mediterráneo.

With its four large bedrooms, the townhouse also offers sufficient space for guests.

Dank vier großzügiger Schlafzimmer bietet das Townhouse auch genug Platz für Gäste.

Con cuatro amplios dormitorios, la casa también brinda espacio para los invitados.

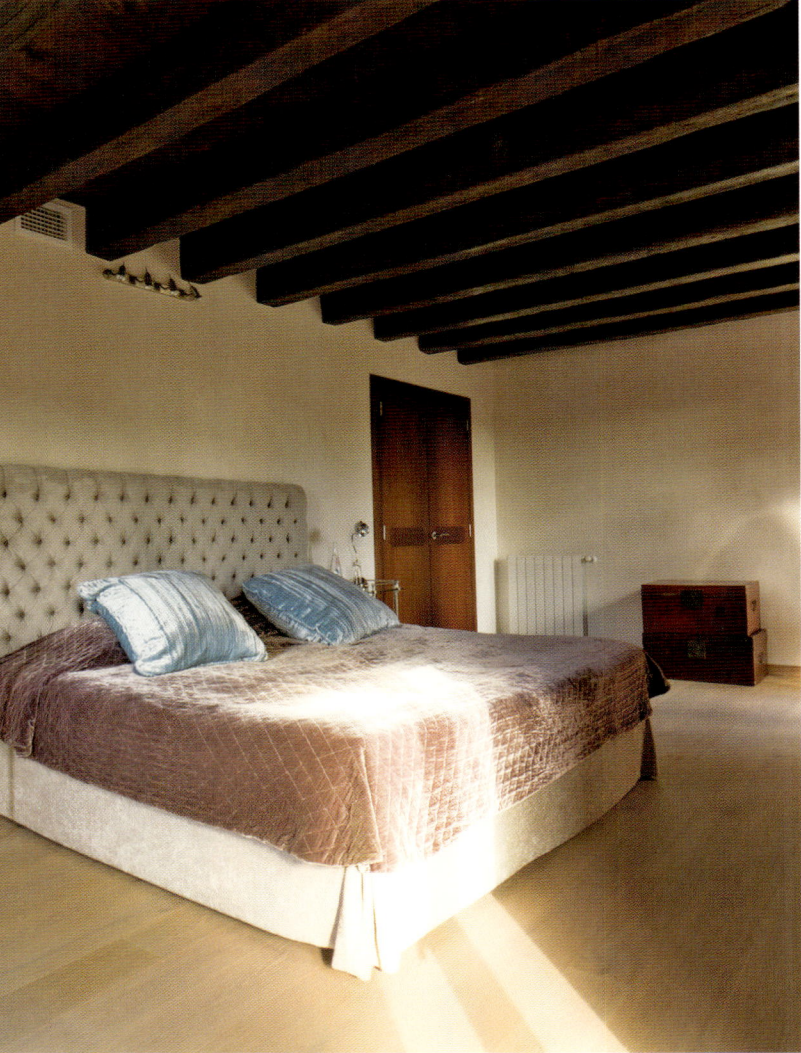

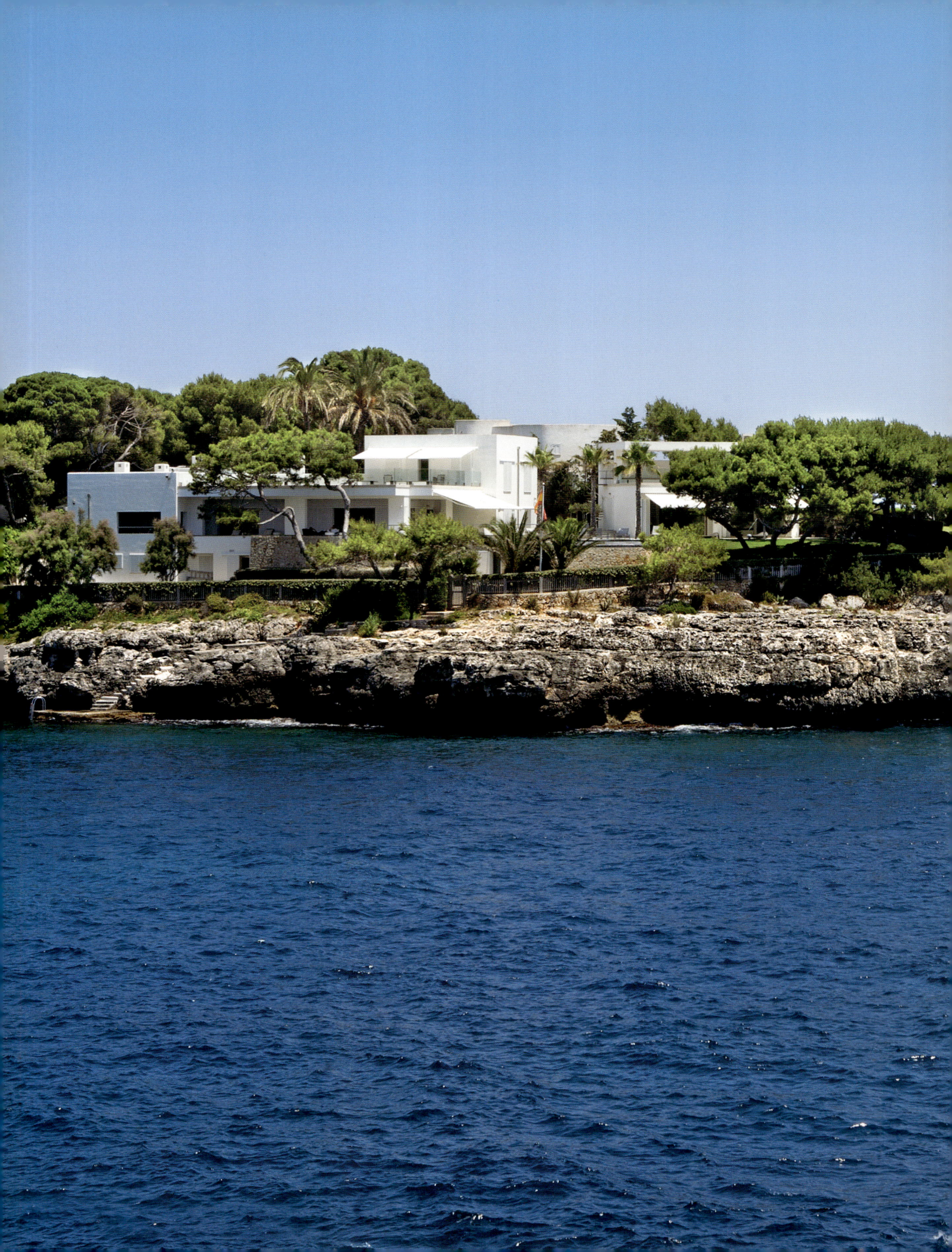

# Cala d'Or in Style

A contemporary architectural masterpiece that will particularly attract lovers of modern design – crowned by an awe-inspiring coastal setting in the prime holiday destination of Cala d'Or on Majorca.

IN TOTAL PRIVACY and with wonderful views of the sea, this precious property enjoys a discreet and protected location by the entrance to the harbour of Cala d'Or in south-east Majorca. Masterfully converted and renovated in 2005 in the style of contemporary design, it is easily one of the island's most beautiful properties today. Welcoming the visitor, an impressive patio behind a wall is surrounded by the gorgeous villa on three sides. The centrepiece of the home is the spacious, stylish living area, graced with a fireplace, that is combined with the dining area – ideal for entertaining and sharing the inimitable views with guests. Four en-suite bedrooms and a fully equipped gourmet kitchen are all located on the ground floor. The top floor accommodates the en-suite master bedroom with a dressing room, as well as a further bedroom and bathroom. The separate guest house comprises two extravagant suites and designer bathrooms. Seafront terraces provide ample space for relaxing and unwinding – at any time of the year.

UNEINSEHBAR GESCHÜTZT, mit einem wunderschönen Blick aufs Meer, versteckt sich dieses Anwesen an der Hafeneinfahrt von Cala d'Or im Südosten Mallorcas. Im Jahr 2005 mit großer Detailliebe im Stil zeitgenössischen Designs umgebaut und renoviert, dürfte es heute zu einer der schönsten Immobilien der Umgebung gehören. Hinter einer Mauer wird man von einem prachtvollen Patio empfangen, den die Villa von drei Seiten umgibt. Ihren Mittelpunkt bildet der repräsentative Wohnbereich mit Kamin, der mit dem Essbereich verbunden ist – perfekt, um auch Gäste an dem unvergleichlichen Ausblick teilhaben zu lassen. Ebenfalls im Erdgeschoss befinden sich vier elegante Schlafzimmer mit Bädern en suite sowie die erstklassig ausgestattete Küche. Das Obergeschoss beherbergt das Hauptschlafzimmer mit Bad und Ankleideraum sowie ein weiteres Schlafzimmer inklusive Bad. Das Gästehaus bietet mit zwei extravaganten Suiten, Design-Bädern und zum Meer ausgerichteten Terrassen ebenfalls viel Platz zum Ausspannen und Wohlfühlen – zu jeder Jahreszeit.

CON TOTAL PRIVACIDAD y maravillosas vistas al mar, esta preciosidad goza de una ubicación discreta y protegida en la bocana del puerto de Cala d'Or, al sudeste de Mallorca. Magistralmente reformada y renovada en 2005 con la estética del diseño contemporáneo, hoy es, probablemente, una de las más bellas propiedades de la isla. Tras un muro, el impresionante patio, que la villa rodea por tres de sus lados, da la bienvenida al visitante. La pieza central de la casa es el amplio y elegante salón con chimenea, conectado con la zona de comedor, idónea para compartir las inimitables panorámicas con los invitados. Cuatro elegantes dormitorios con baño privado y la cocina *gourmet* totalmente equipada ocupan la planta baja, mientras la superior aloja el dormitorio principal con baño en *suite* y vestidor, así como otro dormitorio con baño. La casa de invitados consta de dos sofisticadas *suites* con baños de diseño. Las extensas terrazas con vistas al mar proveen un espacio de lujo para relajarse y dejarse llevar, en cualquier época del año.

SPAIN, MAJORCA **PURCHASE PRICE** EUR 7.5 MILL. **INTERIOR APPROX.** 732 m² **NO. OF BEDROOMS** 11
**LAND APPROX.** 1,839 m² **E&V ID** W-0136C6 **CONTACT** SANTANYI (ES), ENGEL & VÖLKERS MALLORCA SOUTH-EAST S.L.,
LICENCE PARTNER OF ENGEL & VÖLKERS BALEAREV GMBH **TEL.** +34 971 64 21 01
**E-MAIL** SANTANYI@ENGELVOELKERS.COM

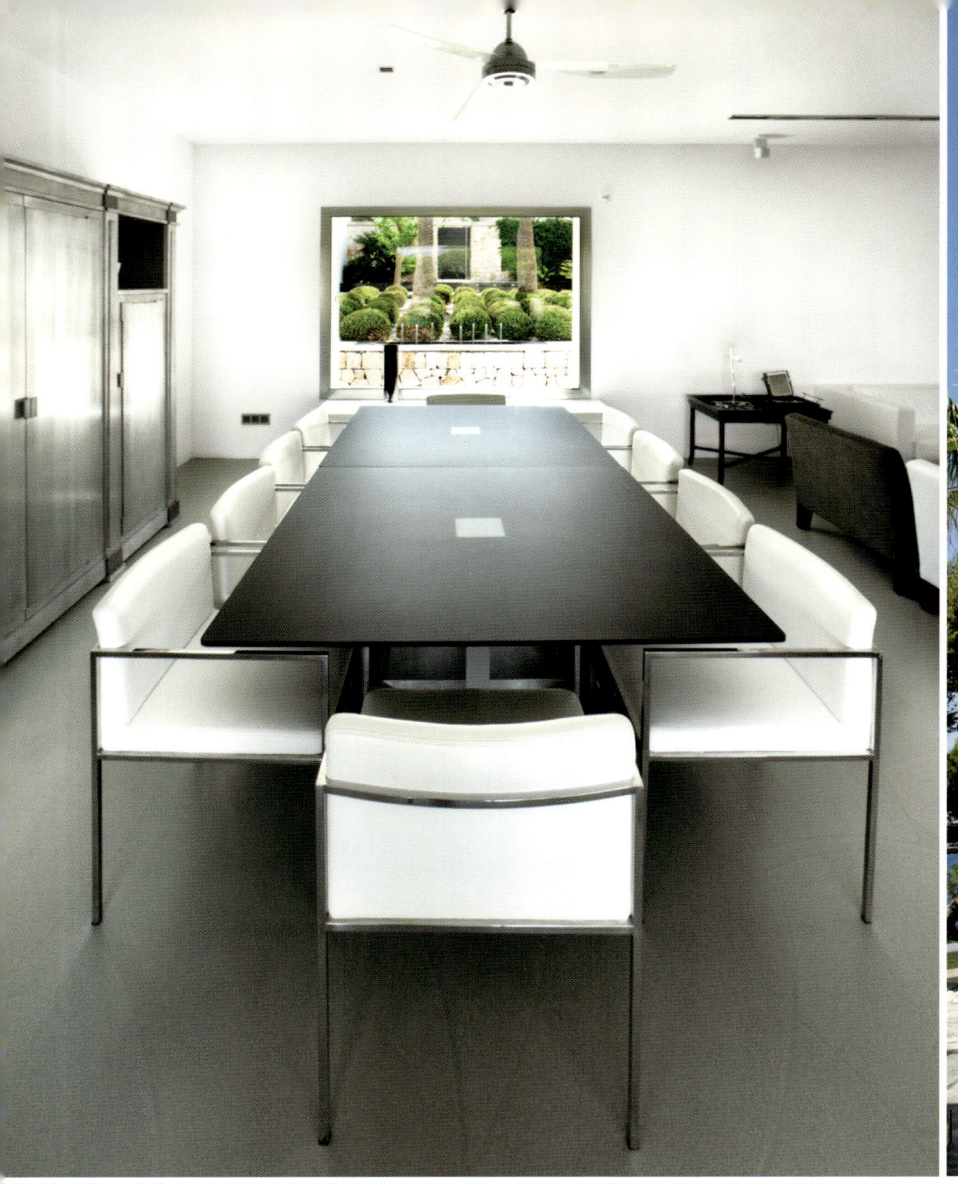

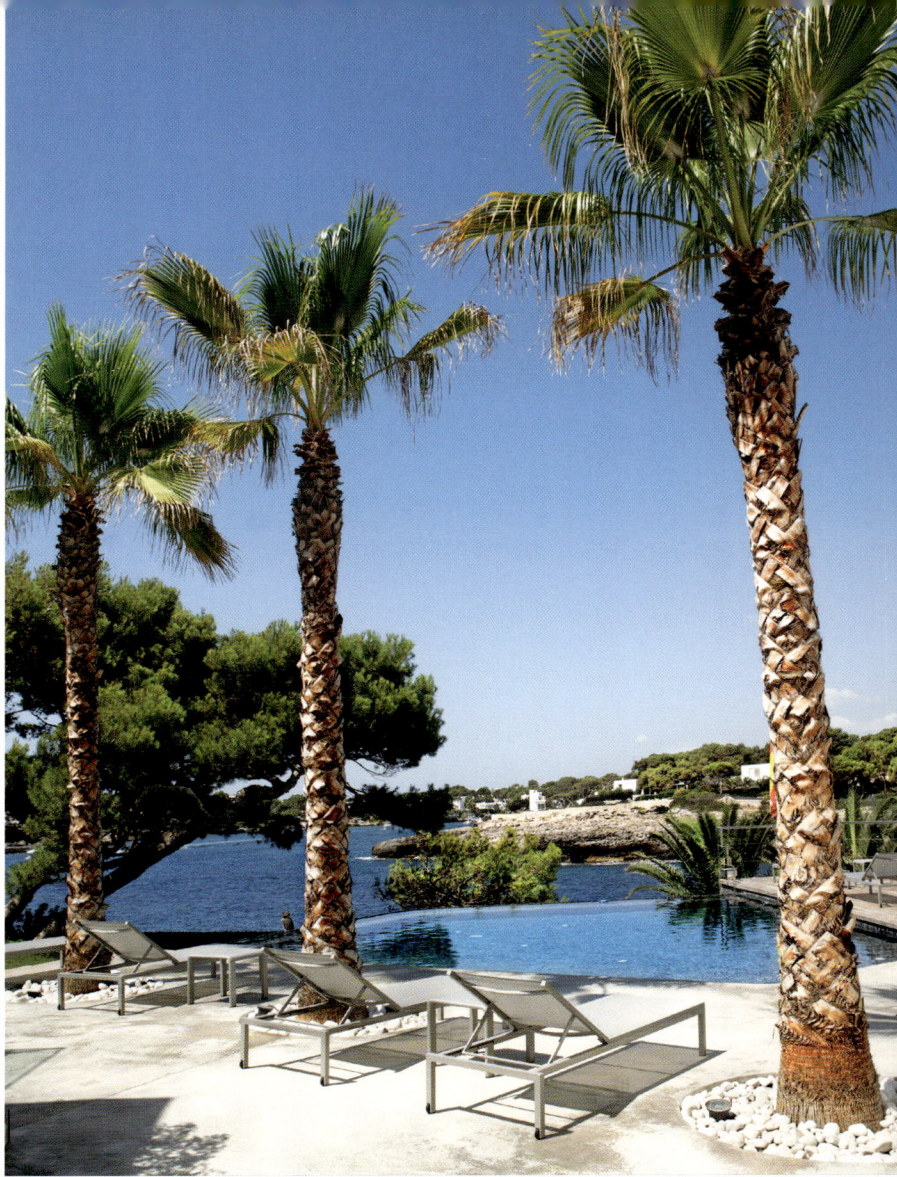

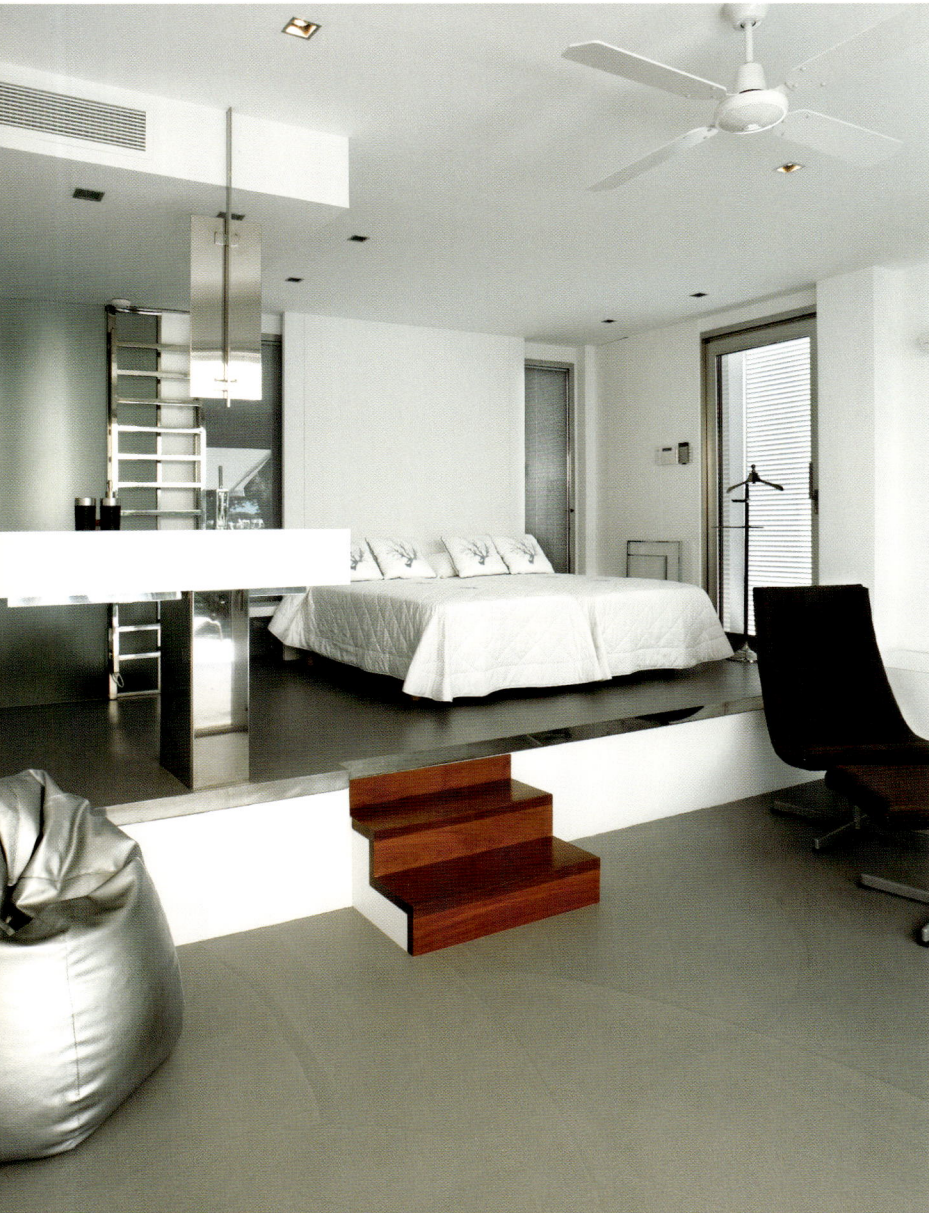

The interiors show that purism and cosiness complement each other perfectly.

Das Interieur beweist: Hier ergänzen sich Purismus und Behaglichkeit perfekt.

Los interiores demuestran que purismo y comodidad se llevan perfectamente juntos.

Clear lines meet with highest comfort – and
windows that do justice to the views.

Klare Linien treffen auf höchsten Komfort –
und Fenster, die den Traum-Ausblick würdigen.

Líneas claras que casan con el mayor confort
y ventanales que hacen justicia a las vistas.

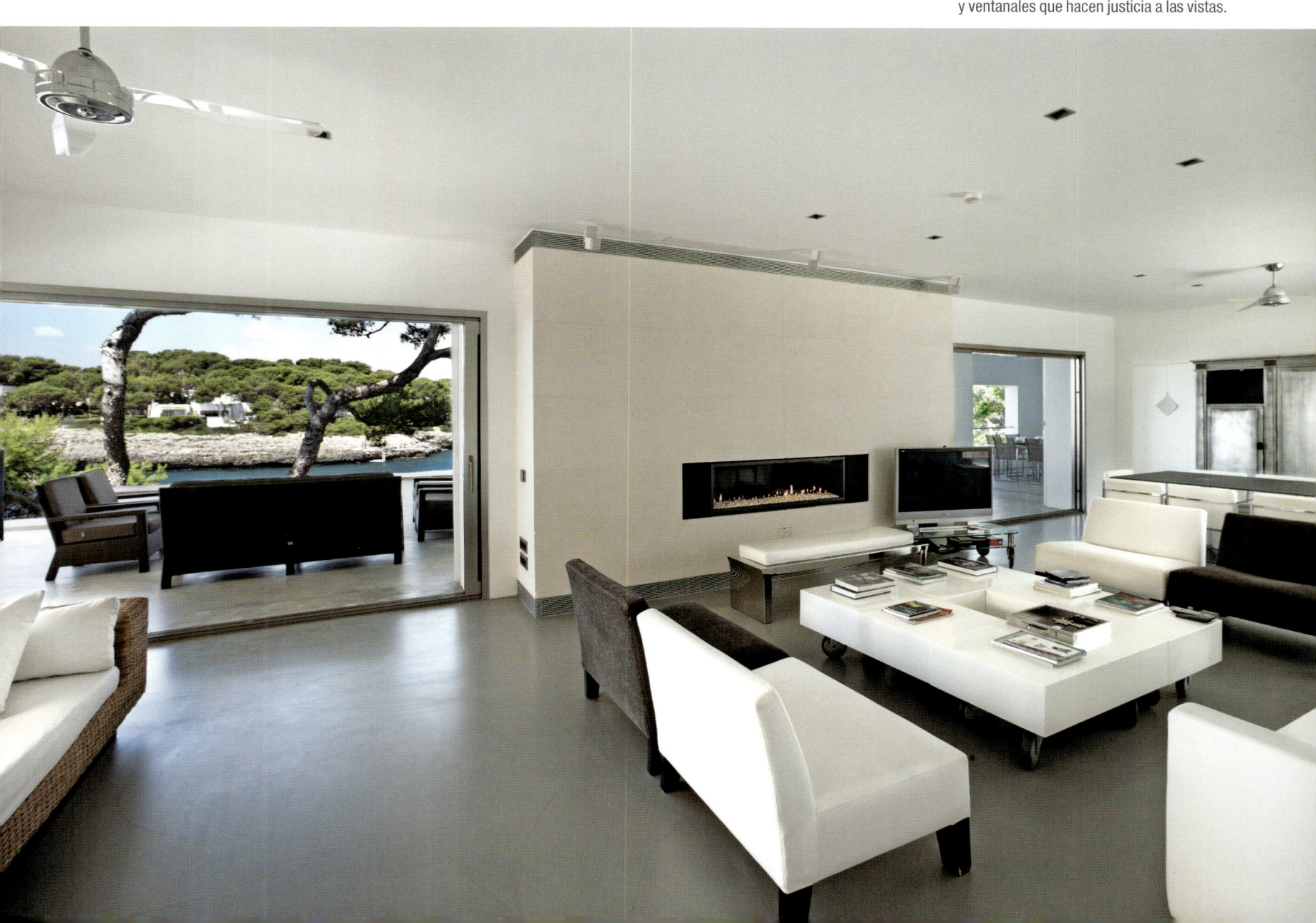

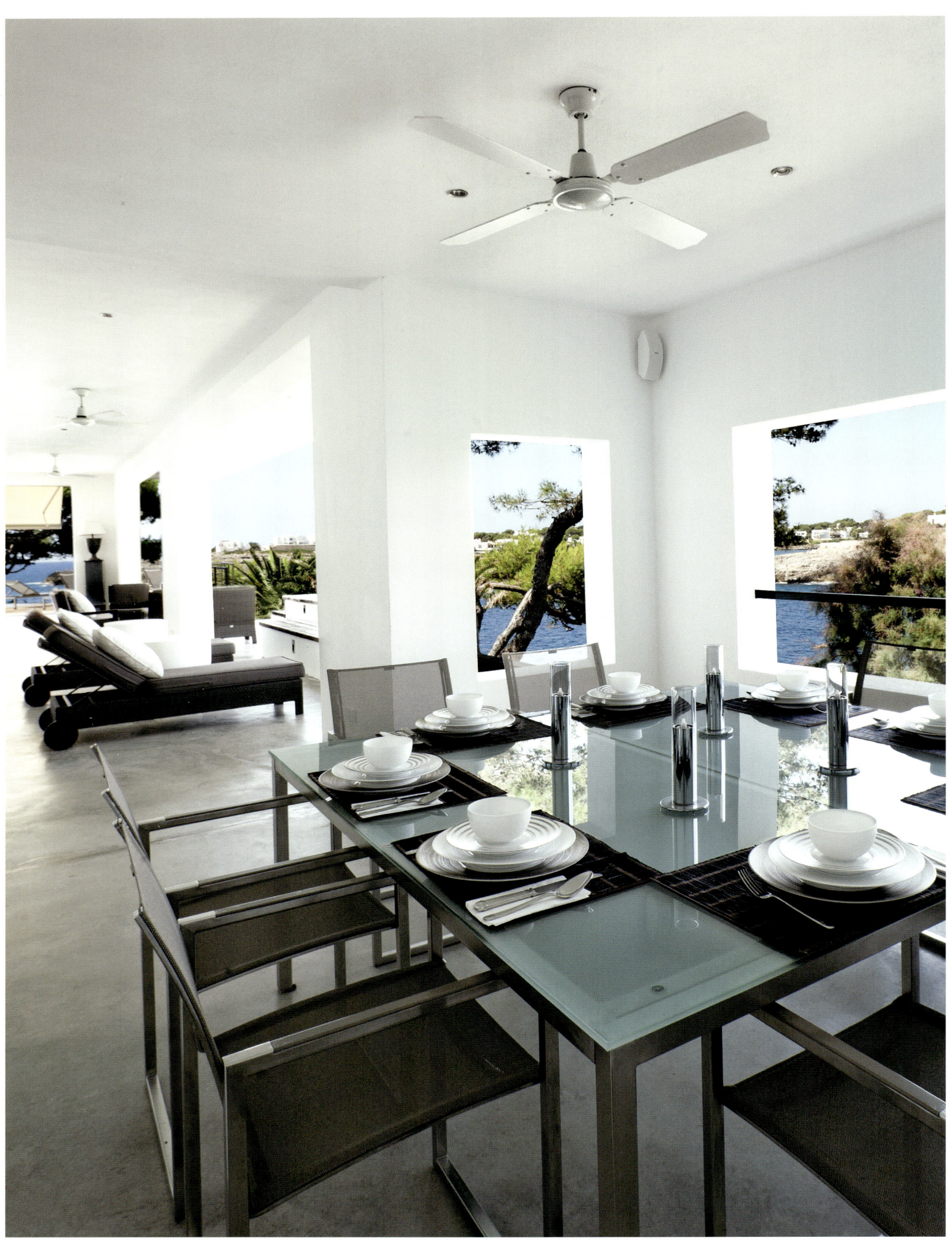

<

Take a seat and enjoy: entertaining guests
in such a setting is a true pleasure.

Platz nehmen und genießen: Vor einer solchen
Kulisse empfängt man Gäste besonders gern.

Tome asiento y disfrute: entretener a los
invitados en un ambiente así es un placer.

A swim at any time of day: the fantastic pool
with spectacular views of the sea.

Lädt zu jeder Tageszeit zum Baden ein: der
fantastische Pool mit Blick aufs Meer.

Un baño a cualquier hora del día: la fantástica
piscina con espectaculares vistas al mar.

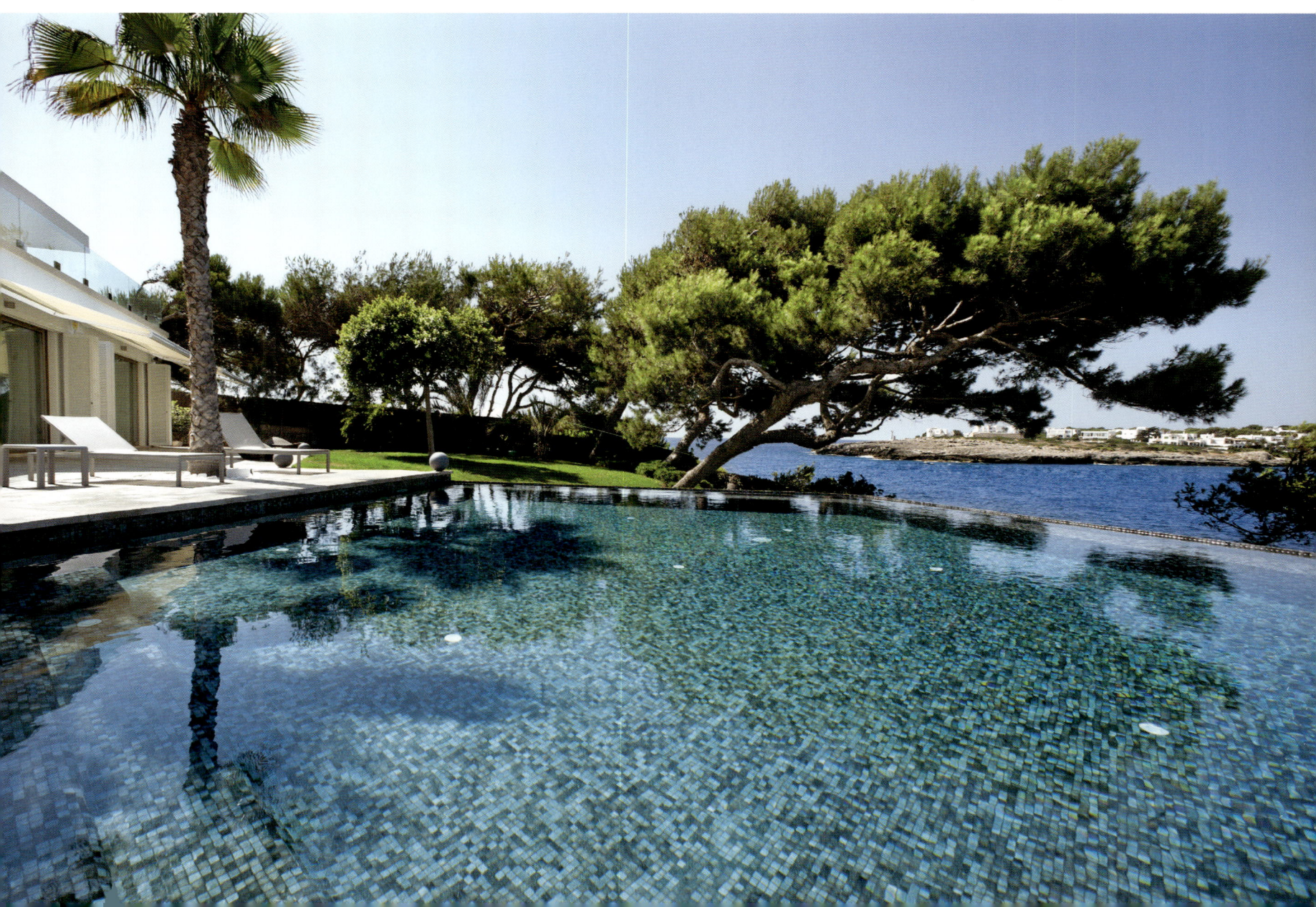

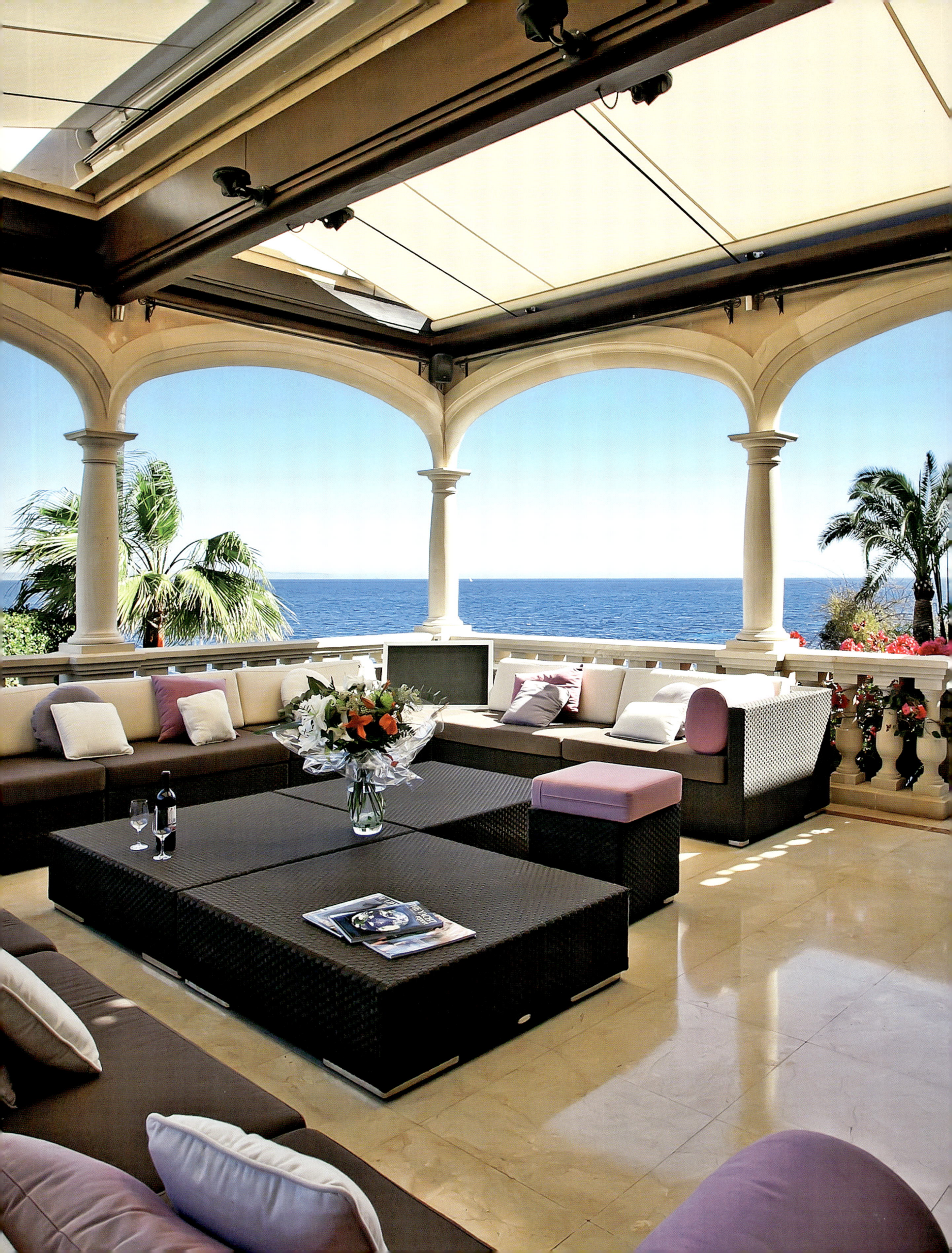

# Gem in Cas Català

This stunning villa has abundant Spanish flair and enjoys a deluxe waterfront setting: perfect for a peaceful holiday yet only minutes from the Majorcan capital.

WITH ITS TYPICAL Spanish architecture and fantastic surroundings, this spacious residence is located in Cas Català, a tranquil suburb of Calvià which belongs to one of the most affluent communities on the island of Majorca. Located directly by the small picturesque harbour Calanova, it offers total privacy and interiors with a high degree of living comfort. The villa was completely renovated with great attention to detail in 2008 and boasts a spacious living area which has a fireplace and also leads out onto a fabulous covered terrace with unrivalled views of the azure-blue sea. The top floor comprises six elegant en-suite bedrooms and the basement level has a spa and a fitness area with a pool, a home cinema, an office and two staff bedrooms. All three storeys are conveniently connected by an internal lift. Magnificent for relaxing and entertaining, the beautiful Balinese-style garden has a saltwater pool, a separate Jacuzzi and a delightful gazebo with a lounge bar – the ideal venue for enjoying pleasant summer evenings with family and friends.

DIESE VILLA in typisch spanischem Baustil besticht vor allem durch ihre einzigartige Lage im mallorquinischen Cas Català, einem beschaulichen Vorort der Gemeinde Calvià. Direkt neben dem kleinen Yachthafen Calanova gelegen, lassen sich hier maximale Privatsphäre und erstklassiger Komfort in erster Meereslinie genießen. Im Jahr 2008 wurde die Villa mit großer Sorgfalt komplett modernisiert und präsentiert sich heute mit einem geräumigen, elegant ausgestatteten Wohnbereich samt Kamin und Zugang zu einer herrlichen überdachten Terrasse. Im oberen Stockwerk befinden sich sechs behagliche Schlafzimmer mit Bädern en suite, im Souterrain ein Spa- und Fitnessbereich mit Pool, ein Heimkino, ein Büro sowie zwei Personalräume. Alle drei Etagen sind durch einen Aufzug verbunden. Zum Entspannen, Feiern und Genießen unter freiem Himmel wie geschaffen ist der wunderschöne Garten im balinesischen Stil mit Salzwasser-Pool und separatem Jacuzzi, ergänzt von einem einladenden Pavillon mit Lounge-Bar für gesellige Sommerabende.

CON SU TÍPICA arquitectura española y un entorno fantástico, esta espaciosa residencia se situa en Cas Català, un tranquilo barrio de Calvià, uno de los municipios más prósperos de la isla de Mallorca. A orillas del pequeño y pintoresco puerto de Calanova y del mar, ofrece total privacidad e interiores singulares con un altísimo nivel de confort residencial. Fue totalmente renovada con gran atención al detalle en 2008 y cuenta con una amplia zona de día con chimenea y acceso a la fabulosa terraza: un porche con sobrias columnas y soberbias vistas al mar. La planta superior aloja seis elegantes dormitorios con baño privado y la planta inferior luce el *spa* y un gimnasio con piscina, sala de cine, despacho y dos dormitorios de servicio. Las tres plantas están cómodamente conectadas mediante un ascensor interno. Magnífico tanto para relajarse como para divertirse, el precioso jardín de estilo balinés se decora con una piscina de agua salada, Jacuzzi independiente y un romántico cenador con su *lounge*-bar: el lugar perfecto para disfrutar de las noches de verano con familia y amigos.

SPAIN, MAJORCA **PURCHASE PRICE** EUR 18 MILL. **INTERIOR APPROX.** 1,091 m² **NO. OF BEDROOMS** 8
**LAND APPROX.** 2,042 m² **E&V ID** W-00ACYQ **CONTACT** PUERTO PORTALS (ES), ENGEL PROPERTIES INVEST SL,
LICENCE PARTNER OF BALEAREV GMBH **TEL.** +34 971 67 68 36 **E-MAIL** PORTALS@ENGELVOELKERS.COM

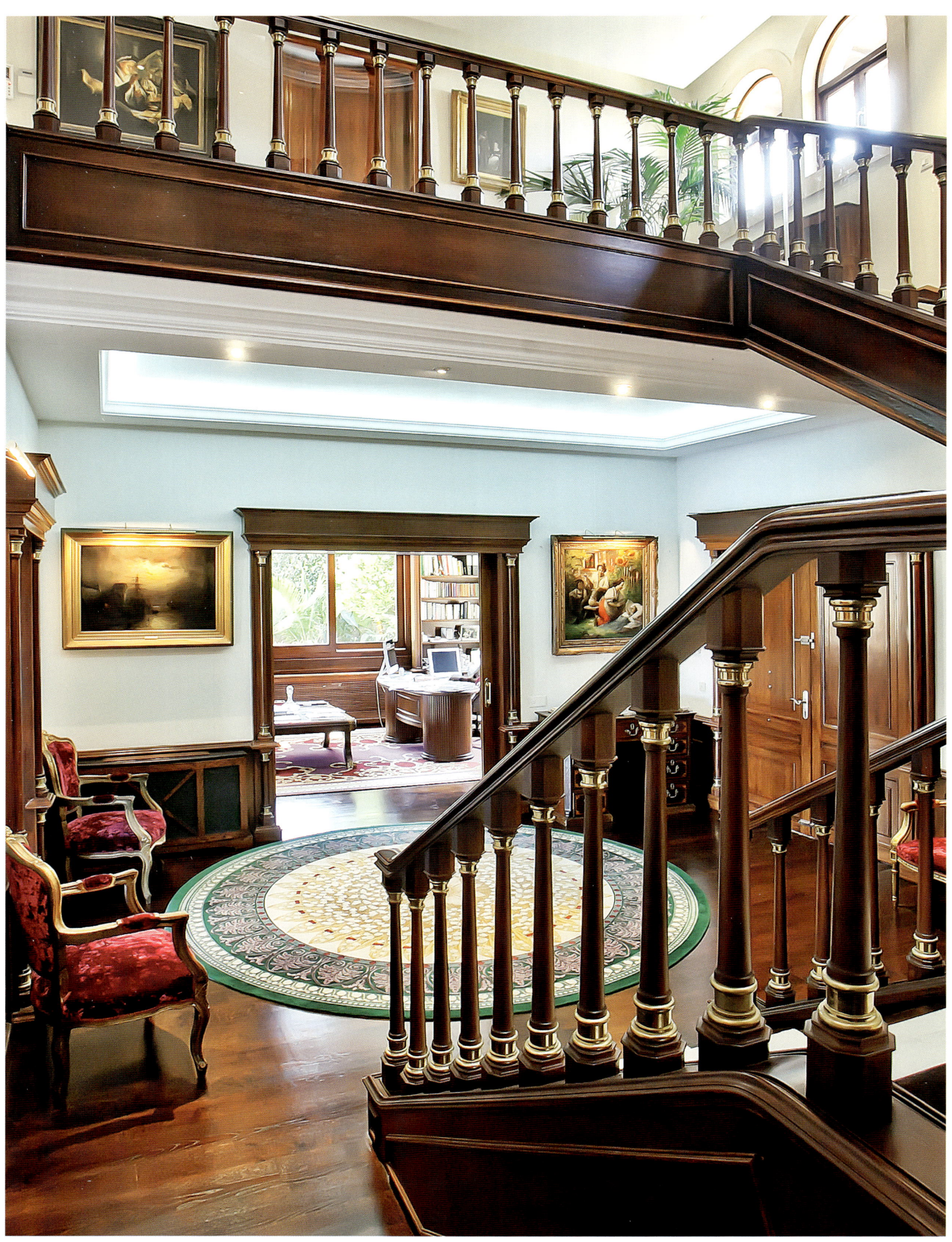

<

A staircase and a lift lead to the upper floor
and the bedrooms of the house.

Zu den Schlafzimmern im oberen Stockwerk
führt neben der Treppe auch ein Aufzug.

Escalera y ascensor: ambos conducen al piso
superior y a los dormitorios de la casa.

The inviting living area is beautifully
enhanced by a spacious terrace.

Der einladende Wohnbereich wird perfekt
ergänzt durch die großzügige Terrasse.

La acogedora zona de día se complementa
a la perfección con la espaciosa terraza.

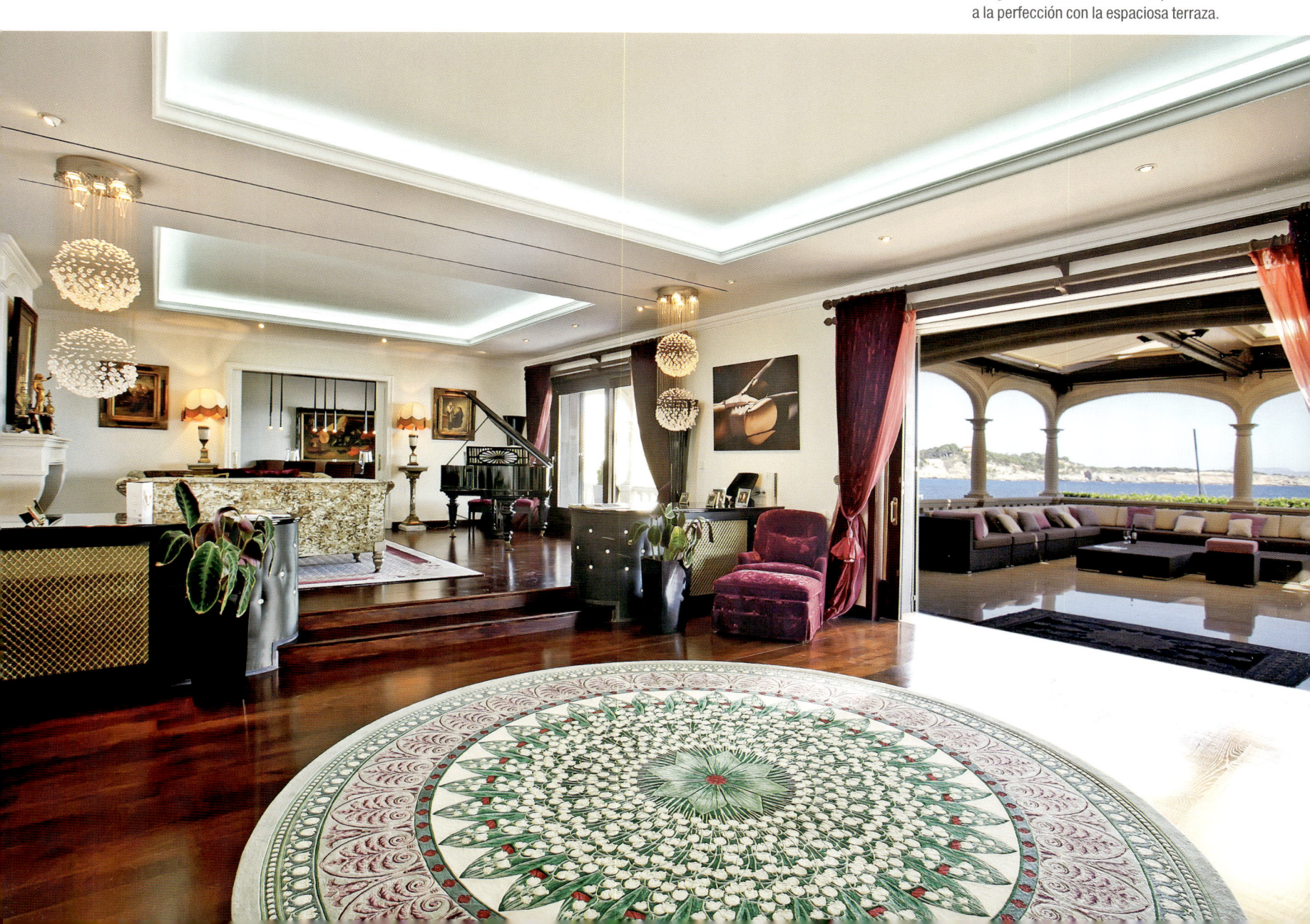

What a view: the location of this property leaves nothing to be desired.

Was für eine Aussicht: Die Lage dieses Anwesens lässt keine Wünsche offen.

Esto sí son vistas: la situación de esta propiedad supera cualquier expectativa.

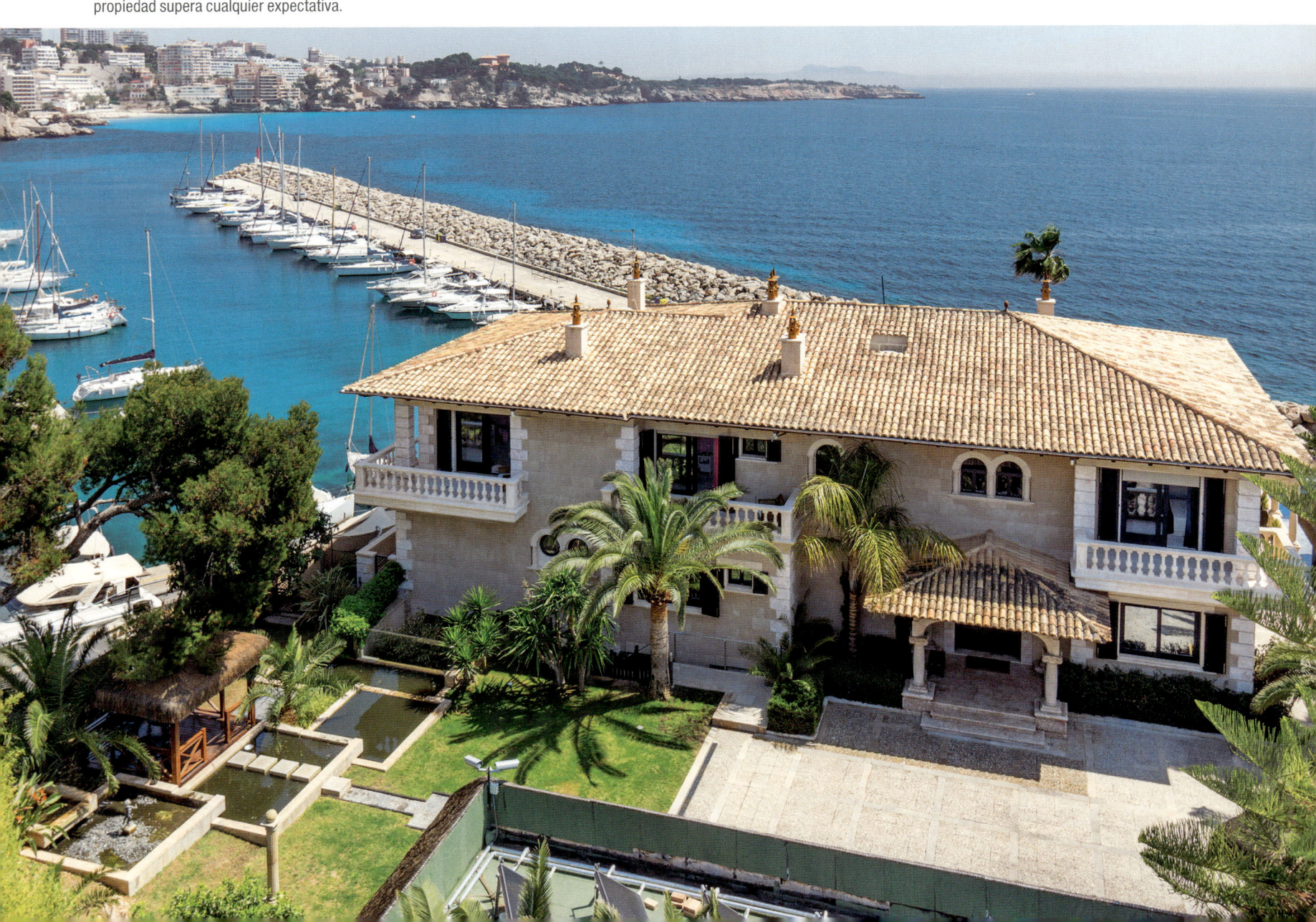

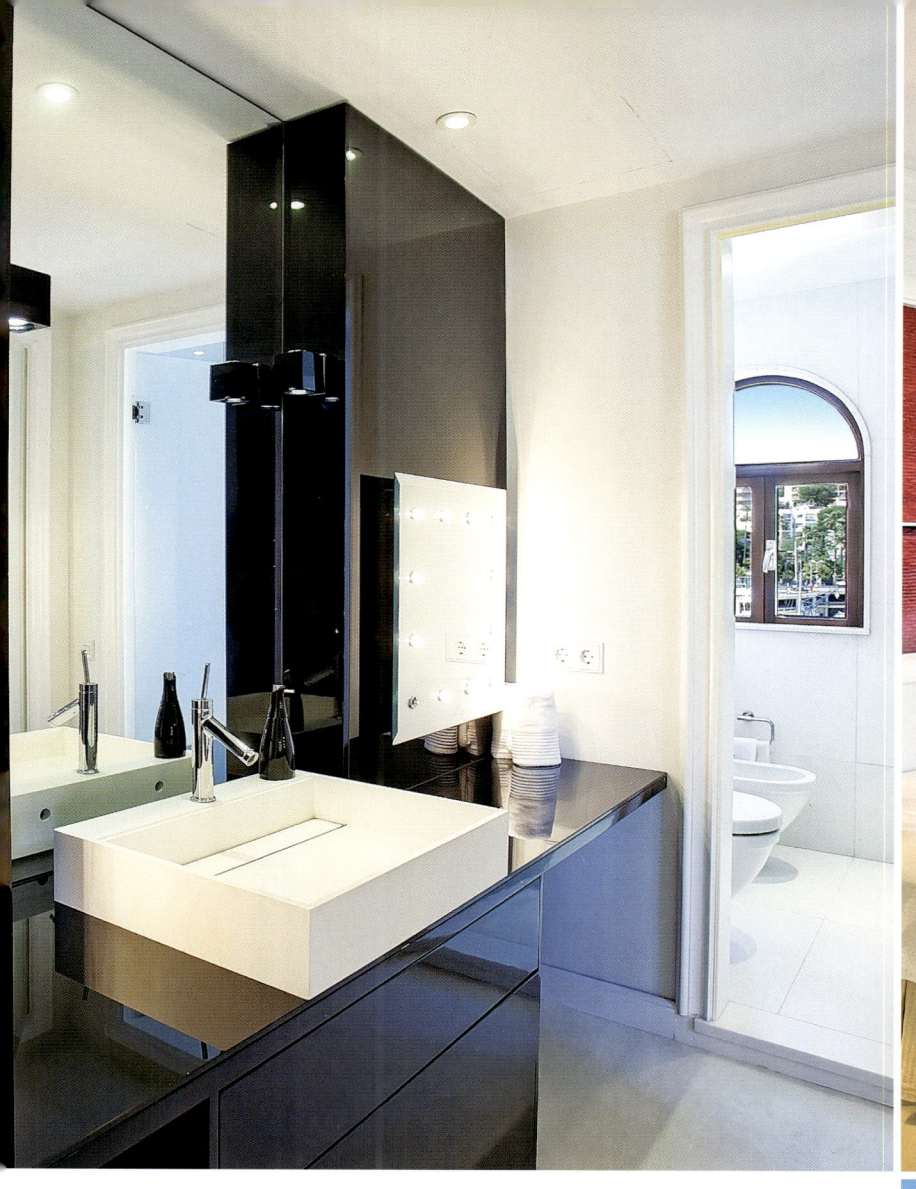

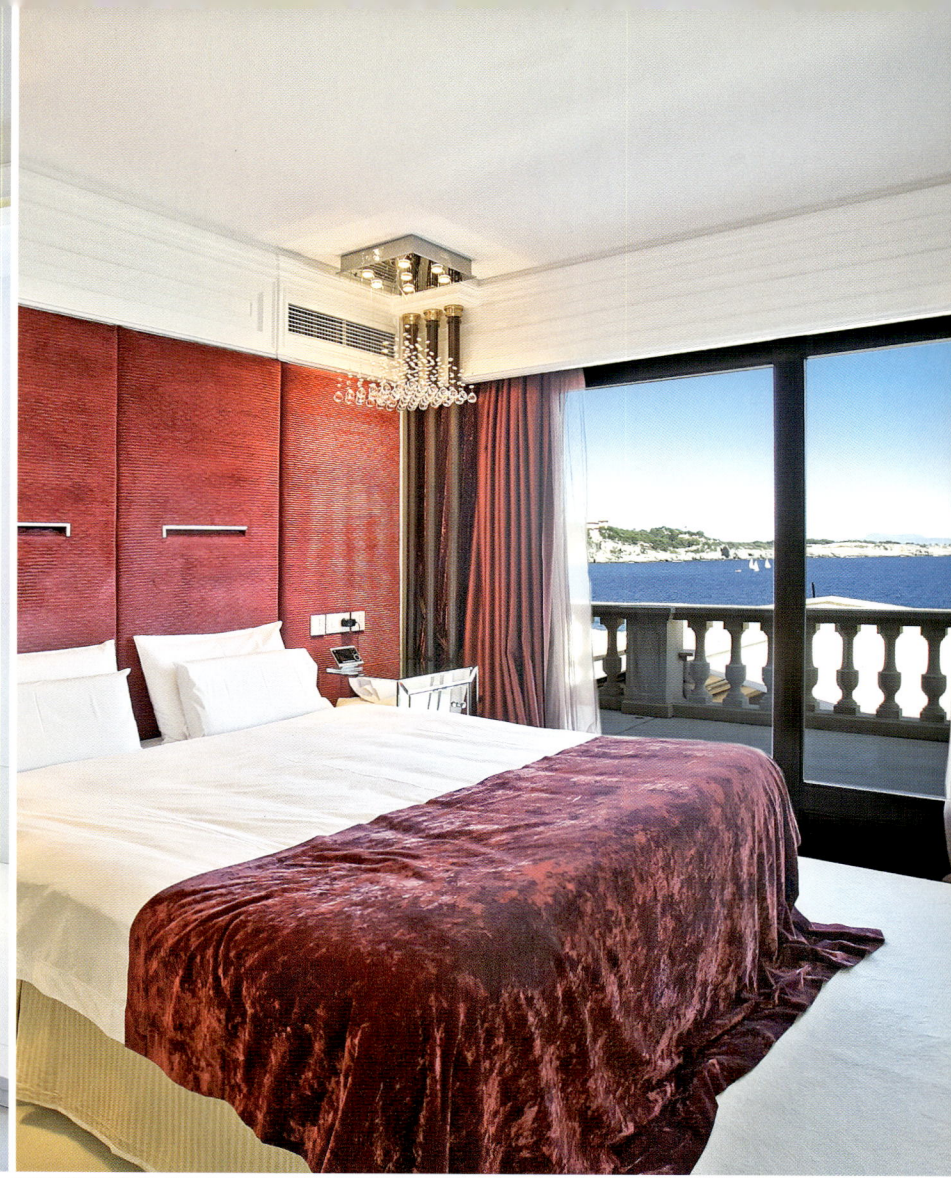

Modern comfort and easy elegance
meet with Mediterranean charm.

Moderner Komfort und behagliche Eleganz
treffen hier auf mediterranen Charme.

Confort, modernidad y serena elegancia
se aúnan con encanto mediterráneo.

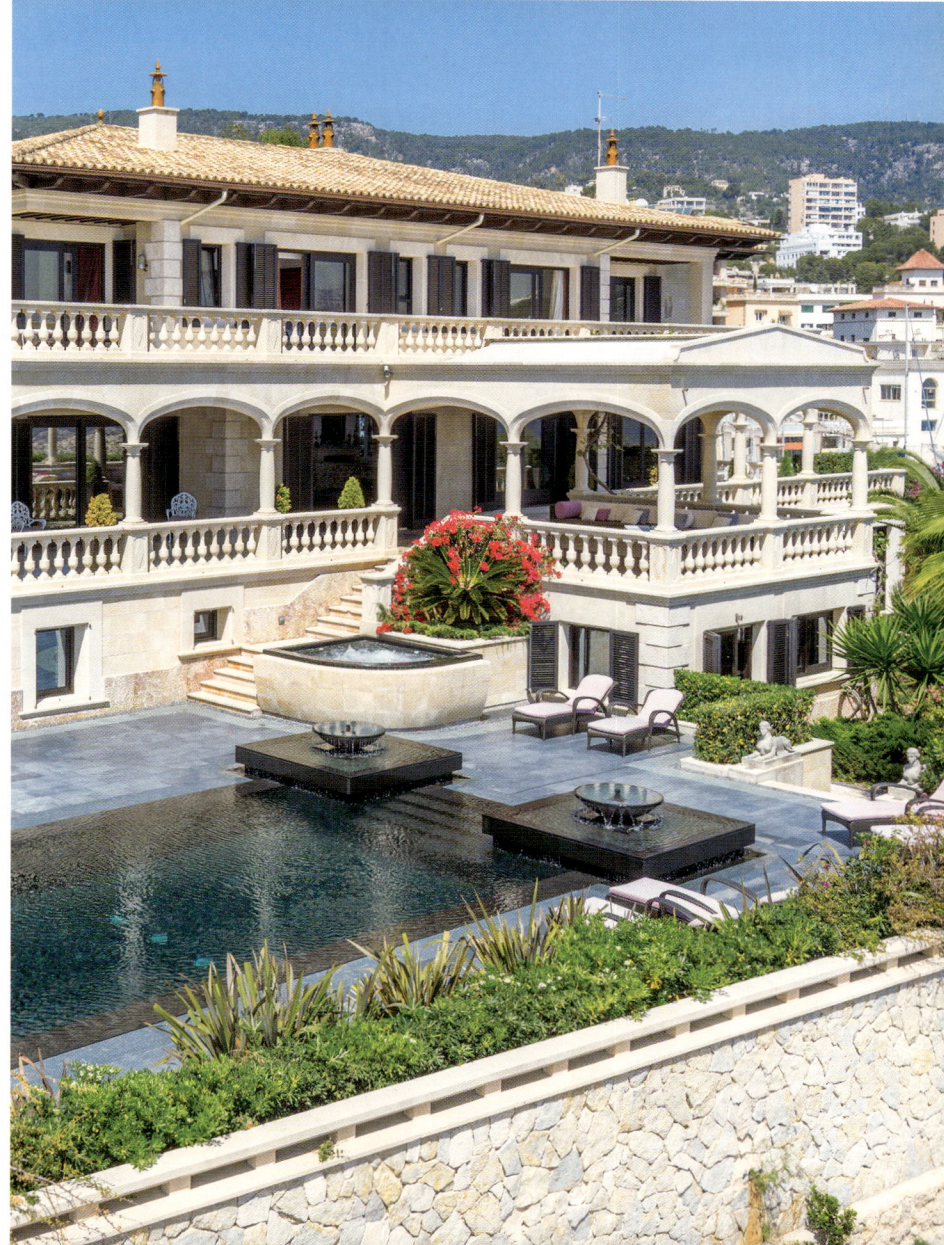

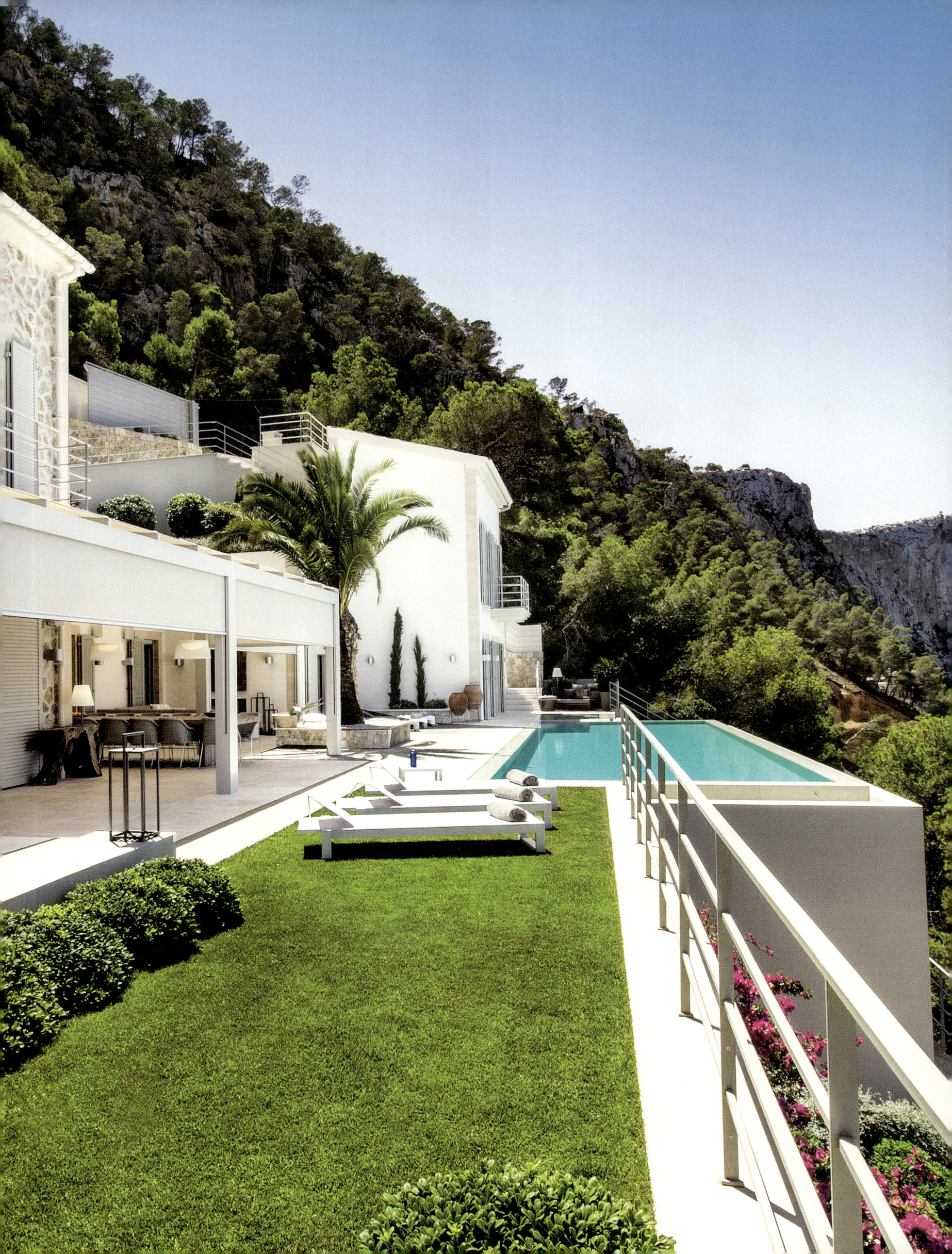

# Luxury Seaside Home

Blessed with a splendid location in Port Andratx,
a natural harbour in south-western Majorca, this home
in a modern finca style is a dream come true.

ENJOYING A PRIME location on a hill directly overlooking the sea, this villa affords breathtaking panoramic views and boasts a level of comfort which meets, and if not exceeds, the most discerning of tastes. With no less than seven bedrooms and bathrooms spread across the main residence, a guest house and a separate apartment, the property is simply perfect for accommodating family, friends and relatives in a highly comfortable fashion. The generous living area of approx. 950 square metres is enhanced by extensive terraced areas, promising hours of relaxation and enjoyment on warm summer days and evenings spent outside. Further highlights include the heated pool, the spa and fitness area and a wine cellar. The bespoke interiors of this dwelling are aesthetically pleasing thanks to the many fine materials, including natural stone and oak flooring, and state-of-the-art technology plus the use of environmentally friendly solar energy. Last but not least, almost every room of this impressive home offers views that are like something straight out of a Majorcan fairy tale ...

AUF EINER ANHÖHE direkt am Meer präsentiert sich dieses einzigartige Villenanwesen, das neben einem sagenhaften, unverbaubaren Meerblick einen Wohnkomfort verspricht, der höchsten Ansprüchen genügt – wenn nicht sogar übertrifft. Das komplett sanierte Anwesen verfügt über sieben Schlafzimmer und Bäder, die sich auf das Haupt- und das Gästehaus sowie ein separates Apartment verteilen – ideal, um auch Freunde oder Verwandte komfortabel unterbringen zu können. Die Wohnfläche von ca. 950 Quadratmetern wird von offenen und überdachten Terrassen ergänzt, die zum Verweilen an warmen Tagen und lauen Sommerabenden einladen. Zu den weiteren Highlights zählen der beheizte Pool, der Spa- und Fitnessbereich sowie ein Weinkeller. Die erstklassige Innenausstattung besticht durch die Verwendung edler Materialien, darunter z. B. Naturstein und Eichenböden, modernste Technik und den Einsatz umweltschonender Solarenergie. Last but not least bietet nahezu jeder Raum einen Ausblick, der immer wieder aufs Neue zum Träumen einlädt ...

EN UNA EXCELENTE ubicación sobre una colina con exquisitas vistas al mar, la villa ofrece fabulosas panorámicas y un nivel de confort que alcanza, si no supera, el más exigente de los gustos. Con nada menos que siete dormitorios y cuartos de baño entre la casa principal, la casa de invitados y el apartamento independiente, la propiedad pone el marco perfecto donde recibir a familiares y amigos de manera cómoda y privada. La generosa zona de día de unos 950 metros cuadrados se realza con las extensas terrazas que prometen entretenidas horas de relajación y disfrute al aire libre durante los cálidos días y noches de verano, al igual que la piscina climatizada, el *spa*, el gimnasio y la bodega. Los interiores a medida lucen materiales nobles tales como la piedra natural y suelos de roble, además de tecnología de última generación y empleo de energía solar. Por último, pero no menos importante, casi cada habitación de esta impresionante residencia ofrece ensoñadoras panorámicas que parecen sacadas de un cuento de hadas mallorquín...

Energy consumption certificate · Energy consumption: 35.7 kWh/m²a · Energy source: heating pump · Year of construction: 2013 · Energy efficiency class: A.

SPAIN, MAJORCA **PURCHASE PRICE** EUR 12.9 MILL. **INTERIOR APPROX.** 950 m² **NO. OF BEDROOMS** 7
**LAND APPROX.** 1,890 m² **E&V ID** W-00Y3TD **CONTACT** ANDRATX (ES), ENGEL & VÖLKERS PUERTO DE ANDRATX,
LICENCE PARTNER OF BALEAREV GMBH **TEL.** +34 971 67 47 80 **E-MAIL** ANDRATX@ENGELVOELKERS.COM

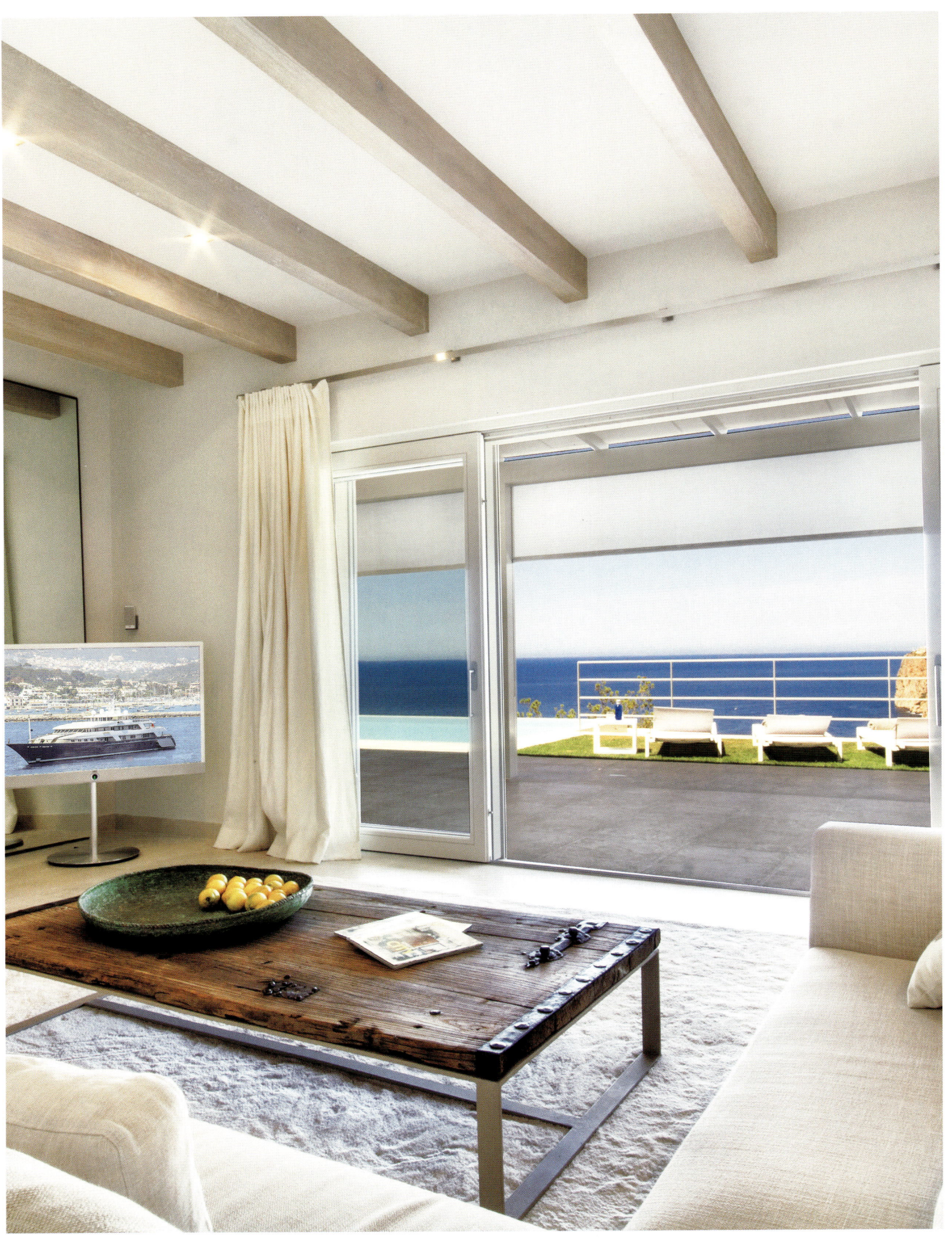

<

Both the living room and the terrace afford
heavenly panoramic vistas of the sea.

Vom Wohnzimmer und von der Terrasse aus
genießt man einen wahren Traumausblick.

Tanto el salón como la terraza ofrecen
paradisíacas vistas panorámicas al mar.

Modern, airy and Mediterranean: the stylish
colour scheme in cream and sand tones.

Modern, luftig und mediterran: die stilvolle
Innenausstattung in Creme- und Sandtönen.

Moderna, ligera y mediterránea: la estilosa
combinación de colores crema y arena.

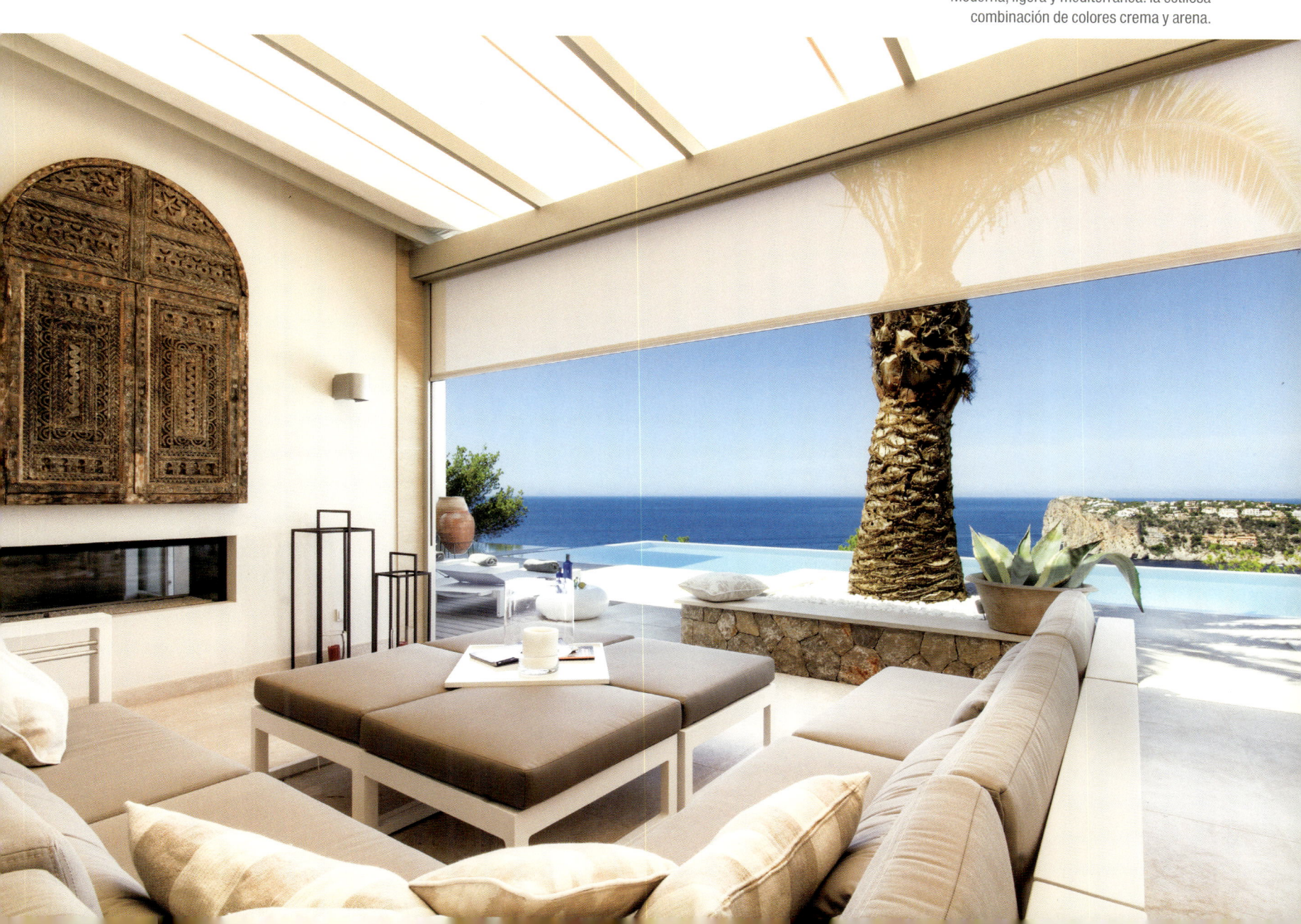

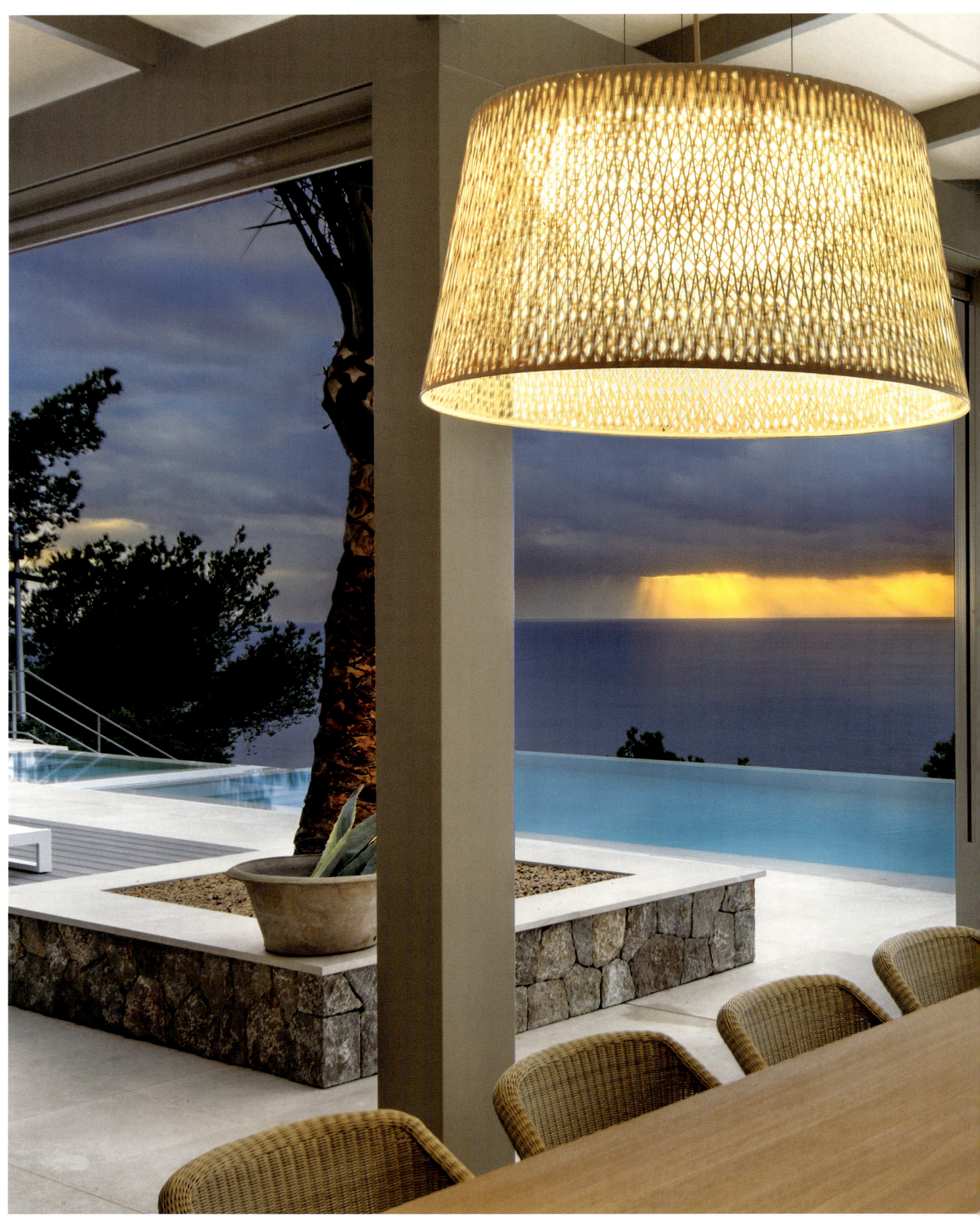

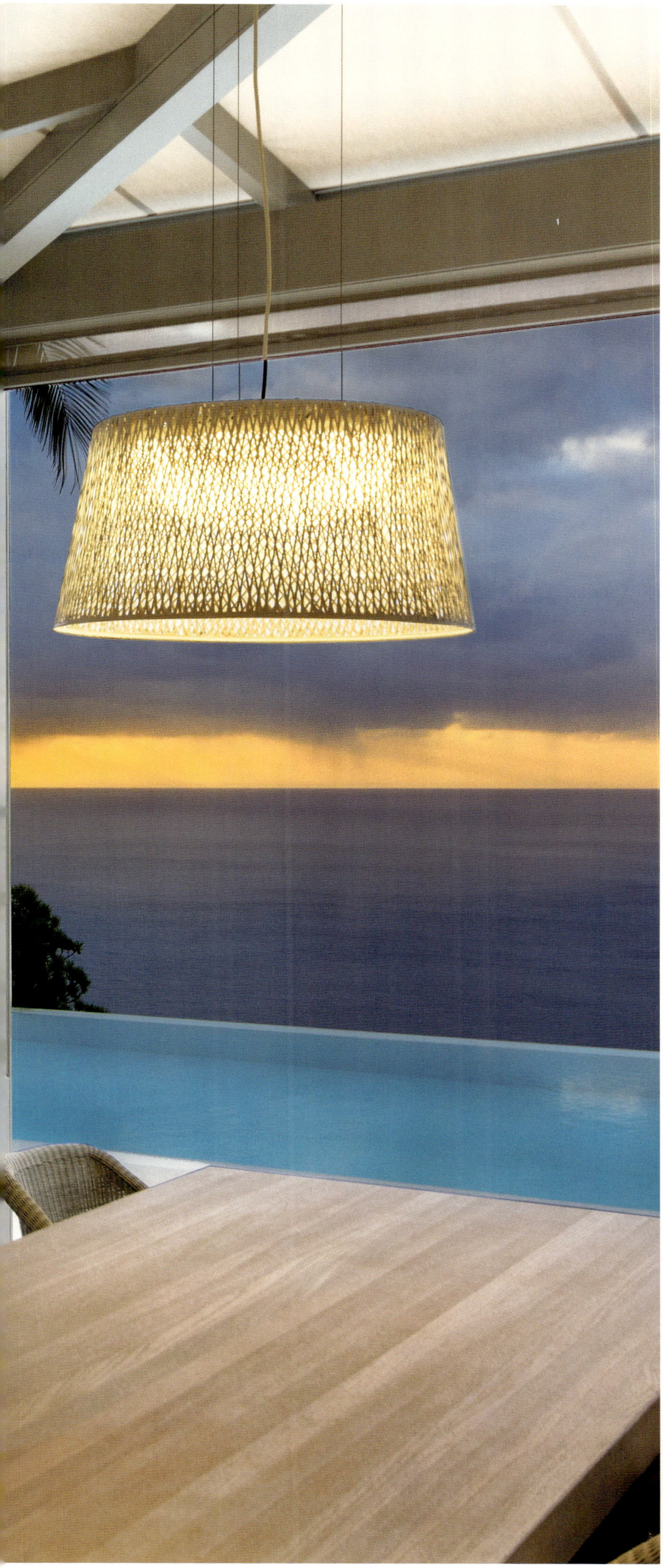

A quick dip in the pool before dinner:
swimming has never been more beautiful ...

Vor dem Dinner noch ein Sprung in den Pool:
Schöner kann man kaum baden gehen ...

Un chapuzón en la piscina antes de la cena:
nadar como bello y refrescante aperitivo...

Opportunities abound for enjoying a
sundowner amidst a spectacular setting.

Gelegenheiten für einen Sundowner vor
spektakulärer Kulisse gibt es hier genügend.

Abundan las ocasiones de disfrutar la puesta
de sol en un entorno natural espectacular.

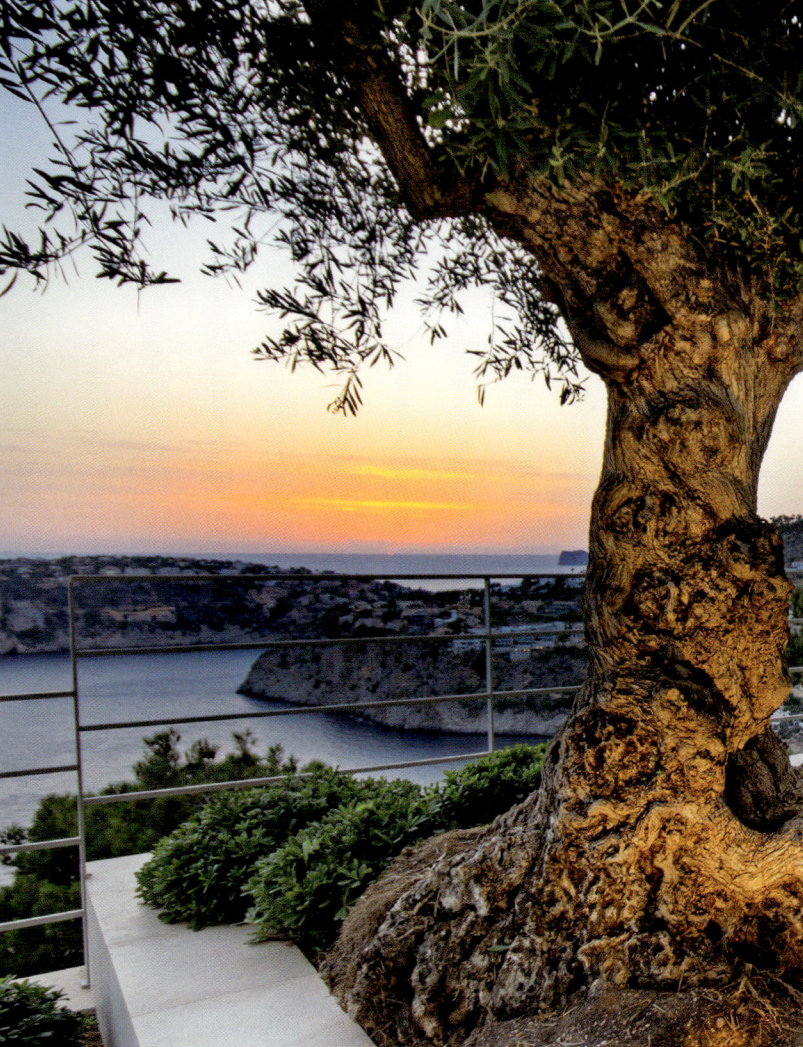

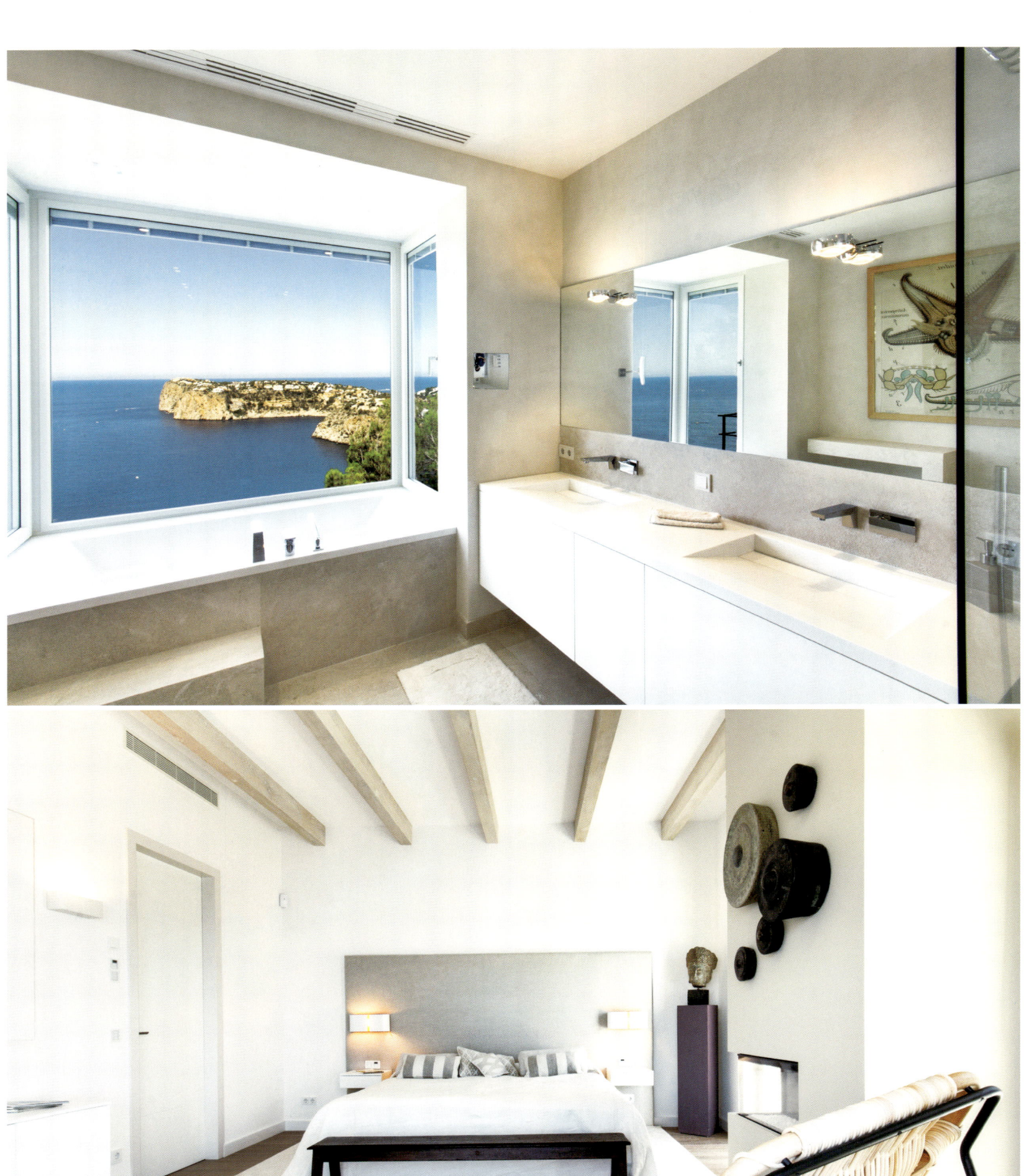

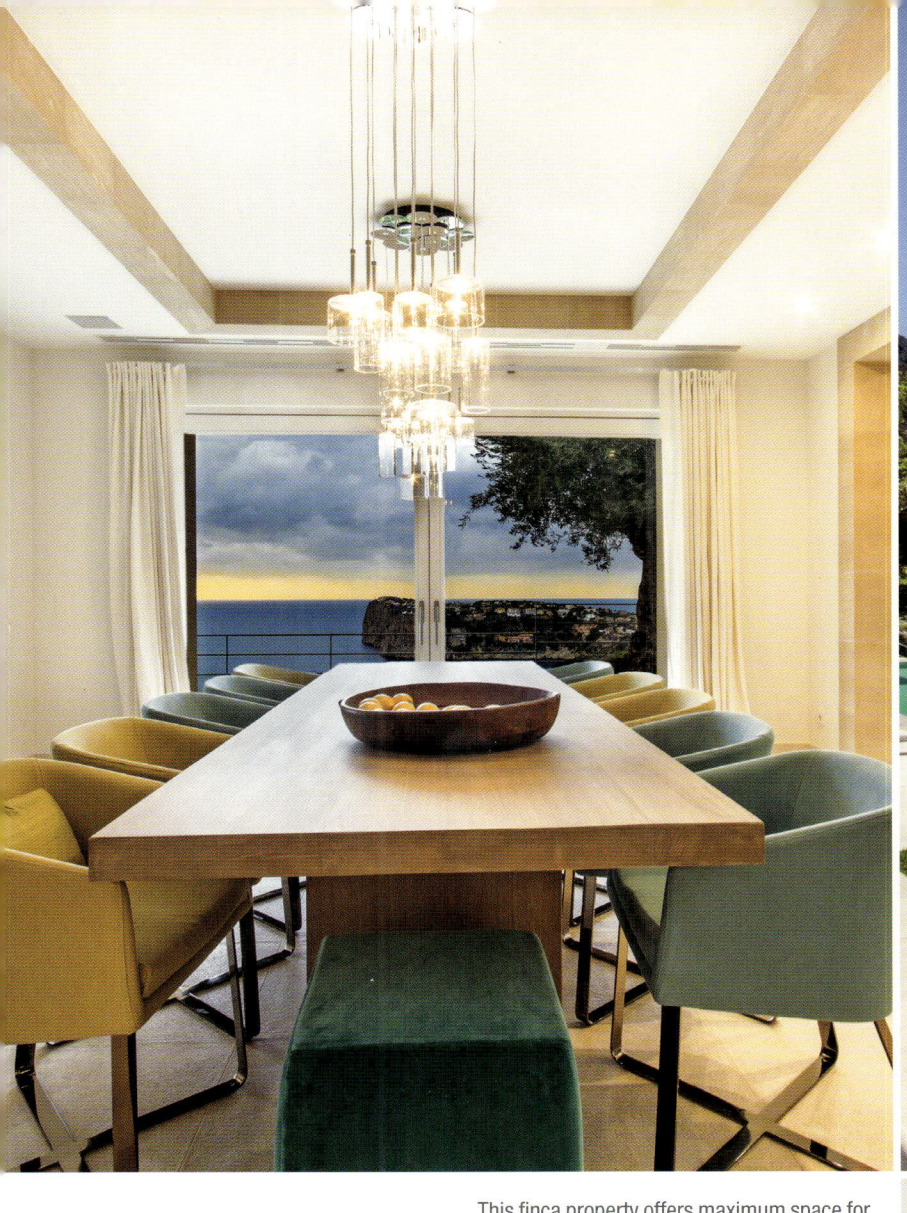

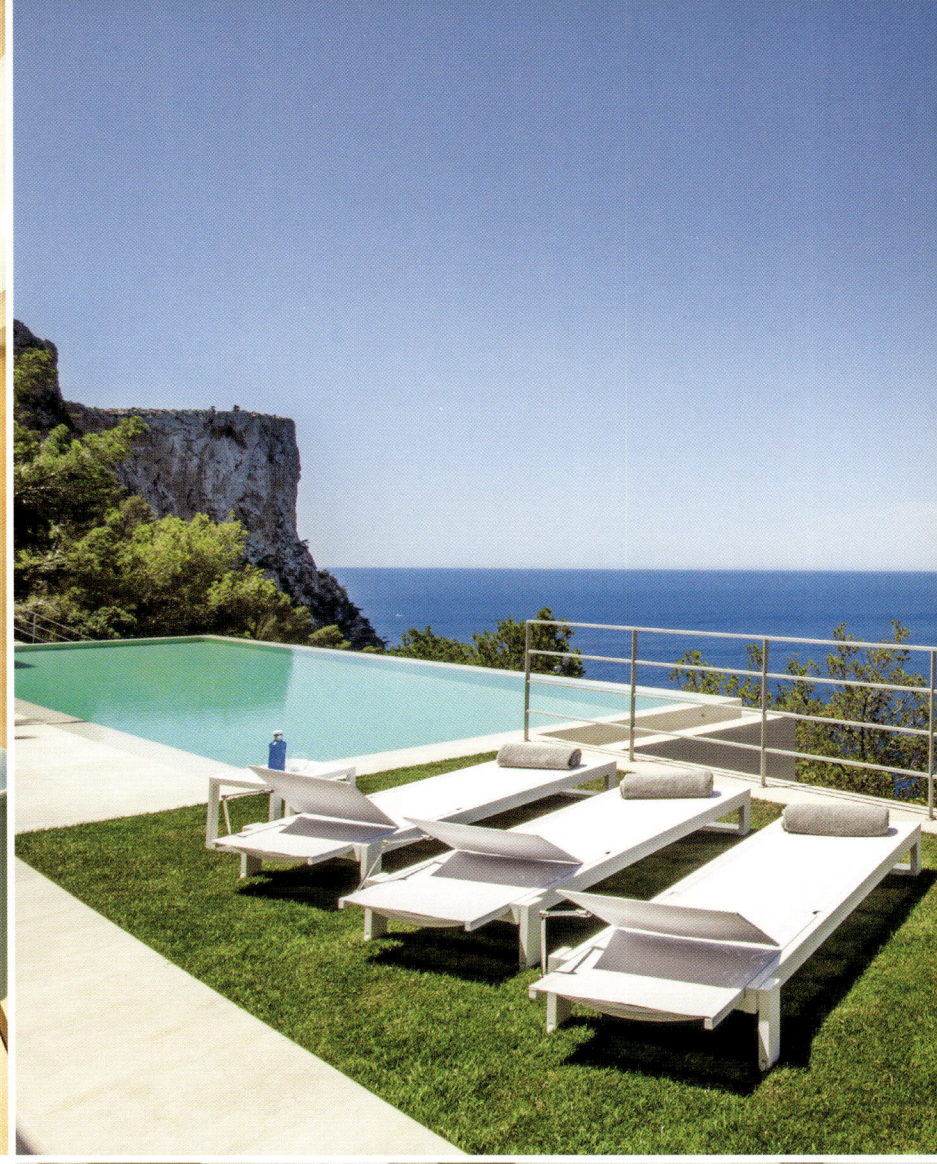

This finca property offers maximum space for the highest quality of life in every respect.

Raum für maximale Lebensqualität bietet dieses Finca-Anwesen in jeglicher Hinsicht.

Esta finca ofrece el máximo espacio para la más alta calidad de vida, en todos los sentidos.

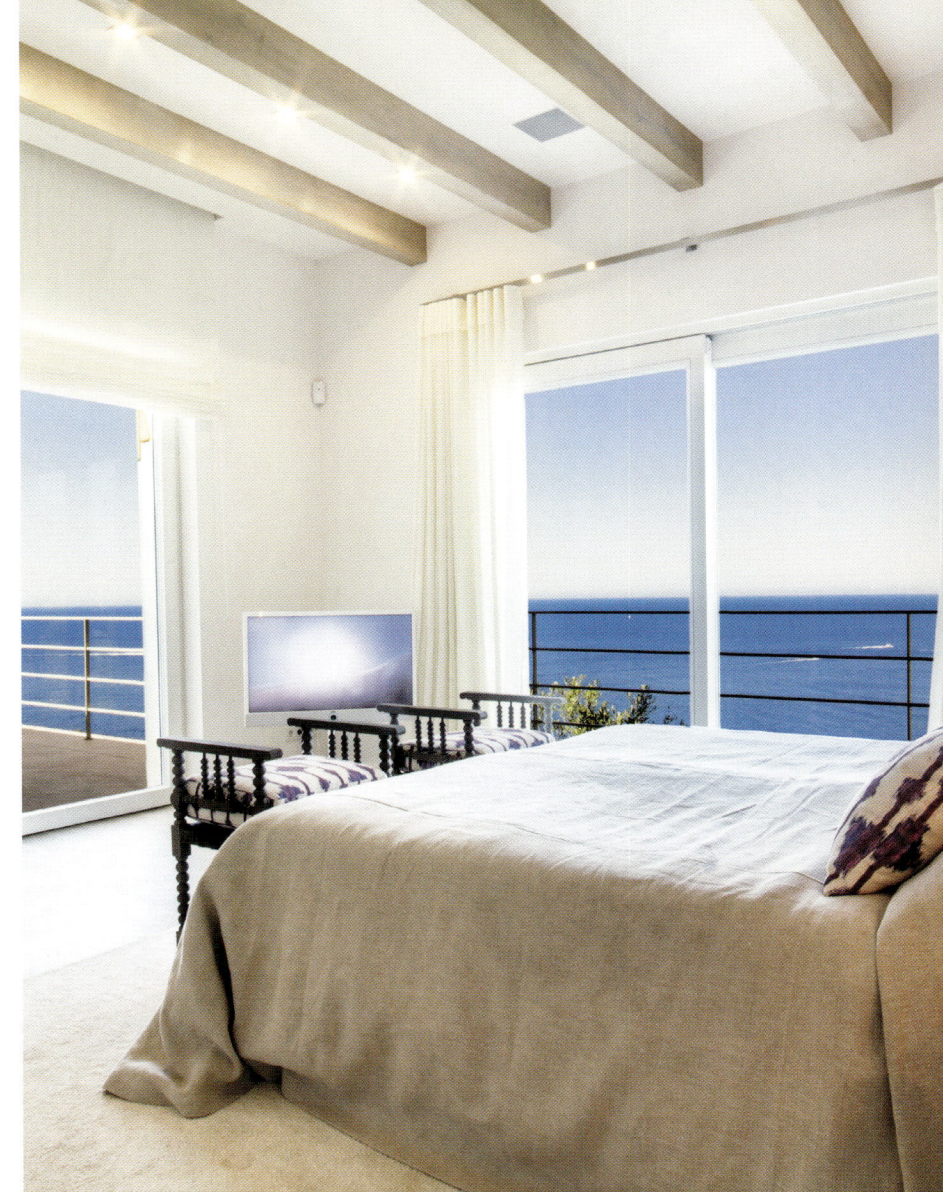

<

The bathrooms and bedrooms are graced with elegant purist flair and lots of comfort.

Auch die Bäder und Schlafzimmer bestechen durch eleganten Purismus und viel Komfort.

Baños y dormitorios lucen en su ambiente estiloso, elegante y purista con todo el confort.

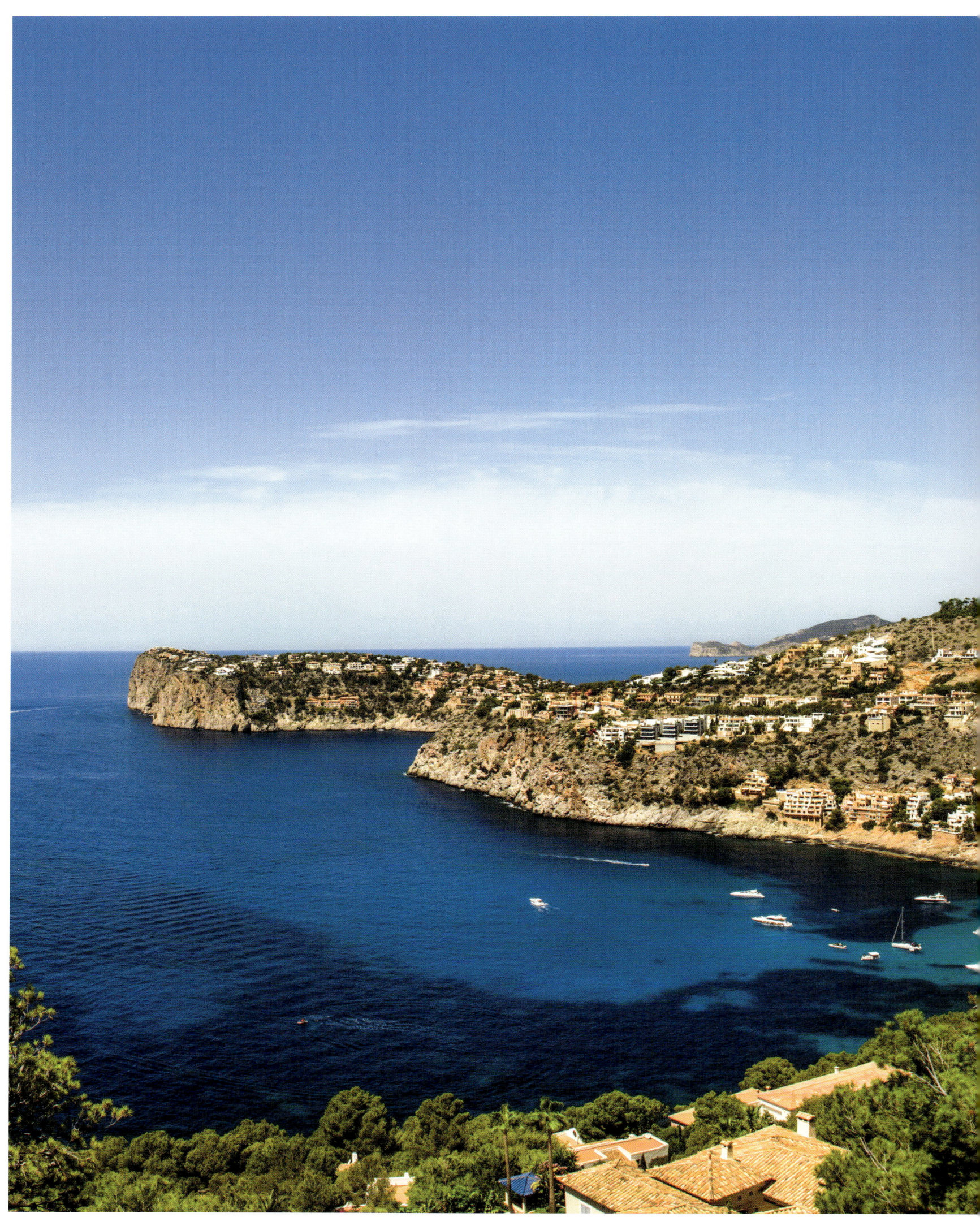

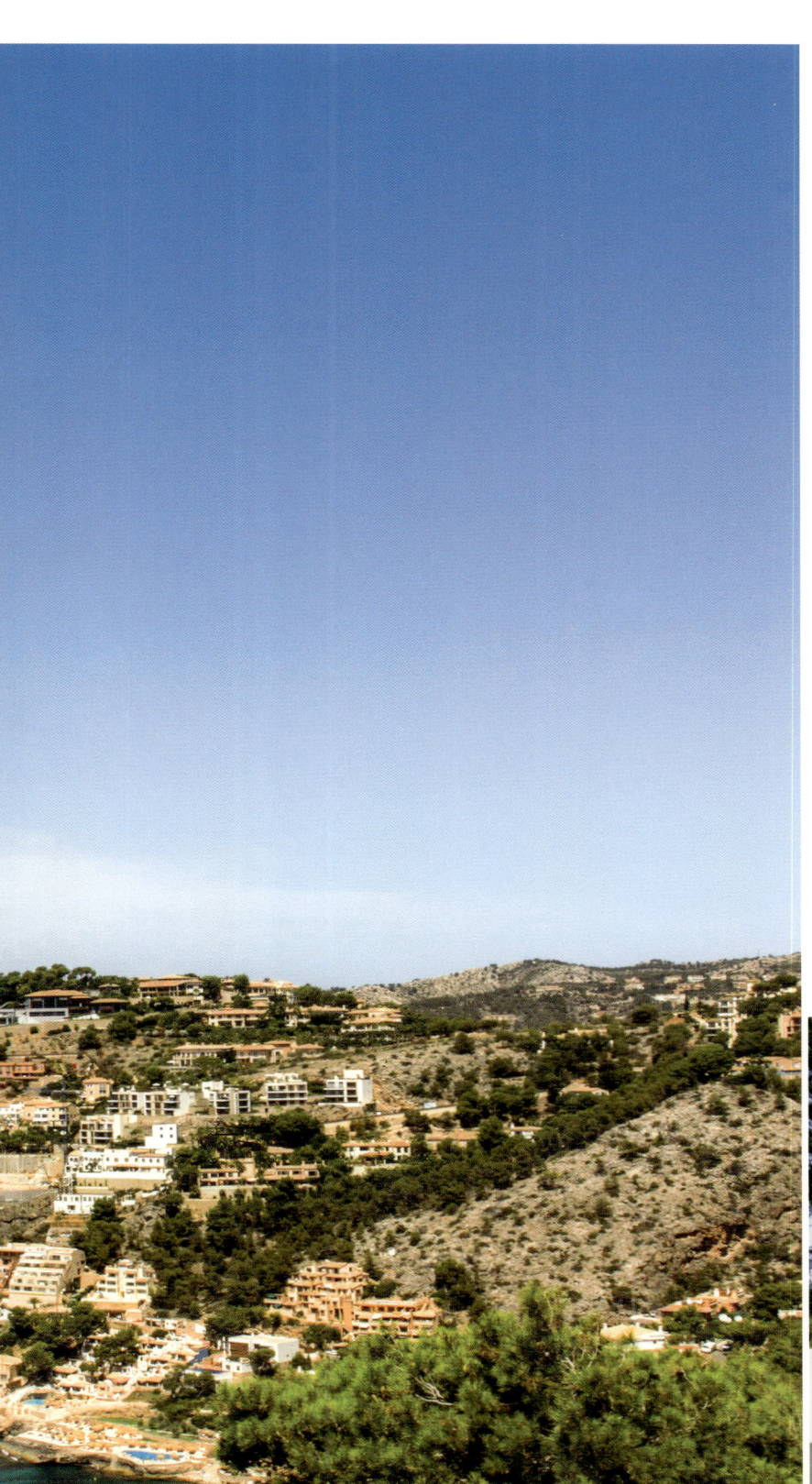

<

Port Andratx in south-western Majorca is one of the island's most coveted addresses.

Port Andratx im Südwesten Mallorcas zählt zu den begehrtesten Adressen der Insel.

Port Andratx, al sudoeste de Mallorca, es una de las localidades más codiciadas de la isla.

The beautifully landscaped gardens are an invitation to relax and unwind.

Die schön gestaltete Gartenanlage lädt zum Verweilen unter spanischer Sonne ein.

Los hermosos jardines son una contínua invitación a relajarse y descansar.

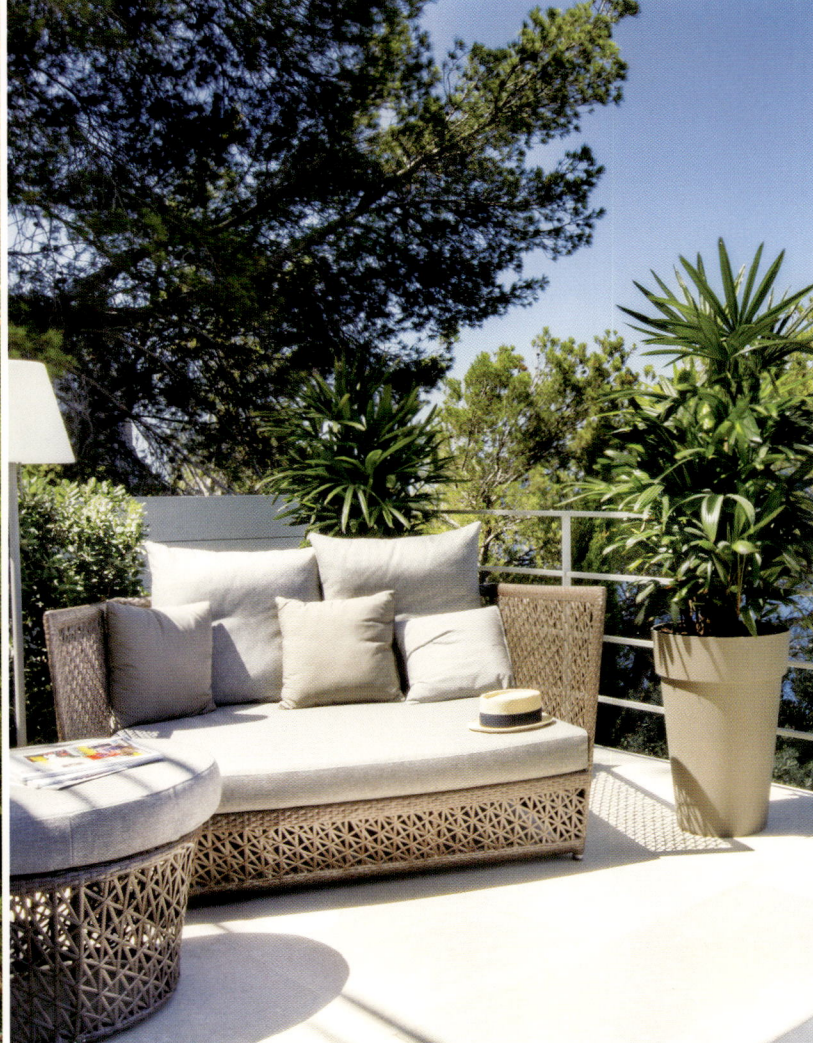

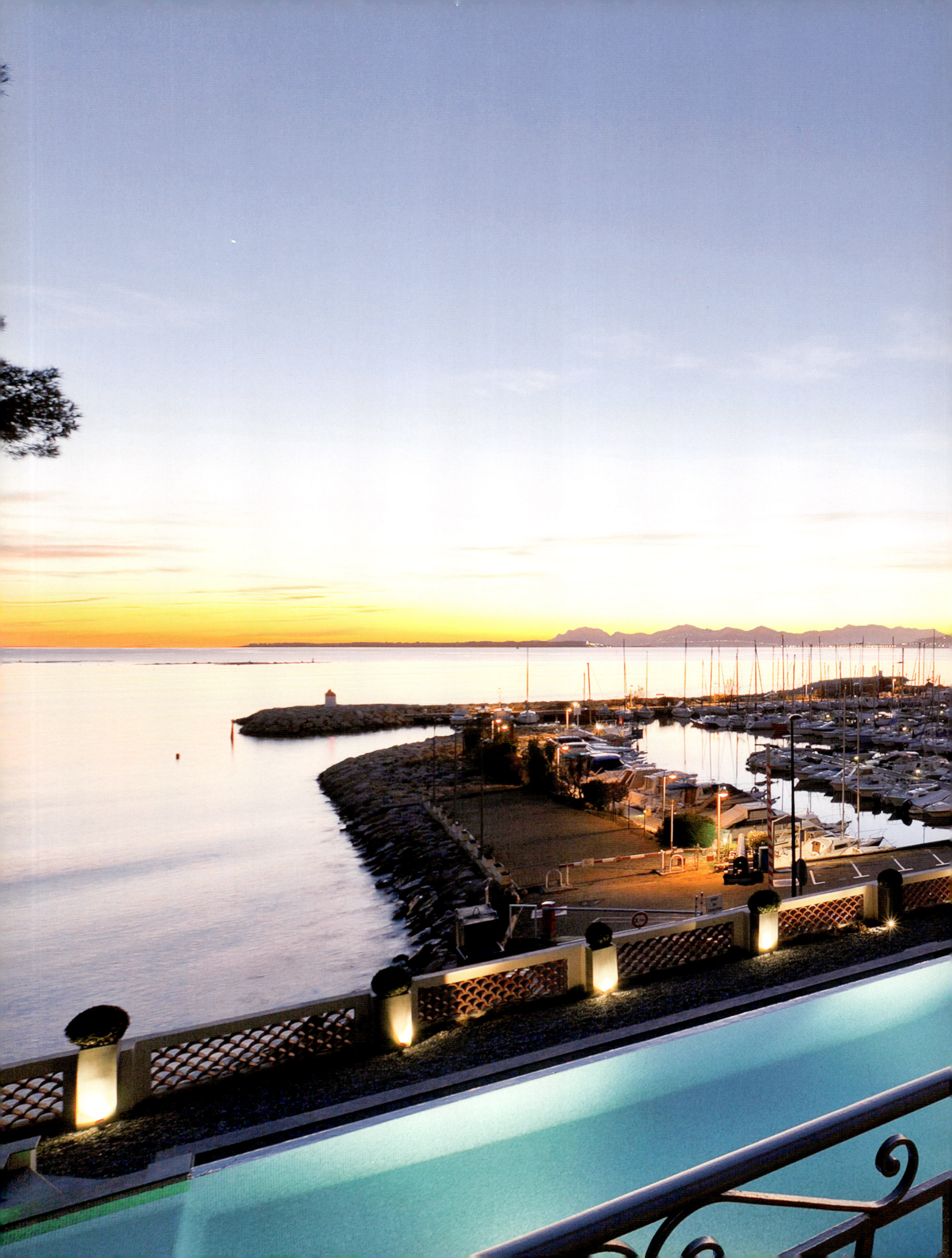

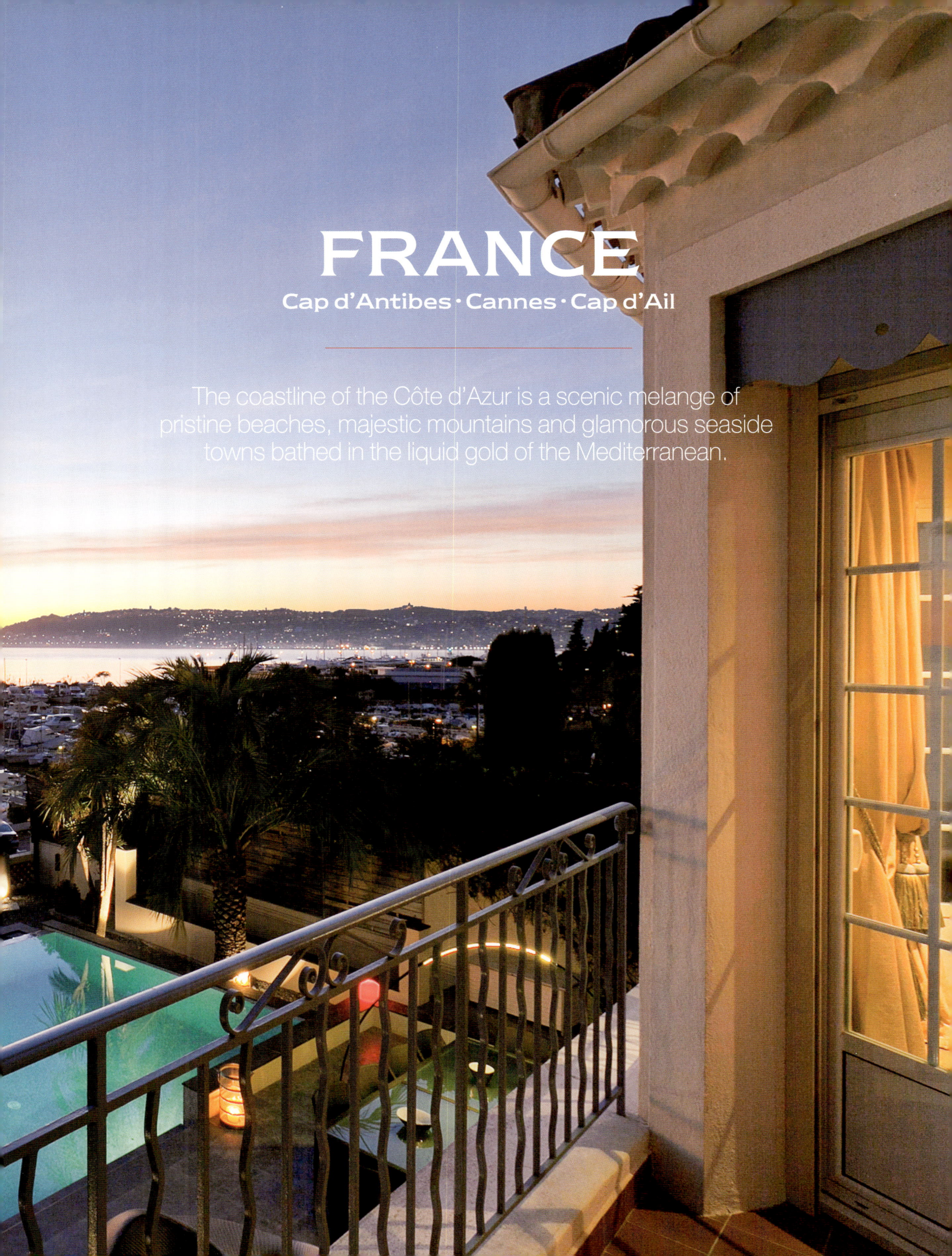

# FRANCE
### Cap d'Antibes · Cannes · Cap d'Ail

The coastline of the Côte d'Azur is a scenic melange of pristine beaches, majestic mountains and glamorous seaside towns bathed in the liquid gold of the Mediterranean.

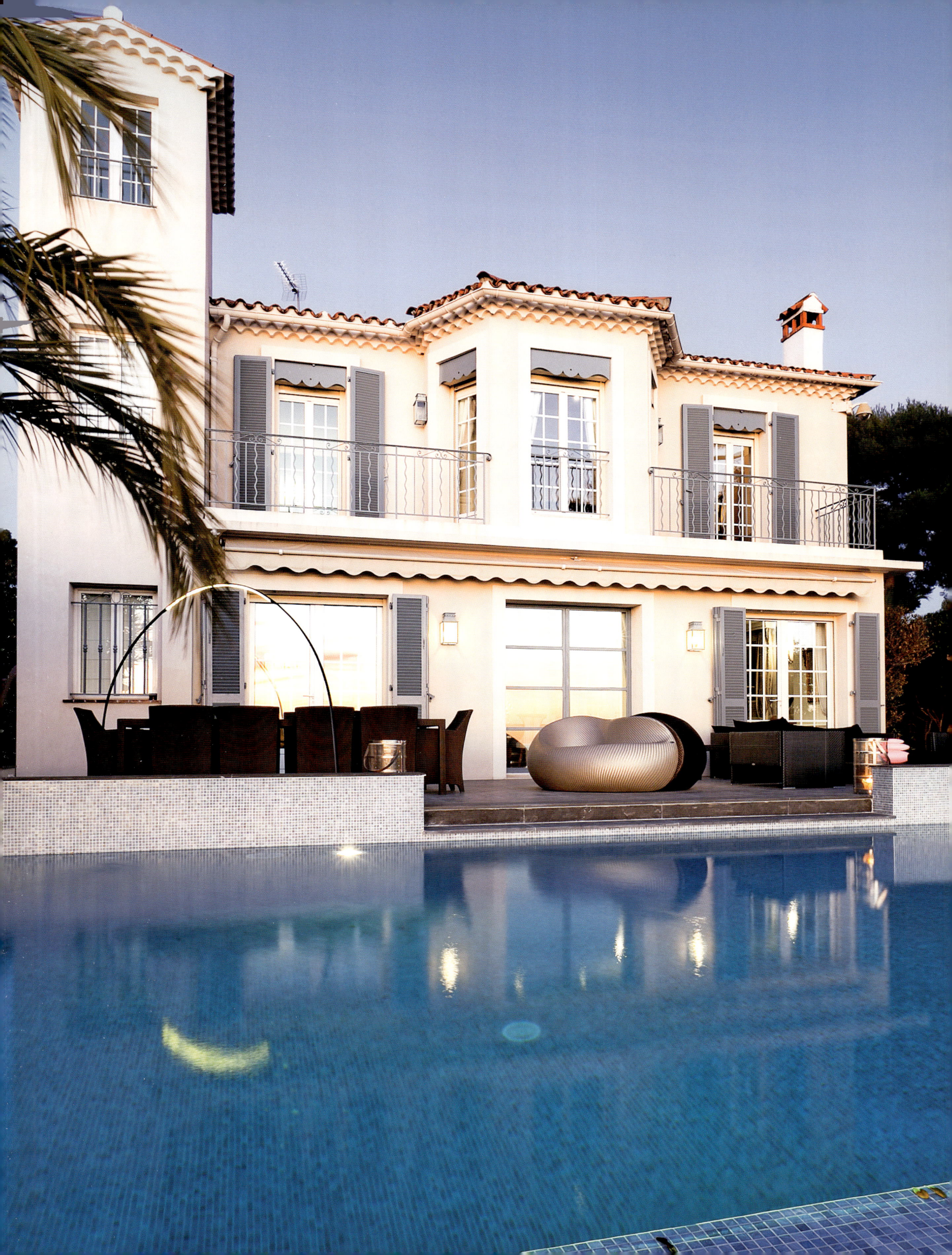

# Côte d'Azur Dream

This refined villa in Cap d'Antibes promises
French perfection on the doorstep and is an ideal place
to celebrate a dazzling Mediterranean lifestyle.

THANKS TO ITS mild climate, fabulous sea views and a pinch of glamour, Cap d'Antibes is one of the most exclusive spots on the French Riviera. Even F. Scott Fitzgerald, in his famous novel *Tender Is the Night*, paid homage to this very special flair. The noble oceanfront mansion offered here provides an opulent level of comfort as well as modern, state-of-the art details such as full air conditioning and an audio/ video system that is controllable via iPad and enables listening to music underwater in the pool. However, the greatest luxury of this refurbished home is most certainly its first-sea-line location, with fantastic vistas of the bay, the Lérins islands and the Estérel hills on the horizon. Opening directly onto the terrace with a splendid infinity pool, the large living room is a true gem. Providing around 360 square metres of living space, the villa comprises three en-suite bedrooms. What is more, a guest cottage for up to four people and a separate studio for domestic staff top off an ensemble that surely would even have impressed Fitzgerald.

DANK SEINEM MILDEN Klima, fantastischen Meerpanoramen und einer Prise Glamour zählt Cap d'Antibes zu den exklusivsten Orten an der Französischen Riviera. Diesem ganz besonderen Flair hatte bereits F. Scott Fitzgerald in seinem Roman *Zärtlich ist die Nacht* ein Denkmal gesetzt. Die hier angebotene, komplett sanierte Villa bietet höchsten Wohnkomfort samt modernster Technik nach heutigem Top-Standard – inklusive Vollklimatisierung und einem vom iPad gesteuerten Audio-/Video-System, über das man auch im Pool unter Wasser Musik hören kann. Das beste Argument für dieses Anwesen ist aber sicherlich die Lage direkt am Meer, mit Traumaussicht auf die Lérins-Inseln und das Estérel-Gebirge am Horizont. Diese hat man auch vom großen Wohnzimmer aus, das sich direkt zur Terrasse samt Infinity Pool öffnet. Auf insgesamt rund 360 Quadratmetern befinden sich zudem drei Schlafzimmer mit En-suite-Bad und ein Gästehaus für bis zu vier Personen. Ein separates Personal-Apartment komplettiert dieses Ensemble, das sicher auch Fitzgerald beeindruckt hätte.

GRACIAS A SU clima suave, fabulosas vistas al mar y una pizca de *glamour*, Cap d'Antibes es uno de los lugares más exclusivos de la Riviera francesa. Incluso F. Scott Fitzgerald, en su famosa novela *Suave es la noche*, rindió homenaje a ese aura tan especial. La noble villa frente al mar provoca una sensación de opulenta comodidad con detalles de vanguardia, como el aire acondicionado o el sistema de audio y vídeo controlado con iPad y que permite escuchar música bajo el agua en la piscina. La máxima expresión del lujo de la villa reformada es sin duda su ubicación en primera línea de mar con fantásticas vistas a la bahía azul celeste, las islas Lerins y las montañas Esterel en el horizonte. Abriéndose directamente a la terraza con la espléndida piscina, la gran sala de estar resulta una verdadera joya. Cerca de 360 metros cuadrados habitables incluyen tres dormitorios en suite, a los que se suman la casita de invitados para cuatro personas y un estudio independiente para el personal o el servicio, rematando un conjunto que seguramente habría impresionando al mismísimo Fitzgerald.

FRANCE, CAP D'ANTIBES **PURCHASE PRICE** EUR 13 MILL. **INTERIOR APPROX.** 360 m² **NO. OF BEDROOMS** 3
**LAND APPROX.** 1,360 m² **E&V ID** W-01EKW4 **CONTACT** CANNES (FR), EV FRENCH RIVIERA SAS,
LICENCE PARTNER OF ENGEL & VÖLKERS RESIDENTIAL GMBH **TEL.** +33 493 68 64 72
**E-MAIL** CANNES@ENGELVOELKERS.COM

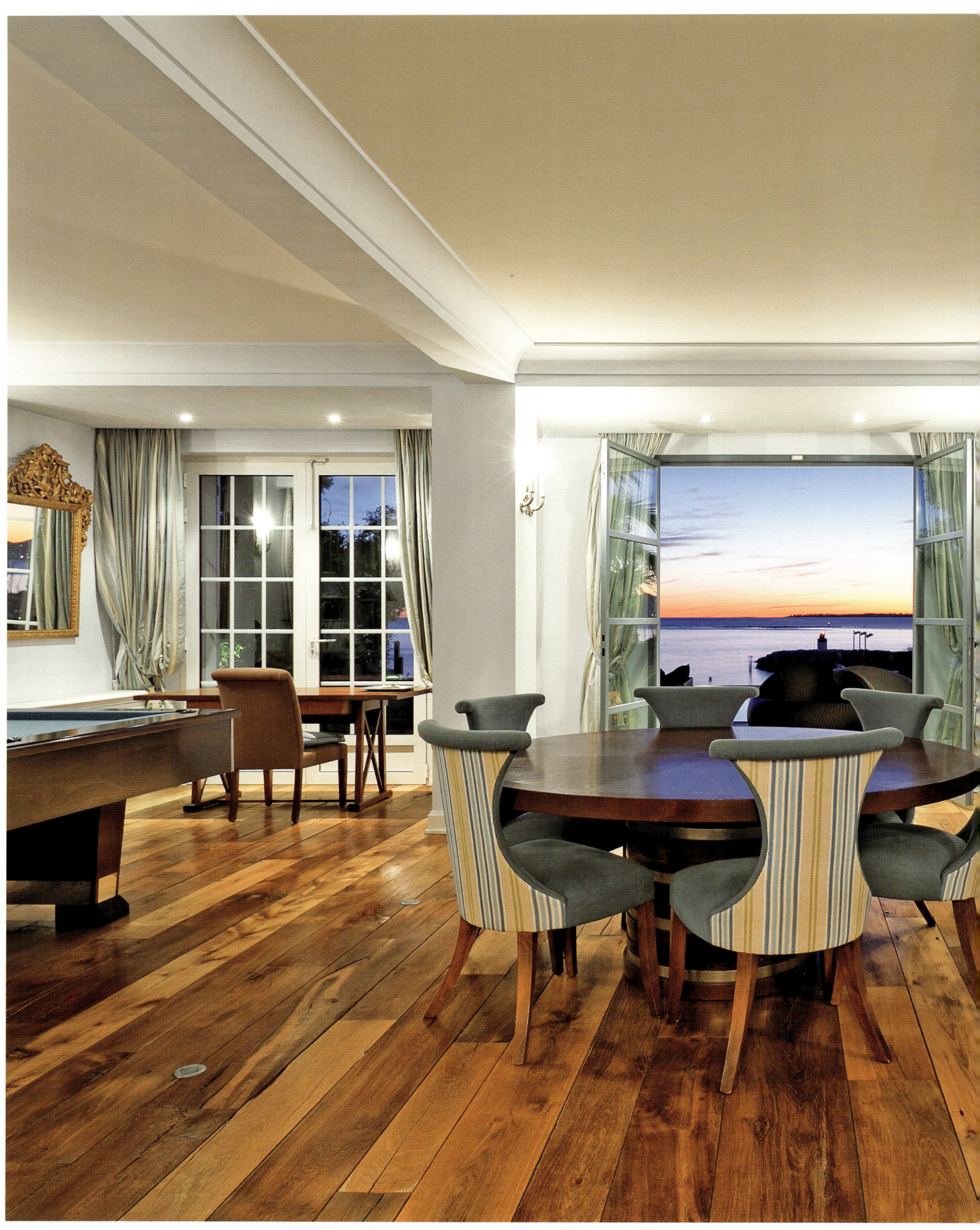

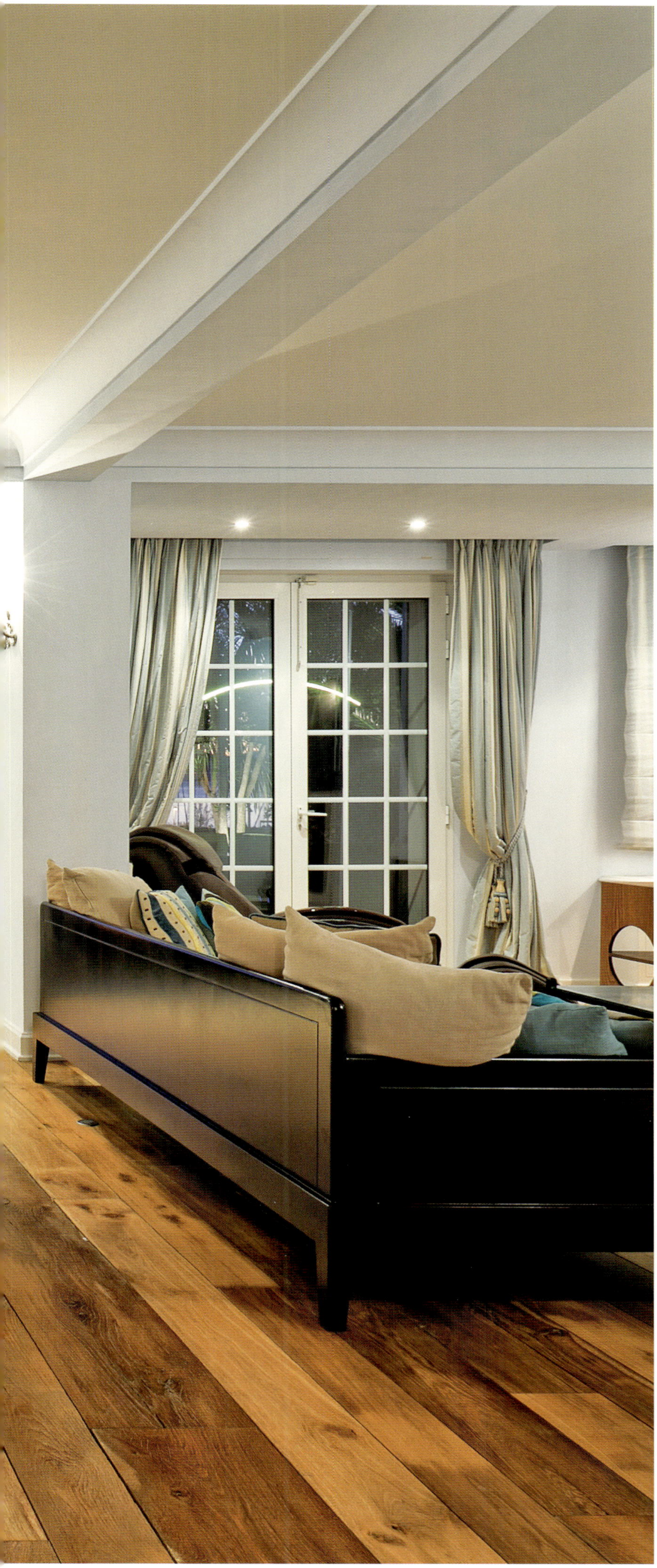

The sea is the perfect backdrop
for this house in Cap d'Antibes.

Das weite Meer bildet die perfekte Kulisse
für dieses Anwesen in Cap d'Antibes.

El mar es el perfecto telón de fondo
para esta casa en Cap d'Antibes.

Endless blue: the glorious infinity pool
certainly does live up to its name.

Unendliches Blau: ein Infinity Pool,
der seinem Namen alle Ehre macht.

Azul sin fin: la piscina de horizonte
sin duda hace honor a su nombre.

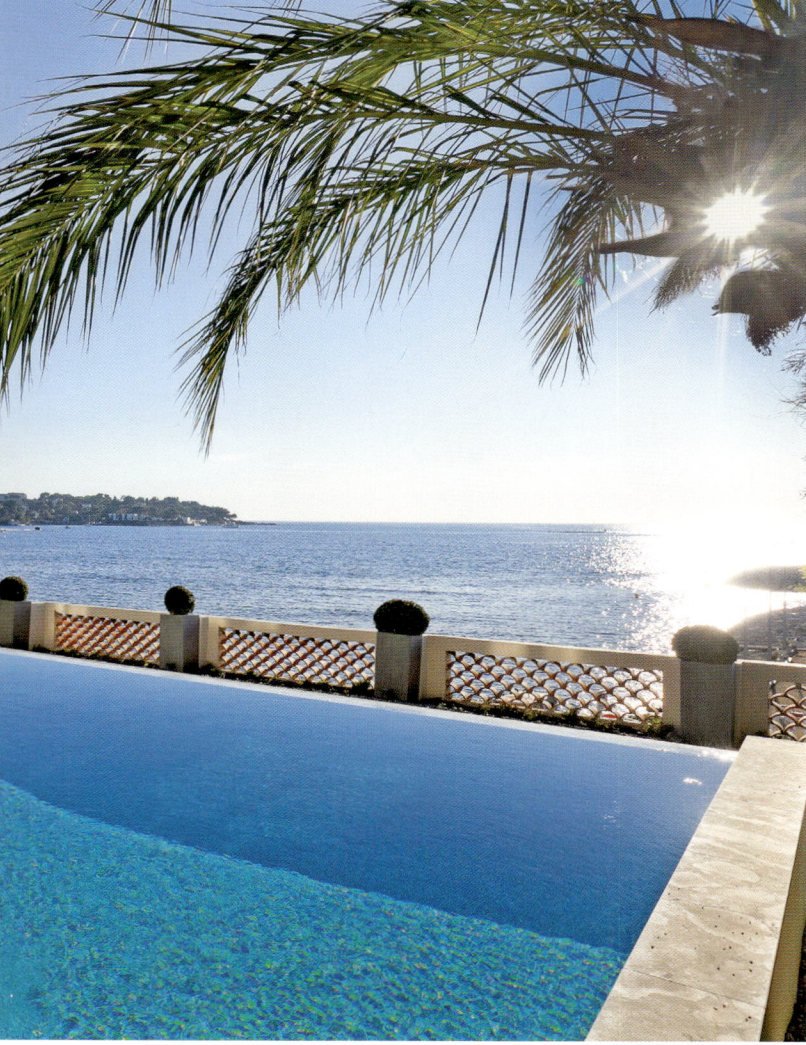

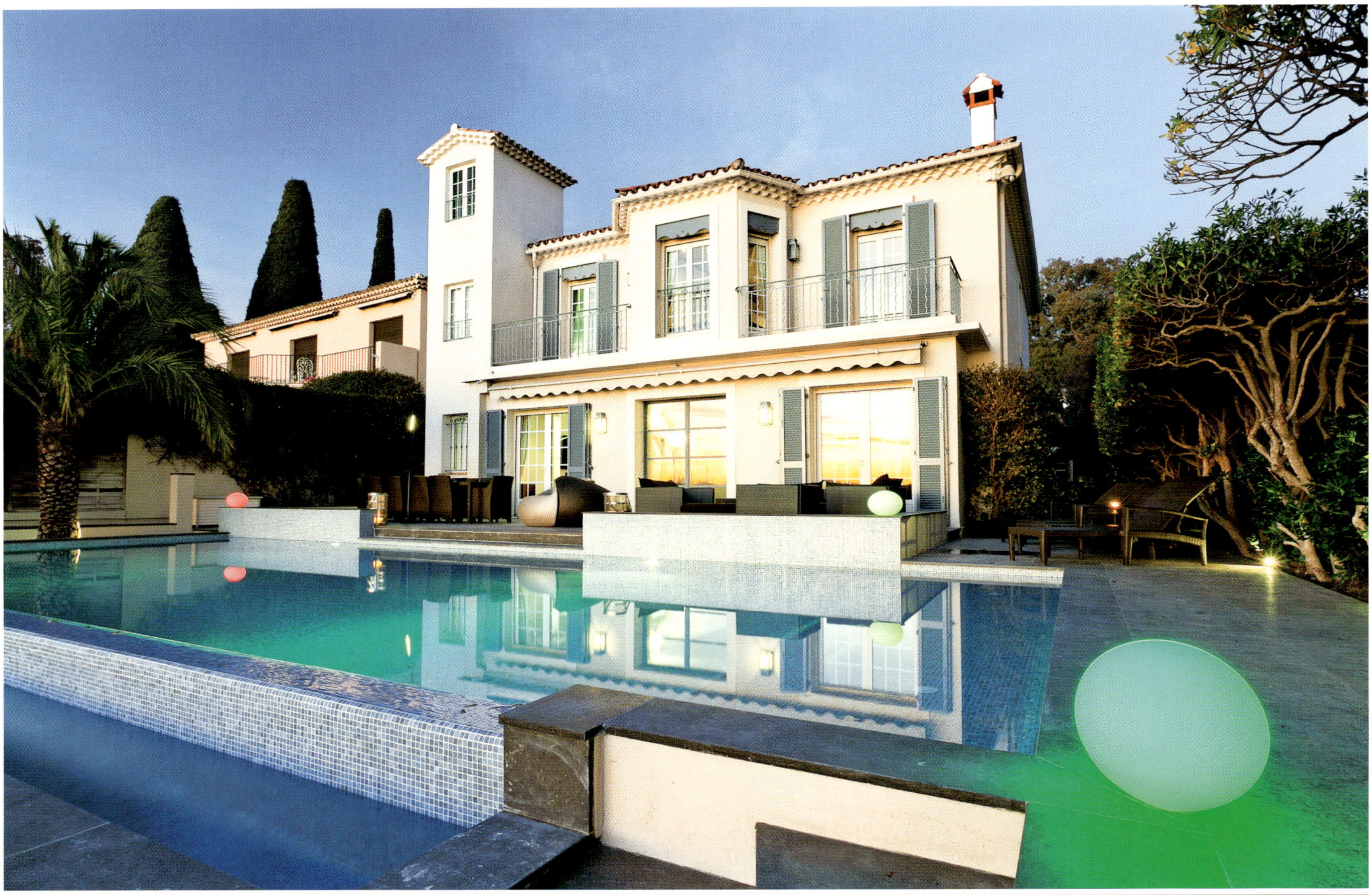

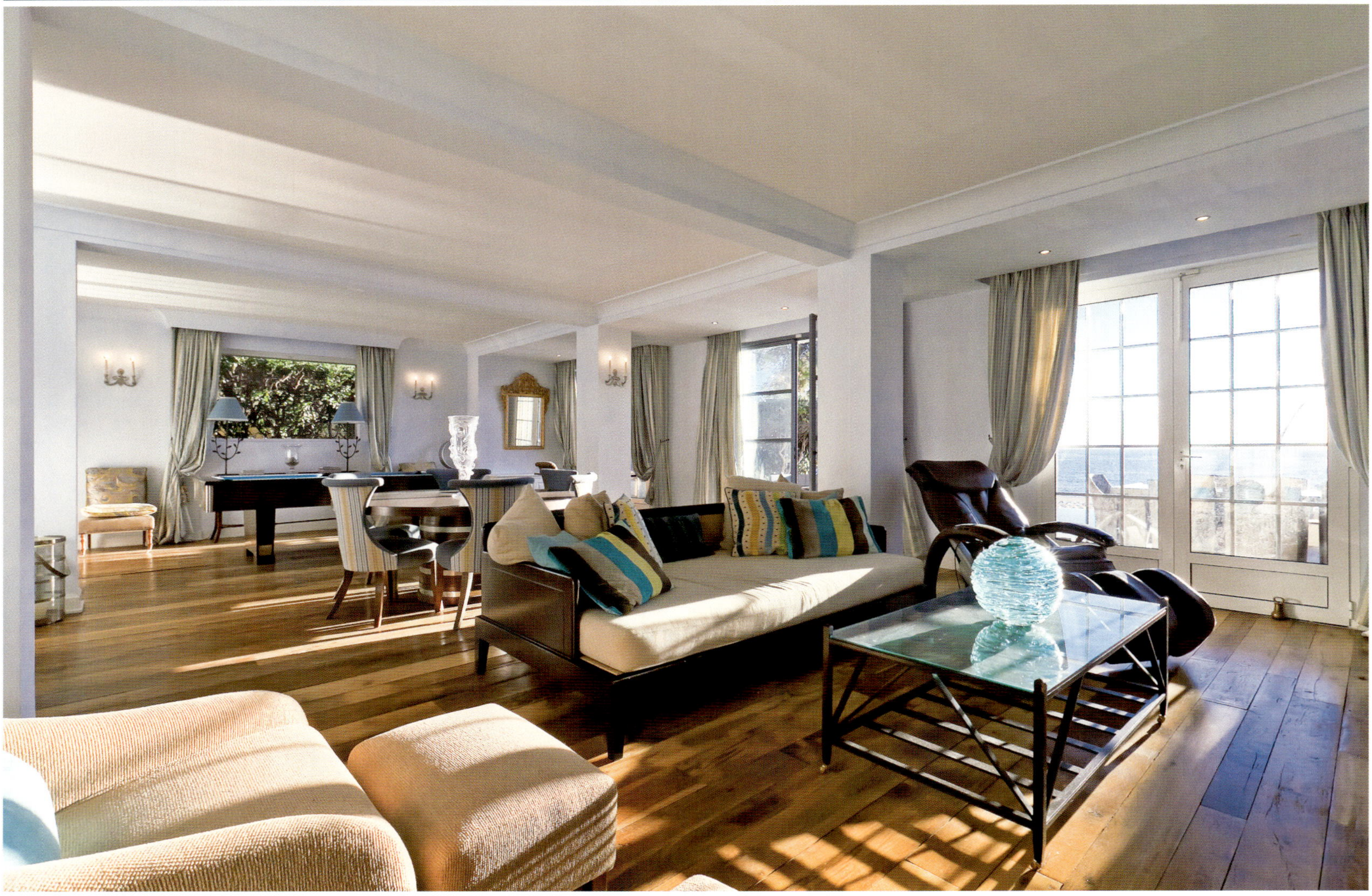

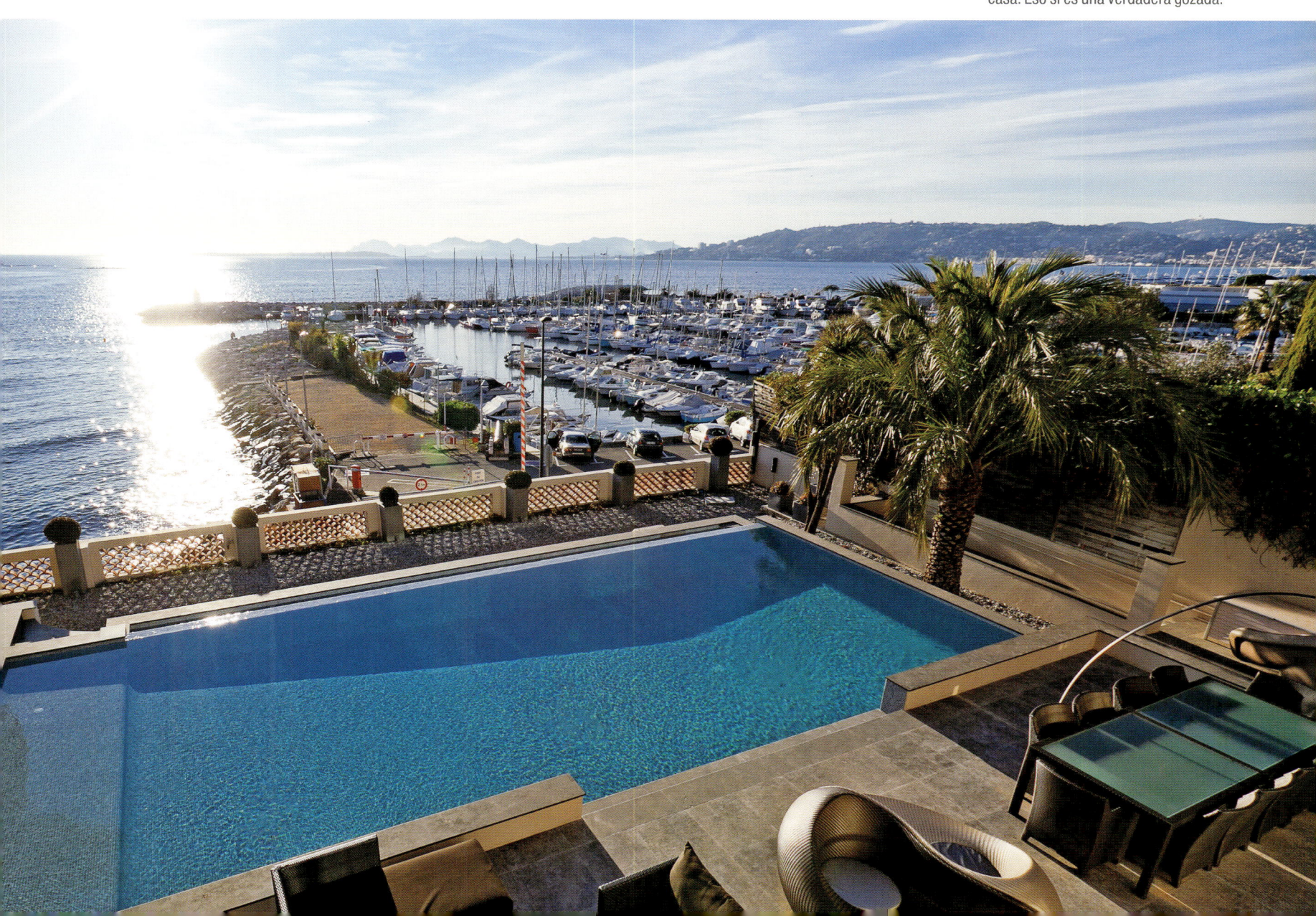

Evening mood on the Côte d'Azur: the
villa was completely renovated in 2005.

Abendstimmung an der Côte d'Azur:
Die Villa wurde 2005 vollständig renoviert.

Cae la tarde en la Costa Azul: la villa
fue completamente renovada en 2005.

With an impressive marina right on the
doorstep, sailing home is pure bliss.

Mit dem Segelboot bis zur Haustür: Am
Fuße der Villa liegt ein großer Yachthafen.

El puerto en el umbral para navegar hasta
casa. Eso sí es una verdadera gozada.

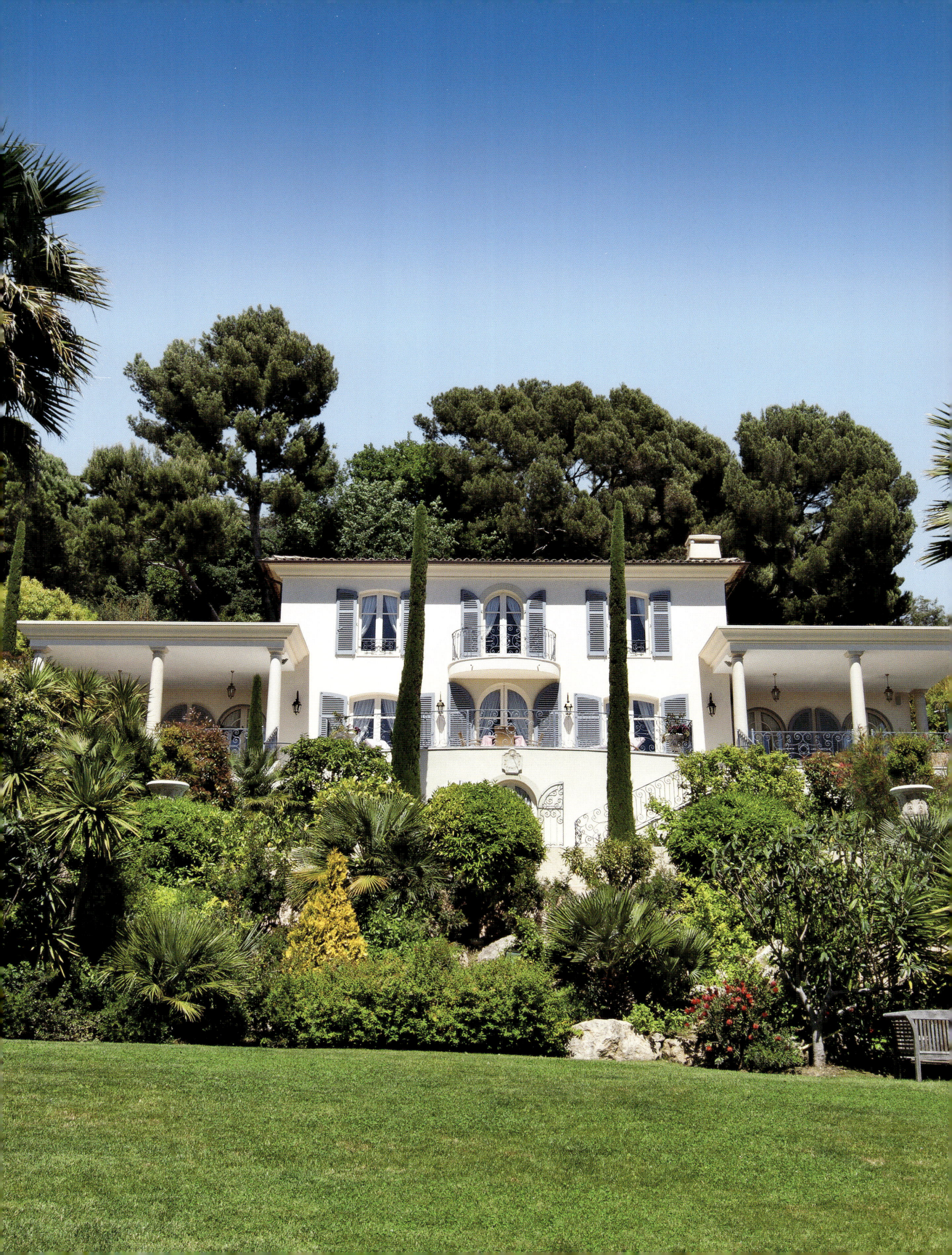

# French Magnificence

With its desirable setting in the heights of Cannes,
this exquisite home on the Côte d'Azur enjoys elegance,
discretion and panoramic sea views aplenty.

SITUATED IN A QUIET and prestigious residential area not far from the centre of Cannes, this spectacular three-storey home radiates a graceful southern French air. With six bedroom suites, five bathrooms and a living area of around 560 square metres, the villa is very spacious and has been completely renovated using premium materials. An immediate highlight is the grand entrance hall with its imperial double-flight staircase – yet the large living room, the dining room and the library with a fireplace are just as stately. The expansive plot of just over 4,000 square metres boasts an infinity pool and a pool house with a sauna as well as lush gardens that are equipped with an automatic watering system. A home cinema, a staff apartment, a triple garage with direct access to the villa, a security camera system and reversible air conditioning complete the range of features. It is easy to live life to the fullest here and in the most beautiful manner possible: "savoir-vivre" – as if the French phrase were conceived with this very dwelling in mind.

IN EINEM RUHIGEN, renommierten Wohnviertel unweit des Zentrums von Cannes, betört diese herrschaftliche dreistöckige Villa durch ihren eleganten südfranzösischen Stil. Das mit sechs Schlafzimmer-Suiten, fünf Bädern und einer Wohnfläche von rund 560 Quadratmetern äußerst komfortable Anwesen wurde unter Verwendung hochwertiger Materialien komplett renoviert. Die imposante Eingangshalle mit ihrer doppelläufigen Treppe präsentiert sich ebenso einladend wie das große Wohn- und Esszimmer und die Bibliothek mit Kamin. Das mehr als 4.000 Quadratmeter große, üppig begrünte Gartenareal ist mit einer automatischen Bewässerungsanlage ausgestattet und verfügt über einen Infinity Pool sowie ein Poolhaus mit Sauna. Ein Heimkino, eine Personalwohnung, eine Dreifachgarage mit direktem Zugang zur Villa, Kameraüberwachung sowie eine umschaltbare Klimaanlage gehören ebenfalls zur Ausstattung – angesichts derer man fast den Eindruck gewinnt, der Begriff „Savoir-vivre" wäre speziell für dieses Traumhaus erfunden worden.

SITUADA EN UNA TRANQUILA y prestigiosa zona residencial cerca del centro de Cannes, esta espectacular casa de tres plantas con el aura del sur de Francia ha sido totalmente renovada con materiales de primera calidad. Con seis *suites*, cinco baños y unos 560 metros cuadrados habitables, la villa resulta muy cómoda. Destaca de inmediato el gran vestíbulo con su escalinata imperial de doble vuelo, aunque el gran salón, el comedor y la biblioteca con chimenea empatan en majestuosidad. El terreno de más de 4.000 metros cuadrados cuenta con una piscina de horizonte infinito y su casita con sauna, envueltas en exuberantes jardines equipados con riego automático. Cine en casa, apartamento para el servicio, garaje triple con acceso directo a la villa, sistema de cámaras de seguridad, aire acondicionado reversible y persianas eléctricas completan su equipamiento. Es fácil vivir la vida al máximo aquí y de la manera más hermosa posible. *Savoir-vivre*, como si la forma francesa para "saber vivir" hubiera sido concebida con esta maravilla inmobiliaria en mente.

FRANCE, CANNES **PURCHASE PRICE** EUR 15.75 MILL. **INTERIOR APPROX.** 560 m² **NO. OF BEDROOMS** 6
**LAND APPROX.** 4,100 m² **E&V ID** W-01GVTE **CONTACT** CANNES (FR), ENGEL & VÖLKERS FRENCH RIVIERA SAS,
LICENCE PARTNER OF ENGEL & VÖLKERS RESIDENTIAL GMBH **TEL.** +33 493 68 64 72
**E-MAIL** CANNES@ENGELVOELKERS.COM

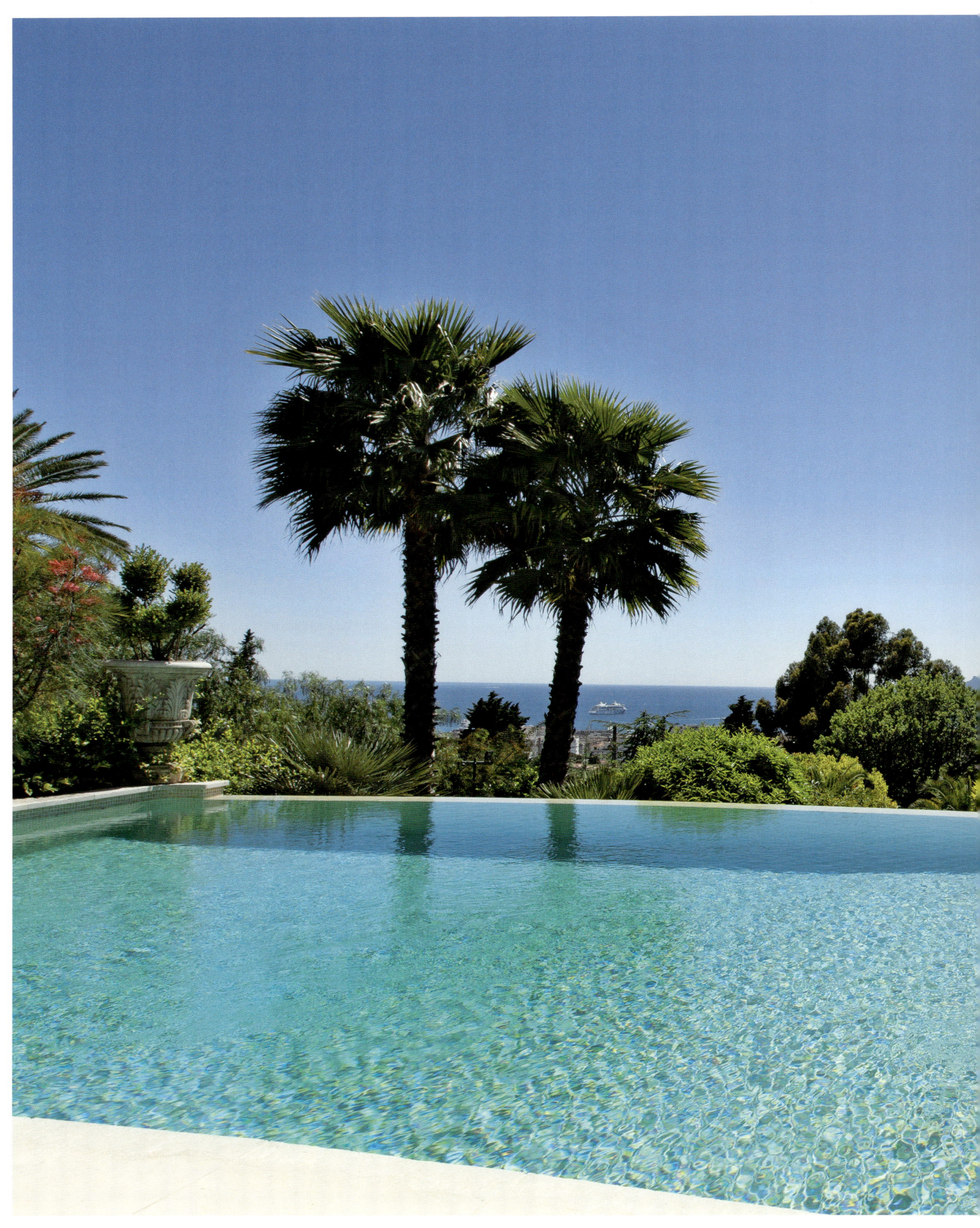

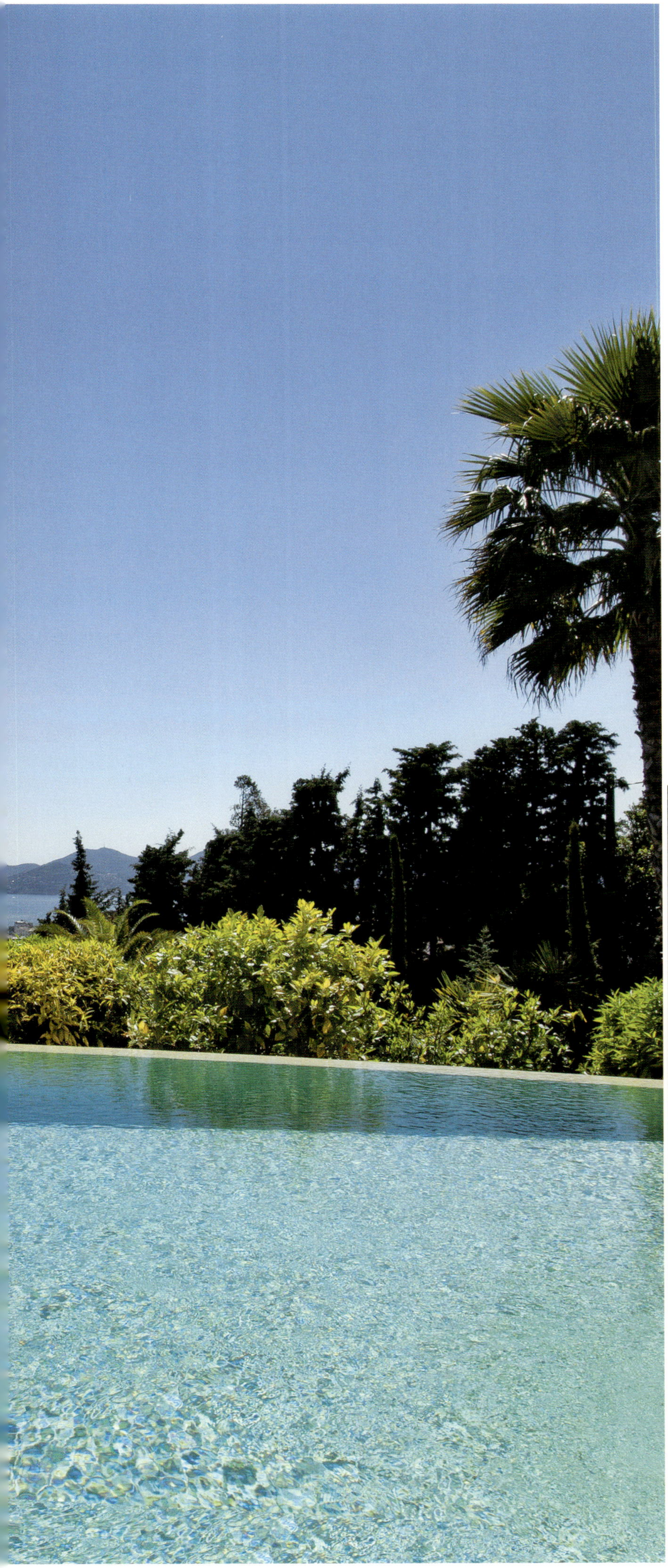

<

One look at the infinity pool in harmony with
the horizon is enough to soothe the the soul.

Hier, wo der Infinity Pool mit dem Horizont
verschmilzt, kommt die Seele zur Ruhe.

Un vistazo a la piscina desbordante en armonía
con el horizonte basta para serenar el alma.

The vast terrace of the villa affords truly
phenomenal panoramic sea views.

Die große Terrasse der Villa bietet einen
phänomenalen Panoramablick aufs Meer.

La gran terraza de la villa ofrece vistas
panorámicas realmente fenomenales al mar.

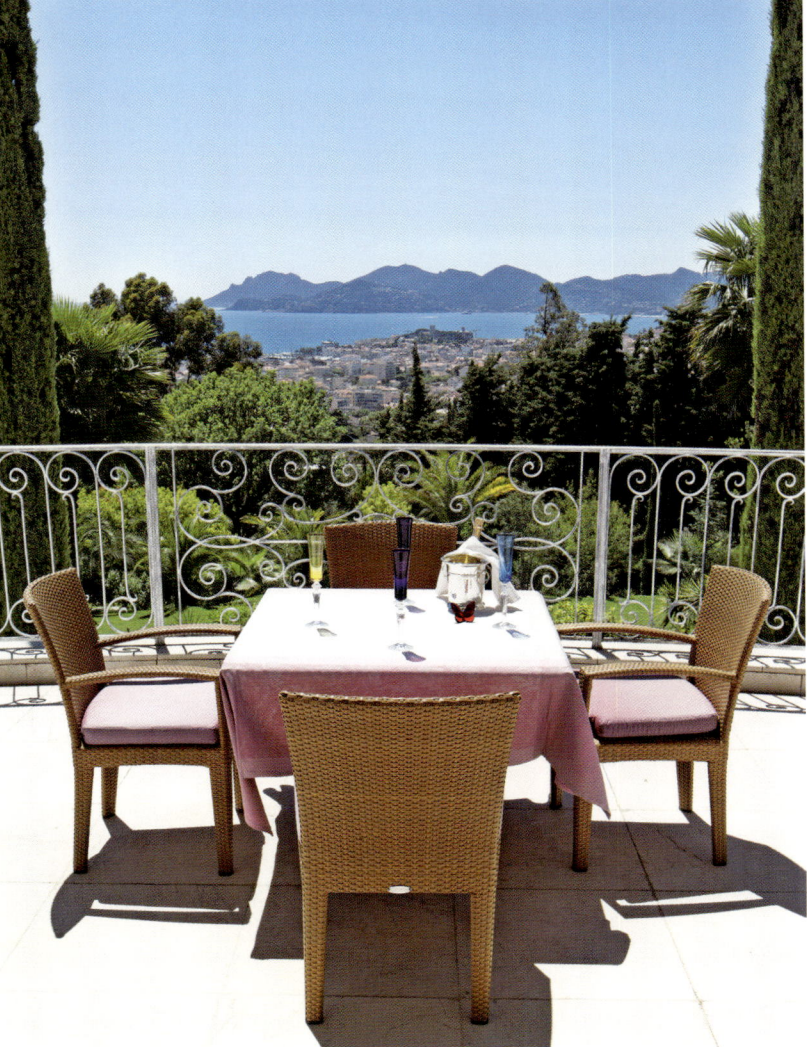

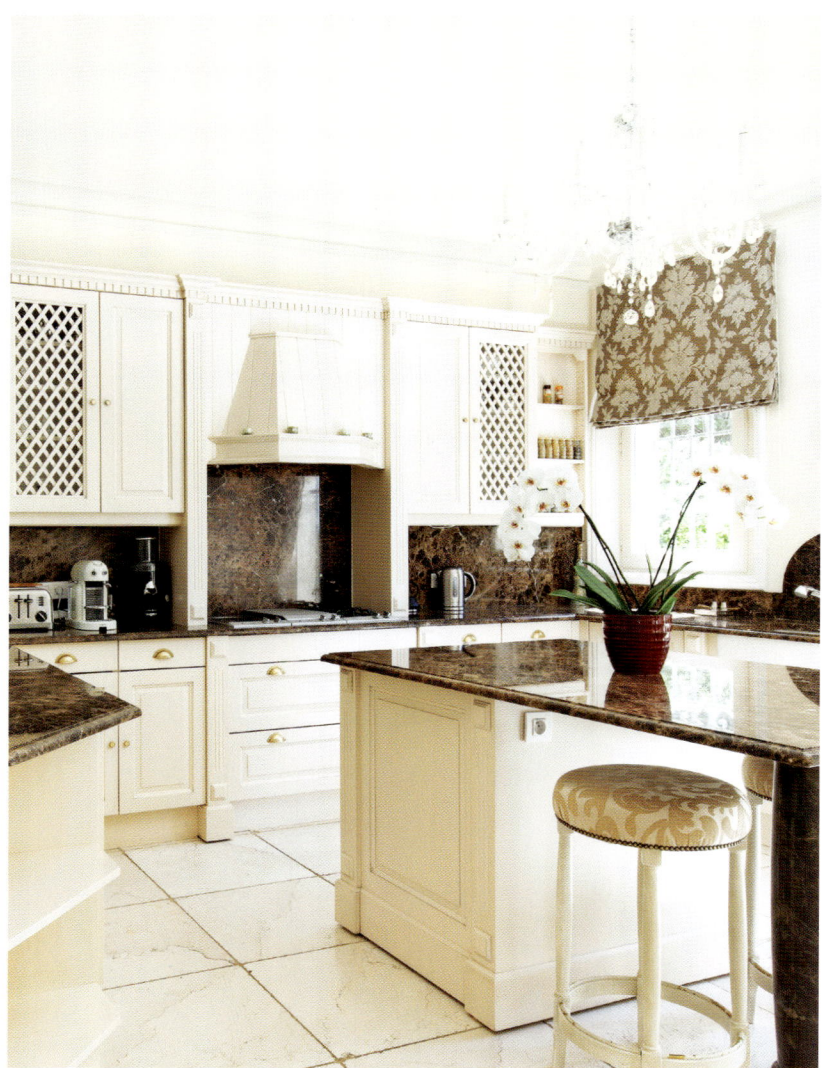

Because first impressions count:
the stunning imperial dual-flight staircase.

Eindrucksvoll und repräsentativ:
die herrschaftliche doppelläufige Treppe

Por que las primeras impresiones cuentan:
la llamativa escalinata imperial de doble vuelo.

The charming country-style kitchen perfectly
matches the radiant and elegant dining room.

Die charmante Landhausküche harmoniert
perfekt mit dem eleganten Speisezimmer.

La coqueta cocina rústica combina idónea-
mente con el luminoso y elegante comedor.

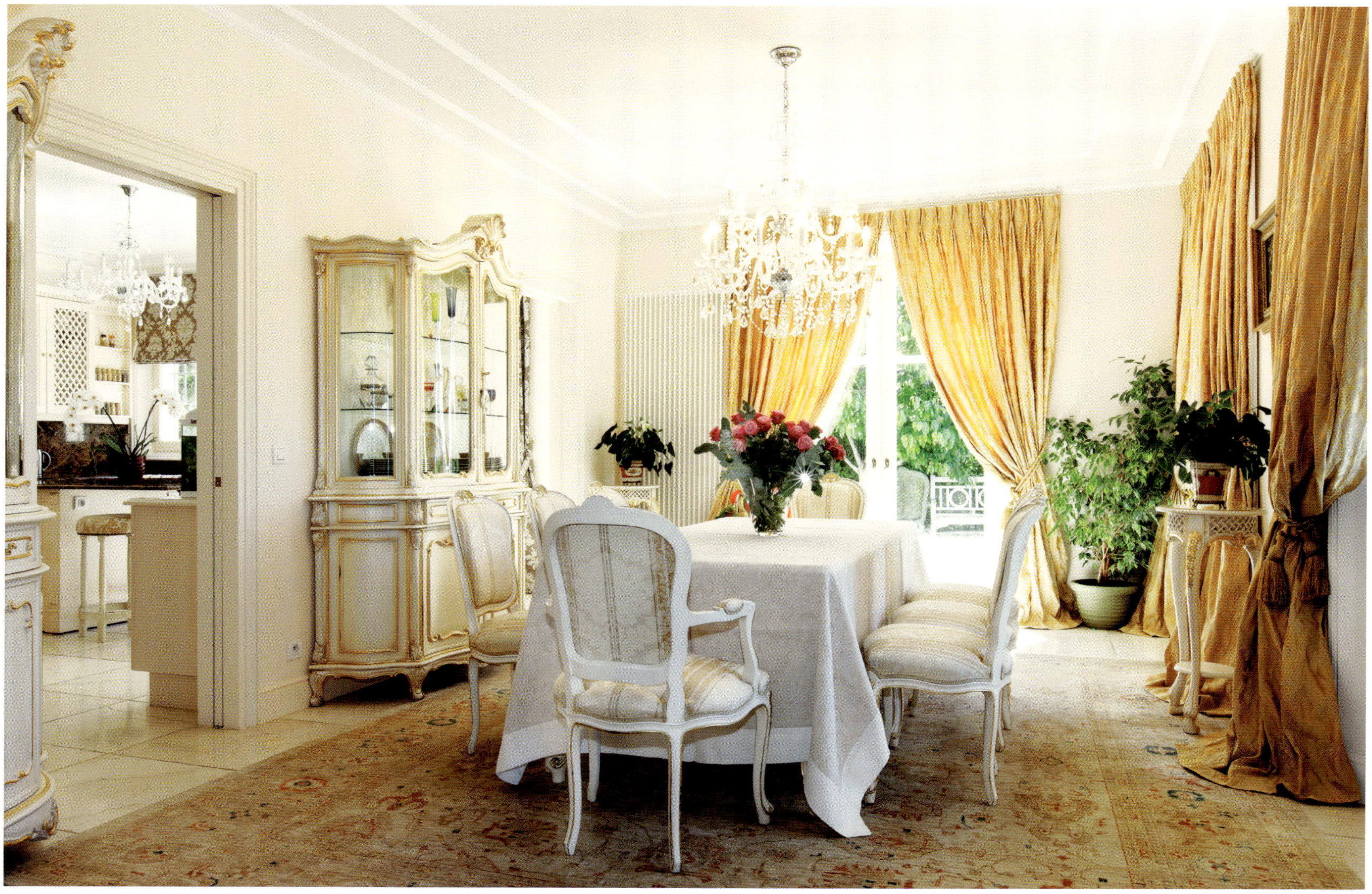

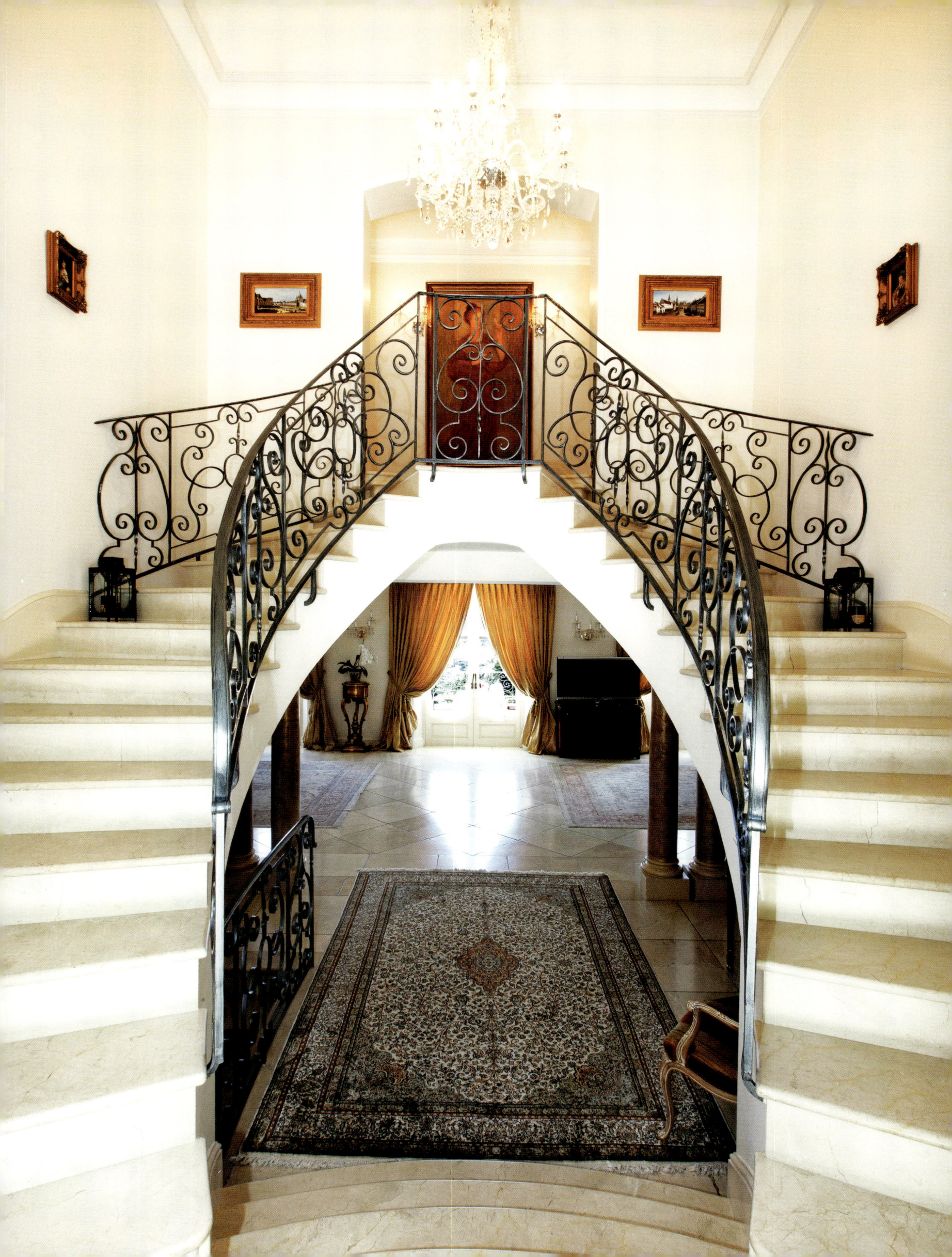

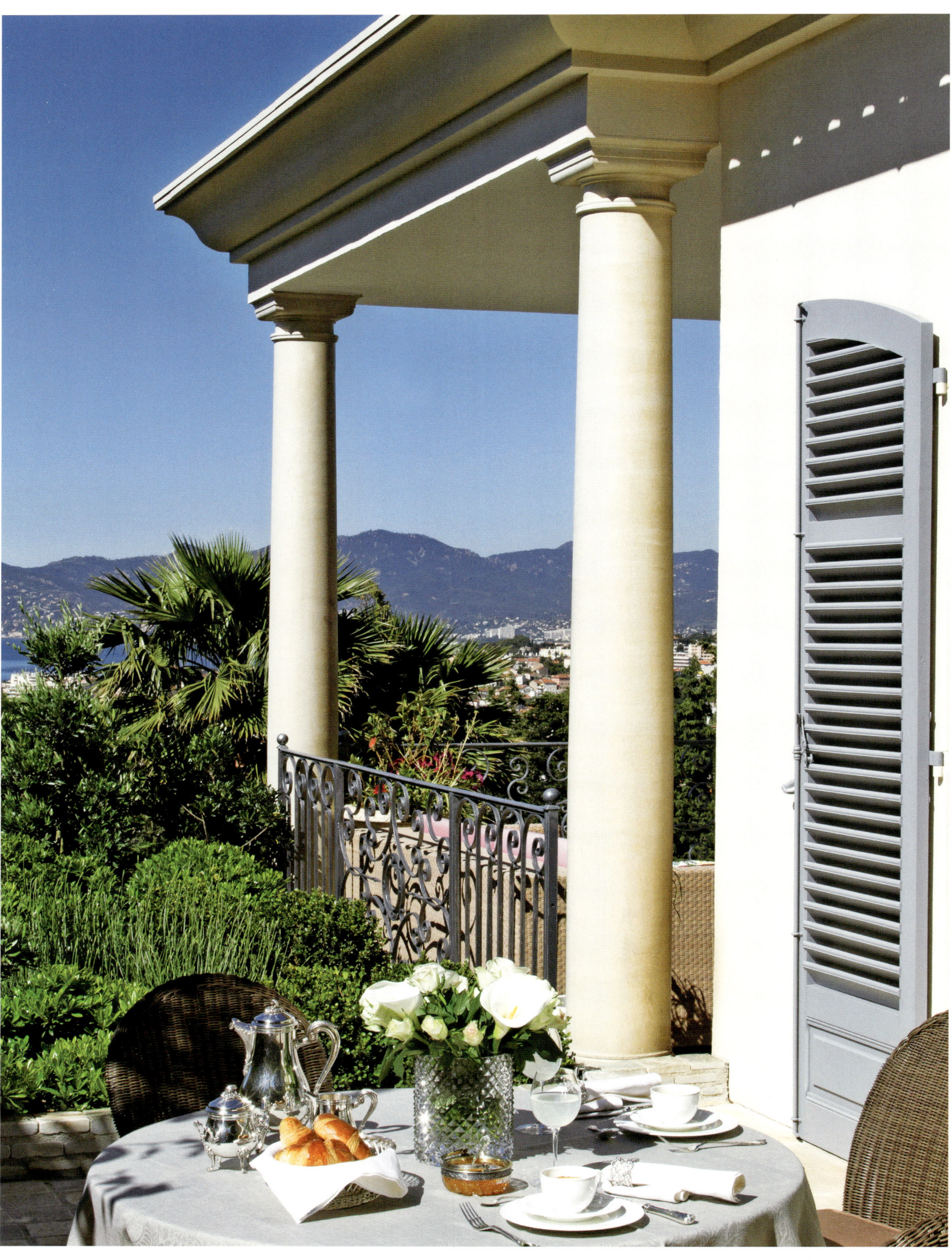

<

Who would not want to enjoy a typical
French breakfast in such a pretty setting?

Wer möchte in einer solchen Umgebung nicht
ein typisch französisches Frühstück genießen?

¿Quién no querría disfrutar de un típico
desayuno francés en un ambiente tan bonito?

The joy of poolside living amidst the privacy
of the lush and well-kept garden.

Am Pool inmitten des prachtvollen Gartens
lässt es sich himmlisch entspannen.

Gozar la bondad de la piscina en la intimidad
del exuberante jardín verde y bien cuidado.

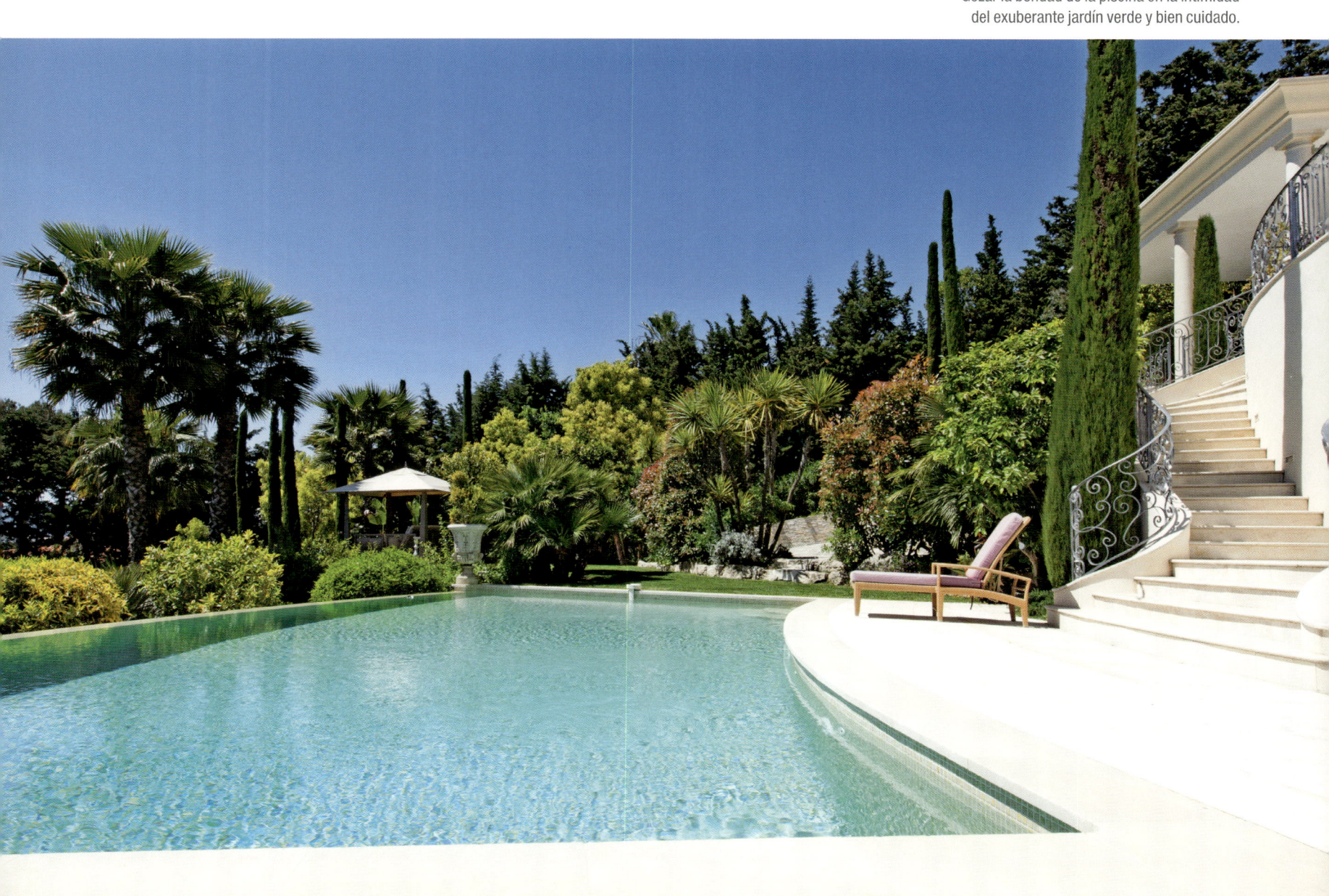

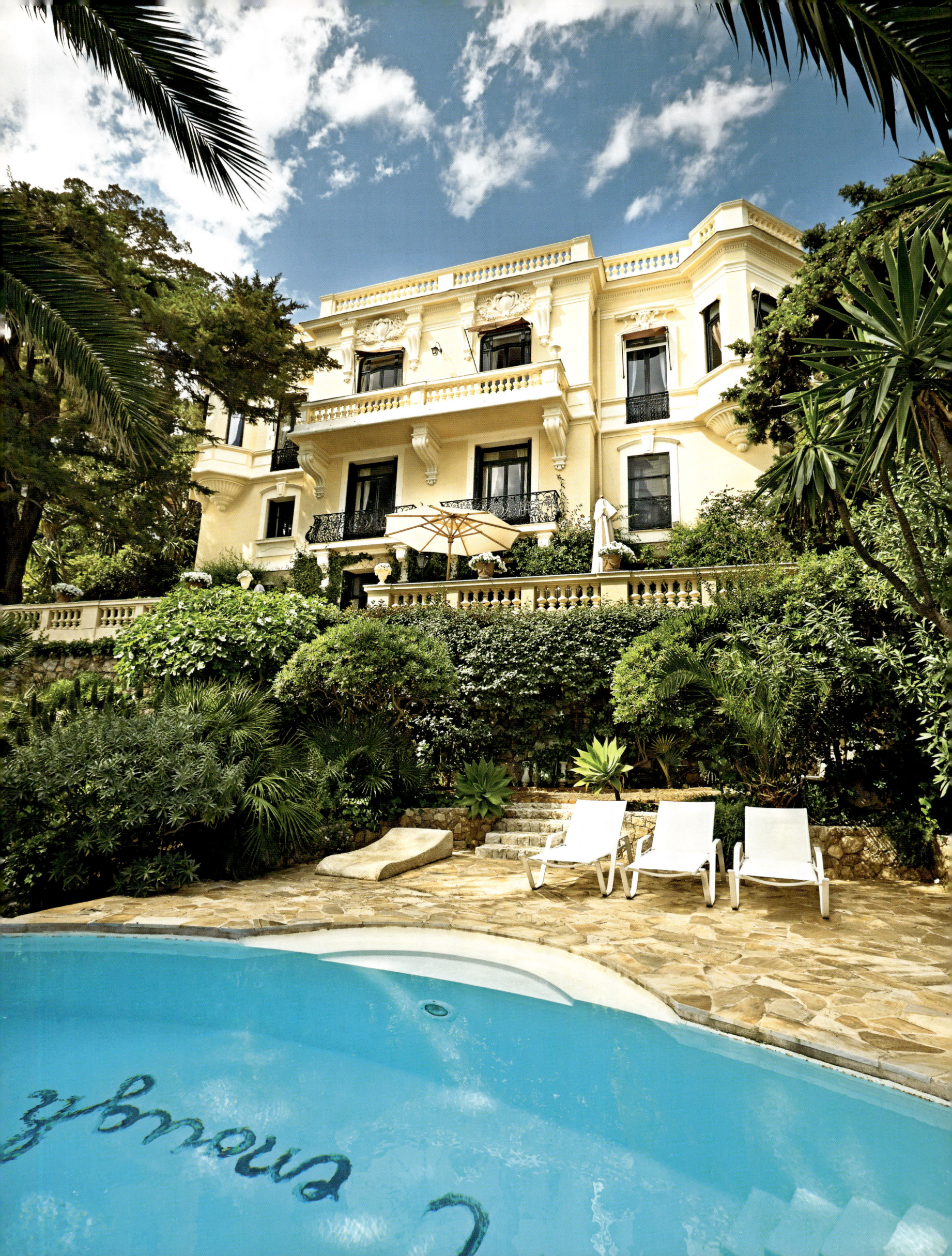

# Belle Epoque Beauty

Rich in charm and history, this gracious abode
dating back to the early twentieth century enjoys
a supreme location on the French Riviera.

THE HISTORIC RESIDENCE exudes an enchanting aura that can be sensed upon very first sight. Whether this is due to its architectural splendour or the privileged seaside location lies in the eyes of the beholder or, rather, its future residents. Built around 1900 as one of the very first palaces in Cap d'Ail, the villa – in which Queen Beatrix also spent some time during her childhood – has remained in the very same family for generations. Indeed, the majestic property with its idyllic gardens as well as the residence interiors still radiate a gracious aristocratic flair today. Offering around 700 square metres of exquisite living space spread across three levels in the main villa, there is also a separate house to accommodate staff or guests. The palatial dwelling features an entrance hall, a large living area with terrace access, a television room, several bedrooms, some with en-suite facilities, as well as a spacious dining room with an adjacent kitchen that leads onto a further terrace – boasting panoramic views that will never cease to fascinate.

DIESE HISTORISCHE RESIDENZ strahlt auf den ersten Blick eine magische Aura aus. Ob dies an ihrer architektonischen Pracht oder der traumhaften Lage direkt am Mittelmeer liegt, bleibt dem Betrachter oder vielmehr den künftigen Bewohnern überlassen. Um 1900 als eines der ersten Schlösser in Cap d'Ail errichtet, ist das Anwesen, in dem unter anderem schon Königin Beatrix einige Zeit während ihrer Kindheit verbracht hat, über Generationen im Besitz derselben Familie geblieben. Das imposante Grundstück mit seinen idyllischen Gärten verströmt ebenso wie die Innenräume auch heute noch aristokratisches Flair. Rund 700 Quadratmeter Wohnfläche verteilen sich auf drei Ebenen im Haupthaus sowie eine Gäste- bzw. Personalunterkunft. Die Villa verfügt unter anderem über eine Eingangshalle, einen großen Wohnbereich mit Terrassenzugang, ein TV-Zimmer, mehrere Schlafzimmer, teils mit En-suite-Bad, sowie ein repräsentatives Esszimmer mit angrenzender Küche und Zugang zu einer weiteren Terrasse – mit einer Aussicht, die immer wieder aufs Neue fasziniert.

LA RESIDENCIA HISTÓRICA exuda un aura encantadora que se puede percibir a primera vista. Si esto se debe a su esplendor arquitectónico o a su privilegiada ubicación junto al mar dependerá de los ojos del espectador o, mejor dicho, de sus futuros moradores. Construida alrededor de 1900 como uno de los primeros palacios de Cap d'Ail, la propiedad donde la reina Beatriz pasó cierto tiempo durante su infancia ha permanecido en manos de la misma familia durante generaciones. De hecho, la majestuosa propiedad con sus idílicos jardines así como sus interiores todavía irradian cierto aire aristocrático aún a día de hoy. Dispone de cerca de 700 metros cuadrados habitables exquisitamente repartidos en los tres niveles de la villa principal, además de una casa aparte para acomodar al personal o los invitados. La vivienda palaciega luce un vestíbulo, el gran salón con acceso a la terraza, sala de televisión, varias habitaciones -algunas con su baño-, así como un amplio comedor con cocina adyacente que conduce a otra terraza con panorámicas eternamente fascinantes.

FRANCE, CAP D'AIL **PURCHASE PRICE** ON REQUEST **INTERIOR APPROX.** 700 m² **NO. OF BEDROOMS** 7
**LAND APPROX.** 1,480 m² **E&V ID** W-0159YW **CONTACT** CAP FERRAT (FR), EV FRENCH RIVIERA SAS,
LICENCE PARTNER OF ENGEL & VÖLKERS RESIDENTIAL GMBH **TEL.** +33 493 54 93 42
**E-MAIL** CAPFERRAT@ENGELVOELKERS.COM

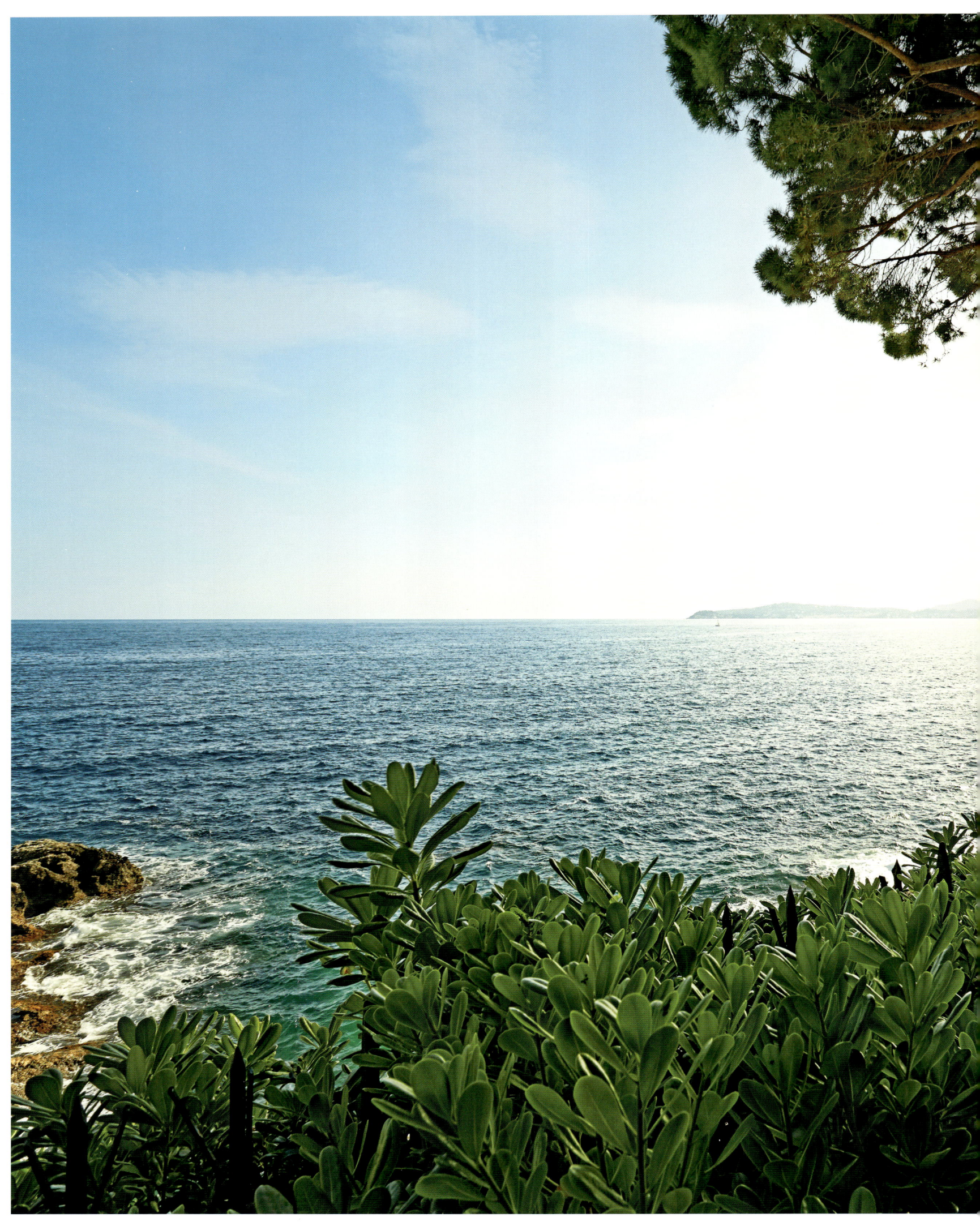

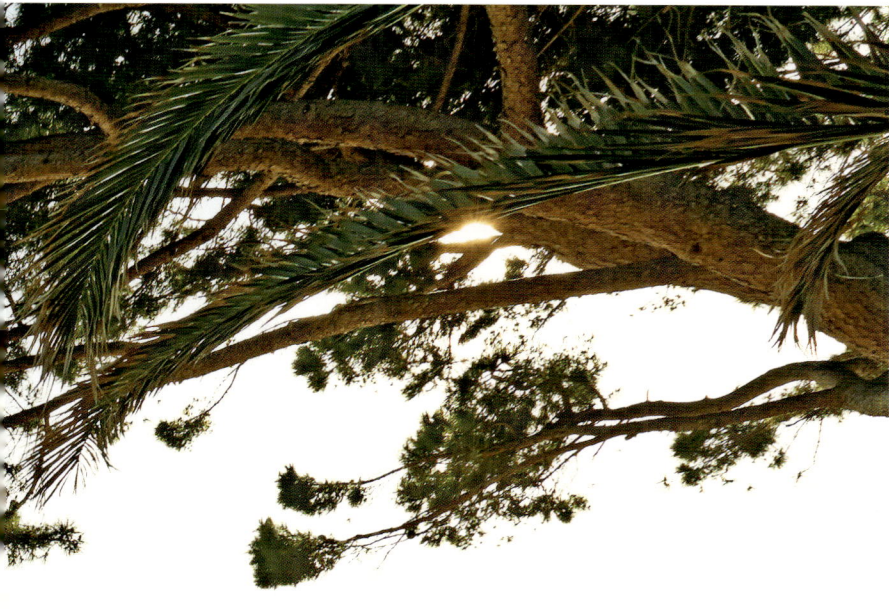

The villa's privileged location between Nice and Monaco is befitting of its rank.

Standesgemäß: die einzigartige Lage des Anwesens zwischen Nizza und Monaco.

La privilegiada ubicación de la villa, entre Niza y Mónaco, avala su clase por sí misma.

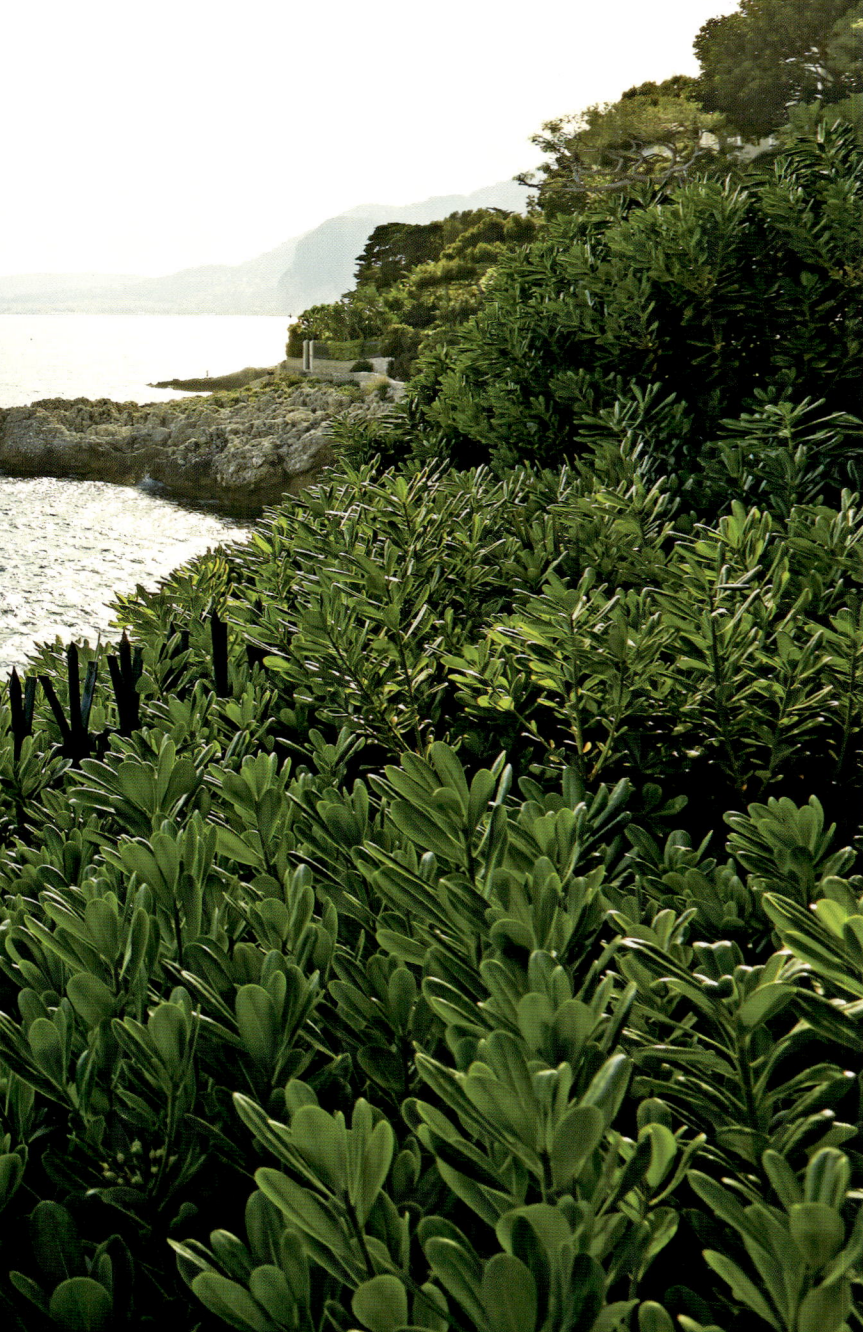

A place where impressions steeped in history meet upon stately comfort.

Ein Ort, an dem historische Impressionen auf herrschaftlichen Komfort treffen.

Un lugar donde los rasgos llenos de historia se amalgaman con el confort señorial.

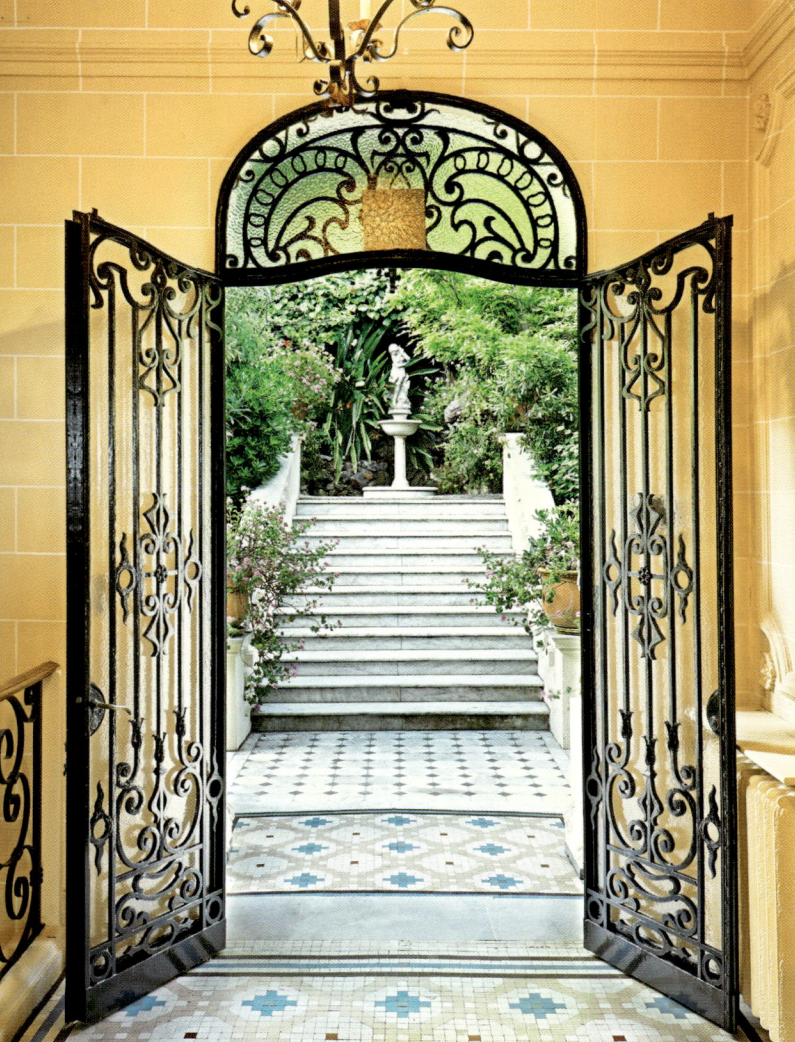

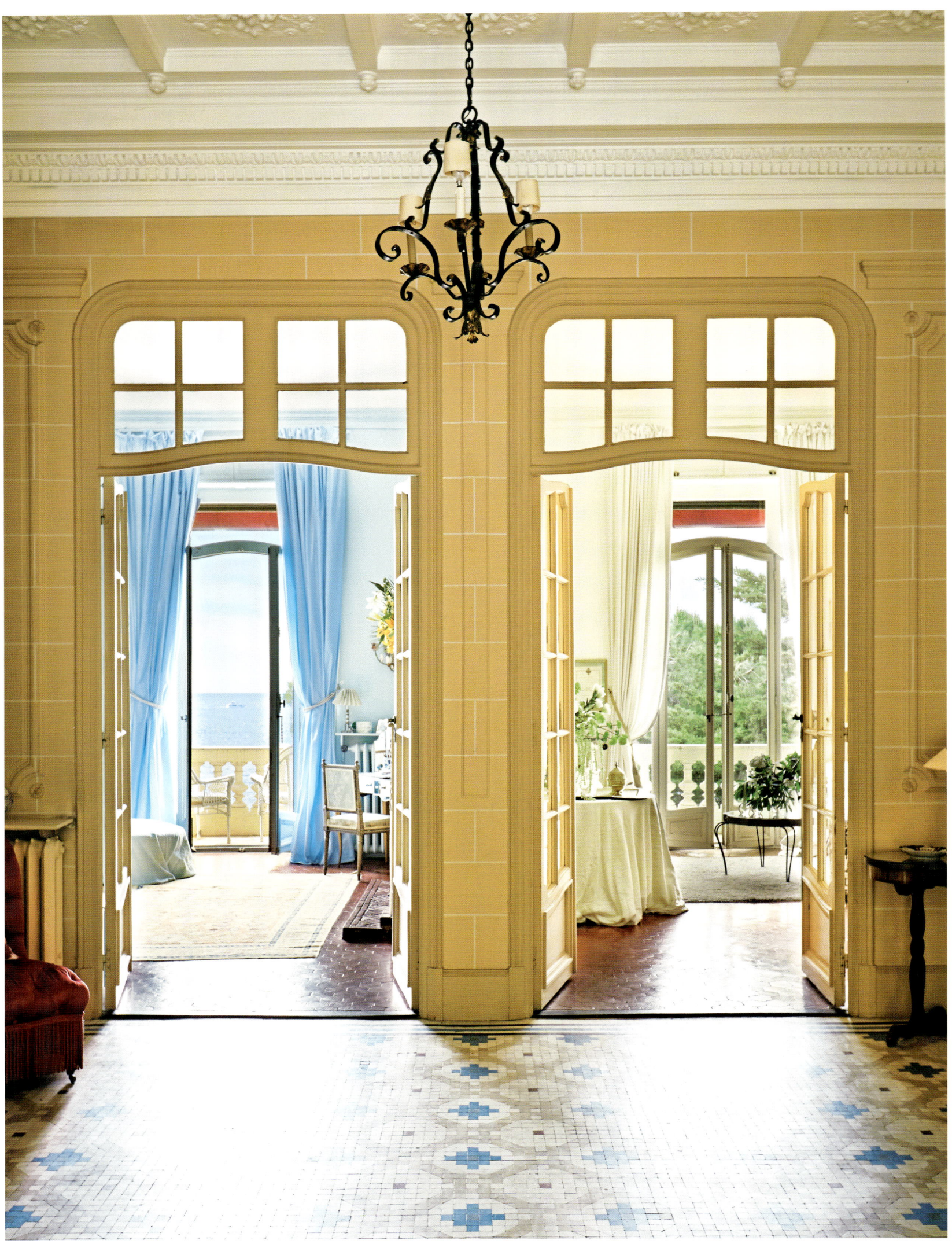

Inviting: the elegant belle époque style with
lofty ceilings and double-wing doors.

Einladend: der elegante Belle-Epoque-Stil
mit seinen hohen Decken und Flügeltüren.

Atractivo: el elegante estilo "belle époque" con
techos altos, molduras y puertas de doble ala.

Much loving attention to detail has been
paid to the appointment of the rooms.

Viel Liebe zum Detail wurde hier bei der
Gestaltung der Räumlichkeiten bewiesen.

El diseño de las estancias ha sido ejecutado
con una primorosa atención al detalle.

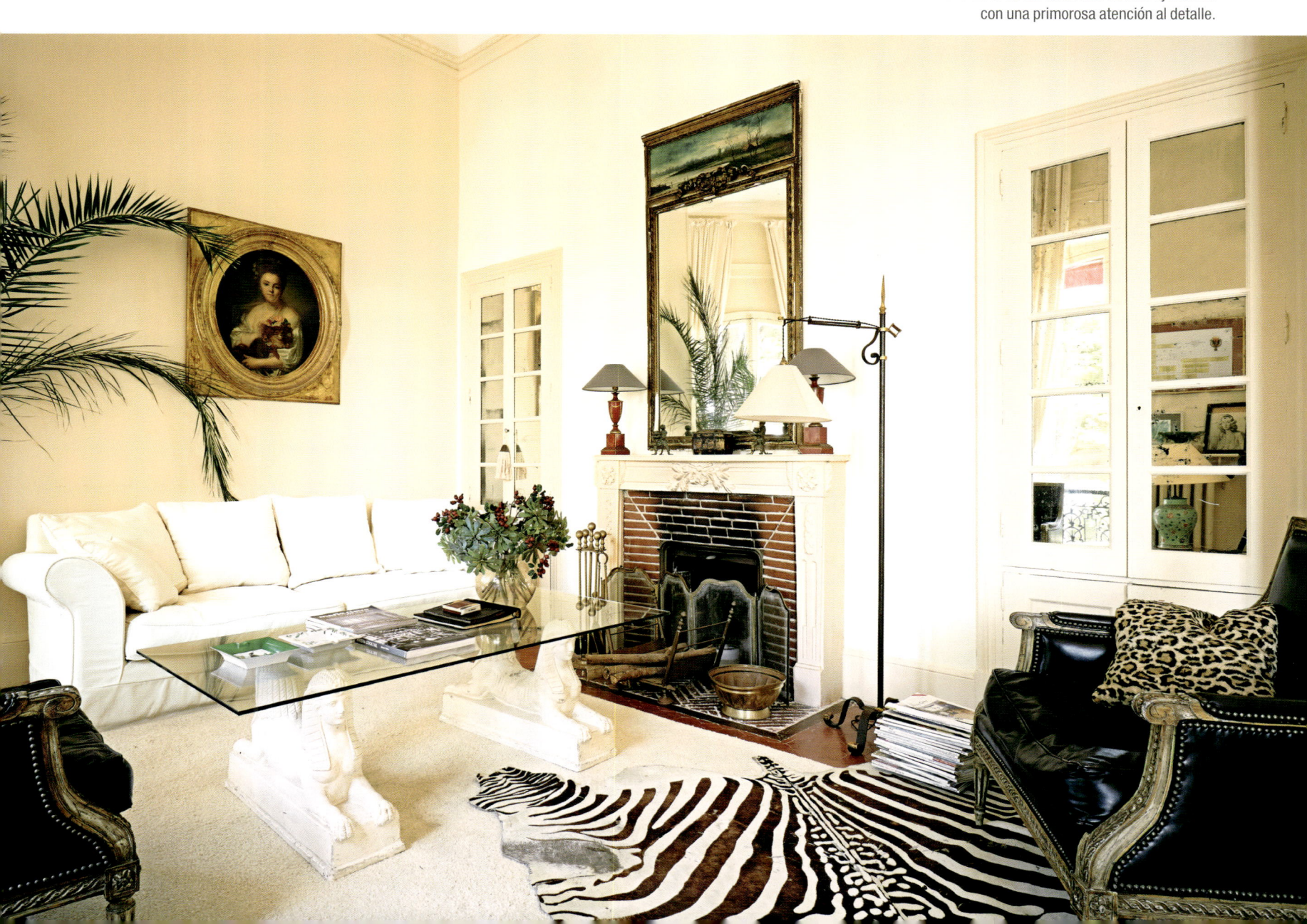

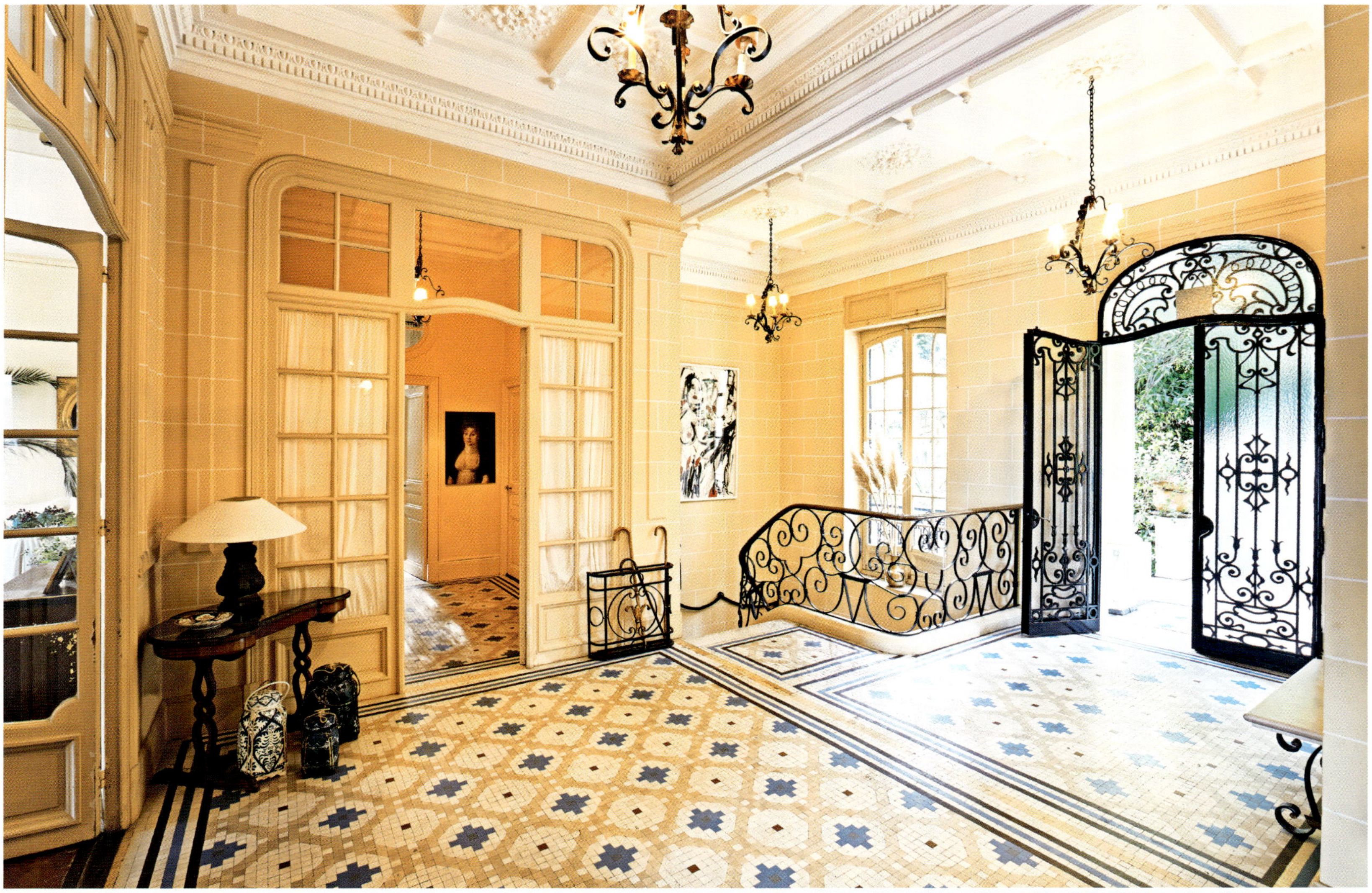

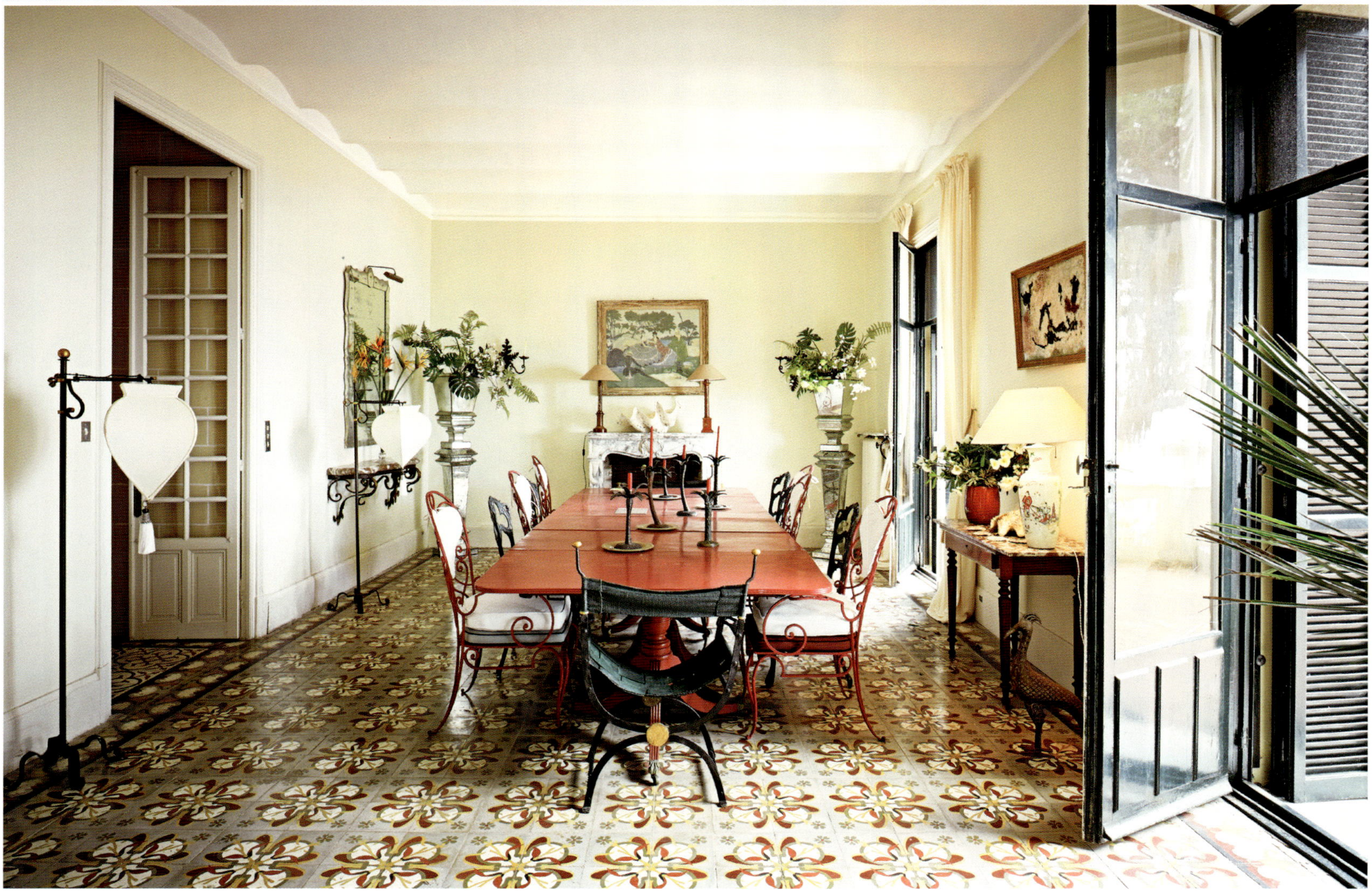

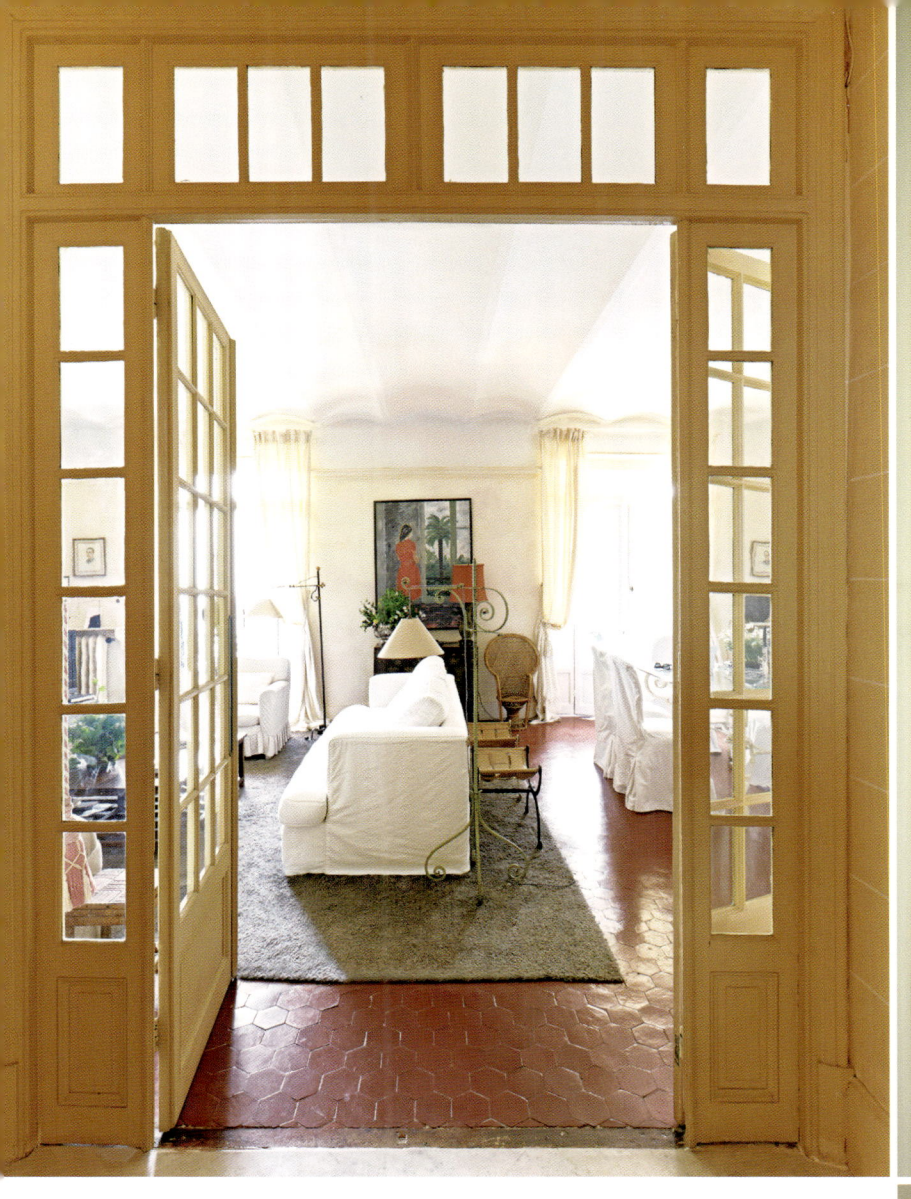

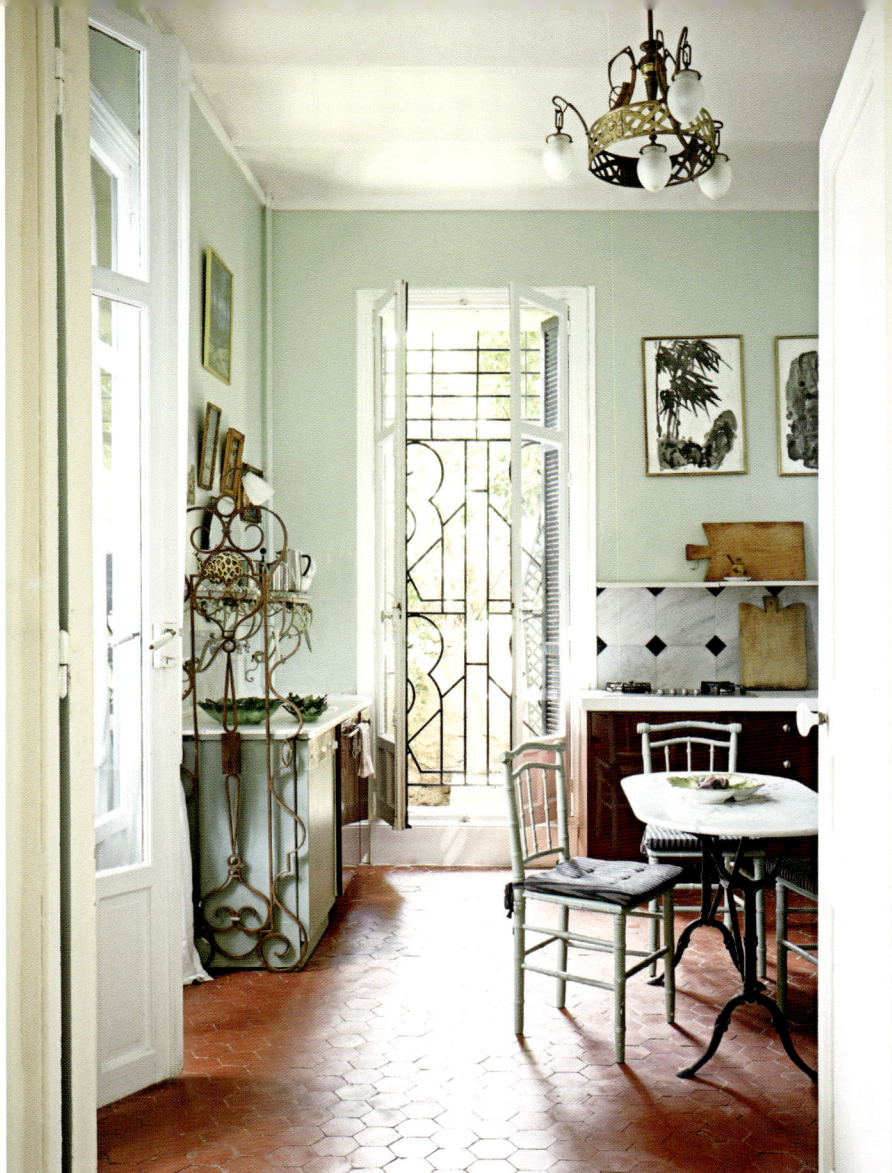

Aristocratic flair and southern French charm – a simply irresistible liaison.

Aristokratisches Flair und südfranzösischer Charme – eine unwiderstehliche Liaison.

Estilo aristocrático y encanto del sur de Francia: una pareja simplemente irresistible.

<

Dining in a regal fashion – accompanied by absolutely glorious vistas of the sea.

Hier diniert man auf königlichem Niveau – und genießt dabei die Aussicht aufs Meer.

Sobremesas regias adornadas con las magníficas panorámicas sobre el mar.

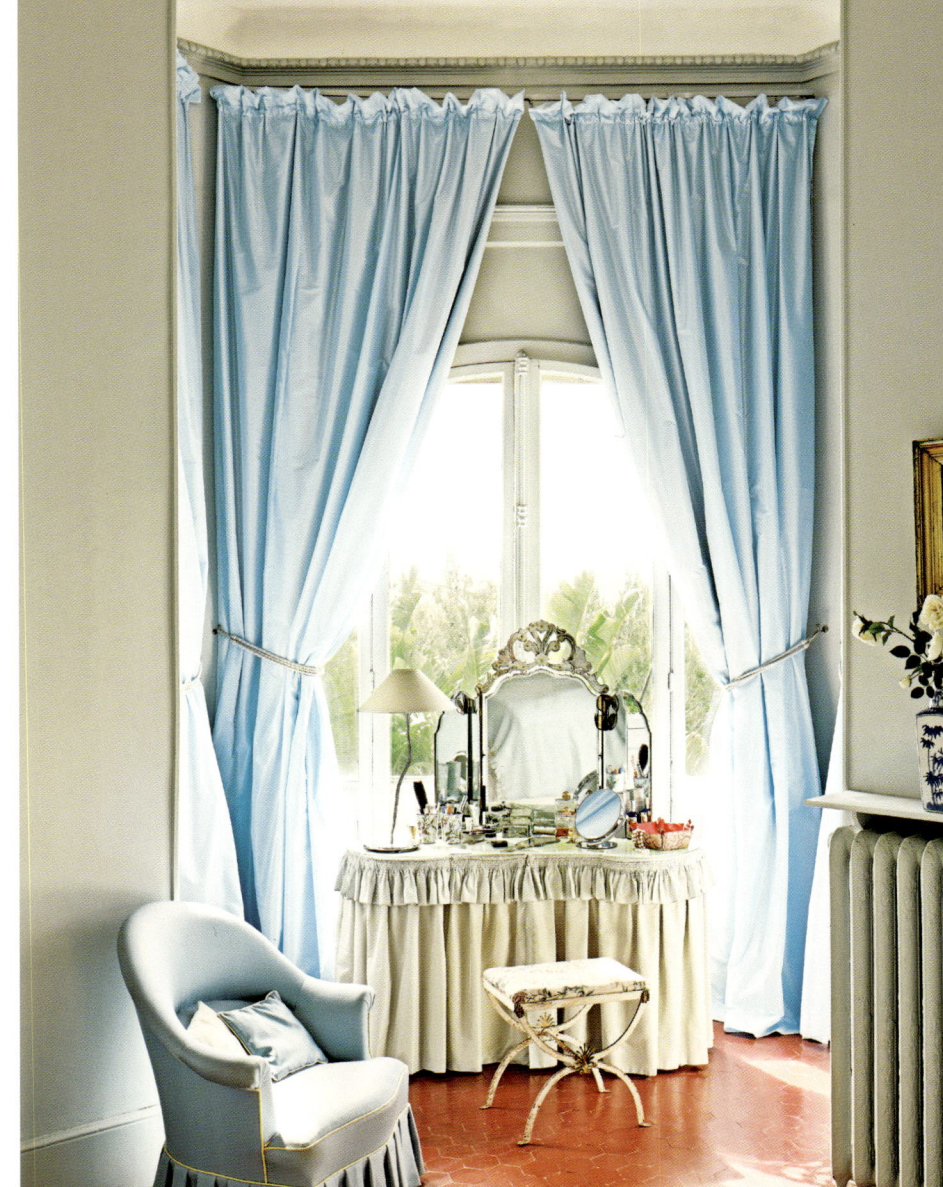

The terrace of this palatial villa affords
views that are a real dream come true.

Der Blick von der Terrasse dieses Villen-
anwesens – ein wahr gewordener Traum.

La terraza de esta villa palaciega luce
vistas que parecen un sueño hecho realidad.

Sublime and impressive, this historic
residence presides on the Côte d'Azur.

Erhaben thront diese geschichtsträchtige
Residenz über der Côte d'Azur.

Sublime e impresionante, la residencia
histórica corona la Costa Azul.

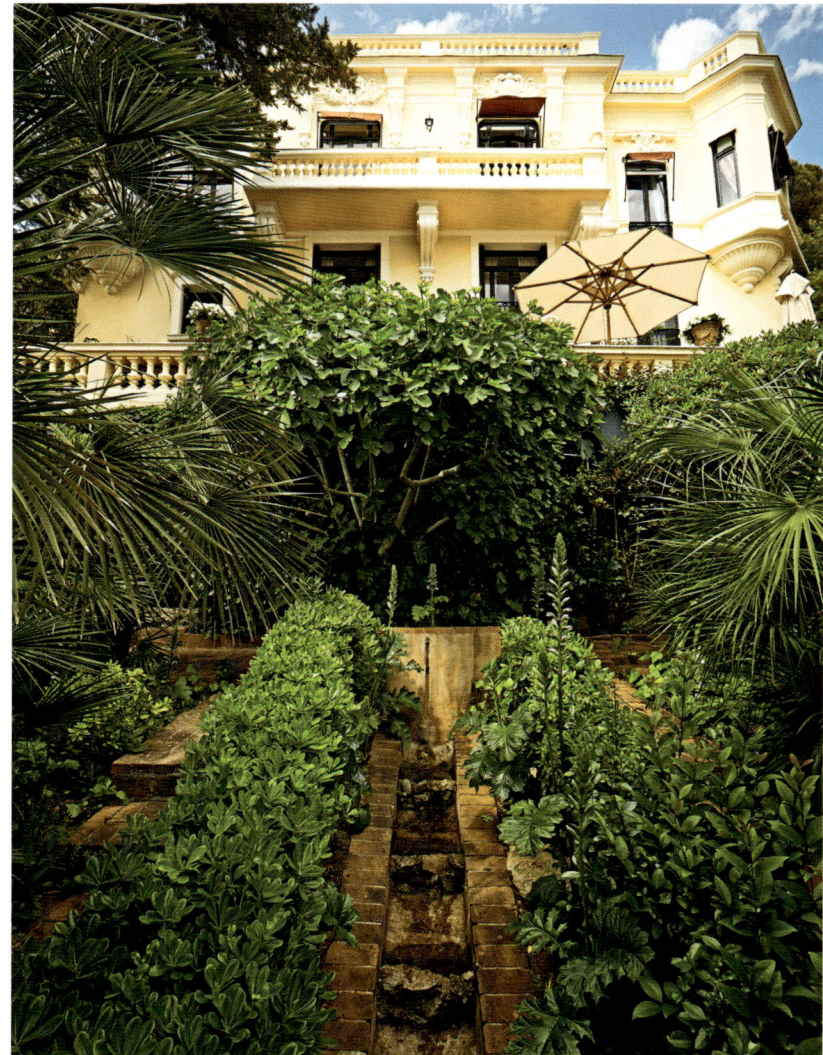

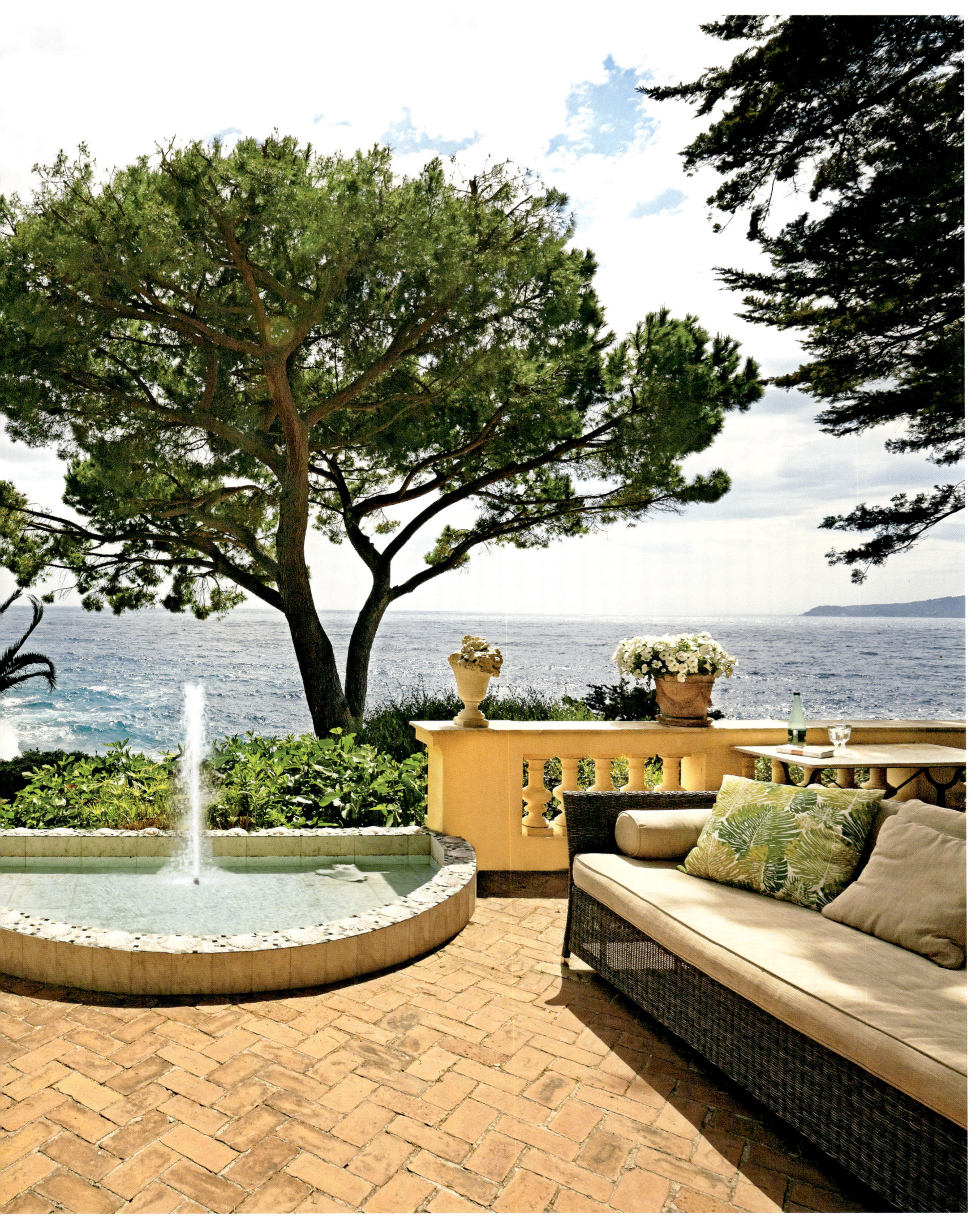

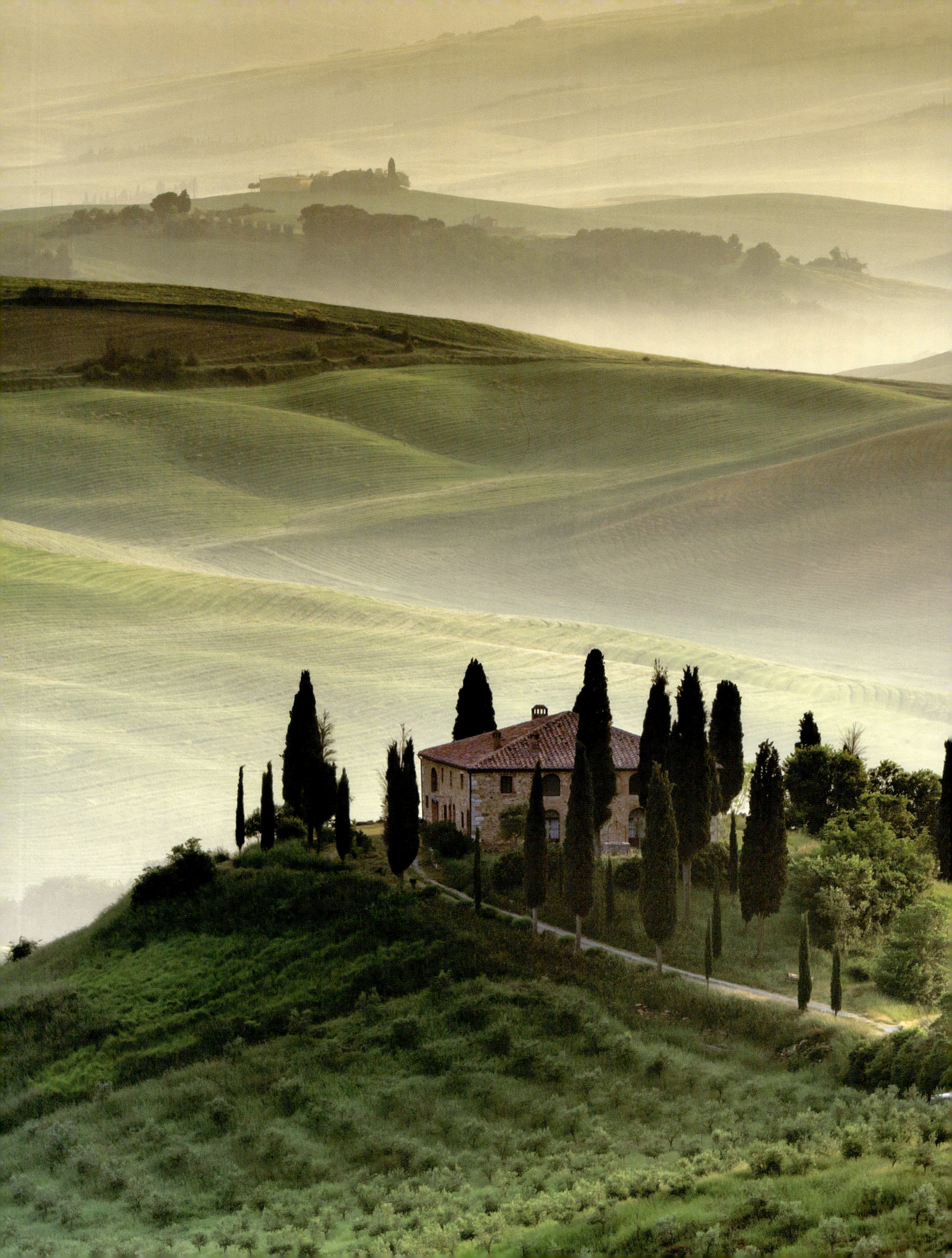

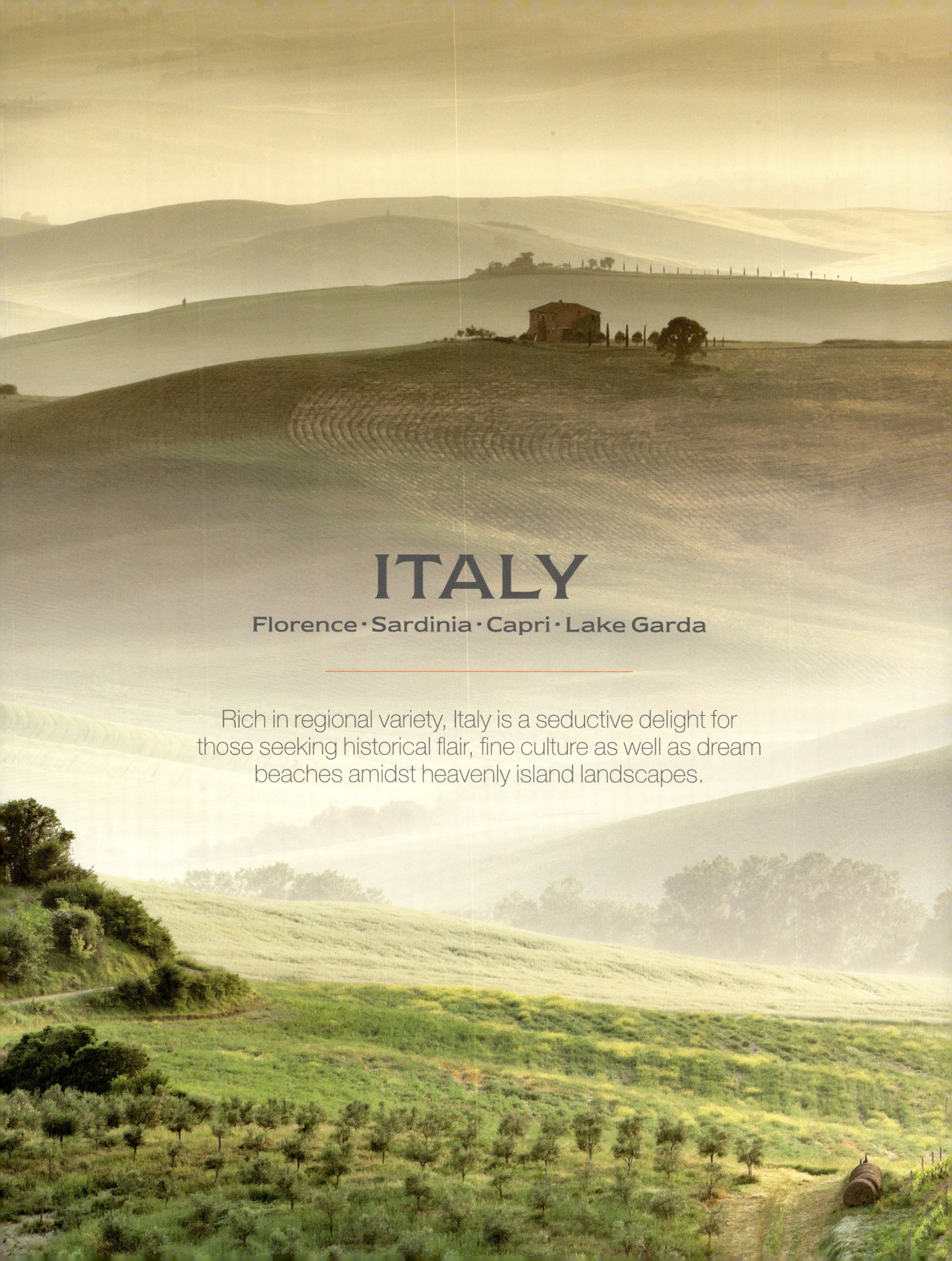

# ITALY
### Florence · Sardinia · Capri · Lake Garda

Rich in regional variety, Italy is a seductive delight for those seeking historical flair, fine culture as well as dream beaches amidst heavenly island landscapes.

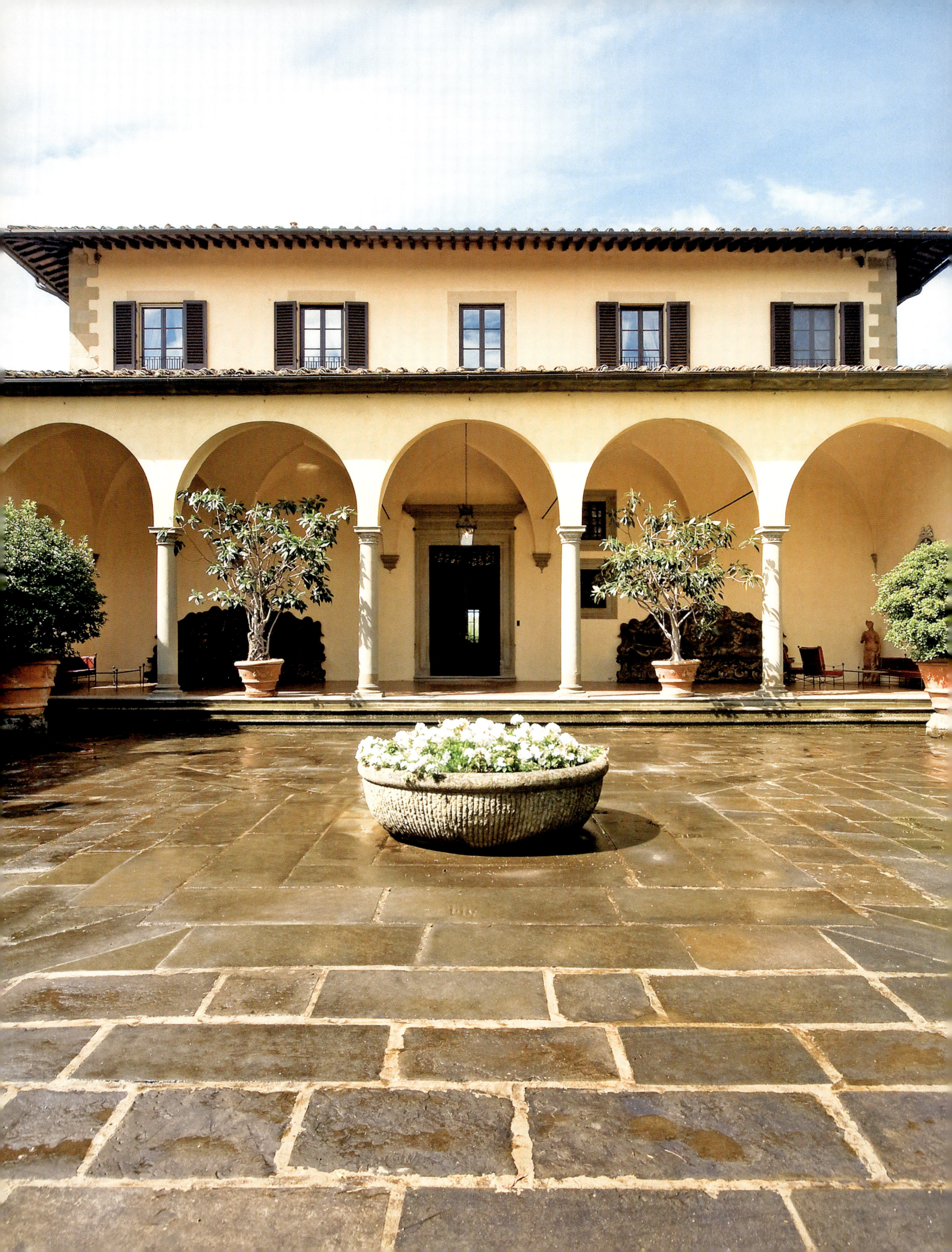

# Renaissance Manor

Presiding over the gently rolling hills south of Florence, an opulent Medici villa with an artistic soul invokes a rare combination of noble grandeur and family warmth.

COMMISSIONED BY THE Marchese Niccolò Antinori in the fifteenth century, "Villa le Rose" is a marvellous example of an aristocratic Renaissance residence. Nestled in the Tuscan landscape amidst the Chianti wine-growing region only minutes from Florence, this countryside retreat in Tavarnuzze is ideal for an exclusive holiday for up to twelve guests. Lovingly refurbished, the villa has all the modern comforts that the discerning traveller might wish for, whilst attention has been paid to maintain the home's historical features. Standing at the end of a long private driveway lined with cypress trees, the dwelling is built around a courtyard and is surrounded by gardens with fragrant olive groves, rose bushes, lemon trees, giant azaleas, laurel and boxwood shrubs and a 300-year-old Lebanese cedar; an outdoor pool and a private lake also grace the property. The manor itself exudes endless beauty, seen in the period frescoed walls, the grand ballroom, ornate ceilings, exquisite antique furnishings and seven lavish bedrooms as well as the bathrooms with finest amenities.

IM AUFTRAG DES Marquis Niccolò Antinori im 15. Jahrhundert erbaut, präsentiert sich die „Villa le Rose" als Prachtexemplar einer Adelsresidenz aus der Renaissancezeit. Im reizvollen Chianti-Weinanbaugebiet nahe Florenz gelegen, präsentiert sich das ländliche Refugium in Tavarnuzze als Feriendomizil der Superlative. Liebevoll mit Blick auf den Erhalt historischer Details restauriert, bietet der Besitz nicht nur Platz für bis zu zwölf Gäste, sondern auch alle Annehmlichkeiten, die anspruchsvolle Reisende zu schätzen wissen. In geschützter Lage am Ende einer langen, von Zypressen gesäumten Einfahrt fasziniert das Anwesen nicht zuletzt durch seine weitläufige Parklandschaft mit Olivenhainen, Rosenstöcken, Azaleen, Zitronen-, Buchs- und Lorbeerbäumen sowie einer 300 Jahre alten Libanonzeder. Ein Außenpool und ein privater See gehören ebenfalls zu dieser Residenz, die mit ihren Freskomalereien und reich verzierten Decken, einem großen Ballsaal, sieben opulenten Schlafgemächern und edel ausgestatteten Badezimmern ihresgleichen sucht.

ENCARGADA POR EL marqués Niccolò Antinori en el siglo XV, Villa le Rose es un maravilloso ejemplo de residencia aristocrática del Renacimiento. Decorada con el paisaje de Toscana, en el corazón de la región vinícola de Chianti a pocos minutos de Florencia, esta finca señorial en Tavarnuzze promete disfrutar vacaciones exclusivas, con capacidad para hasta doce personas. Cuidadosamente restaurada, dispone de todas las comodidades que puede desear el viajero más exigente, al tiempo que se han preservado las características históricas de la casa. Culminando un largo camino privado flanqueado de cipreses, la mansión está construida alrededor de un patio y envuelta en fragantes y antiguos olivares, rosales, limoneros, azaleas gigantes, laureles, setos de boj y un cedro libanés de 300 años; la piscina al aire libre y un lago privado completan la propiedad. La mansión en sí rezuma belleza, como se aprecia en los frescos de época, techos ornados, exquisitas antigüedades, el gran salón de baile, los aposentos de lujo y los baños con los más refinados complementos.

ITALY, FLORENCE **RENTAL PRICE/WEEK** EUR 30,000–42,000 **INTERIOR APPROX.** 800 m² **NO. OF BEDROOMS** 7 **LAND APPROX.** 120,000 m² **E&V ID** W-01VNQB **CONTACT** FLORENCE (IT), M. & M. IMPERIALE IMMOBILIARE S.R.L., LICENCE PARTNER OF ENGEL & VÖLKERS ITALIA S.R.L. **TEL.** +39 055 28 10 76 **E-MAIL** FIRENZEMICHELANGELO@ENGELVOELKERS.COM

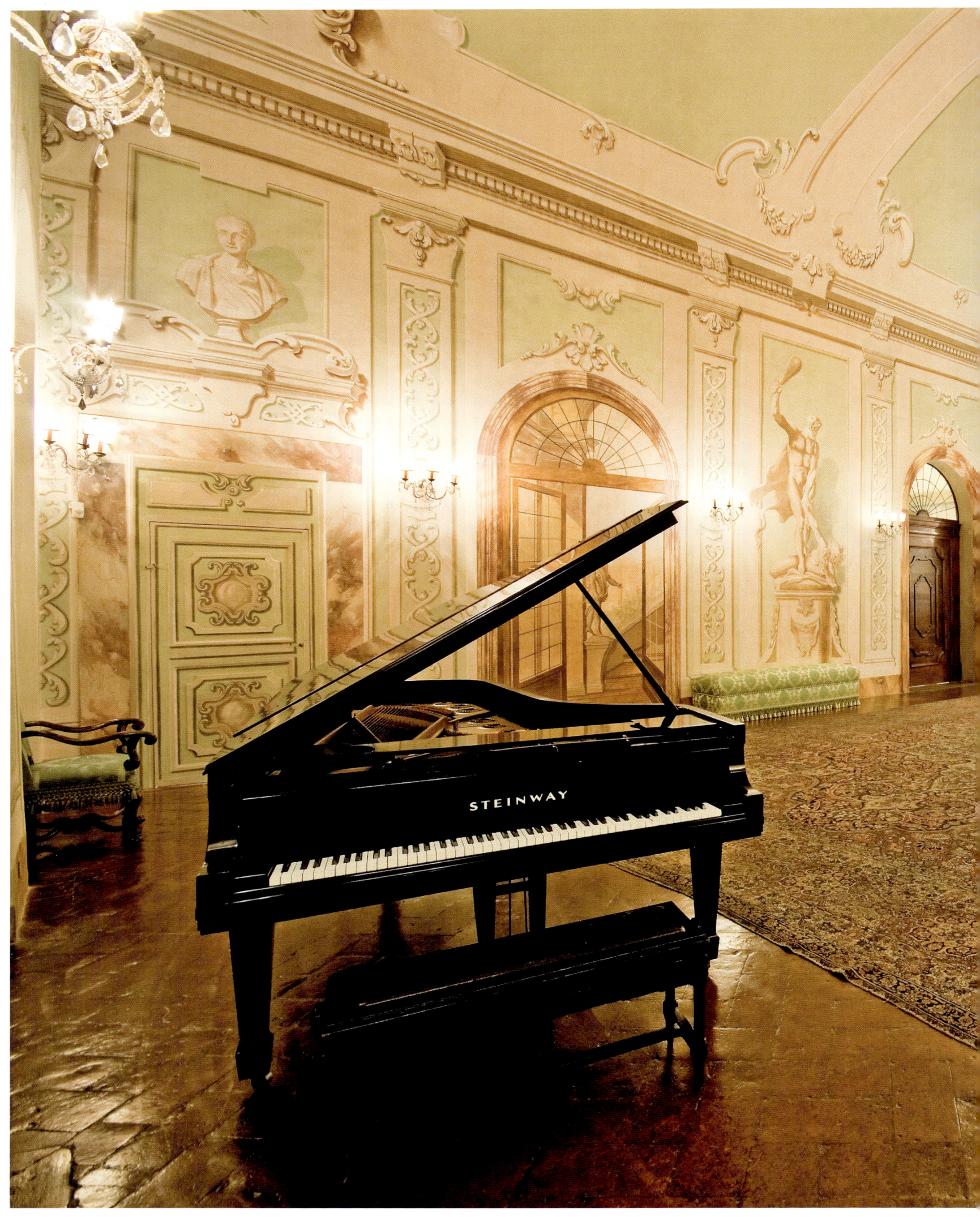

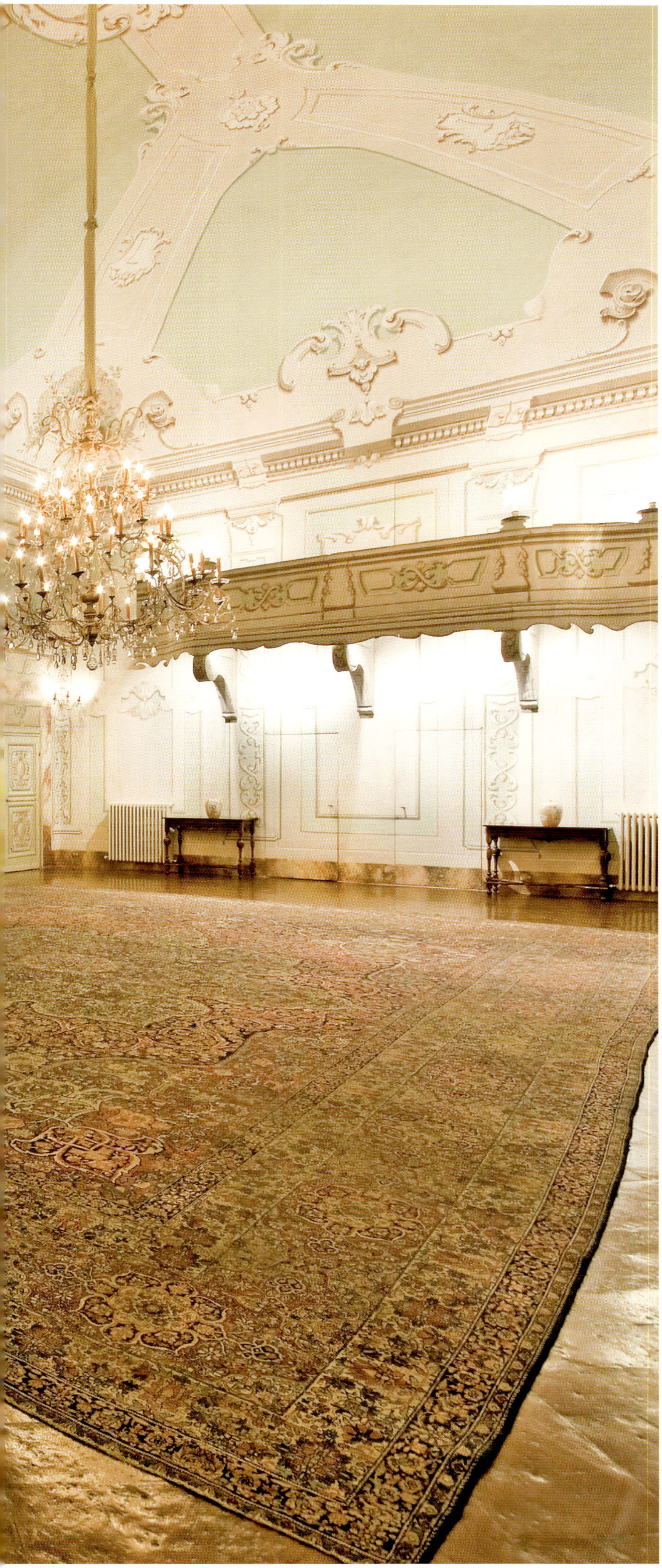

A feast for all the senses: the ballroom with its stunning frescoes and a Steinway grand piano.

Ein Fest für die Sinne: der Ballsaal mit prachtvollen Freskomalereien und Steinway-Flügel.

Un festín para los sentidos: el salón de baile con soberbios frescos y un Steinway a punto.

An inviting welcome to a truly aristocratic estate and the best of Tuscan beauty.

Hier öffnet sich das Tor zu einem wahrhaft herrschaftlichen Aufenthalt in der Toskana.

Una cálida bienvenida a una finca aristocrática y lo mejor de la belleza de Toscana.

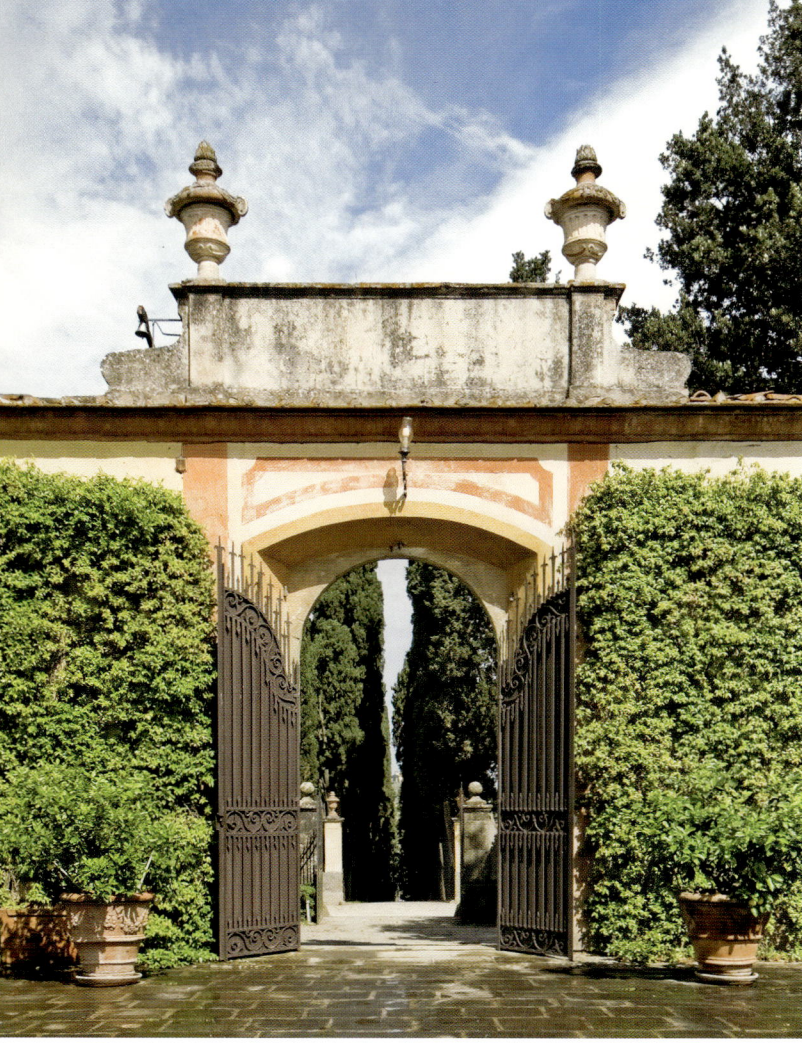

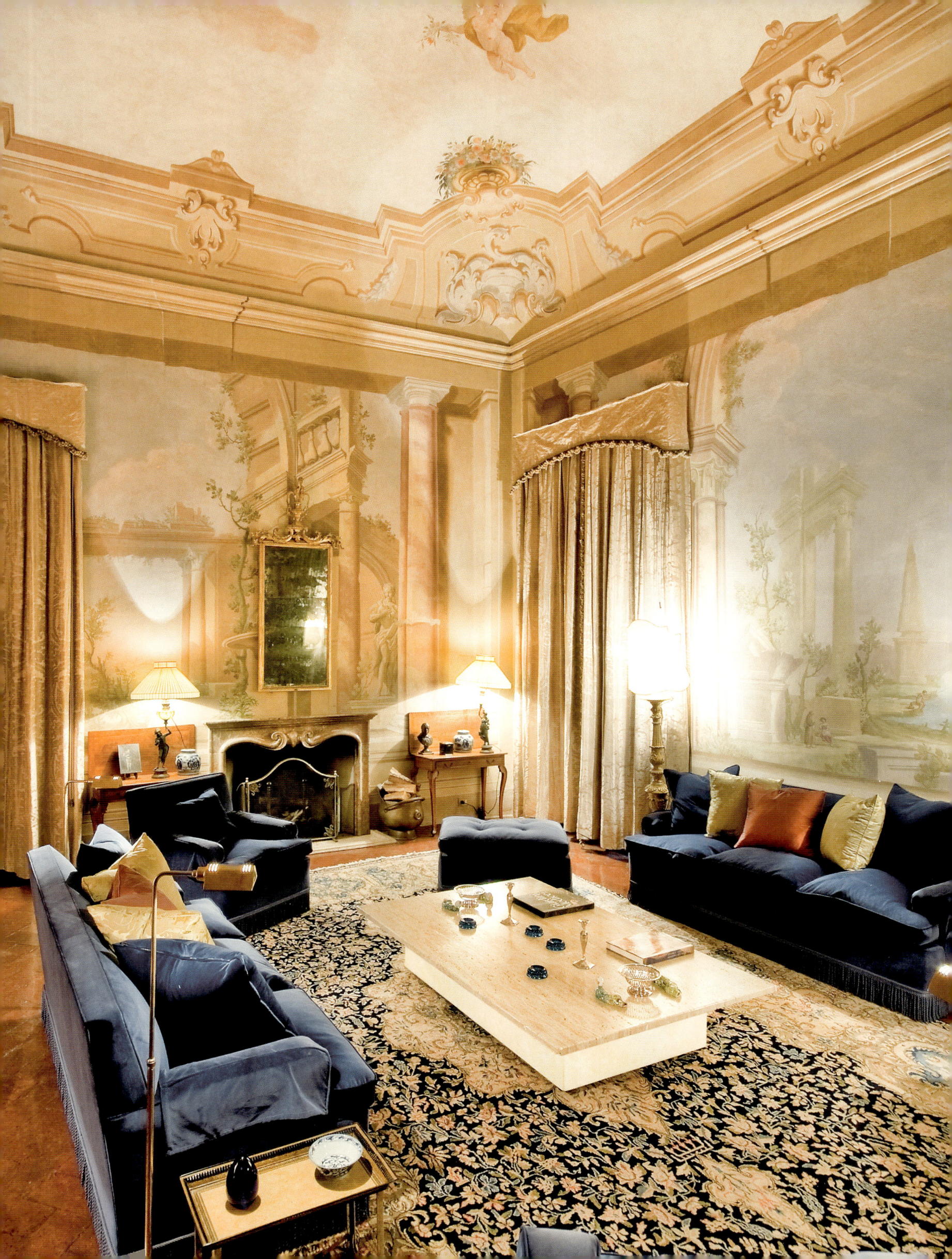

Opulent, stylish and comfortable: every room in this villa breathes a sense of history.

Opulent, stilvoll und behaglich: Jedes Zimmer dieses Anwesens atmet historisches Flair.

Opulencia, elegancia y comodidad: todas las estancias de la villa destilan historia.

As if time had stood still: one of the seven bedrooms with unique period furnishings.

Wie aus vergangenen Zeiten: eines der sieben Schlafzimmer mit eleganten Stilmöbeln.

Como si se parase el tiempo: una de las siete estancias con muebles de época únicos.

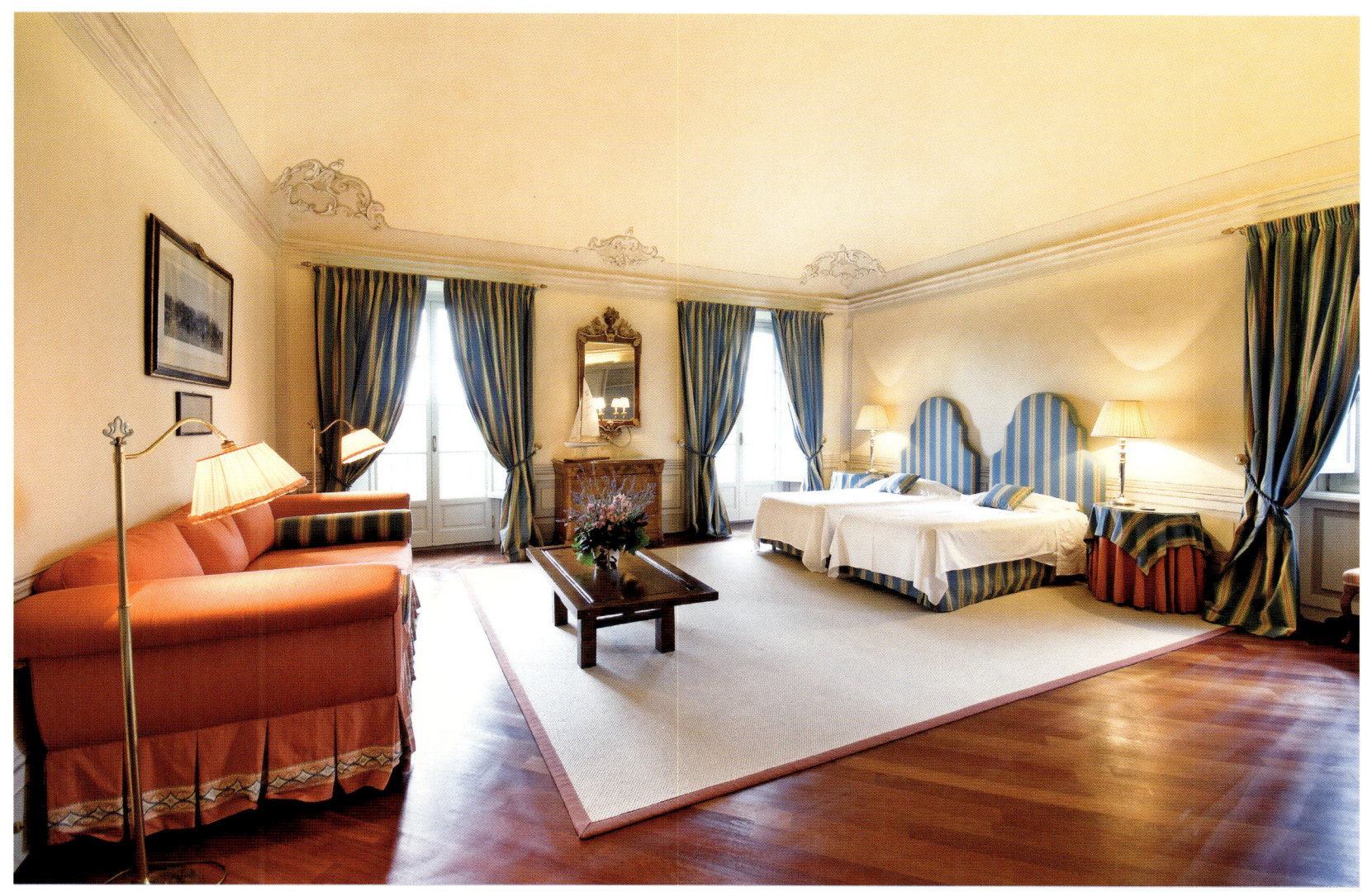

Remarkable: the formal dining room and
a marble bathroom, replete with fireplace.

Eindrucksvoll: das gediegene Speisezimmer
und das große Marmorbad mit Kamin.

Sobresalientes: el comedor formal y el cuarto
de baño en mármol, con su sobria chimenea.

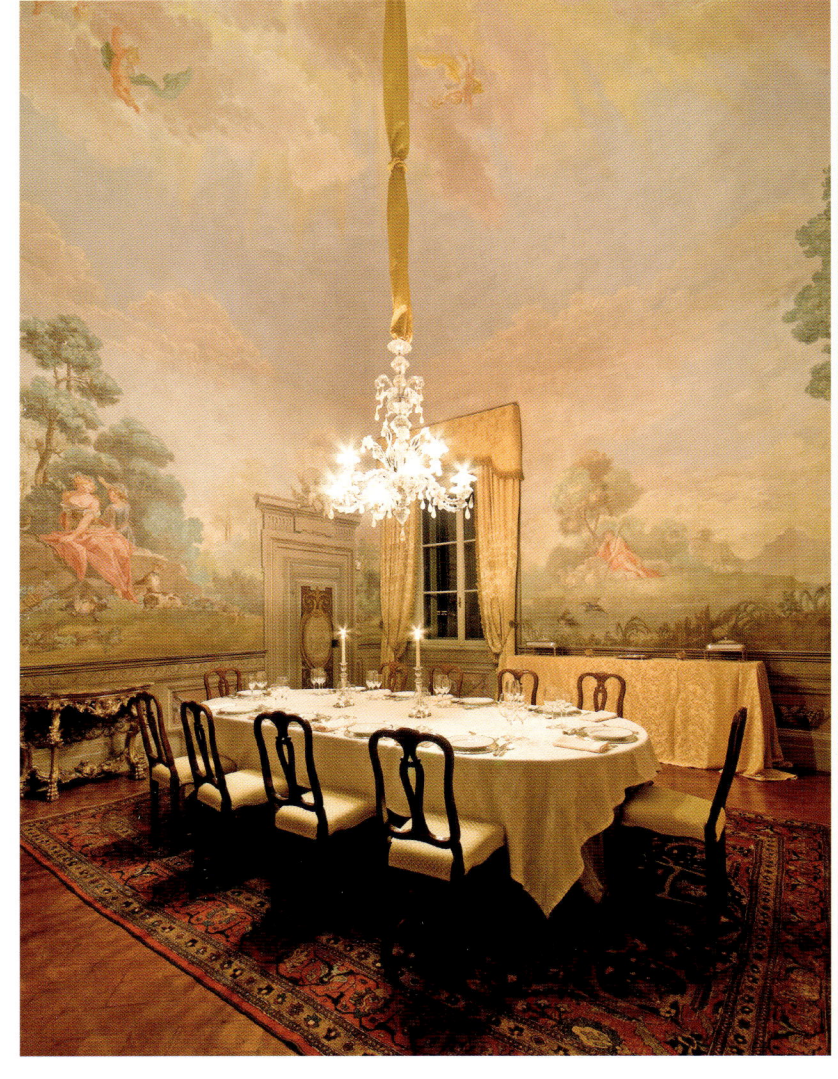

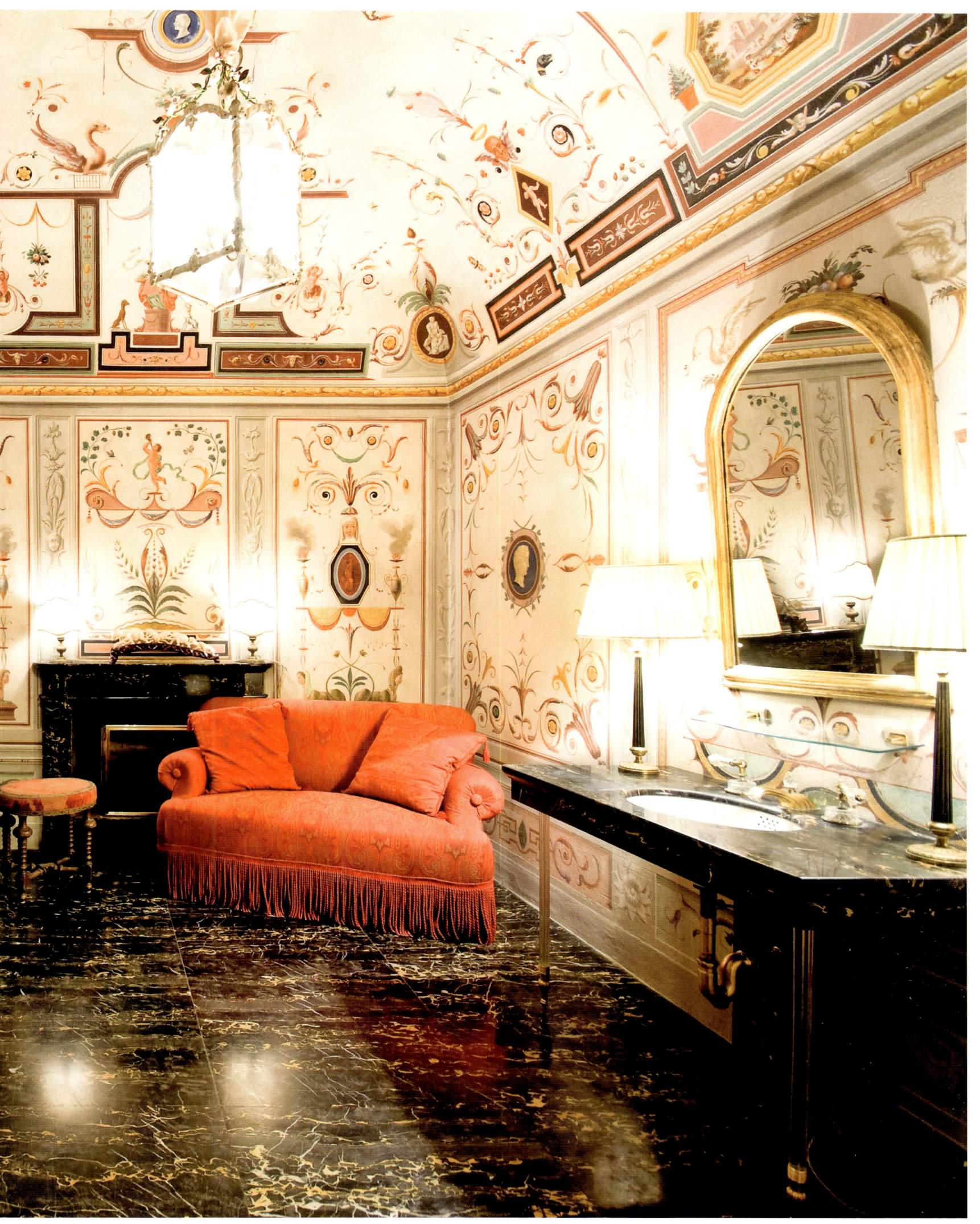

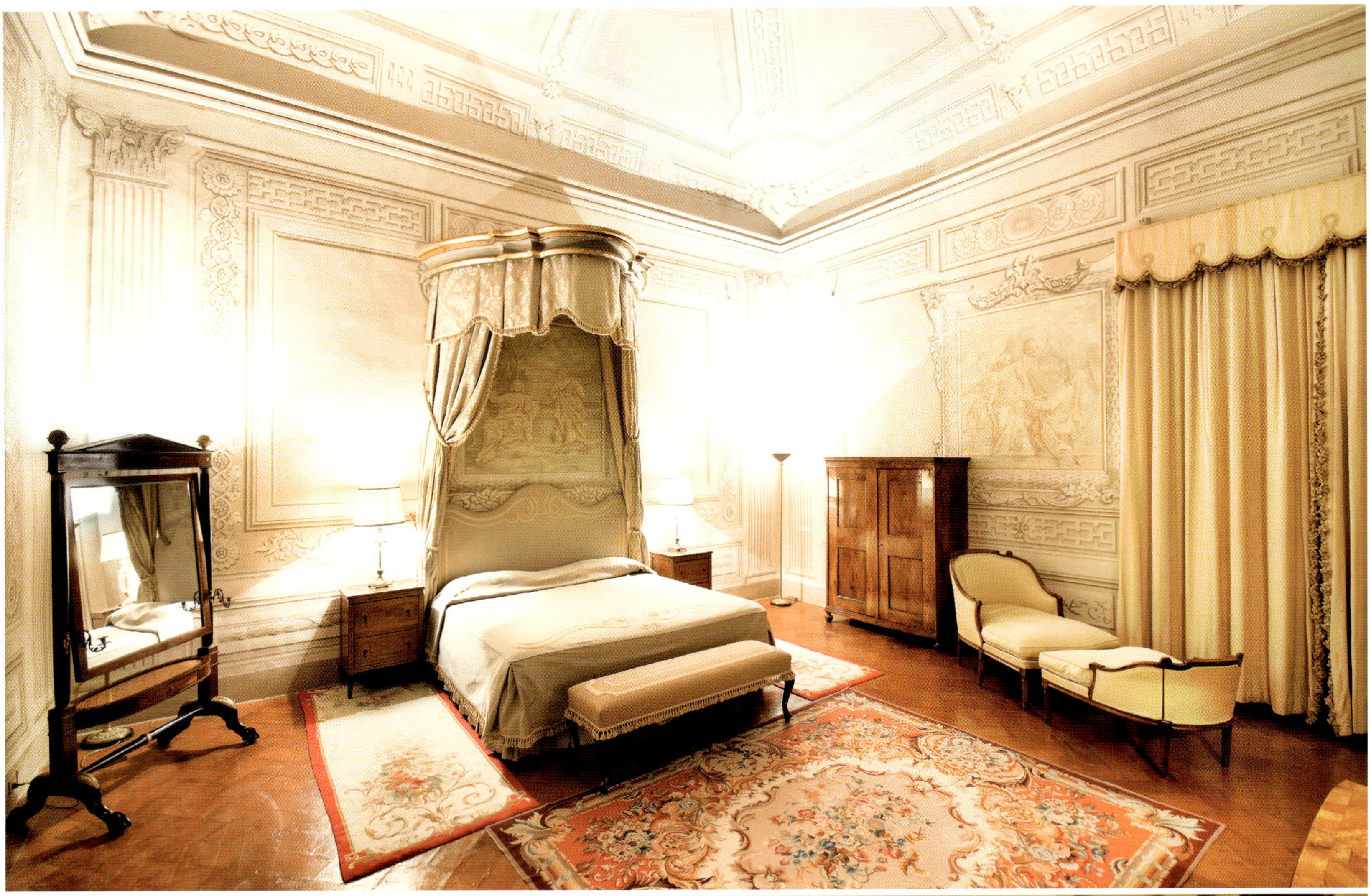

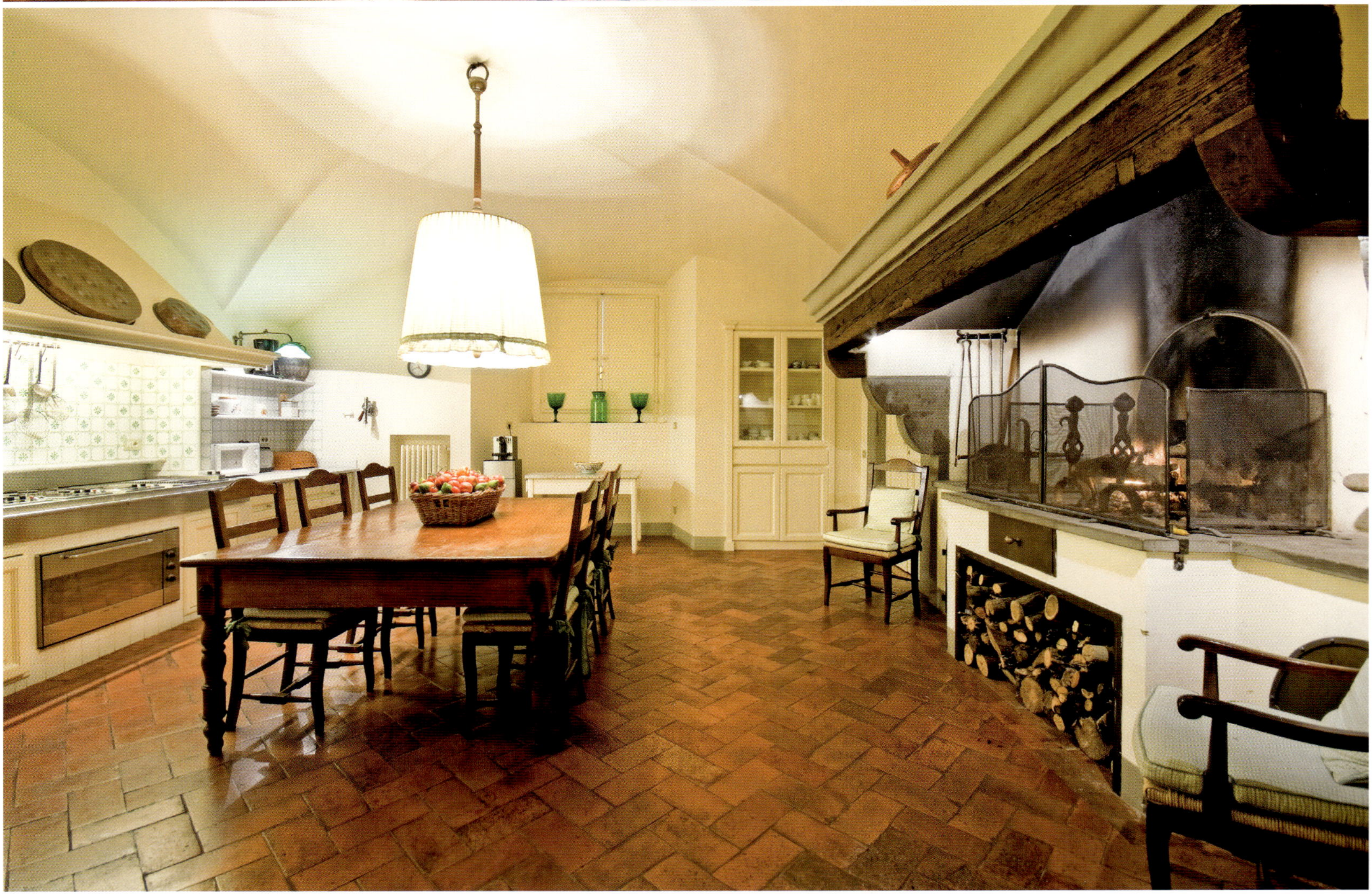

Fit for a royal night's sleep: a night in this lavish canopied bed will be unforgettable.

Prädestiniert für eine königliche Nachtruhe ist dieses Schlafgemach mit Himmelbett.

A punto para el descanso real: esta majestuosa cama con dosel lo hará inolvidable.

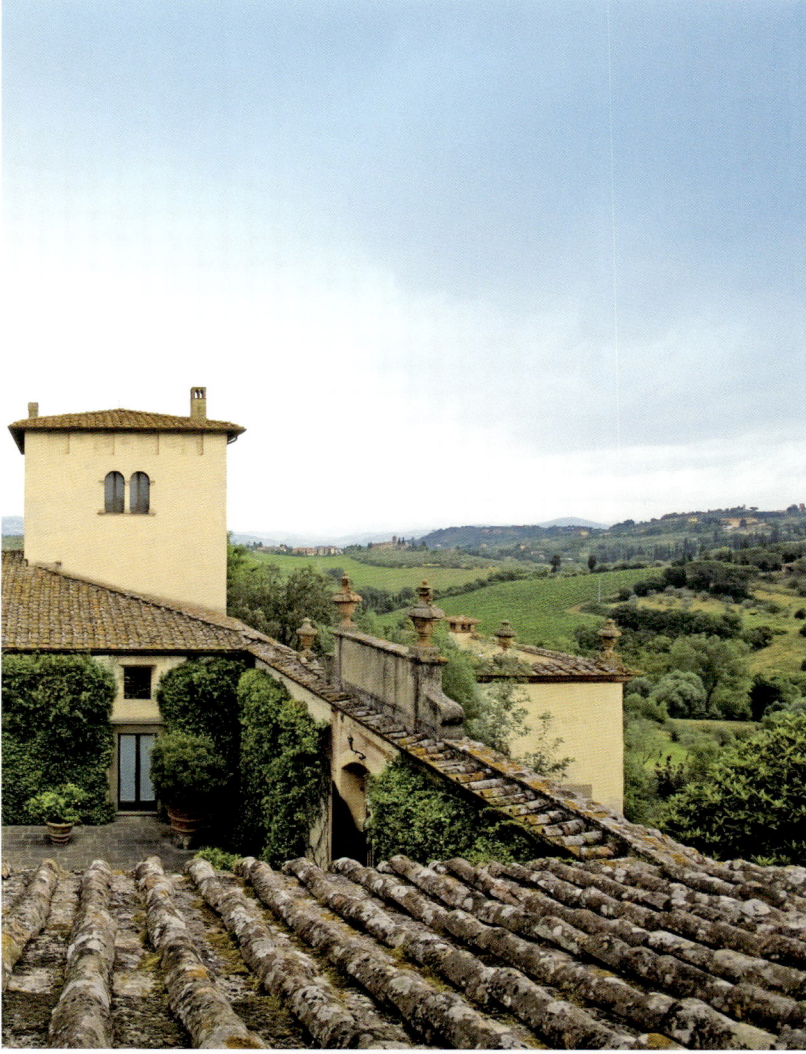

Picture-perfect vignettes of Tuscany as far as the eye can see.

Malerische Ausblicke über die toskanische Landschaft, so weit das Auge reicht.

Vistas como imágenes de Toscana sencillamente perfectas hasta el horizonte italiano.

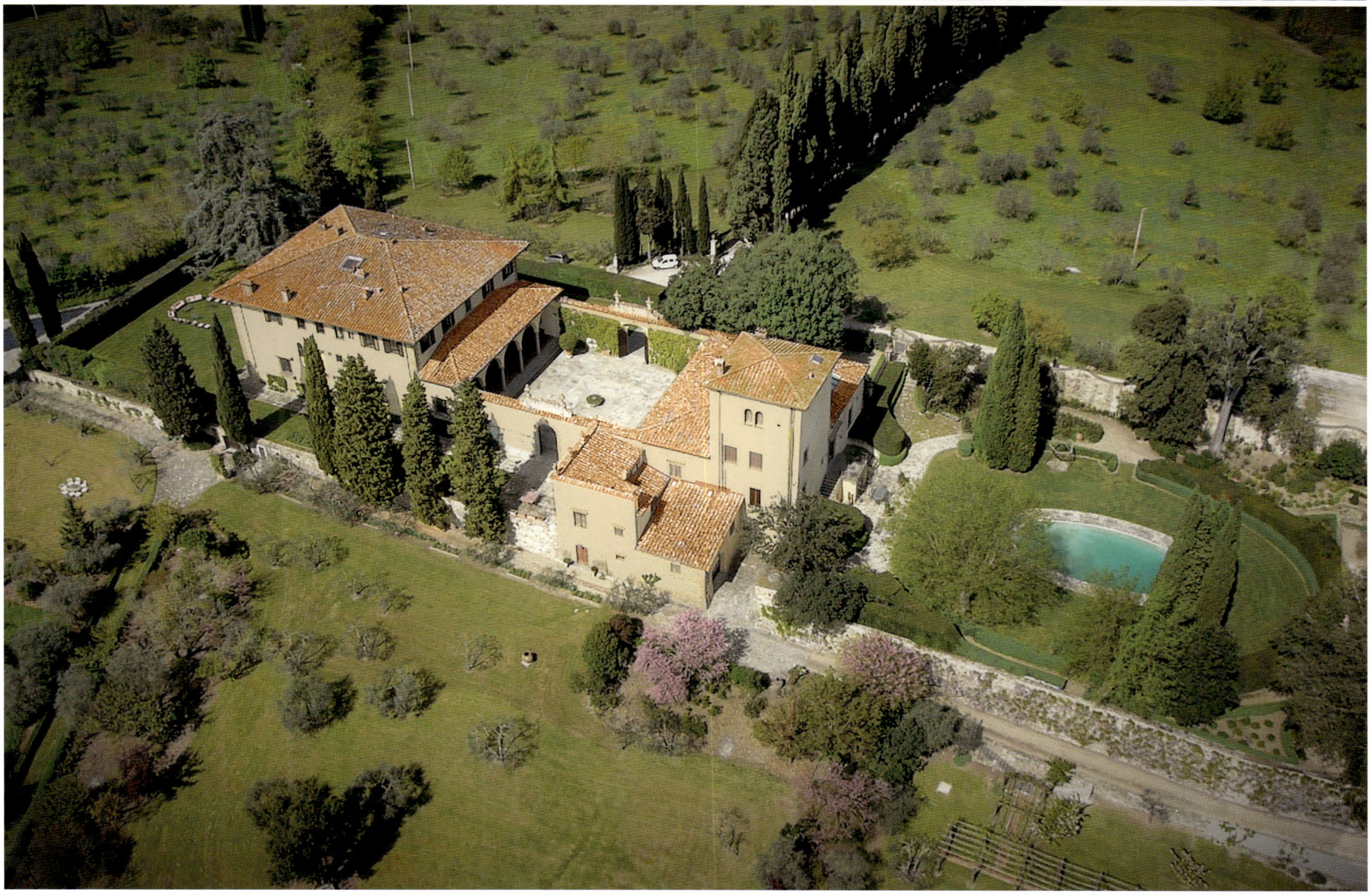

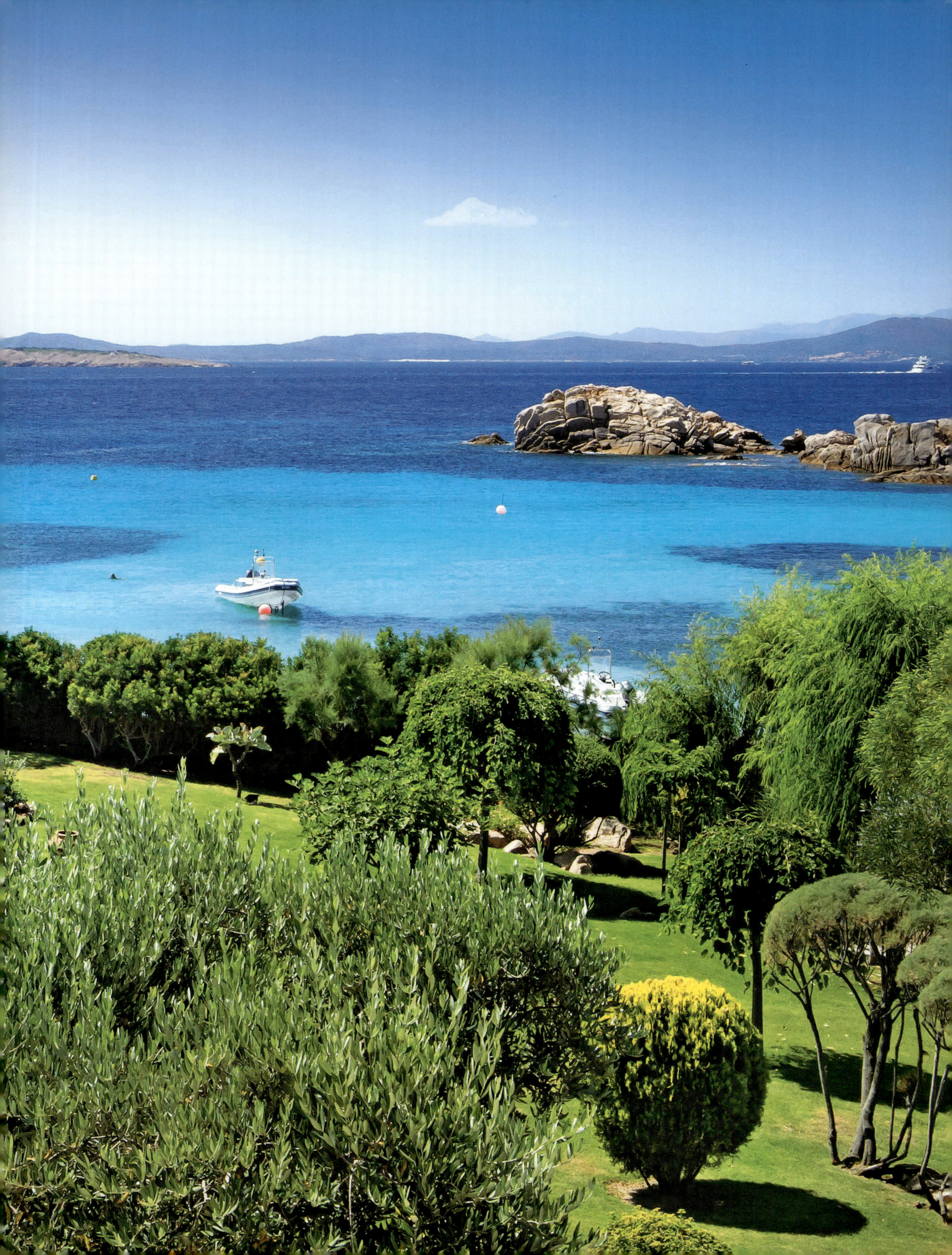

# Villa by Porto Cervo

Out of this world: a Mediterranean masterpiece promising luxury comforts and memorable holidays in an idyllic and delightfully picturesque cove.

NESTLED AMIDST a sprawling garden, this spectacular residence on a private beach enjoys a peaceful location with maximum privacy and breathtaking views. Built in a traditional architectural style typical for the Costa Smeralda, the seaside retreat has a warm and welcoming character with a comfortable and highly spacious ambience throughout. The villa has numerous living areas and lounges, splendidly enhanced with a sense of fine Italian craftsmanship and many loving details. The six beautifully furnished bedrooms and seven bathrooms provide sufficient space to accommodate a large family, affording privacy for several guests as well. A true delight to behold are the property's extensive outside areas, including an open-air kitchen and barbecue area, terraced spaces for outside dining and the wonderful pool with an adjacent Jacuzzi – ideal for relaxing and entertaining friends and relatives. This architectural treasure is undoubtedly one of the most prestigious properties on the Costa Smeralda: a dream holiday home ready to appreciate and enjoy.

EINGEBETTET IN ein paradiesisches Gartenareal, profitiert dieses prachtvolle Anwesen von seiner ruhigen Lage mit viel Privatsphäre und einem kaum zu übertreffenden Meerblick. Die Villa, zu der ein kleiner Privatstrand gehört, wurde im traditionellen Architekturstil der Costa Smeralda erbaut. Ihr einladendes, sehr großzügiges Ambiente macht sie zum perfekten Rückzugsort am Meer. Die Räumlichkeiten wurden allesamt mit viel Liebe zum Detail und Sinn für feine italienische Handwerkskunst gestaltet. Sechs wunderschön möblierte Schlafzimmer und insgesamt sieben Bäder bieten ausreichend Platz für eine größere Familie und die Unterbringung mehrerer Gäste. Überaus beeindruckend sind auch die weitläufigen Außenbereiche des Anwesens, die mit einer Open-Air-Küche samt Grillplatz, verschiedenen Terrassen sowie einem Pool plus Jacuzzi zum Entspannen und Genießen unter sardischer Sonne einladen. Damit dürfte dieses architektonische Kleinod zweifellos zu den exklusivsten Ferienimmobilien an der gesamten Costa Smeralda gehören.

EN EL CORAZÓN de un vasto jardín, esta espectacular residencia en una tranquila playa privada disfruta de serenidad con la máxima privacidad y vistas que quitan el aliento. En el tradicional estilo arquitectónico típico de la Costa Smeralda, este retiro playero destila carácter y calidez con un ambiente cómodo y muy espacioso. La villa cuenta con numerosas estancias y salones, espléndidamente complementados con fina artesanía italiana y muchos detalles de buen gusto. Los seis dormitorios bellamente decorados y los siete baños ofrecen espacio generoso para una gran familia y la máxima privacidad para sus invitados. Una verdadera delicia para la vista: los inmensos exteriores de la propiedad, incluyendo la cocina al aire libre y zona de barbacoa, terrazas para comer al fresco y la maravillosa piscina con Jacuzzi adyacente, perfectos tanto para los amigos como para la relajación y disfrute de toda la familia. Este tesoro arquitectónico es sin duda uno de los inmuebles más prestigiosos de toda la Costa Smeralda, un sueño de hogar para las vacaciones, a punto para ser apreciado y disfrutado.

ITALY, SARDINIA **RENTAL PRICE/WEEK** EUR 45,000–65,000 **INTERIOR APPROX.** 700 m² **NO. OF BEDROOMS** 6
**LAND APPROX.** 8,000 m² **E&V ID** W-0IH4B0 **CONTACT** PORTO CERVO (IT), FIRST SARDEV S.R.L.,
LICENCE PARTNER OF ENGEL & VÖLKERS ITALIA S.R.L. **TEL.** +39 078 99 41 83
**E-MAIL** PORTOCERVO@ENGELVOELKERS.COM

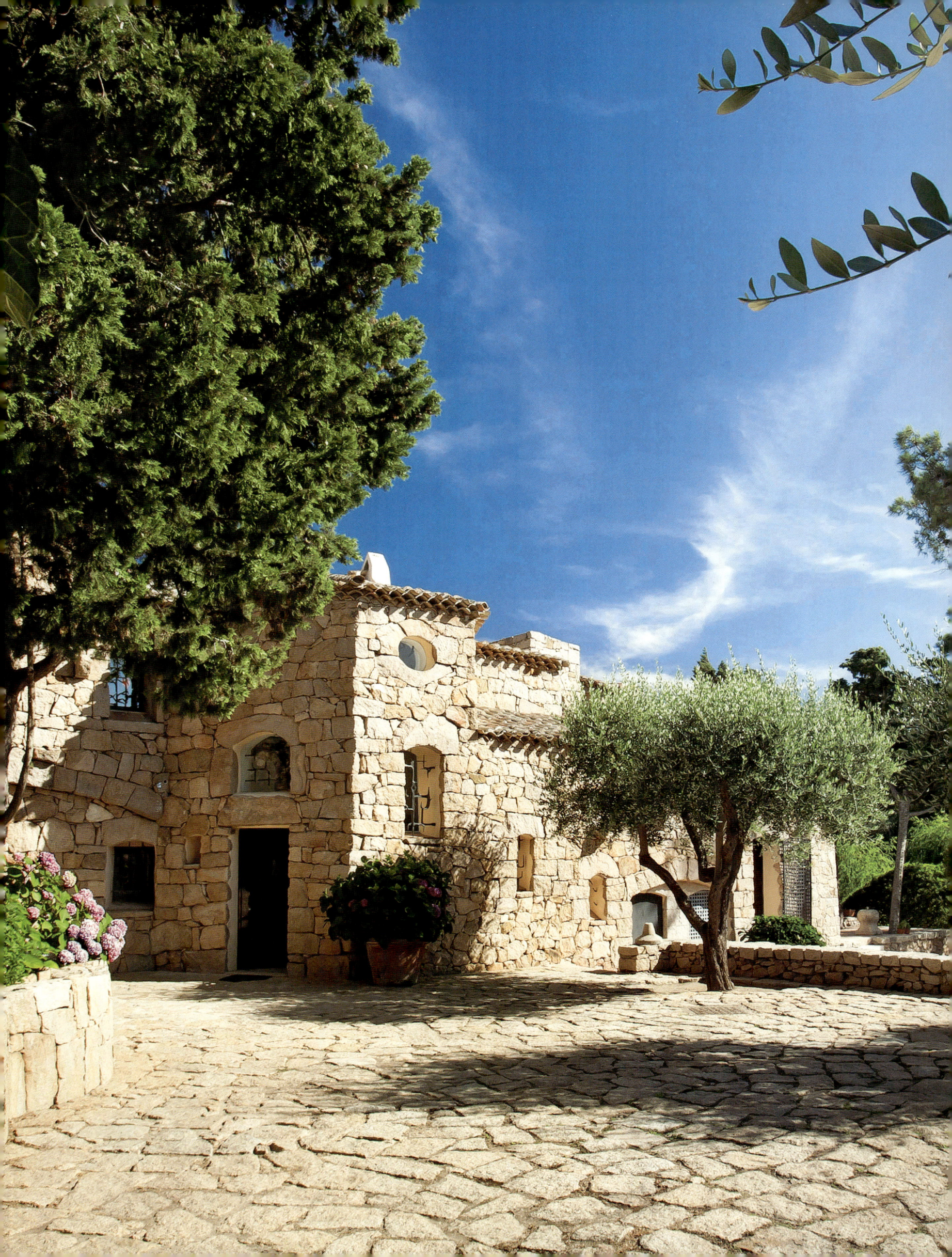

Simply perfect: an inviting holiday hideway
with authentic Sardinian charm.

Einfach perfekt: ein Urlaubsrefugium mit
authentischem Sardinien-Charme.

Es perfecto: un atractivo refugio de vacaciones
con el genuino encanto de Cerdeña.

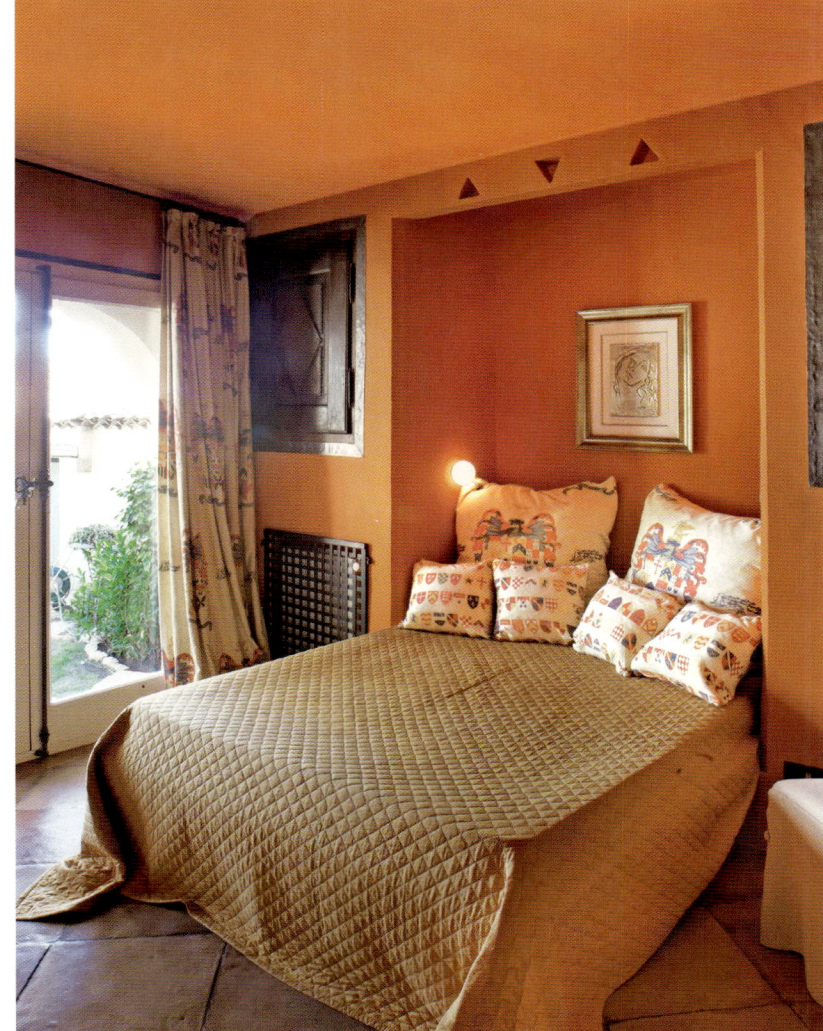

Gently vaulted ceilings and terracotta floors
create a graceful Mediterranean ambience.

Sanft gewölbte Decken und Terrakottaböden
unterstreichen das mediterrane Ambiente.

Techos con suaves bóvedas y suelos de barro
dan aires mediterráneos llenos de estilo.

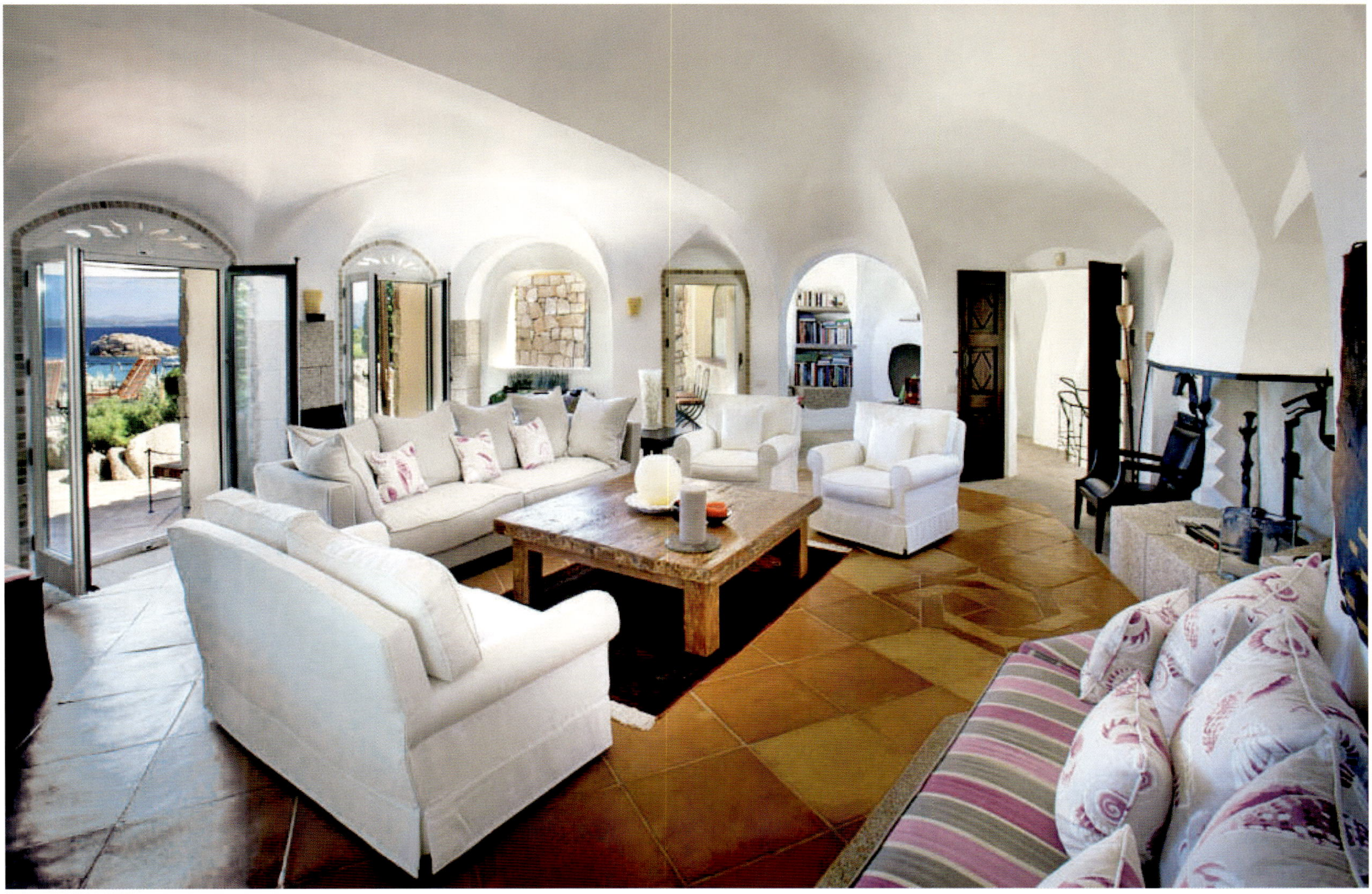

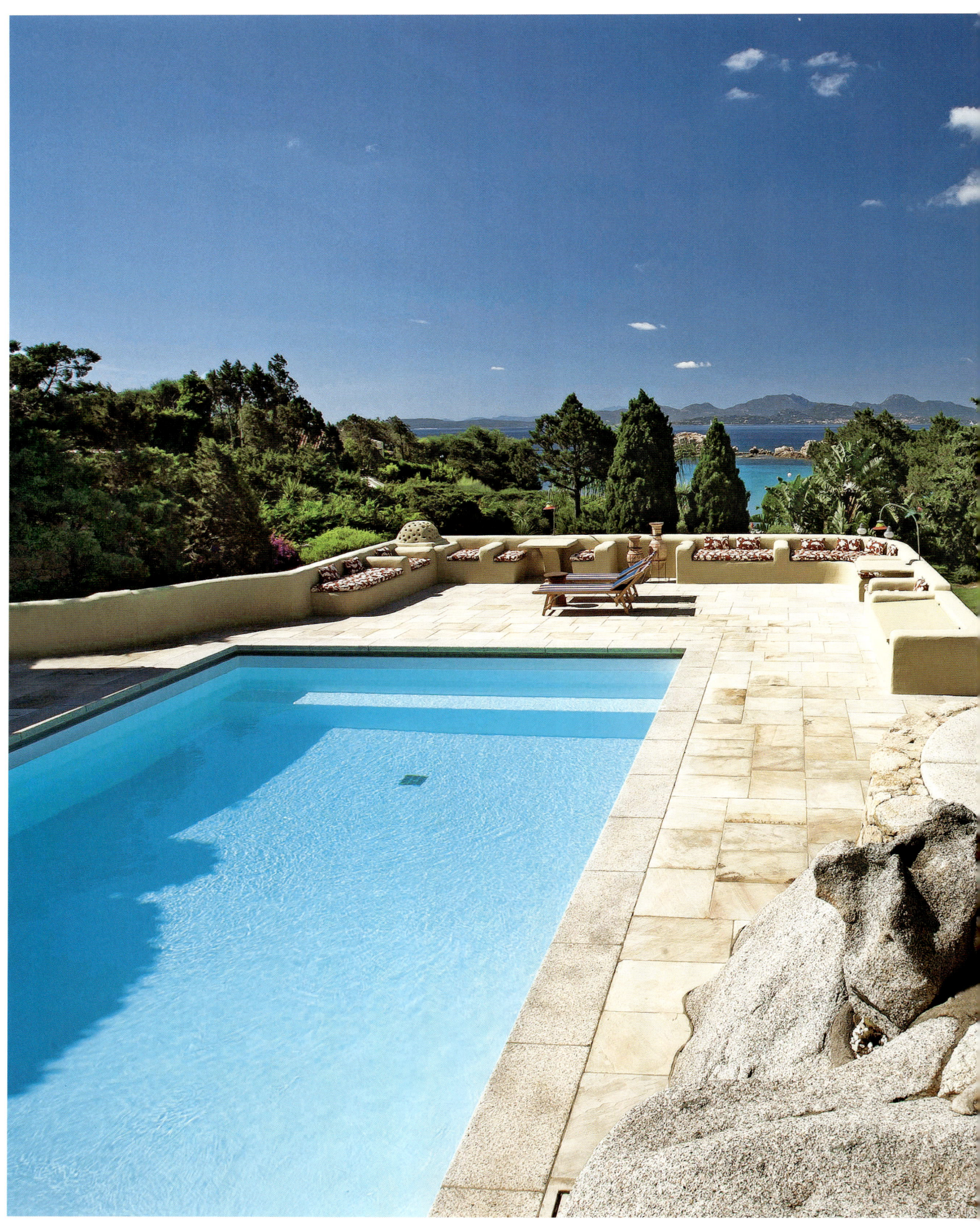

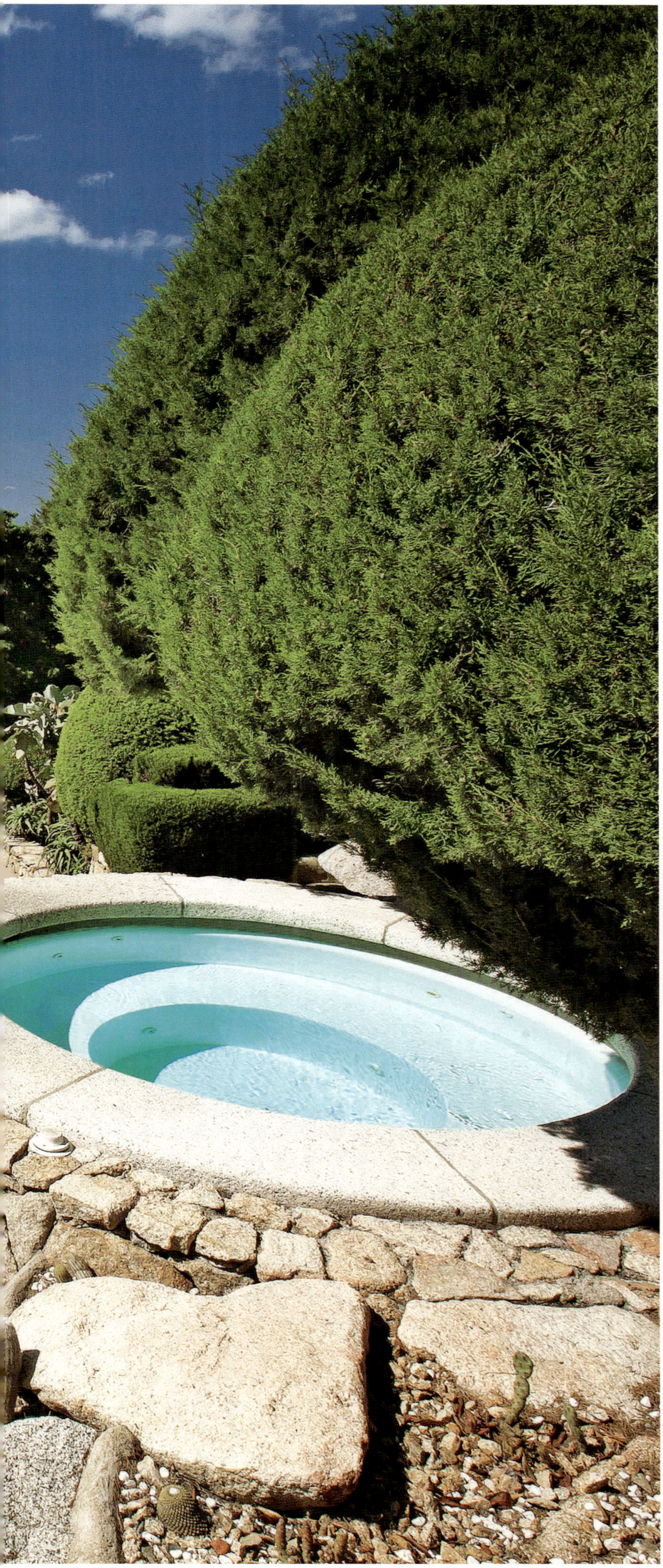

<

Life at its very best: glorious poolside
bliss under the dazzling Mediterranean sun.

So lässt es sich leben: am schönsten bei
einem Sonnenbad am Swimmingpool.

La vida en su máxima expresión: gozar la
piscina bajo el deslumbrante sol de Cerdeña.

Carefully conceived sitting areas in
the garden ensure the best views possible.

Durchdacht konzipierte Sitzecken im Garten
ermöglichen die besten Aussichten.

Rinconcitos en el jardín concebidos con primor
para disfrutar las mejores vistas posibles.

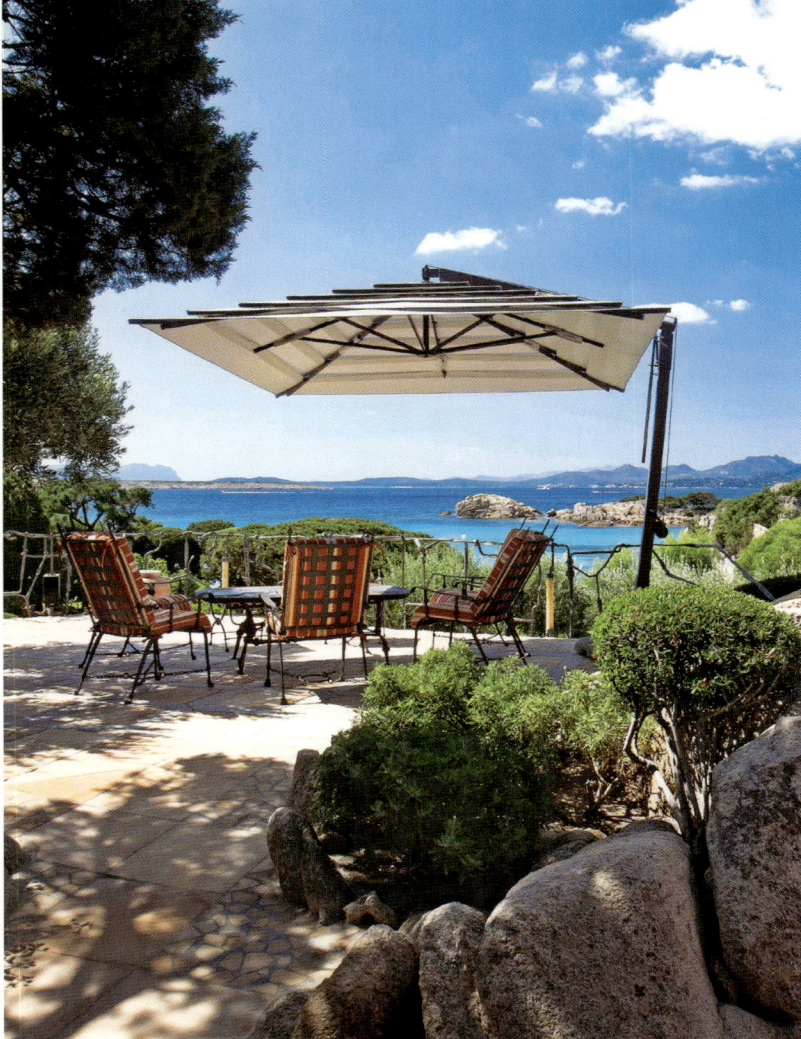

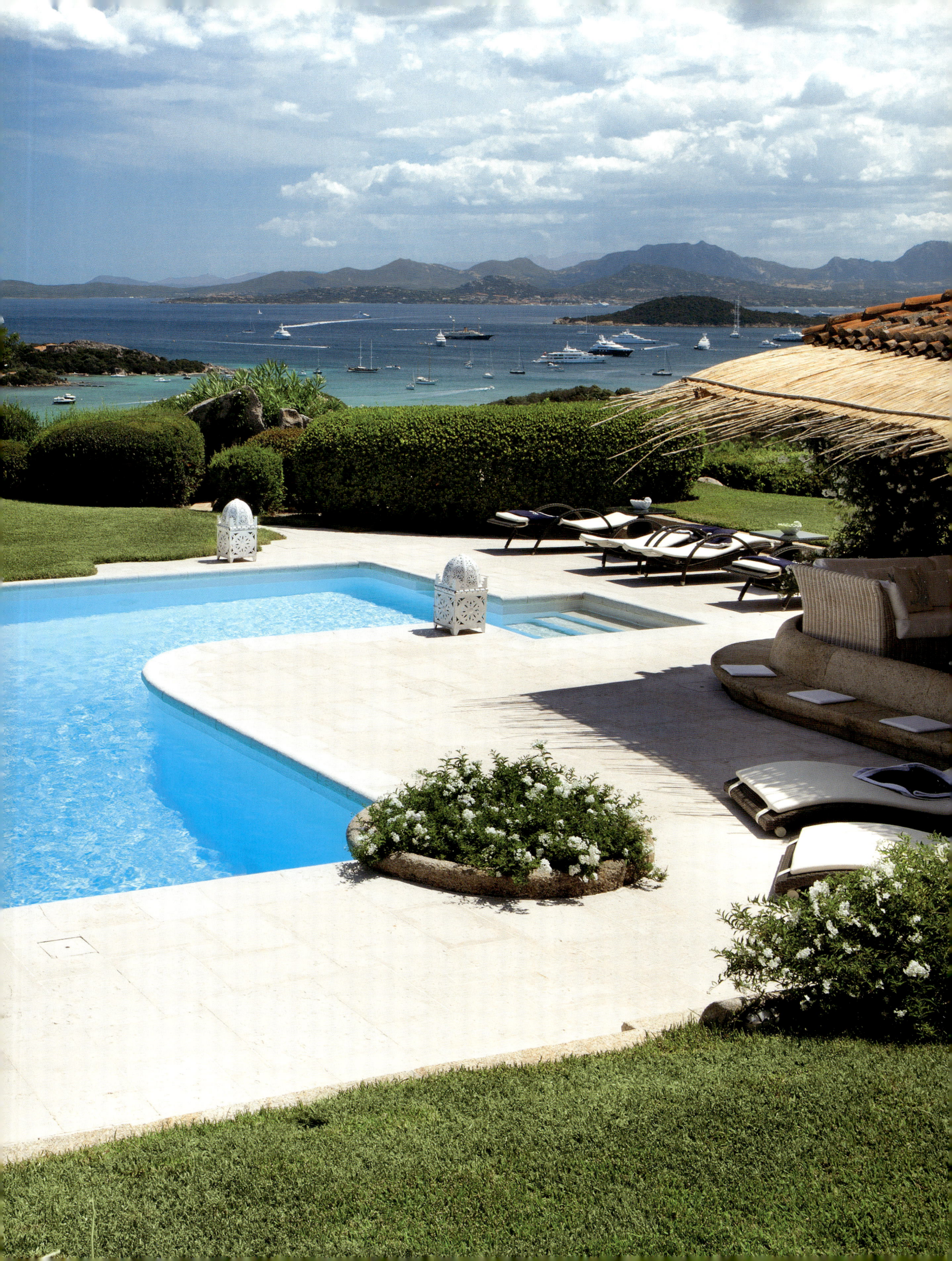

# Sardinian Jewel

It is easy to succumb to the Mediterranean magic
and to fall in love with this truly unforgettable holiday home
overlooking Cala di Volpe bay on the Costa Smeralda.

SIMPLY EVERYTHING about the beautifully landscaped gardens, the architecture of this estate and its distinctive interior design is harmonious and a delight for the senses. With its stylish Mediterranean details, the bright and commodious living room leads guests into the dining area and the large country-style kitchen. The four bedroom suites of this holiday domicile radiate subtle folkloric flair, each boasting their own private bathroom. Looking onto the pool and the coastline, the beautiful terraced areas are an invitation to enjoy convivial hours of al fresco dining. And when the heat of the day subsides, ushering in the pleasant coolness of the evening, the outdoor areas are ideal for taking in the beauty of Porto Cervo by night – with the starry heavens above and the lovely lights of the yachts dotting the bay. The spacious basement comprises a wine cellar, a laundry room and a staff area, and parking for up to three cars completes the many amenities of this holiday home, leaving absolutely nothing to be desired.

ALLES FÜGT SICH bei diesem Anwesen harmonisch ineinander – die wunderschönen Gärten, die charakteristische Architektur, das charmante Interieur. Mit seinen stilvollen mediterranen Details führt das helle und geräumige Wohnzimmer in den einladenden Essbereich und in die große Landhausküche. In den vier Schlafzimmer-Suiten mit dezent-folkloristischem Flair und En-suite-Bädern lässt es sich herrlich träumen und entspannen, während die überdachten Terrassen zu genussvollen Stunden bei einem Dinner im Freien einladen. Und wenn die Hitze des Tages in die angenehme Kühle des Abends übergeht, kann man hier wunderbar die nächtliche Schönheit Porto Cervos mit seinem unendlichen Sternenhimmel und den Lichtern der Yachten bestaunen, die sich über die ganze Bucht verteilen. Zu den weiteren Vorzügen dieses Domizils gehören unter anderem ein Weinkeller, eine Waschküche und ein Personalbereich sowie Parkplätze für bis zu drei Autos. Damit verspricht dieses sardische Anwesen eine Ferienzeit, die wunschlos glücklich macht.

SIMPLEMENTE TODO acerca de los preciosos jardines, la arquitectura y su distintivo diseño interior es armonioso y una delicia para los sentidos. Con elegantes detalles mediterráneos, el salón luminoso y cómodo conduce a los invitados a la zona de comedor y a la amplia cocina de estilo rústico. Las cuatro *suites* de esta casa de vacaciones están decoradas con un sutil toque folclórico, cada una con su cuarto de baño privado. Guarnecidas con vistas a la piscina y la costa, las diversas terrazas cubiertas son una invitación para disfrutar de pantagruélicas horas en compañía al aire libre. Y, cuando el calor del día se desvanece y llega la agradable temperatura de la noche, las zonas al fresco son ideales para admirar la belleza nocturna de Porto Cervo, con el cielo estrellado en lo alto y las luces de los yates salpicando la bahía. La espaciosa planta inferior cuenta con una bodega, cuarto para la colada y una zona para el personal, además de aparcamiento para tres coches, completando las muchas amenidades de este hogar de vacaciones, sin dejar ningún deseo por cumplir.

ITALY, SARDINIA **RENTAL PRICE/WEEK** EUR 18,000–25,000 **INTERIOR APPROX.** 300 m² **NO. OF BEDROOMS** 4
**LAND APPROX.** 2,400 m² **E&V ID** W-00KBFO **CONTACT** PORTO CERVO (IT), FIRST SARDEV S.R.L.,
LICENCE PARTNER OF ENGEL & VÖLKERS ITALIA S.R.L. **TEL.** +39 078 99 41 83
**E-MAIL** PORTOCERVO@ENGELVOELKERS.COM

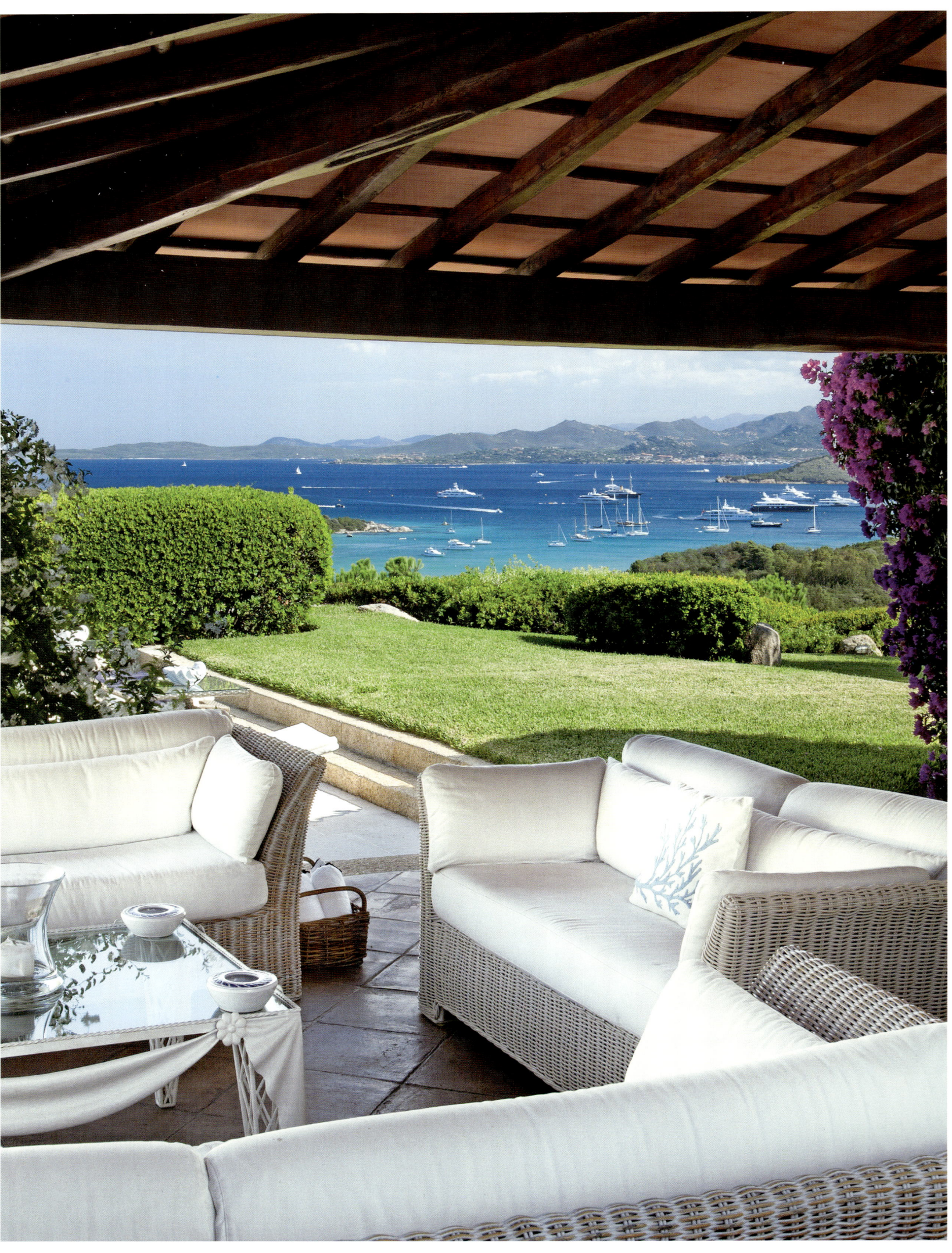

Shady outdoor terraces are the perfect spot to relax with a refreshing cool drink – and a view.

Schattige Terrassen laden zum Relaxen bei einem kühlen Drink ein – Meerblick inklusive.

Terrazas sombreadas al fresco donde relajarse con algo refrescante… como las vistas al mar.

A bright Mediterranean flair and curved contours sweep through the villa's interiors.

Lichtes mediterranes Flair und geschwungene Linien prägen die Räumlichkeiten der Villa.

Claridad mediterránea y contornos curvos caracterizan el interior de la villa.

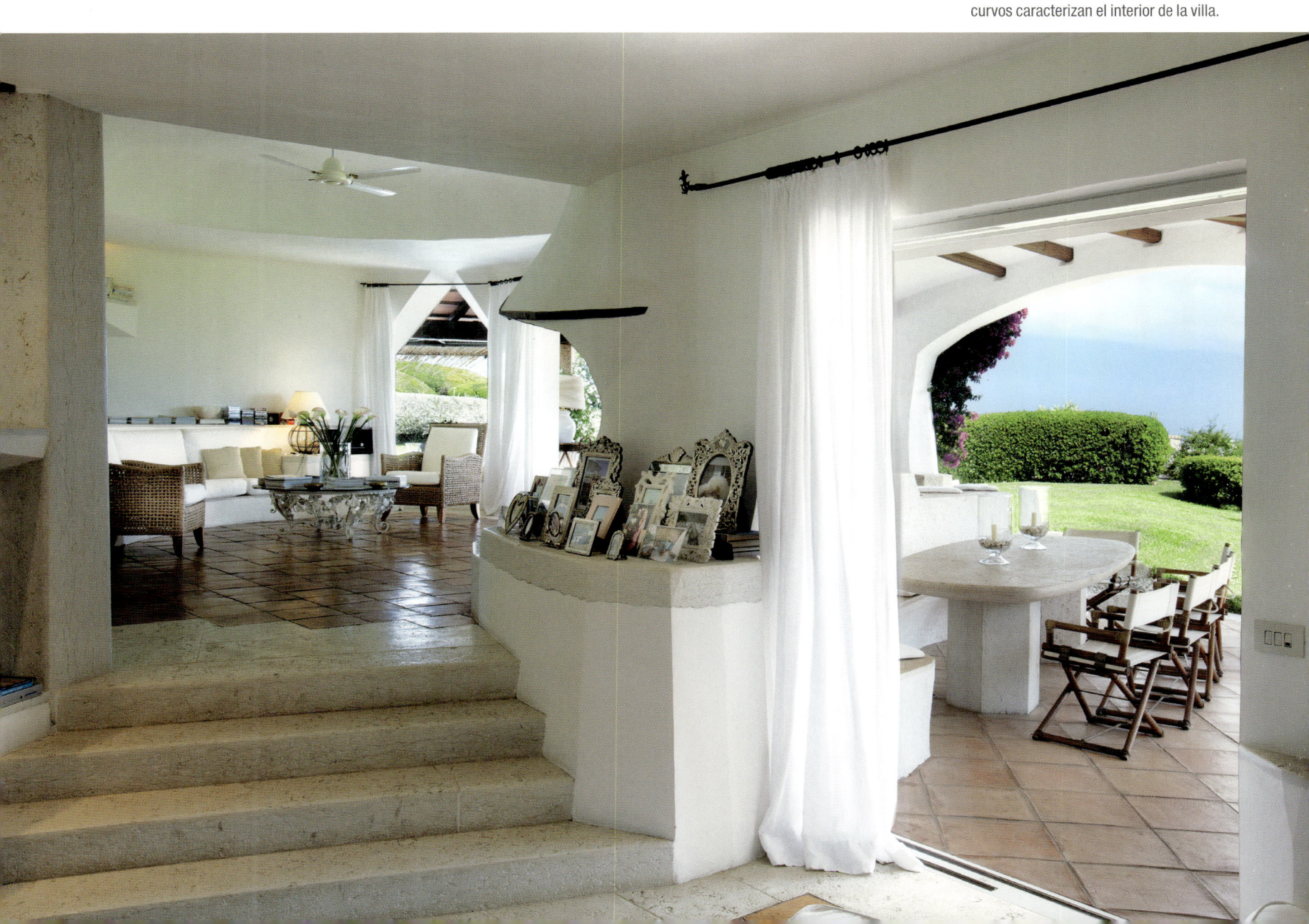

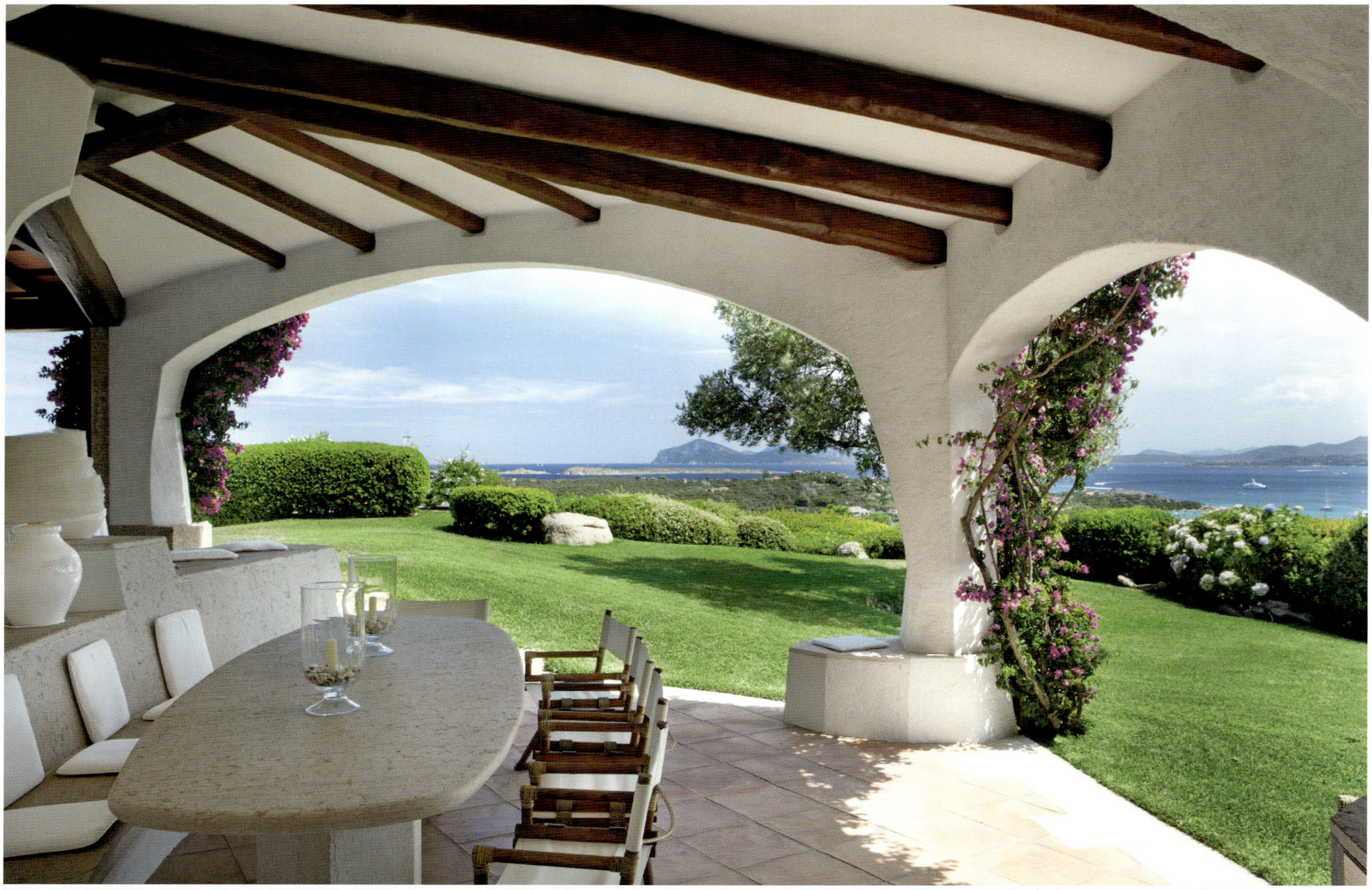

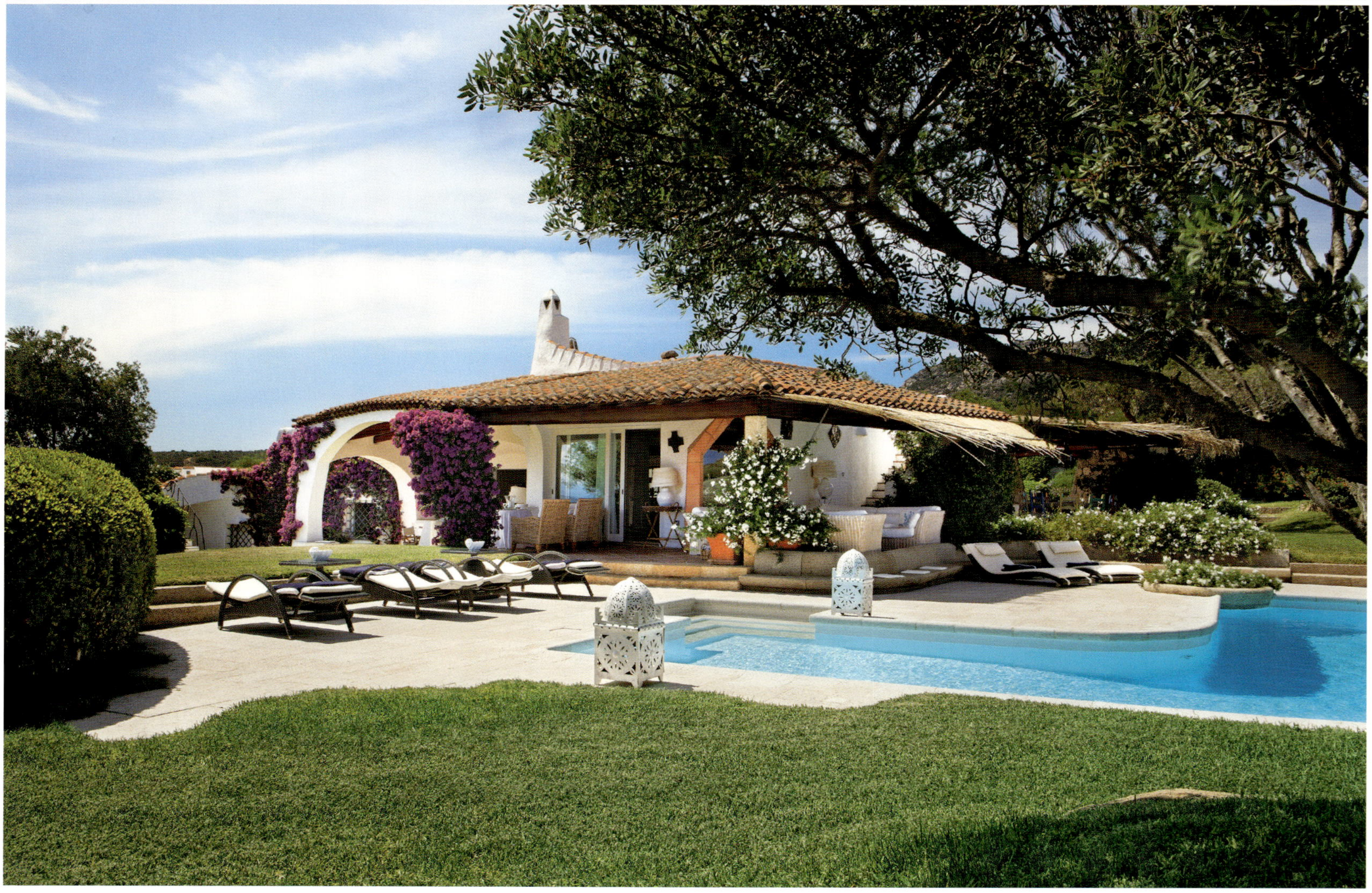

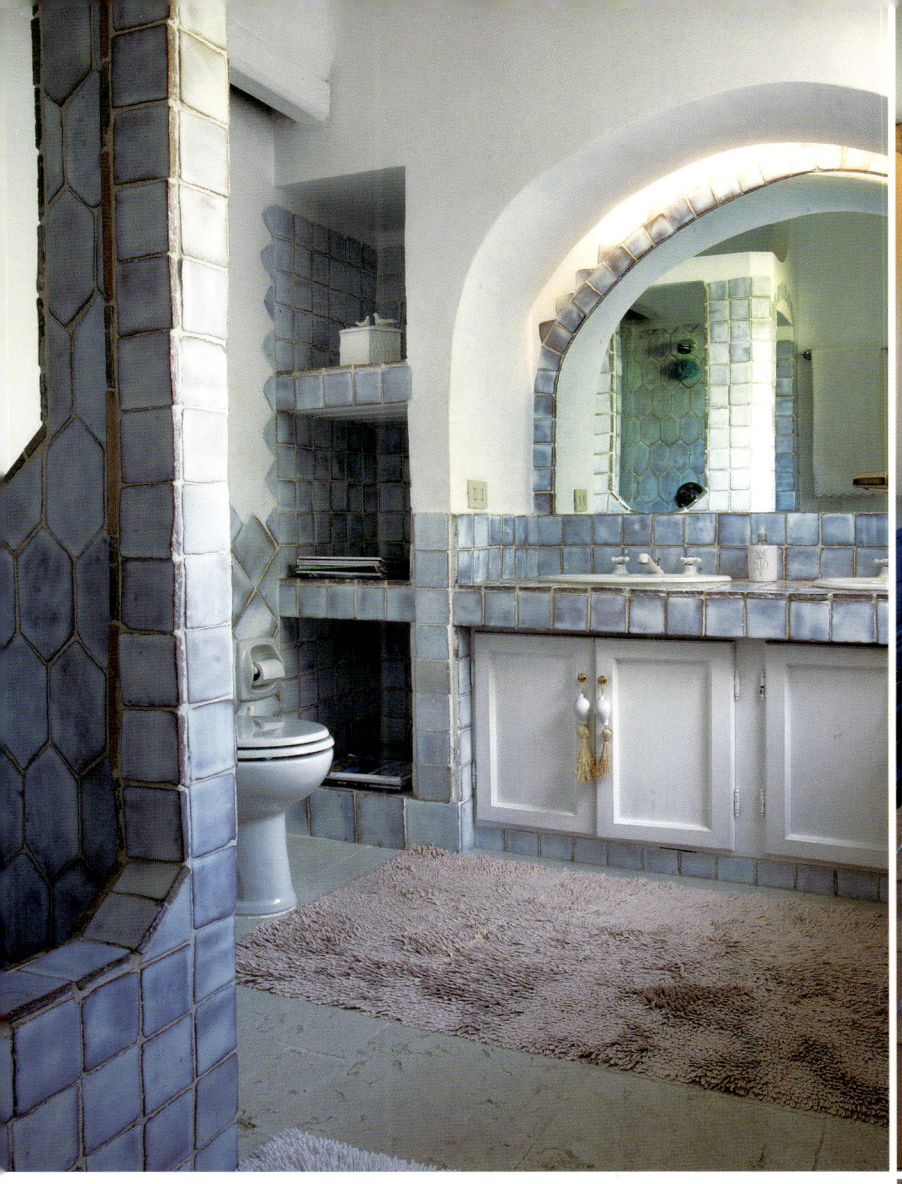

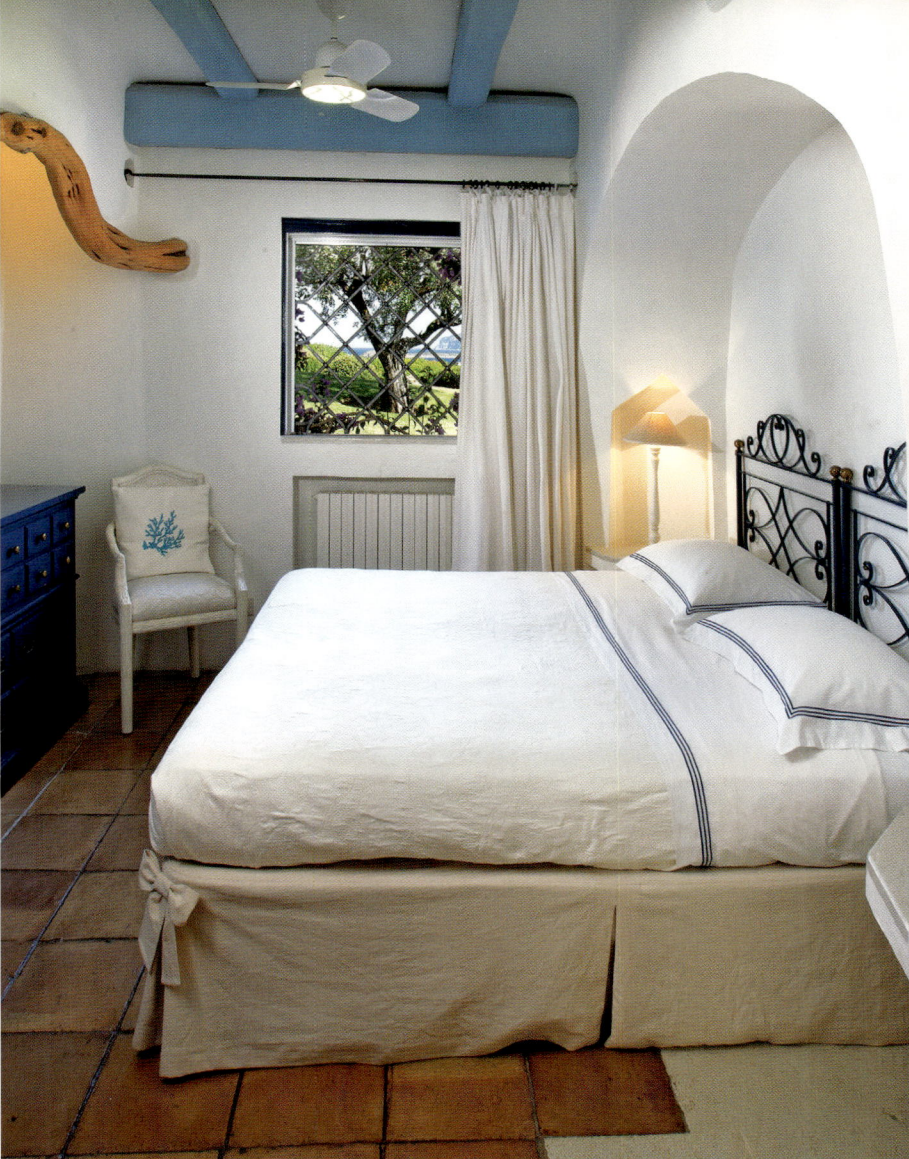

The pretty bathroom and romantic suite have been conceived with a loving eye for detail.

Das hübsche Bad und die romantische Suite wurden mit viel Liebe zum Detail gestaltet.

La bonita y romántica *suite* y su baño han sido concebidos con mucho amor por el detalle.

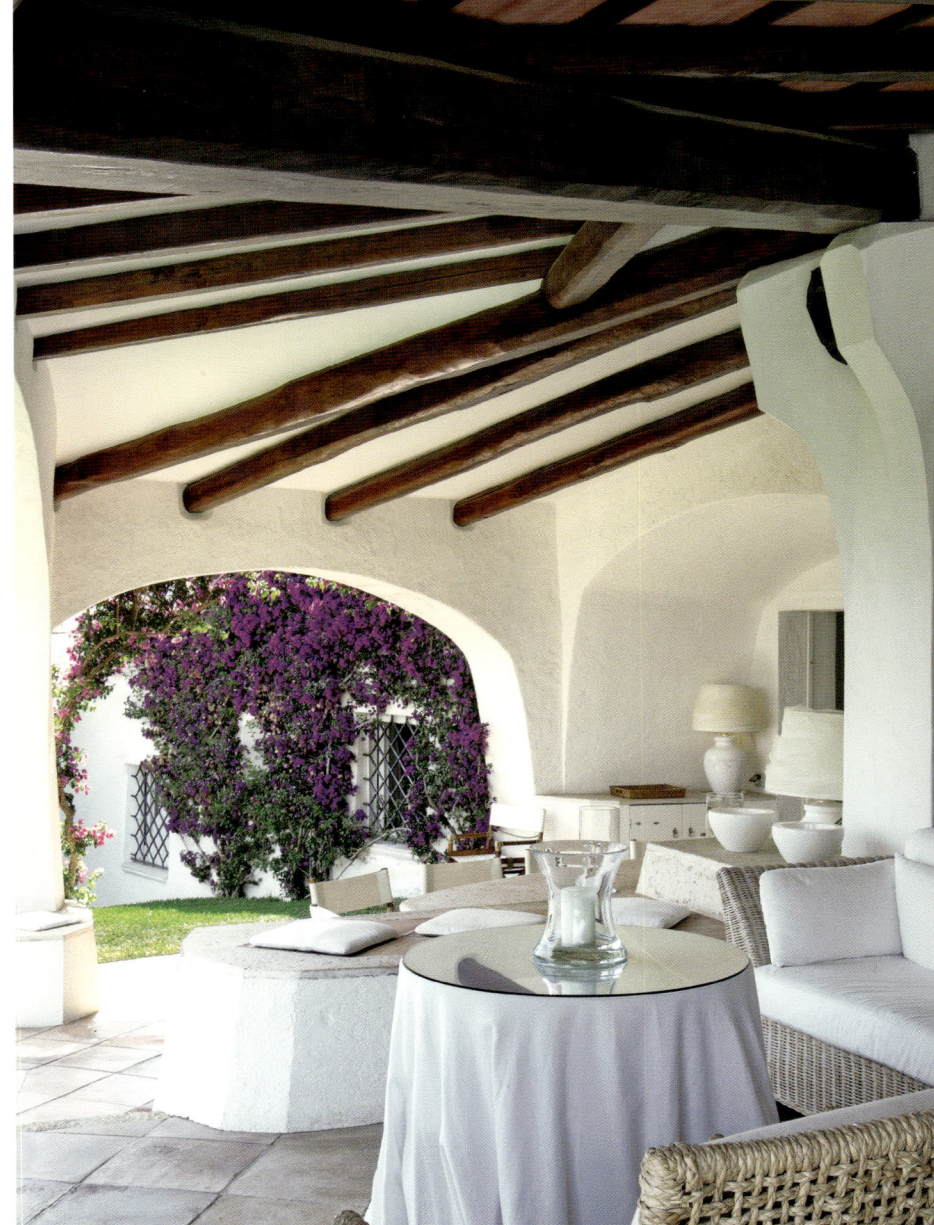

<
With such a splendid poolside oasis, what more could one wish for in life?

Was könnte es Schöneres geben, als an einem Pool wie diesem zu entspannen?

Con tan espléndido santuario junto a la piscina, ¿qué más se puede desear en la vida?

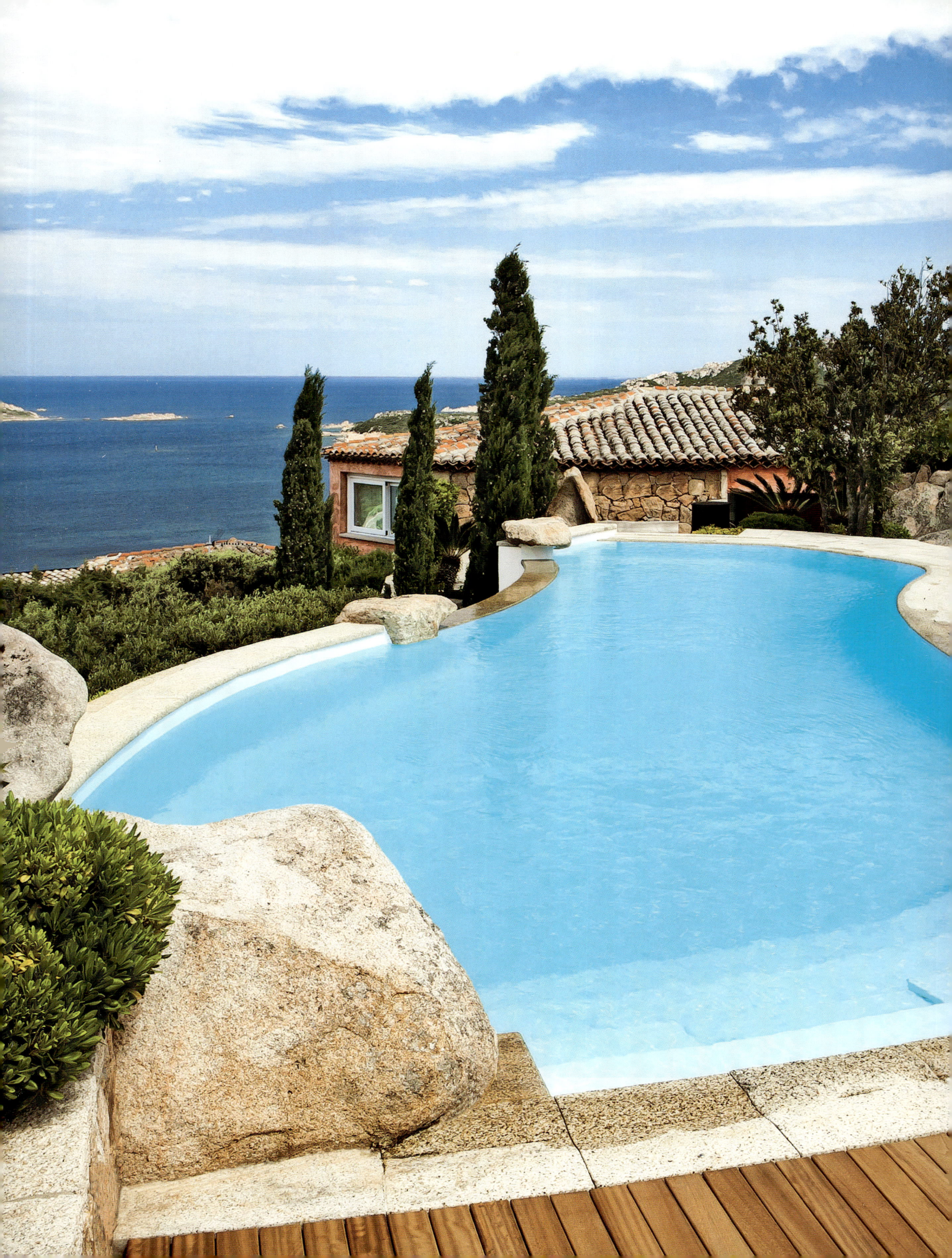

# Seaside Perfection

Set against the breathtaking scenery of Sardinia's north-eastern coastline, this designer dwelling reinvents the essence of stylish living in a harmonious fashion.

SPECTACULARLY LOCATED on the hill of Pantogia not far from Porto Cervo, this oasis of calm and tranquillity makes for a heavenly holiday retreat. The spacious interiors of the completely renovated two-level villa are dominated by the soothing colour white, radiating a clean and minimal feel that is perfectly offset by the emerald ocean outside. Affording stunning views and with their natural hues and purist design, the three bedroom suites of this holiday home create a lovely sense of well-being. The living area is equally impressive with its commodious open-plan atmosphere and modern, upmarket furnishings. Highlights are the infinity pool, the extensive outside spaces including terraced zones and a barbecue as well as an open-air dining area. With many amenities such as air conditioning in all rooms, satellite television, Wi-Fi and covered parking for up to four automobiles, a stay in this glorious abode is exceptionally comfortable indeed – simply perfect for enjoying life to the full on the sunny island of Sardinia!

SPEKTAKULÄR AUF DEM Hügel von Pantogia nahe Porto Cervo gelegen, dürfte diese Oase der Ruhe vor allem Liebhaber modernen Designs begeistern. Die Innenräume der komplett renovierten, zweistöckigen Villa werden von wohltuendem Weiß dominiert, wodurch eine klare, reduzierte Atmosphäre entsteht – ein reizvoller Kontrast zum smaragdfarbenen Meer. Mit ihren natürlichen Farbnuancen, dem puristischen Design und der überwältigenden Aussicht sorgen die drei Schlafzimmer-Suiten für ein wunderbar entspannendes Ambiente, ebenso wie der offen gestaltete Wohnbereich mit seinem hochwertigen Interieur. Zu den weiteren Highlights zählen der Infinity Pool und die großflächigen, teilweise terrassenartigen Außenbereiche mit Grill und Open-Air-Essplatz. Nicht zuletzt sind es auch die vielen Annehmlichkeiten wie Airconditioning in allen Zimmern, Sat-TV, WLAN sowie die überdachten Parkplätze für bis zu vier Autos, die den Aufenthalt hier besonders komfortabel machen. Beste Bedingungen also, um die Ferien im sonnigen Sardinien in vollen Zügen zu genießen!

ESPECTACULARMENTE SITUADO en la colina de Pantogia, cerca de Porto Cervo, este inmenso oasis de calma y tranquilidad se traduce en un paraíso de vacaciones. Los interiores de la villa en dos niveles, totalmente renovada, están dominados por el sereno color blanco, irradiando pulcritud y minimalismo en perfecto contrapunto con el mar color esmeralda en el exterior. Con vistas impresionantes, los tres dormitorios también destilan bienestar con sus tonos naturales y puros. El salón es igualmente impresionante, con su cómodo ambiente de distribución abierta y los modernos muebles de lujo. Destacan la piscina de horizonte desbordante y los extensos exteriores que incluyen terrazas y la zona de barbacoa y comedor al aire libre. Con aire acondicionado, TV vía satélite, conexión *wifi* y aparcamiento cubierto para cuatro coches formando parte de su completo equipamiento, una estancia en esta fabulosa morada contemporánea resulta realmente confortable, perfecta para disfrutar de la vida al máximo en la soleada isla italiana de Cerdeña.

ITALY, SARDINIA **RENTAL PRICE/WEEK** EUR 9,000–13,000 **INTERIOR APPROX.** 250 m² **NO. OF BEDROOMS** 3
**LAND APPROX.** 3,500 m² **E&V ID** W-01GJXA **CONTACT** PORTO CERVO (IT), FIRST SARDEV S.R.L.,
LICENCE PARTNER OF ENGEL & VÖLKERS ITALIA S.R.L. **TEL.** +39 078 99 41 83
**E-MAIL** PORTOCERVO@ENGELVOELKERS.COM

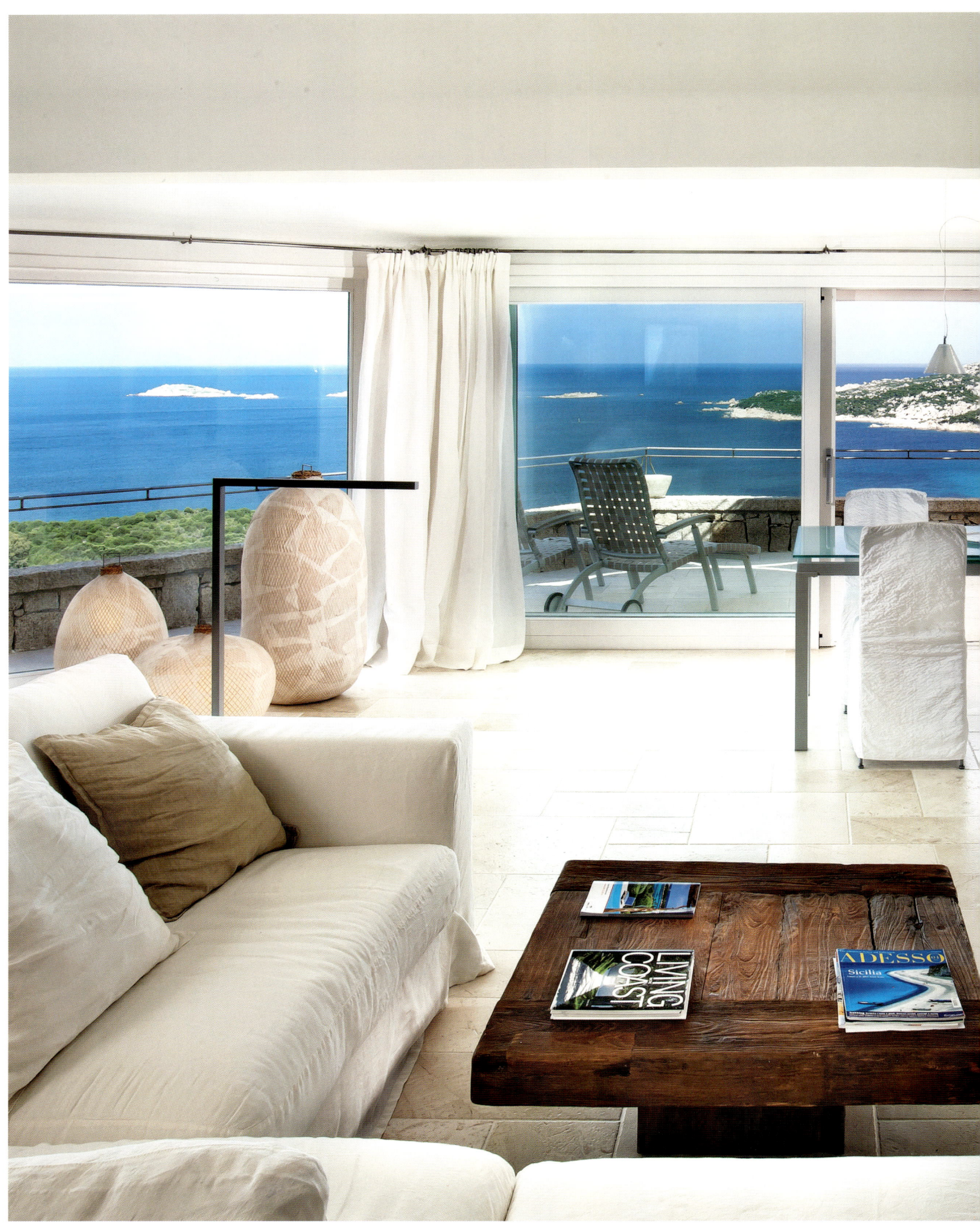

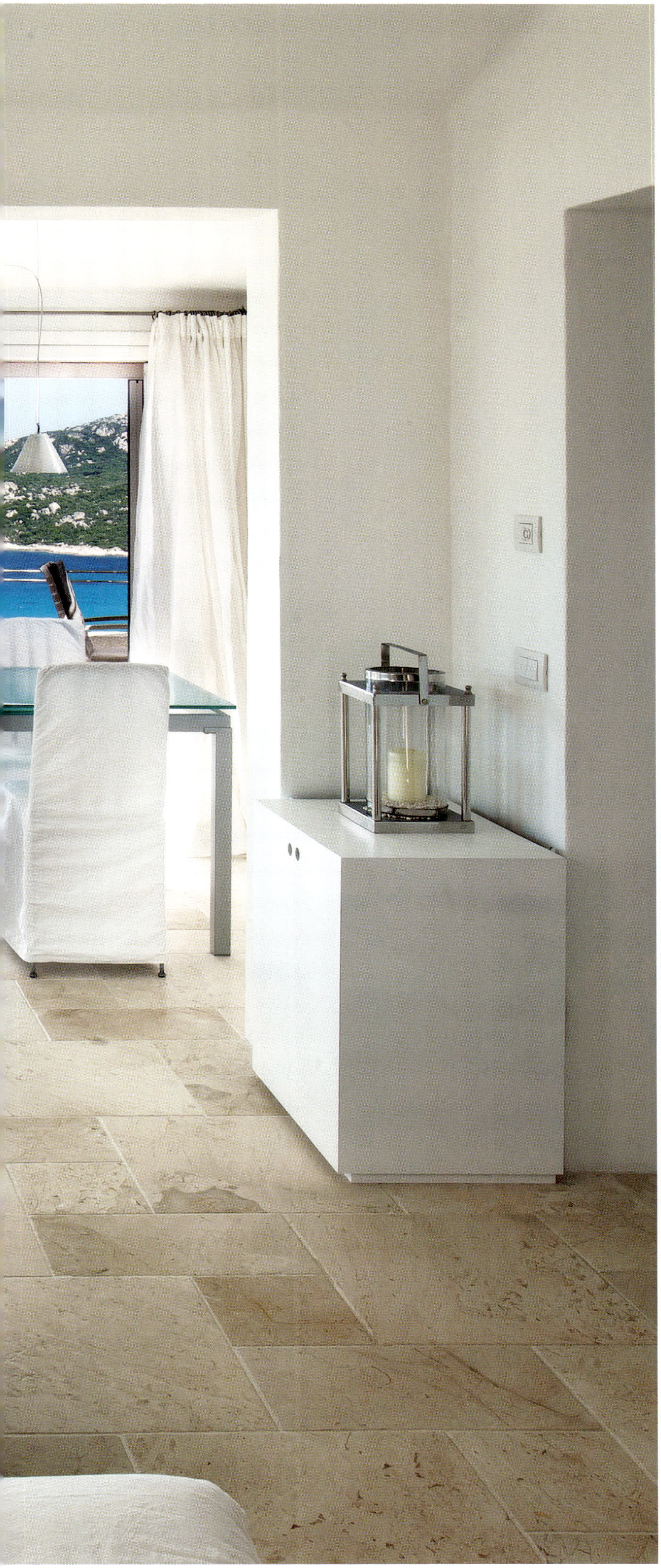

A room with a view: panoramic vistas of
Pevero bay as far as the eye can see.

Zimmer mit Aussicht: Der Blick über die
Pevero Bay reicht bis zum Horizont.

Habitación con vistas: panorámicas a la bahía
de Pevero hasta donde alcanza la mirada.

A refreshing dip in the elegantly landscaped pool is an experience unto itself.

Ein erfrischender Sprung in den schön angelegten Infinity Pool ist ein Erlebnis für sich.

Darse un chapuzón en la piscina desbordante
entre bellos jardines resulta inolvidable.

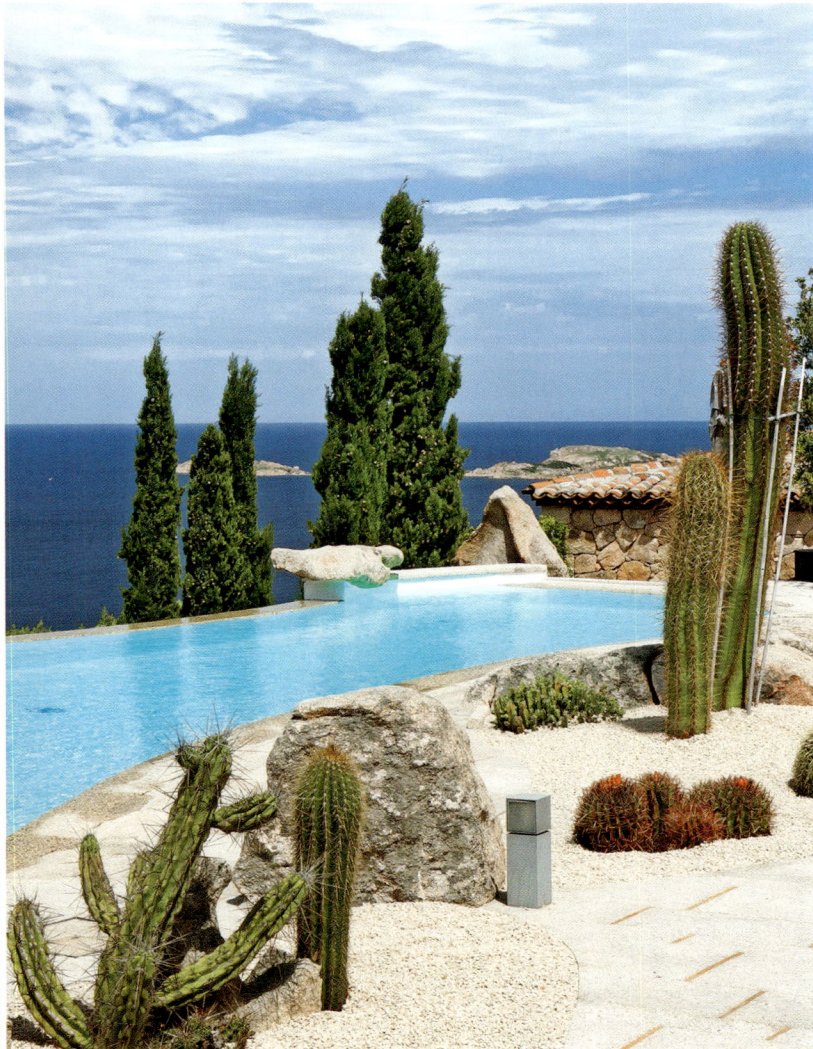

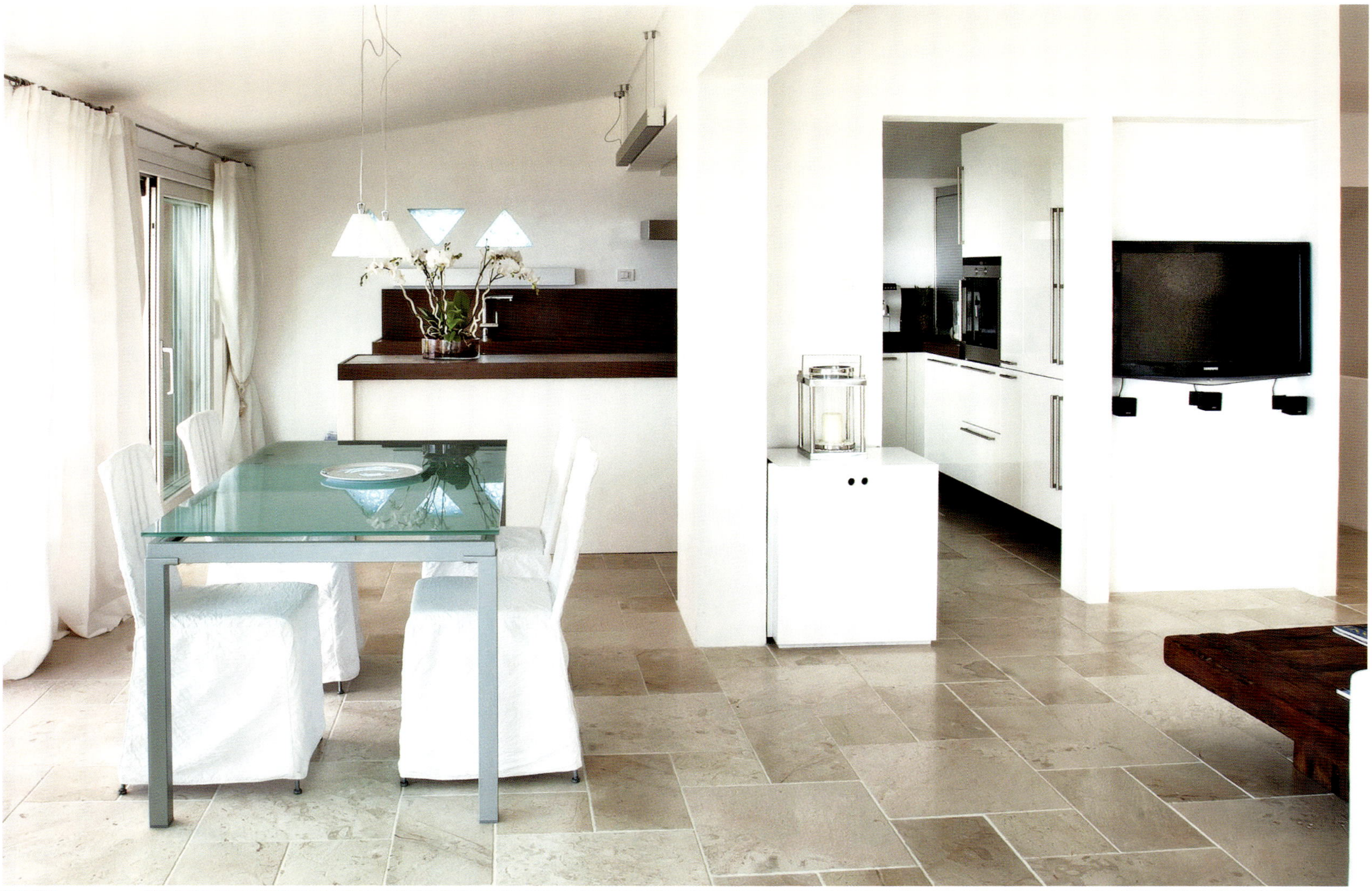

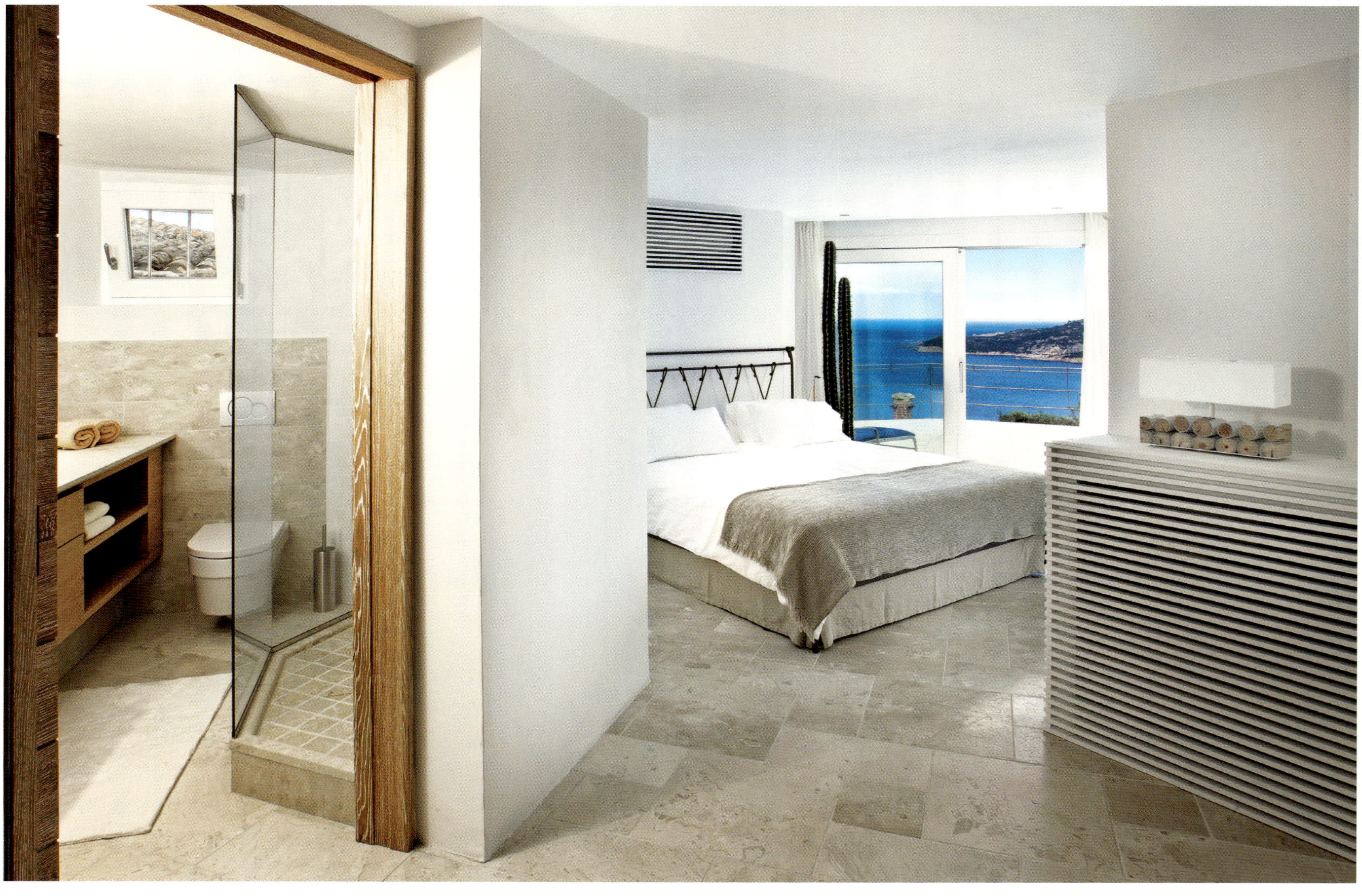

The bright open-plan kitchen with adjacent
dining area promises truly enjoyable hours.

Die helle, offene Küche mit angrenzendem
Essbereich verspricht genussvolle Stunden.

La luminosa cocina abierta y el comedor
adyacente prometen horas deleitosas.

With such an outlook, it is easy to see why the
Costa Smeralda is a top holiday destination.

Diese Aussicht ... kein Wunder, dass die Costa
Smeralda zu den Top-Ferienzielen gehört.

Tal perspectiva define por qué Costa Smeralda
es un destino vacacional de primera categoría.

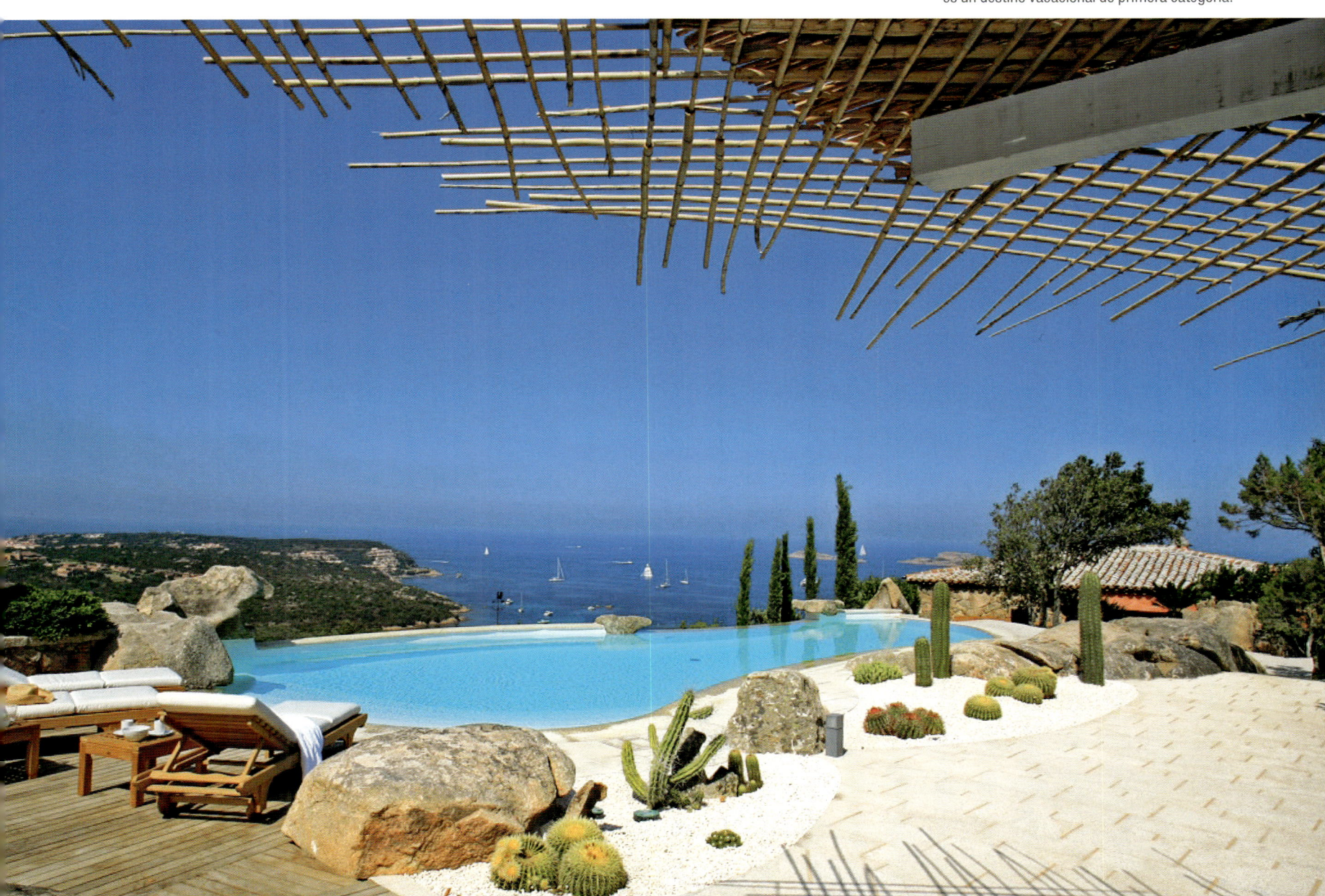

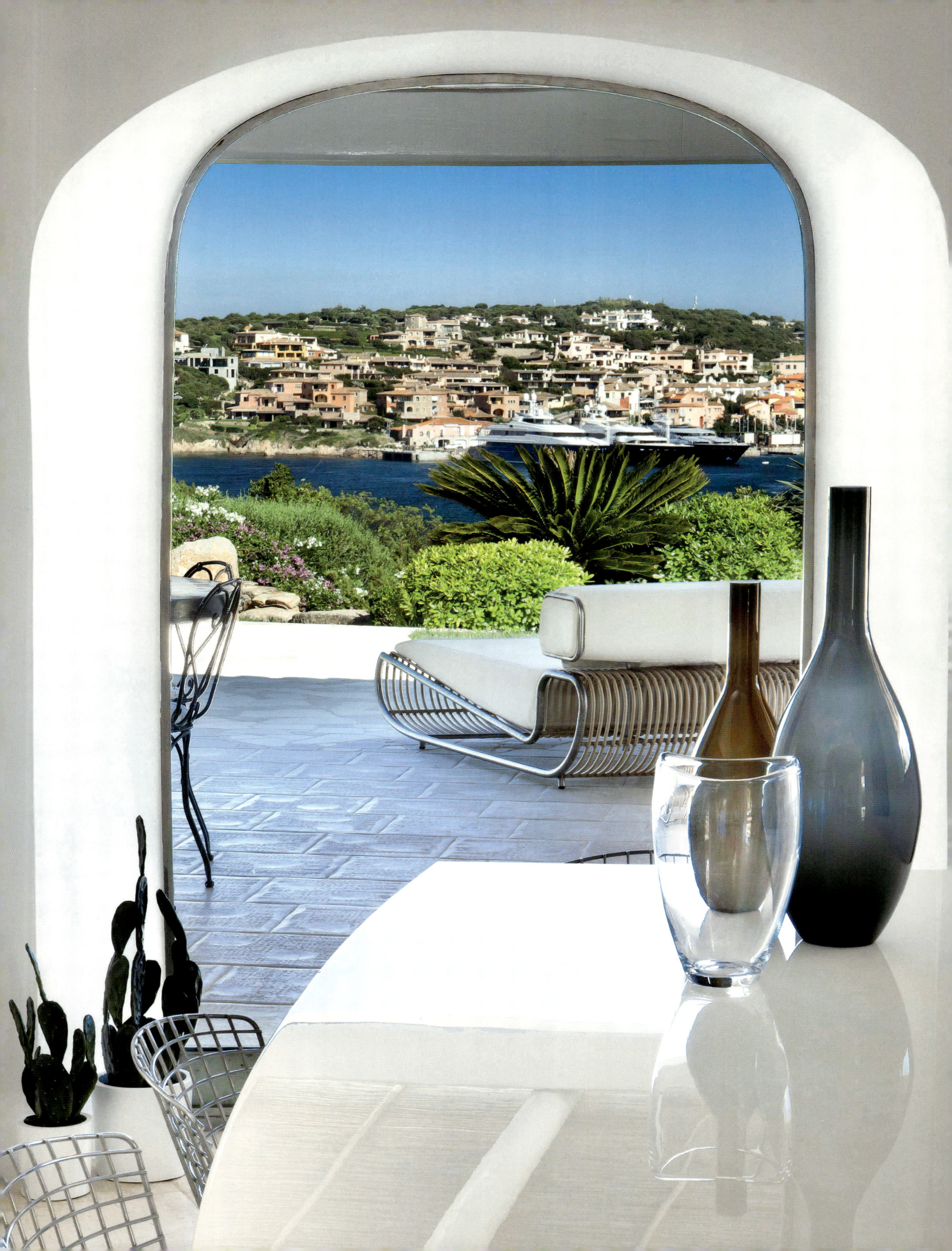

# Superb Marina Flair

The epitome of a luxury lifestyle and the ultimate Italian holiday feeling are guaranteed in this impressive domicile with views of Porto Cervo marina.

AS AN EXCLUSIVE Mediterranean hotspot and glamorous home to the international jet set, Porto Cervo is quite easily one of the most sought-after locations in the world. In this precious setting, a spectacular residence plays host to the most sophisticated holidays ever. The discreet architecture of this lovely whitewashed villa is inspired by the Mediterranean landscape, gently curved and rolling, and the interior design is kept decidedly simple yet stylish. The marble floors have been customised of Orosei stone, with white, beige and sand-coloured tones dominating – again inspired by the colours of nature. The large living room boasts a fireplace, and the beautiful patio offers an additional outdoor dining area. With five bedrooms, four of which open onto the terraces and a mature landscaped garden, guests enjoy maximum independence, and a glorious pool makes paradise complete. This is the perfect dwelling to indulge in pure Costa Smeraldan luxury, with stunning vistas of the glittering ocean – and the occasional superyacht sailing past.

ALS EXKLUSIVER Mittelmeer-Hotspot und glamouröse Heimat des internationalen Jetsets gehört Porto Cervo mit Recht zu den begehrtesten Feriendestinationen der Welt – und bildet somit den perfekten Rahmen für diese wunderschöne, weiß getünchte Villa mit ihrer typisch mediterranen Architektur, inspiriert durch die umgebende Landschaft mit ihren sanft geschwungenen Hügeln. Die Innenausstattung ist stilvoll-puristisch und in Weiß, Beige- und Sandtönen gehalten – ebenfalls inspiriert durch die Farben der Natur. Ein Highlight sind dabei die individuell angepassten Marmorböden aus Orosei-Stein. Das geräumige Wohnzimmer verfügt über einen großen Kamin, die schöne Terrasse über einen zusätzlichen Essbereich. Mit fünf behaglichen Zimmern, von denen vier auf die Terrassen und den traumhaft angelegten Garten blicken, genießt man hier ein Höchstmaß an Privatsphäre. Der wunderschöne Pool macht dieses paradiesische Hideaway mit seiner sagenhaften Aussicht auf das glitzernde Meer, den Hafen und die vorüberziehenden Yachten schließlich komplett.

MEDITERRÁNEO Y EXCLUSIVO, *hotspot* y glamoroso hogar de la *jet set* internacional, Porto Cervo se cuenta sin duda entre los lugares más codiciados del mundo. En este precioso entorno, una espectacular residencia puede ser anfitriona de las vacaciones más sofisticadas que se puedan imaginar. Su discreta arquitectura encalada se inspira en el impresionante paisaje mediterráneo, suavemente curvo y ondulante. El diseño interior es sencillo pero elegante, con suelos de mármol personalizados con piedra de Orosei y dominio de blancos, beige y arena, tonos de nuevo inspirados por la naturaleza. La gran sala de estar cuenta con una gran chimenea, y el bello patio con un comedor adicional al aire libre. Con cinco dormitorios, cuatro de los cuales se abren a las terrazas y al jardín maduro, los invitados disfrutan de la máxima independencia. Una gloriosa piscina completa el paraíso de esta vivienda, idónea para disfrutar del puro lujo de la Costa Smeralda y con impresionantes vistas al mar centelleando alrededor, surcado por la estela de algún que otro superyate.

ITALY, SARDINIA **RENTAL PRICE/WEEK** EUR 20,000–35,000 **INTERIOR APPROX.** 300 m² **NO. OF BEDROOMS** 5
**LAND APPROX.** 3,000 m² **E&V ID** W-01GXEF **CONTACT** PORTO CERVO (IT), FIRST SARDEV S.R.L.,
LICENCE PARTNER OF ENGEL & VÖLKERS ITALIA S.R.L. **TEL.** +39 078 99 41 83
**E-MAIL** PORTOCERVO@ENGELVOELKERS.COM

The place to enjoy dinner Porto Cervo style –
crowned by incredible views of the marina.

Hier genießt man Dinner à la Porto Cervo –
gekrönt von einem sensationellen Hafenblick.

Las comidas aquí siempre se acompañan de
soberbias panorámicas al puerto deportivo.

In a league of its own: a dream property that
simply oozes Mediterranean charm.

Eine Klasse für sich: Diese Traumimmobilie
besticht durch ihren mediterranen Charme.

En su propia liga: una propiedad de ensueño
desbordante de encanto mediterráneo.

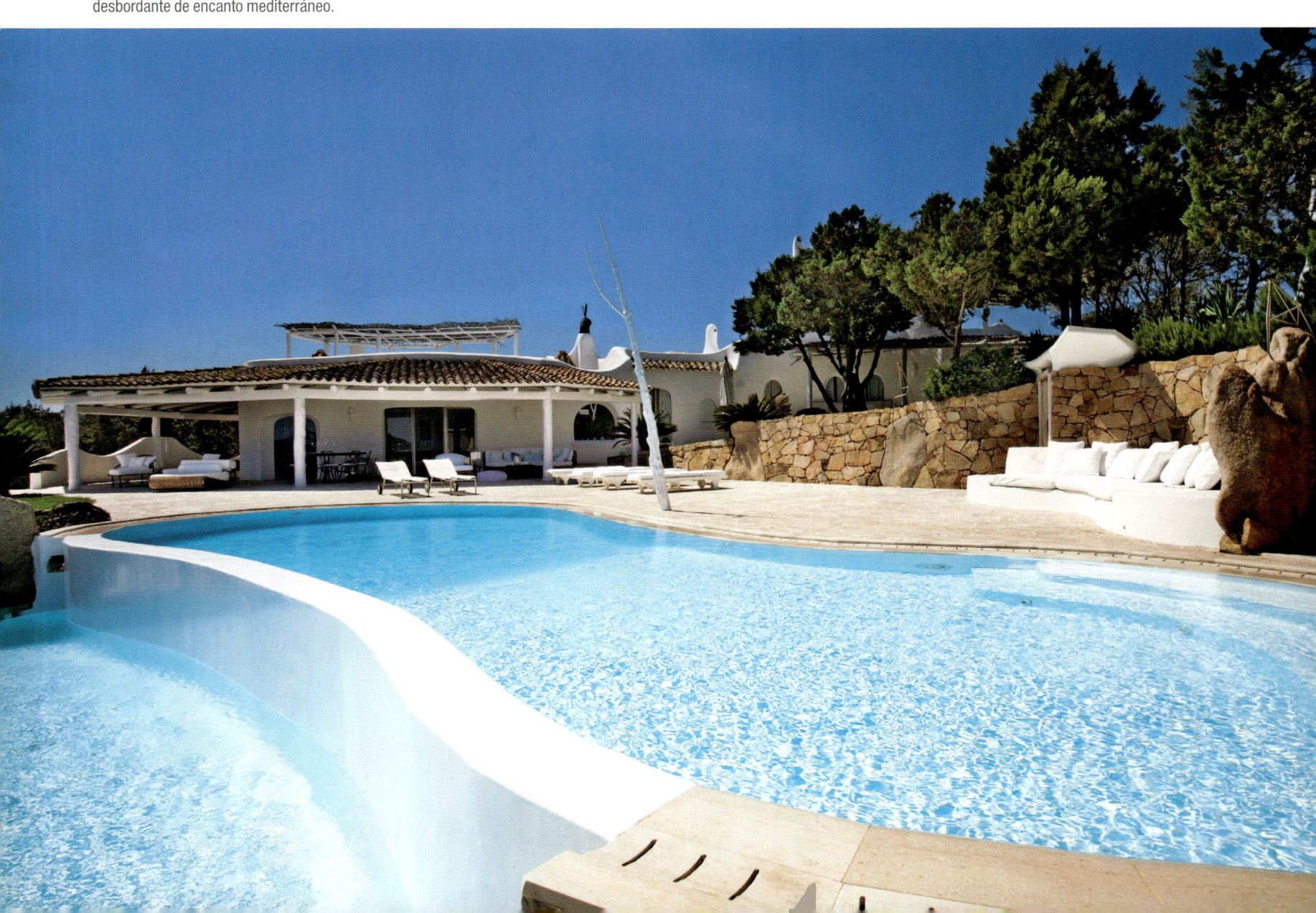

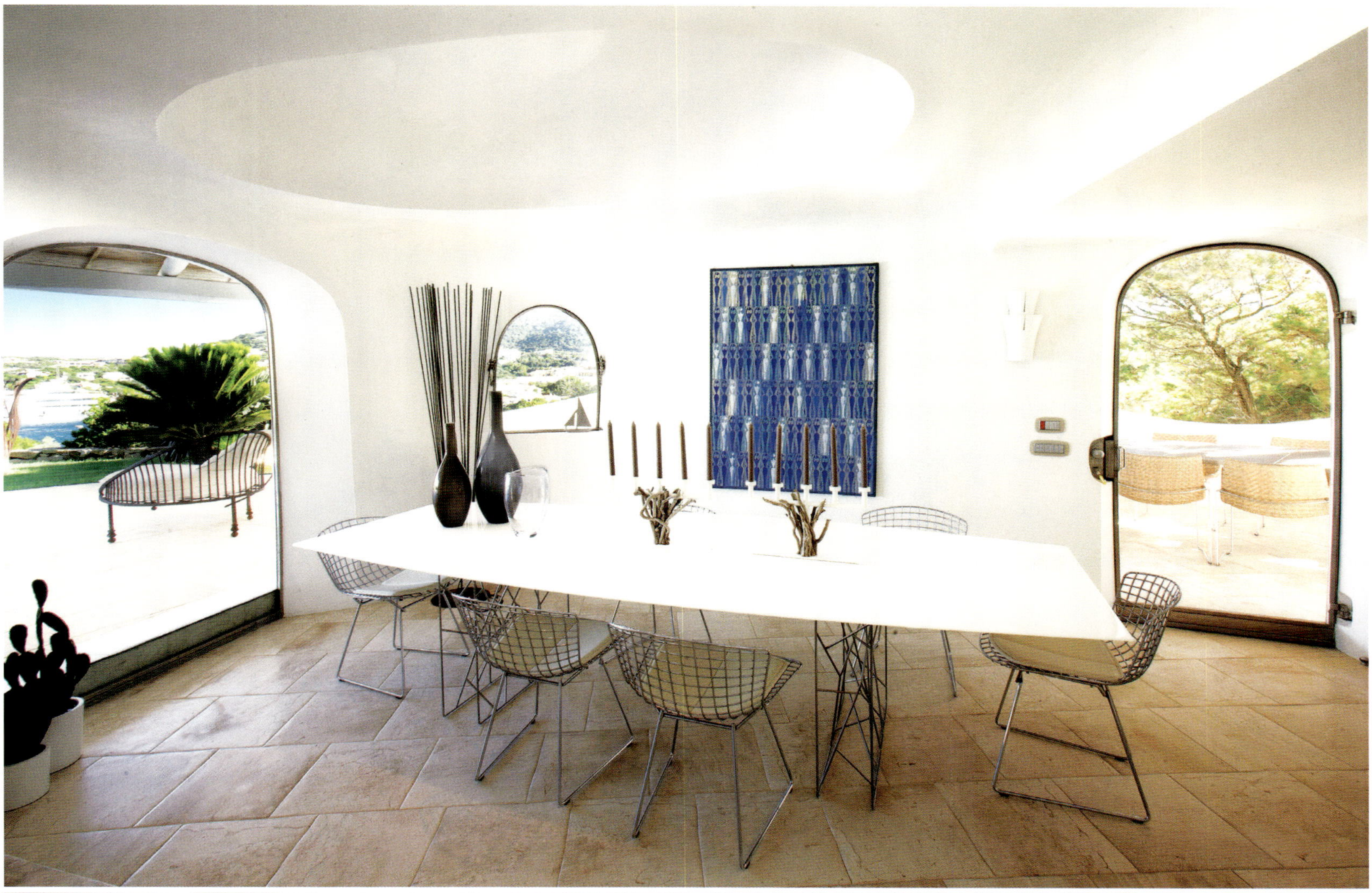

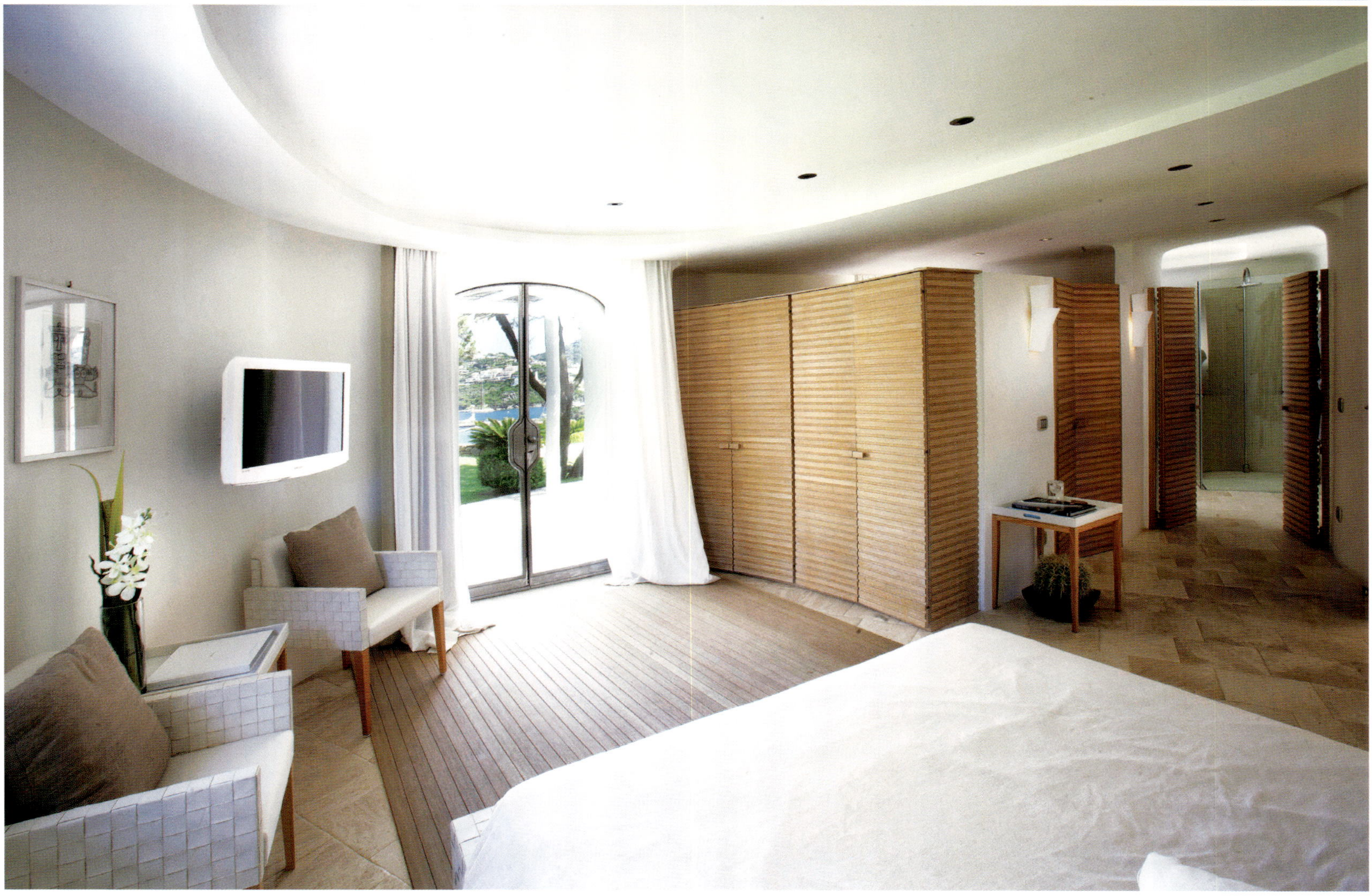

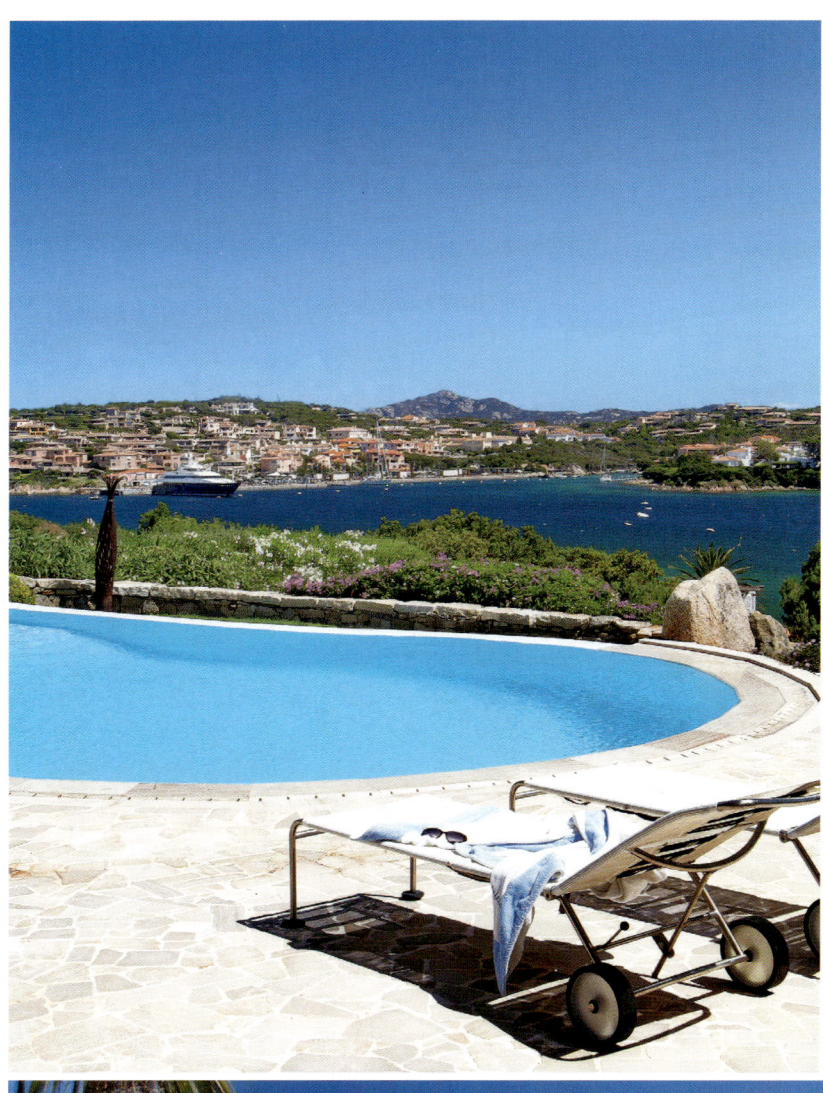

A top location for catching some rays and admiring the luxury yachts as they pass by.

Von der Sonne verwöhnt: der ideale Ort, um die vorbeiziehenden Yachten zu beobachten.

Un palco privilegiado donde tomar el sol y admirar de cerca el paso de los yates de lujo.

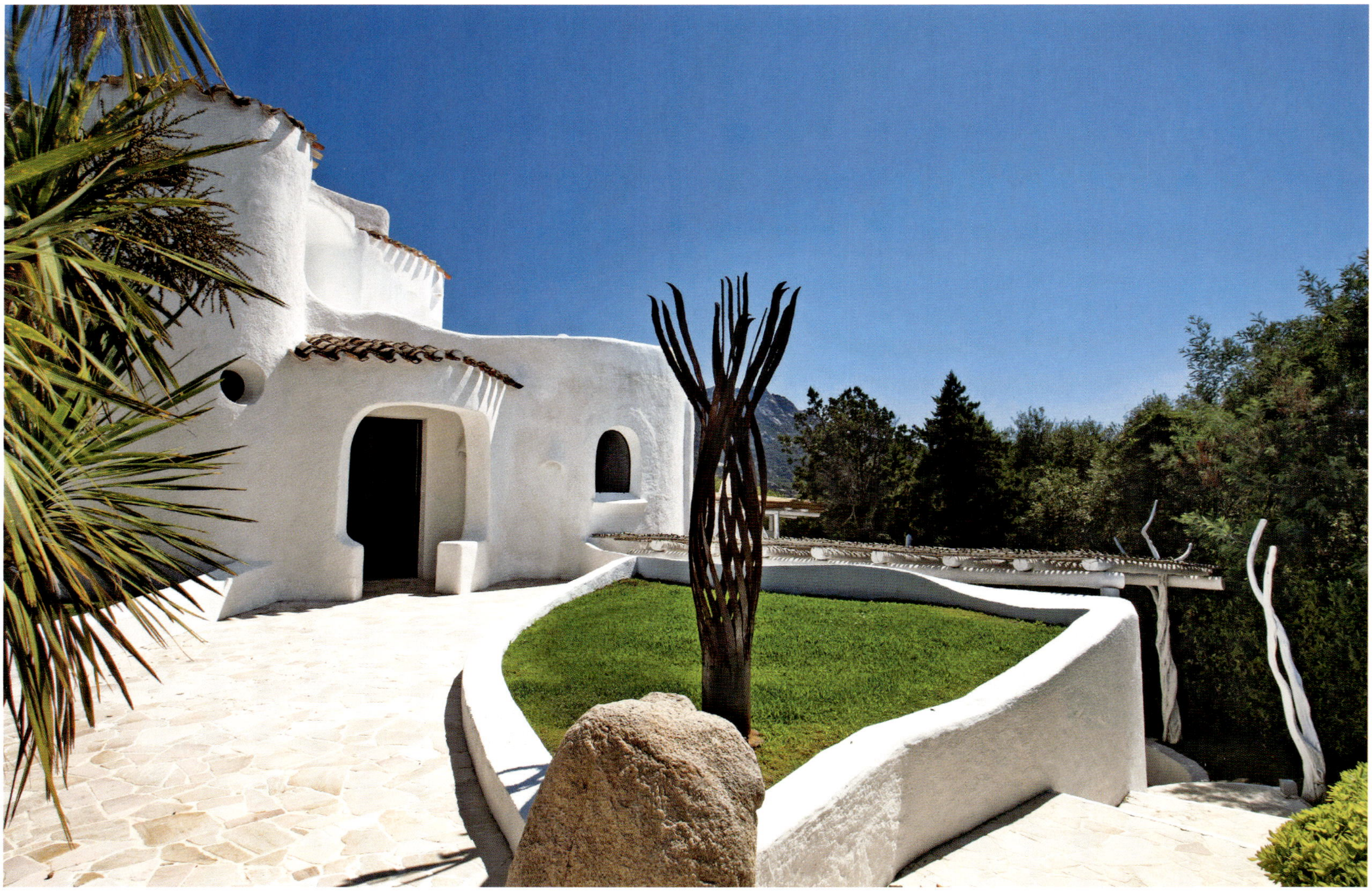

Interiors with a truly uplifting concept:
clean, comfortable, modern – yet homely.

Ein stimmiges Wohlfühl-Konzept: clean,
komfortabel, modern – und sehr behaglich.

Edificante concepto interior de bienestar:
limpio, cómodo, moderno… y acogedor.

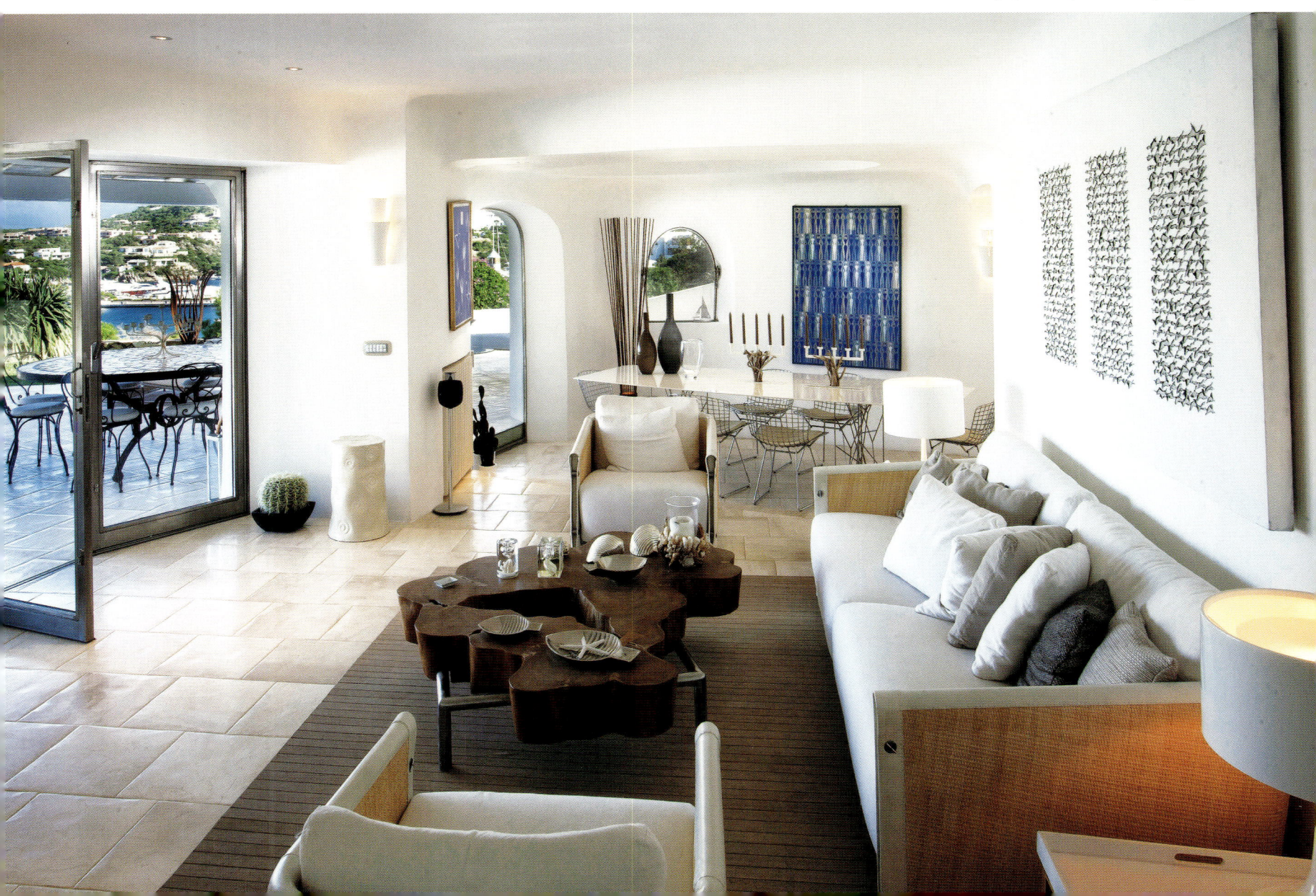

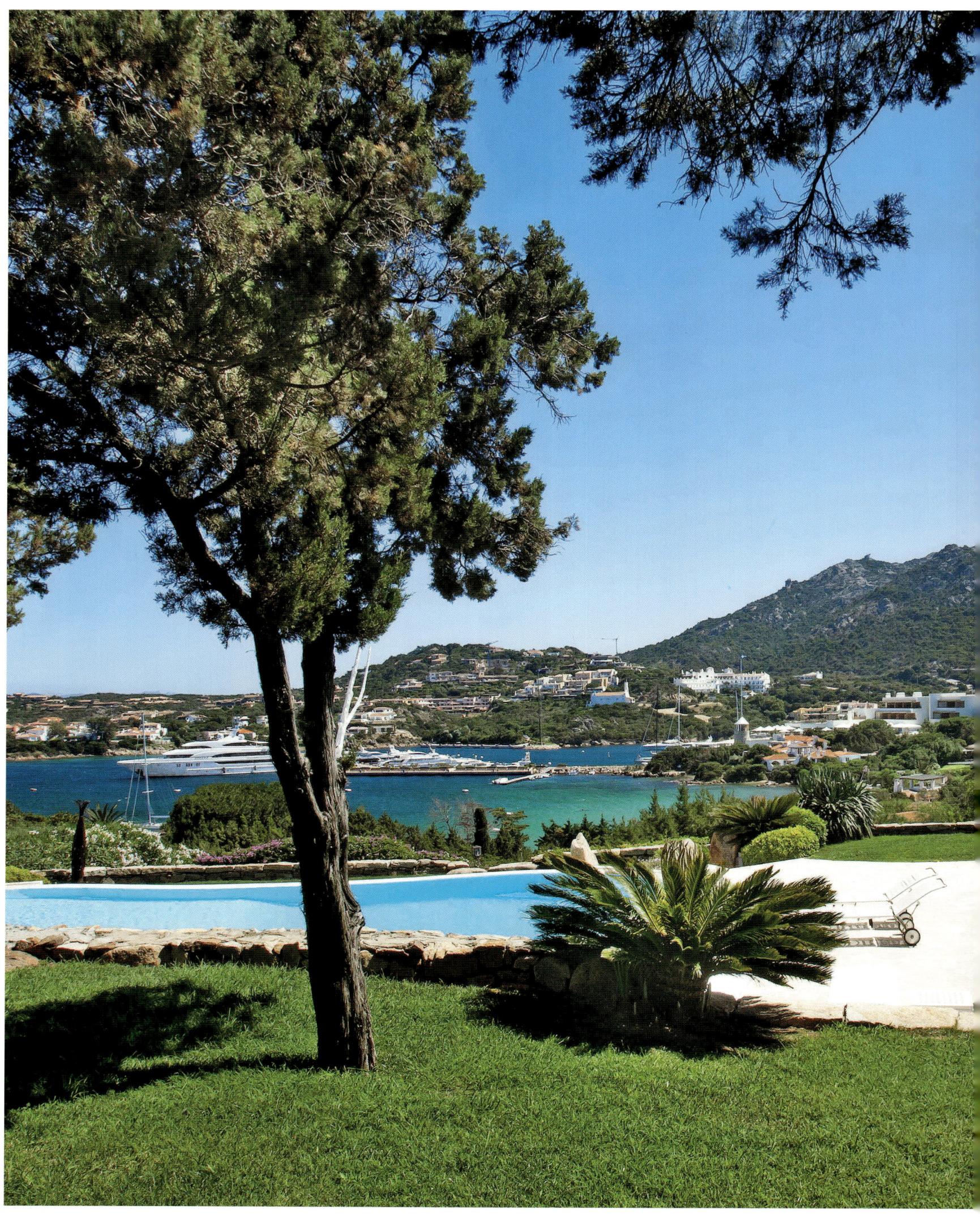

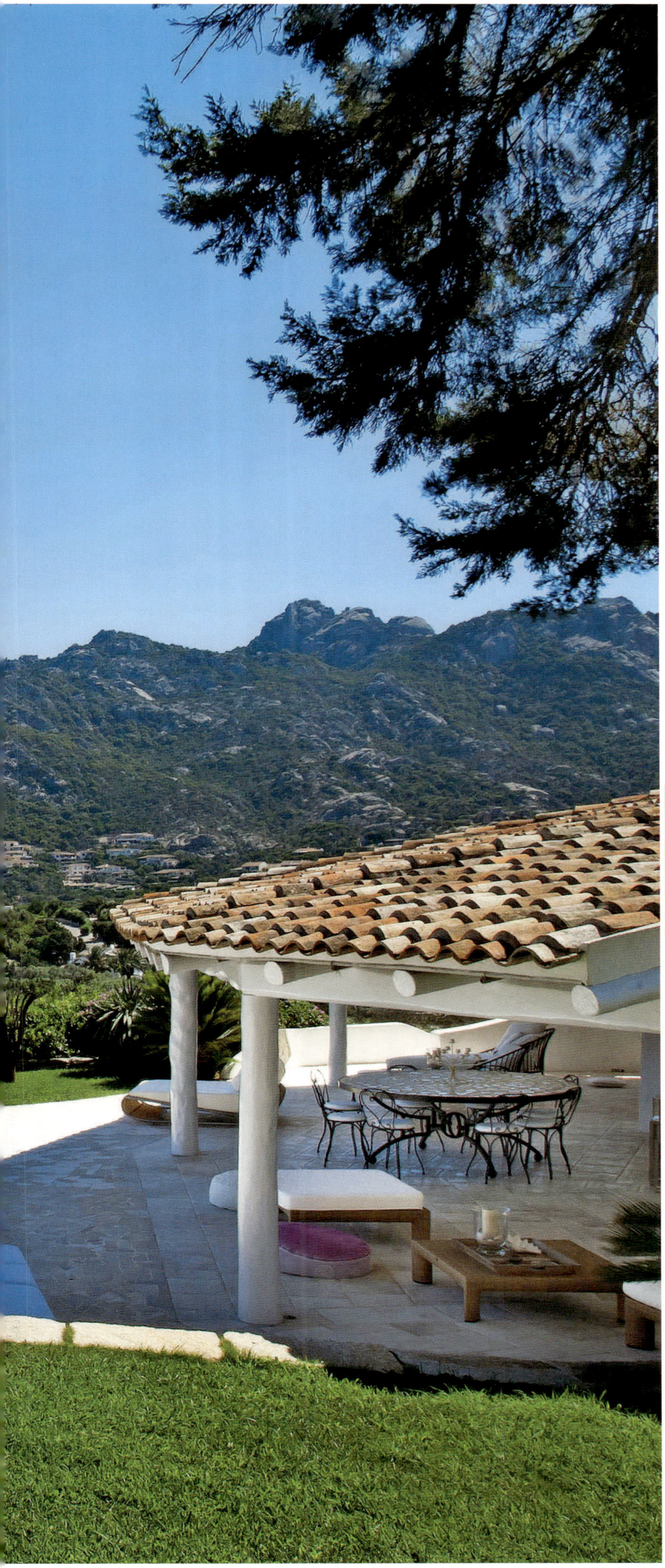

<

This villa soaks up the vibrant flair and international sophistication of Porto Cervo.

Die Villa reflektiert das lebendige Flair und die kosmopolitische Lebensart von Porto Cervo.

Esta villa embebe el ambiente vibrante y la sofisticación internacional de Porto Cervo.

Plenty of shady outdoor areas make this beautiful Sardinian property so special.

Die schattigen Außenbereiche machen diese wunderschöne sardische Villa so besonders.

El abundante espacio al fresco hace esta hermosa propiedad sarda tan especial.

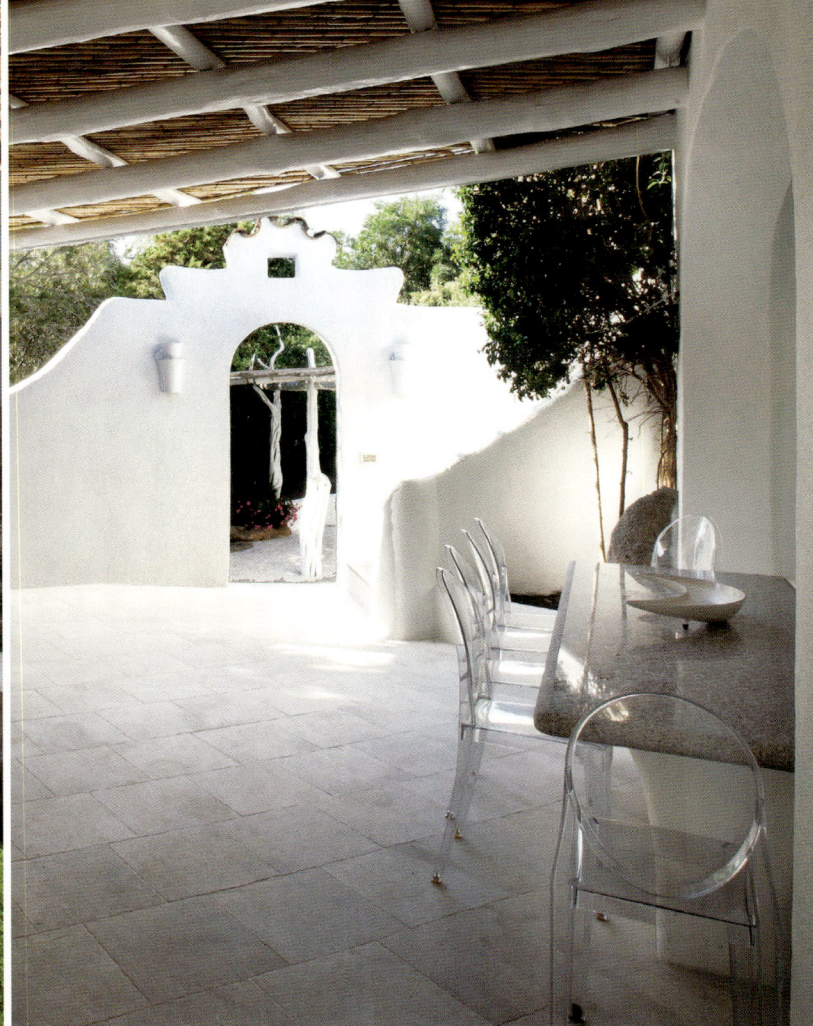

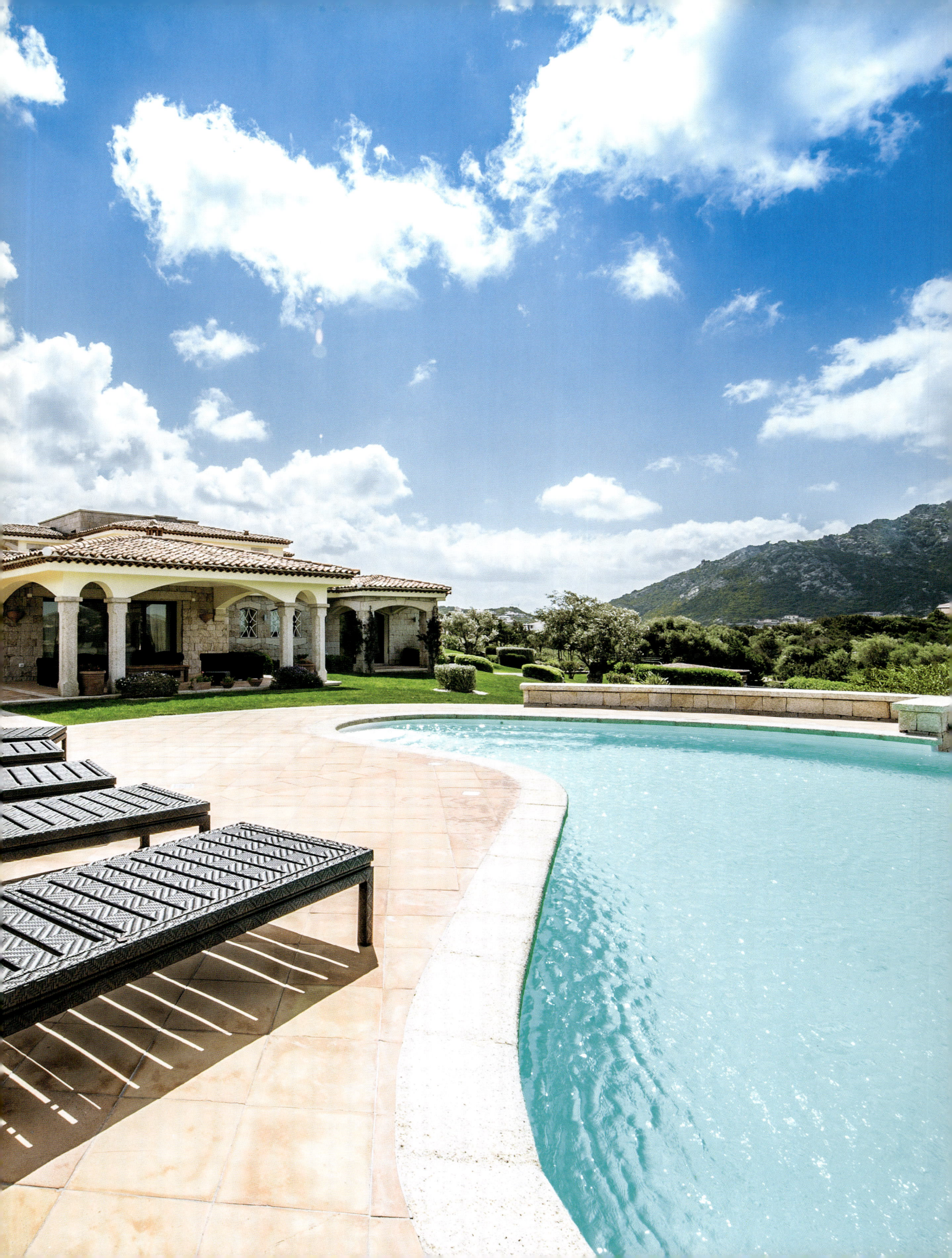

# Stately Holiday Home

With glorious vistas of La Maddalena archipelago, this majestic estate with a truly captivating garden offers a supreme level of comfort for a dream holiday.

LOCATED ONLY FIVE MINUTES by foot from Porto Cervo's famous marina and the Yacht Club Costa Smeralda, established by Aga Khan in the late 1960s, this prestigious dwelling is one of a kind. Presiding on a plot of around 4,000 square metres with a mature garden, an expansive lawn and a beautifully landscaped swimming pool, this magnificent mansion promises a high degree of residential excellence in terms of quality and style. The luminous open-plan living and dining area provides direct access to the outside terrace, replete with a poolside barbecue area that is perfect for wining and dining with friends and guests. The large, comfortable sofas and the fireplace in the living room create a relaxed and highly inviting indoor ambience. With a total of eight attractively furnished bedrooms and nine bathrooms, there is space aplenty in this villa boasting approx. 520 square metres of luxurious living area. A staff suite with a separate entrance ensures extra privacy and discretion. Welcome to a truly refined Costa Smeraldan lifestyle!

NUR FÜNF GEHMINUTEN von Porto Cervos berühmtem Yachthafen und dem Yachtclub Costa Smeralda entfernt, präsentiert sich dieses von Aga Khan in den späten Sechzigerjahren errichtete, prestigeträchtige Villenanwesen. Auf einem rund 4.000 Quadratmeter umfassenden Grundstück samt weitläufigem Garten, sattgrünen Rasenflächen und schön angelegtem Swimmingpool begeistert diese stilvolle Residenz durch ihr besonderes Wohlfühl-Ambiente. Vom lichtdurchfluteten, offenen Wohn- und Essbereich mit Kamin und herrlich bequemen Sofas gelangt man direkt auf die überdachte Außenterrasse mit Grillplatz, die zu entspannten Nachmittagen und geselligen Barbecues an lauen Sommerabenden einlädt. Mit einer Wohnfläche von rund 520 Quadratmetern samt acht geschmackvoll eingerichteten Schlafzimmern, neun Bädern und einer Personal-Suite bietet die Villa zudem jederzeit ausreichend Privatsphäre und Platz für Familie und Freunde. Willkommen in einem Feriendomizil, in dem der Lifestyle der Costa Smeralda zu Hause ist!

A SÓLO CINCO MINUTOS a pie del famoso puerto deportivo de Porto Cervo y del Yacht Club Costa Smeralda, fundados por el Aga Khan a finales de los 60, esta prestigiosa mansión es única en su clase. Dominando un gran terreno de unos 4.000 metros cuadrados, con frondosos jardines y extenso césped de estilo inglés y una piscina paisajística, ofrece un alto grado de excelencia residencial en términos de calidad y estilo. La luminosa zona de estar y comedor de diseño abierto dispone de acceso directo a la terraza, dotada de una zona de barbacoa junto a la piscina, perfecta para agasajar a amigos e invitados. Los amplios y cómodos sofás y la soberbia chimenea del salón crean un ambiente interior relajado y muy acogedor. Con un total de ocho atractivos dormitorios y nueve cuartos de baño hay abundancia de espacio en esta villa con unos 520 metros cuadrados habitables de puro lujo. Una *suite* para el personal con entrada independiente proporciona privacidad y discreción añadida. ¡Bienvenido a un estilo de vida verdaderamente refinado en la Costa Esmeralda!

ITALY, SARDINIA **RENTAL PRICE/WEEK** EUR 20,000–35,000 **INTERIOR APPROX.** 520 m² **NO. OF BEDROOMS** 8
**LAND APPROX.** 4,000 m² **E&V ID** W-01YERV **CONTACT** PORTO CERVO (IT), FIRST SARDEV S.R.L.,
LICENCE PARTNER OF ENGEL & VÖLKERS ITALIA S.R.L. **TEL.** +39 078 99 41 83
**E-MAIL** PORTOCERVO@ENGELVOELKERS.COM

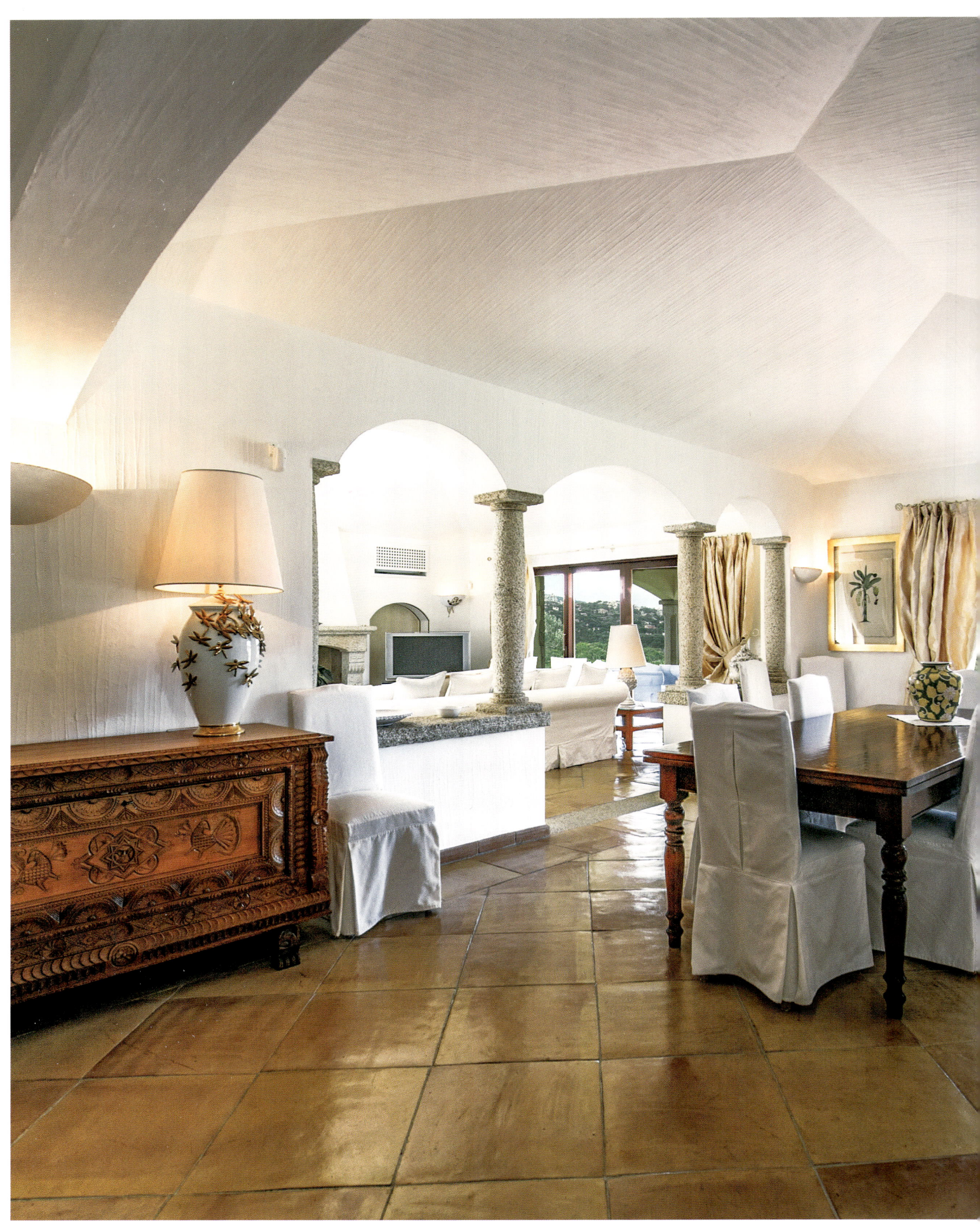

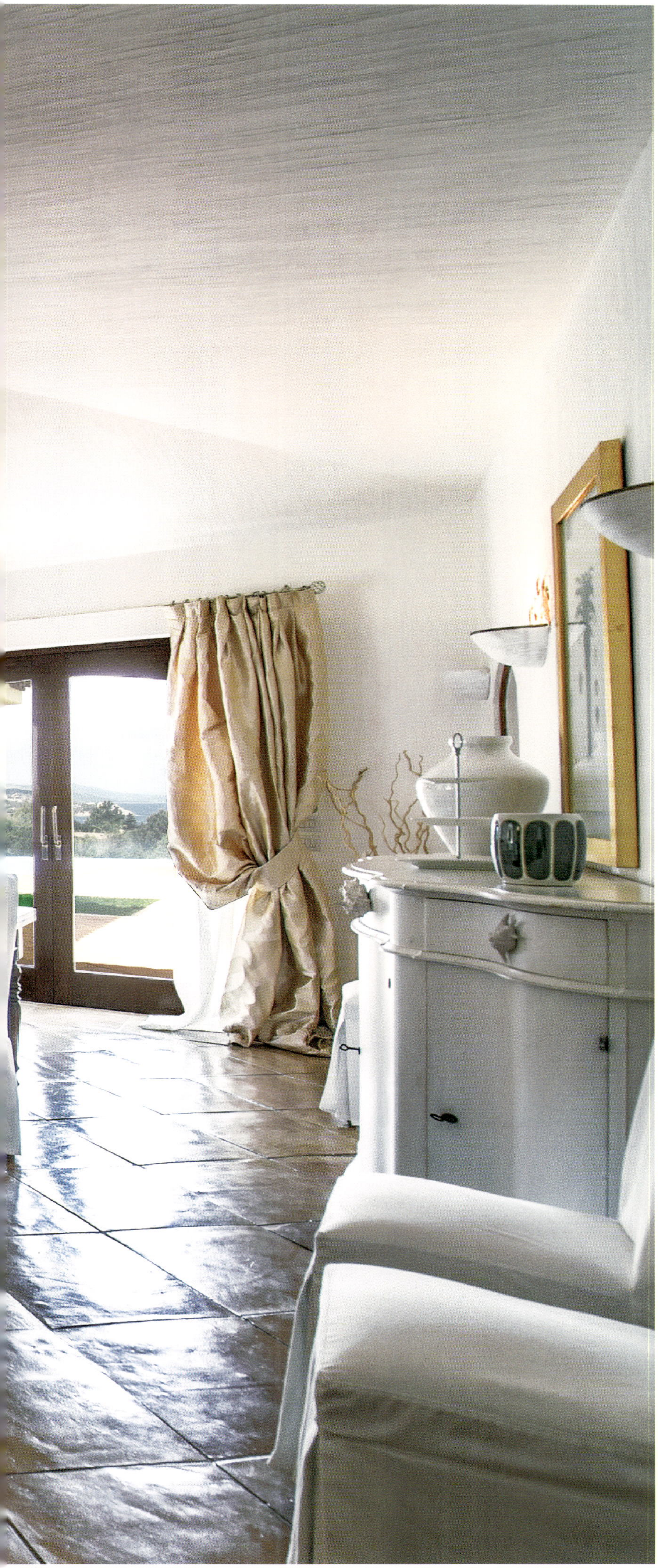

Perfect for a relaxing holiday:
the elegant country-style interiors.

Umgeben von urbanem Landhaus-Chic:
die stilvolle Art zu entspannen.

Interiores elegantes con un toque campestre:
ideales para combinar vacaciones y relajación.

A joy to discover: charming details
abound in this inviting Sardinian villa.

Eine Entdeckung wert: die vielen
charmanten Details dieser einladenden Villa.

Un tesoro por descubrir: los encantadores
detalles de esta atractiva villa sarda.

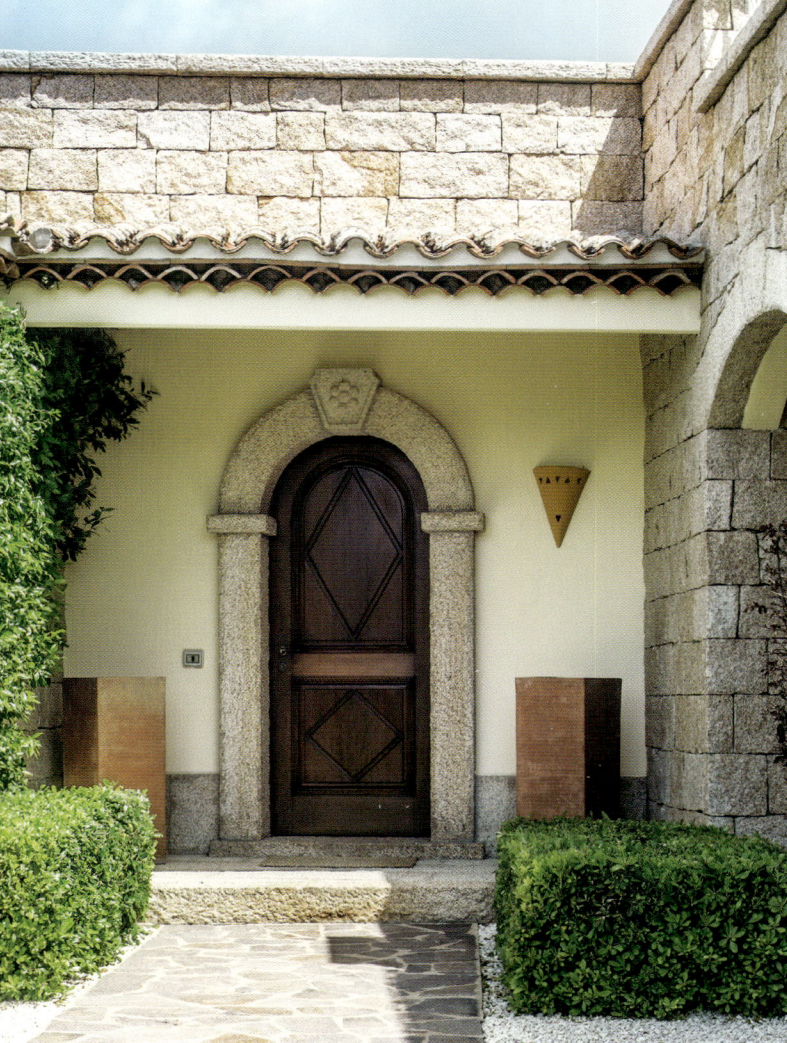

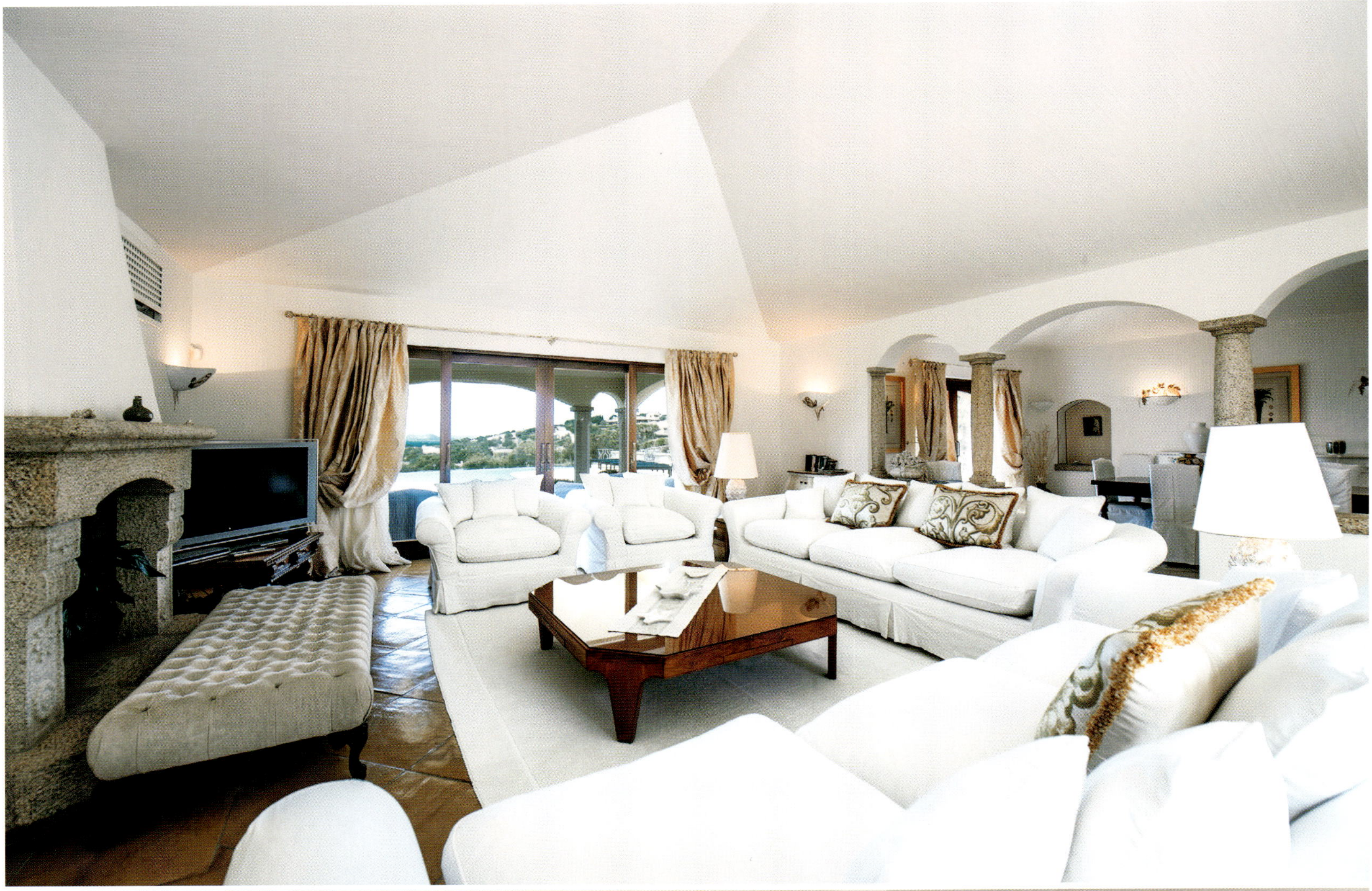

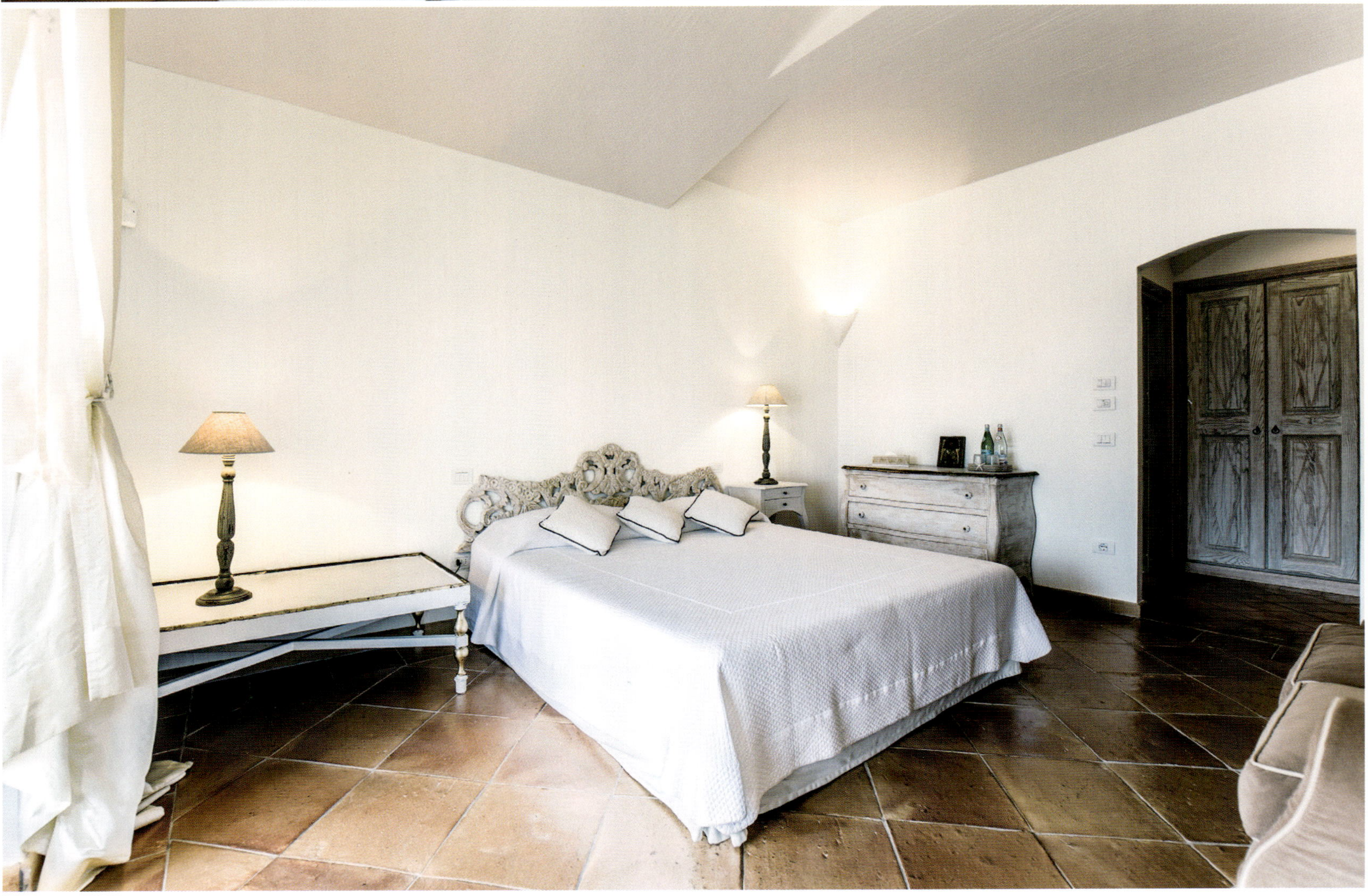

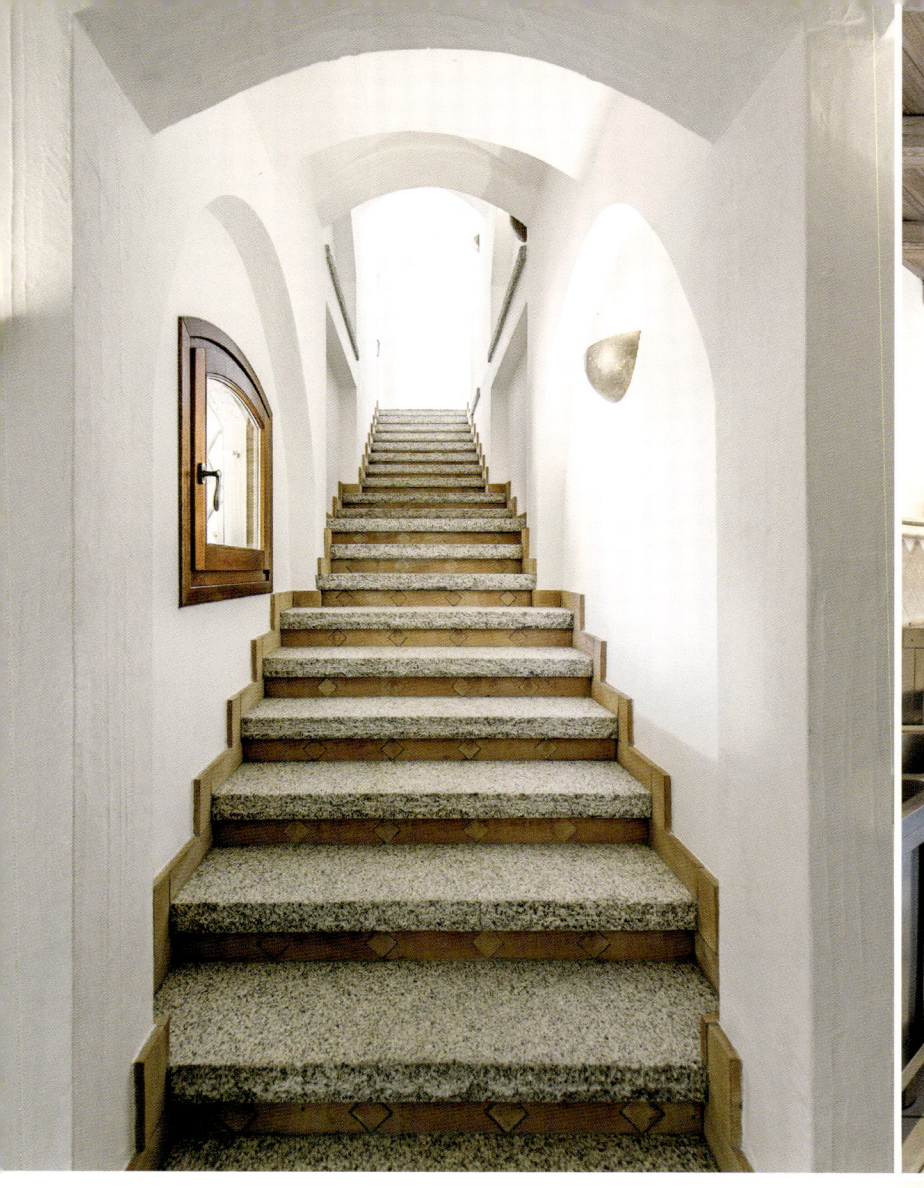

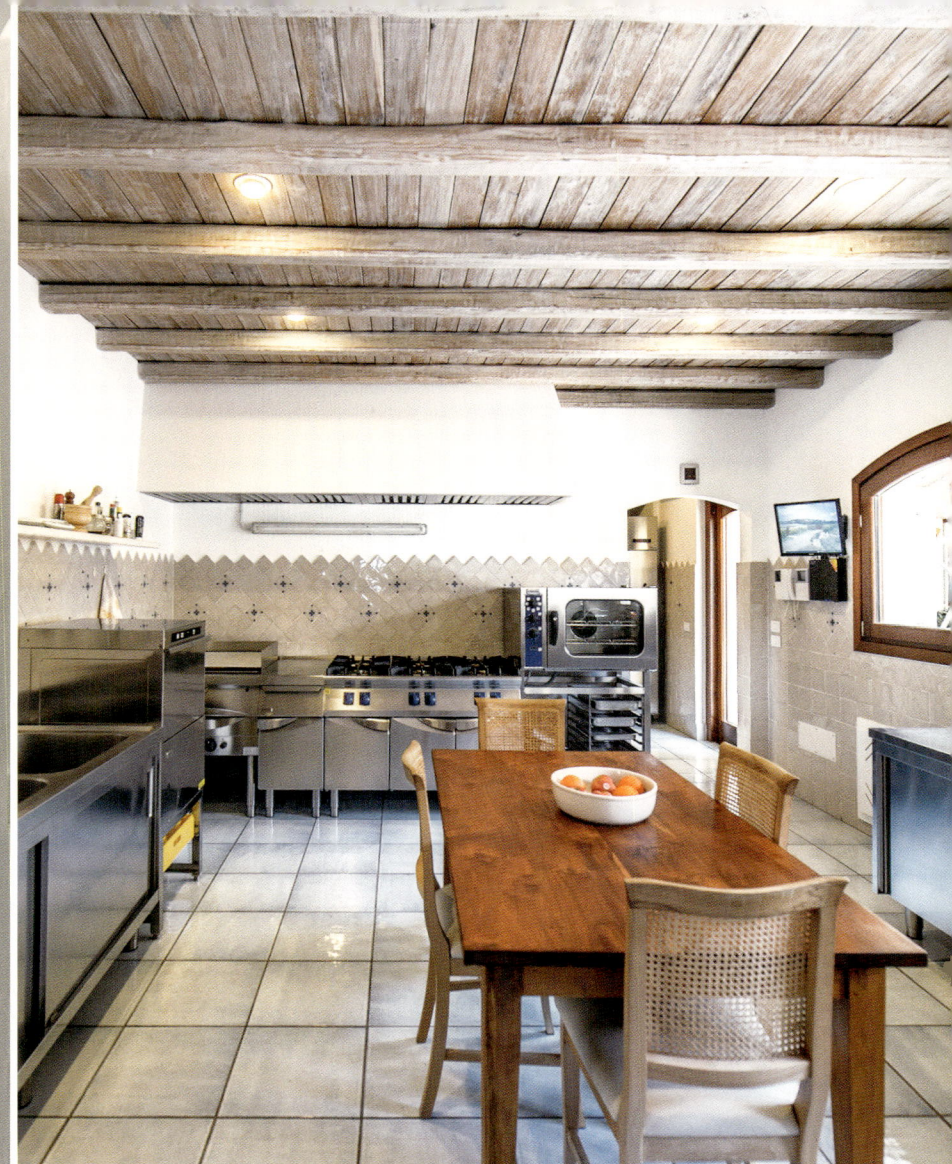

A muted colour scheme and abundant authentic touches are found everywhere.

Schmeichelnde Farbtöne und edle Materialien vereinen sich hier aufs Schönste.

Suave combinación de colores tenues y muchos toques tradicionales por doquier.

<

Cool, airy and with a spacious atmosphere, the villa is a delight for body and soul.

Das lichte, großzügige Ambiente im ganzen Haus lässt Körper und Seele aufatmen.

Los interiores frescos, aireados y espaciosos serenan tanto el cuerpo como el alma.

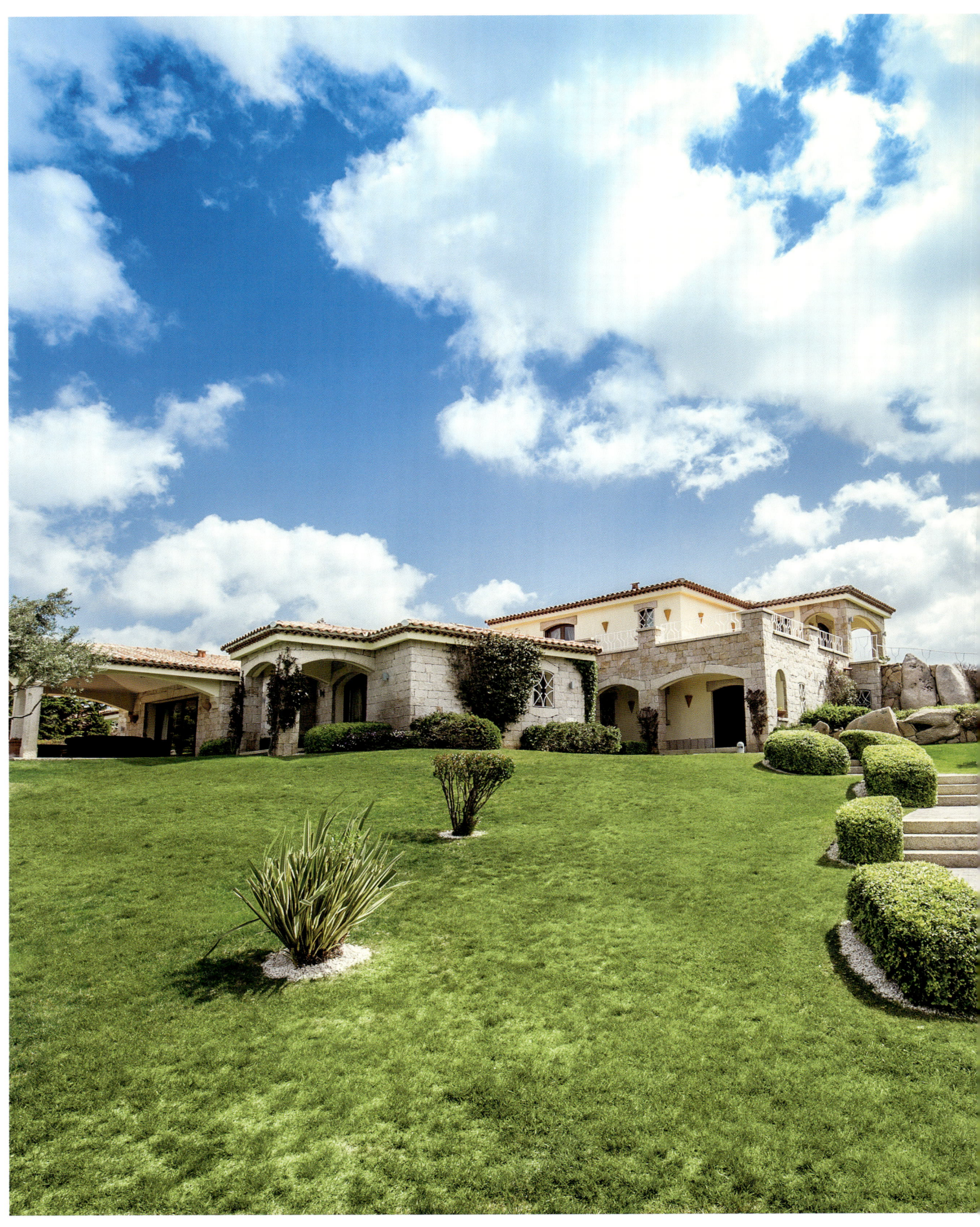

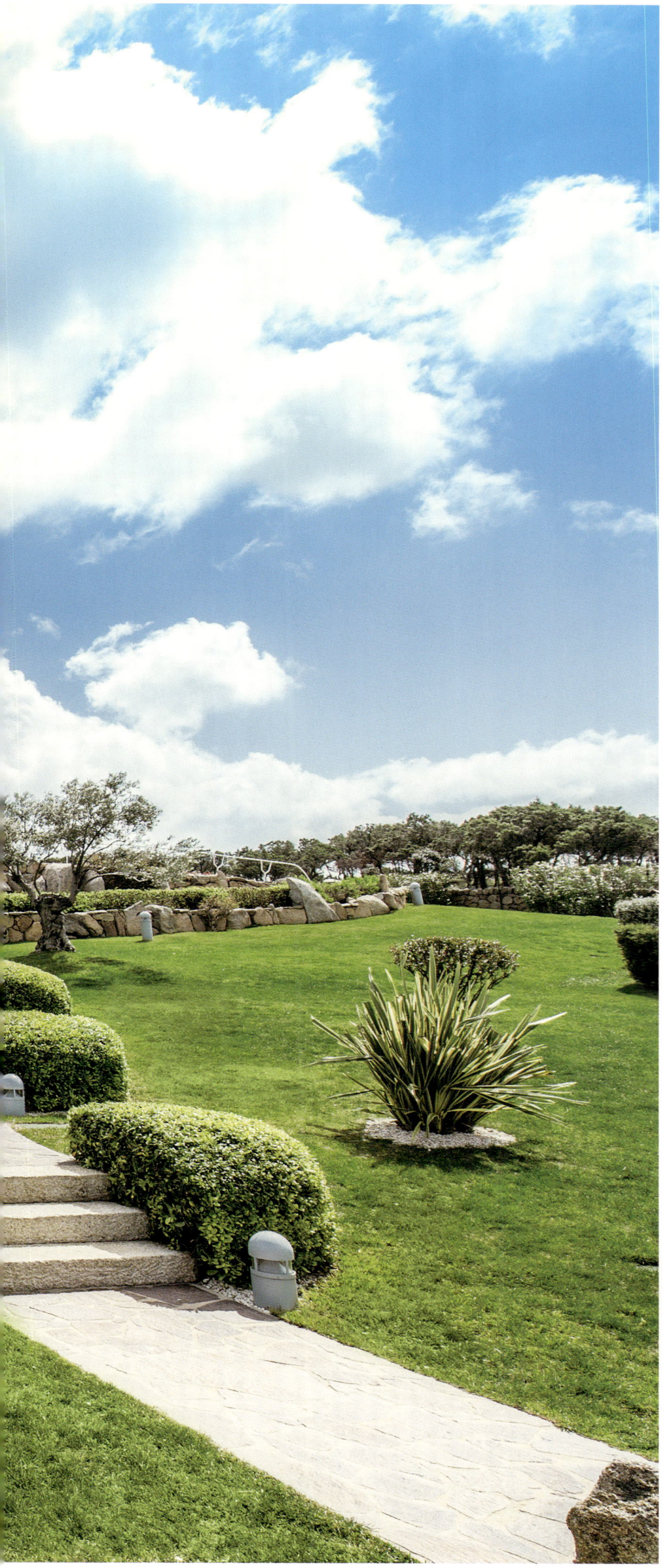

&lt;

Simply magnificent: the villa with its
beautiful garden and sprawling lawn.

Einfach himmlisch: das imposante Gartenareal mit seinen weitläufigen Rasenflächen.

Simplemente magnífica: la villa, envuelta en
sus exquisitos jardines y un mar de césped.

Exceptional views of the Sardinian landscape
can be taken in when relaxing by the pool.

Vom Pool aus genießt man unvergleichliche
Ausblicke auf die sardische Landschaft.

La atractiva piscina paisajística
ofrece vistas totalmente incomparables.

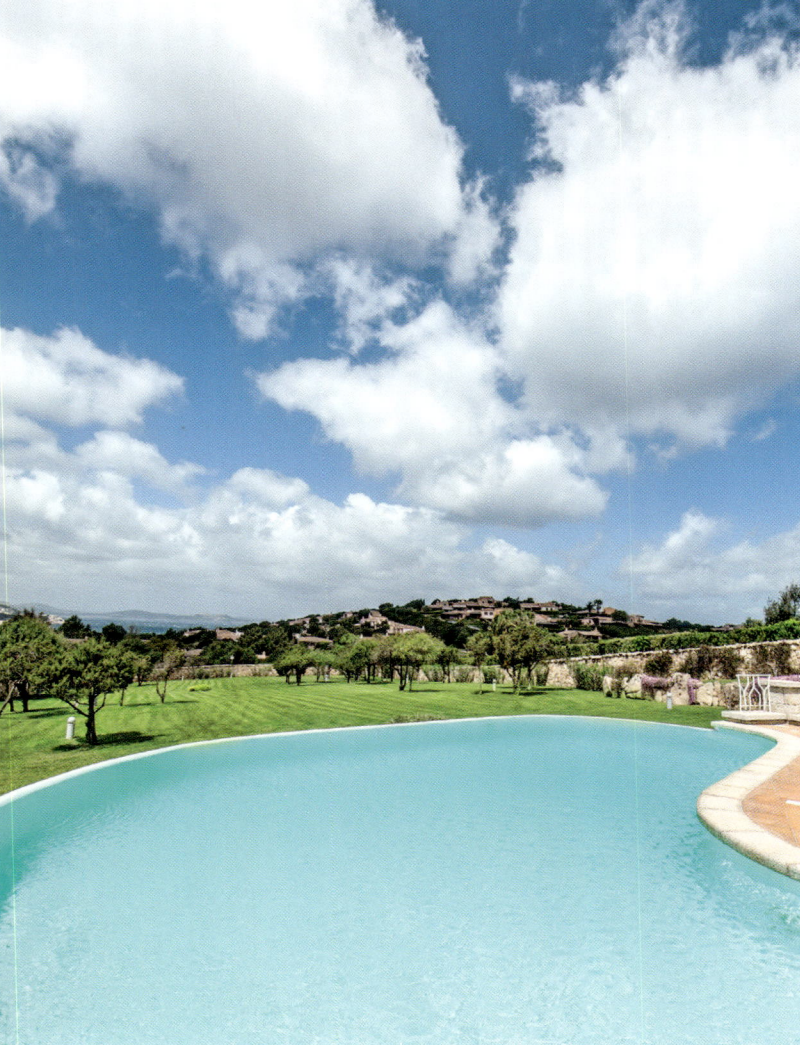

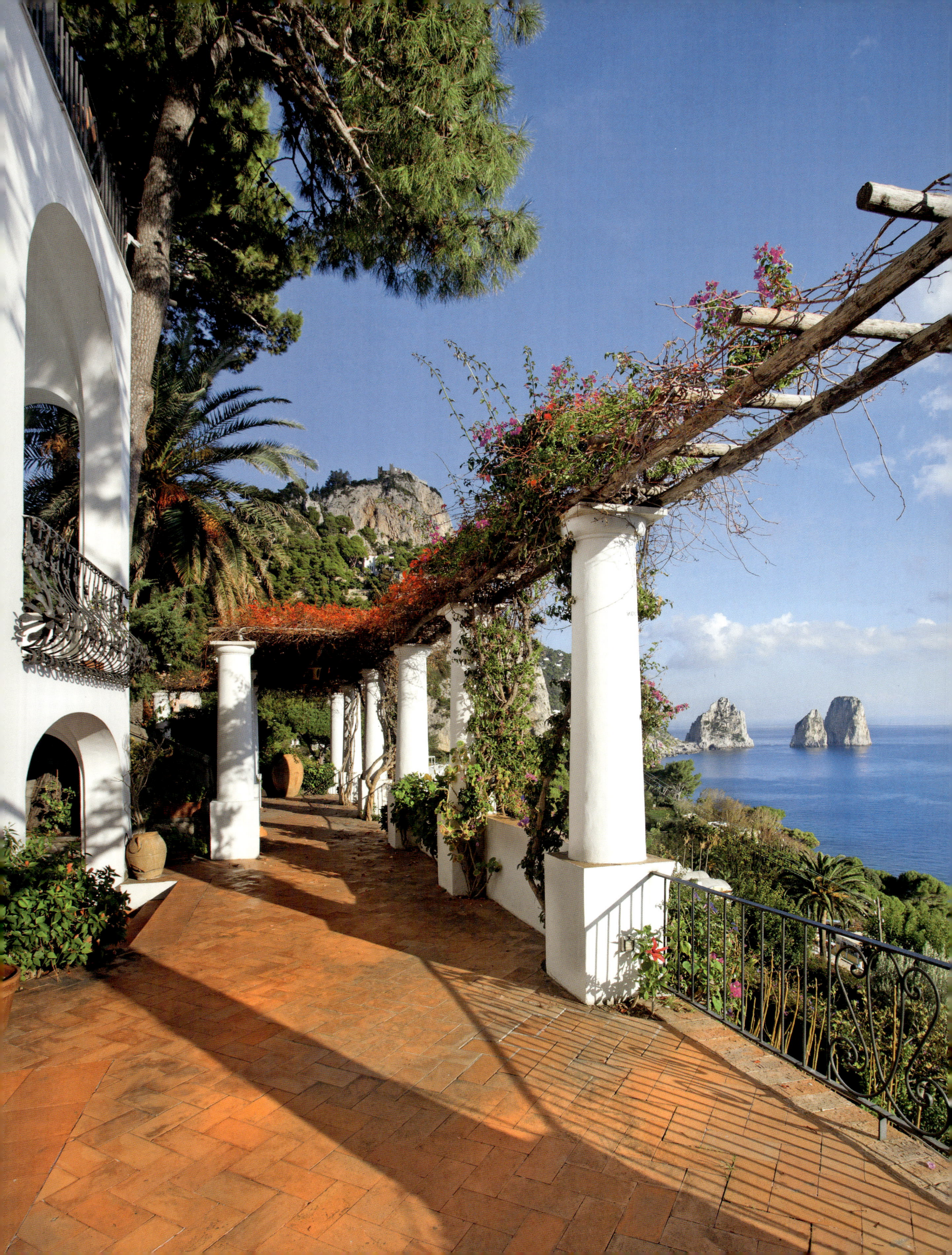

# Scenic Capri Charm

This enchanting villa with picture-perfect appeal and unrivalled ocean views lies in Marina Piccola, only a short stroll from the celebrated lively "piazzetta" of Capri.

THE FABULOUS ISLE of Capri: a famous site since the ancient Roman times, the legendary setting for countless films and literary works, and fragrant home of the delicious Limoncello liqueur. With its mild year-round climate and many hills, vineyards, cliffs and gardens amidst a spectacular Mediterranean backdrop, Capri is a perfect holiday destination. This attractive three-level villa dating from 1900 boasts spectacular views of the renowned "Faraglioni", three vertical rocks protruding from the azure-blue sea. With its luminous living room, spacious dining area and a kitchen that opens onto a terrace of around 120 square metres, the delightful holiday home ensures a pleasurable ambience. The residence has six bedrooms, all with vistas of the sea, and six bathrooms exuding abundant Italian charm. Alongside the high ceilings and ornate flooring, the furnishings are tasteful and chosen with an eye for detail. The property has driveway access with space for two cars. Finally, a pretty garden immerses the villa in a sea of Mediterranean perfumes surrounded by the magic of Capri.

DIE BERÜHMTE INSEL Capri ist dank ihrer pittoresken Mittelmeerlandschaft mit Hügeln, Felsen und Weinbergen nicht nur Schauplatz zahlreicher Werke aus Film und Literatur, sondern auch Heimat des köstlichen Limoncello-Likörs. Eine wunderbare Kulisse für diese dreistöckige Villa aus dem Jahr 1900, die neben einer spektakulären Aussicht auf die berühmten „Faraglioni", drei aus dem Meer herausragende Felsformationen, über ein einladendes Wohnzimmer, einen geräumigen Essbereich, eine Küche, die sich zu einer ca. 120 Quadratmeter großen Terrasse öffnet, sechs Schlafzimmer mit Meerblick sowie sechs Bäder verfügt. Neben den hohen Decken und kunstvoll verzierten Böden fällt hier vor allem das mit viel Detailliebe ausgewählte Mobiliar ins Auge, das den typisch italienischen Charme dieser Immobilie noch unterstreicht. Eine eigene Auffahrt mit Platz für zwei Autos sowie ein romantischer Garten, der herrlichste mediterrane Düfte verströmt, machen diese Villa zu einem Domizil für unvergessliche Ferien – umgeben vom magischen Panorama Capris.

LA FABULOSA ISLA de Capri: famoso retiro vacacional desde los tiempos de los antiguos romanos, célebre escenario para incontables películas y obras literarias y fragante hogar del delicioso Limoncello. Con su suave clima durante todo el año y eternas colinas, acantilados, viñedos y jardines ante el telón de fondo del Mediterráneo, Capri es un destino de vacaciones perfecto. Esta atractiva villa en tres niveles que data de 1900 cuenta con fabulosas vistas a los famosos Faraglioni, tres rocas verticales que surgen del mar azul celeste. La encantadora casa de vacaciones garantiza serenidad con su luminoso salón, la gran zona de comedor y la generosa cocina que se abre a la terraza de 120 metros cuadrados, y suma seis dormitorios, todos con vistas al mar, y seis baños que destilan abundante encanto italiano. Techos altos y suelos intrincados redondean la decoración de buen gusto y con ojo para el detalle. La propiedad cuenta con acceso rodado para dos coches. Como colofón, un bello jardín sumerge la villa en un mar de aromas mediterráneos, envueltos en la magia de Capri.

ITALY, CAPRI **RENTAL PRICE/WEEK** ON REQUEST **INTERIOR APPROX.** 570 m²
**NO. OF BEDROOMS** 6 **LAND APPROX.** 600 m² **E&V ID** W-01V1UK **CONTACT** ISCHIA (IT), LUXURY IN S.R.L.,
LICENCE PARTNER OF ENGEL & VÖLKERS ITALIA S.R.L. **TEL.** +39 081 333 10 58
**E-MAIL** ISCHIA@ENGELVOELKERS.COM

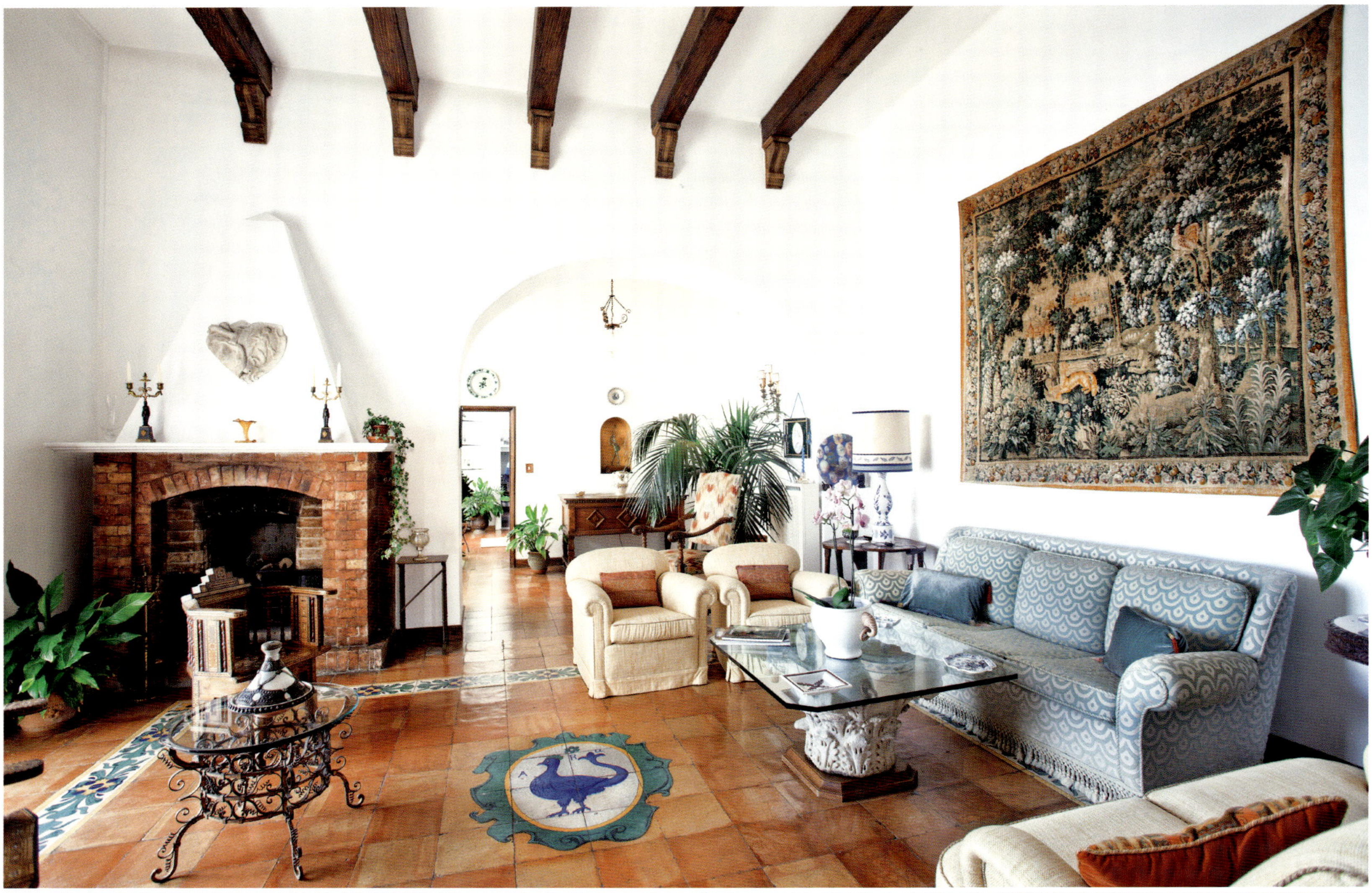

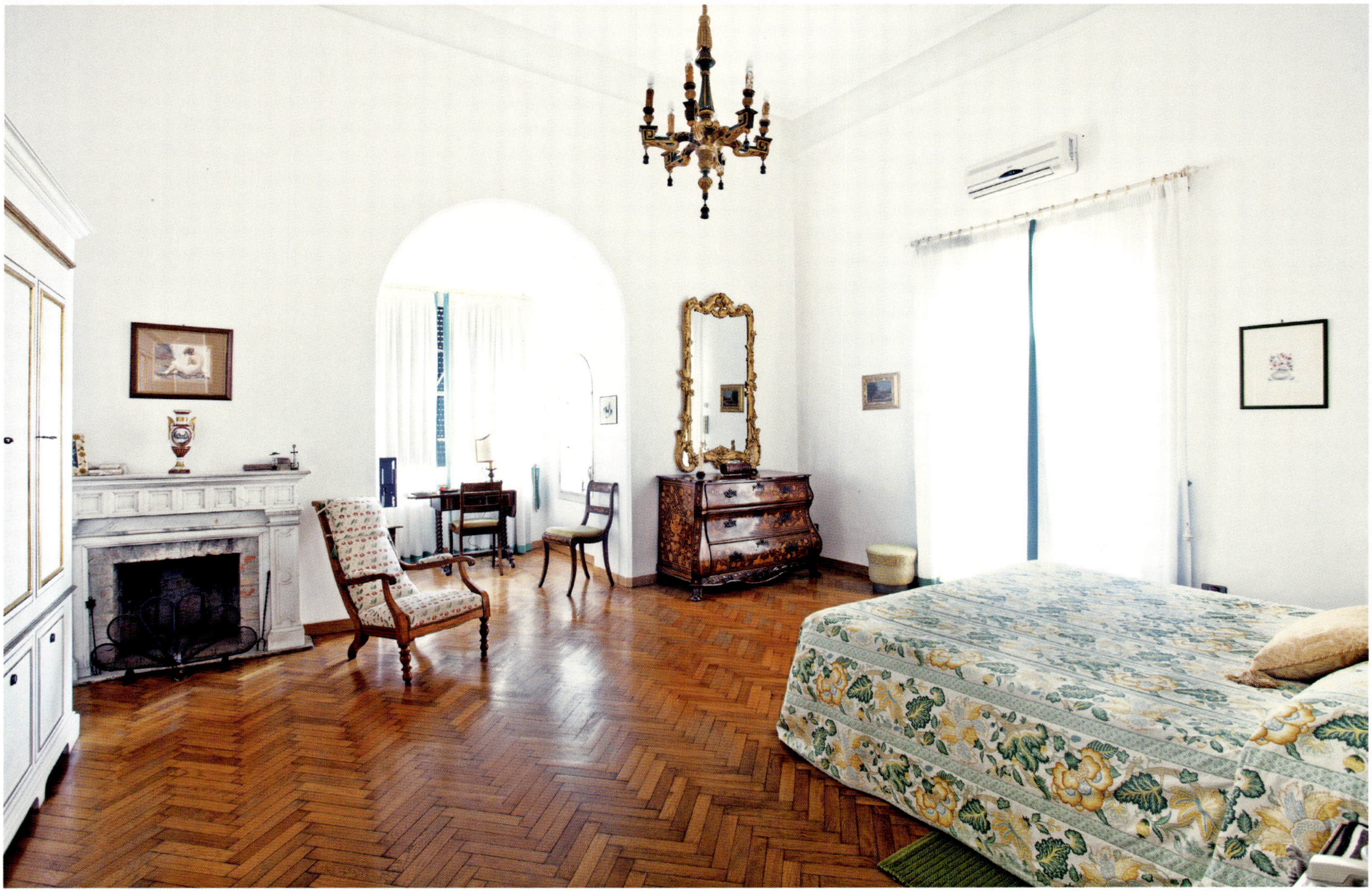

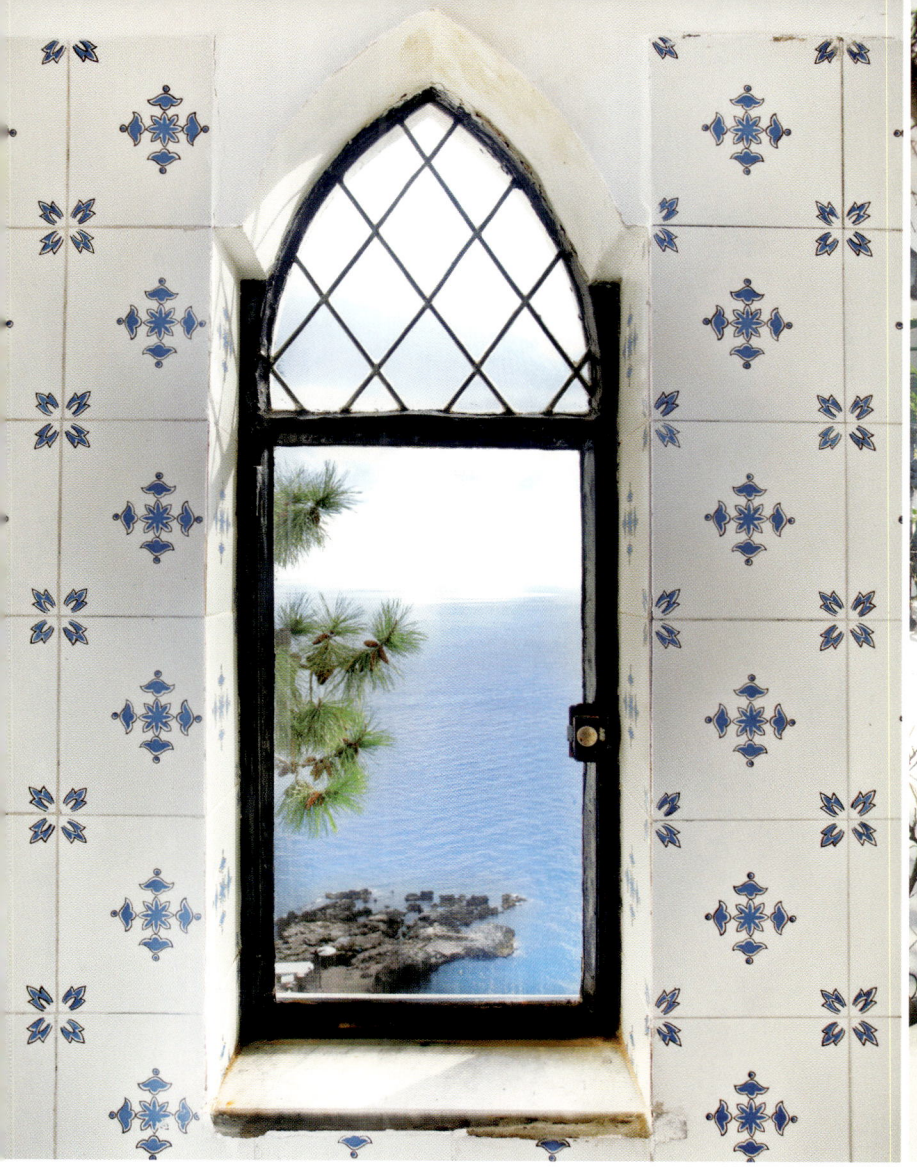

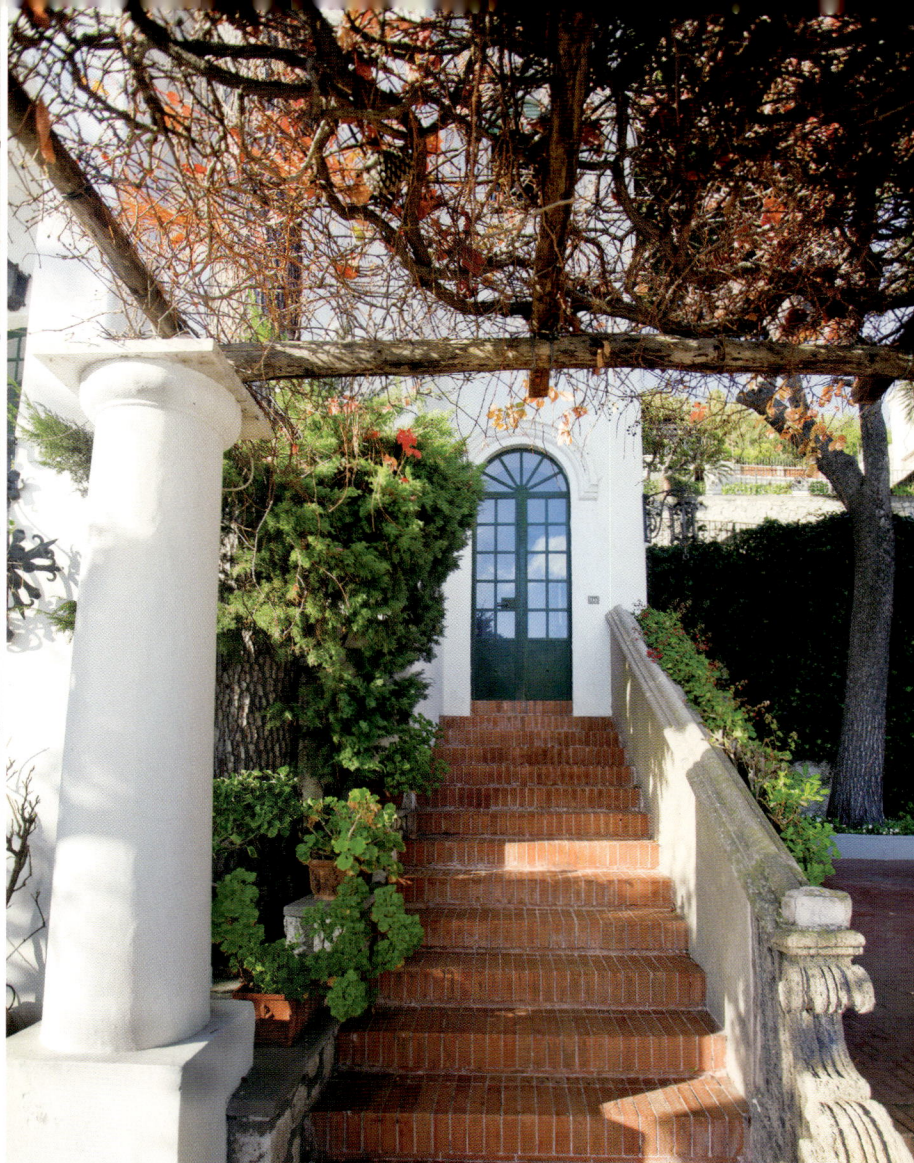

Enchanting details abound in this holiday villa,
affording captivating vistas of the sea.

Die zauberhaften Details der Villa werden
gekrönt von einem sagenhaften Ausblick.

Los detalles con encanto abundan en esta villa
de vacaciones con seductoras vistas al mar.

<

Spacious, light-flooded interiors with a
timeless appeal and Italian finesse.

Die großzügigen, lichtdurchfluteten Räume
strahlen zeitlosen italienischen Charme aus.

Interiores amplios y luminosos con un sinfín de
atractivo atemporal y refinamiento italiano.

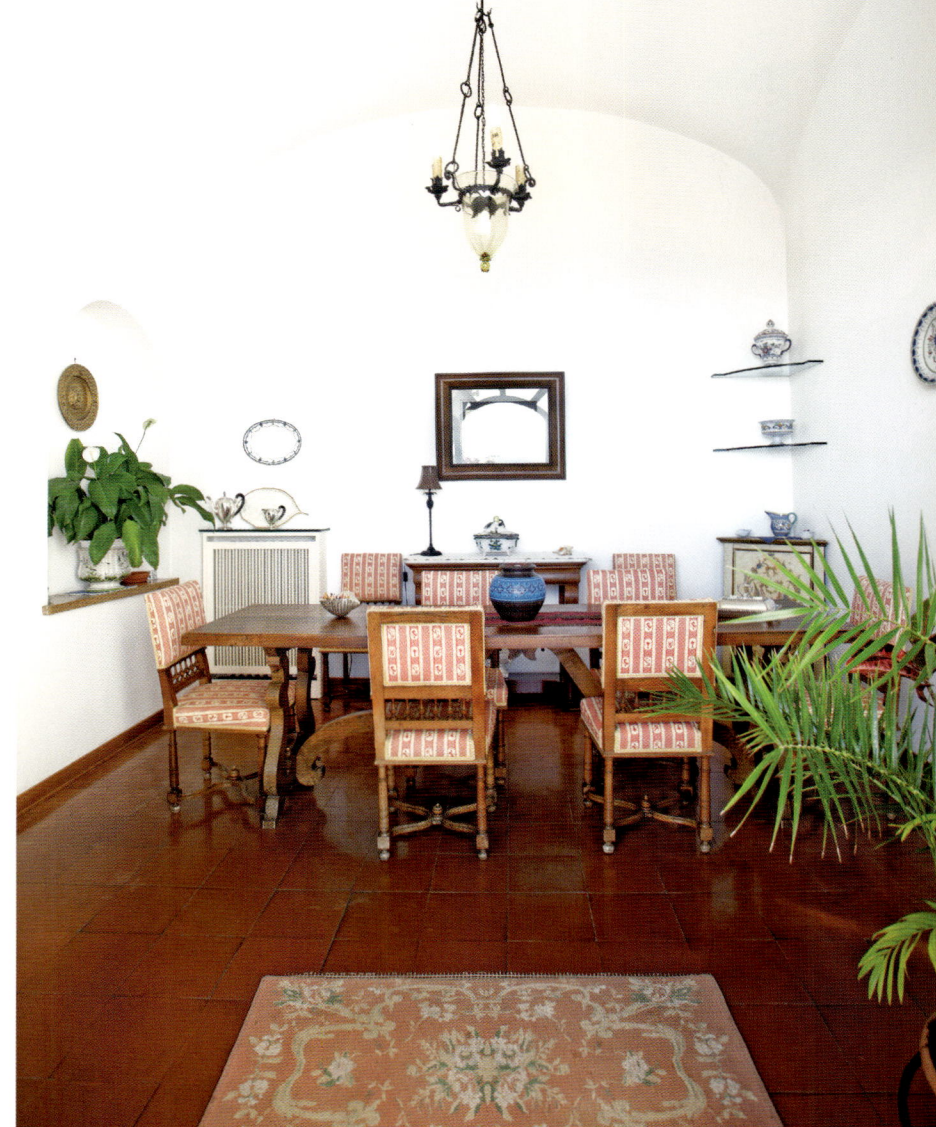

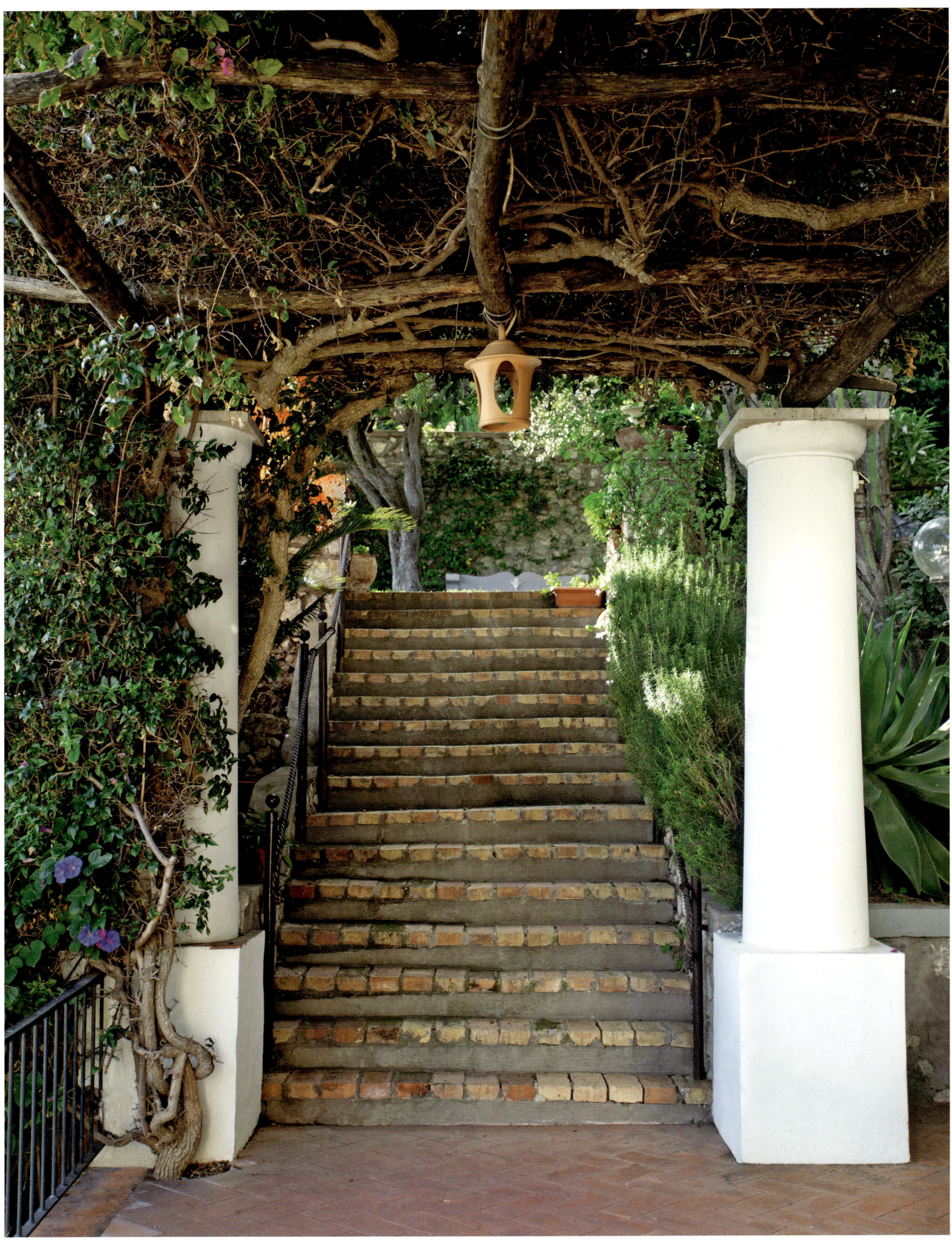

Secluded and romantic, the villa's fragrant
garden casts its Mediterranean magic.

Der geschützte, wildromantische Garten
verströmt mediterran duftende Magie.

Íntimo y maduro, el romántico jardín de la villa
destila toda su seductora magia mediterránea.

With around 120 square metres, the terrace
offers heavenly views of the coast.

Die rund 120 Quadratmeter große Terrasse
bietet himmlische Ausblicke auf die Küste.

Con 120 metros cuadrados, la terraza también
brinda vistas celestiales de postal a la costa.

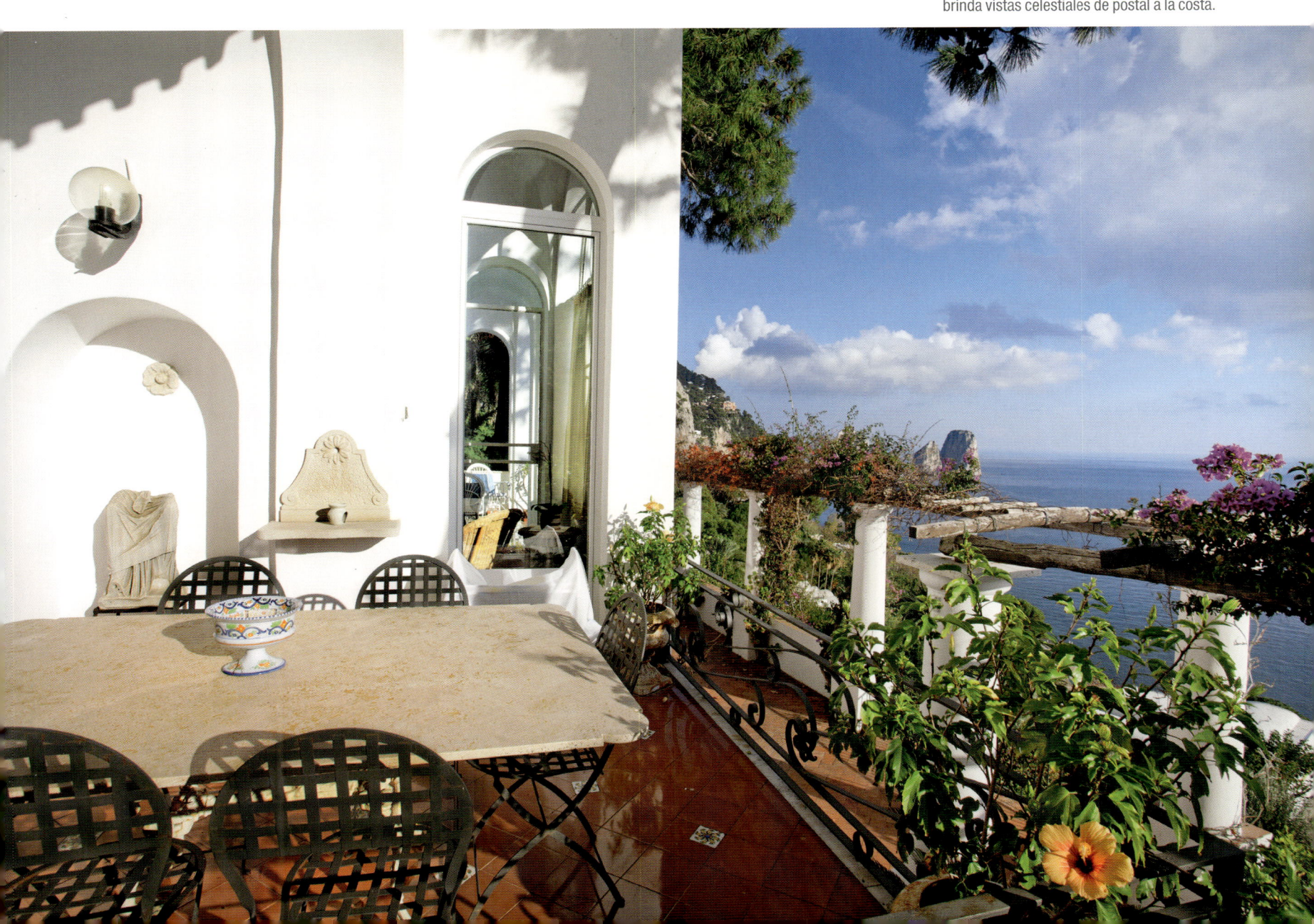

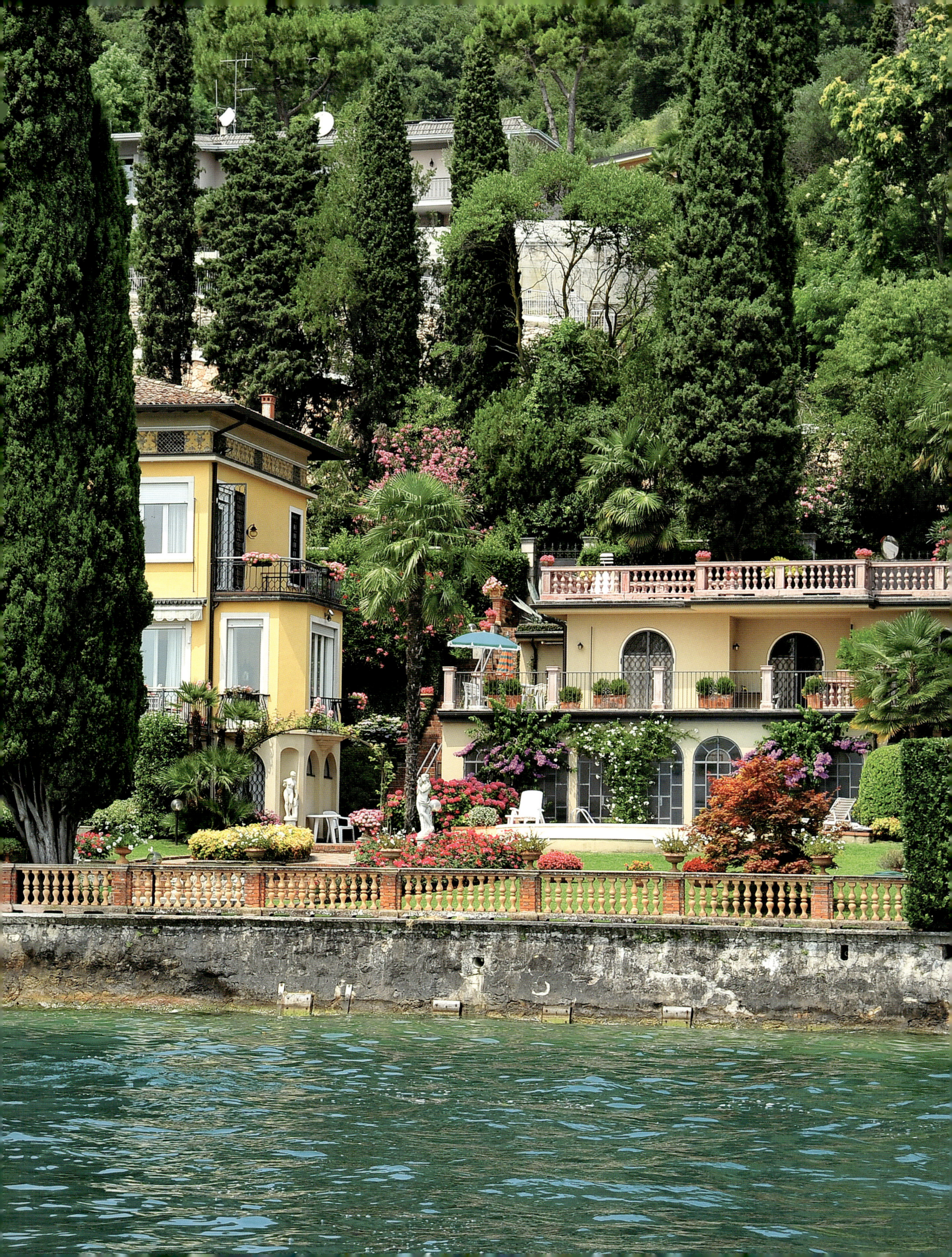

# Historic Villa in Salò

A charming property graced with a top location directly on the banks of Lake Garda – ideal as a family residence or as a magnificent second home.

THE ELEGANT TOWN of Salò lies protected on the south-western shores of legendary Lake Garda in Italy. Its lively historic centre, with its many designer boutiques and inviting restaurants, is nestled behind a long water-front promenade – and only a kilometre away from the centre resides this delightful historic villa with a self-contained smaller building at its side. Encompassed by a large and well-kept park, which – 1,500 square metres in size – also has a swimming pool and an enchanting historic fountain, the three-storey period residence boasts two living rooms, five bedrooms, four bathrooms, a fully fitted kitchen and a large portico covered by an impressive panoramic terrace. Built in 1910, the villa has been fully restored and renovated. The lovely adjacent house contains a fitness area with direct access to the pool and a separate apartment for a custodian or for guests, including a large terrace that overlooks the scenic lake. All in all, this early-twentieth-century villa in Salò is a sensational dwelling for all those who wish to enjoy "il dolce far niente" in their very own fashion!

DAS ELEGANTE STÄDTCHEN Salò befindet sich in erstklassiger, geschützter Lage am südwestlichen Gardasee. Hinter einer langen Uferpromenade erstreckt sich seine lebendige Altstadt mit vielen Designer-Boutiquen und einladenden Restaurants – und nur einen Kilometer entfernt lädt diese nicht minder charmante, historische Villa mit zugehöriger Dependance zum Rundum-Wohlfühlen und Entspannen ein. Umgeben von einem 1.500 Quadratmeter großen Garten mit Swimmingpool und einem denkmalgeschützten Brunnen, verfügt das dreistöckige, im Jahr 1910 erbaute und komplett sanierte Anwesen über zwei Wohn- und fünf Schlafzimmer, vier Bäder, eine Einbauküche sowie einen großen Portico mit darüberliegender Panorama-terrasse. In der Dependance befinden sich ein Fitnessbereich mit Zugang zum Pool sowie eine separate geräumige Personal- bzw. Gästeunterkunft samt Terrasse mit Blick auf den malerischen See. Alles in allem ein ideales Domizil für all jene, die „il dolce far niente" auf ihre ganz eigene Weise genießen wollen!

LA ELEGANTE LOCALIDAD de Salò queda resguardada en la ensoñadora costa sudoeste del legendario lago de Garda. Su vibrante casco antiguo, con numerosas *boutiques* de diseño y coquetos restaurantes, corre paralelo al largo paseo marítimo, y a sólo un kilómetro del centro se alzan esta preciosa villa histórica y su casita aparte. Envuelta en un gran y bellamente atendido terreno de unos 1.500 metros cuadrados que luce la piscina y una en-cantadora fuente histórica, la residencia de tres plantas cuenta con dos salas de estar, cinco dormitorios, cuatro baños, la cocina totalmente equipada y un amplio pórtico con una impresionante terraza panorámica. Construi-da en 1910, la villa ha sido completamente restaurada y renovada. El igualmente romántico edificio adyacente al-berga hoy una zona de *fitness* con salida a la piscina y un apartamento independiente para el guarda o invitados, además de una gran terraza con vistas al pintoresco lago. Con todo, esta villa de principios del siglo XX en Salò resulta el hogar idóneo para quienes deseen disfrutar del *dolce far niente* a su manera y estilo.

ITALY, LAKE GARDA **PURCHASE PRICE** EUR 7.5 MILL. **INTERIOR APPROX.** 480 m² **NO. OF BEDROOMS** 6 **LAND APPROX.** 2,070 m²
**E&V ID** W-0197CD **CONTACT** DESENZANO DEL GARDA (IT), GOLDEN HOUSE REAL ESTATE S.R.L.,
LICENCE PARTNER OF ENGEL & VÖLKERS ITALIA S.R.L **TEL.** +39 030 990 73 76
**E-MAIL** DESENZANODELGARDA@ENGELVOELKERS.COM

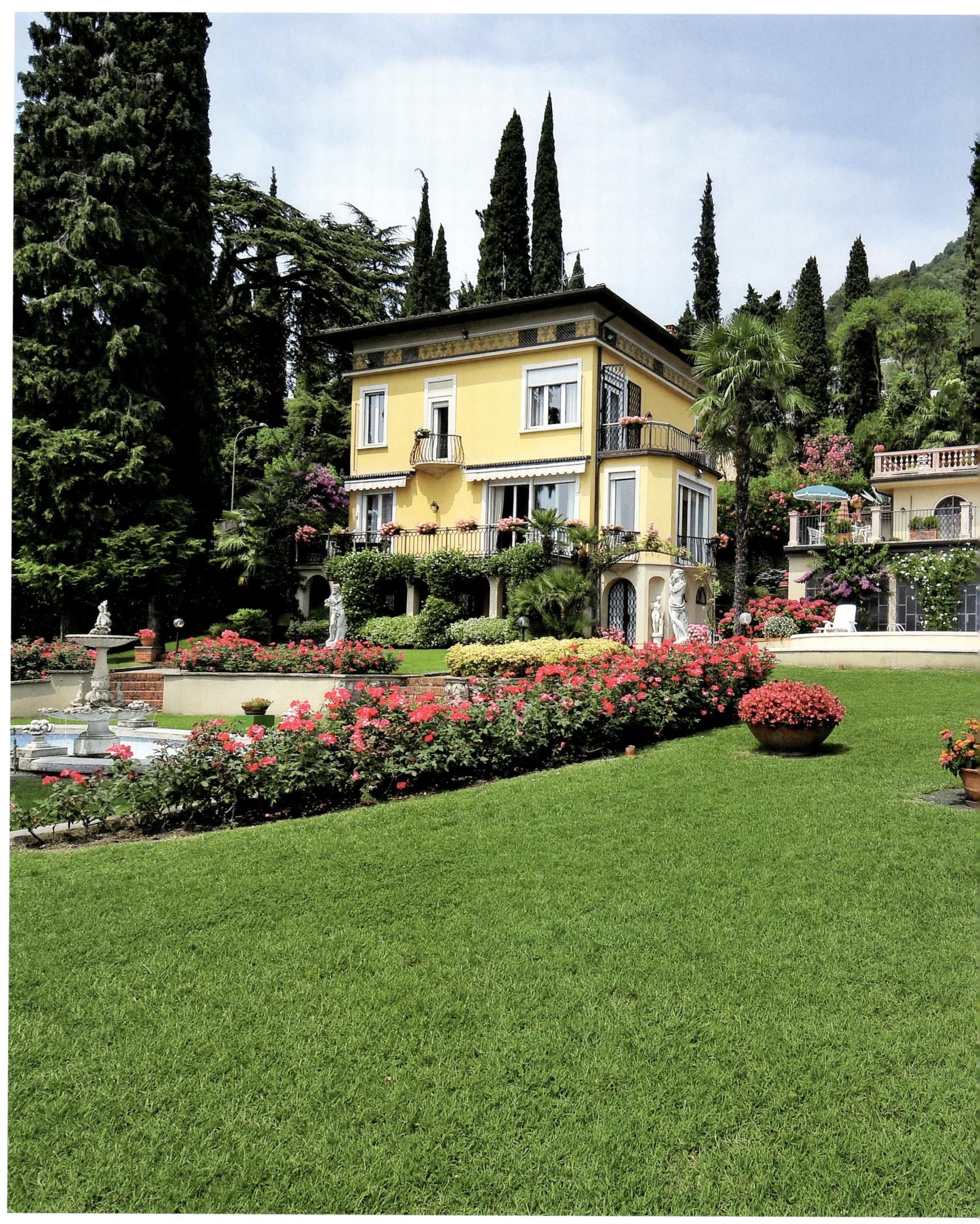

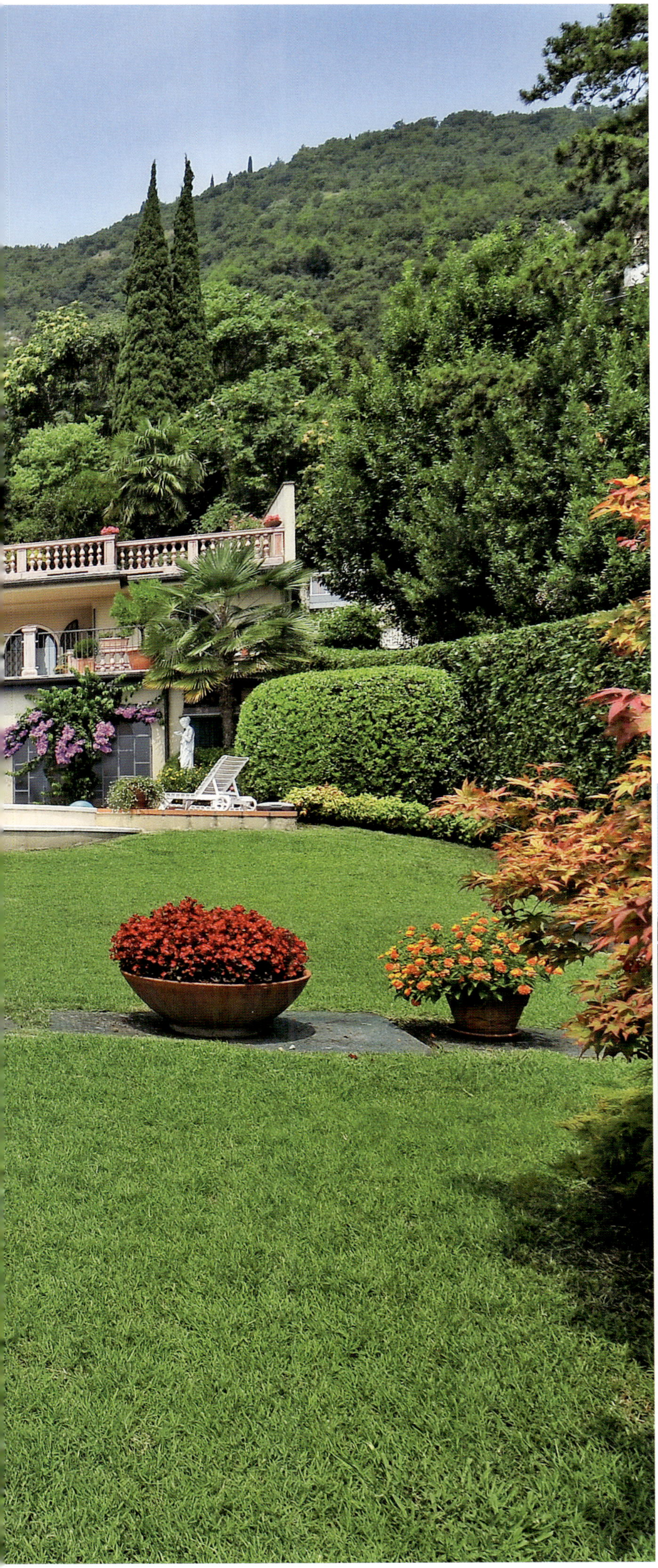

<

The gorgeous villa and landscaped park
radiate extensive Italian charm.

Die wunderschöne Villa mit ihrem prachtvollen
Garten besticht durch ihr italienisches Flair.

La preciosa villa y el terreno ajardinado en
todo su esplendor irradian encanto italiano.

For utmost enjoyment: the oval pool is located
as close to the lake's edge as possible.

Dem Himmel so nah: Der ovale Pool
befindet sich fast unmittelbar am Seeufer.

Para mayor disfrute: la piscina oval no podría
estar más cerca de la orilla del lago.

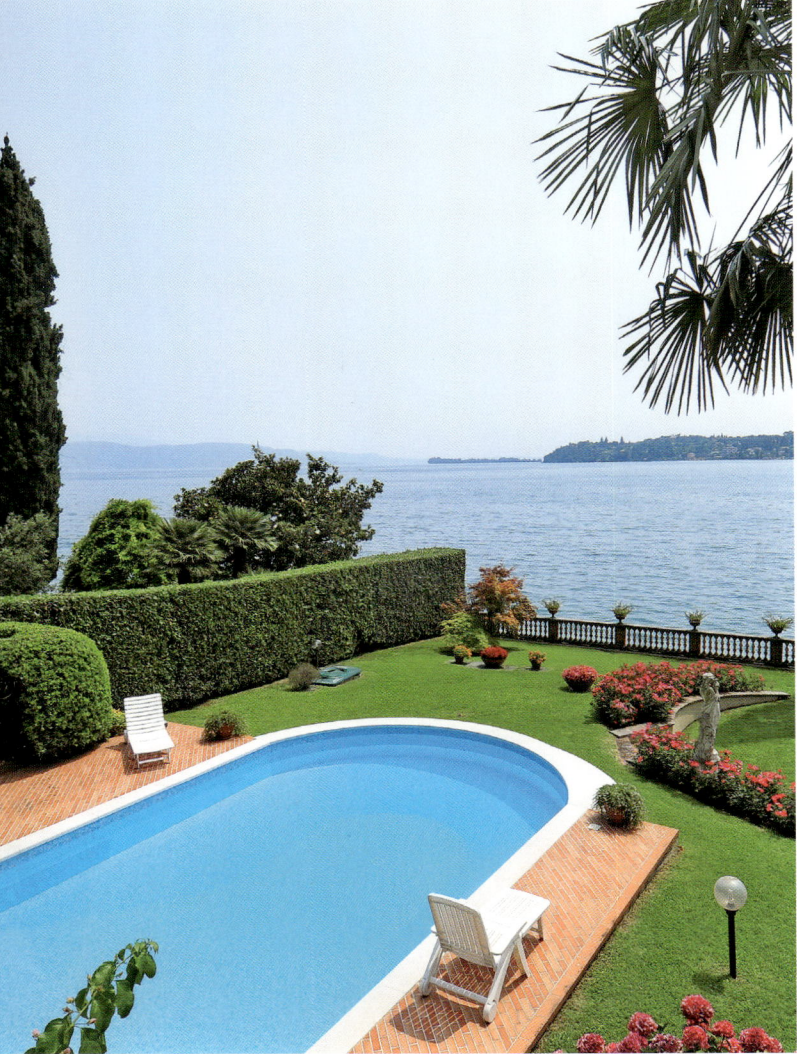

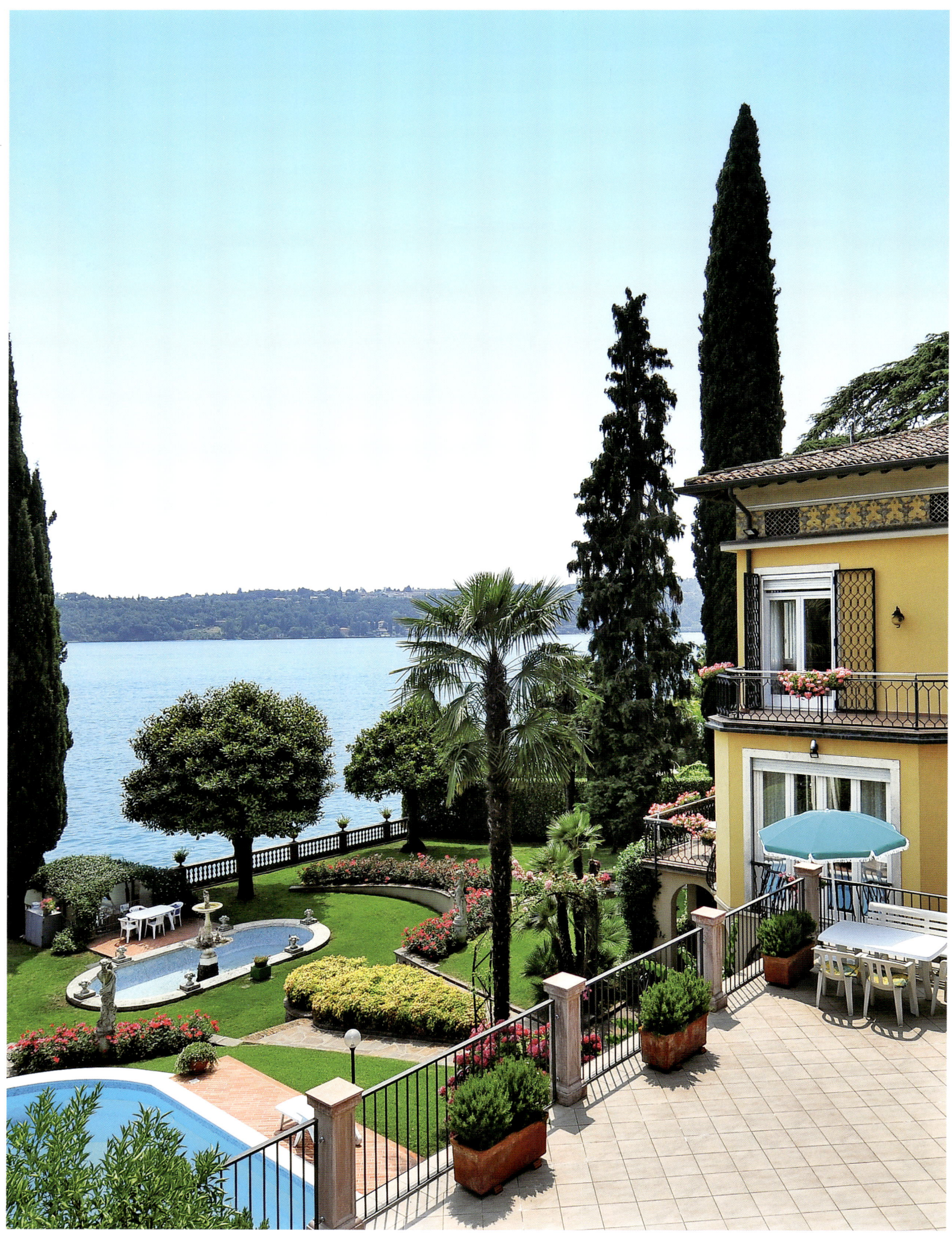

<

The rooftop terrace is the best place for enjoying views across Lake Garda.

Von der Dachterrasse lässt sich die Aussicht über den Gardasee am besten genießen.

La azotea es el mejor sitio para disfrutar las irrepetibles panorámicas al lago de Garda.

Admirers of romantic gardens will never tire of strolling through this lakefront paradise.

Auch und gerade für Liebhaber romantischer Gärten ist dieses Anwesen wie geschaffen.

Los fans de los jardines románticos no se cansarán jamás de pasear por este paraíso.

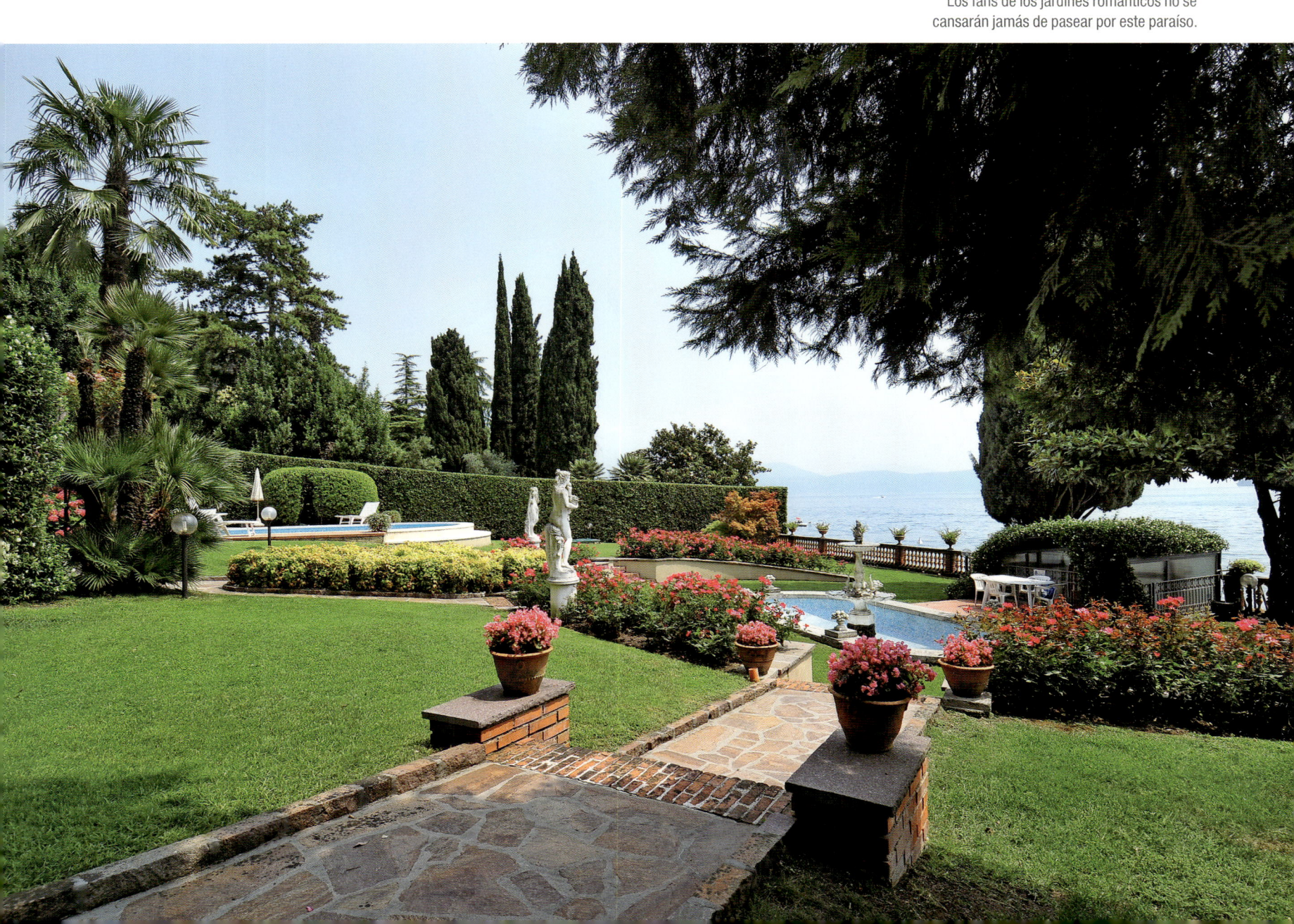

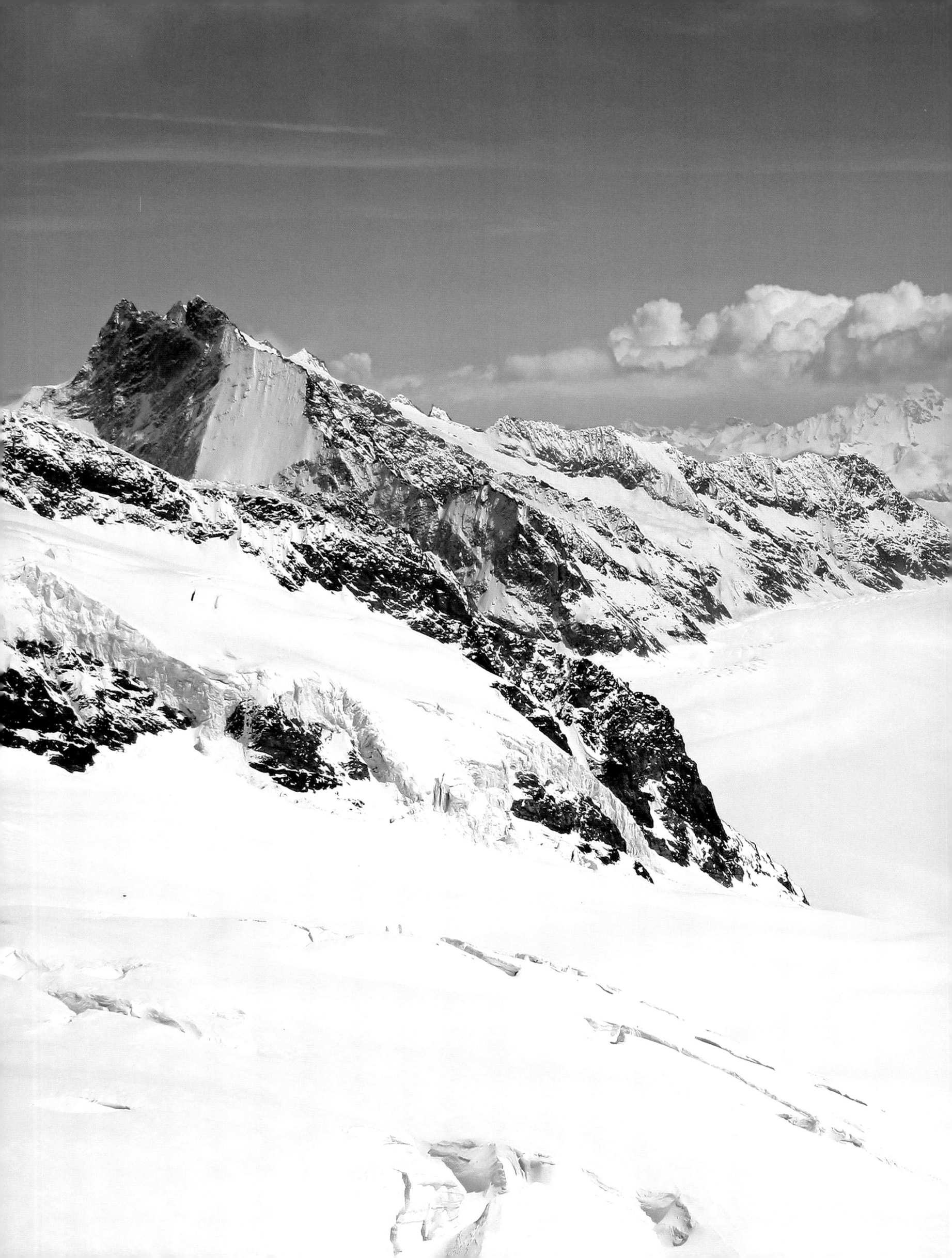

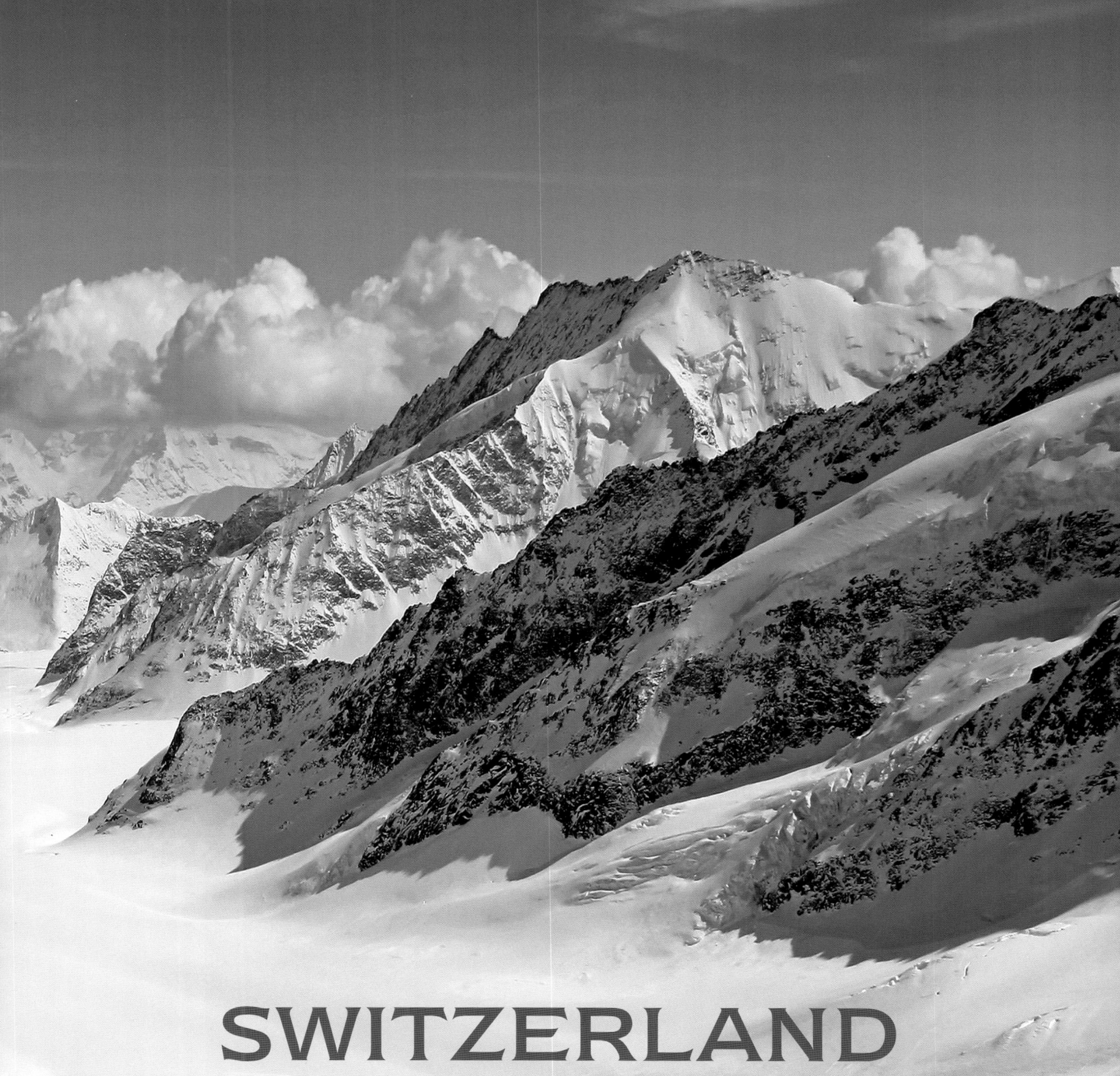

# SWITZERLAND

### Gstaad · St. Moritz

A hotspot not just for the international jet set, Switzerland
is captivating with its sublime Alpine landscapes, prestigious
chalet villages and a mix of tradition and glamour.

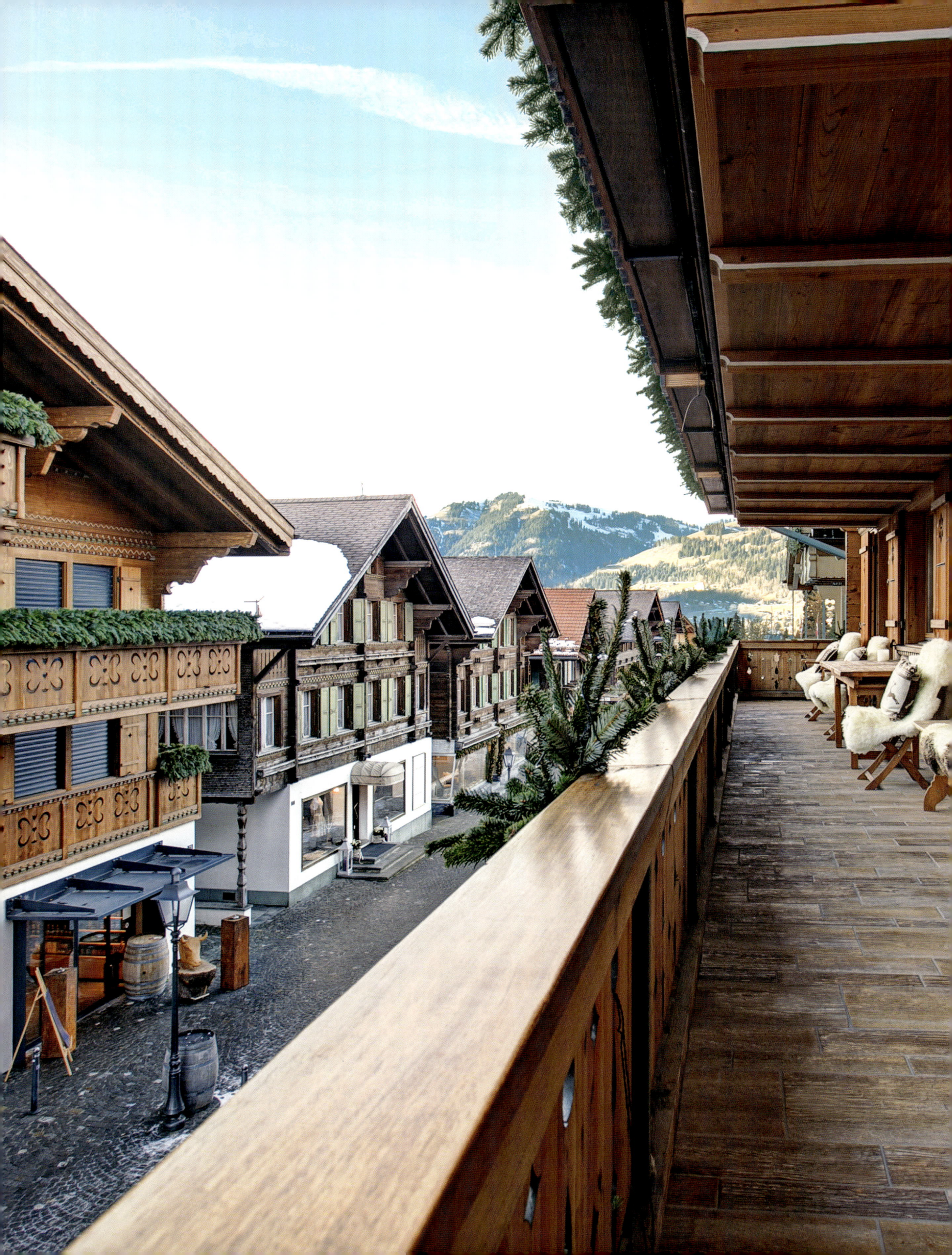

# Luxury Village Flat

Situated directly on the promenade of Gstaad, this exquisite apartment cannot fail to impress, ensuring an extraordinary quality of life in the midst of the Alps.

PICTURESQUE MOUNTAIN PANORAMAS, first-class skiing areas, exquisite restaurants and excellent shopping – Gstaad enjoys the worldwide reputation of an exclusive and prestigious holiday region that is certainly worth visiting. This fine apartment in one of the typical chalets not only profits from its prime location in the heart of the famous promenade of Gstaad. The interiors also do justice to the most discerning of standards in stylish living; with their high-quality wood panelling and muted colours, they exude a wonderful sense of comfort and warmth. The fully appointed open-plan kitchen and the living room with a cosy fireplace create the perfect setting for relaxing hours spent with friends and family. Furthermore, the apartment boasts four comfortable bedrooms, three of them with en-suite bathrooms. The large-sized balcony, offering plenty of space as well as absolutely breathtaking views of the surrounding mountains, makes a stay in this Alpine dream dwelling even more unforgettable.

MALERISCHE BERGPANORAMEN, Skigebiete auf Weltklasse-Niveau, exquisite Restaurants und erstklassige Shopping-Möglichkeiten – Gstaad genießt weit über die Grenzen der Schweiz hinaus den Ruf einer überaus erlebenswerten, prestigeträchtigen Ferienregion. Dieses Apartment in einem der typischen Chalets punktet jedoch nicht nur durch seine Lage im Herzen der bekannten Promenade von Gstaad. Auch die Räumlichkeiten werden höchsten Ansprüchen an stilvollem Wohnkomfort gerecht und strahlen mit ihren hochwertigen Holzverkleidungen und gedeckten Farben eine ganz besondere Wärme aus. Die offene, komplett eingerichtete Küche und das Wohnzimmer mit Kamin laden zu entspannten Stunden mit Freunden und Familie ein. Das Apartment verfügt darüber hinaus über vier behagliche Schlafzimmer, drei davon mit En-Suite-Bädern. Der großzügige Balkon, der viel Platz und eine wahrhaft atemberaubende Aussicht auf die umliegenden Berge bietet, macht den Aufenthalt in diesem alpinen Traumdomizil noch unvergesslicher.

PINTORESCOS PANORAMAS DE MONTAÑA, estaciones de esquí de primera clase, restaurantes exquisitos y excelentes tiendas y *boutiques*: Gstaad goza de la mejor reputación a nivel mundial y de ser un destino vacacional tan exclusivo como prestigioso, digno merecedor de una visita. Este apartamento forma parte de un típico chalet de los Alpes y se beneficia de su ubicación más que privilegiada en el corazón del famoso paseo de Gstaad, y de interiores que también hacen justicia a los más exigentes estándares del estilo. Paneles de madera de alta calidad y colores neutros exudan sensación de confort y calidez; la cocina de plano abierto y totalmente equipada y el salón con chimenea crean el escenario perfecto donde disfrutar durante horas en compañía de amigos y en familia. Además, cuenta con cuatro cómodos dormitorios, tres de ellos con su cuarto de baño. Pero lo que hace de una estancia aquí algo excepcional e inolvidable es el gran balcón, que ofrece muchísimo espacio así como vistas de ensueño a las montañas que lo rodean por todas partes.

SWITZERLAND, GSTAAD **RENTAL PRICE/WEEK** ON REQUEST **INTERIOR APPROX.** 220 m² **NO. OF BEDROOMS** 4
**E&V ID** W-01T223 **CONTACT** GSTAAD (CH), E&V GSTAAD PROPERTIES AG,
LICENCE PARTNER OF ENGEL & VÖLKERS WOHNEN SCHWEIZ AG **TEL.** +41 33 655 65 05
**E-MAIL** GSTAAD@ENGELVOELKERS.COM

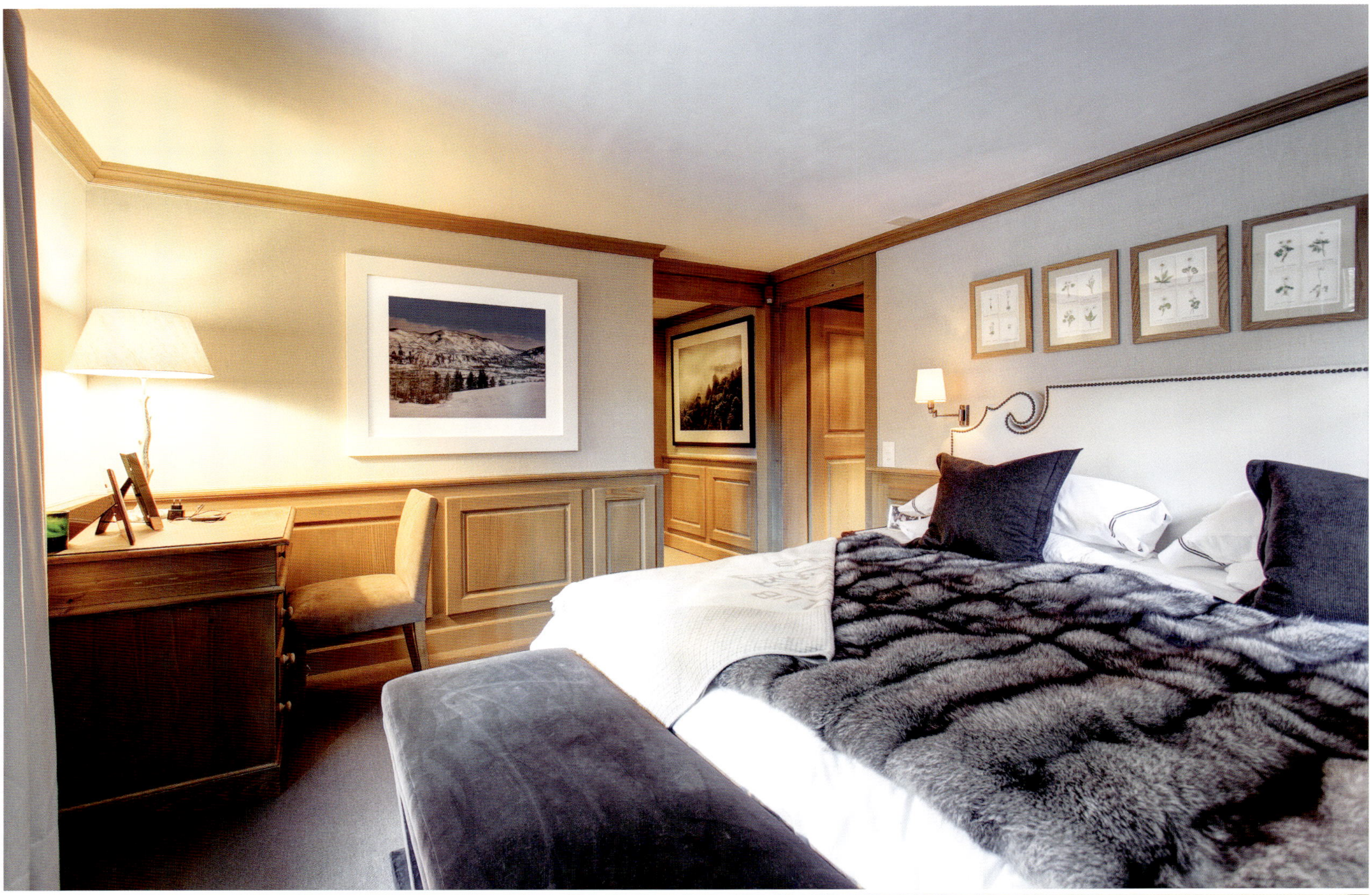

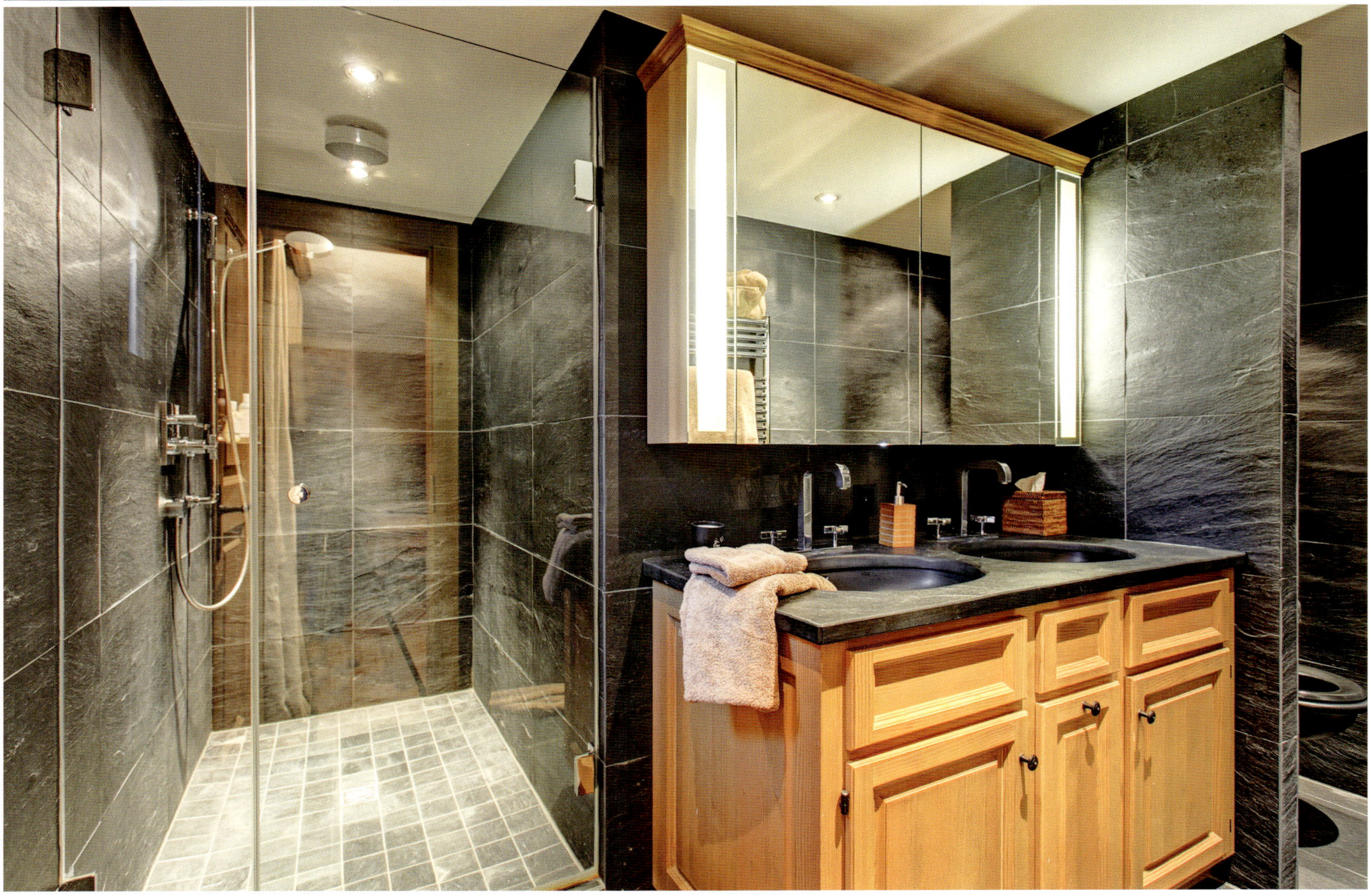

<

Cosiness and comfort were key elements
considered when designing this apartment.

Behaglichkeit und Komfort standen bei der
Gestaltung dieses Apartments an erster Stelle.

Comodidad y confort fueron elementos clave a
considerar en el diseño de este apartamento.

Open spaces, lots of light and real wood
create an inimitable atmosphere.

Offene Räume, viel Licht und edles Holz
schaffen eine einzigartige Atmosphäre.

Espacios abiertos, con mucha luz y madera
maciza, crean una atmósfera inimitable.

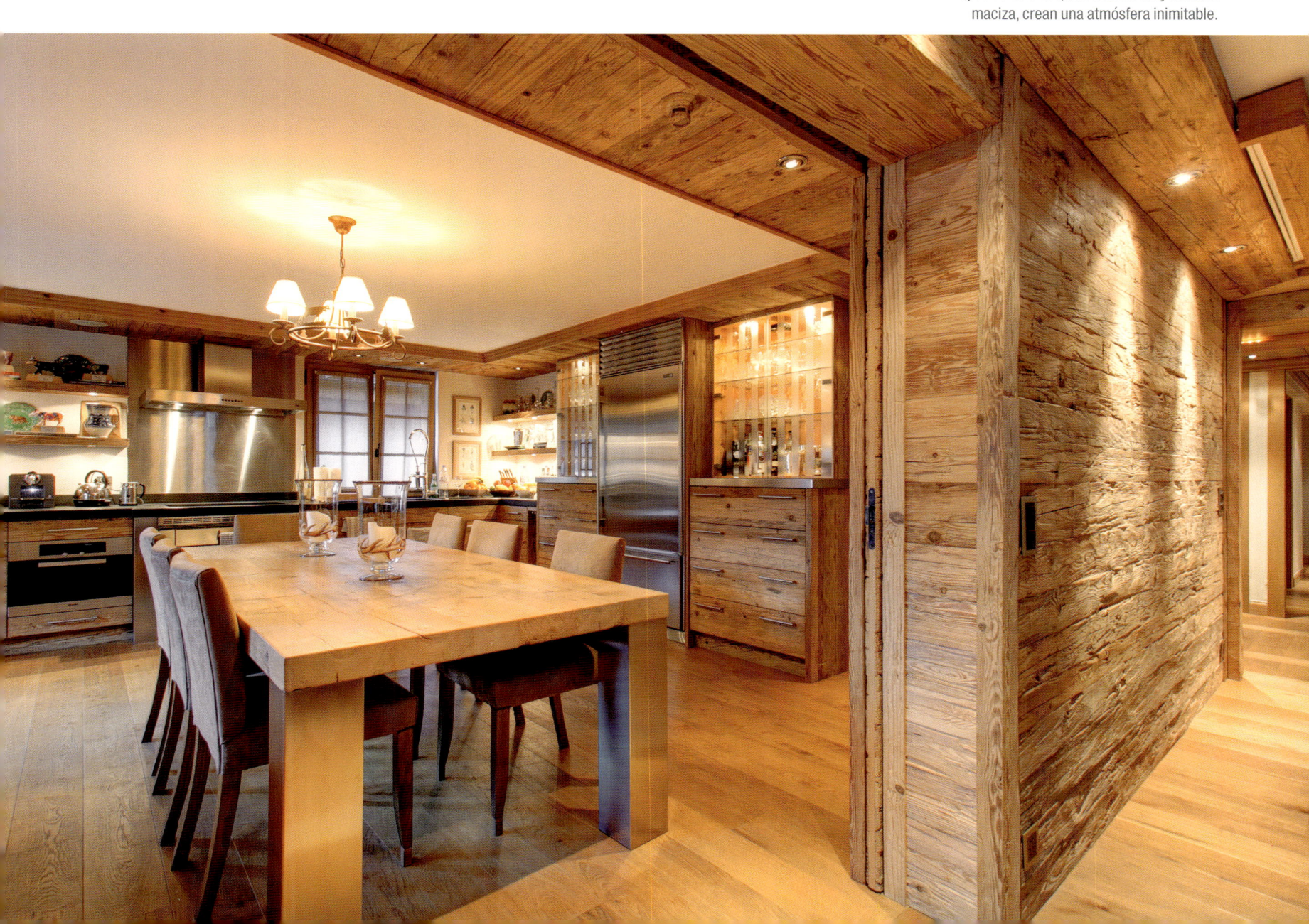

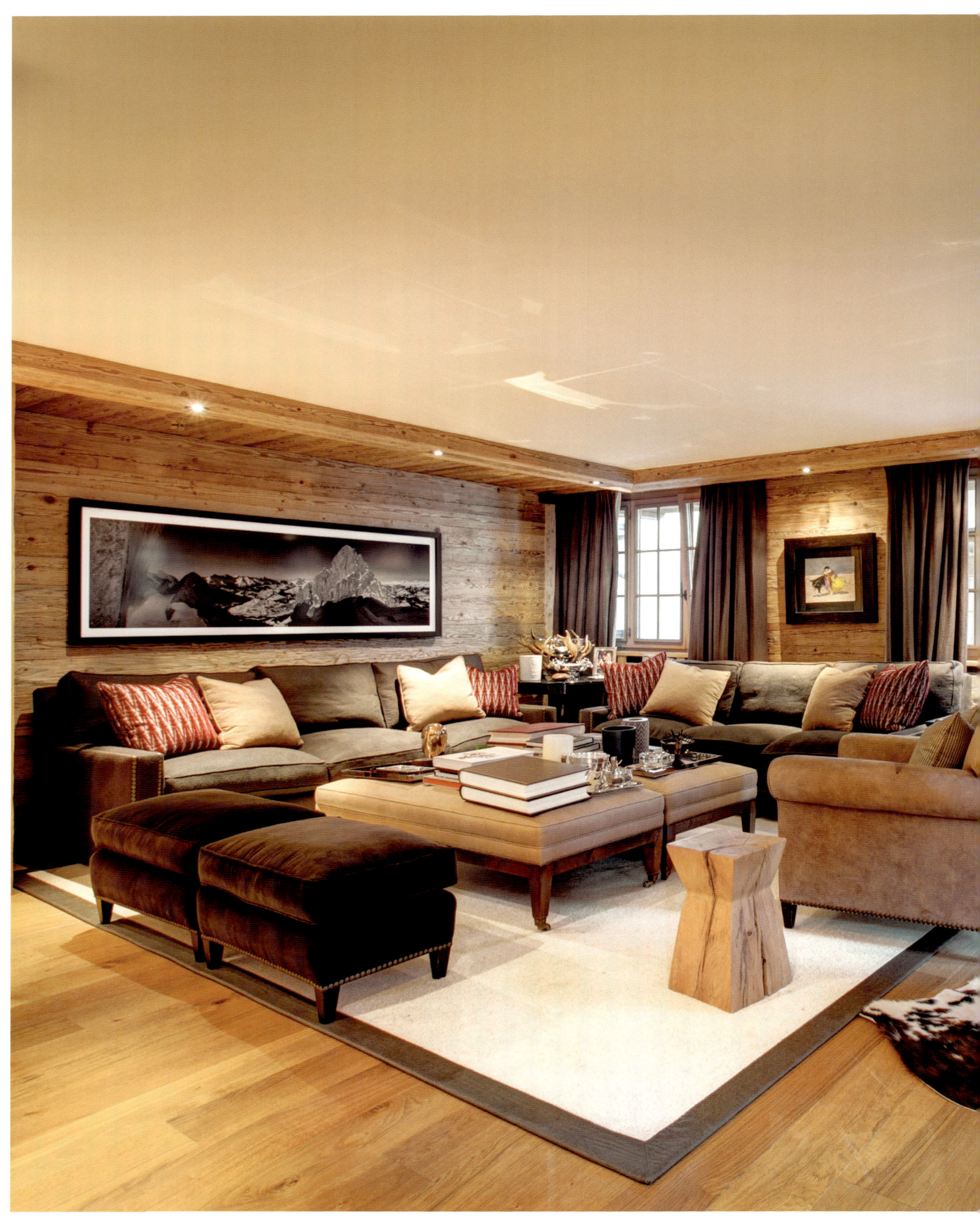

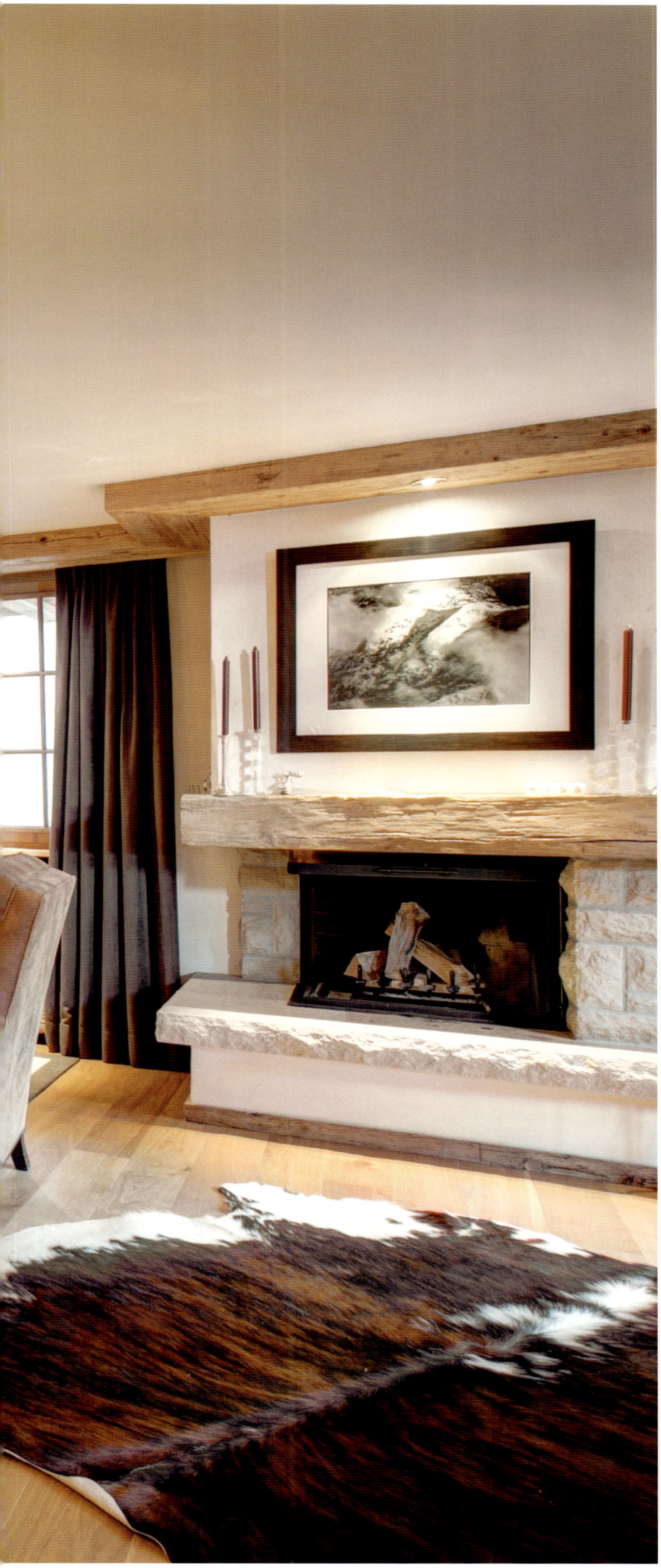

The living area: perfect for social evenings
with friends or romantic hours as a couple.

Der Wohnbereich: perfekt für gesellige Abende
oder romantische Stunden zu zweit.

La sala de estar: perfecta para las noches con
amigos o veladas románticas de a dos.

The large dressing room offers space for
clothing as well as shoes and accessories.

Der geräumige Ankleideraum bietet viel Platz
für Kleidung, Schuhe und Accessoires.

El amplio vestidor ofrece mucho espacio para
la ropa, el calzado y los accesorios.

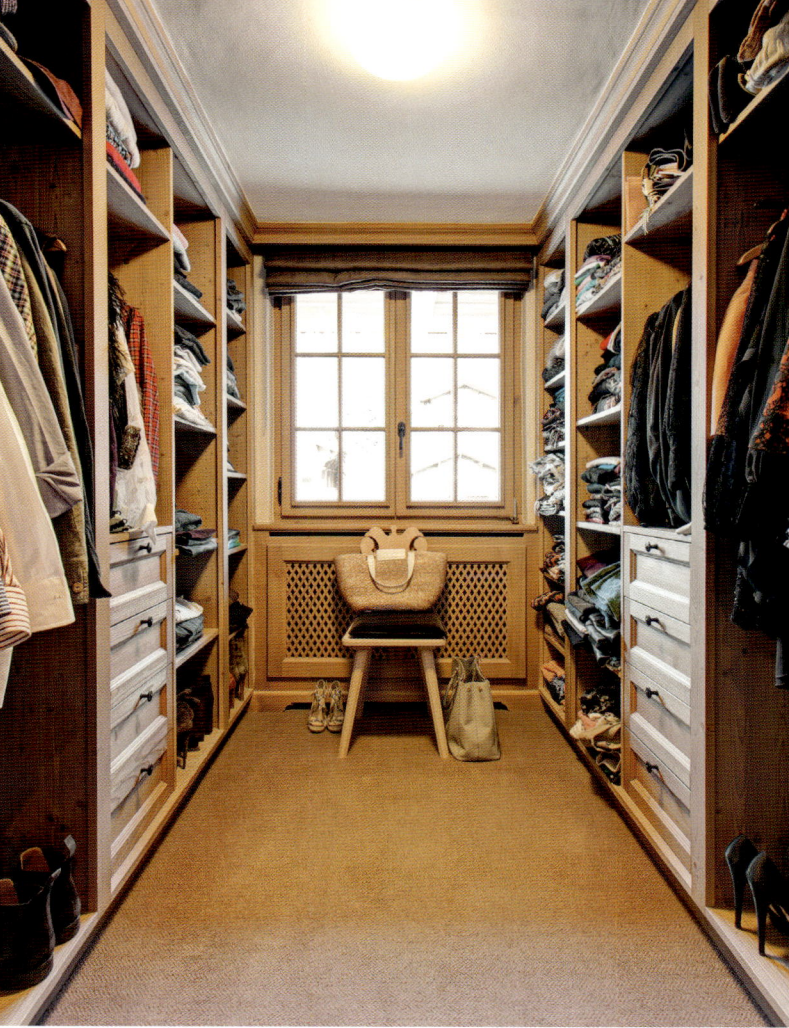

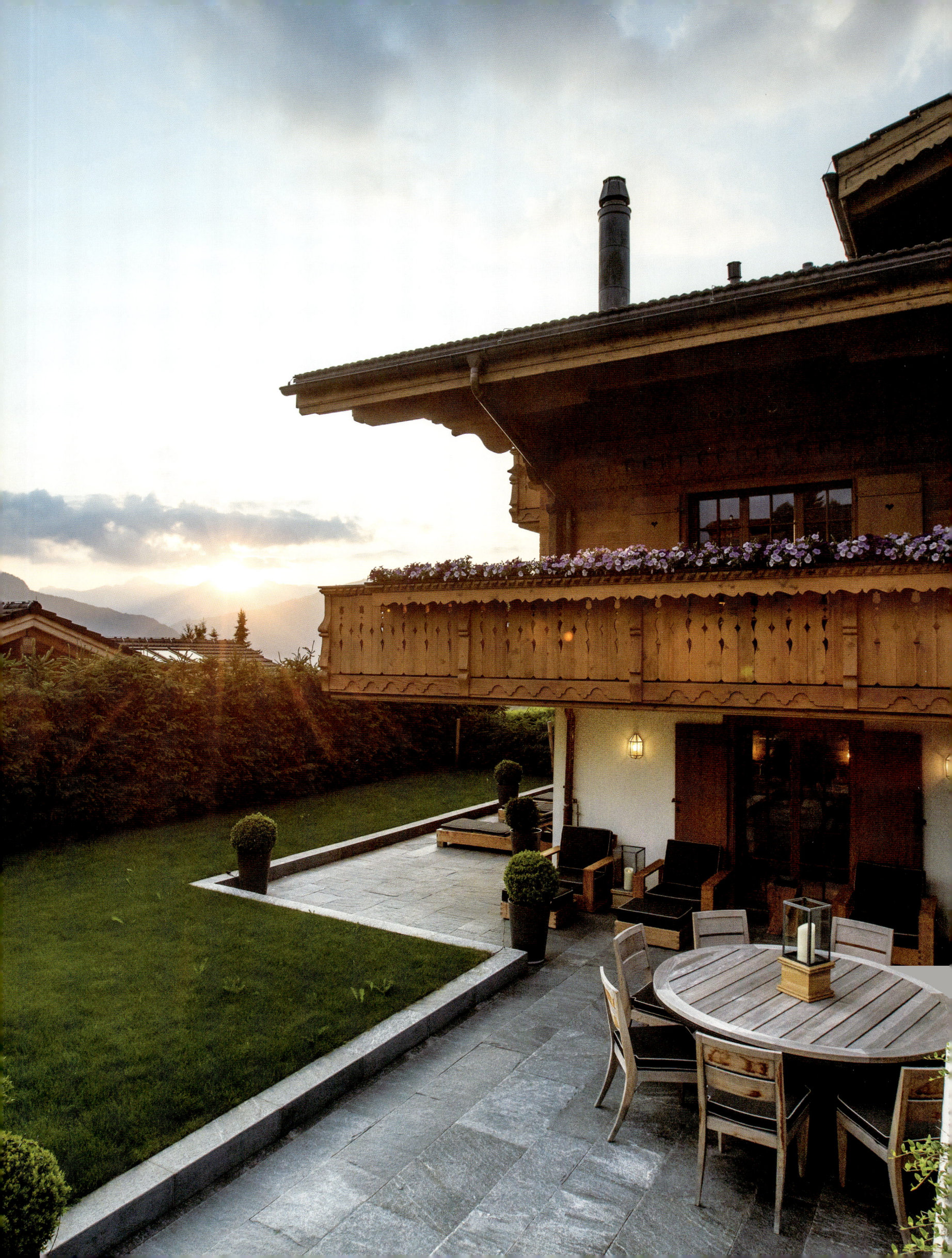

# Swiss Dream Chalet

Leaving nothing to be desired, Alpine charm meets contemporary interior design in this stylish chalet which radiates the epitome of a refined homely lifestyle.

WITH AN EXTERIOR design that is based on traditional architecture with lots of wood, this mountain chalet reveals the many aspects of its beauty inside – thanks to the tasteful, high-end interiors comprising a magnificent melange of valuable antiques and contemporary art. The ceiling and wall panelling made of real wood creates a pleasant atmosphere, and the well-thought-out lighting concept effectively accentuates the cosy yet distinctly modern Alpine flair. With its living space of around 450 square metres spread across three floors, the chalet offers a generously sized living room with a fireplace and a total of seven en-suite bedrooms. Further comforts include the swimming pool and a hammam as well as the garden with a barbecue area. Stunning views of the renowned Gstaad Palace Hotel and the surrounding mountains can be enjoyed from the terrace and the balconies of the chalet. Guests will hardly miss the vibrant village life of Gstaad – and if so, this can very easily be reached within a mere five minutes by car.

VON AUSSEN traditionell gestaltet, mit viel Holz und in charakteristischer Architektur, entfaltet dieses Chalet im Inneren seinen ganzen Facettenreichtum – was dem geschmackvollen, hochwertigen Interieur mit seinen kostbaren Antiquitäten in Kombination mit zeitgenössischer Kunst zu verdanken ist. Die mit edlem Holz verkleideten Wände und Decken schaffen eine äußerst angenehme Atmosphäre, das durchdachte Lichtkonzept unterstreicht dabei das behaglich-moderne Alpenflair. Auf einer Wohnfläche von 450 Quadratmetern, verteilt auf drei Etagen, bietet das Chalet neben einem großzügigen Wohnbereich mit Kamin insgesamt sieben Schlafzimmer mit En-suite-Bädern. Zu den weiteren Annehmlichkeiten gehören unter anderem ein Hammam, ein Pool sowie ein Garten mit Grillplatz. Von der Terrasse und den Balkonen lässt sich wunderbar der Blick auf die Berge und das berühmte Palace Hotel genießen. Das pulsierende Leben im Dorfkern von Gstaad wird man dabei kaum vermissen – und falls doch, ist man in nur fünf Autominuten mittendrin.

DESDE EL EXTERIOR luce tradicional, con mucha madera y en la arquitectura típica, mientras en su interior, este chalet despliega toda su gloria multifacética: belleza, buen gusto y calidad conseguidos con valiosas antigüedades en acertado equilibrio con arte contemporáneo hacen el resto. Las paredes y techos revestidos con maderas preciosas crean un ambiente de serena calidez donde un sofisticado concepto de iluminación destaca el acogedor a la vez que moderno estilo alpino. En unos 450 metros cuadrados habitables en tres plantas, el chalet aloja la espaciosa zona de día con chimenea y un total de siete dormitorios con cuartos de baño en *suite*. Se añaden otros elementos para el disfrute, como la piscina, el *hammam* y el jardín con zona de barbacoa, entre muchas más comodidades. Desde la terraza y los balcones son impecables las vistas al famoso Palace Hotel y a las eternas montañas circundantes. La animada vida del pueblo de Gstaad no se echa de menos, o sí, pero basta una vuelta de cinco minutos en coche para disfrutarla.

SWITZERLAND, GSTAAD **RENTAL PRICE/2 WEEKS** CHF 140,000 **INTERIOR APPROX.** 400 m² **NO. OF BEDROOMS** 7
**E&V ID** W-00LL4V **CONTACT** GSTAAD (CH), E&V GSTAAD PROPERTIES AG,
LICENCE PARTNER OF ENGEL & VÖLKERS WOHNEN SCHWEIZ AG **TEL.** +41 33 655 65 05
**E-MAIL** GSTAAD@ENGELVOELKERS.COM

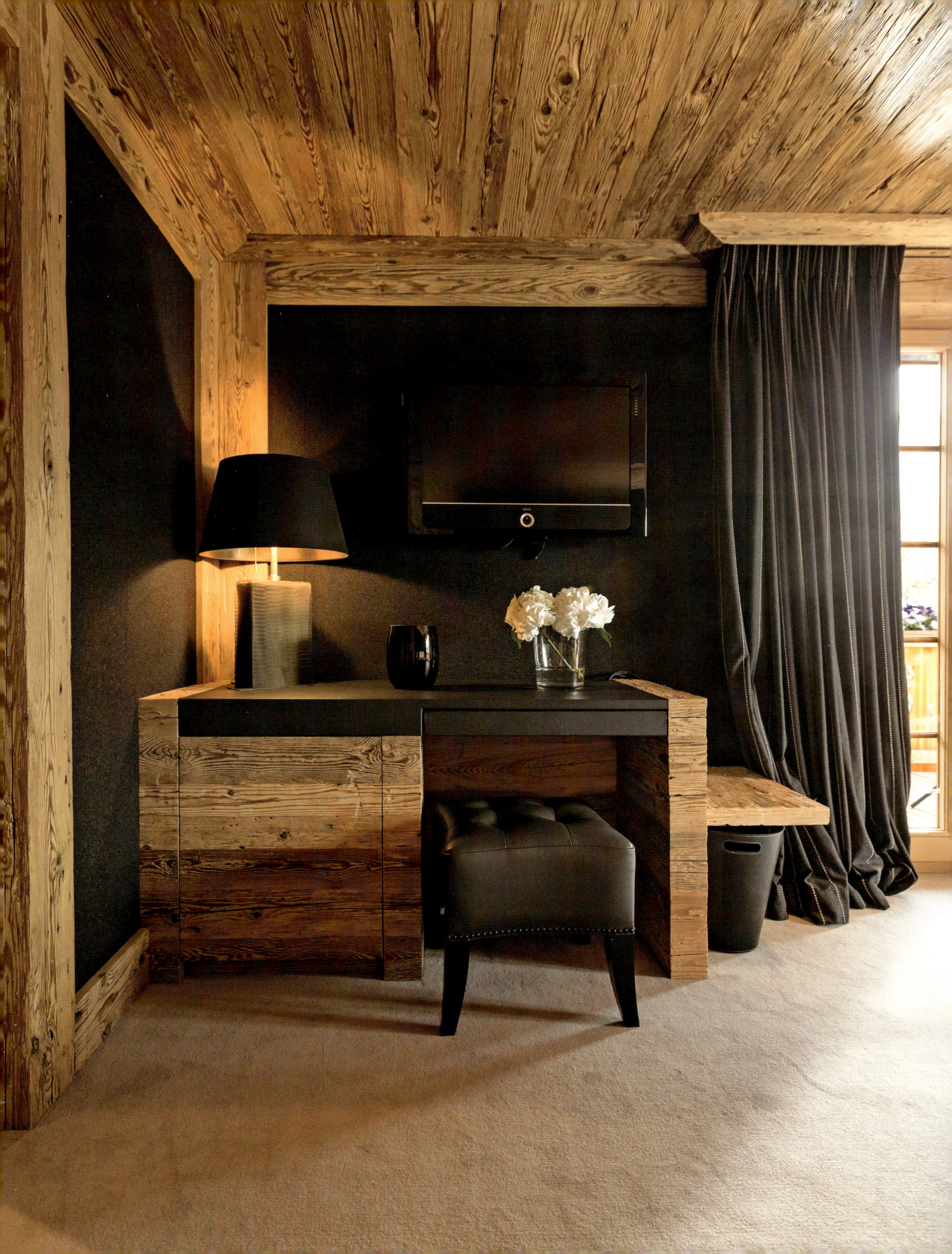

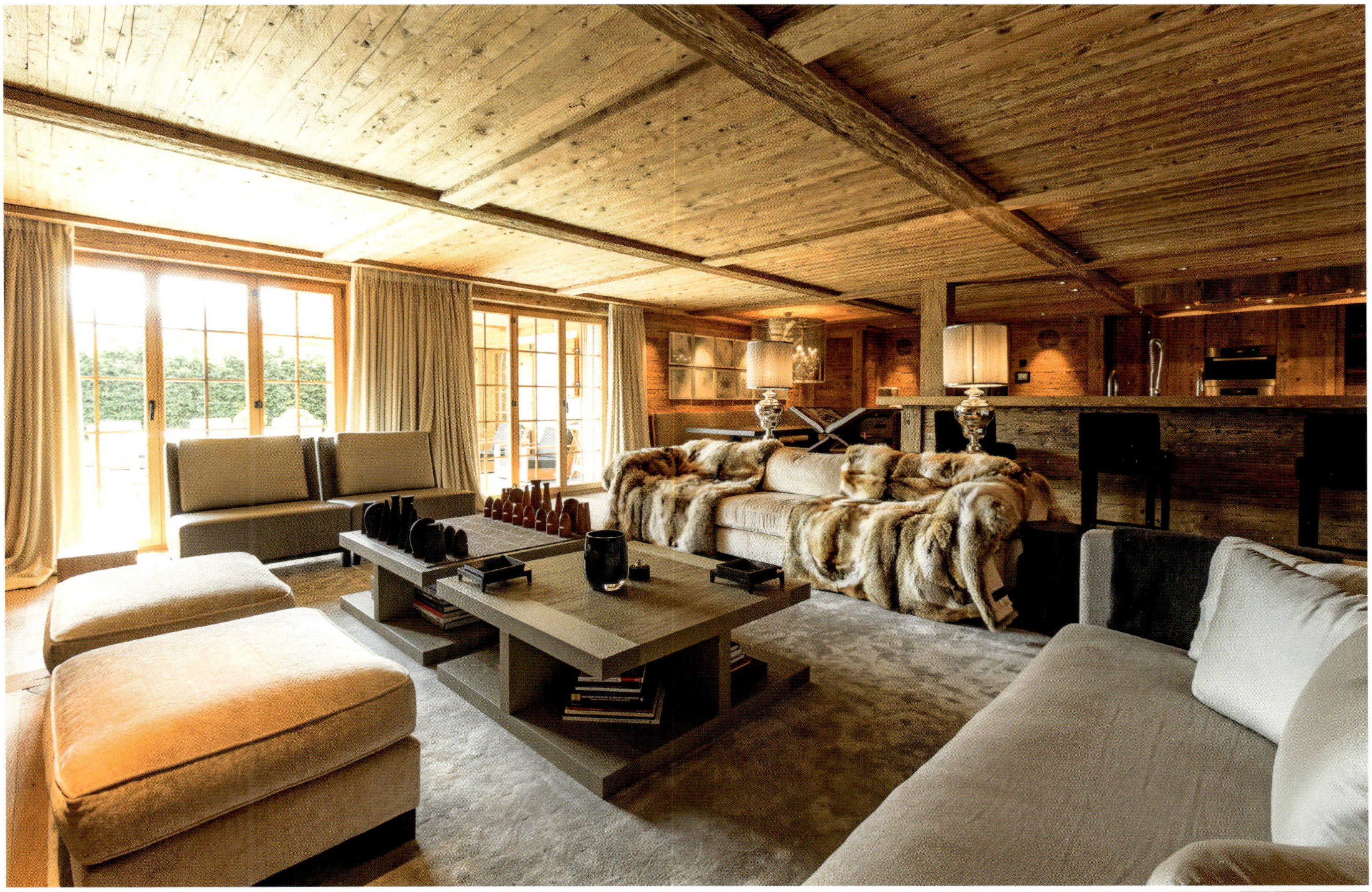

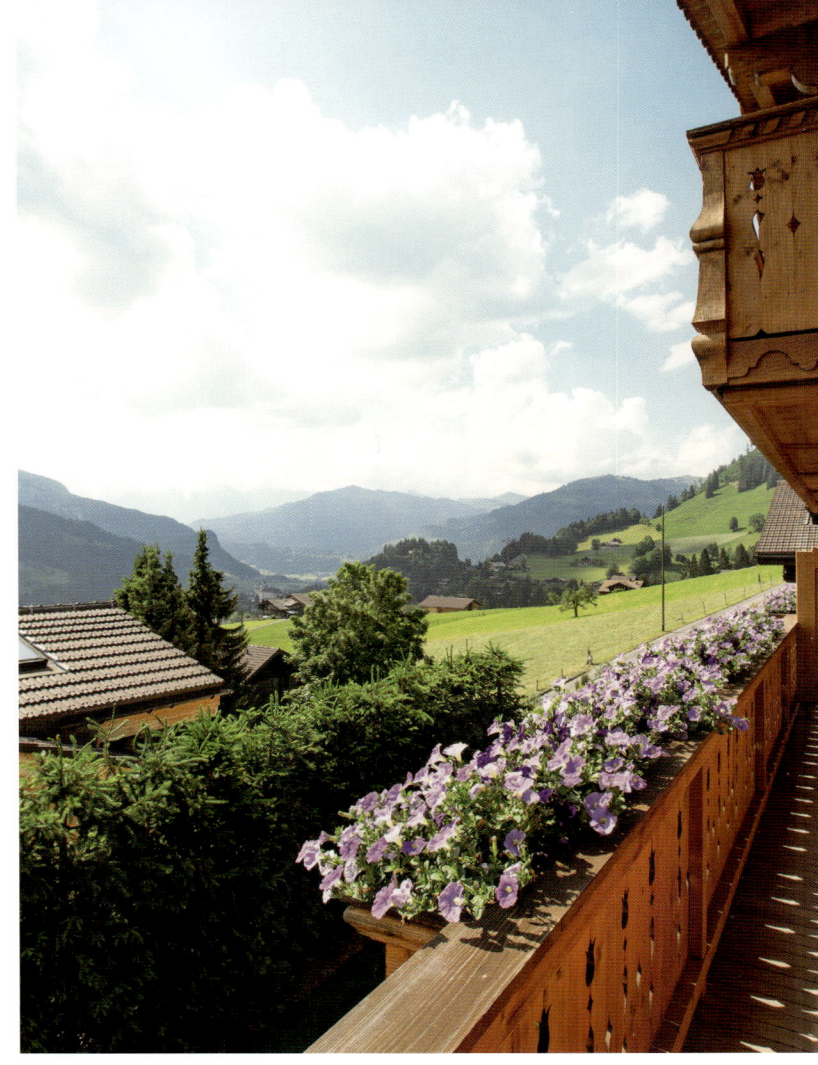

Alpine lifestyle in its most beautiful form –
aesthetic and stylish in equal measure.

Alpiner Lifestyle zeigt sich hier in seiner
schönsten Form – so kunstvoll wie stilsicher.

El estilo de vida de los Alpes se muestra en su
forma más bella, tan artística como elegante.

<

The homogeneous, discreet colour scheme
of the interiors creates a relaxing ambience.

Die homogene, unaufdringliche Farbgebung
des Interieurs trägt zur Entspannung bei.

La acertada gama tonal discreta y homogénea
de sus interiores contribuye a la relajación.

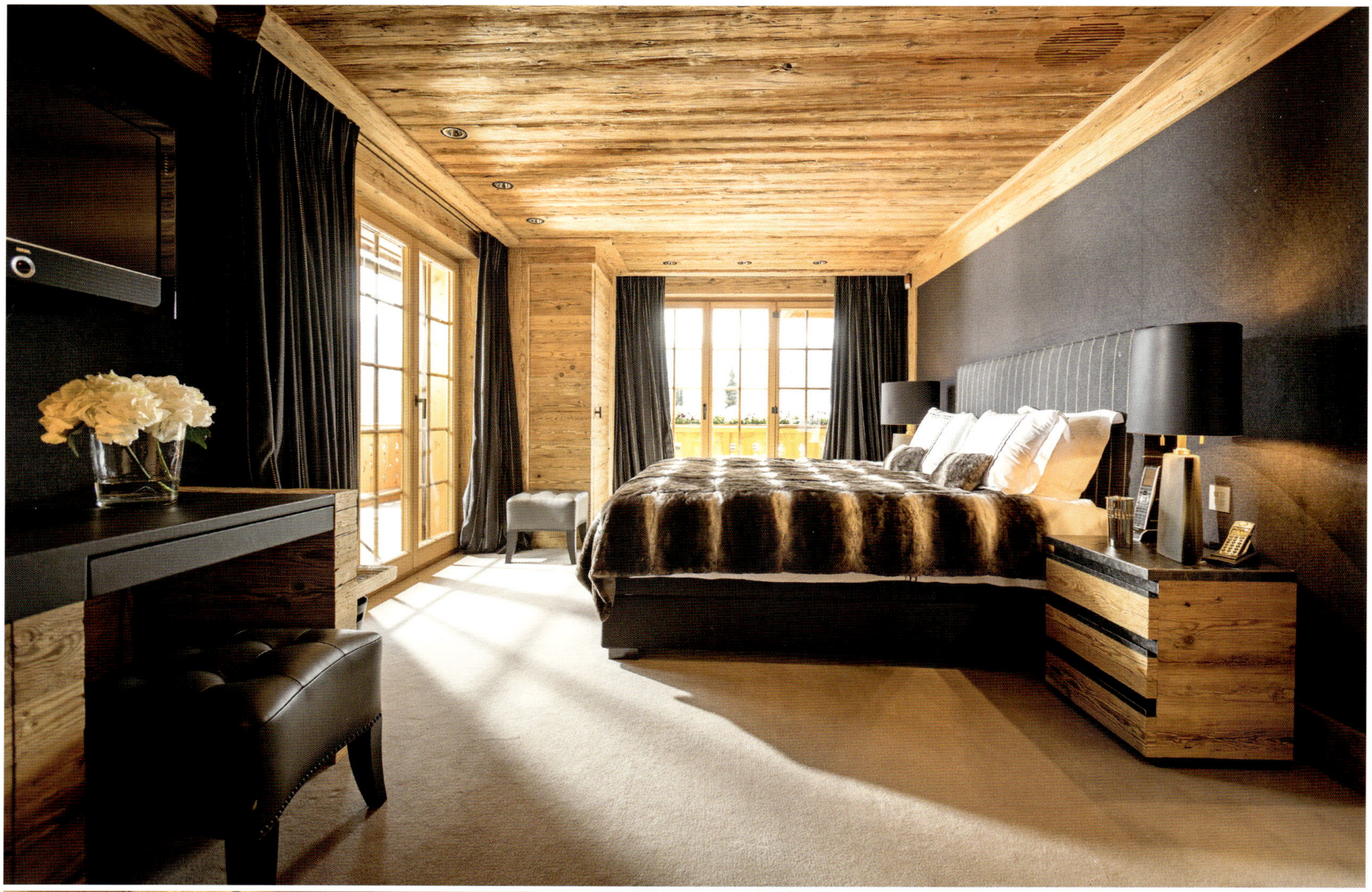

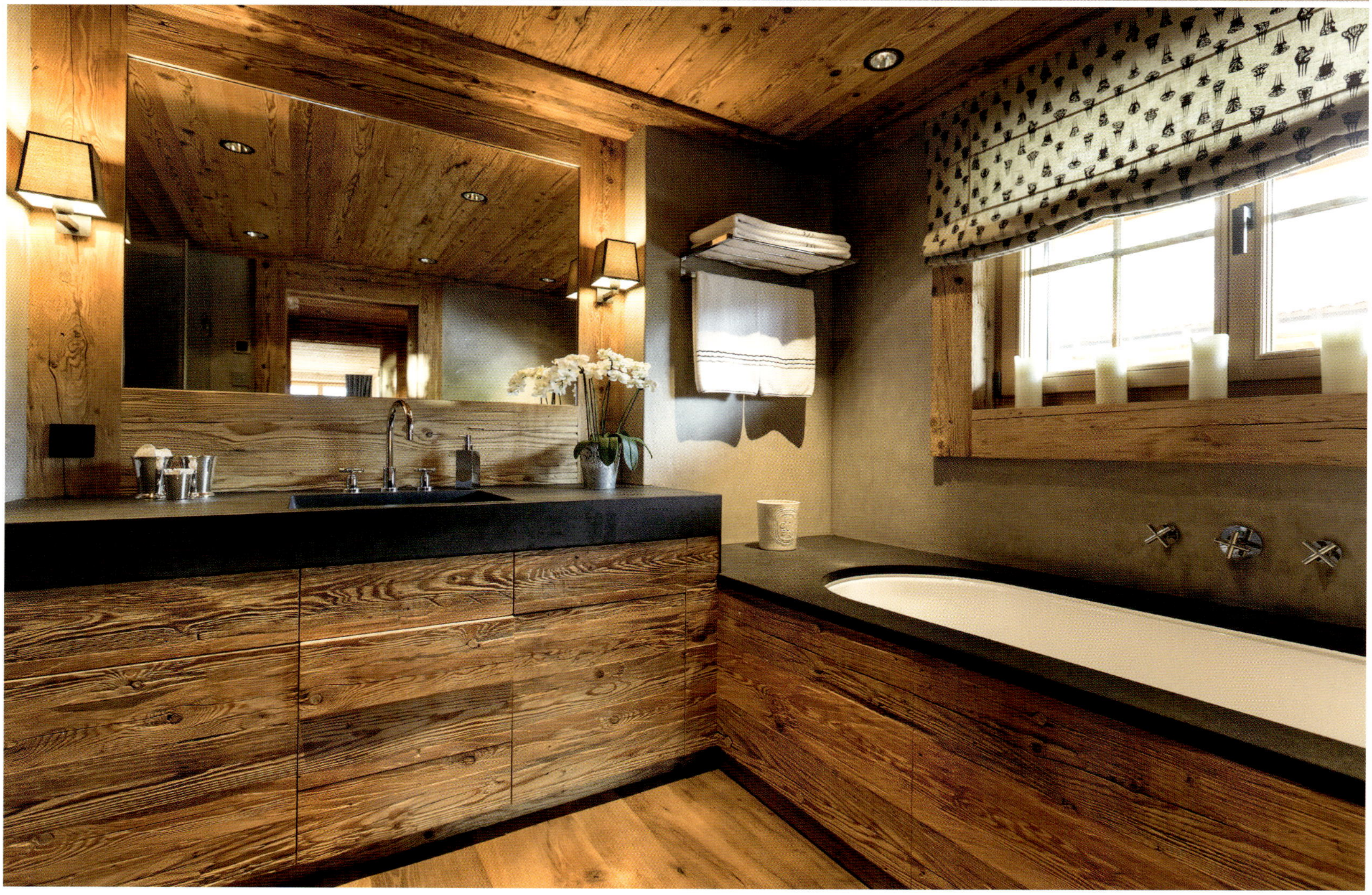

<

A maximum of space and comfort: every bedroom has its own private bathroom.

Ein Maximum an Platz und Komfort: Jedes Schlafzimmer verfügt über ein eigenes Bad.

Lo máximo en espacio y comodidad: cada dormitorio tiene su cuarto de baño privado.

Simply divine: the hillside location and the large garden – perfect for a barbecue.

Einfach himmlisch: die Hanglage und der große Garten – perfekt für ein Barbecue.

Sencillamente divino: el sitio en la colina y con el gran jardín, perfecto para una barbacoa.

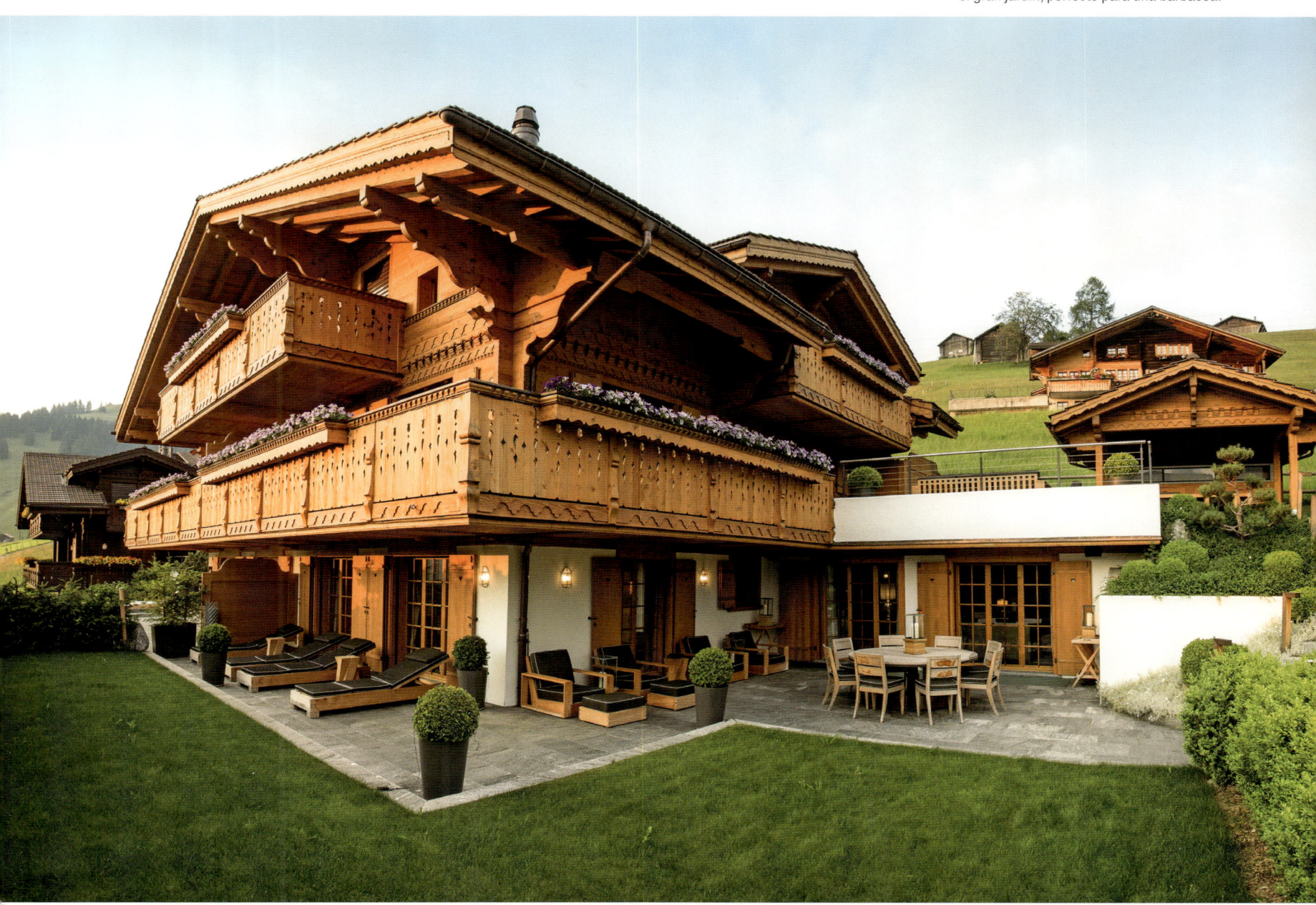

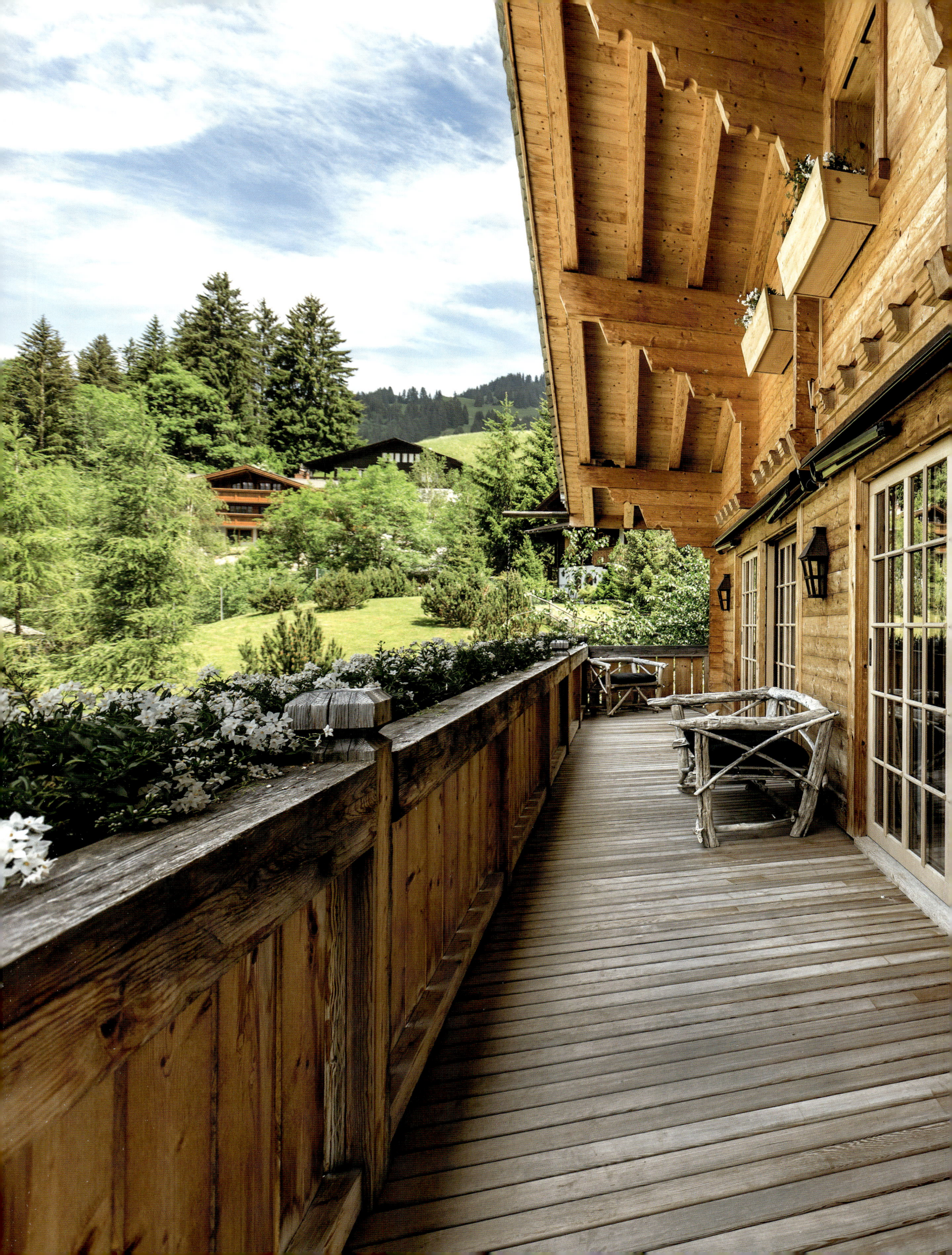

# Exclusive Alpine Chic

Set amidst a majestic mountain landscape, this stylish Swiss chalet is an elegant symbiosis of traditional architecture and modern interior design.

AS A HOLIDAY DESTINATION, Gstaad has much to offer for nature lovers and sports enthusiasts alike – and the region can be enjoyed in a particularly stylish manner when staying in this chalet. Located close to the village centre and a range of hiking paths, ski pistes, shops, boutiques and restaurants, the domicile features a highly exclusive, modern Alpine interior. Typical of chalet-style architecture, the wooden ceilings, walls and floors ensure a cosy feel and create an intriguing contrast to the contemporary interior design. The four-level chalet comprises five bedrooms and bathrooms, a generously sized living area replete with lofty ceilings and a fireplace, and an inviting dining room plus gourmet kitchen. All the rooms are surrounded by a magnificent balcony, which – together with the barbecue area and the lovely garden – affords spectacular vistas of the surrounding Alpine panorama. A sauna, a fitness room and a well-stocked library also belong to the appointments of this holiday home, rounding off the many features of this feel-good chalet.

ALS FERIENZIEL hat Gstaad insbesondere für Naturliebhaber und Sportfreunde vielfältige Freizeitaktivitäten zu bieten – und mit diesem Chalet als Unterkunft lassen sich diese auf höchst stilvolle Weise genießen. Unweit des Dorfzentrums und diverser Wanderwege, Skipisten, Einkaufsmöglichkeiten und Restaurants, präsentiert es sich mit einer modern-alpinen, exklusiven Innenausstattung. Die chalettypische, hochwertige Holzverkleidung strahlt Behaglichkeit aus und bildet einen spannenden Kontrast zum stylishen Interieur. Auf vier Etagen beherbergt das Chalet jeweils fünf Schlafzimmer und Bäder sowie einen großzügigen Wohnbereich mit hohen Decken und Kamin, der ins einladende Esszimmer und die Küche übergeht. Die Räume sind ringsum von einem Balkon umgeben, der schlichtweg atemberaubende Aussichten bietet – ebenso wie der Barbecue-Bereich und der Garten. Eine Sauna, ein Fitnessraum sowie eine gut sortierte Bibliothek gehören ebenfalls zur Ausstattung und runden den Aufenthalt in diesem Wohlfühldomizil perfekt ab.

COMO DESTINO DE VACACIONES Gstaad ofrece una gran variedad de actividades de ocio, en especial para los aficionados a los deportes y los apasionados por la naturaleza; alojados en este chalet, ambos gozarán de la manera más elegante imaginable, y no sólo éstos. Cerca del centro del pueblo y con diversidad de rutas de senderismo, pistas de esquí, tiendas y restaurantes a tiro de piedra, el magnífico chalet luce diseño interior alpino, moderno y exclusivo. El típico revestimiento de madera de techos, suelos y muros de los chalets irradia aquí comodidad y calidez, en estimulante contraste con el estilismo contemporáneo. En cuatro pisos brinda cinco dormitorios con sus baños y una espaciosa zona de día con techos altos y chimenea, que se funde con el acogedor comedor y la cocina. Las estancias acceden al balcón circundante con impresionantes panorámicas a las montañas, la zona de barbacoa y el jardín. Sauna, gimnasio y una biblioteca bien surtida redondean el equipamiento y también la estancia en este inmueble para un perfecto bienestar.

SWITZERLAND, GSTAAD **RENTAL PRICE/3 WEEKS** CHF 120,000 **INTERIOR APPROX.** 350 m² **NO. OF BEDROOMS** 5
**E&V ID** W-0155OQ **CONTACT** GSTAAD (CH), E&V GSTAAD PROPERTIES AG,
LICENCE PARTNER OF ENGEL & VÖLKERS WOHNEN SCHWEIZ AG **TEL.** +41 33 655 65 05
**E-MAIL** GSTAAD@ENGELVOELKERS.COM

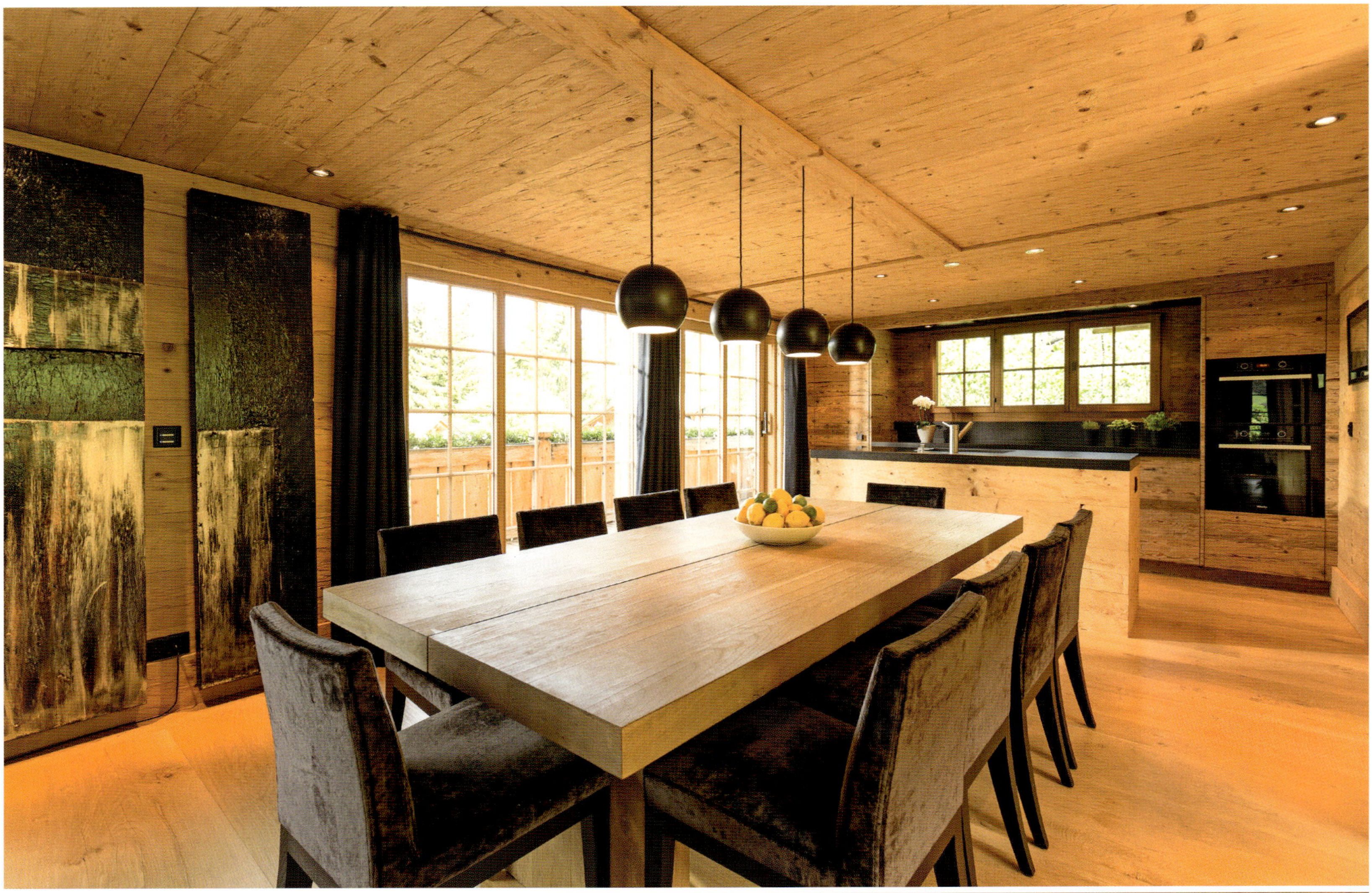

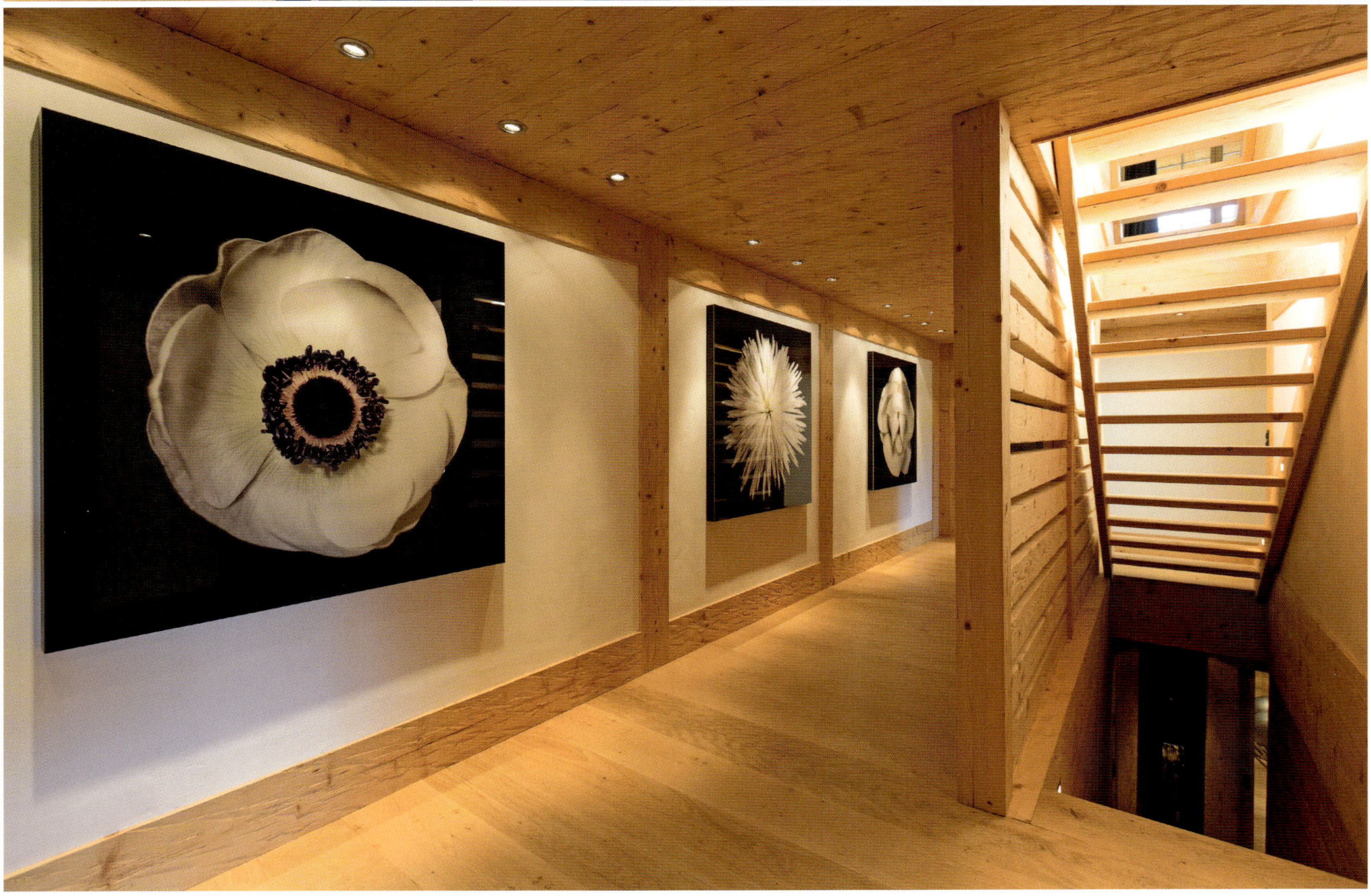

<

The modern interiors and first-class amenities promise a superlative level of comfort.

Das moderne Interieur und die erstklassige Ausstattung versprechen höchsten Komfort.

El máximo confort queda garantizado con mobiliario moderno y de primera calidad.

The characteristic wood panelling in all the chalet rooms creates a cosy Alpine flair.

Die charakteristische Holzverkleidung in allen Räumen sorgt für behagliches, alpines Flair.

La calidez de la característica madera en todos los espacios destaca el acogedor toque alpino.

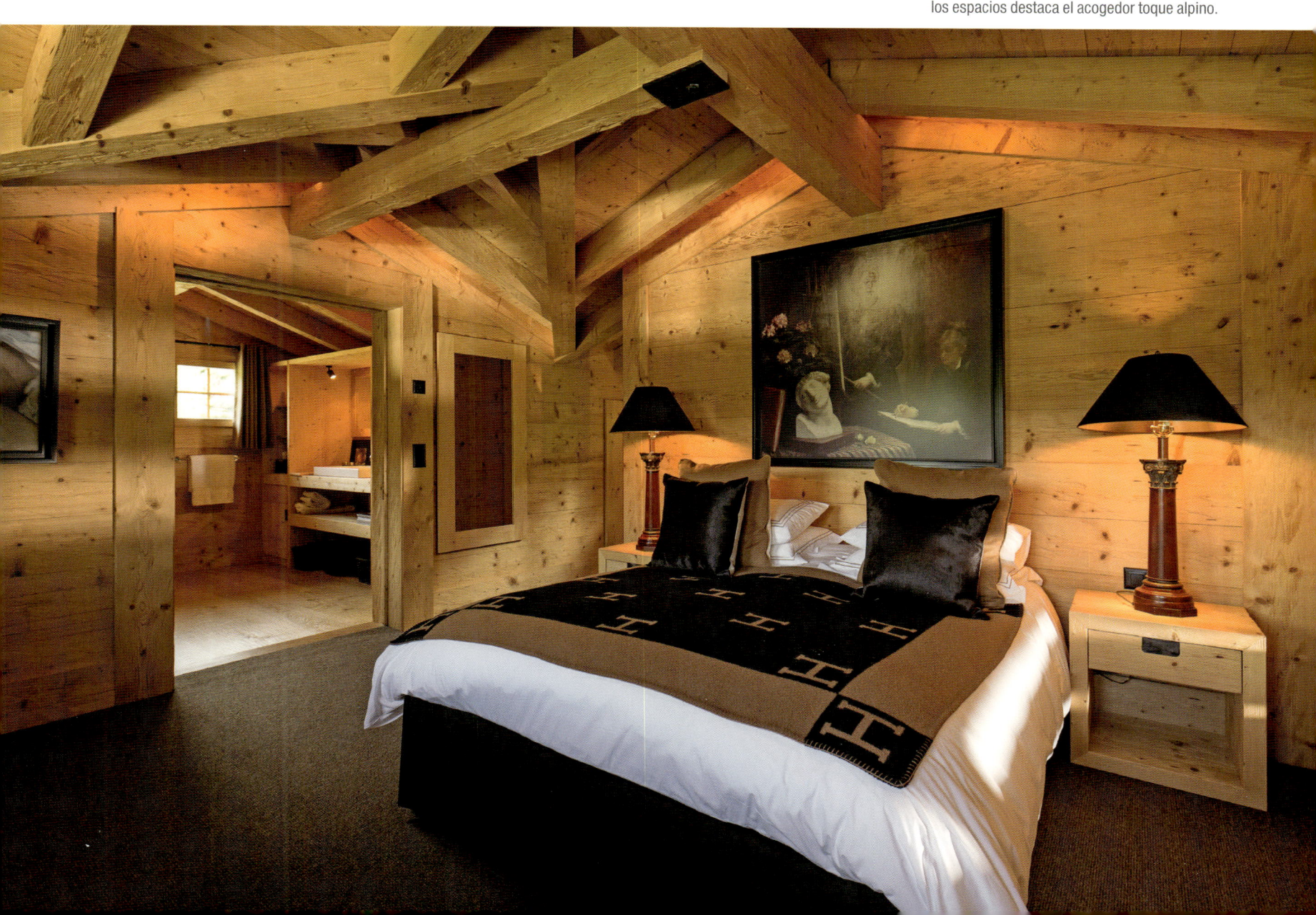

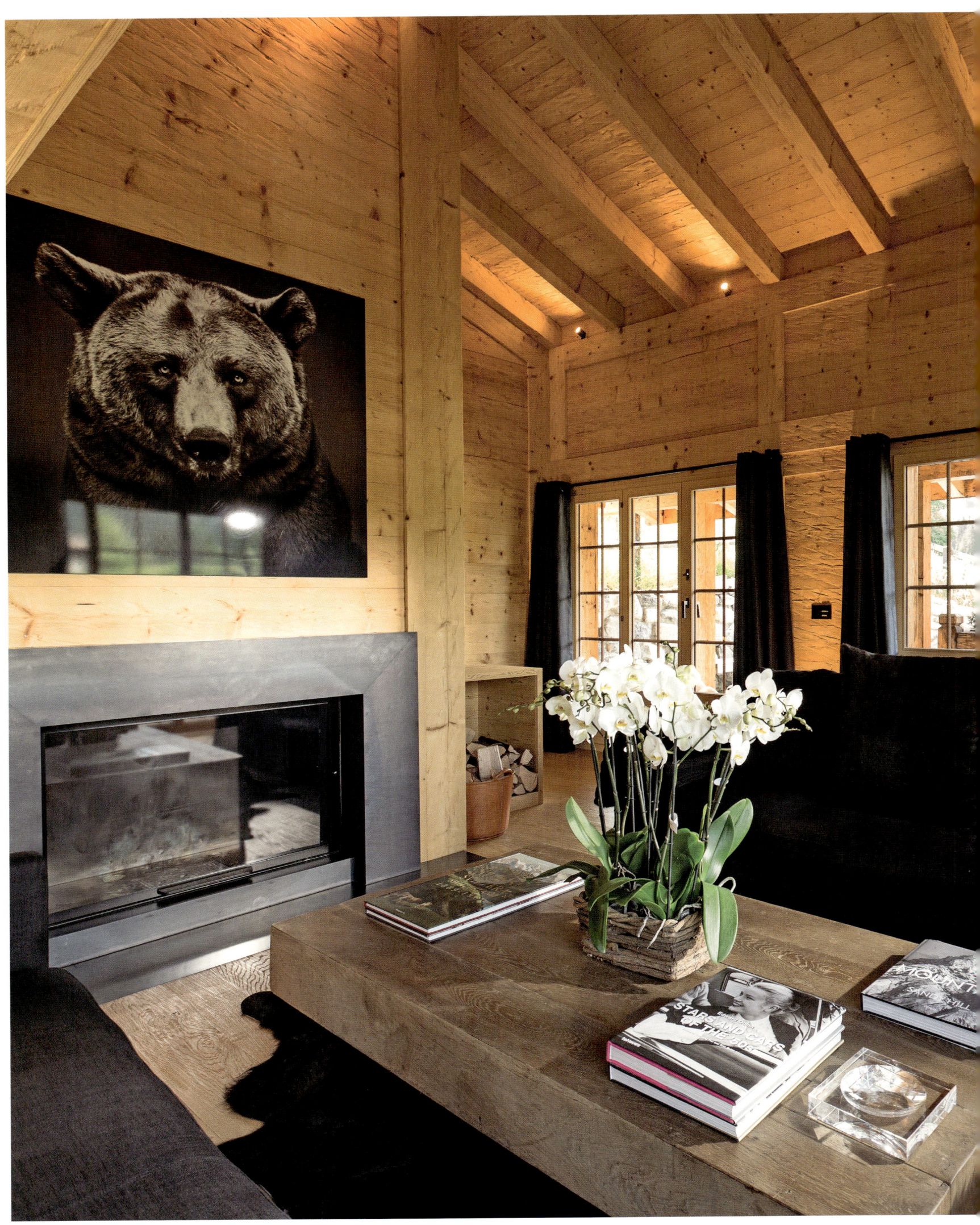

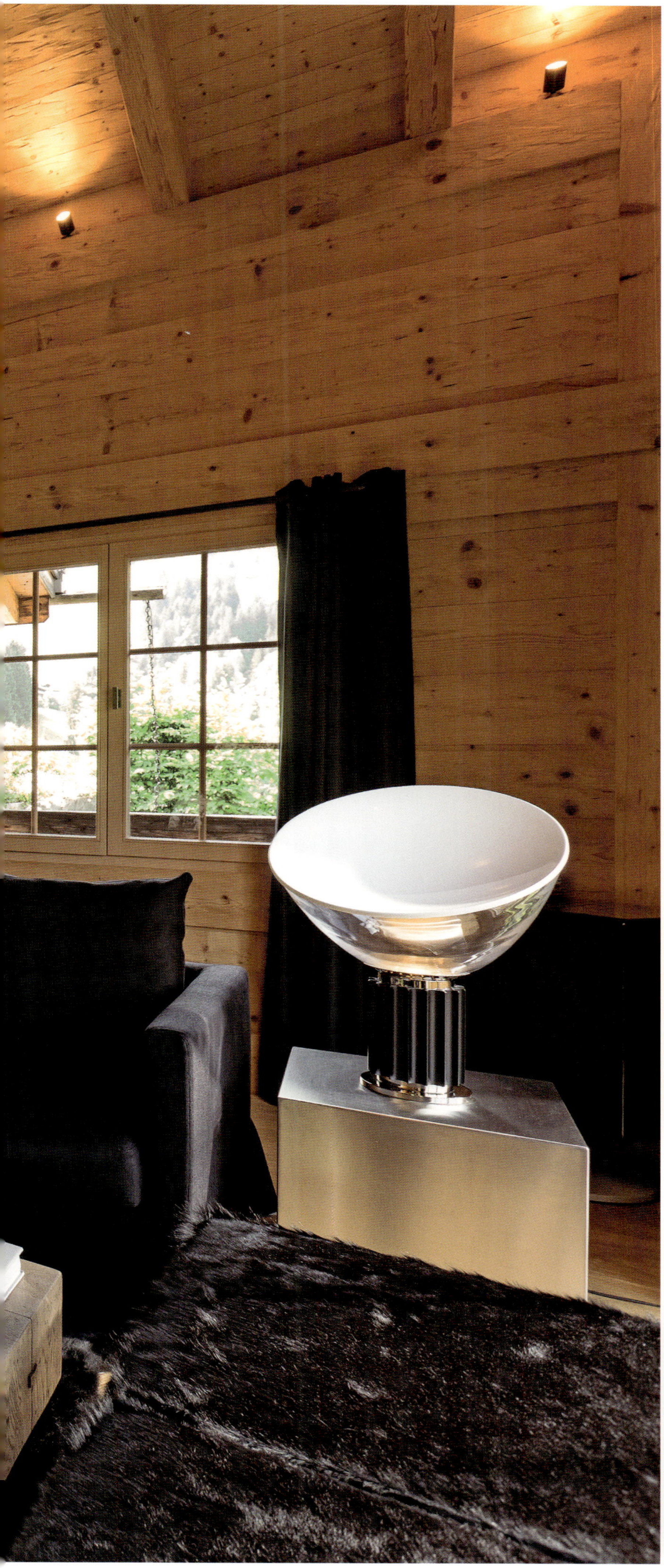

<

Relaxing in this chalet after an active day
in the mountains is simply wonderful.

Nach einem aktiven Tag in den Bergen lässt es
sich in diesem Chalet wunderbar entspannen.

Tras un activo día en la montaña qué mejor
lugar para relajarse que el fabuloso chalet.

Perfect for social evenings with friends:
the spacious living and dining area.

Perfekt für gesellige Abende mit Freunden:
der großzügige Wohn- und Essbereich.

Perfecta para las amenas veladas con
amigos: la gran zona de estar y comedor.

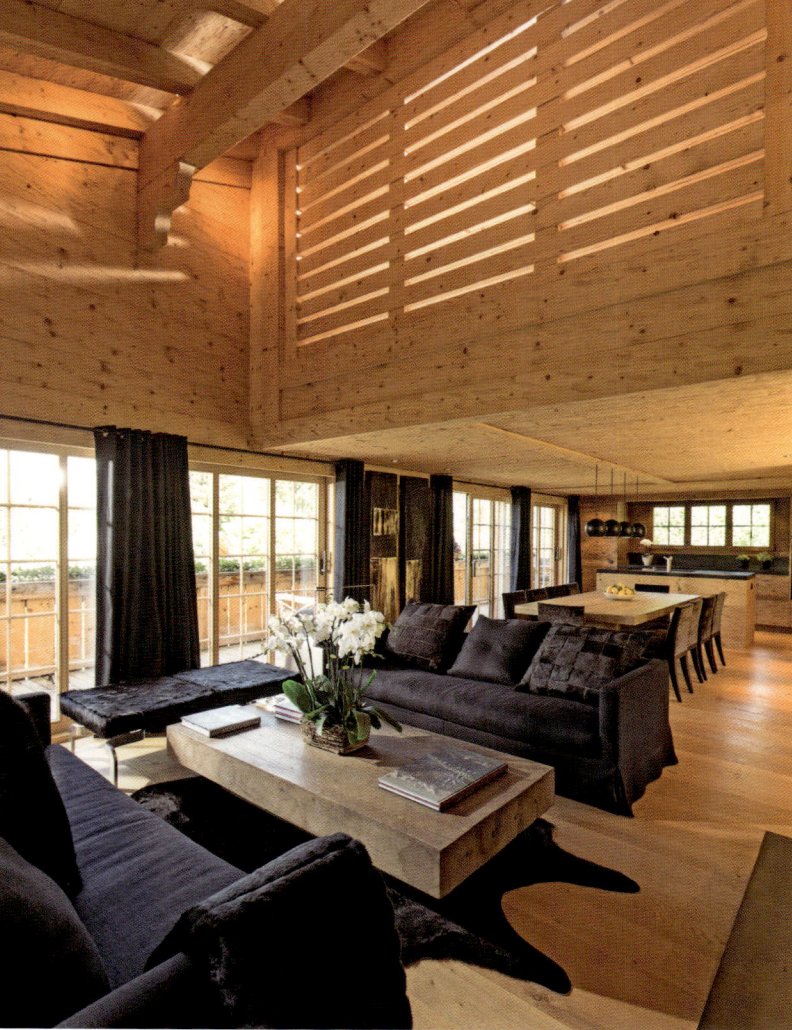

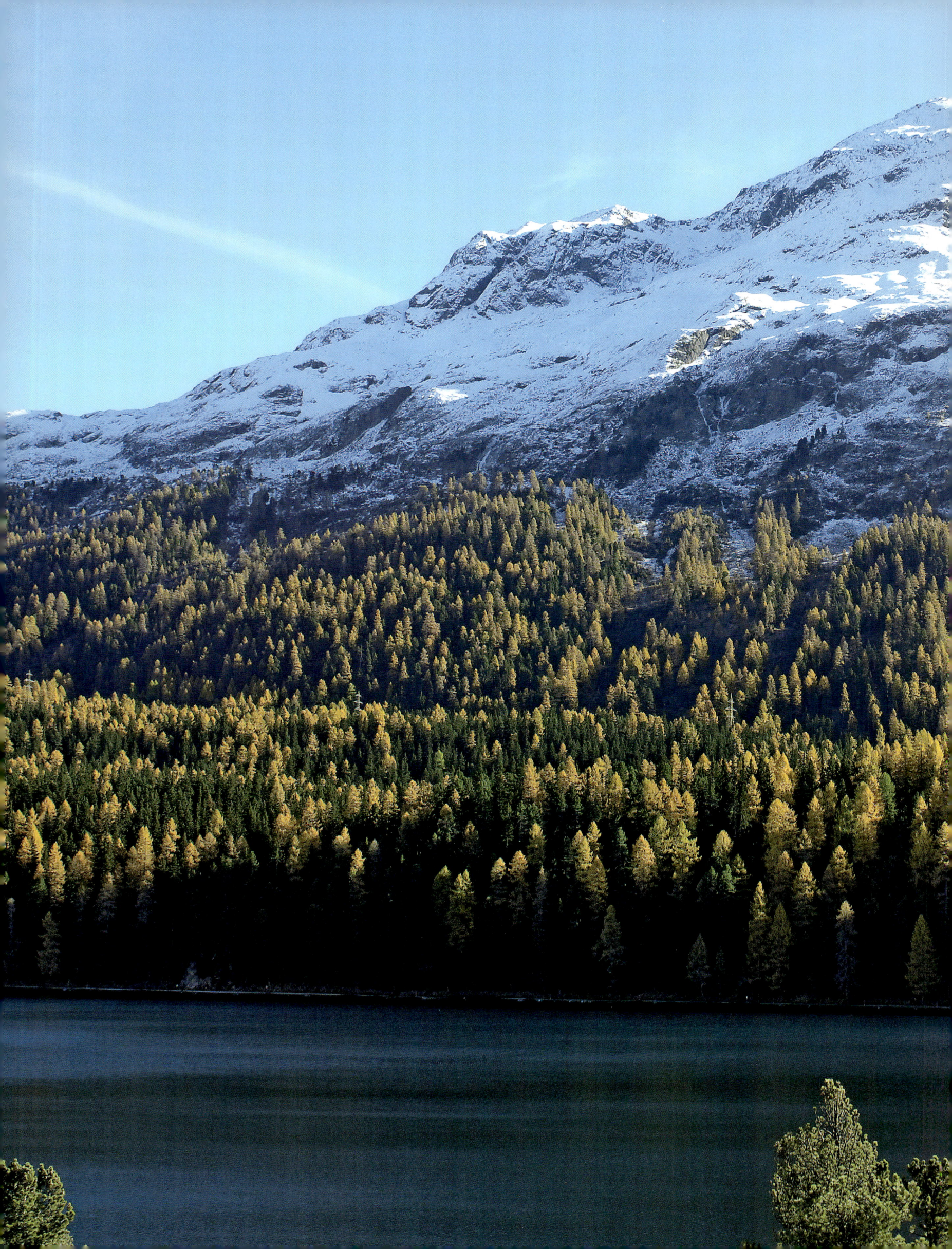

# St. Moritz Spirit

Stylish flamboyance with a chic modern twist makes this apartment an outstanding place to live – a domicile that fits perfectly with the cultured savoir-vivre of St. Moritz.

GLAMOROUS, ELEGANT, COSMOPOLITAN: St. Moritz is one of the most desirable travel destinations worldwide frequented by celebrities and the international jet set – and this for a good reason: promising a sophisticated lifestyle, it is crowned by a sparkling "Champagne climate" and the celebrated St. Moritz sun that shines an average of 322 days a year. The perfect setting for an extravagant apartment like this, which reflects the lifestyle of the region. Clear lines create a sense of stylish elegance enhanced by beautiful decorative elements and fine materials used for the appointments. The heart of the exclusive apartment is the generous living and dining area with a fireplace and views of the Engadine mountain scenery. The open-plan, real-wood kitchen is fully equipped with state-of-the-art appliances, while the four sumptuous bedrooms each boast an en-suite bathroom, one of them with a personal hammam – ensuring nothing but pure relaxation after an active day spent hiking or skiing in the mountains of the region.

MONDÄN, ELEGANT, KOSMOPOLITISCH: St. Moritz zählt nicht umsonst zu den begehrtesten Reisezielen von Prominenz und Jetset – atmet es doch den Charme von Weltläufigkeit und gehobenem Lebensstil, gekrönt vom prickelnden „Champagnerklima" und der berühmten St. Moritzer Sonne, die durchschnittlich 322 Tage im Jahr scheint. Die passende Umgebung für dieses Apartment, das die Lebensart der Region perfekt widerspiegelt. Klare Linien prägen eine stilvolle Eleganz, die von überraschenden Deko-Elementen belebt und durch die edlen Materialien, welche für die Ausstattung verwendet wurden, betont wird. Herzstück des Apartments ist der großzügige Wohn- und Essbereich mit Kamin und Ausblick auf die Engadiner Bergwelt. Die offene, aus Edelholz gefertigte Küche ist mit modernsten Geräten ausgestattet, während die vier Schlafzimmer jeweils über ein En-suite-Bad verfügen, eines davon mit eigenem Hammam – so steht der Entspannung nach einem aktiven Wander- oder Ski-Tag in den Bergen nichts mehr im Wege.

GLAMUROSO, ELEGANTE, COSMOPOLITA: St. Moritz es uno de los destinos turísticos más deseados, frecuentado por celebridades y la *jet set* internacional, y con motivo: además del sofisticado y exclusivo estilo de vida que promete, está coronada por el centelleante "clima Champagne" y el celebrado sol de St. Moritz, que brilla un promedio de 322 días al año, siendo el escenario perfecto para un apartamento sofisticado como es éste, fiel reflejo del estilo de vida de la región. Las líneas claras crean una estilosa elegancia realzada con los preciosos elementos decorativos y los materiales nobles de sus acabados. El corazón de la propiedad es la generosa sala de estar y comedor con chimenea y vistas al escenario de montaña de la Engadina. La cocina abierta de madera maciza está equipada con electrodomésticos de última generación, mientras que los cuatro suntuosos dormitorios cuentan cada uno con su baño en *suite* y uno de ellos con un *hammam*, garantizando nada más que pura relajación tras un activo día de senderismo o esquí en las montañas de los alrededores.

SWITZERLAND, ST. MORITZ **RENTAL PRICE/WEEK** ON REQUEST **INTERIOR APPROX.** 305 m²
**NO. OF BEDROOMS** 4 **E&V ID** W-00IBXQ **CONTACT** ST. MORITZ (CH), EV RESIDENCES SUISSE SA,
LICENCE PARTNER OF ENGEL & VÖLKERS WOHNEN SCHWEIZ AG **TEL.** +41 81 837 51 51
**E-MAIL** STMORITZ@ENGELVOELKERS.COM

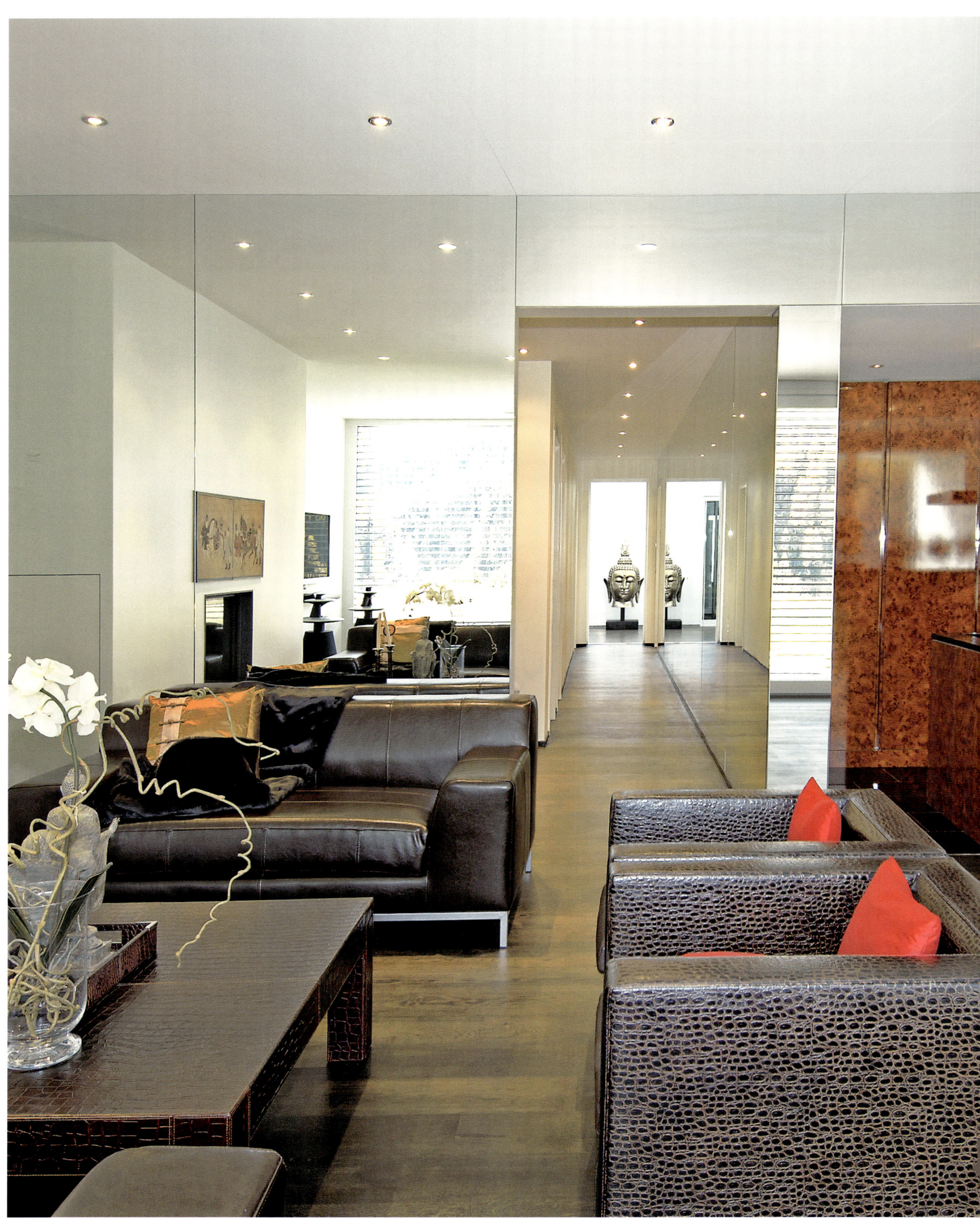

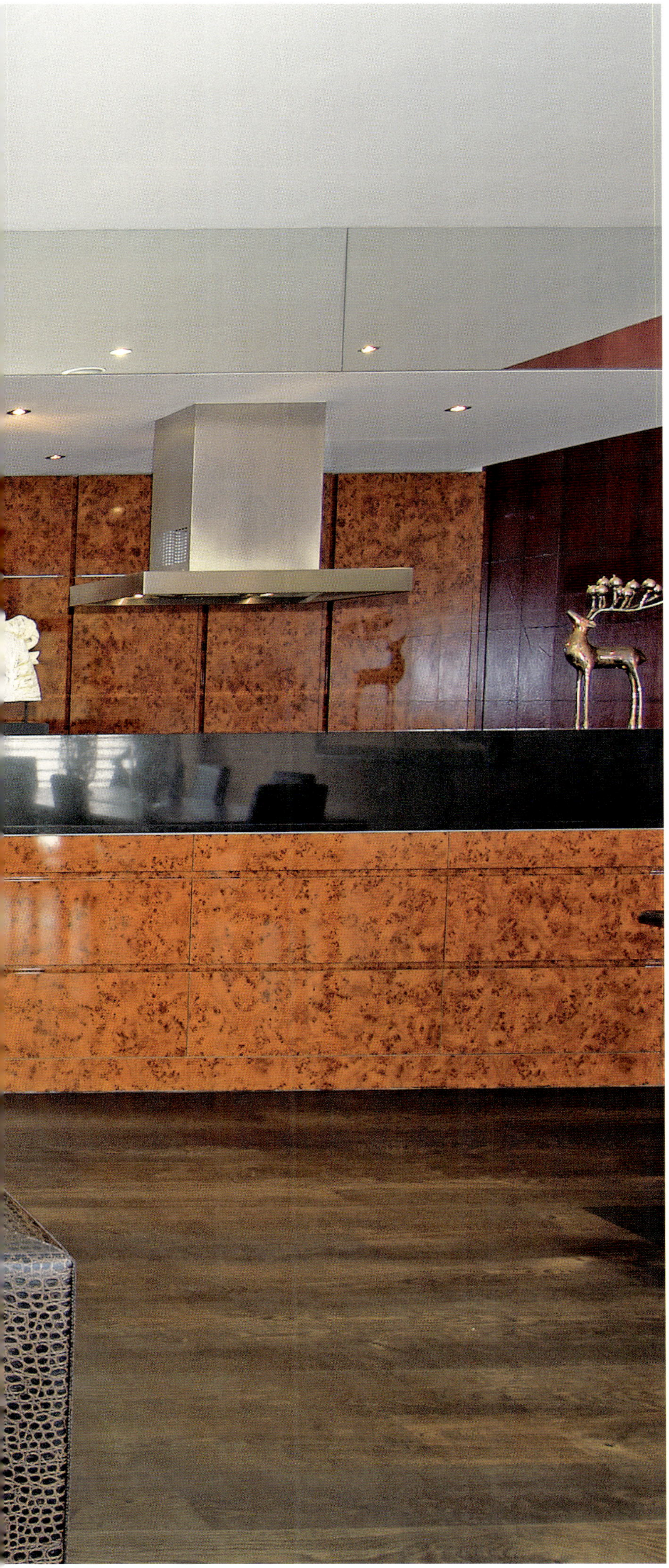

Modern design and top functionality
complement each other in the open kitchen.

In der offenen Küche ergänzen sich modernes
Design und erstklassige Funktionalität.

Diseño contemporáneo y alta funcionalidad se
complementan en la cocina abierta.

Decorative Asian elements create an attractive
contrast to the Swiss mountain scenery.

Asiatische Deko-Elemente schaffen einen
reizvollen Kontrast zur Schweizer Bergwelt.

El estilismo asiático crea un atractivo
contraste con la Suiza más montañosa.

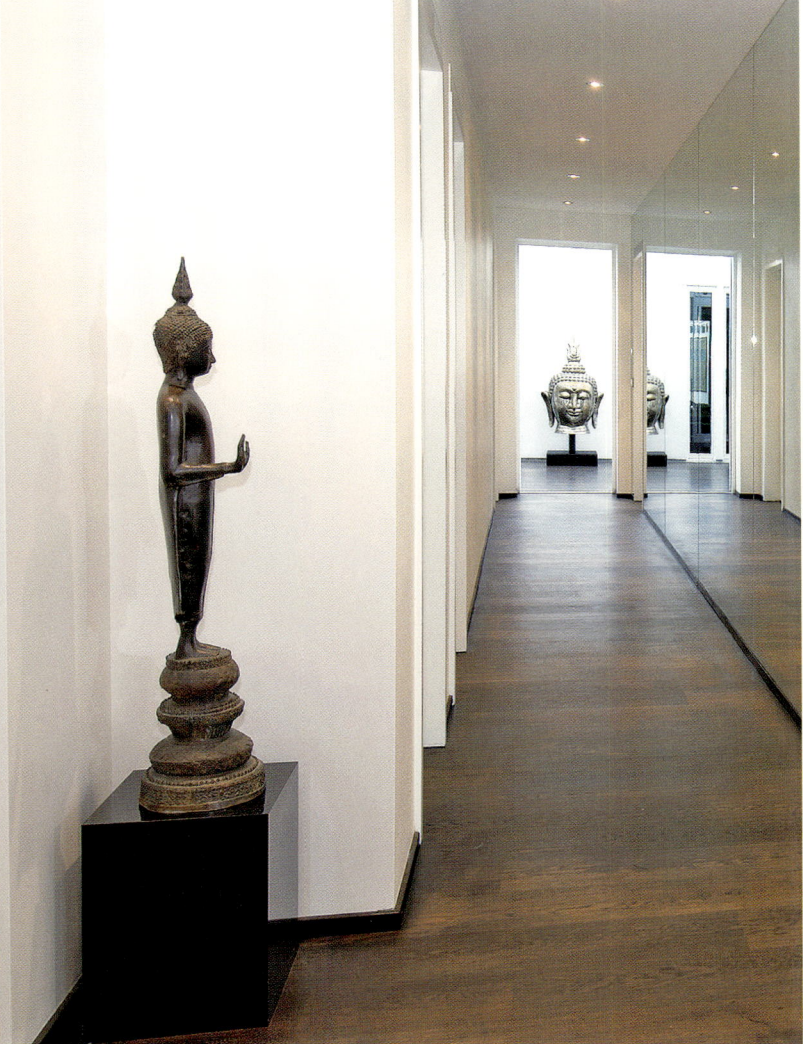

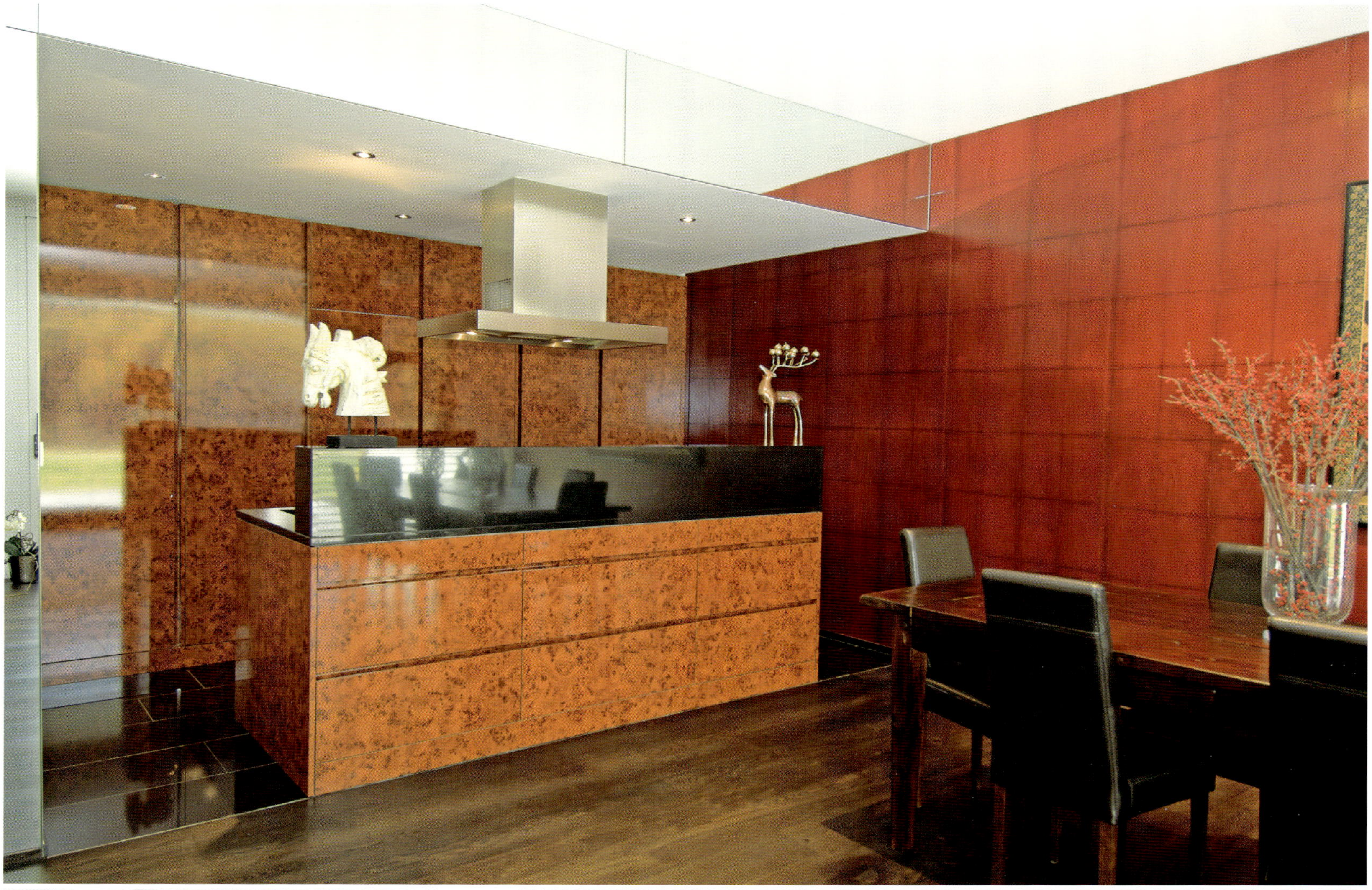

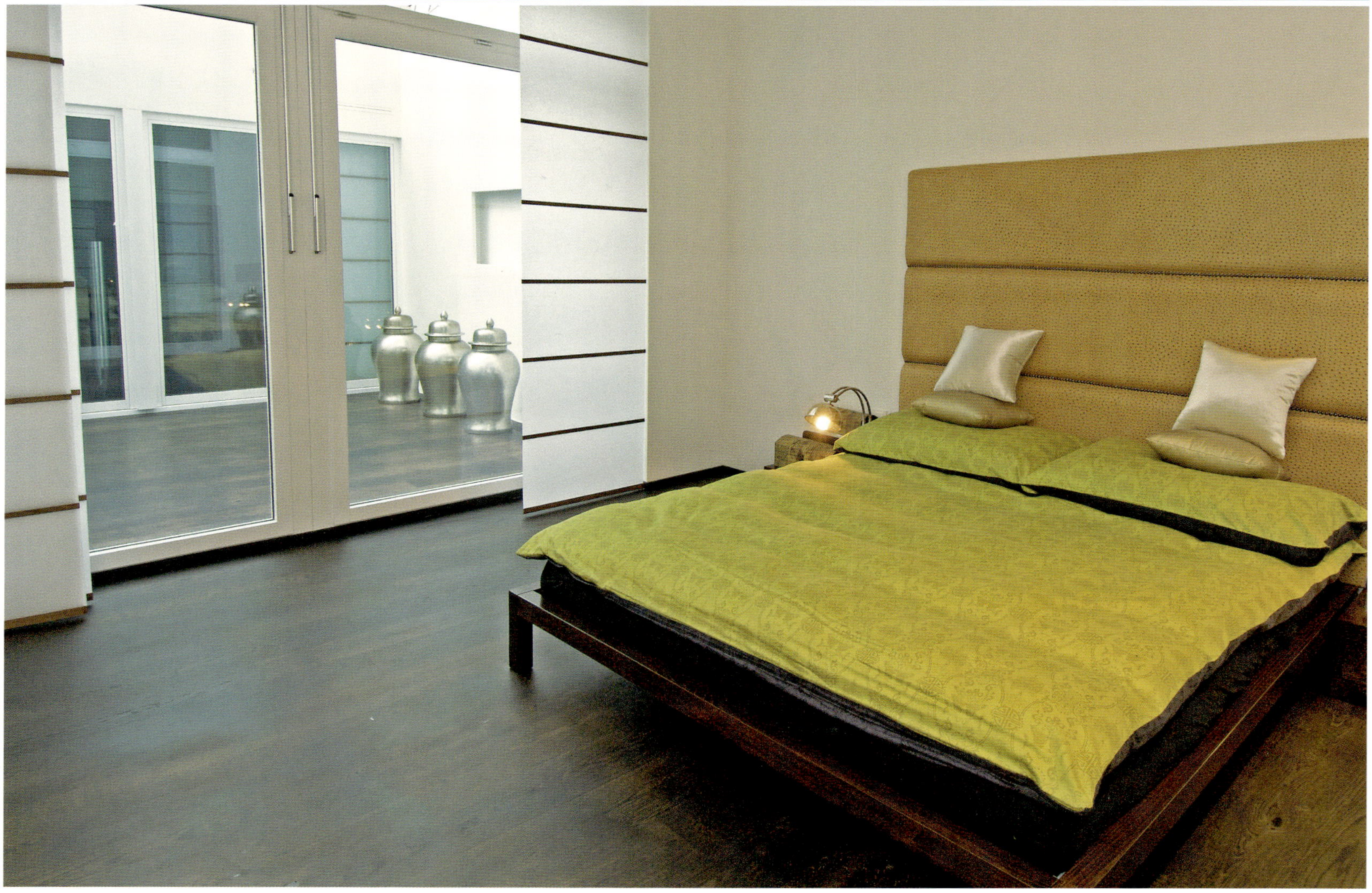

<

The well-appointed layout of the apartment ensures a high level of comfort.

Die durchdachte Raumaufteilung des Apartments sorgt für besonderen Komfort.

La óptima distribución espacial del aparta-mento garantiza un alto nivel de confort.

Wellness with style: the beautiful spacious bathrooms are made of fine marble.

Wellness mit Stil: Die geräumigen Bäder sind in edlem Marmor gehalten.

Wellness con estilo: los preciosos y amplios baños lucen esplendorosos en fino mármol.

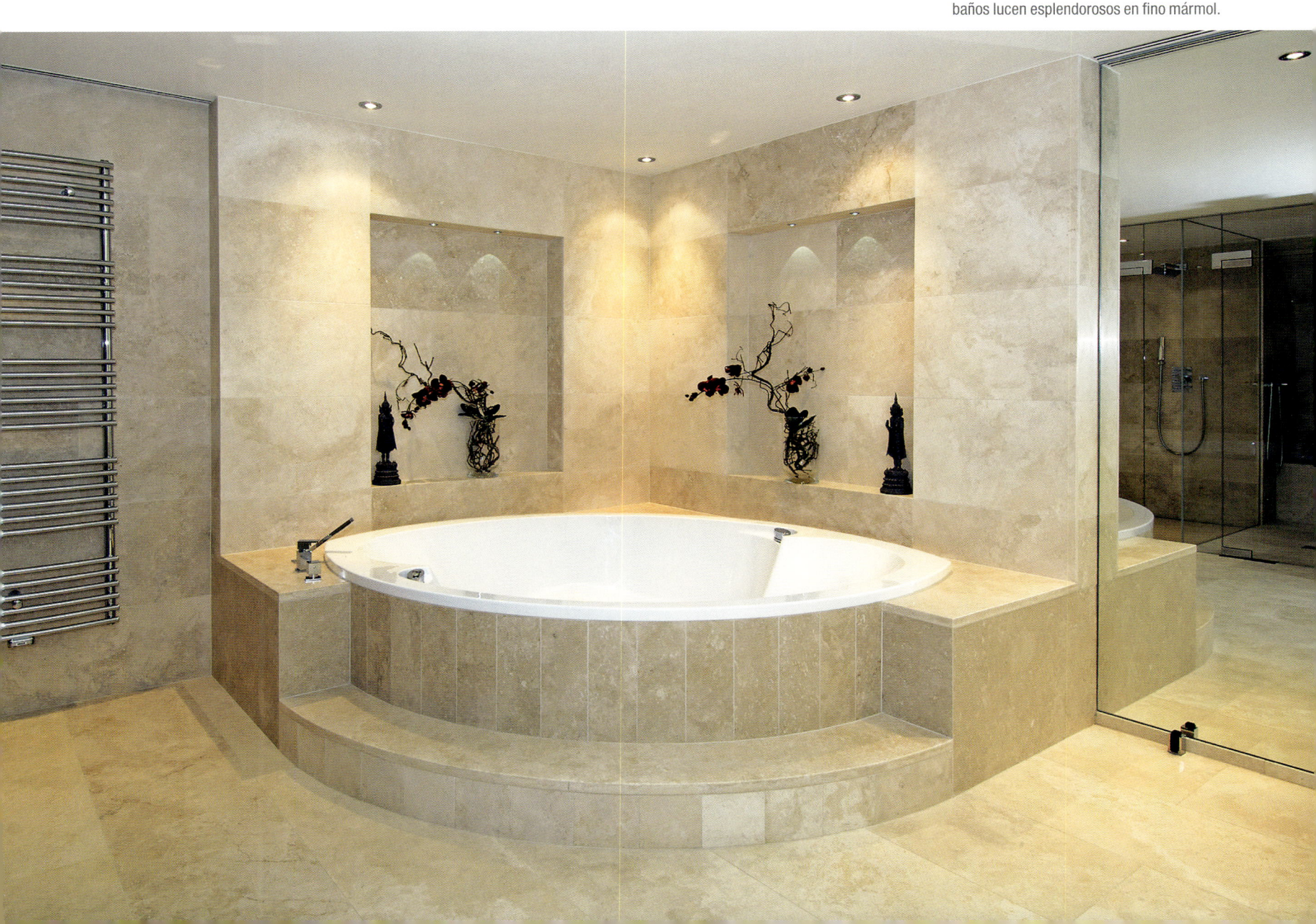

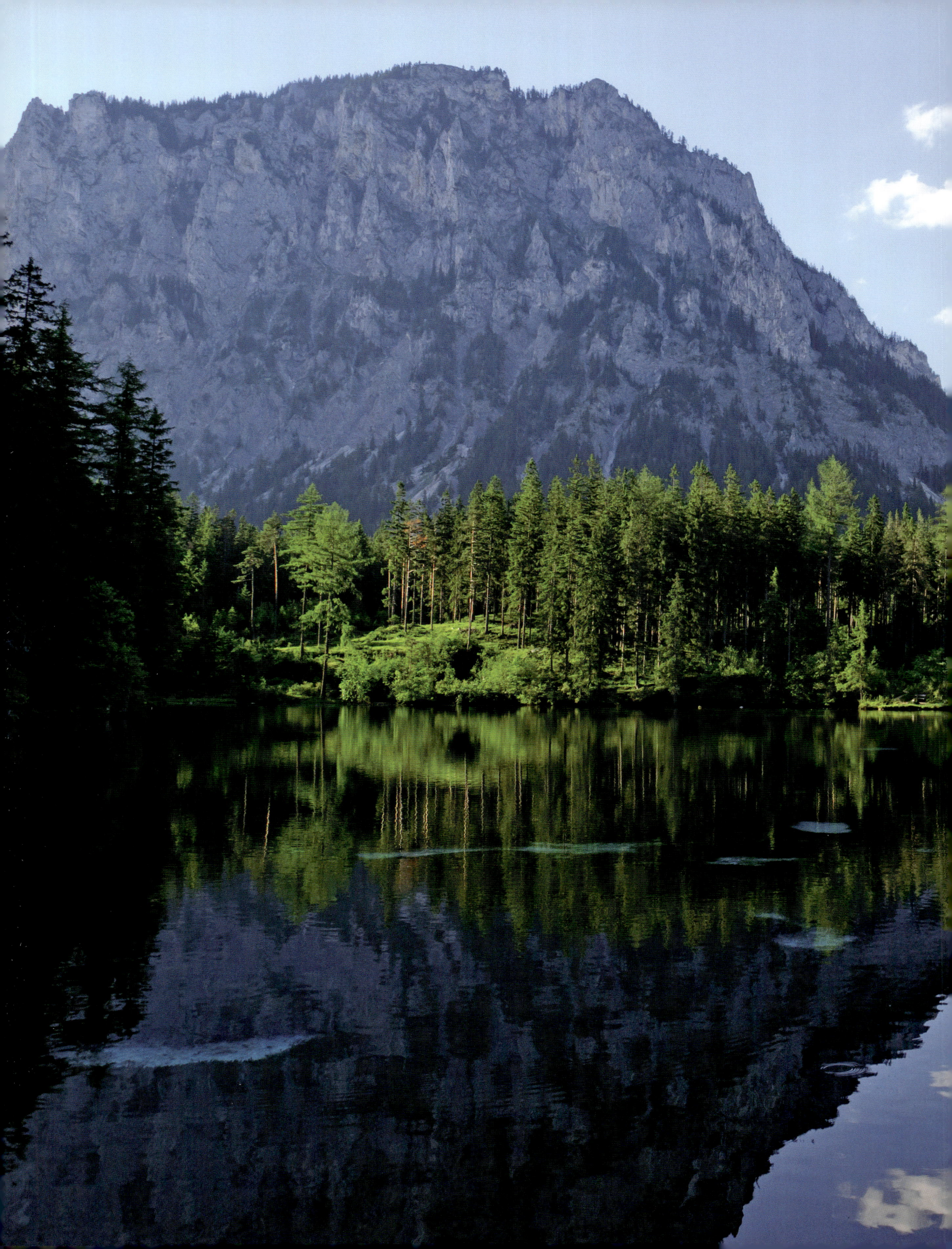

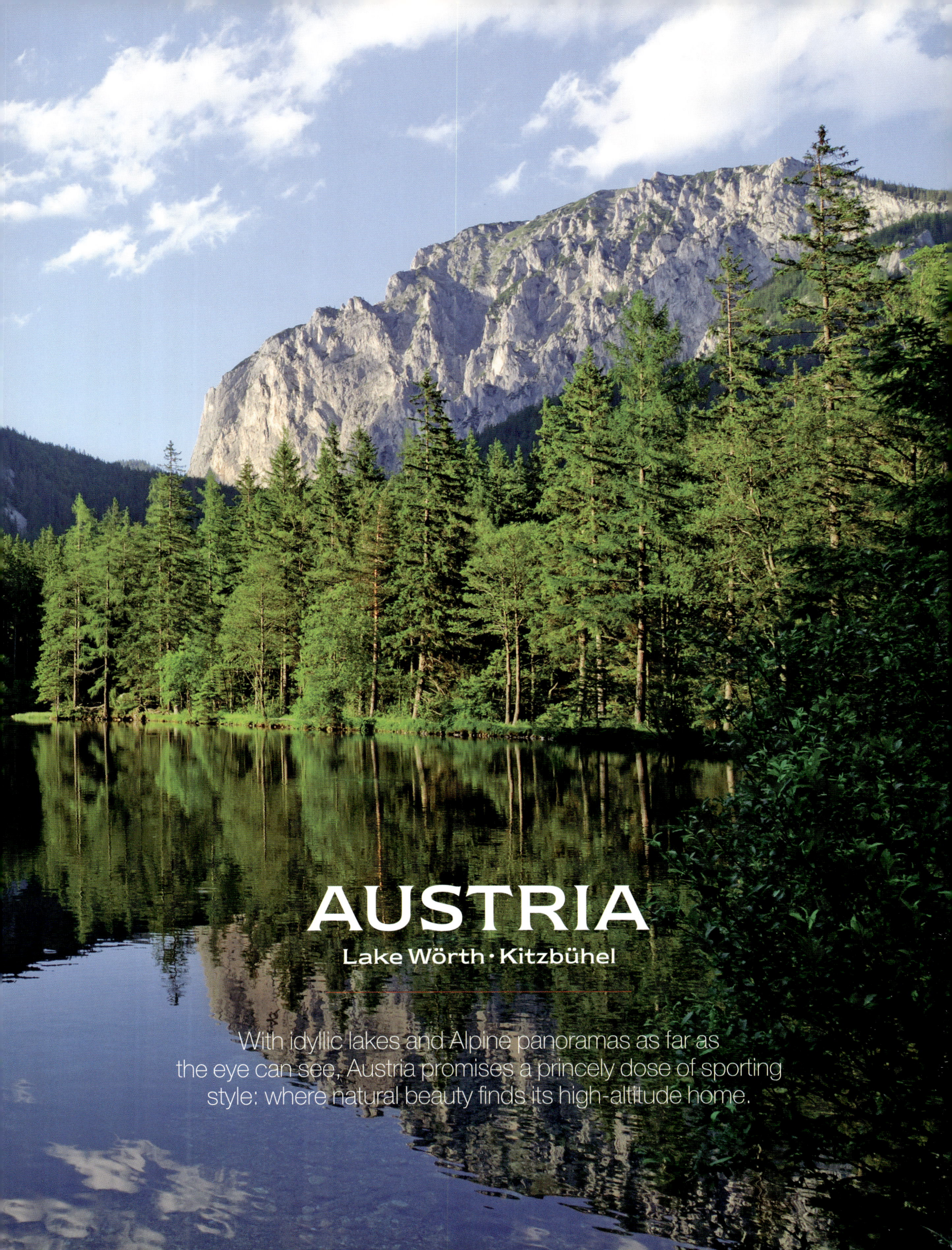

# AUSTRIA
Lake Wörth · Kitzbühel

With idyllic lakes and Alpine panoramas as far as
the eye can see, Austria promises a princely dose of sporting
style: where natural beauty finds its high-altitude home.

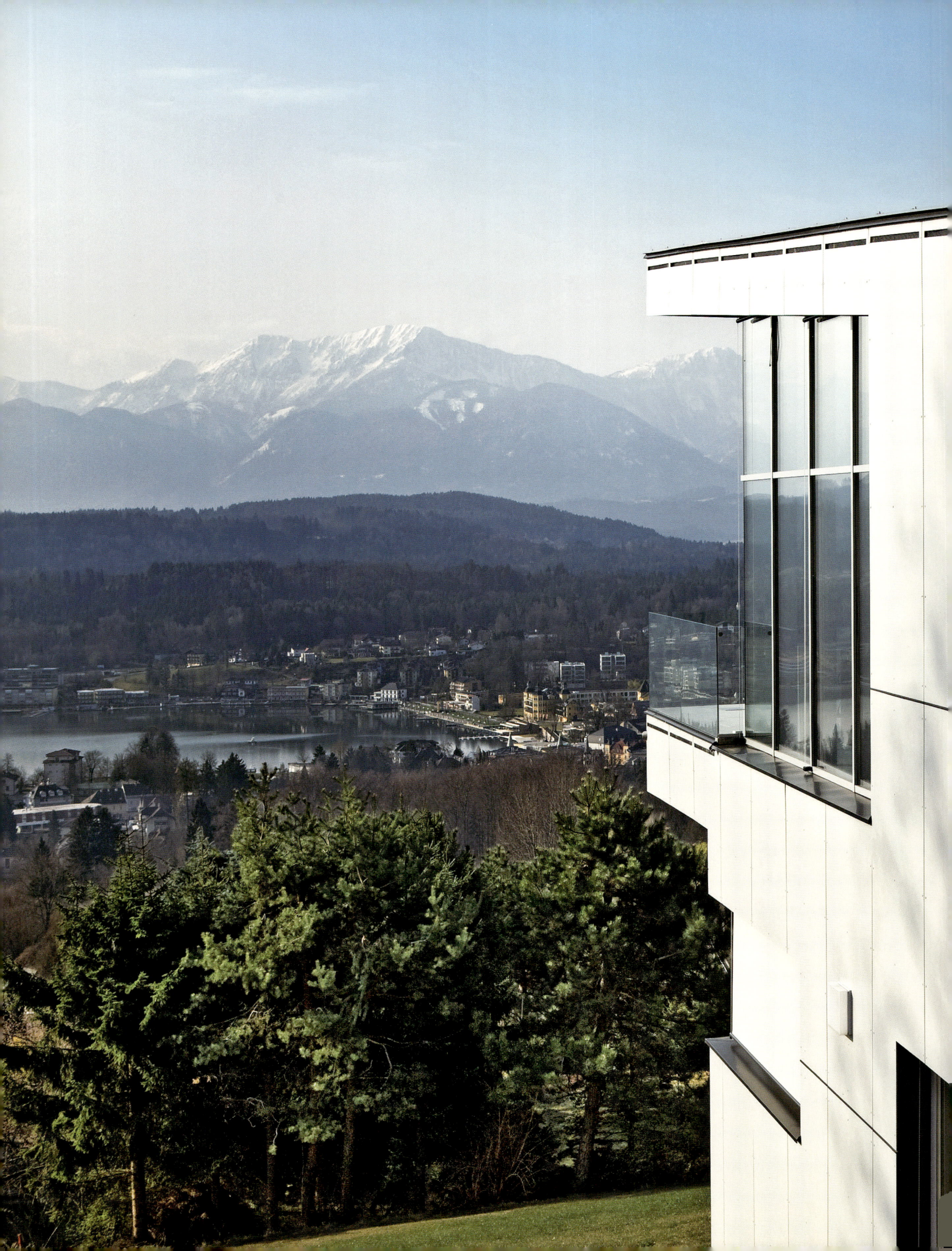

# Lakefront Design Villa

Together with spectacular panoramic views of
Lake Wörth, this phenomenal dwelling has a presence
and appointments that are truly second to none.

THE LOCATION ALONE is superior in every respect – set on the picturesque northern banks of Lake Wörth, this property enjoys a high degree of privacy and excellent connections to the town centre of Velden, together with the wide range of recreational and sightseeing delights that the region has to offer. Yet what is truly unrivalled is the residence, built in 2006, particularly in terms of its architecture and interior design: lovers of modern design will enjoy a supreme quality of life on approx. 750 square metres of living space. Thanks to the floor-to-ceiling panoramic windows, the rooms are bathed in glorious light, and the elegant puristic furnishings are included in the purchase price. The contemporary villa comprises an inviting lounge and dining area, a library, a modern kitchen, three bedroom suites and a large dressing room as well as two bathrooms, an office and three conference rooms. Several terraces for enjoying the outlook and, last but not least, the fantastic infinity pool make living in this high-class home simply perfect.

ALLEIN DIE LAGE ist kaum zu übertreffen – bietet dieses Anwesen am Nordufer des Wörthersees doch neben viel Privatsphäre auch eine hervorragende Anbindung an das Zentrum von Velden, ergänzt von einem vielfältigen Ausflugs- und Freizeitangebot in der Umgebung. Doch als absolut unvergleichlich kann man die im Jahr 2006 erbaute Villa im Hinblick auf ihre Architektur und die Innenausstattung bezeichnen: Auf rund 750 Quadratmetern Wohnfläche genießen anspruchsvolle Design-Liebhaber hier Lebensqualität auf höchstem Niveau. Die Räume bestechen dank bodentiefer Panoramafenster durch ihr lichtdurchflutetes Ambiente und das elegant-puristische, im Kaufpreis inbegriffene Design-Mobiliar. Neben dem einladenden Lounge- und Essbereich nebst Bibliothek verfügt die Villa über eine moderne Küche, drei Schlaf- und ein großes Ankleidezimmer, zwei Bäder, ein Büro sowie drei Besprechungsräume. Mehrere Terrassen und, last but not least, der fantastische Infinity Pool machen das Wohnerlebnis in dieser High-Class-Immobilie perfekt.

LA UBICACIÓN EN sí misma es superior en todos los sentidos: en las pintorescas orillas septentrionales del lago Wörthersee, esta propiedad goza de gran privacidad y excelentes conexiones con el centro de la ciudad de Velden, junto con el amplio abanico de delicias turísticas y recreativas que ofrece la región. Aunque lo ciertamente incomparable es la residencia, construida en 2006, sobre todo en cuanto a su arquitectura y concepto de interiores se refiere: quienes gustan del diseño moderno disfrutarán de la suprema calidad de vida que se extiende en unos 750 metros cuadrados habitables. Gracias a los ventanales panorámicos de suelo a techo las estancias están bañadas en luz; el mobiliario, elegante y purista, viene incluido en el precio de compra. La villa cuenta con una acogedora zona de estar y comedor, biblioteca, la moderna cocina, tres *suites* y un amplio vestidor, así como dos cuartos de baño, un despacho y tres salas de conferencia. Varias terrazas y, por último, pero no menos importante, la fantástica piscina desbordante hacen de la vida aquí una experiencia de nivel superior.

AUSTRIA, LAKE WÖRTH **PURCHASE PRICE** EUR 3.5 MILL. **INTERIOR APPROX.** 750 m² **NO. OF BEDROOMS** 3
**LAND APPROX.** 1,264 m² **E&V ID** W-01668U **CONTACT** VELDEN (AT), H&H PREMIUM IMMOBILIENVERMITTLUNG GMBH,
LICENCE PARTNER OF ENGEL & VÖLKERS RESIDENTIAL GMBH
**TEL.** +43 4274 23 55 51 00 **E-MAIL** WOERTHERSEE@ENGELVOELKERS.COM

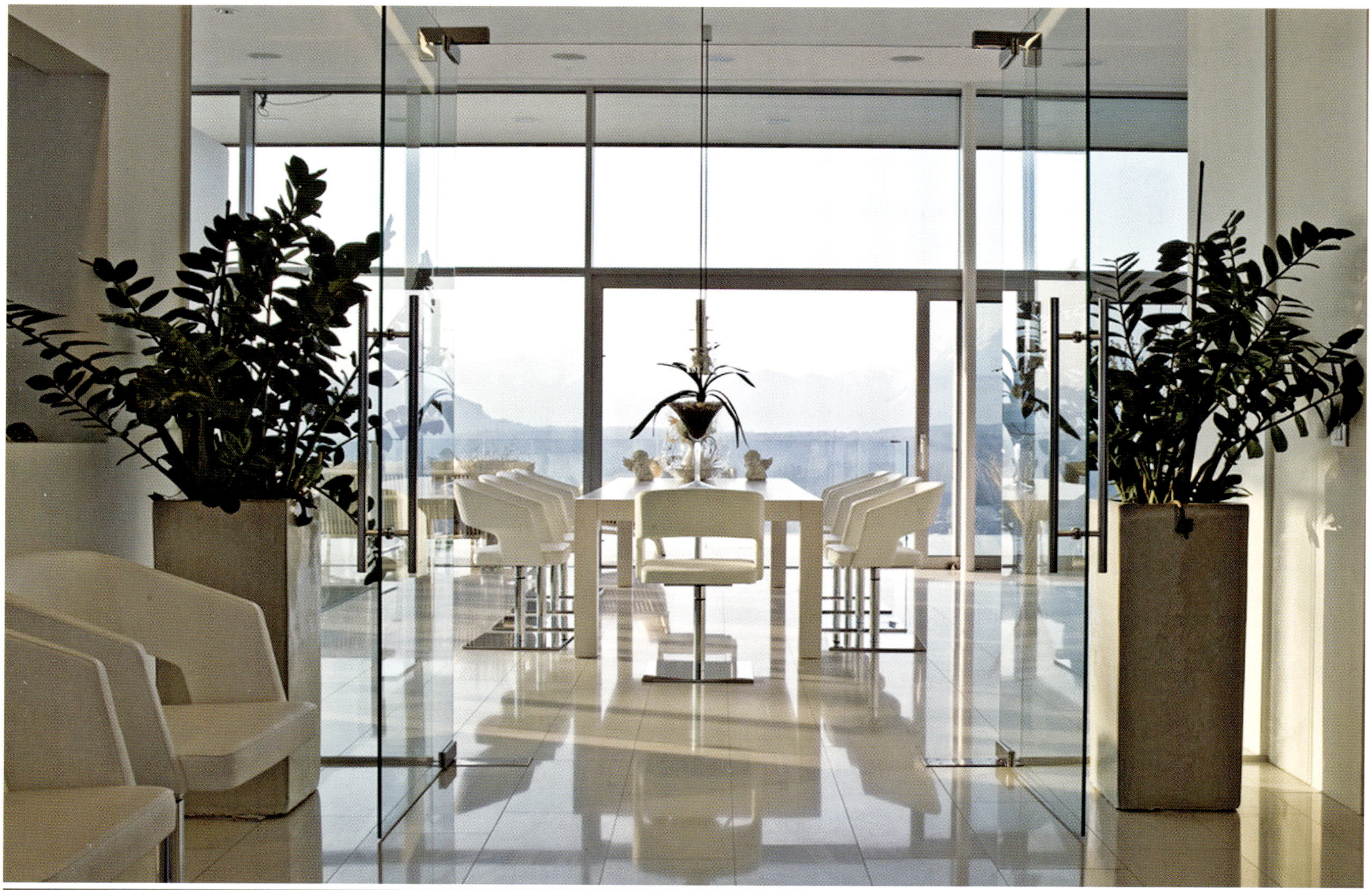

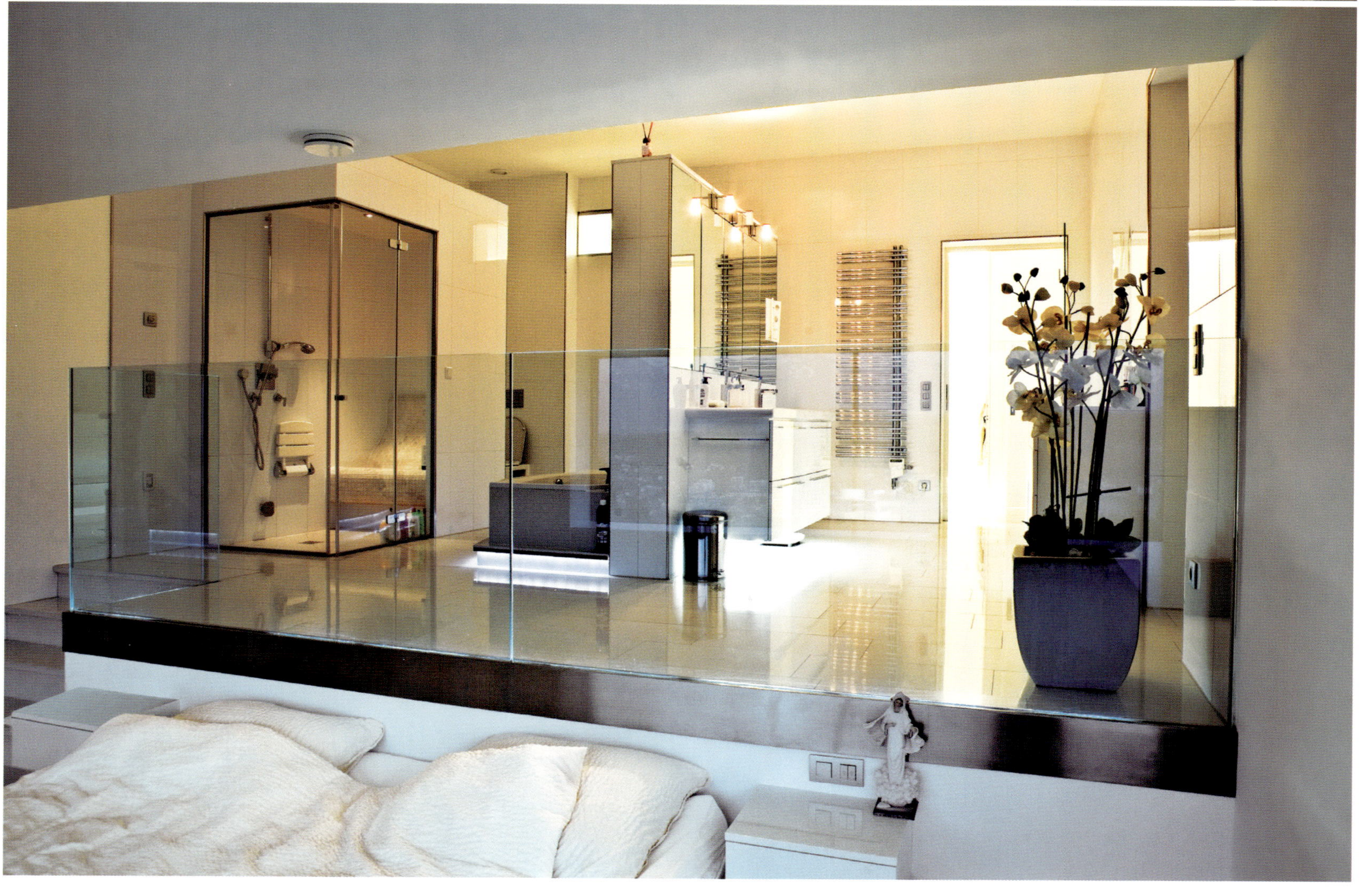

<

Lots of light, plenty of space and a high degree
of comfort spread across three floors.

Viel Licht, viel Raum und maximalen Wohnkomfort genießt man hier auf drei Etagen.

Mucha luz, cantidad de espacio y un alto grado
de confort se reparten en tres plantas.

The floor-to-ceiling panoramic windows
ensure absolutely sensational vistas.

Für wahrhaft spektakuläre Aussichten
sorgen die bodentiefen Panoramafenster.

Los ventanales de suelo a techo garantizan
vistas absolutamente sensacionales.

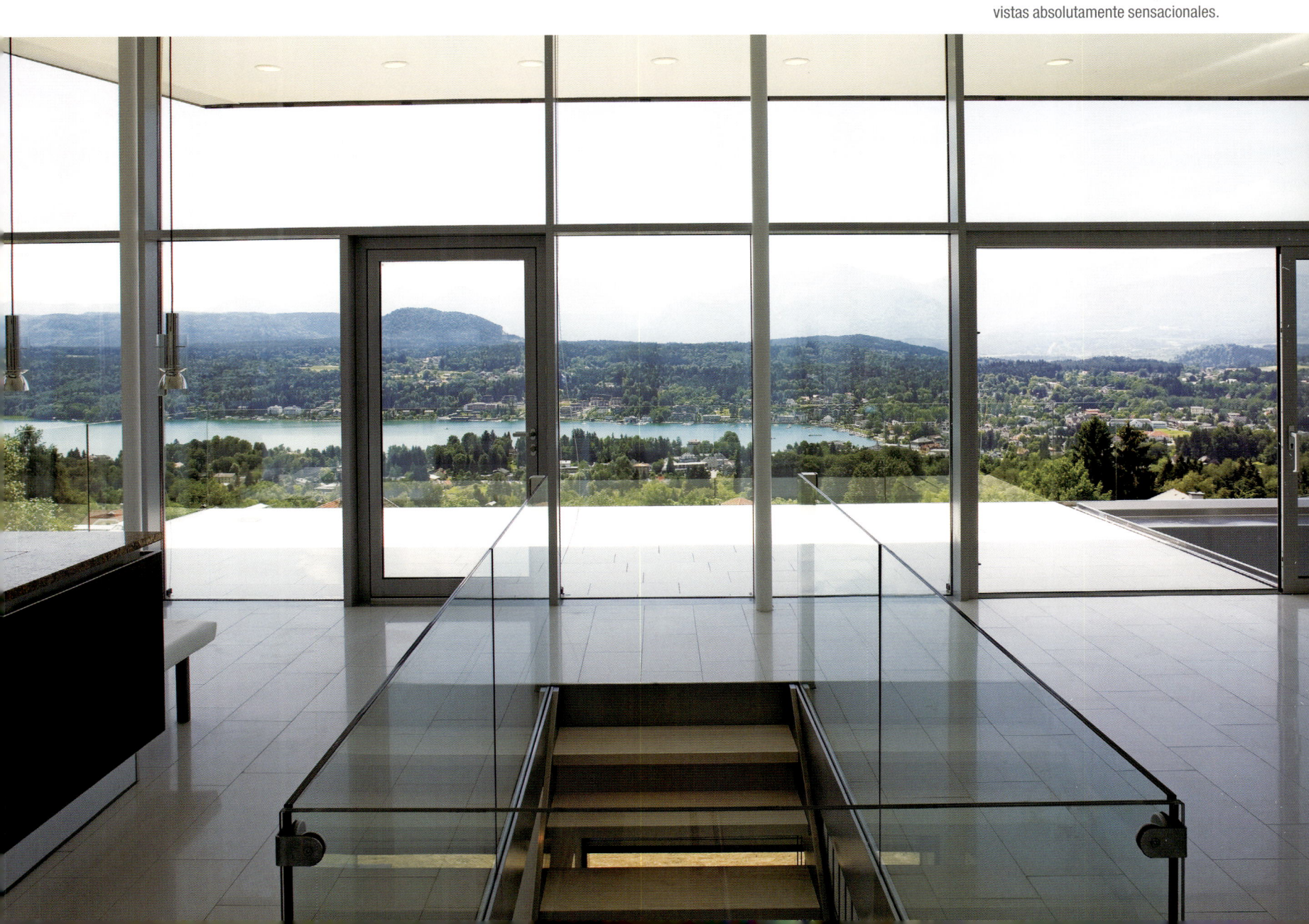

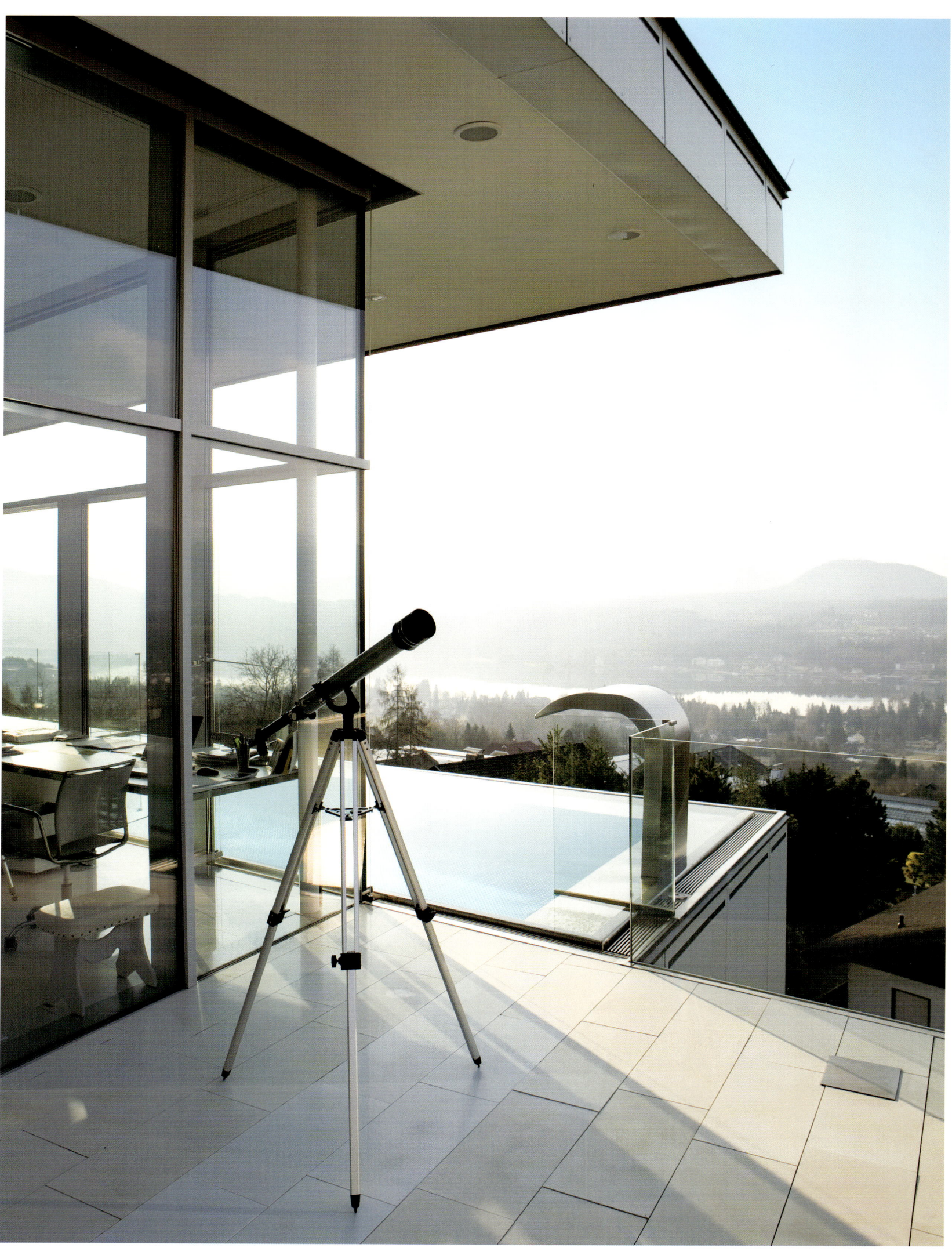

Unrivalled: the 360-degree views of
Lake Wörth and the surrounding region.

Unvergleichlich: der Rundumblick über
die Umgebung und den Wörthersee.

Incomparables: las vistas panorámicas
integrales al Wörthersee y los alredededores.

A stunning example of modern architecture
that is unsurpassed in many respects.

Ein Prachtexemplar moderner Architektur, das
in vielerlei Hinsicht seinesgleichen sucht.

Un impresionante ejemplo de arquitectura
moderna, sin igual en muchos aspectos.

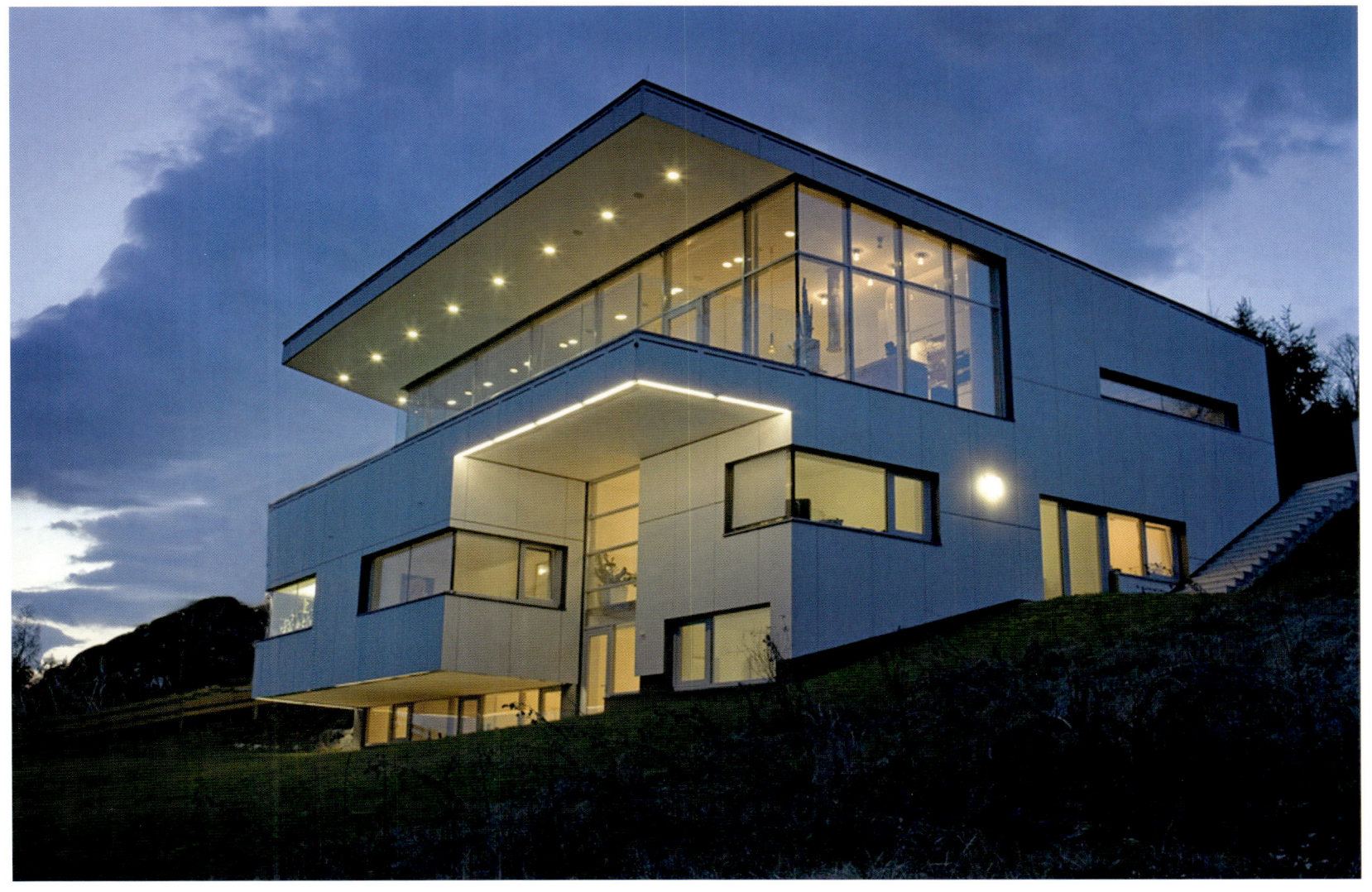

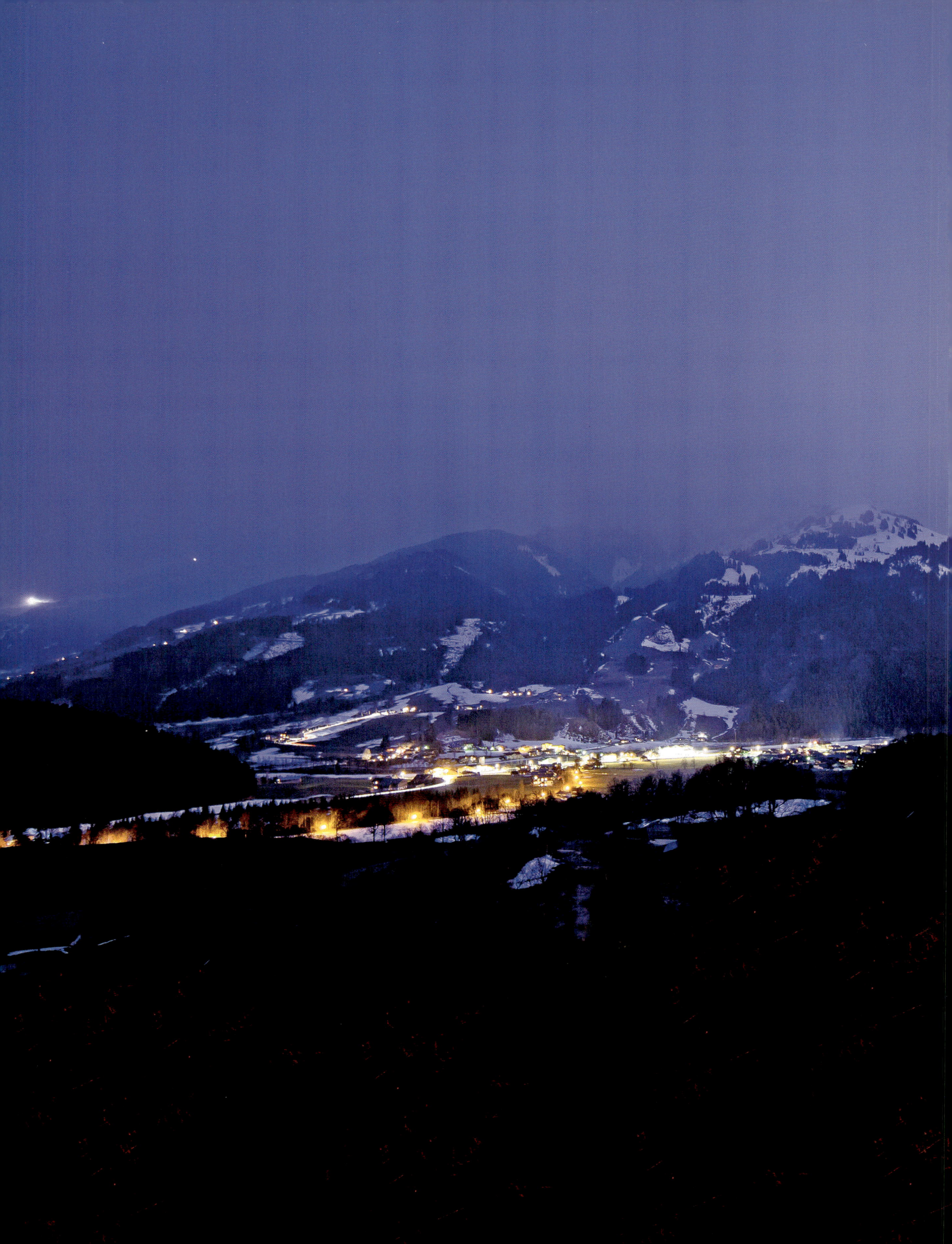

# Cosy Mountain Home

The unique sweeping scenery of the Tyrolean
Alps provides the backdrop for this chalet, combining
a luxurious sense of space with maximum privacy.

AT THE END of a private road on the Kitzbühel Bichlalm, this property offers exclusivity and utter peace and tranquillity – for families, in particular. At the same time, breathtaking views over the entire valley can be enjoyed, thanks to the chalet's large panoramic windows. The factors of light and spaciousness played a central role in the design and layout of the rooms, such as in the large open-plan living room of around 140 square metres with a fireplace or the spacious roofed balcony that wraps itself around the entire dwelling. Facing the south, the warm rays of the sun can be enjoyed on the terrace until the late afternoon. The interior design is impressive with its nuanced combination of traditional and modern elements, enhanced by family- and guest-friendly extras such as the terrace dining area for 18 persons or the climbing wall for children. Thanks to several guest bedrooms, there is also sufficient space to accommodate friends and relatives – and this amidst spectacular Alpine scenery and only ten minutes away from the town centre.

AM ENDE EINES kleinen Privatweges auf der Kitzbüheler Bichlalm gelegen, verspricht dieses besonders für Familien geeignete Anwesen vollkommene Ruhe und Exklusivität. Gleichzeitig sorgen die großen Panoramafenster für atemberaubende Ausblicke über das gesamte Tal. Licht und Weite spielten auch bei der Gestaltung der Räume eine zentrale Rolle, so z. B. beim offenen, ca. 140 Quadratmeter großen Wohnzimmer mit Kamin oder dem ebenfalls sehr großzügigen, überdachten Balkon, der sich um das gesamte Gebäude zieht. Dank der Südlage strahlt hier bis zum späten Nachmittag die Sonne. Die Inneneinrichtung besticht durch eine gekonnte Kombination traditioneller und moderner Elemente, ergänzt von familien- und gastfreundlichen Extras wie dem Essbereich für 18 Personen auf der überdachten Terrasse oder der Kletterwand für Kinder. Darüber hinaus gibt es dank mehrerer Schlaf- bzw. Gästezimmer genügend Platz, um Freunde und Verwandte zu beherbergen – und das vor schönster Alpenkulisse und nur zehn Minuten vom Stadtzentrum entfernt.

AL FINAL DE una calle privada en el Kitzbühel Bichlalm, esta propiedad ofrece la máxima exclusividad y la paz y la tranquilidad más absolutas, en especial para familias, pero gozando a la vez de unas vistas impresionantes a todo el valle, gracias a los ventanales panorámicos del chalet. Los factores de luz y amplitud jugaron un papel fundamental en el diseño y la distribución de los espacios, como la gran sala de estar abierta de 140 metros cuadrados con su chimenea, o la amplia terraza cubierta que rodea toda la vivienda. Mirando al sur, la calidez de los rayos del sol inunda la terraza hasta caer la tarde. El interiorismo es magnífico, con su matizada combinación de elementos tradicionales y modernos realzados por detalles para la familia y sus invitados, como el comedor para 18 personas en la terraza cubierta o el muro de escalada para los niños. Además, al disponer de varios dormitorios para invitados, hay espacio suficiente para alojar a los amigos y los parientes, siempre rodeados por el espectacular paisaje alpino y a tan sólo diez minutos del centro de la localidad.

AUSTRIA, KITZBÜHEL **RENTAL PRICE/WEEK** EUR 13,500 **INTERIOR APPROX.** 540 m² **NO. OF BEDROOMS** 5
**LAND APPROX.** 2,200 m² **E&V ID** W-01VPAK **CONTACT** KITZBÜHEL (AT), ENGEL & VÖLKERS KITZBÜHEL GMBH,
PARTNER OF ENGEL & VÖLKERS RESIDENTIAL GMBH **TEL.** +43 5356 716 15
**E-MAIL** KITZBUEHEL@ENGELVOELKERS.COM

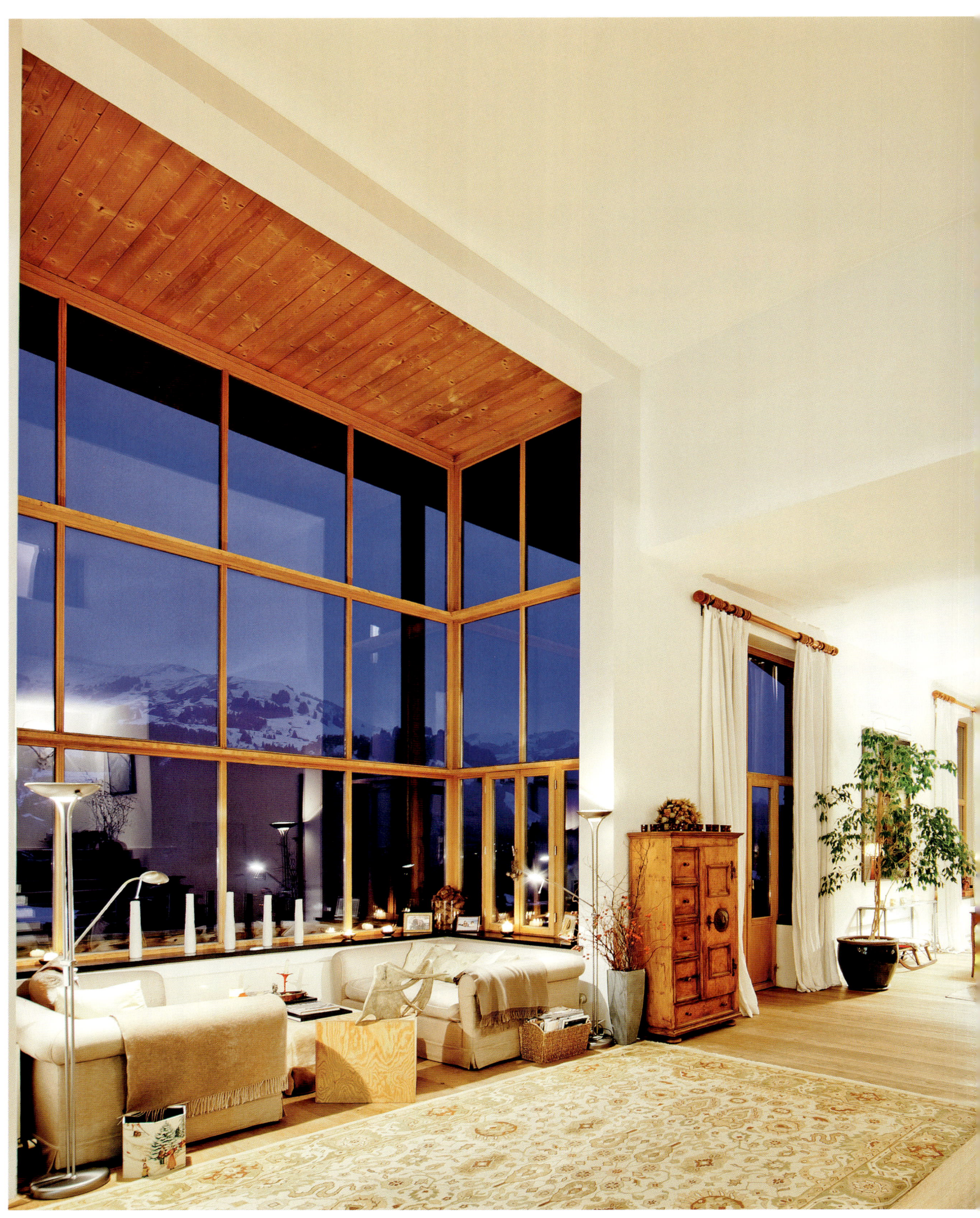

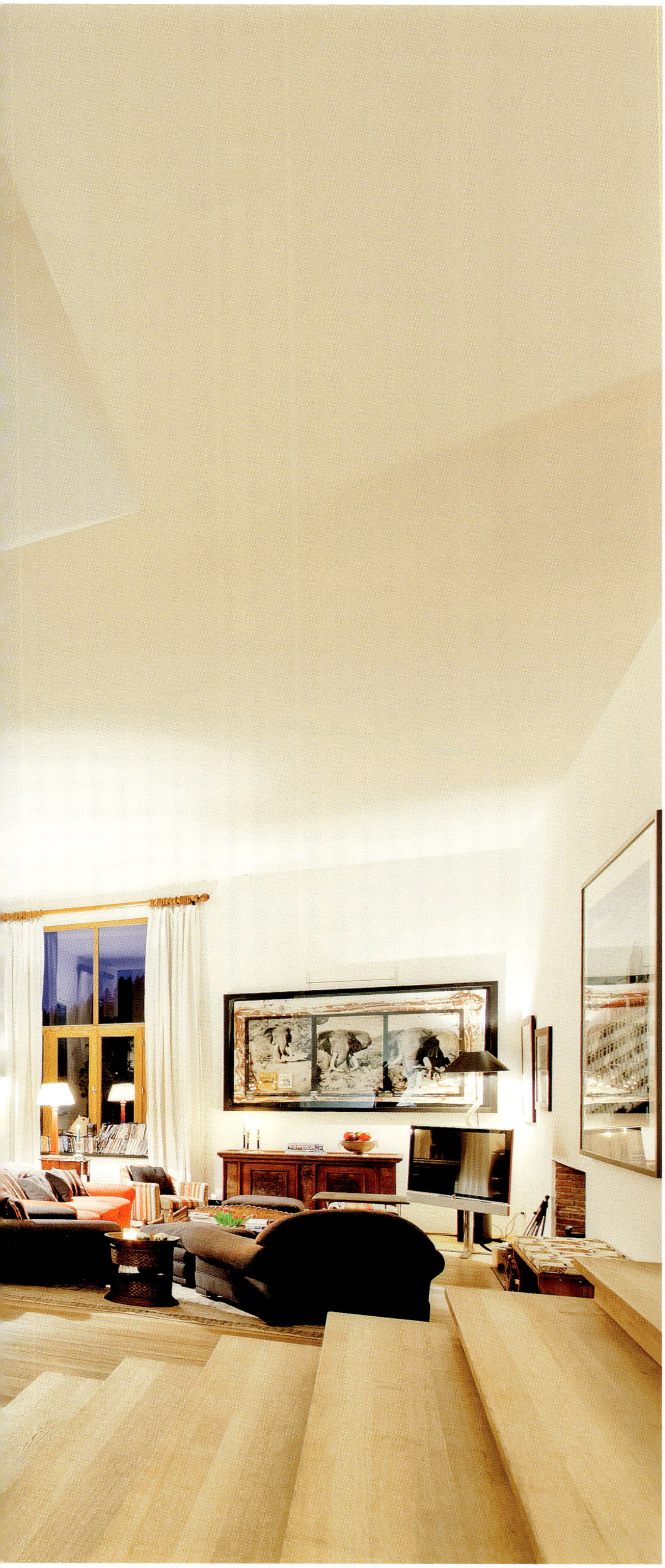

The large panoramic windows do splendid
justice to the stunning mountain scenery.

Die großen Panoramafenster setzen die
imposante Bergkulisse gebührend in Szene.

Los ventanales panorámicos hacen justicia al
siempre impresionante paisaje de montaña.

The bedrooms are all quiet, and their design
consciously avoids a wall-to-wall layout.

Die Schlafzimmer sind allesamt ruhig und
bewusst nicht Wand an Wand gelegen.

Todos los dormitorios son tranquilos,
diseñados evitando compartición de paredes.

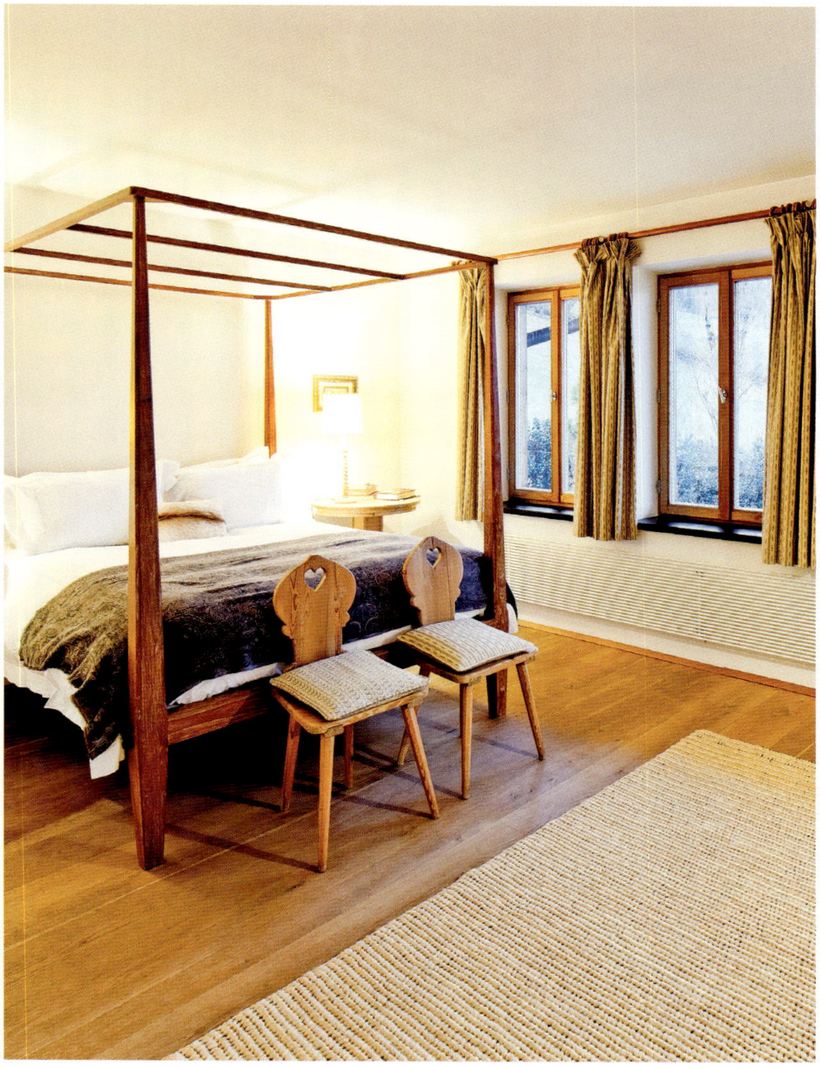

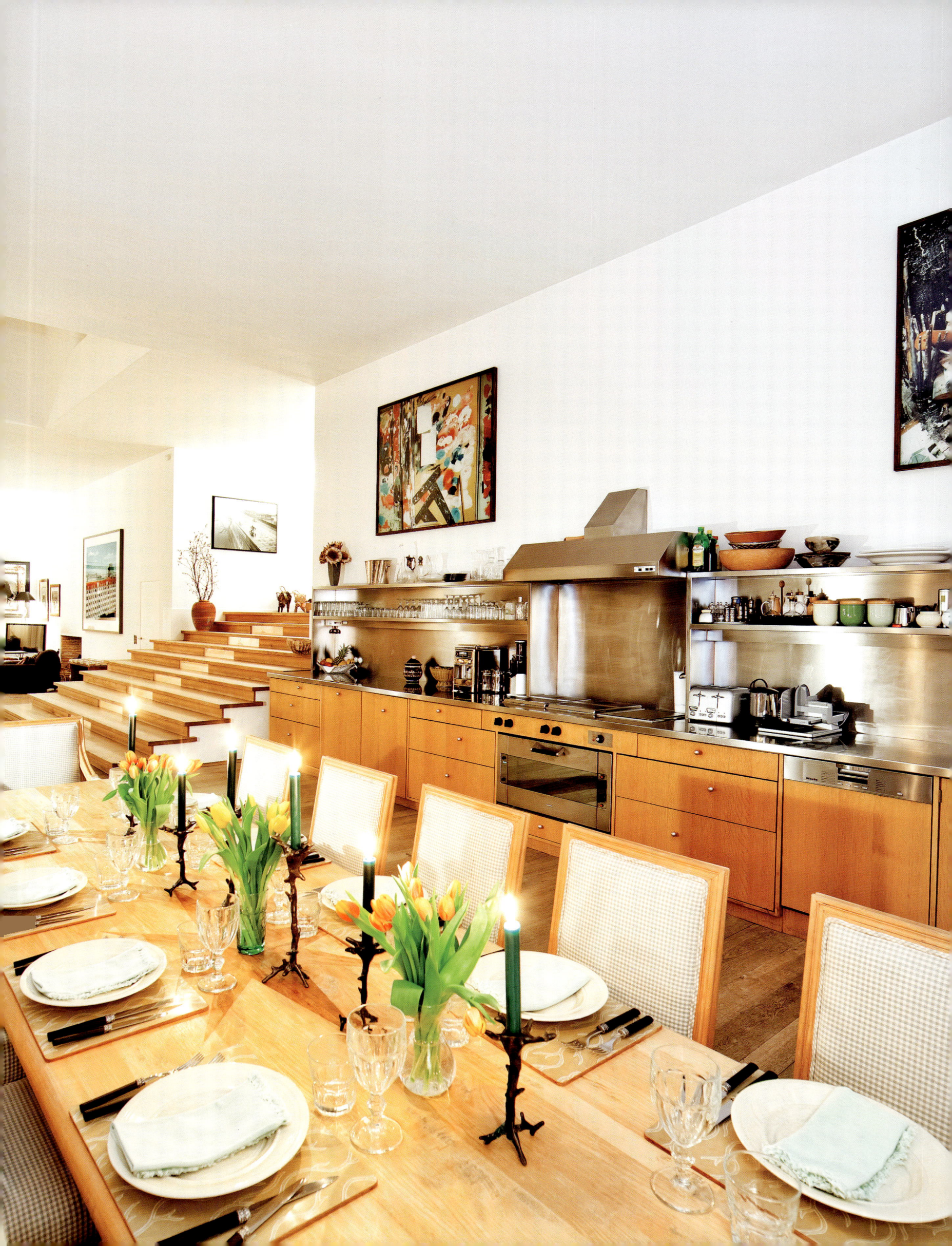

<

The open-plan kitchen, dining and living areas provide ample space for guests.

Küche, Ess- und Wohnbereich gehen ineinander über und bieten viel Platz für Gäste.

En plano abierto, cocina, comedor y salón brindan un amplio escenario a los invitados.

The living spaces provide a cosy sense of comfort and great technical refinement.

Die Wohnräume verfügen über behaglichen Komfort mit allen technischen Raffinessen.

Las zonas de día destilan una acogedora comodidad y gran refinamiento técnico.

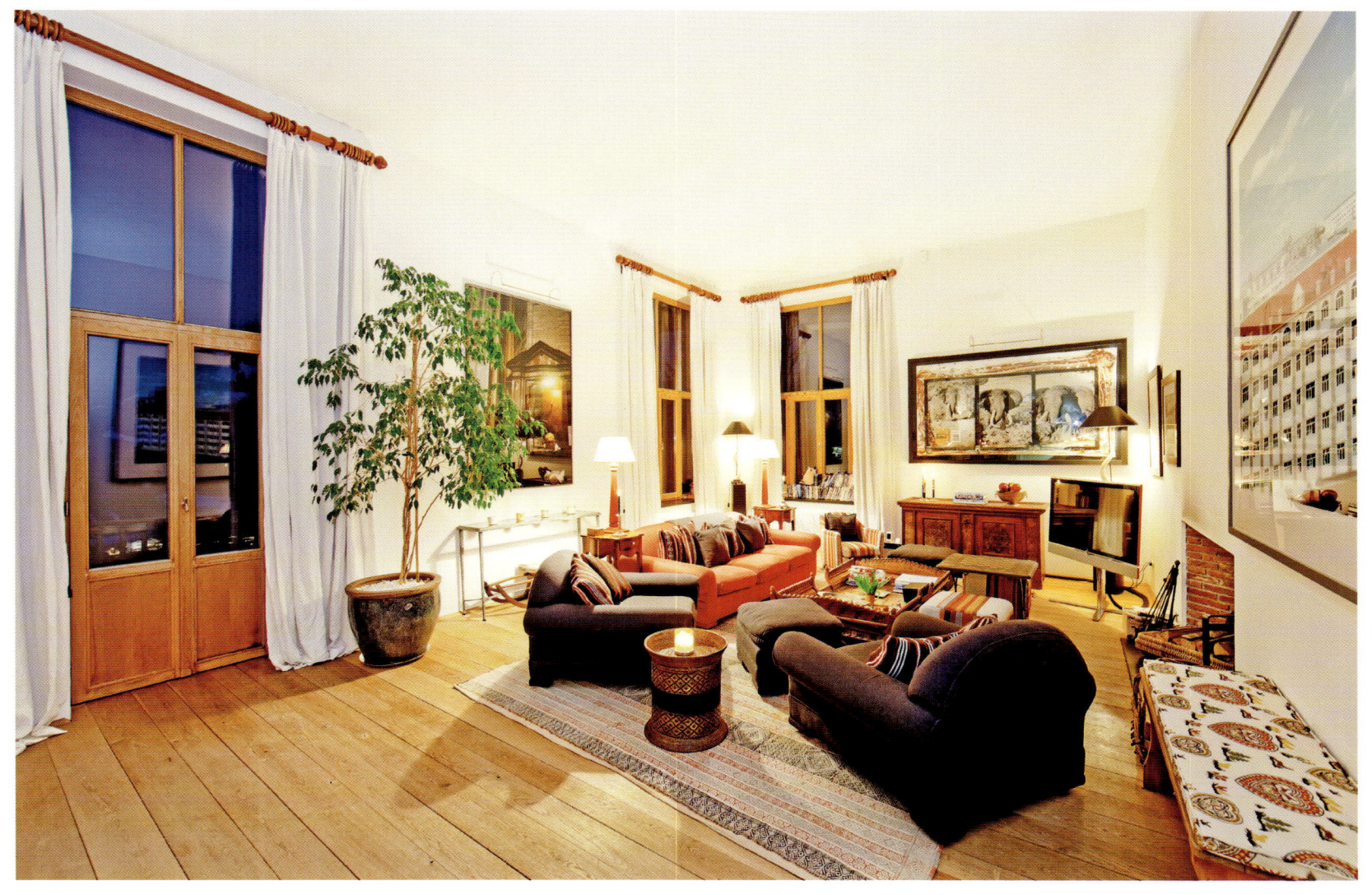

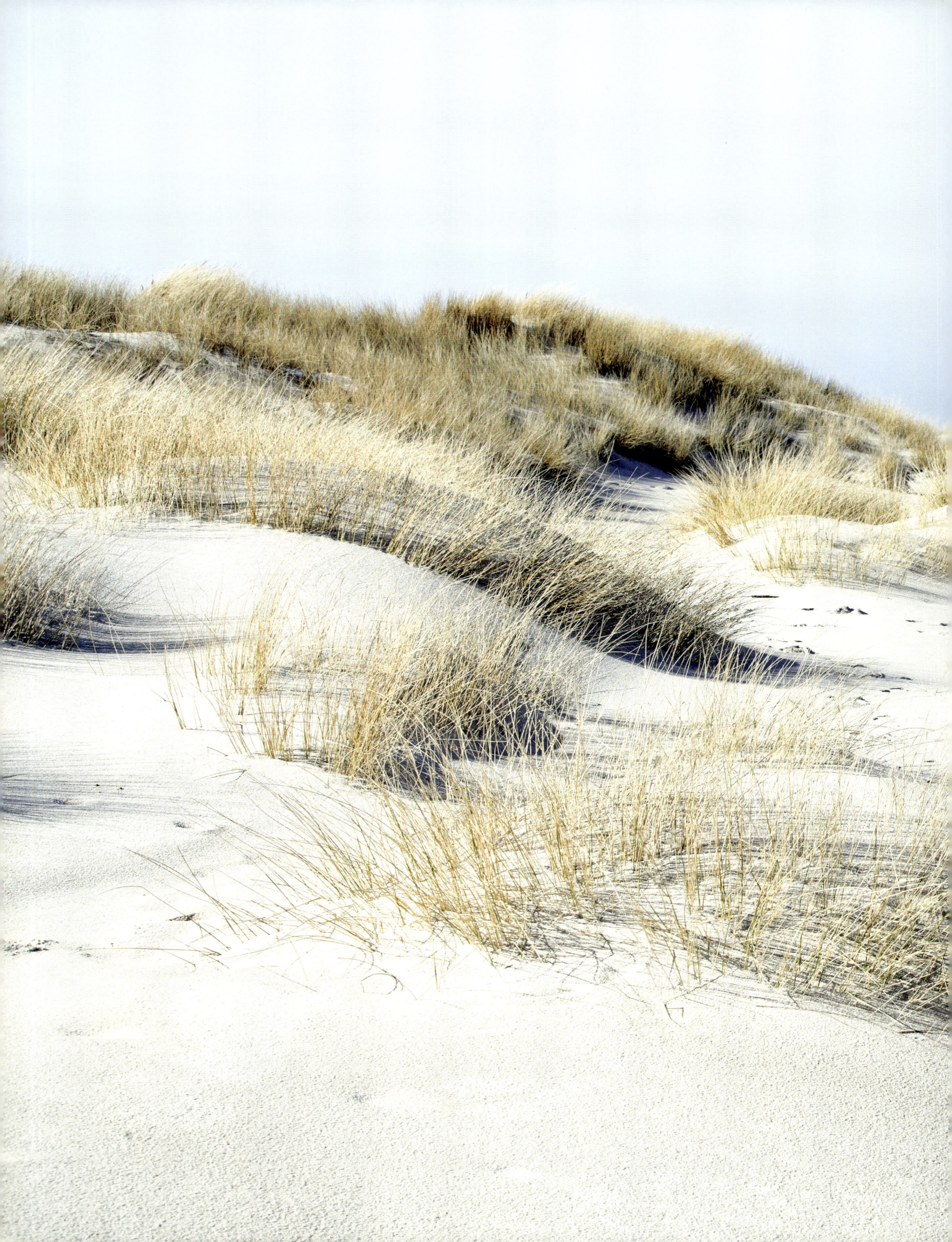

# GERMANY

## Sylt · Föhr · Lake Ammer

From the charm of the North Frisian islands to the lovely
lake and mountain panoramas of Bavaria, Germany's diversity
is not only fascinating but also worth exploring.

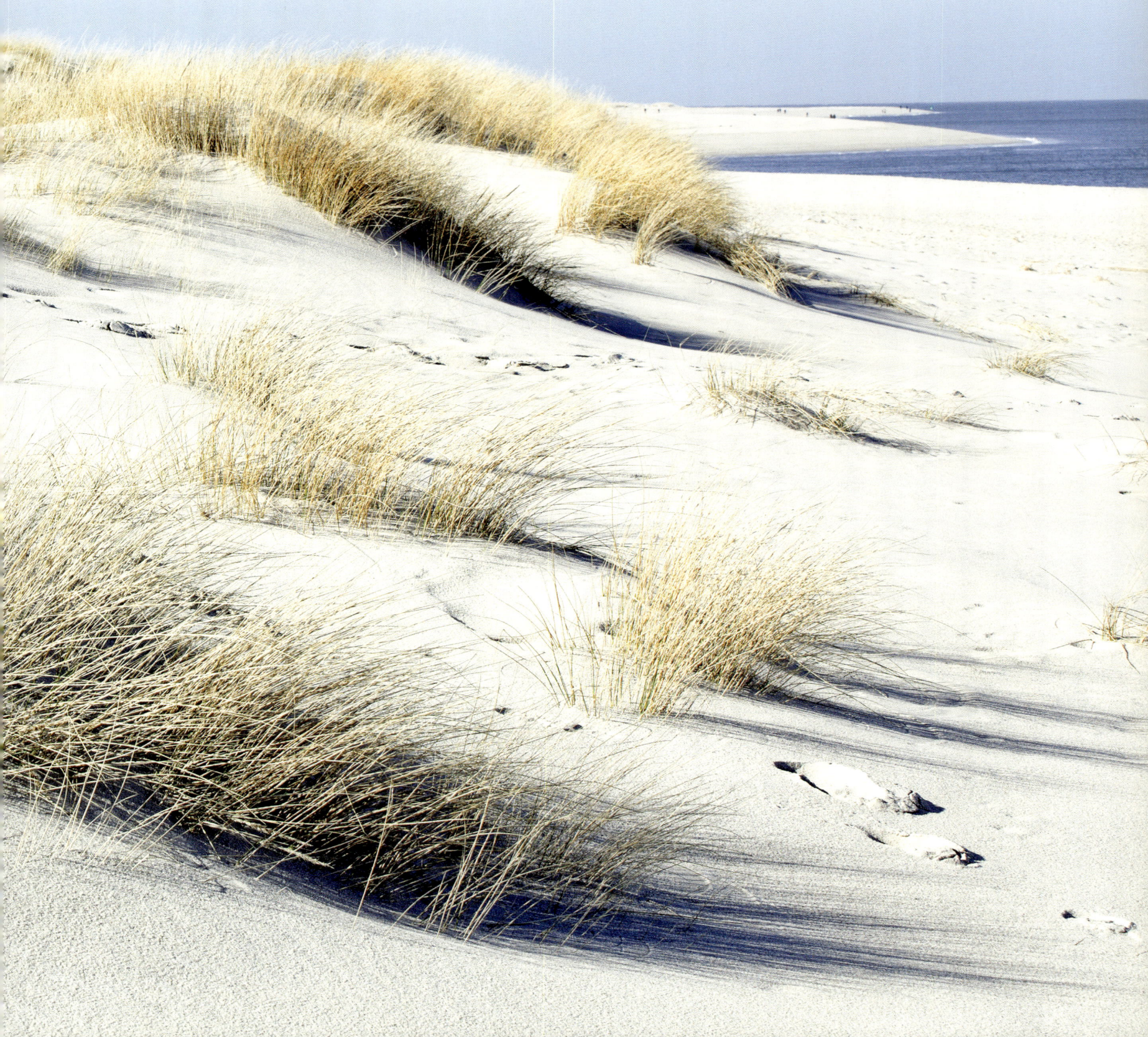

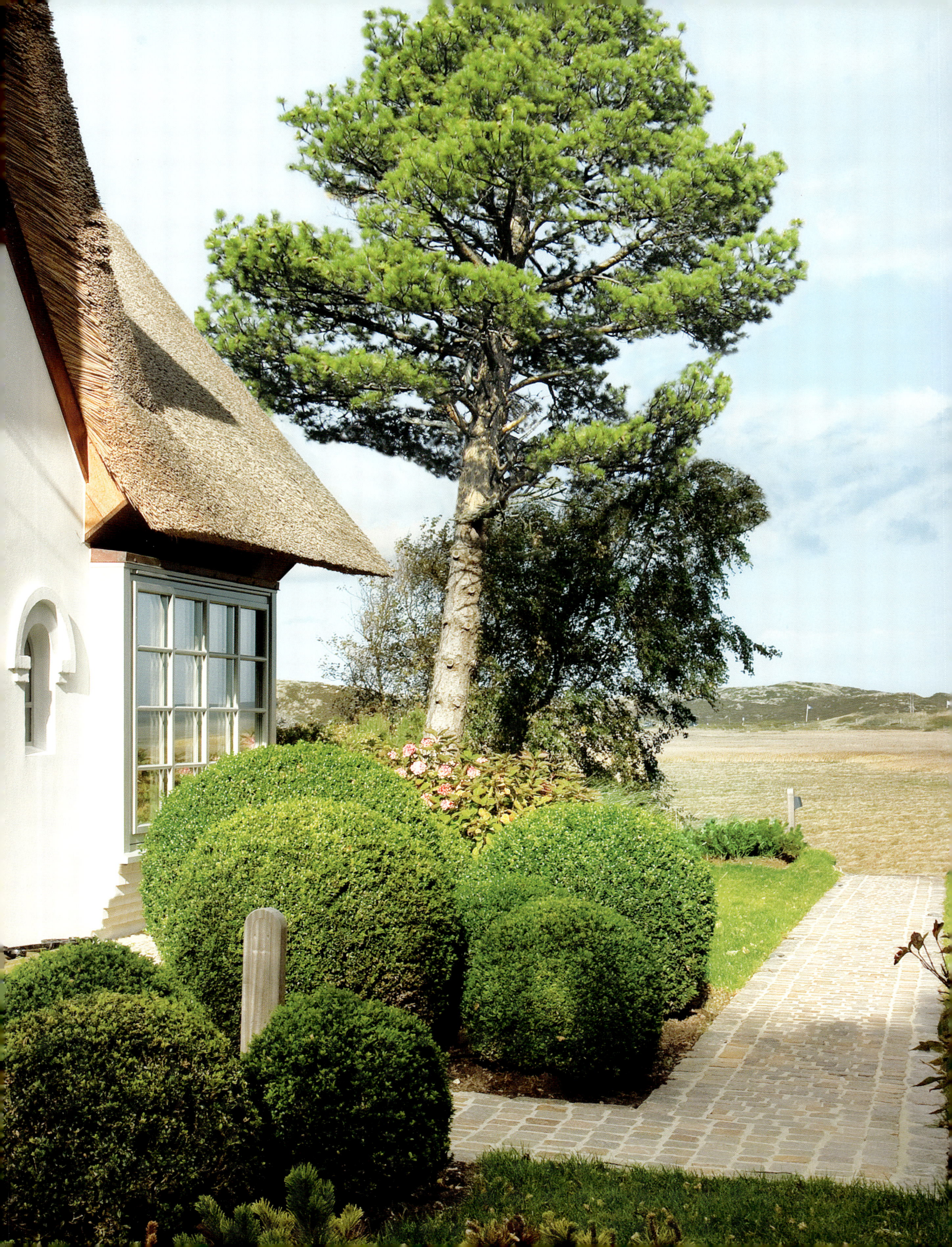

# North Frisian Cottage

Boasting a seafront location in the exclusive town of Kampen on Sylt, this romantic thatched home exudes a wonderful Nordic sense of style and serenity.

SYLT, THE LARGEST of the North Frisian islands, is an ideal place to visit for those who wish to get away from it all: endless dunes and white sandy beaches, the mudflats of the Wadden Sea National Park, and the fresh North Sea air to restore one's soul. Set on a large property, this beautiful detached house in Kampen could almost be paradise on earth: enjoying a prime location directly by the dunes with spectacular oceanfront views, the idyllic property is both quiet and protected – yet only minutes from the exclusive boutiques and famous star-quality cuisine of Kampen. Originally built in 1930 and recently renovated with loving attention to detail, this holiday home is tastefully appointed, featuring a large and inviting entrance area, open-plan living space with panoramic windows, a comfortable lounge and a sophisticated dining area, as well as a luxury kitchen with a separate breakfast corner. Three beautiful en-suite bedrooms, which are ideal for six persons, ensure a peaceful rest and sweet dreams – all in all, the perfect base for an exclusive island getaway!

SYLT, DIE GRÖSSTE der nordfriesischen Inseln, ist wie geschaffen für eine entspannte Auszeit am Meer: Die endlosen, feinsandigen Dünenstrände des Wattenmeers und die frische Nordseeluft sind eine Wohltat für Körper, Geist und Seele. Als exklusiver Hotspot der Insel bildet die Gemeinde Kampen die perfekte Kulisse für dieses Kleinod mit Reetdach. Ruhig und geschützt, mit spektakulärem Blick über das Watt, liegt das idyllische Anwesen dennoch nur wenige Minuten von den edlen Boutiquen und der sternegekrönten Gastronomieszene Kampens entfernt. Ursprünglich im Jahre 1930 erbaut und erst kürzlich mit viel Liebe zum Detail renoviert, verfügt es über großzügige, geschmackvoll eingerichtete Räumlichkeiten. Dazu gehören ein einladender Eingangs- und ein offener Wohn- und Essbereich mit Panoramafenstern, eine hochwertig ausgestattete Küche samt separater Frühstücksecke sowie drei behagliche Zimmer mit Bad, die sechs Personen ausreichend Platz zum Wohlfühlen bieten. Das perfekte Domizil, um die vielfältigen Reize Sylts in vollen Zügen zu genießen!

SYLT, LA MAYOR de las islas del norte de Frisia, es un destino de vacaciones idóneo para quienes desean alejarse de todo: interminables dunas y playas de arena blanca, las marismas del Parque Nacional del Mar de Wadden y el aire fresco del Mar del Norte restaurant el alma. En un gran terreno, esta hermosa casa en Kampen casi podría considerarse un paraíso en la tierra, dada su ubicación privilegiada en las dunas con espectaculares vistas frente al mar, idílica, tranquila y protegida, pero a sólo unos minutos de las exclusivas *boutiques* y la famosa gastronomía de Kampen. Construida en 1930 y renovada recientemente con amor al detalle, la generosa zona de día de esta casa de vacaciones luce su buen gusto: cuenta con una cálida y espaciosa entrada, la sala de estar abierta con ventanales panorámicos, un cómodo salón y la sofisticada área de comedor, así como una cocina de lujo con zona separada para desayunos. Tres preciosos dormitorios en *suite*, perfectos para seis personas, garantizan un descanso tranquilo y dulces sueños en este destino perfecto para una exclusiva escapada isleña.

GERMANY, SYLT **RENTAL PRICE/NIGHT** EUR 590–1,490 **INTERIOR APPROX.** 220 m² **NO. OF BEDROOMS** 3 **LAND APPROX.** 1,000 m²
**E&V ID** W-01MTFW **CONTACT** KAMPEN (DE), BLUME & HAGENAH IMMOBILIEN GMBH & CO. KG,
LICENCE PARTNER OF ENGEL & VÖLKERS RESIDENTIAL GMBH **TEL.** +49 4651 985 70
**E-MAIL** SYLT@ENGELVOELKERS.COM

Energy Performance Certificate is not available.

An atmospheric dining experience by the
cosy warmth of the modern fireplace.

Ein moderner Kamin unterstützt das elegante,
stimmungsvolle Ambiente im Essbereich.

Gozar la sobremesa junto a la acogedora
calidez de la chimenea de vanguardia.

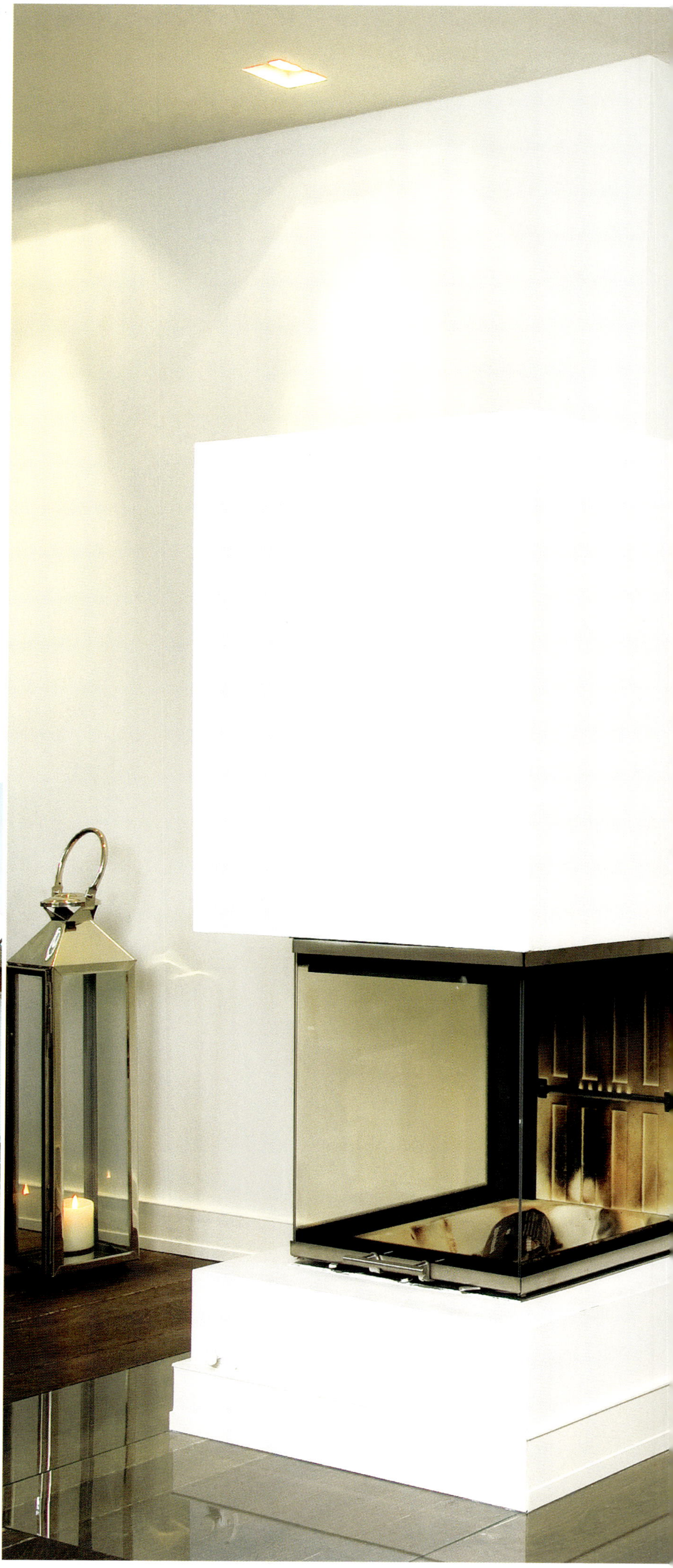

A little idyll: the lovingly tended cottage garden
basking in the glorious late-afternoon sun.

Ein wahres Idyll in schönster Nachmittags-
sonne: der liebevoll angelegte Garten.

Un idilio: el jardín amorosamente atendido
resplandece bajo el glorioso sol de la tarde.

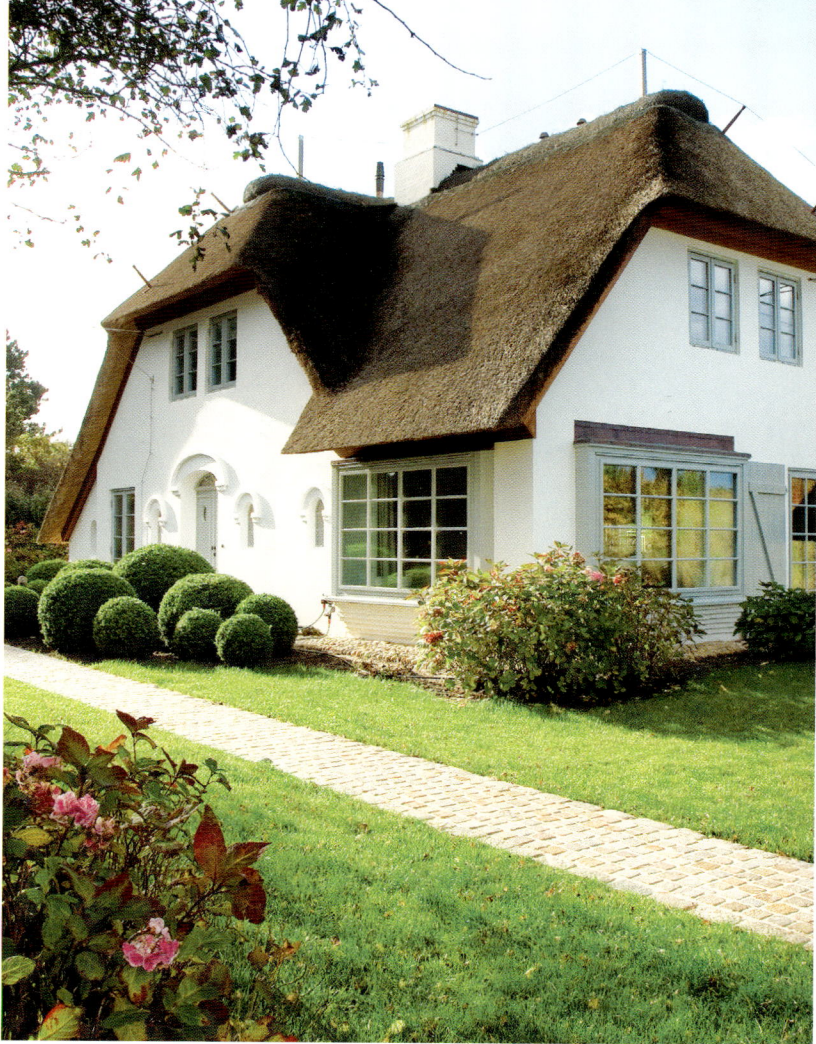

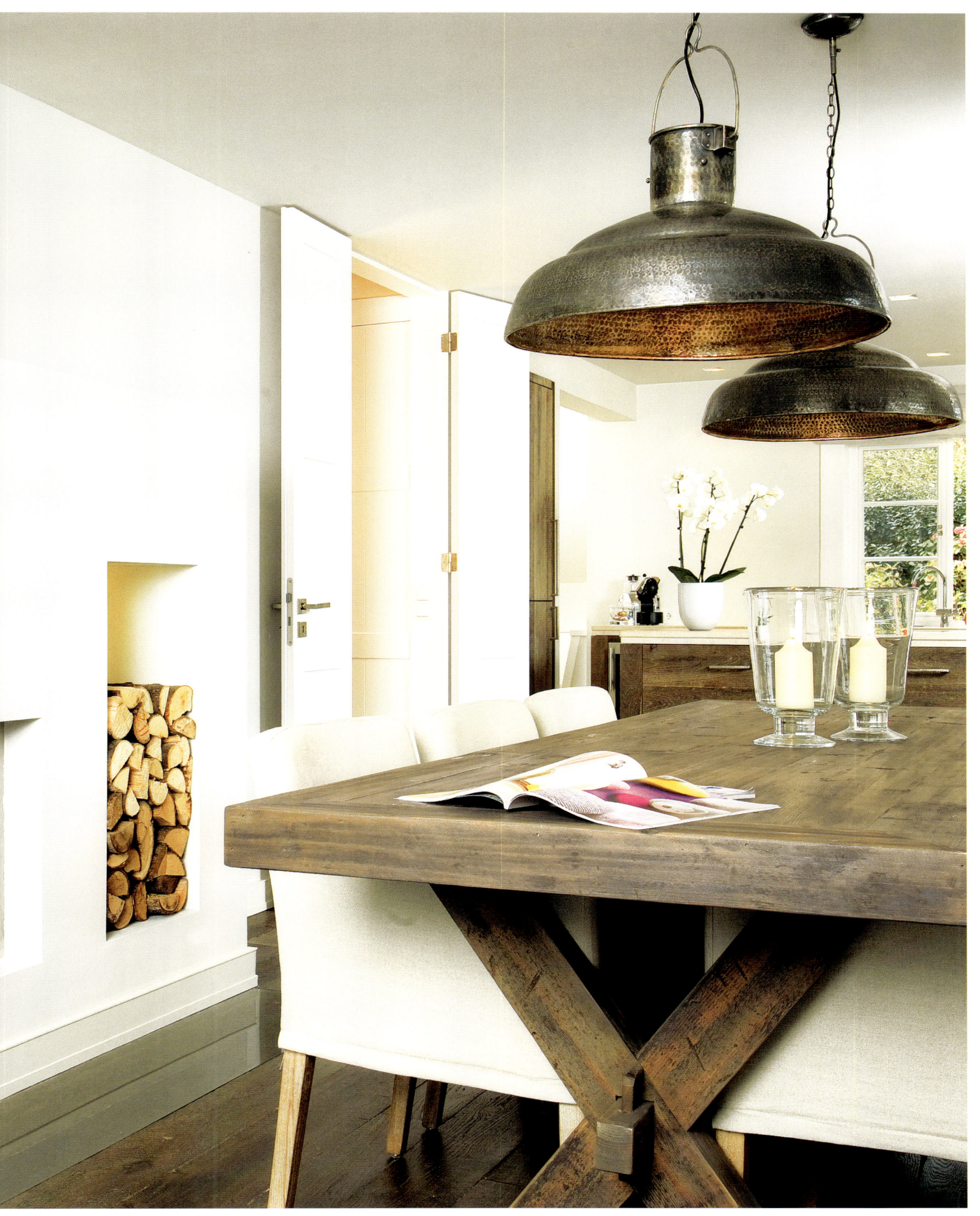

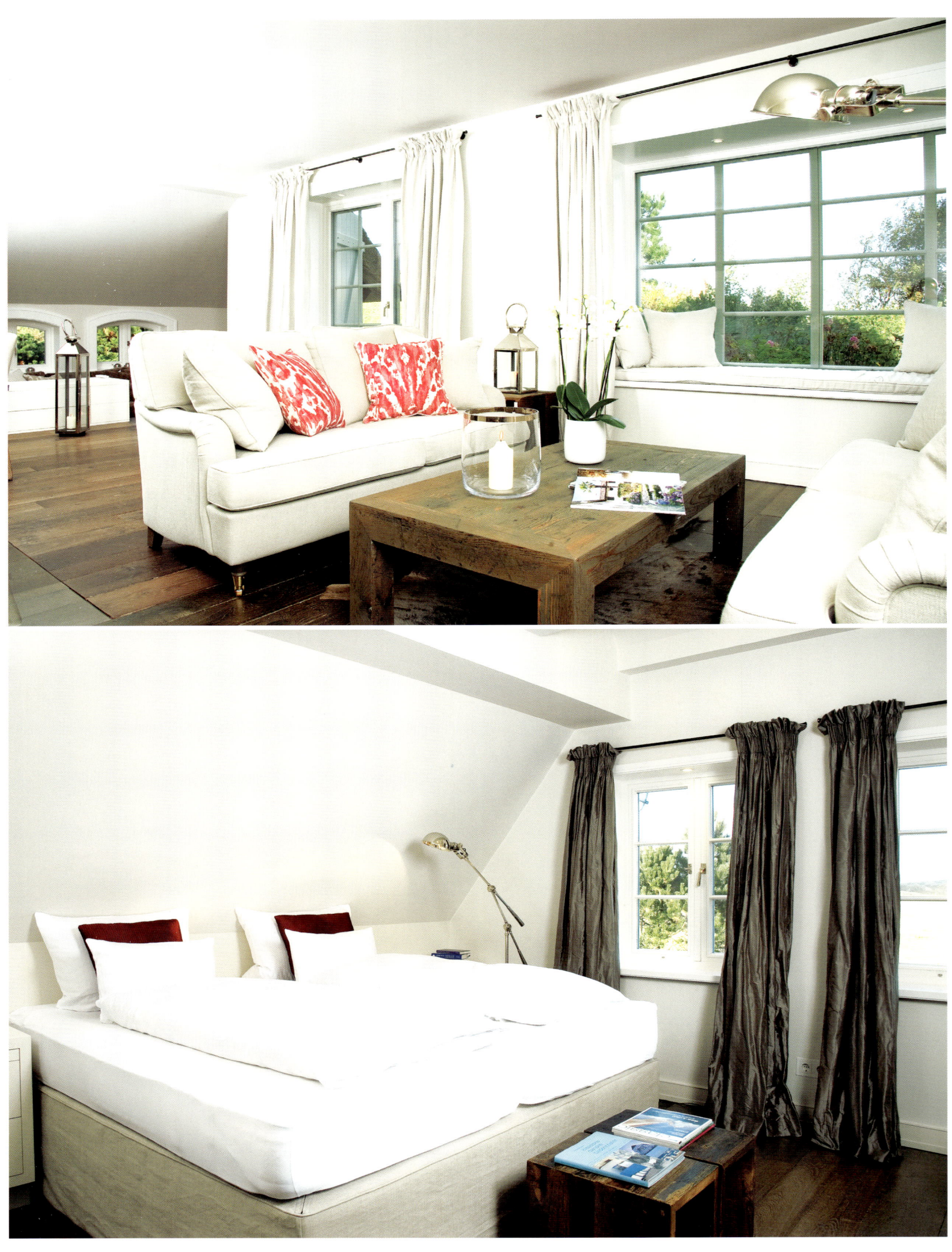

Echoing the sandy hues of the beautiful dunes, the interiors are light and airy.

Inspiriert von den Farben der Dünenlandschaft: das helle, geschmackvolle Interieur.

Haciéndose eco de los tonos de las dunas, los refinados interiores son amplios y luminosos.

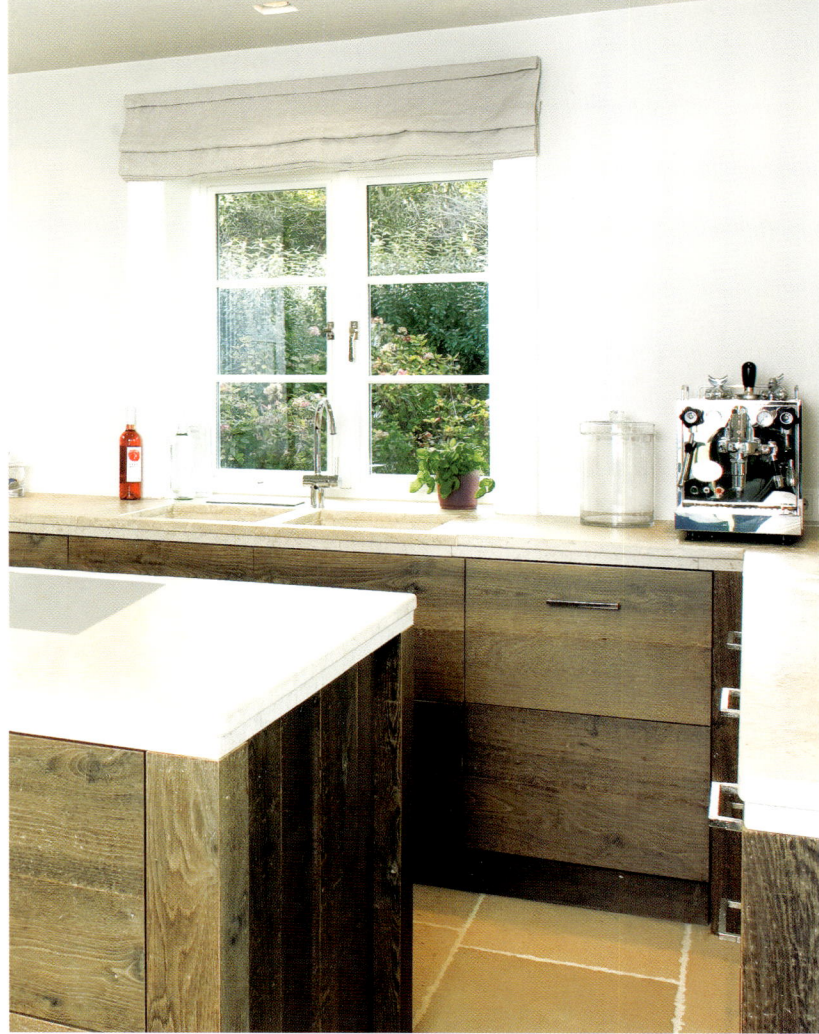

The state-of-the-art luxury kitchen is a dream come true for culinary enthusiasts.

Lässt die Herzen von Hobbyköchen höher schlagen: die luxuriös ausgestattete Küche.

La estilosa cocina de vanguardia es un sueño hecho realidad para los fans de los fogones.

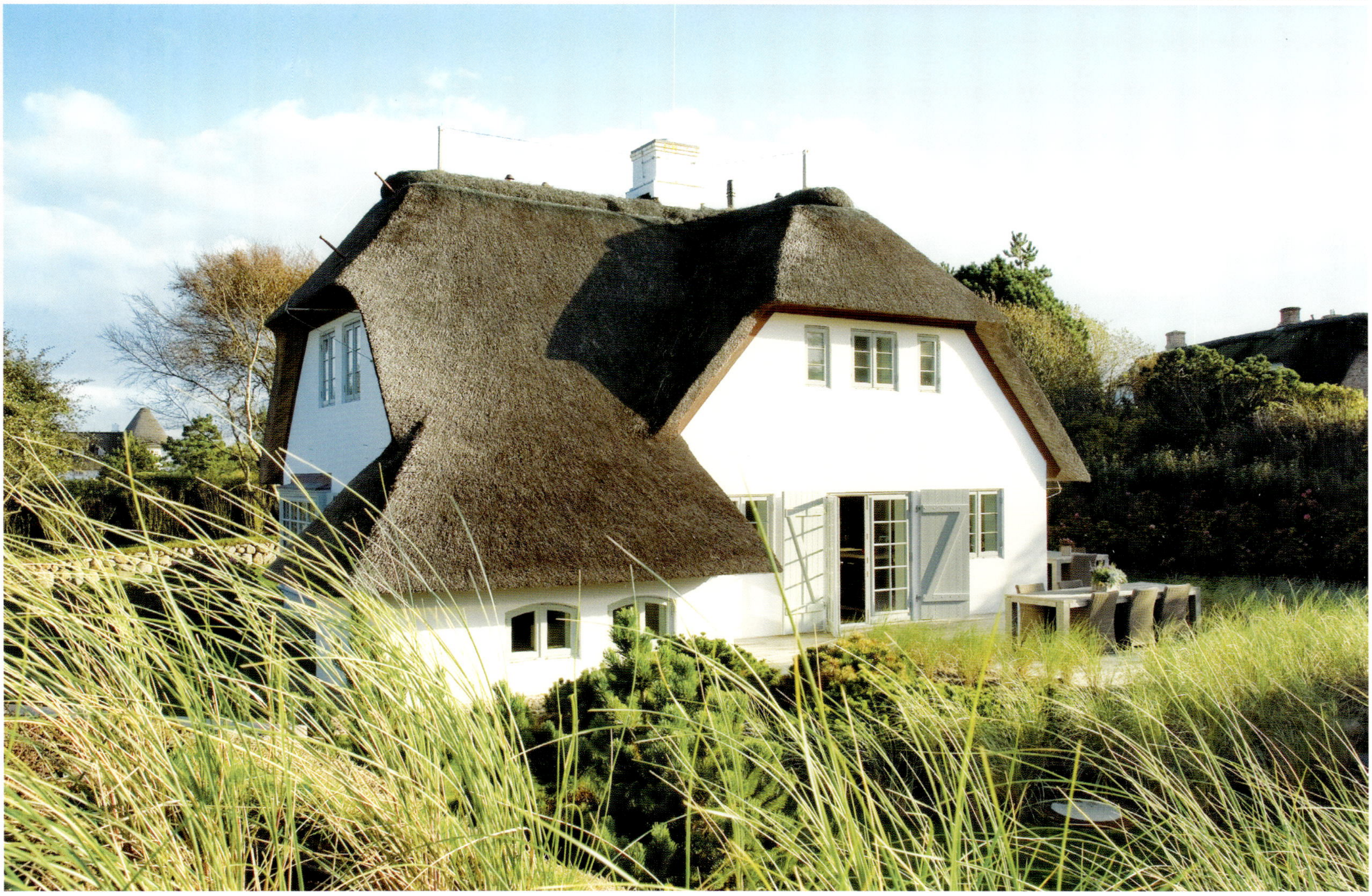

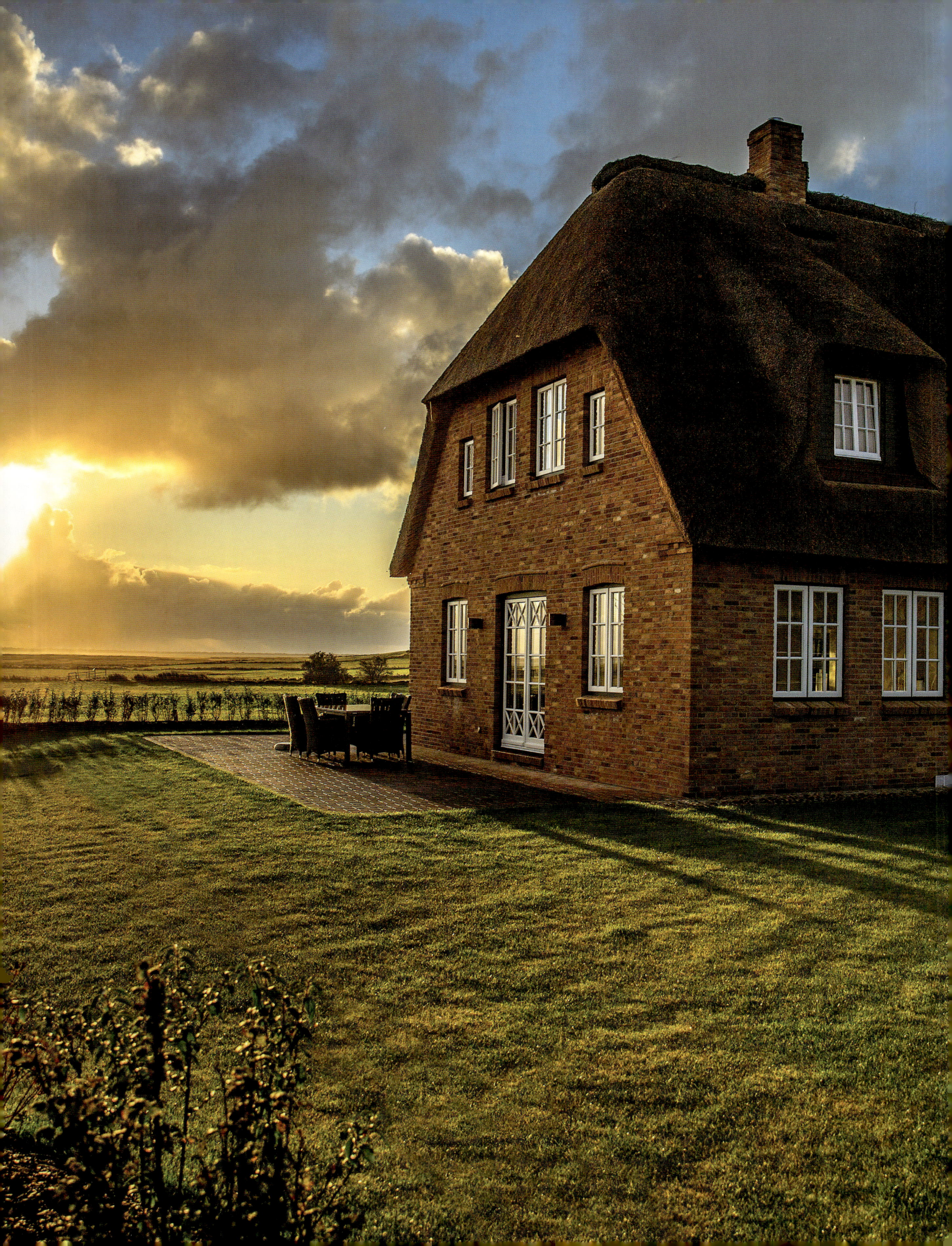

# Thatched Treasure

With its light, airy design and supreme views over the wide salt marshes, this lovely thatched cottage on Föhr is just perfect for those seeking rest and relaxation.

A MILD MARITIME climate, pristine nature in abundance and kilometre-long sandy beaches make Föhr one of the most popular holiday destinations in Germany. This beautiful thatched cottage is located in Witsum, the smallest village on the island. With around 230 square metres of living space, it has a living room with a dining area and a separate kitchen as well as three bedrooms with adjacent bathrooms. The luminous Nordic interior design is stylish and radiates a special feel-good atmosphere – details like the fireplace, the high-tech appointments and the sauna with an external window all provide additional comfort. And the many scenic attractions of the island can easily be reached within a short period of time: the beach, for instance, is only 200 metres away, and the nearest golf course lies a mere seven kilometres away. However, guests are bound to spend a considerable amount of time on the terrace of this pretty cottage, affording glorious views across the wide salt marshes and the mudflats as far as the island of Amrum – relaxation the North Frisian way.

MILDES SEEKLIMA, viel ursprüngliche Natur und kilometerlange Sandstrände machen Föhr zu einem der beliebtesten Ferienziele Deutschlands. In Witsum, dem kleinsten Dorf der Insel, befindet sich dieses wunderschöne Reetdachhaus mit ca. 230 Quadratmetern Wohnfläche, die sich auf drei Schlafzimmer mit angrenzenden Bädern sowie ein Wohnzimmer mit Essecke und separater Küche verteilen. Die nordisch-helle und ausgesprochen stilvolle Raumgestaltung verströmt dabei überall ein besonderes Wohlfühl-Ambiente, während Details wie der Kamin, die Hightech-Ausstattung und die Sauna mit Außenfenster für besonderen Komfort sorgen. Zudem sind die Vorzüge und landschaftlichen Reize der Insel in kürzester Zeit erreichbar – so ist der Strand gerade mal 200 Meter, der nächste Golfplatz nur sieben Kilometer entfernt. Viel Zeit wird man hier jedoch sicherlich auch auf der eigenen Terrasse verbringen, von der sich der Blick über die Salzwiesen und das Wattenmeer bis hin nach Amrum erstreckt – Entspannung auf nordfriesische Art.

SUAVE CLIMA MARÍTIMO, naturaleza virgen por doquier y kilométricas playas de arena hacen de Föhr uno de los destinos turísticos más populares de Alemania. Esta preciosa casa de campo con techo de brezo se encuentra en Witsum, el pueblo más pequeño de la isla. En unos 230 metros cuadrados habitables cuenta con sala de estar y comedor, cocina independiente y tres dormitorios con baños adyacentes. El interiorismo de estilo nórdico resulta luminoso y elegante, destilando un ambiente realmente especial de bienestar y disfrute, con detalles como la chimenea, el equipamiento de alta tecnología y la sauna con ventana exterior, para mayor comodidad adicional. Además, los muchos lugares de interés de la isla quedan bien cerca: la playa, por ejemplo, a sólo 200 metros, y el campo de golf más cercano a tan sólo siete kilómetros de distancia. Sin embargo, nadie puede evitar pasar el máximo tiempo posible en la terraza, embelesado con las maravillosas vistas que cruzan las llanuras saladas y marismas hasta la isla de Amrum: relajación pura a la manera de Frisia del Norte.

GERMANY, FÖHR **RENTAL PRICE/NIGHT** FROM EUR 180 **INTERIOR APPROX.** 230 m² **NO. OF BEDROOMS** 3
**LAND APPROX.** 1,100 m² **E&V ID** W-01YM3I **CONTACT** WYK (DE), HC HORST CHRISTOPHERSEN –
FÖHR-AMRUMER IMMOBILIEN E.K., LICENCE PARTNER OF ENGEL & VÖLKERS RESIDENTIAL GMBH
**TEL.** +49 4681 74 86 90 **E-MAIL** FOEHR@ENGELVOELKERS.COM

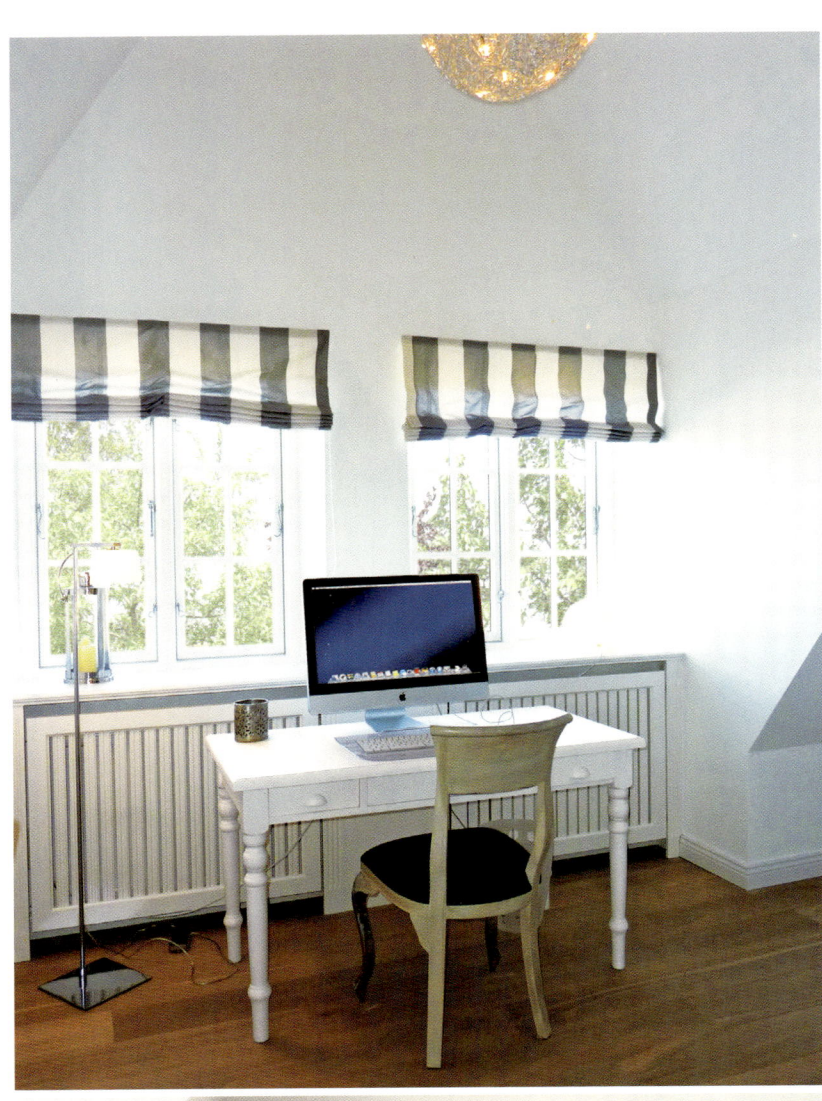

The refined maritime interiors create
a decidedly relaxed atmosphere.

Die gediegen-maritime Raumgestaltung
sorgt für eine entspannte Atmosphäre.

Refinado y marítimo, el diseño interior crea
una atmósfera decididamente relajada.

Beautiful views: the large windows let plenty of
light into the stylishly decorated rooms.

Schöne Aussichten: Die großen Fenster lassen
viel Licht in die stilvoll eingerichteten Zimmer.

Vistas espectaculares: los grandes ventanales
iluminan los elegantes y románticos interiores.

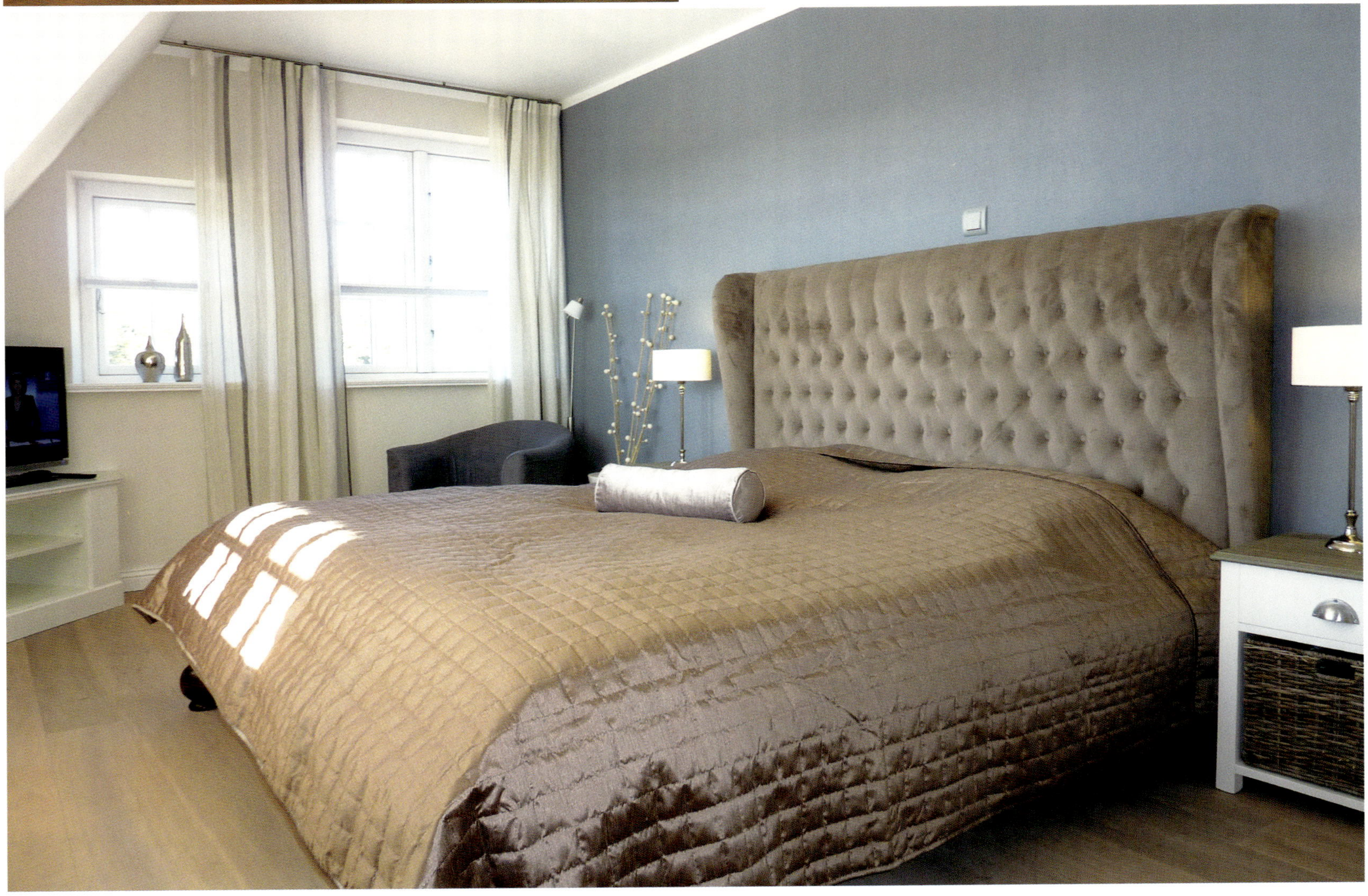

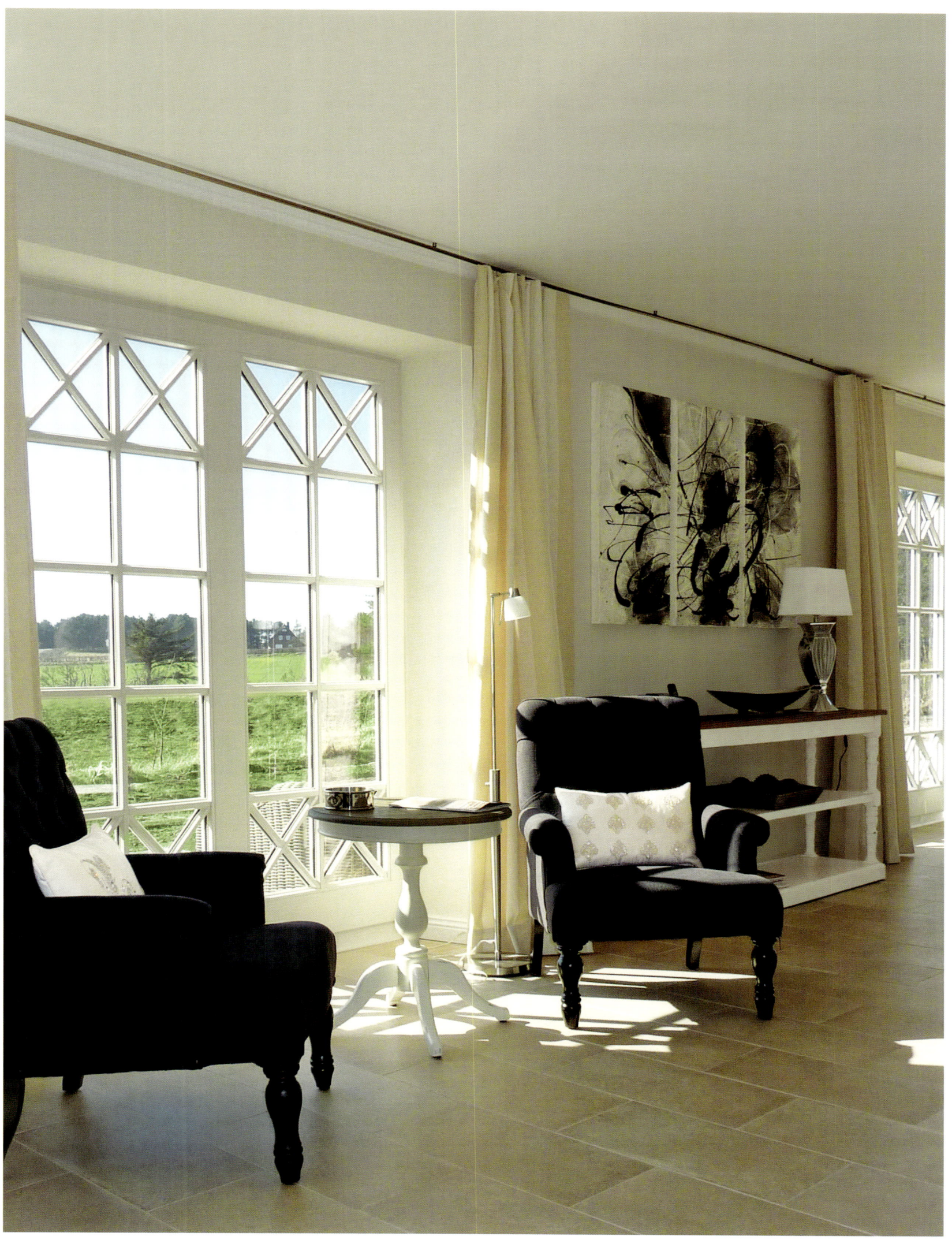

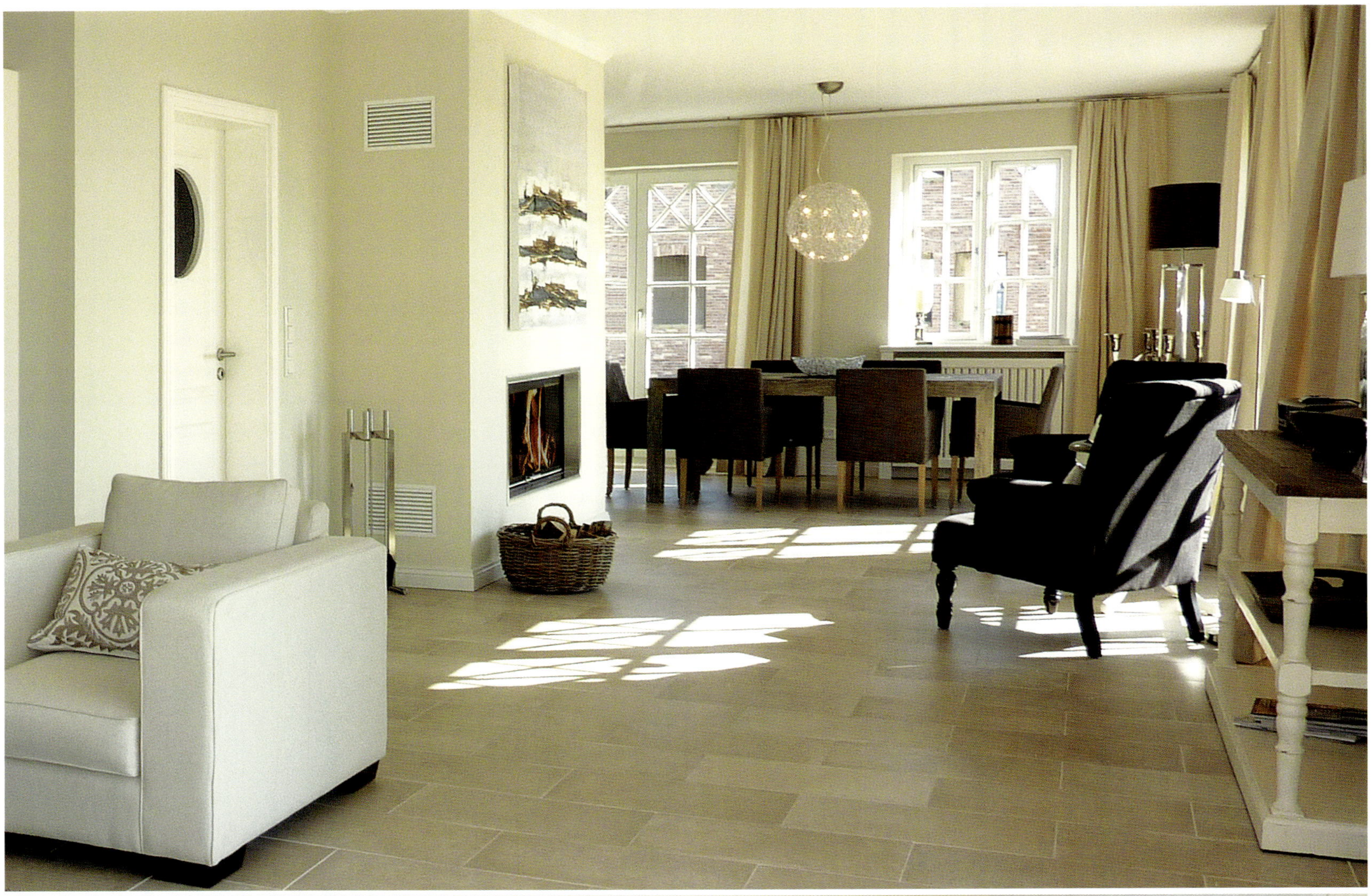

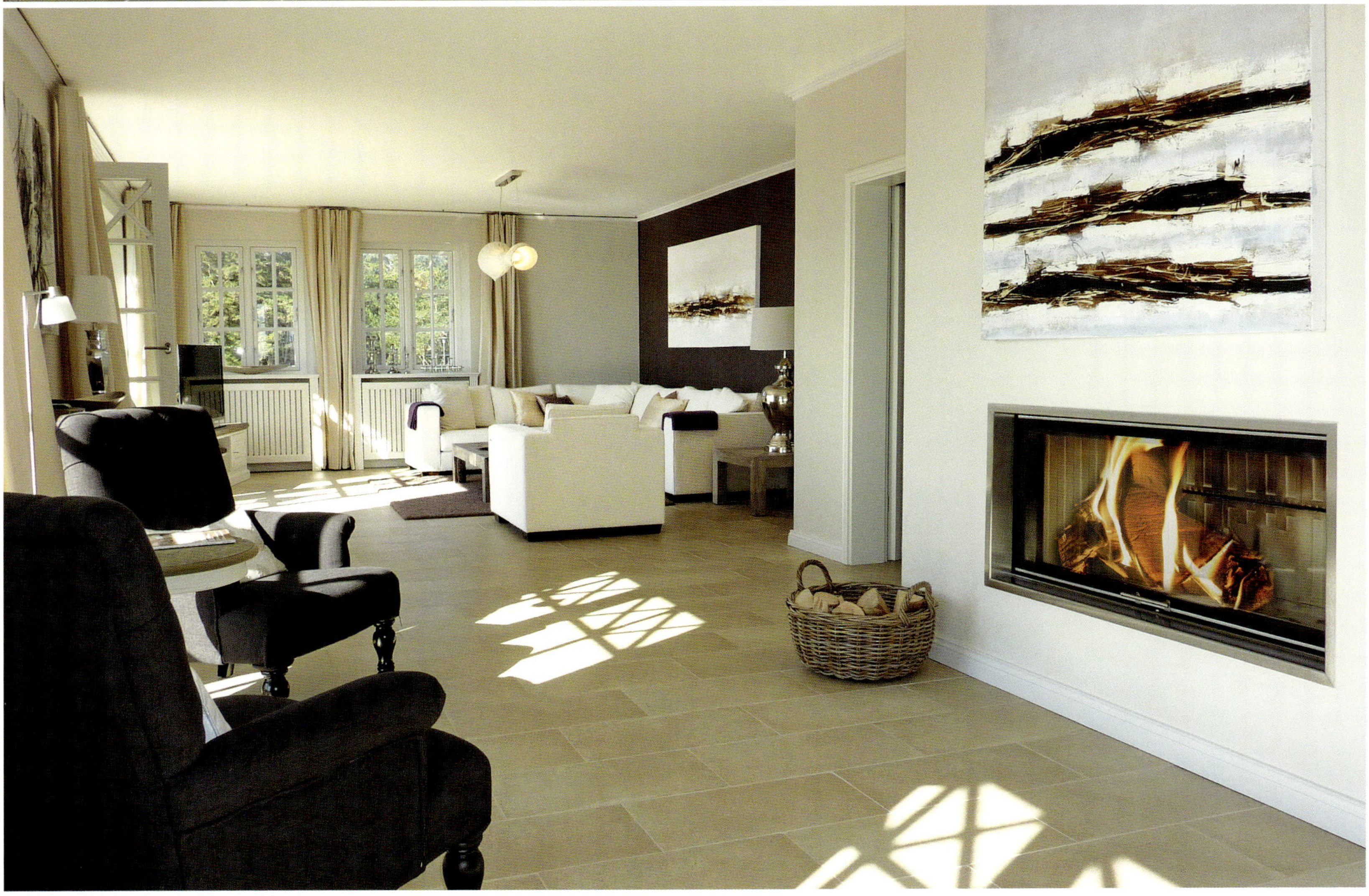

<

The spacious living and dining area
shows extensive attention to detail.

Viel Liebe zum Detail zeigt sich auch im
großzügigen Wohn- und Essbereich.

La espaciosa zona de estar y comedor muestra
una gran y exquisita atención al detalle.

The stunning sunsets on Föhr cast the
landscape in a sea of golden light.

Die herrlichen Sonnenuntergänge von Föhr
tauchen die Landschaft in goldenes Licht.

Las impresionantes puestas de sol sumen el
paisaje de Föhr en un mar de luz dorada.

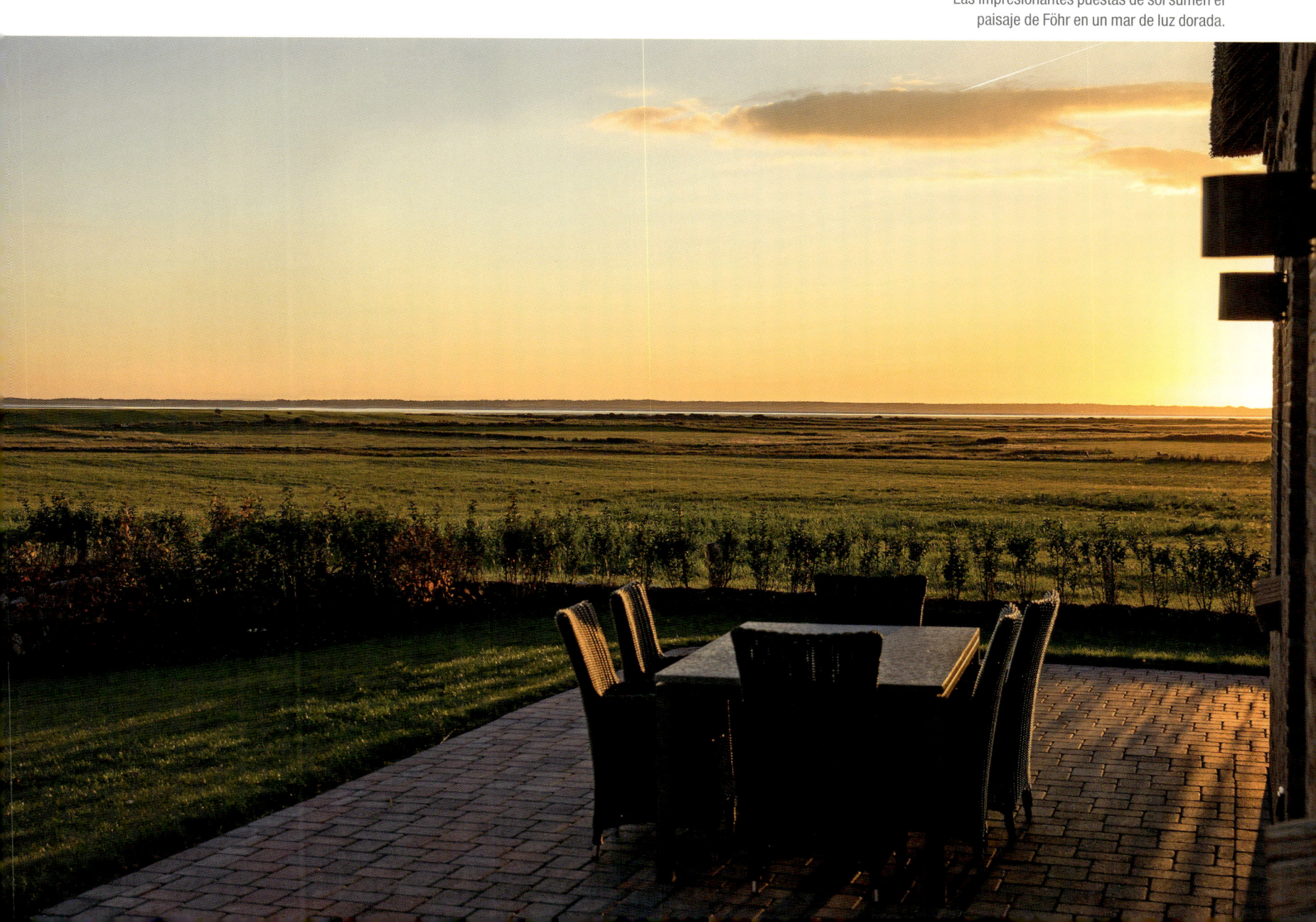

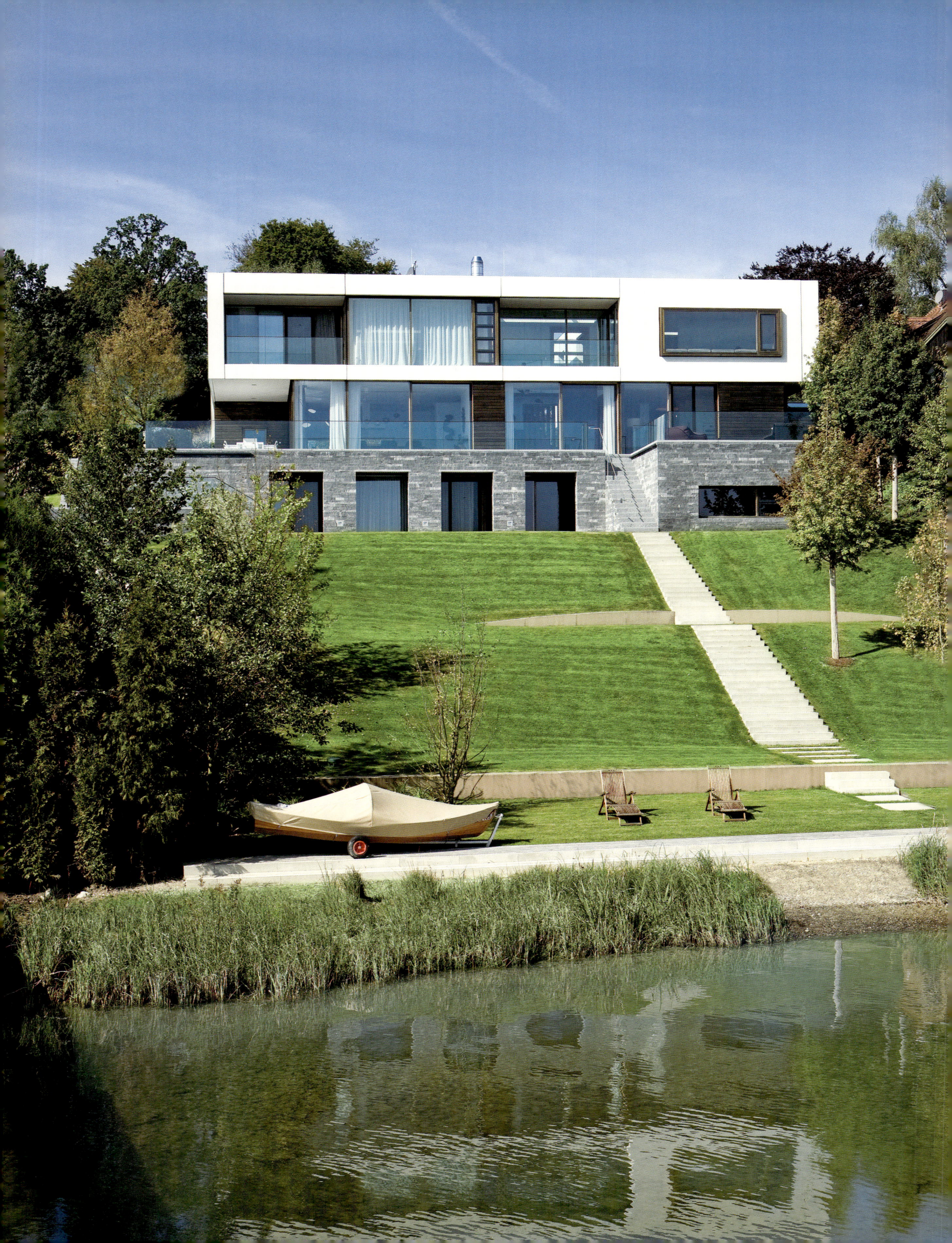

# Modern Masterpiece

An idyllic position on the banks of Lake Ammer
and an ultra-modern design concept make this villa
a truly superlative lakefront treasure.

A SMALL COMMUNITY in Upper Bavaria, Schondorf is the ideal hideaway for those wishing to savour the peaceful joys of Lake Ammer and its picturesque environs – without having to forego the convenient connections to nearby cities like Munich or Zurich. Discreetly hidden from the roadside, this modern design villa offers sensational panoramic views across the lake. The stylish interior design is no less impressive, however, thanks to the many fine materials used such as architectural bronze, natural stone and oak wood. Boasting seamless transitions from one area to the next, the open-plan interiors create an ample sense of space with a clean and contemporary ambience. The many attractive features of the lakefront home include an open-plan gallery above the living area, a central fireplace, comfortable bedroom suites with separate dressing areas, a designer kitchen, bespoke features and fittings and, last but not least, the spectacular spa complex with a waterfall, a sauna, a wellness shower and a fitness and relaxation room – to ensure an all-round sense of well-being.

DAS KLEINE ÖRTCHEN Schondorf in Oberbayern ist ein idealer Rückzugsort, um die landschaftlich reizvolle Umgebung rund um den Ammersee in Ruhe zu genießen, ohne dabei auf eine gute Anbindung an Metropolen wie München oder Zürich verzichten zu müssen. Zur Straße hin diskret verborgen, bietet das modern gestaltete Anwesen einen märchenhaft schönen Panoramablick über den See. Nicht weniger beeindruckend ist die stilvolle Ausstattung, die unter anderem durch die Verwendung edler Materialien wie Baubronze, Naturstein und Eichenholz besticht. Alle Wohnbereiche gehen fließend ineinander über, wodurch eine weitläufige Atmosphäre mit einem klaren, modernen Flair entsteht. Zu den vielen attraktiven Besonderheiten gehören die offene Galerie über dem Wohnbereich mit Kamin, die komfortablen Schlafzimmer mit separaten Ankleideräumen, eine Design-Küche, maßgefertigte Schreinereinbauten und last, but not least der Spa-Bereich mit Wasserfall, Sauna, Wellnessdusche sowie Fitness- und Ruheraum – für vollendetes Wohlbefinden.

UNA PEQUEÑA LOCALIDAD de la Alta Baviera, Schondorf, es un lugar ideal donde refugiarse para disfrutar de los frondosos y serenos paisajes alrededor del precioso Ammersee, sin renunciar a las facilidades, incluso de conexión, de las metrópolis de Múnich o Zúrich. Discreta, retirada de la calle, la propiedad de estilo moderno ofrece unas magníficas panorámicas sobre el lago. No menos impresionante es el diseño contemporáneo del interior: el uso de materiales nobles como el bronce, la piedra arenisca y madera de roble destila sobriedad por doquier. Todas las estancias son abiertas y con transiciones suaves entre sí, creando un ambiente de auténtica amplitud, aireado y actual. Entre sus muchas y atractivas características se cuentan la galería abierta por encima de la sala de estar con chimenea, los confortables dormitorios con vestidores aparte, cocina de diseño, carpintería a medida y, por último pero no menos importante, la zona de *spa* con cascada, sauna, ducha de hidromasaje, gimnasio y sala de relajación, cumpliendo su papel para el perfecto bienestar.

GERMANY, LAKE AMMER **PURCHASE PRICE** ON REQUEST **INTERIOR APPROX.** 515 m² **NO. OF BEDROOMS** 4 **LAND APPROX.** 1,985 m²
**E&V ID** W-00MT38 **CONTACT** STARNBERG (DE), EuV RESIDENTIAL STARNBERG FÜNF SEEN LAND GMBH,
LICENCE PARTNER OF ENGEL & VÖLKERS RESIDENTIAL GMBH
**TEL.** +49 8151 36 89 70 **E-MAIL** STARNBERGERSEE@ENGELVOELKERS.COM

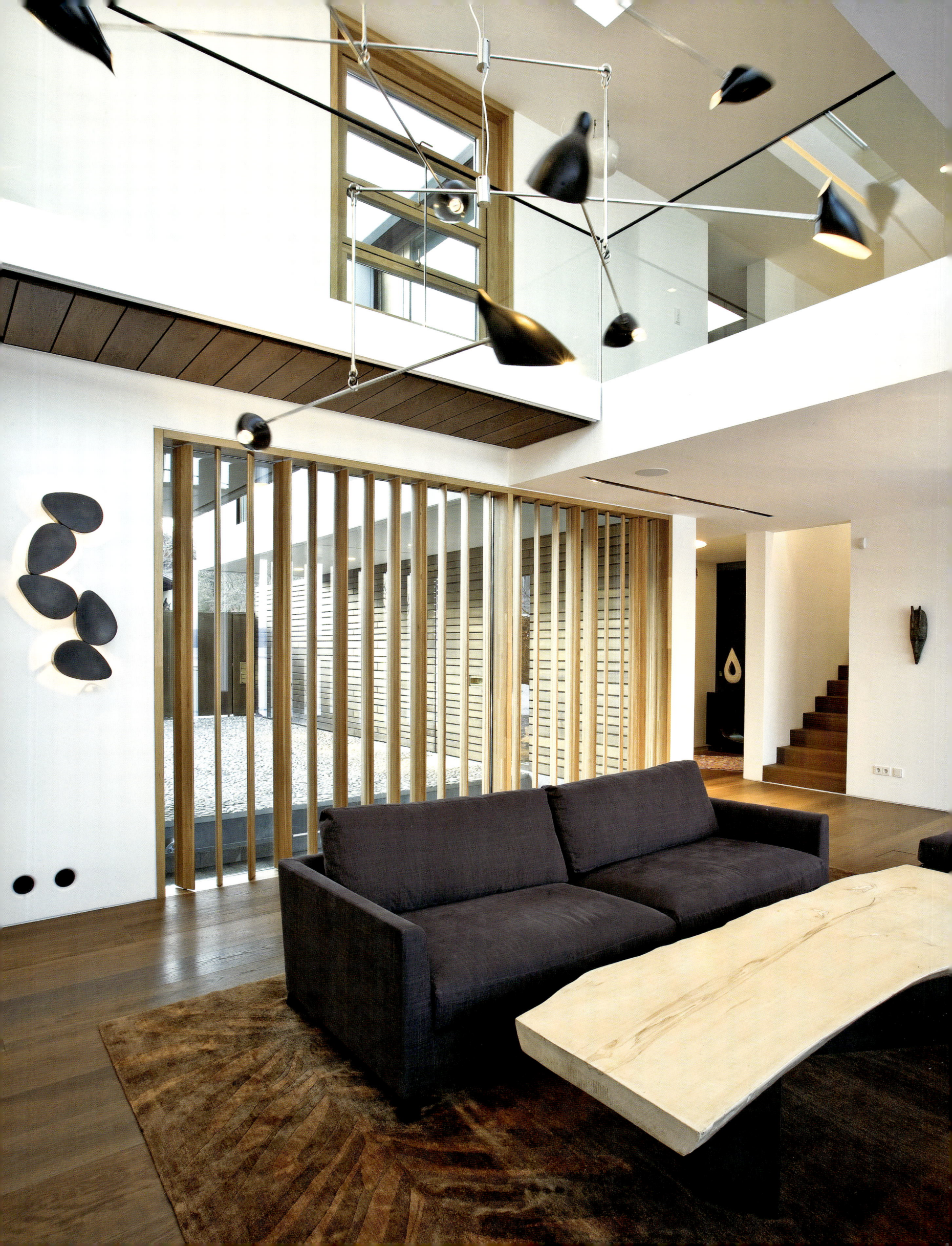

Inviting: the modern interiors with the gallery and generous open-plan living area.

Einladend: die moderne Innenausstattung mit Galerie über dem offenen Wohnbereich.

Atractivo: el moderno diseño interior con la galería y la zona de día de plano abierto.

Sophisticated lifestyle for aesthetes – created by the renowned architects Fuchs, Wacker.

Urbaner Lifestyle für Genießer – kreiert von den renommierten Architekten Fuchs, Wacker.

*Lifestyle* sofisticado para estetas creado por los renombrados arquitectos Fuchs, Wacker.

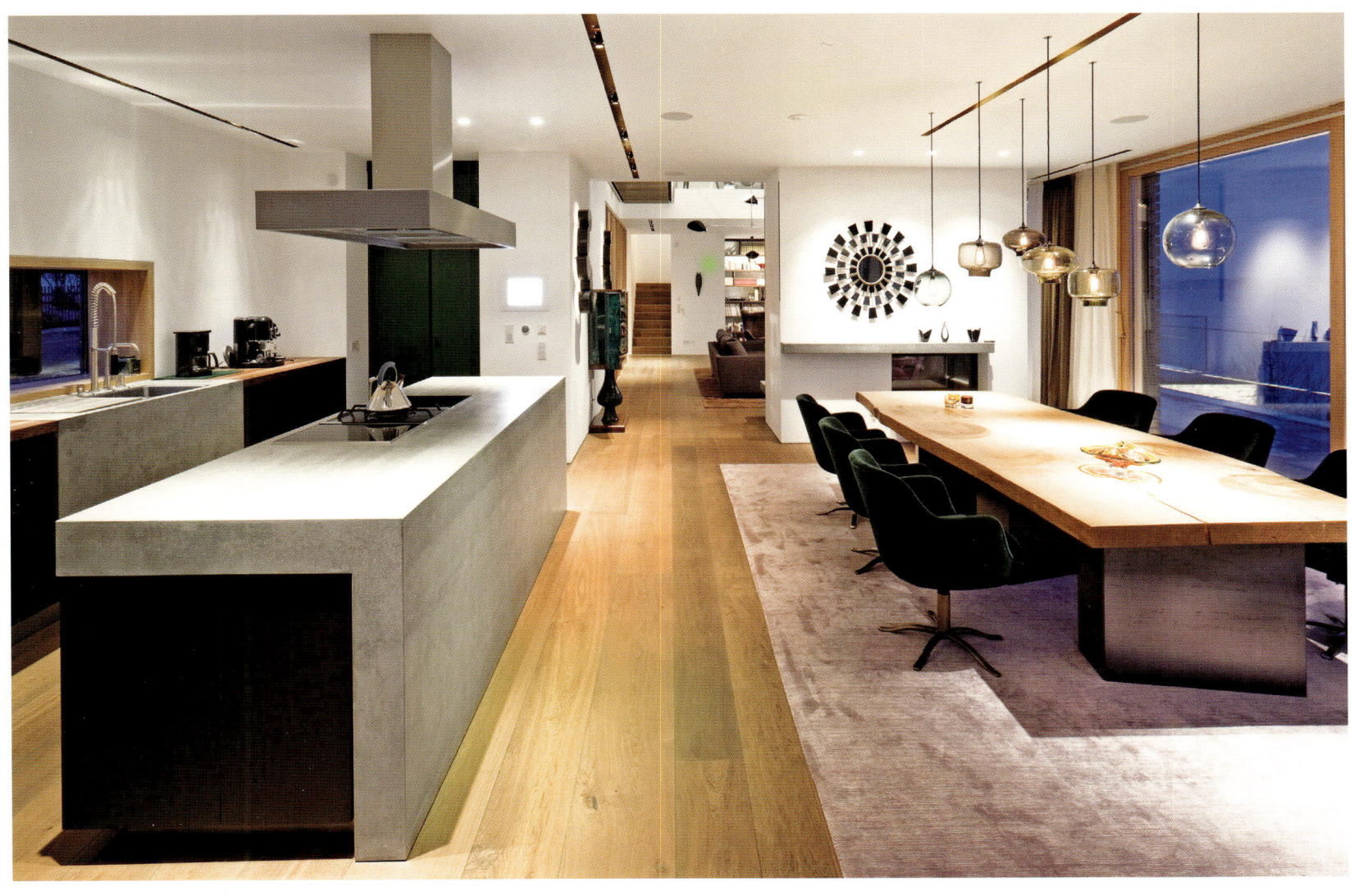

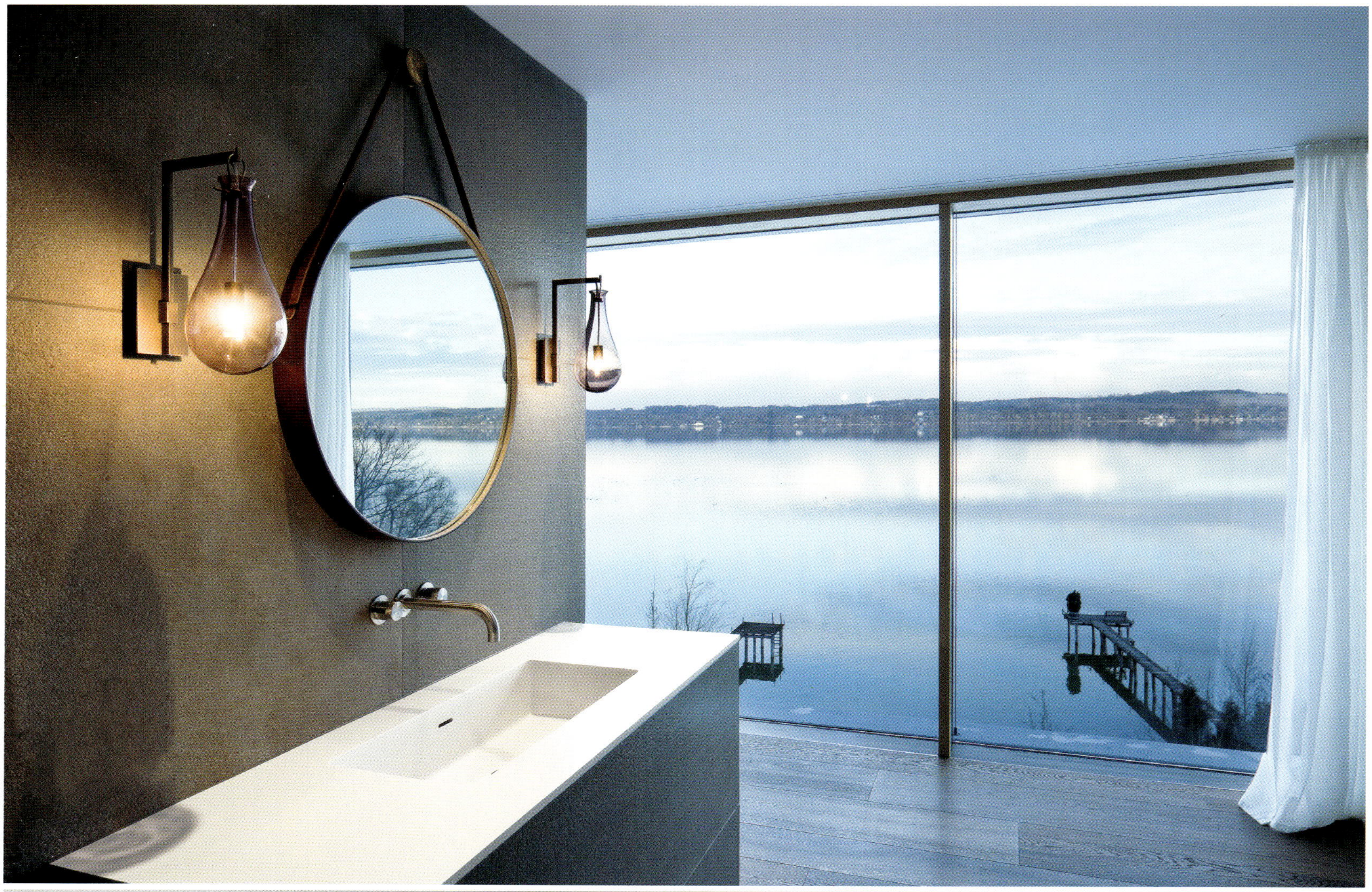

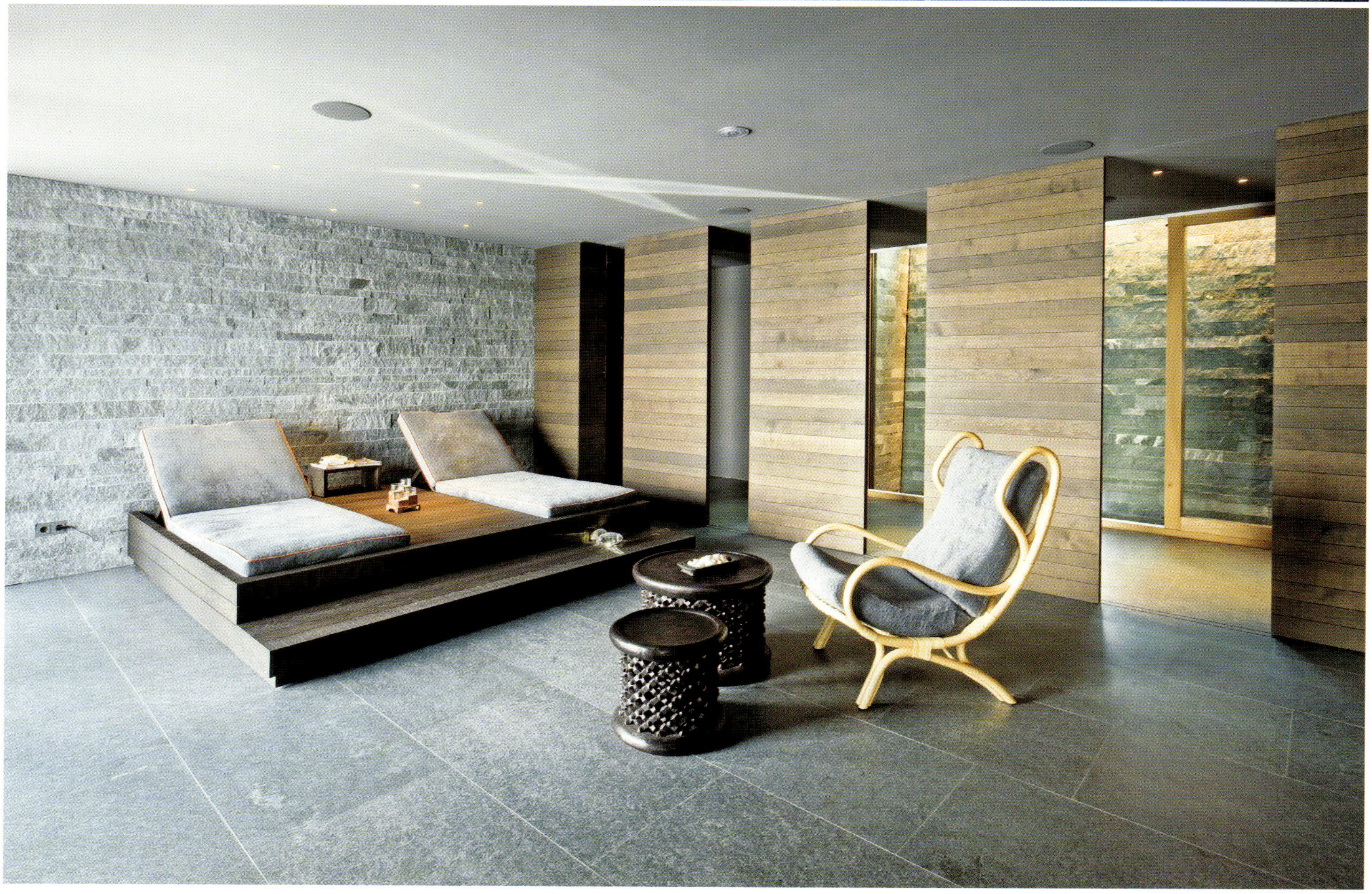

<

Wellness in the bathroom with lakefront
vistas: no better way to start the day ...

Wellness im Bad mit Blick auf den Ammersee:
Besser kann der Tag kaum beginnen ...

*Wellness* en el baño con vistas al lago:
no hay mejor manera de empezar el día...

A new dimension of domestic comfort – with
a multifunctional lighting and sound system.

Wohnkomfort in neuer Dimension – mit
multifunktionalem Licht- und Soundsystem.

Una nueva dimensión en confort residencial: el
sistema multifuncional de sonido e iluminación.

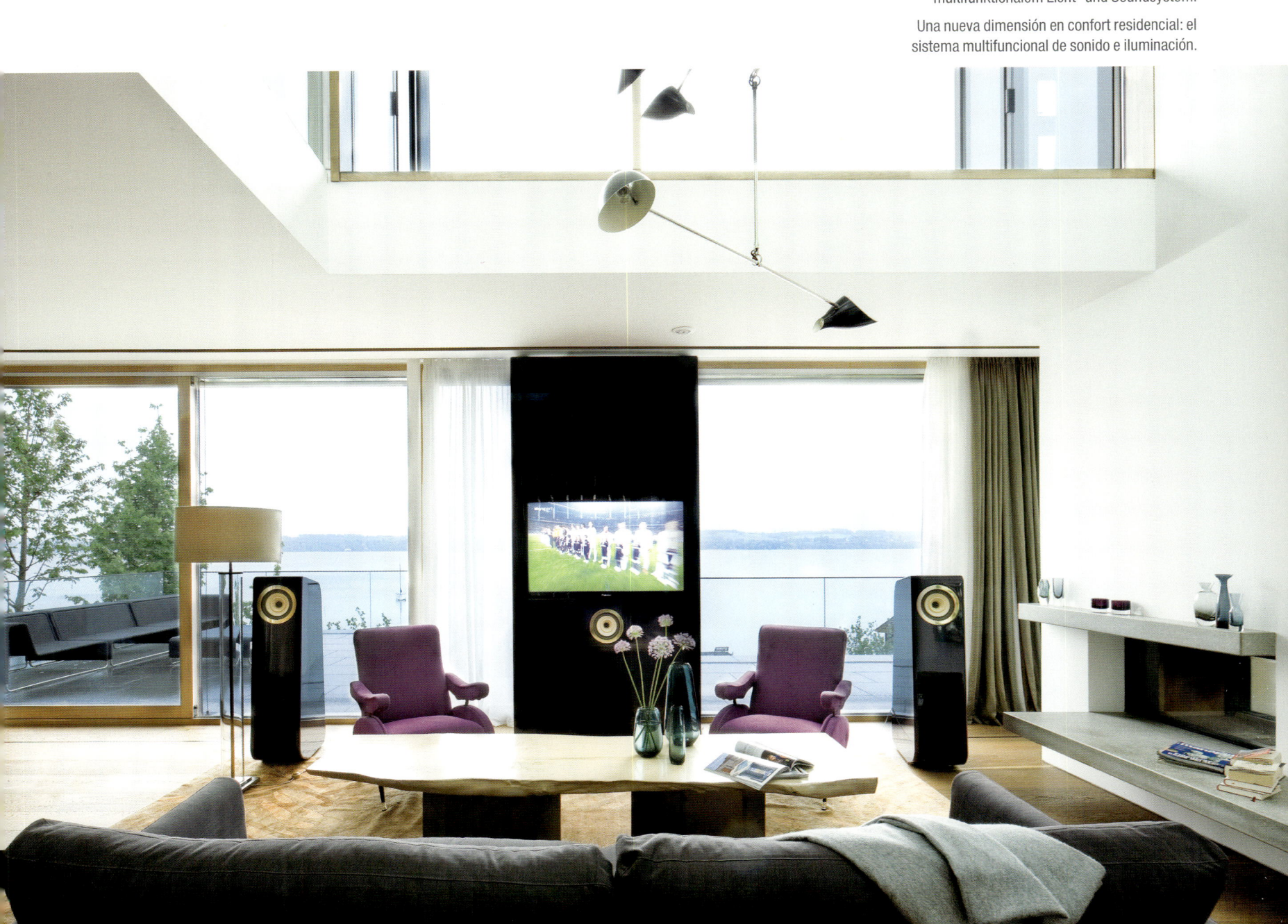

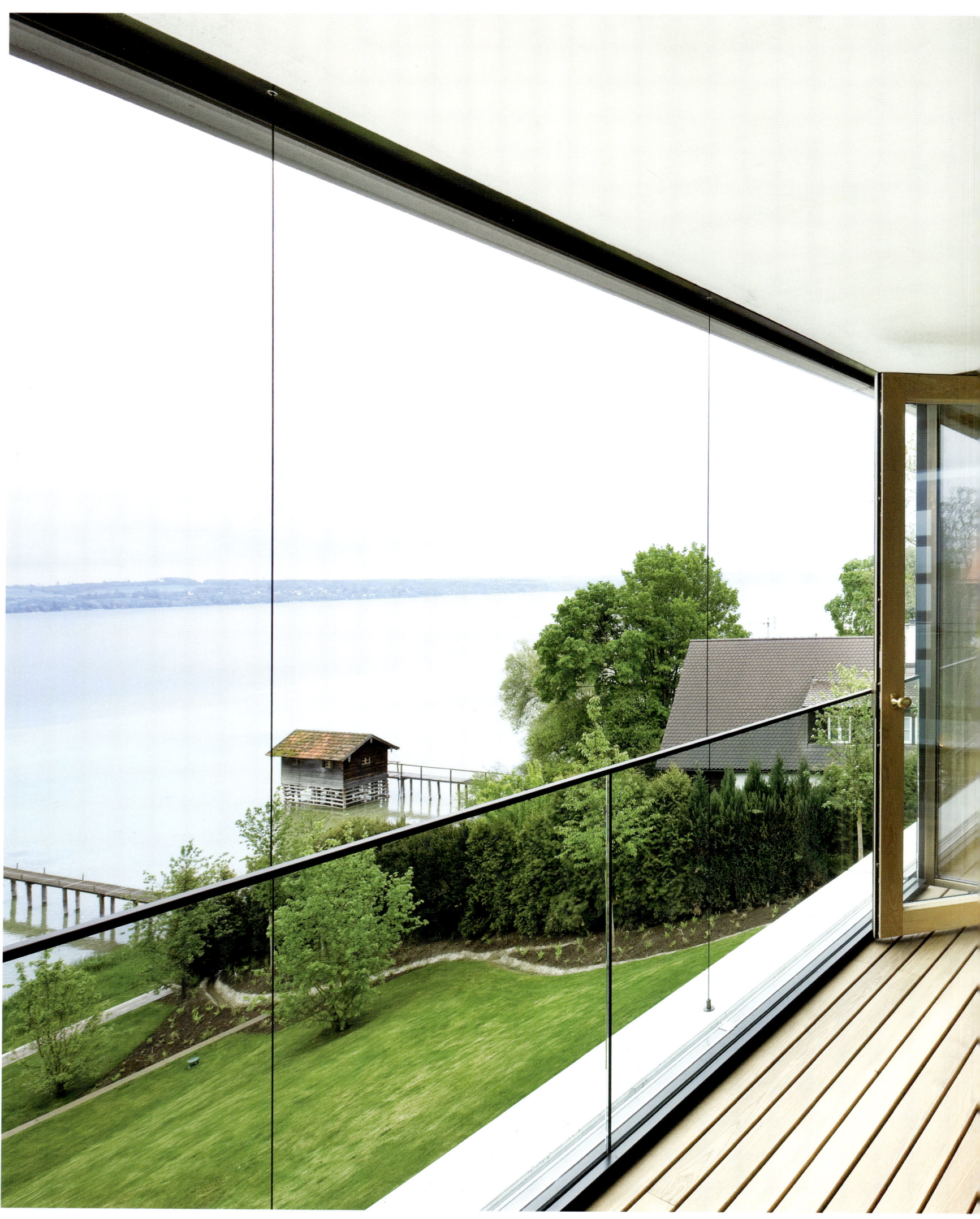

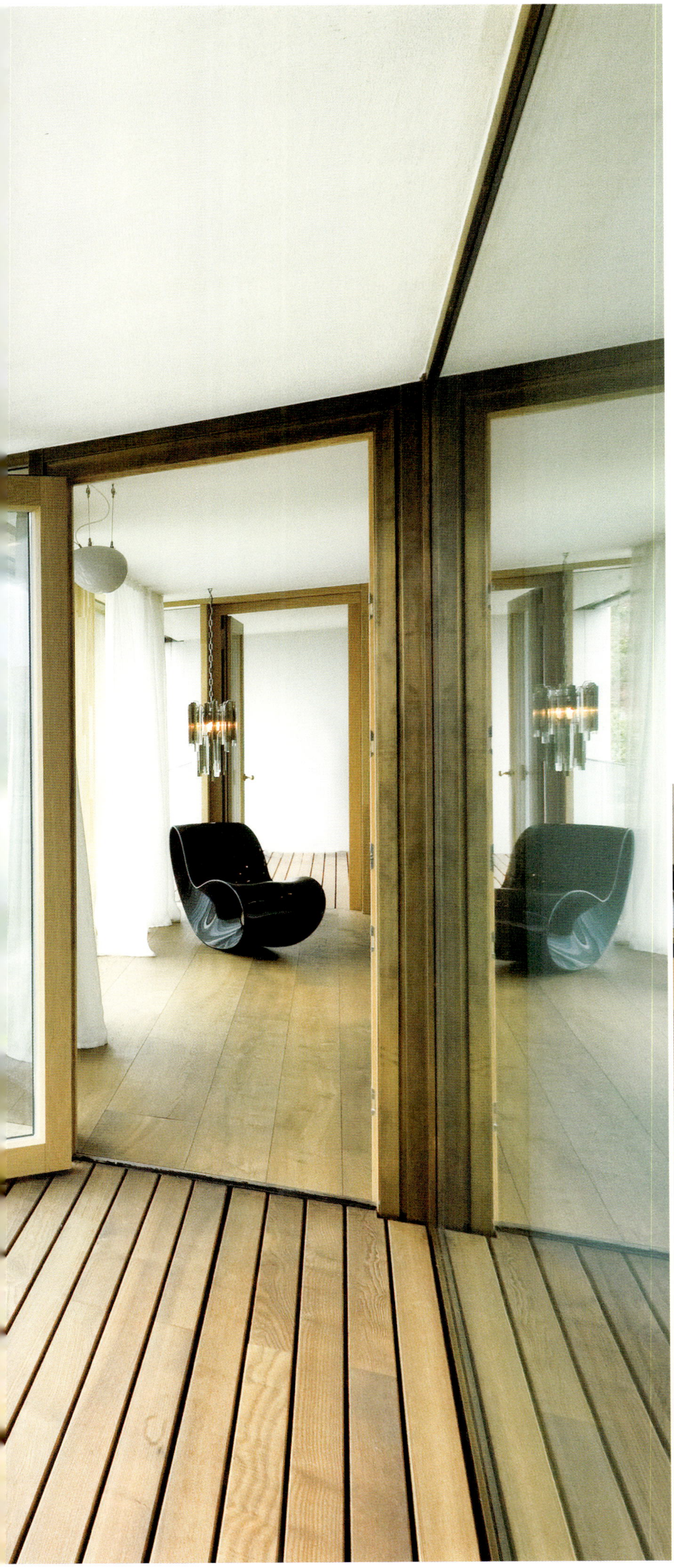

<

Floor-to-ceiling glass ensures captivating
views of the picturesque environs.

Raumhohe Glasfronten sorgen für herrliche
Ausblicke über die reizvolle Umgebung.

Fachadas acristaladas de suelo a techo
garantizan las panorámicas más pintorescas.

The interior design of the villa is enhanced
by the careful use of many fine materials.

Bei der Raumgestaltung wurde viel Wert auf
die Verwendung edler Materialien gelegt.

El diseño interior de la villa se ha resaltado con
especial atención al uso de materiales nobles.

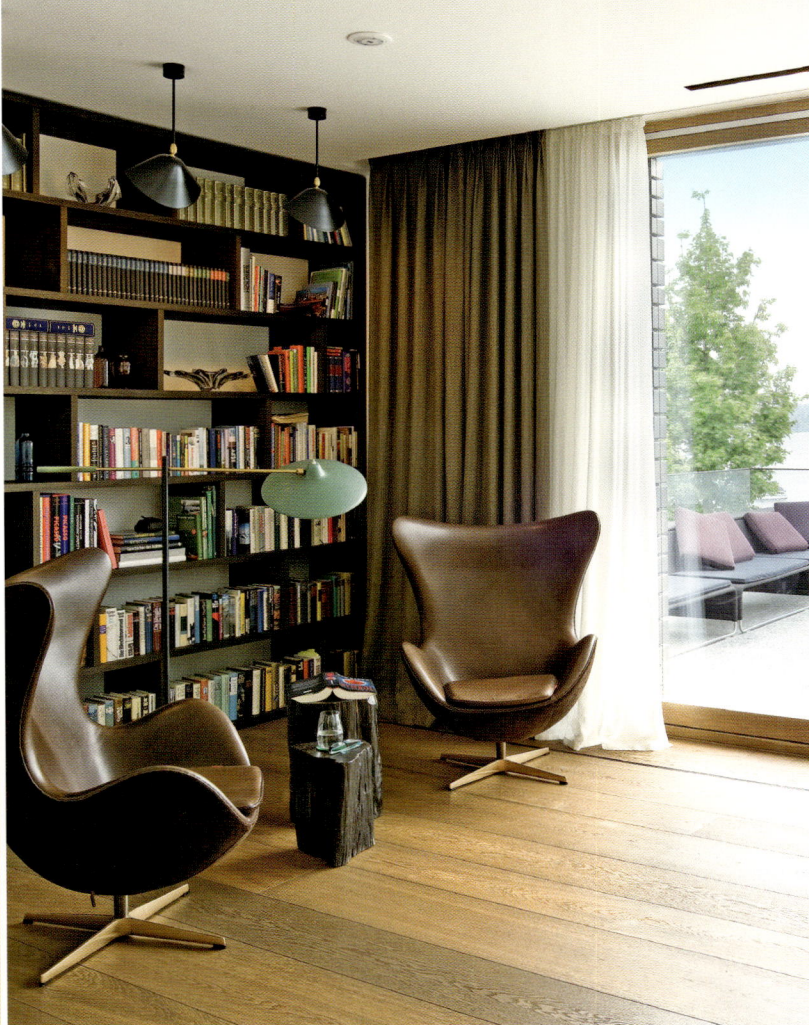

# WELCOME

## to the World of Engel & Völkers

Engel & Völkers is one of the world's leading service companies specialised in the brokerage of high-end real estate. With over 35 years' experience and a global network of more than 500 residential shops and 50 commercial offices in 38 countries, the company offers an exceptional level of service and a first-class property and client portfolio.

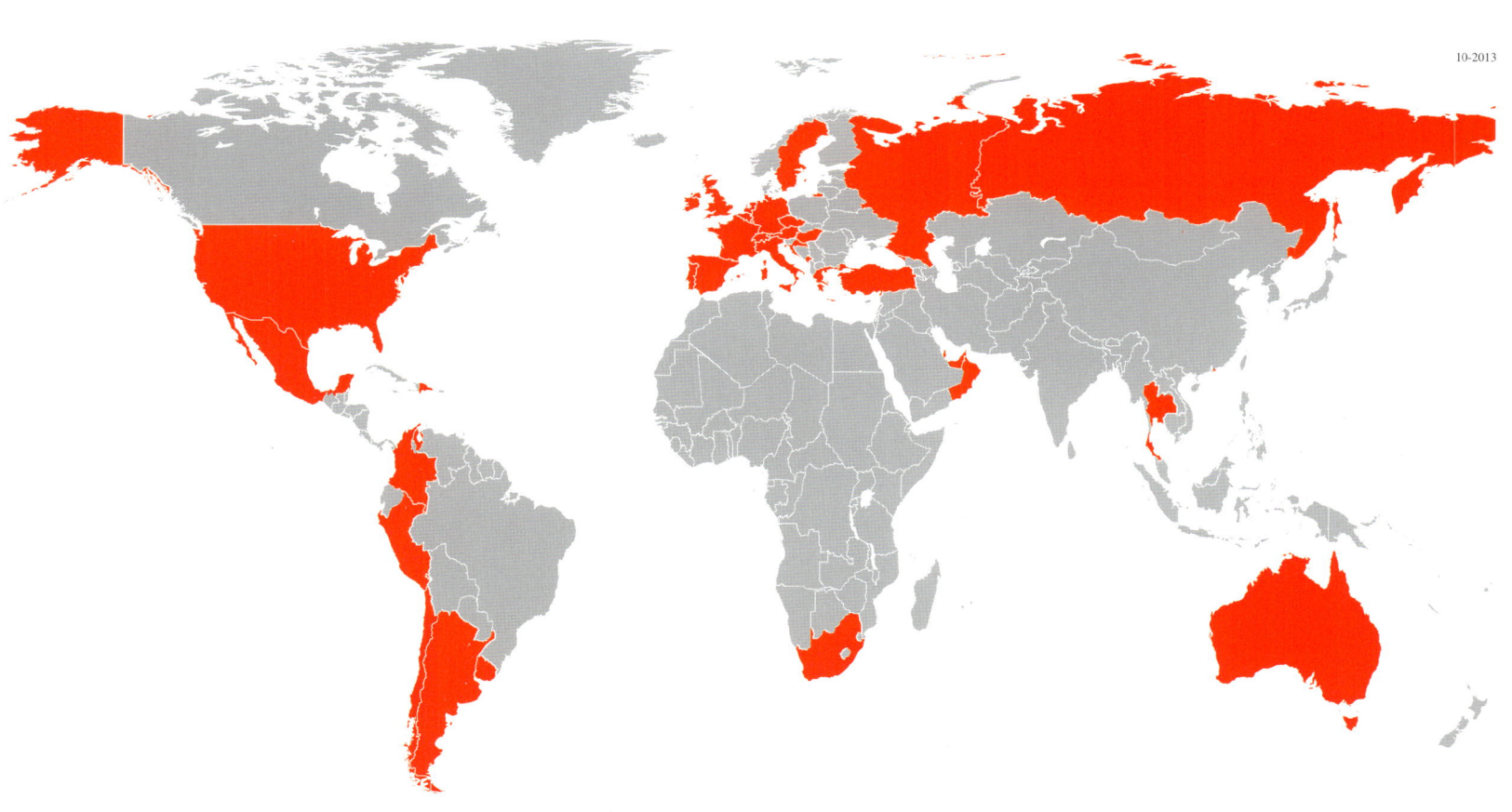

10-2013

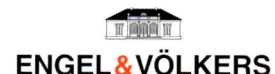

**ENGEL&VÖLKERS**

**ENGEL&VÖLKERS**
**COMMERCIAL**

**ENGEL&VÖLKERS**
**YACHTING**

ARGENTINA · AUSTRALIA · AUSTRIA · BAHRAIN · BELGIUM ·

CHILE · CHINA · COLOMBIA · CROATIA · CZECH REPUBLIC ·

DOMINICAN REPUBLIC · FRANCE · GERMANY · GREECE ·

HUNGARY · IRELAND · ITALY · LIECHTENSTEIN · LUXEMBOURG ·

MALTA · MEXICO · MONTENEGRO · NETHERLANDS · OMAN ·

PERU · PORTUGAL · QATAR · RUSSIA · SOUTH AFRICA · SPAIN ·

SWEDEN · SWITZERLAND · THAILAND · TURKEY · UNITED ARAB

EMIRATES · UNITED KINGDOM · URUGUAY · USA

 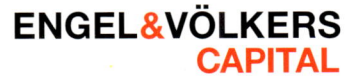 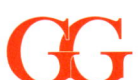

# IMPRINT

## Edition 2014/2015

---

**EDITED BY** CHRISTIAN VÖLKERS

**MARKETING DIRECTOR** MELANIE KLUSMEIER

**ART DIRECTOR** PETRA WEHLING

**AUTHORS & COPY EDITORS** CLAUDIA BÖHME, ARIANE KOSSACK

**TRANSLATORS** CLAUDIA BÖHME, ARIANE KOSSACK, SUSANA SILVA OLLET, SVEN WEISS

**PROJECT COORDINATOR** SASKIA HERRMANN

**PRE-PRESS** BERTHEAU DRUCK GMBH, NEUMÜNSTER, GERMANY

**PRINTING** TESINSKA TISKARNA A.S., CESKY TESIN, CZECH REPUBLIC

Published by Engel & Völkers

Engel & Völkers AG
Stadthausbrücke 5
20355 Hamburg, Germany
Tel. +49 40 36 13 10
www.engelvoelkers.com

Photo credits
Jordi Folch (pp. 38–43), Bartomeu Amengual (p. 50), Oliver Neilson (pp. 62–67), Mark Seelen (pp. 94–103), Tiziano Canu (pp. 116–141), Andrea Mignogna (pp. 142–149), Sebastian Devenish (pp. 164–169), Mark Nolan (pp. 170–181), Marc van Swoll (pp. 182–187), Thomas Trinkl (pp. 196–201), Gerhard Blank (pp. 216–223), Thinkstock (pp. 16–17), Shutterstock (pp. 104–105, 162–163, 188–189, 202–203)

Disclaimer of liability
All information covered in this book is based upon data provided by the respective Engel & Völkers licence partners. Therefore, Engel & Völkers Residential GmbH assumes no liability for the accuracy and completeness of information. Errors and omissions are explicitly reserved.
All photographic material in this book was provided to Engel & Völkers Residential GmbH by the respective advertising licence partners. Therefore, Engel & Völkers Residential GmbH is not liable for any infringement caused by publication of this photographic material.

In cooperation with teNeues Publishing Group

teNeues Media GmbH + Co. KG
Am Selder 37, 47906 Kempen, Germany
Phone: +49 (0)2152 916 0 · Fax: +49 (0)2152 916 111
E-mail: books@teneues.com
Press Department: Andrea Rehn · Phone: +49 (0)2152 916 202 · E-mail: arehn@teneues.com
teNeues Digital Media GmbH
Kohlfurter Straße 41–43, 10999 Berlin, Germany · Phone: +49 (0)30 700 77 65 0
teNeues Publishing Company
7 West 18th Street, New York, NY 10011, USA · Phone: +1 212 627 9090 · Fax: +1 212 627 9511
teNeues Publishing UK Ltd.
12 Ferndene Road, London SE24 0AQ, UK · Phone: +44 (0)20 3542 8997
teNeues France S.A.R.L.
39, rue des Billets, 18250 Henrichemont, France · Phone: +33 (0)2 4826 9348 · Fax: +33 (0)1 7072 3482

www.teneues.com
© 2014 teNeues Media GmbH + Co. KG, Kempen
ISBN: 978-3-8327-9853-6

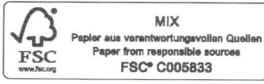